CYCLING ATLAS EUROPE

UNIVERSE

Created by Olo Éditions
www.oloeditions.com

ORIGINAL CONCEPT : Nicolas Marçais / Philippe Marchand
EDITORIAL DIRECTION : Nicolas Marçais
ART DIRECTION : Philippe Marchand
ROUTES DESIGN : Alexandre Vermersch
LAYOUT : Thomas Hamel
PROOFREADER : Catherine Decayeux
ENGLISH TRANSLATION : Rolland Glasser

First published in the United States of America in 2023 by
Universe Publishing
A division of Rizzoli International Publications, Inc.
300 Park Avenue South
New York, NY 10010
www.rizzoliusa.com

For Rizzoli
Publisher: Charles Miers
Editor: Klaus Kirschbaum
Assistant Editor: Meredith Johnson
Managing Editor: Lynn Scrabis

Printed in Bosnia & Herzegovina

2023 2024 2025 2026 / 10 9 8 7 6 5 4 3 2 1

ISBN: 978-0-7893-3953-9
Library of Congress Control Number: 2020931897

Visit us online:
Facebook.com/RizzoliNewYork
Twitter: @Rizzoli_Books
Instagram.com/RizzoliBooks
Pinterest.com/RizzoliBooks
Youtube.com/user/RizzoliNY
Issuu.com/Rizzoli

CLAUDE DROUSSENT

CYCLING ATLAS EUROPE

THE 350 MOST BEAUTIFUL CYCLING ROUTES IN EUROPE

WITH ROUTES PROVIDED BY

STRAVA

UNIVERSE

BEYOND THE TOUR DE FRANCE

From London to Heraklion, Reykjavik to Palermo, Tenerife to Tampere, the Lofoten Islands to Montenegro, the Stelvio to the Carpathians, the dry stone walls of Yorkshire to the Cretan peaks, and from the Atlantic coast to the Balkan Lakes, *Cycling Atlas Europe* is an extraordinary voyage through thirty-four countries, seen through the prism of 350 of their finest cycling routes. It covers all aspects of Europe—cities laden with history; extraordinary heritage; and thousands of kilometers of coast, plains, hills, endless valleys, and mountains. While this Atlas does trace the well trodden routes of the Tour de France, it also encourages you to discover new adventures all around the continent.

Millions of sports enthusiasts in Europe share their efforts on Strava, a social network for endurance sports. The total content helps the other members of the community realize their inner potential, as well as stir a sense of curiosity and desire to explore. Strava cyclists appreciate and share demanding routes—particularly if they lead to superb viewpoints or to a rare or enjoyable destination. The routes chosen for *Cycling Atlas Europe* reflect that mindset.

It was no easy task to pick routes for inclusion in the Atlas, and the list is certainly not exhaustive. Europe is blessed with an extraordinary breadth and depth of cycling terrain, related not only to the beauty of the regions traversed, but also to the local food, drink, and customs. Most of these routes feature opportunities to explore additional roads and trails. Everyone is free to make the journey their own and to pursue a unique experience there.

Some large regions, and even some countries, are excluded from the *Cycling Atlas Europe*, either because of a topography that is not appealing for cycling or because of roads that are too dangerous to be cycled.

Before setting out, you should check your itinerary in detail. Routes that appear in this book may, in a few weeks or months, be modified because of roadwork, bad weather, or other circumstances. They will be updated on Strava as much as possible.

Happy cycling!

HOW TO USE THIS ATLAS

FOR CYCLISTS WHO ENJOY A CHALLENGE AND INSPIRING VISTAS

Every route included in *Cycling Atlas Europe* is aimed at cyclists with an active profile, regardless of whether they are already Strava users. There are three ability levels (Intermediate, Advanced, and Expert), which allow riders to choose routes according to their own physiological capacities. The routes have been planned with an eye to safety—staying away from motor traffic as much as possible—and with a focus on pleasure, whether from a purely cycling point of view or in terms of relaxation, culture, and food.

Cycling Atlas Europe is all about the joy of riding and exploring, whether on your own or with friends. A number of the roads are world-famous; most are less well-known and full of surprises. Some of them involve unsurfaced sections (generally indicated in the text) that may require the use of a gravel bike. It goes without saying that you should always check the weather forecast before setting out.

1

STARTING POINT
For reasons of accessibility, most of the routes leave from the main train station of the departure city.

2

ABILITY LEVELS
Three ability levels are specified to make it easier for you to pick a route that suits your capacities and aims. They are "Intermediate," for cyclists who have ridden a minimum of 3,000 km (1,865 mi) over the last six months; "Advanced," for cyclists who have ridden a minimum of 6,000 km (3,730 mi); and "Expert," for cyclists who have ridden a minimum of 10,000 km (6,215 mi).

3

STRAVA ROUTE LINK
Each route has been created on the Strava website. To use it during your ride, download the GPX file and transfer it to your bike's GPS device before you set off.

4

ROUTE HIGHLIGHTS
This text summarizes the main arguments in favor of each route (e.g., sporting, fun, touristy).

5

CARTOGRAPHY
The route is traced on a map, accompanied by its profile, just as it appears online on the Strava website.

6

DIRECTION
The arrow indicates the suggested direction of the route.

7

DISTANCE AND ELEVATION GAIN (E+)
The total distance and the total elevation gain (E+) are those calculated by Strava (rounded to the nearest 50 m/165 ft for the E+). The elevation gain can sometimes be overestimated, particularly in the mountains.

8

KEY INFORMATION

This section contains key information on how to get to the route's start town.

9

KEY SEGMENTS
For some routes, we suggest two Strava segments that you can add to your favorites for easy identification as you approach them on your ride. You can compare your times with those of your friends and the whole of the Strava community, including professional riders and top-level athletes who have also ridden the segments.

10

DESCRIPTION
This describes the general context and atmosphere of the route. It includes information regarding its difficulty and appeal, as well as related anecdotes.

11

DIFFICULTY AND APPEAL
The physical difficulty and the physical/contemplative appeal of a route are graded out of five.

12

TOP TIPS

Each route features a selection of the following top tips:
- A bike store and workshop
- Somewhere to eat
- A place to visit
- An exceptional viewpoint

Bike cafes may be indicated in either of the first two categories. The top tips are indicated by pictograms on the route map in the Atlas, but they are not online.

1 MONREAL

FULL GAS AT THE NÜRBURGRING

2 *Very hilly / Advanced*

3 *Map strava.com/routes/22267681*

Test yourself km 55 (mi 34) strava.com/segments/8038832

Test yourself km 68 (mi 42) strava.com/segments/2091505 9

4 **The Rad am Ring is a cycle racing festival held at the legendary motorsport complex, the Nürburgring, every July. The 20 km (12 mi) Nordschleife track has nearly 500 m (1,640 ft) of elevation gain, and is also open to cyclists at several other times of the year.**

5 6

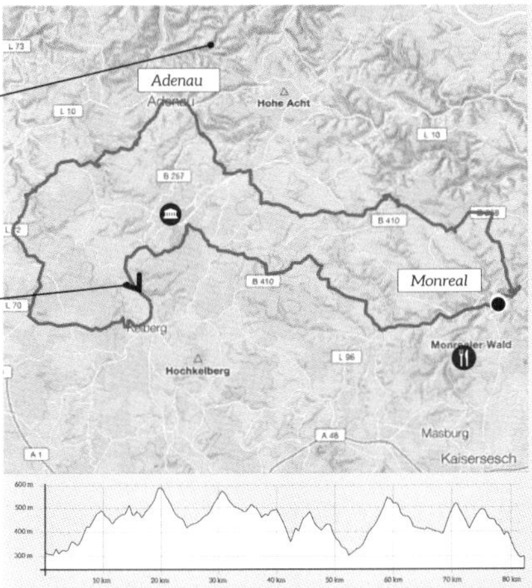

We are not in the mountains proper but, just as in the neighboring Belgian Ardennes, there is a lot of up and down to attract cyclists here in Rhineland-Palatinate. The Nürburgring motor racing track (nearly a century old) is renowned for its undulating terrain. Sadly, it is only open to cyclists a few times a year. However, this 82 km (51 mi) route around it provides an opportunity to appreciate the topography and charm of the Eifel mountains: 1,500 m (4,920 ft) of elevation gain by the end. You will pass the race track, at km 20 (mi 12) and km 59 (mi 37), at the top of the long but irregular Adenau climb, with its 7 km (4.5 mi) at an average gradient of 4%—having already tackled three similar hills near Bermel, Welcherath, and Kelberg, so it is a brisk workout for the legs. The road often passes through beech woods, with glimpses of narcissuses or orchids in the clearings, and the occasional roar of sports cars. 10

Distance **82 km** (51 mi) | E+ **1,500 m** (4,920 ft) | Difficulty **3/5** | Appeal **4/5** 11

7

12

8 Monreal (pop. 900) lies 40 km (25 mi) west of Koblenz. It is 2h30 by train from Düsseldorf, or 1h30 by car (140 km/87 mi). Frankfurt is 3h15 by train or 1h30 by car (160 km/100 mi). Brussels is 5h by train or 2h45 by car (280 km/174 mi).

Cafe Plüsch is the perfect spot for a snack when you return to Monreal. Amazing local cakes and delicious waffles in a friendly atmosphere.

Obertorstrasse 14, 56729 Monreal cafe-plüsch-monreal.de

Even if you are not a motor racing specialist, the Nürburgring has a wide range of events and activities all year round, including tours, drives around the track with a pro, lessons, sports car hire, and virtual races.

nuerburgring.de

227

CONTENTS

Snowdonia National Park in Wales, United Kingdom.

UK & IRELAND

LONDON & HOME COUNTIES

YORKSHIRE

MOORS & LAKES

SCOTLAND

WALES

NORTHERN IRELAND

IRELAND

LONDON
NORTHEAST SURPRISES

⊕ *Hilly / Intermediate*
⊕ *Map strava.com/routes/22130474*
⊕ *Test yourself km 12 (mi 7) strava.com/segments/3753318*
⊕ *Test yourself km 23 (mi 14) strava.com/segments/7185454*

Away from the clichés of Big Ben, Buckingham Palace, and Tower Bridge, northeast London may surprise anyone who has not paid attention to the city's twenty-first century metamorphosis—especially on a bike, as you ride out into the Essex countryside.

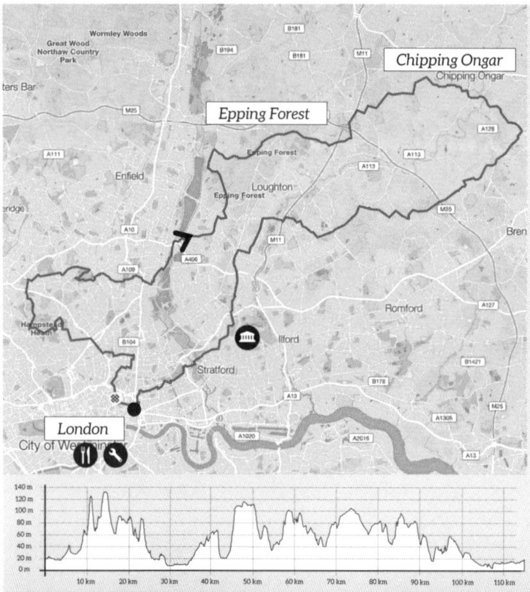

This route, which begins and ends at the hip bike cafe Look Mum No Hands!, provides a snapshot of edgy twenty-first century London, heading out of the city center to the county of Essex and back with no difficulties. At first, we ride north past Highbury (and Arsenal F.C.'s Emirates Stadium), Holloway, and on up to Highgate with some short ramps at gradients of between 7% and 10% by Waterlow Park and through Hampstead Heath, then Alexandra Park, where there is a stunning panorama across Greater London. The countryside is getting closer: Tottenham Marshes (close to Tottenham Hotspur Stadium), reservoirs, and steep little Beach Hill, the gateway to gorgeous Epping Forest. We turn before Chelmsford, returning via Hainault Forest, Stratford (and the Olympic Park), then through the colorful, creative quarters of Hackney, Brick Lane, Spitalfields, and Old Street.

Distance	E+	Difficulty	Appeal
114 km (71 mi)	1,100 m (3,600 ft)	3/5	3/5

London is highly accessible from across Europe via its several airports. London is 2h15 from Paris and 3h from Brussels by Eurostar, and 6h from Cologne by connecting train.

Rapha, the brand that has restored a certain chicness to cycling, has two London Clubhouses: one in Soho and the other in picturesque Old Spitalfields Market (km 113/mi 70).

Old Spitalfields Market, 61-63
London E1 6AA
rapha.cc

On the Olympic Park of the 2012 Games, the Lee Valley VeloPark (km 105/mi 65) holds the Six Day London race every fall. Track and BMX events for all throughout the year.

Queen Elizabeth Olympic Park,
Abercrombie Road
London E20 3AB
visitleevalley.org.uk

DORKING

SURREY WORKOUT

Very hilly / Advanced

Map strava.com/routes/22749488

Distance	E+	Difficulty	Appeal
101 km (63 mi)	1,900 m (6,200 ft)	4/5	4/5

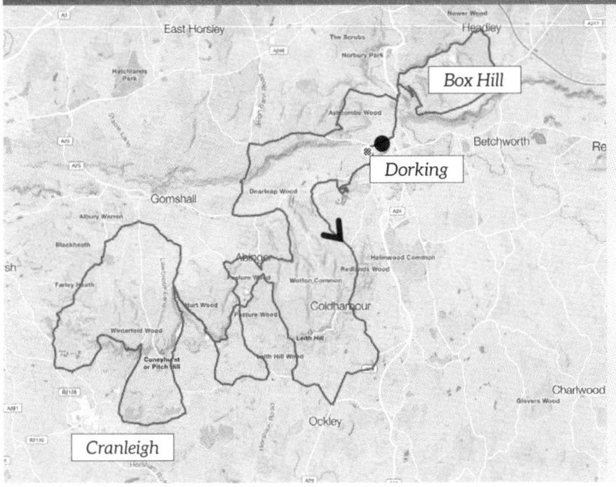

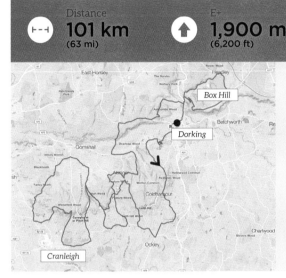

Cyclists flock to the Surrey hills, an hour by train southwest of London, perhaps because they are so challenging to ride, although you are not obliged to tackle the whole of this difficult loop. There is a dizzying succession of ramps—one every 10 km (6 mi): short, but with average gradients of 7% or 8%—between Dorking and Guildford: Coldharbour, Leith Hill, Holmbury Hill, Barhatch, Radnor, Broadmoor, and White Down. It is enough to make you dizzy. One climb that should not be missed is the longer (and very popular) Box Hill, a key obstacle in the 2012 Olympic road race.

LONDON

CHIC AND GREEN

Fairly flat / Intermediate

Map strava.com/routes/22751208

Distance	E+	Difficulty	Appeal
63 km (39 mi)	250 m (820 ft)	2/5	3/5

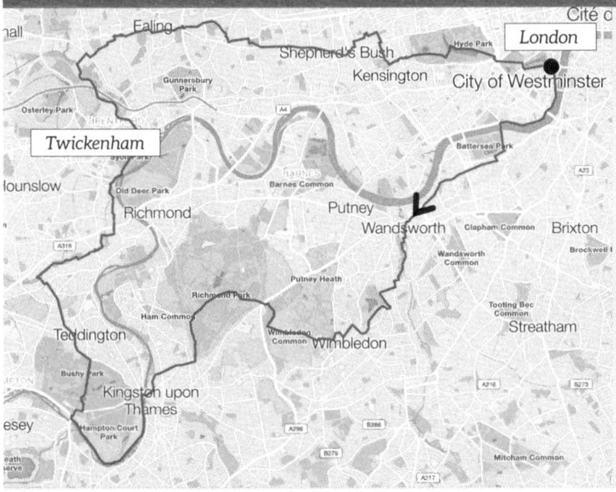

London's western suburbs have several large green spaces that are well suited to cycling. We ride out from Big Ben along dedicated cycle lanes installed since 2010. They lead via Chelsea to hilly Wimbledon, the temple of lawn tennis. At km 18 (mi 11), you will find whole pelotons. The 11.25 km (7 mi) car-free circuit of Richmond Park is very popular with the London fans of Wiggins, Froome, and Cavendish. We cross back over the Thames at Kingston, returning via Hyde Park. Twickenham Stadium is at km 36 (mi 22), and Buckingham Palace at km 62 (mi 38).

LONDON
DAYTRIP TO BRIGHTON

- *Hilly / Intermediate*
- *Map strava.com/routes/22136069*
- *Test yourself km 14 (mi 9) strava.com/segments/7261085*
- *Test yourself km 41 (mi 25) strava.com/segments/15928781*

Ever since the "mod" subculture of the 1960s, Brighton has been popular with young Londoners. Back then, the kids would ride scooters. By bike, it takes a little longer, but it is still an attractive ride through the green, rolling countryside of Surrey and West Sussex.

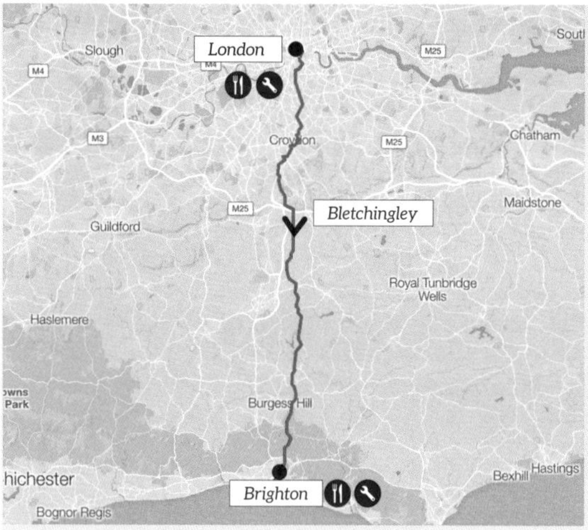

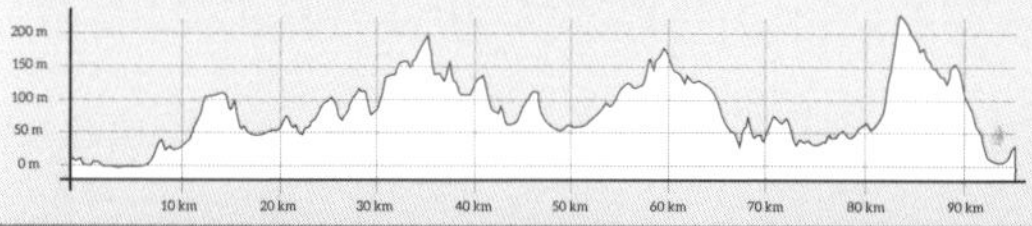

Imagine pedaling off from St. Paul's Cathedral through the City of London onto the East-West cycle path, around the Tower of London, and across the Thames via Tower Bridge. Only 3 km (2 mi), but what fun already! Ahead lies Brighton and the seaside. Riding out via Elephant and Castle, Burgess Park, and the green hills of Dulwich and Crystal Palace, you begin to extricate yourself from the megalopolis. At km 41 (mi 25), you glide through the medieval charm of Bletchingley. After Surrey comes West Sussex. When you look back from Ditchling Beacon (km 83/mi 51) —the final kilometer (0.6 mi) climbs at an average gradient of 9%—there is the most amazing view over this beautiful countryside. The final section is a loop through Brighton center past the Royal Pavilion (km 93/mi 58), Brighton Pier, the British Airways i360 tower and, of course, the seaside itself.

Distance	E+	Difficulty	Appeal
95 km (59 mi)	1,300 m (4,265 ft)	2/5	3/5

London is highly accessible from across Europe via its several airports, including Heathrow and Gatwick. London is 2h15 from Paris, 3h from Brussels by Eurostar, and 6h from Cologne by connecting train. London (Victoria) is 1h by train from Brighton.

Located barely 1 km (0.6 mi) from St. Paul's, Look Mum No Hands! is a cult bike cafe and workshop on historic Old Street. Unique atmosphere.

49 Old St
London EC1V 9HX,
lookmuminohands.com

It is well known that sea air gives you an appetite. Before taking the train back to London, sample some traditional fish and chips at Bankers, located 0.5 km (0.6 mi) from the station.

116A Western Rd, Hove
Brighton BN1 2AB
bankersfishandchips.co.uk

CANTERBURY
HISTORIC & BUCOLIC

Hilly / Advanced — *Map strava.com/routes/22735840*

Distance	E+	Difficulty	Appeal
112 km (70 mi)	1,300 m (4,265 ft)	3/5	3/5

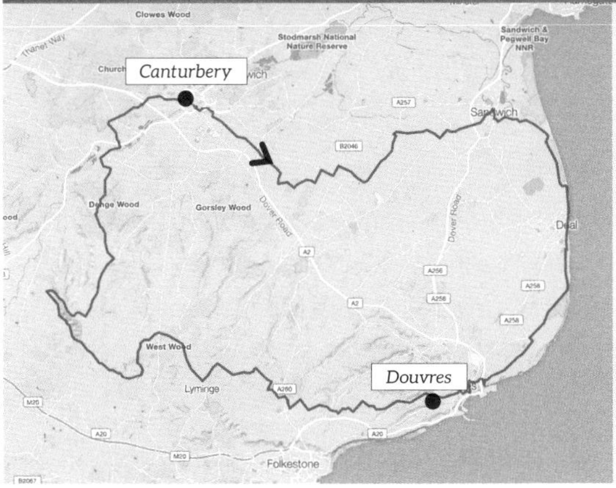

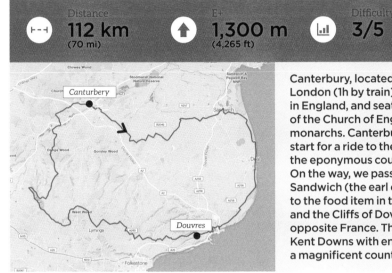

Canterbury, located 100 km (60 mi) east of London (1h by train), is one of the oldest cities in England, and seat of the senior bishop of the Church of England, who crowns British monarchs. Canterbury Cathedral is the ideal start for a ride to the Kent Downs (hills of the eponymous county) above Folkestone. On the way, we pass through medieval Sandwich (the earl of which gave his name to the food item in the eighteenth century), and the Cliffs of Dover (km 45/mi 28), opposite France. Then, it is onto the rolling Kent Downs with endless panoramas across a magnificent countryside.

WINDSOR
THE ROYAL WAY

Fairly flat / Intermediate — *Map strava.com/routes/22135367*

Distance	E+	Difficulty	Appeal
50 km (30 mi)	300 m (980 ft)	1/5	3/5

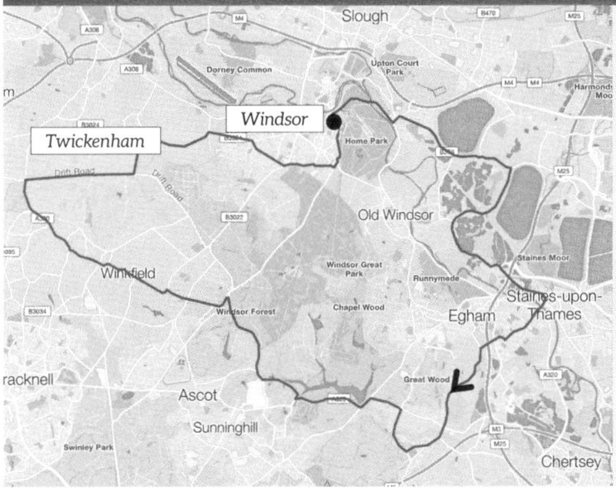

Pedal around something that makes the United Kingdom unique: the nobility of the Crown! Nothing symbolizes it more than medieval Windsor Castle, the Queen's favorite weekend residence, located 40 km (25 mi) west of London (30 min by train). The surrounding parks and forests can be explored by bike, as well as the lakes and reservoirs of Wraysbury and Virginia Water, the River Thames, and the famous Ascot Racecourse. We are close to Eton College, the private school of the elite, such as Princes William and Harry. Ride the royal way!

OXFORD
UNIVERSITY CHALLENGE 1

Fairly flat / Intermediate

Map strava.com/routes/22353222

Distance	E+	Difficulty	Appeal
90 km (56 mi)	700 m (2,295 ft)	2/5	3/5

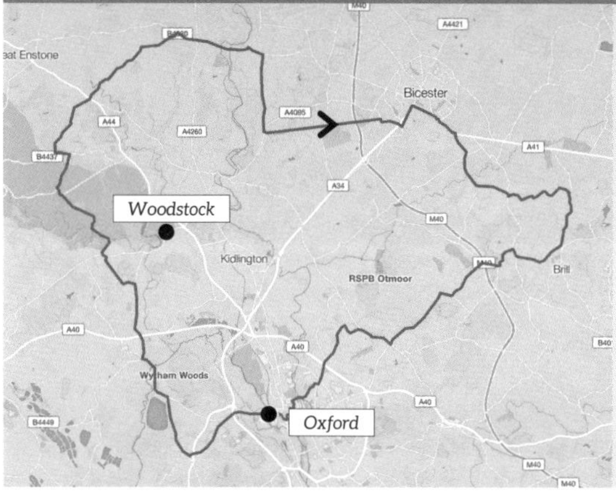

The pleasant, fertile countryside of Oxfordshire is a joy. Oxford is only 100 km (60 mi) from London (1h by train). This loop to the north of the prestigious university city has much to interest the cyclist. We skirt Woodstock and Blenheim Palace (a fine example of English baroque architecture and the ancestral home of Winston Churchill), and Brill with its impressive windmill. Back in Oxford, we ride past stunning buildings in the Gothic style: Trinity College, where King Charles III and thirty-three Nobel Prize winners studied, and St John's and Pembroke Colleges.

CAMBRIDGE
UNIVERSITY CHALLENGE 2

Fairly flat / Intermediate

Map strava.com/routes/22352541

Distance	E+	Difficulty	Appeal
89 km (55 mi)	400 m (1,315 ft)	2/5	3/5

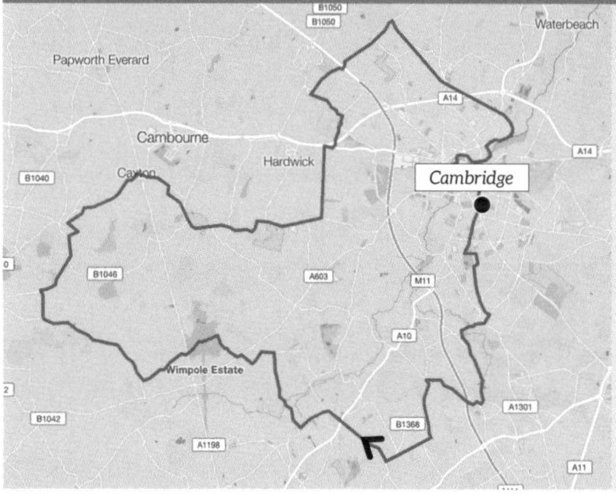

The vast plains surrounding Cambridge, located 100 km (60 mi) north of London (50 minutes by train), never get boring. The colors are so vivid, the seasons so clearly marked, the villages so charming, and the traces of history so well maintained (such as the venerable Wimpole Hall in Arrington). Cambridge, located 140 km (85 mi) east of Oxford, was founded 113 years after the former in the Middle Ages. At km 78 (mi 48), we pass through "Silicon Fen," home to a cluster of high-tech businesses, before a lazy roll along the River Cam, taking in majestic King's College.

NOTTINGHAM
CATCH ROBIN HOOD

Fairly flat / Intermediate
Map strava.com/routes/21940071
Test yourself km 11 (mi 7) strava.com/segments/6503145
Test yourself km 113 (mi 70) strava.com/routes/21940071

Nottingham to Sherwood Forest is Robin Hood country. The city is also home to Raleigh Bicycles, as well as being the birthplace of fashion designer Paul Smith, a huge cycling fan. There are plenty of "gravel" segments to explore here in the East Midlands.

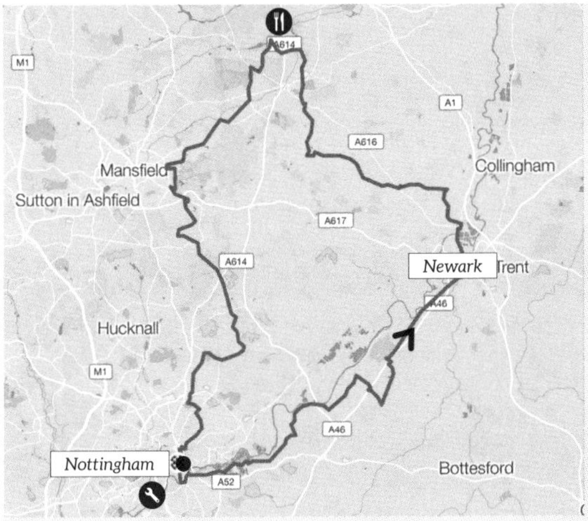

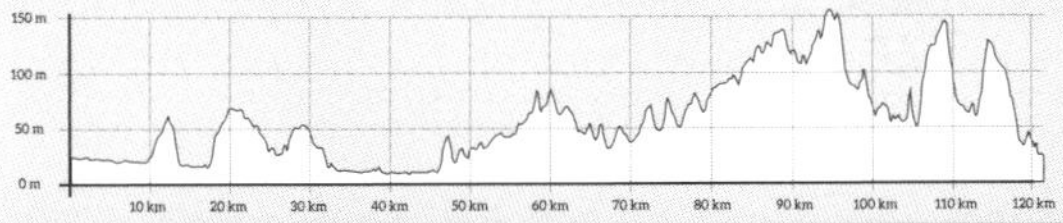

On the edge of Sherwood Forest, just before Edwinstowe, is a sign on the right pointing to the Major Oak, an ancient, majestic oak tree under which Robin Hood and his merry men are said to have slept. The legend alone is worth the 121 km (75 mi) of this route out of Nottingham, an industrial city (textiles and bicycles) with a medieval past, along the River Trent to the South Muskham lakes, after Newark, with its Church of St. Mary Magdalene that boasts an octagonal spire. We reach Sherwood Forest (km 70/mi 43). Traces of the popular heroes—Robin Hood and his Maid Marion—are everywhere. The return through the countryside is somewhat craggier, so keep something in reserve for Bank Hill (km 106/ mi 65) and Woodthorpe Drive (km 114/mi 70). Back in Nottingham, check out the Robin Hood Experience to get a sense of the city in medieval times.

Distance	E+	Difficulty	Appeal
121 km (75 mi)	1,000 m (3,280 ft)	2/5	4/5

Nottingham is 1h50 by train from London (St Pancras or Kings Cross). By car, allow 3h on the M1 (200 km/125 mi). Manchester is 1h50 by train or 2h15 by car (130 km/80 mi).

The Royal Oak (km 75/mi 46) is the main pub in the village of Edwinstowe, which is closely associated with Robin Hood. Good food and fine ales.

High Street
Edwinstowe NG21 9QP
royaloakedwinstowe.co.uk

In the Radford district 2 km (1.25 mi) north of the station, Nottingham Bikeworks is a bike workshop, store, and community educational project.

1 Ayr Street
Nottingham NG7 4FX
nottinghambikeworks.org.uk

MANCHESTER
TO BLACKPOOL FOR FUN

⊕ *Fairly flat / Advanced*

⊕ *Map strava.com/routes/21940309*

Distance	E+	Difficulty	Appeal
161 km (100 mi)	800 m (2,625 ft)	3/5	3/5

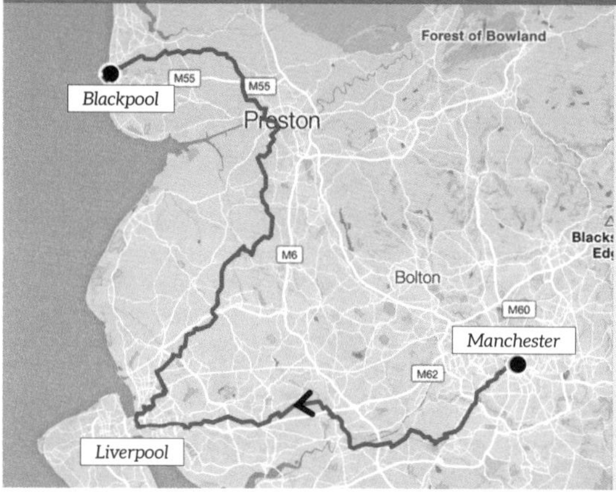

The idea of a 161 km (100 mi) ride from Manchester to Blackpool via Liverpool seems crazy. With distance the only challenge, it is simply fun as we ride along cycle paths with return travel by train in 55 minutes from Liverpool and 1h20 from Blackpool. At km 7 (mi 4.5), we pass Old Trafford, Manchester's "Theatre of Dreams." Warrington on the River Mersey is superb. Anfield Road, proud symbol of Liverpool F.C., is located at km 80 (mi 50). Finally, we pass the resort of Blackpool, where Mancunians and Liverpudlians come in droves to party in the shadow of the stunning (and Eiffel'esque) Blackpool Tower.

NOTTINGHAM
LOVELY MIDLANDS

⊕ *Fairly flat / Intermediate*

⊕ *Map strava.com/routes/22145333*

Distance	E+	Difficulty	Appeal
103 km (64 mi)	900 m (2,950 ft)	2/5	3/5

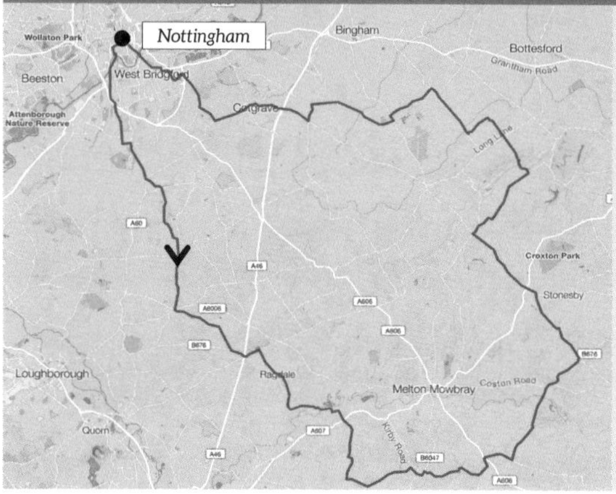

Rolling green hills, dotted with trees, stretching into the distance: this is Leicestershire. Our loop heads south from Nottingham toward Leicester on the bucolic roads of the Midlands with barely any difficulty to disturb your smooth cadence. The trees and hedges provide shelter from the wind as you glide through scenery that could not be more English: little villages of cozy nestled houses, the proud church towers of Ragdale, Great Dalby, Saxby, and Waltham on the Wolds. Back in Nottingham, after 103 km (64 mi), enjoy a pint of ale at The Vat and Fiddle, closed from the railway station.

HAWES
WILD YORKSHIRE

🌐 *Very hilly / Advanced*
🌐 *Map [strava.com/routes/21265876]*
⊕ *Test yourself km 2 (mi 1) strava.com/routes/21265876*
⊕ *Test yourself km 29 (mi 18) strava.com/segments/7095134*

The first stage of the 2014 Tour de France was a revelation. TV viewers across the world were able to discover the wild, arresting beauty of the Yorkshire countryside, a cradle of British cycling culture. If you are a serious cyclist, you must visit Yorkshire.

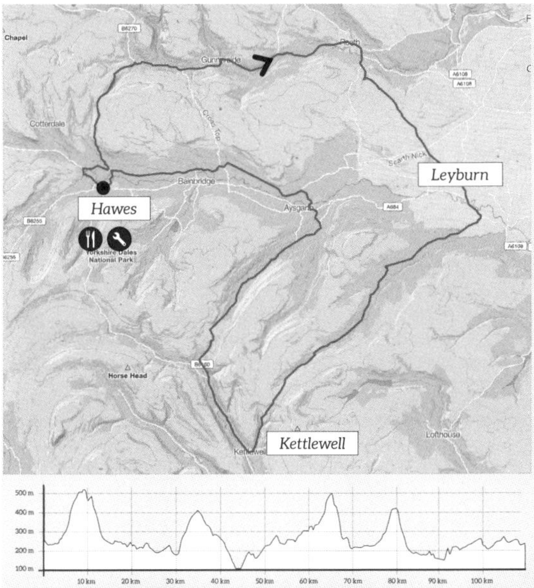

Hawes has barely a thousand inhabitants, but this town northwest of Leeds is a bastion of Yorkshire cycling. It is the ideal starting point for a "seventy miler" through the wild, hilly scenery of the Yorkshire Dales, home of the Swaledale—a black-faced sheep with horns in the shape of upside-down drop handlebars. You will roll for miles (on the left) between dry stone walls across desolate moorland without coming across a single car or pub sign. Four key challenges await. Buttertubs Pass hits you straight away: 6 km (3.8 mi) at an average gradient of 5%, with sections at 10%. Grinton Moor is a classic: 4.5 km (2.8 mi) at an average gradient of 7% over the first two-thirds. Then, Cam Gill Road (km 64/mi 40) and the 2 km (1.25 mi) long Kidstones Pass, at km 78 (mi 49), which has sections at 15%, complete the rugged part of this route. What a pleasure though!

Distance	E+	Difficulty	Appeal
105 km (65 mi)	2,000 m (6,600 ft)	4/5	5/5

From London's airports, allow 3h30 by train then bus. By car, allow 5h (400 km/250 mi). Leeds Bradford Airport is 2h by train then bus, or 1h40 by car (120 km/74.5 mi). Manchester is 2h by car (140 km/87 mi).

Best breakfasts in Hawes, butties, burgers, fried chicken and more: Penny Garth Cafe is the place to have something (yummy) to eat before or after a big outdoor day through the Dales.

Market Place
Hawes North Yorkshire
DL8 3RD
pennygarthcafe.co.uk

Stage 1 Cycles—named in homage to the start of the 2014 Tour de France—is more than just a bike store. It is a place for people to meet, chat, and share local expertise.

Station Yard,
Hawes North Yorkshire
DL8 3NT
stage1cycles.co.uk

CHESTERFIELD
FASCINATING PEAK DISTRICT

- *Very hilly / Advanced*
- *Map strava.com/routes/21949405*
- *Test yourself km 7 (mi 4) strava.com/segments/1227026*
- *Test yourself km 45 (mi 28) strava.com/segments/612982*

Derbyshire and the surprising landscape of the Peak District provide a vision of England far removed from clichés of industrial scenes and quaint cottages. The views are spectacular, and the cycling will really test your legs. The unusual Winnats Pass is an attraction in itself.

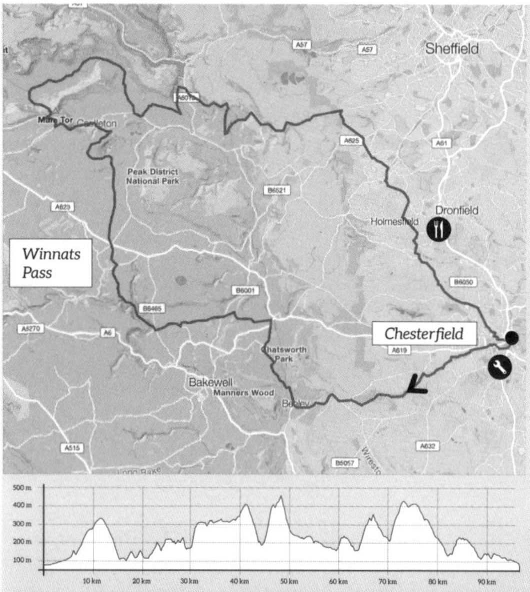

This route is under 100 km (62 mi), but it offers more than 2,000 m (6,560 ft) of climbing and a multitude of steep ascents. Leaving Chesterfield, we cycle through several pleasant parks before warming up the legs on Harewood, with its 5 km (3 mi) at an average gradient of 4%. At km 30 (mi 19), Bottomhill will raise your heart rate: 1.3 km (0.8 mi) at an average gradient of 10%, with one section at 18%. At km 40 (mi 25), Dirtlow Rake ramps up further. Winnats Pass (the name is a corruption of "wind gates") is an absolute must; it is only 2.3 km (1.4 mi) long but has an average gradient of nearly 10%, including one intimidating section at 28%. The ribbon of asphalt winds up between two sheer limestone slopes to a short ramp beneath Mam Tor. At km 71 (mi 44), the spectacular cliff of Stanage Edge is yet another curiosity: 2.3 km (1.42 mi) long at an average gradient of 9%.

Distance	E+	Difficulty	Appeal
97 km (60 mi)	2,100 m (6,890 ft)	3/5	4/5

Chesterfield (pop. 72,000) is only 20 km (12.5 mi) from Sheffield. It is 1h by train or car from Leeds (90 km/55 mi). Manchester is 1h30 by train (via Leeds) or 1h20 by car (80 km/50 mi). London is 2h30 by train (from St Pancras) or 2h45 by car (250 km/155 mi).

At km 86 (mi 53), pop into The Angel, a typical English pub with a fine choice of ales and beers. Gluten-free food available.

Main Road, Holmesfield
Dronfield S18 7WT
facebook.com/TheAngelatHolmesfield

JE James Cycles (close to the station and the route) is Chesterfield's go-to bike store and rental outlet, selling Bianchi, Cannondale, Cervelo, and Focus.

Progress House,
Brimington Road North
Chesterfield S41 9AP
jejamescycles.com

The sun sets over Winnats Pass in Derbyshire, United Kingdom.

HARROGATE

MANX MISSILE'S VACATION

Hilly / Intermediate *Map strava.com/routes/22735163*

Distance	E+	Difficulty	Appeal
94 km (58 mi)	1,500 m (4,920 ft)	3/5	4/5

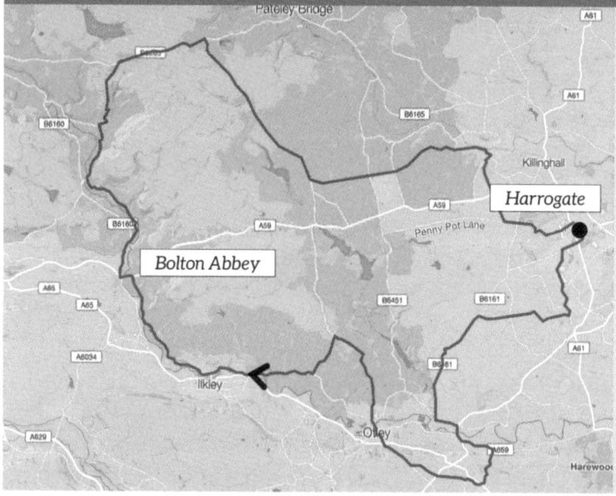

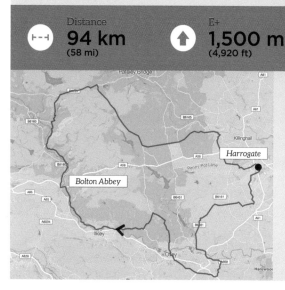

At the turn of the century, Mark Cavendish, a budding young cyclist from the Isle of Man, was on holiday with his family in Harrogate, located 25 km (15 mi) north of Leeds (40 minutes by train). He would go for rides on the Yorkshire roads, principally in the Nidderdale conservation area, through which a large part of this route passes. The future "Manx Missile" built up his muscle on 2 to 4 km (1.25 to 2.5 mi) ramps such as Old Bramhope (km 24/mi 15), Newall Carr (km 30/mi 19), and Greenhow Hill (km 67/mi 42)—from the top of which there is a stunning view over an endless wild landscape.

SETTLE

INFINITE MOORS

Hilly / Intermediate *Map strava.com/routes/22735480*

Distance	E+	Difficulty	Appeal
69 km (43 mi)	1,250 m (4,100 ft)	3/5	3/5

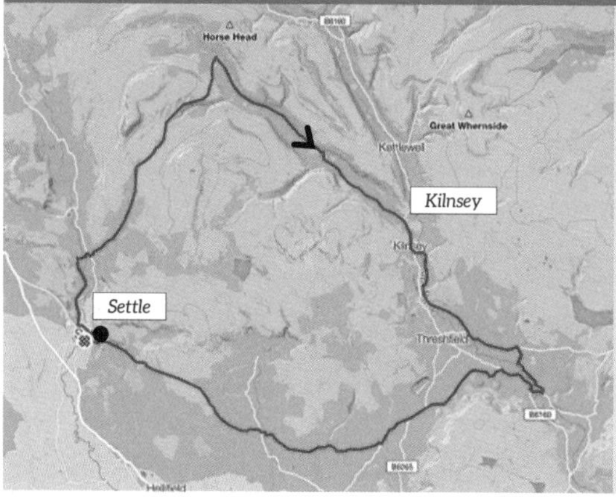

This loop through the southwestern Yorkshire Dales, which starts and ends in Settle (1h by train from Leeds), balances cycling challenge with the pleasure of contemplating the beautiful wild scenery: barren moorland, villages of gray stone houses clustered together at the foot of rocky hills, and dry stone walls lining country roads. There are some stiff gradients too, such as the passages between 8% and 10% on the way up to the highest point of our ride at 435 m (1,420 ft) after Stainforth. We roll on up hill and down dale until the final 4 km (2.5 mi) ramp at 5% before Settle.

WHITBY
MOOR AND MOOR

Very hilly / Advanced
Map strava.com/routes/22100272

Test yourself km 41 (mi 25) strava.com/segments/5077417
Test yourself km 71 (mi 44) strava.com/segments/18337286

The North York Moors National Park is an extraordinary place with a mystical atmosphere. On the wild, bare land, 300 m (1,000 ft) above the North Sea, the horizon is sublime. In short, this paradise is perfect cycling country!

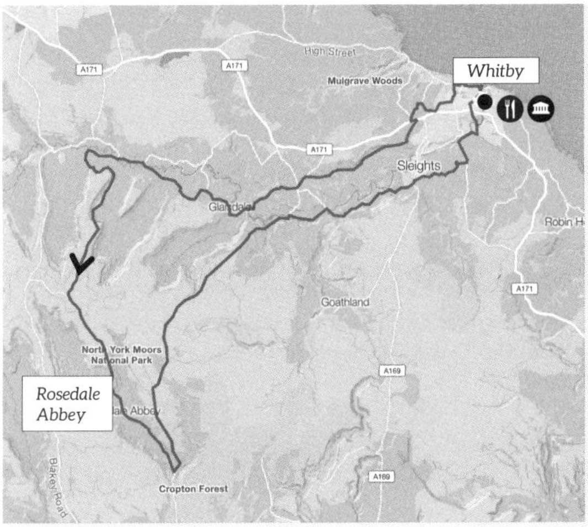

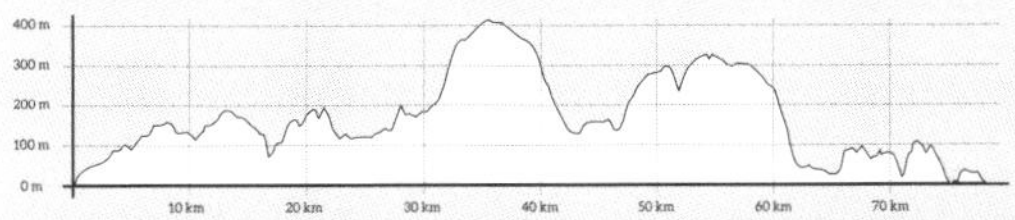

In summer, the vast, rolling hills of the moors are carpeted with heather blossom so intensely mauve, you would think that you were in Provence. The westerly wind, however, rises often enough to remind you that this is northeast England. This loop out from Whitby is not easy, as is evidenced by its 1,500 m (4,920 ft) of elevation gain for less than 80 km (50 mi) of riding. The area has no shortage of testing challenges—the most spectacular of which are suggested here as options just off the route. At km 43 (mi 27), there is Rosedale Chimney Bank: 1.3 km (0.8 mi) at 14% with one switchback section at 33%. At km 54 (mi 33.5), we find Glaisdale Horror: 1.3 km (0.8 mi) dead straight at 14% with sections at 25%. Finally, at km 65 (mi 40), we have Fair Head Lane in Grosmont: 2 km (1.25 mi) at 10%. You can see the sea from up there, sometimes wreathed in spray. This heavenly moor is hellish on the legs!

Distance	E+	Difficulty	Appeal
78 km (48 mi)	1,500 m (4,920 ft)	3/5	4/5

Teesside International Airport, 90 km (55 mi) north of Whitby, is connected to Amsterdam. Middlesbrough, 50 km (31 mi) north of Whitby, is 1h30 by train or 50 minutes by car. Leeds is 2h30 by train or 1h50 by car (120 km/75 mi). London is 5h by train (King's Cross) or by car (430 km/268 mi).

There are few places better than Whitby in which to sample a plate of fish and chips. With its sea view, The Fisherman's Wife is the perfect spot.

Khyber Pass
Whitby YO21 3PZ
thefishermanswife.co.uk

The unique atmosphere of the moors extends to Whitby on the coast. Explore the sumptuous ruins of its Benedictine abbey, a former double monastery (both monks and nuns), which also inspired Bram Stoker for his novel *Dracula*.

visitwhitby.com

MIDDLESBROUGH

UP AND DOWN THE MOORS

Very hilly / Advanced

Map strava.com/routes/22101245

Distance	E+	Difficulty	Appeal
142 km (88 mi)	2,200 m (7,215 ft)	4/5	4/5

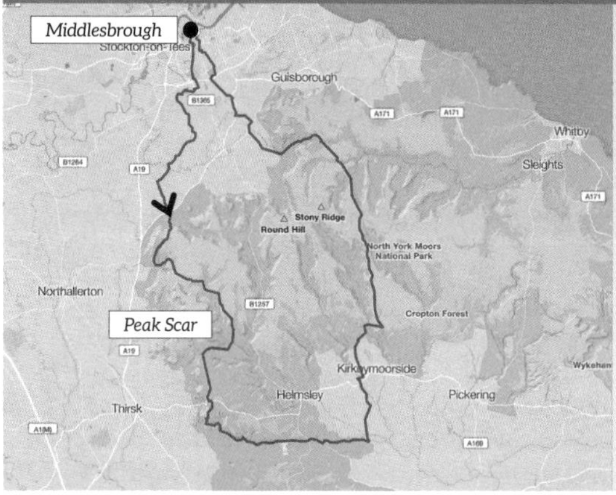

North of Leeds (1h30 by train) and south of Newcastle (1h10), Middlesbrough is well placed for a total immersion in the North York Moors. The elevation gain is high over this kind of terrain: 2,200 m (7,215 ft) in 142 km (88 mi). This route takes a lot of effort, though the climbs are relatively easy (except for the foot of the road up to Peak Scar (km 47/mi 29), a famous cliff for rock climbing that rises at 11% for more than 1 km (0.6 mi). Further on, we pass Ampleforth Abbey and then Nunnington Hall. The views from the top of Ledging Hill (km 106/mi 66) are sublime.

MIDDLESBROUGH

MOOR AND SEA

Hilly / Intermediate

Map strava.com/routes/22089357

Distance	E+	Difficulty	Appeal
86 km (53 mi)	1,000 m (3,280 ft)	3/5	3/5

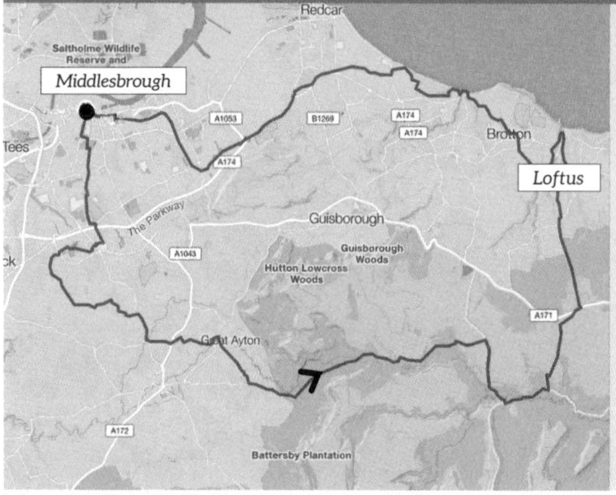

The charm and ruggedness of the North York Moors are embodied by these roads that sweep and roll over the contours, unencumbered by switchbacks, in this loop starting and ending in Middlesbrough. Two climbs of note are Crag Bank (km 31/mi 19) and Sandhill Bank (km 34/mi 21), barely 600 m (2,000 ft) each, but with average gradients of more than 10%. Kilton (km 57/mi 35) will also get your heart pumping with the reward of a lovely sea view. A good third of the route is in the hills, and there are many cycle paths throughout. You will fall in love with the Moors.

INVERNESS
WHERE'S NESSIE?

- *Hilly / Advanced*
- *Map strava.com/routes/21994600*
- *Test yourself km 65 (mi 40) strava.com/segments/723617*
- *Test yourself km 105 (mi 65) strava.com/segments/7152701*

Webcams keep watch over the expanse of Loch Ness, as if the legend of the monster were indeed true. Folks still flock here from Inverness in the hope of seeing something. This is a lovely loop around the loch, particularly the climbs that lift us away from the road traffic.

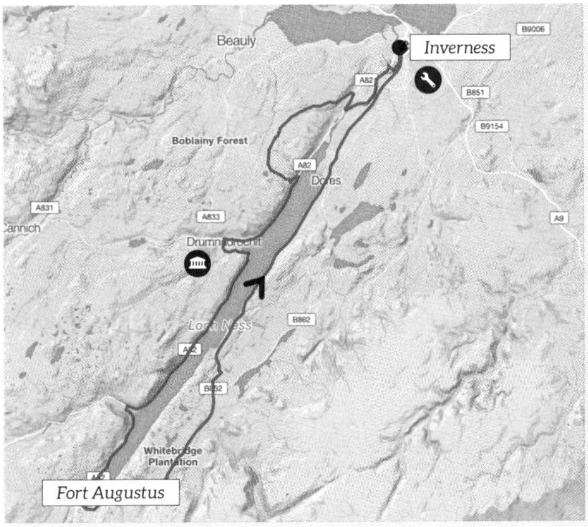

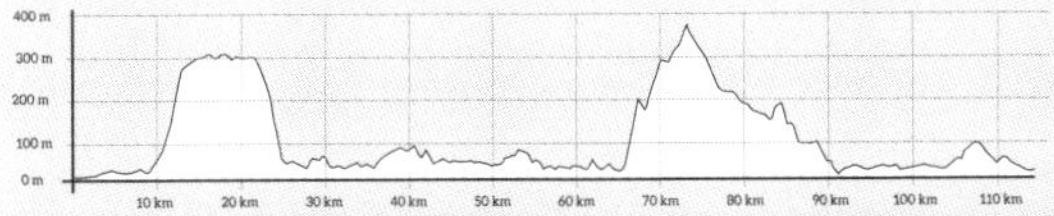

What if Nessie finally appeared? Keep your smartphone within reach and saddle up for a tour of inspection of Loch Ness, which is 40 km (25 mi) long by 1 to 3 km (0.5 to 2 mi) wide, and is renowned for its salmon and trout fishing. Add some climbing: it is good for the heart and leg muscles, and lifts you away from distracted drivers with half an eye on the mysterious waters. Haul yourself up Blackford (km 10/ mi 6)—4 km (2.5 mi) at 7%—and over Carn a'Bhodaich. At the southern end, past Fort Augustus (km 65/mi 40), there is another climb, up to 390 m (1,280 ft): the first section is nearly 2 km (1.25 mi) long at an average gradient of 9.8%, then 5 km (3 mi) at 5%, with sections at 10%. Then it's back to Inverness, the capital of the Highlands with its castle and Victorian Market. If you prefer, you can cut out the Blackford climb, shaving 250 m (850 ft) off the E+ and 9 km (5.5 mi) off the distance.

Distance	E+	Difficulty	Appeal
118 km (73 mi)	1,500 m (4,920 ft)	3/5	4/5

Inverness Airport serves several cities within the UK. The city is equidistant between Edinburgh and Glasgow (280 km/175 mi): 4h30 by train or 3h by car from both. From London (Kings Cross), allow 8h by train or 10h by car (900 km/5620 mi).

The Loch Ness Centre (km 34/mi 21) has a high-tech exhibition that allows you to discover Nessie in 3D. The Cobbs Cafe there is very pleasant.

Drumnadrochit, Loch Ness
Inverness IV63 6TU
lochness.com

Located 500 meters/yards from the train station, Highland Bikes is the go-to road bike specialist in Inverness. Giant and Genesis vendor.

29-31 Shore St
Inverness IV1 1NG
highlandbikes.com

KINBRACE
SCOTTISH STEPPES

Fairly flat / Intermediate

Map strava.com/routes/22733444

Distance	E+	Difficulty	Appeal
102 km (63 mi)	900 m (2,950 ft)	2/5	4/5

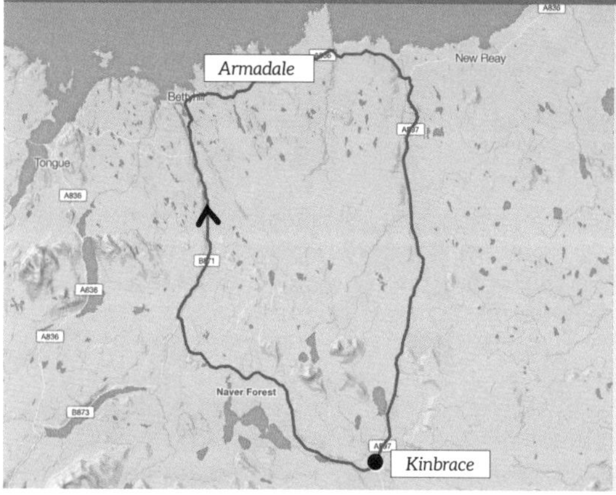

Do you enjoy solitude or riding as a group in the heart of the (very) great outdoors? The Scottish Highlands are an ideal destination for either option. From Kinbrace, the penultimate station before Thurso in the far north of Scotland (dress appropriately), this loop traversing the Forsinard Flows Nature Reserve is a unique experience, passing lakes, rivers, peat bog, bare moorland, little valleys, and the occasional white-walled house. It is a mystical place with wonderful light and fascinating surprises, such as the beaches at Bettyhill and Strathy.

GLASGOW
FROM CITY TO LOCH

Hilly / Advanced

Map strava.com/routes/21995931

Distance	E+	Difficulty	Appeal
141 km (88 mi)	2,000 m (6,560 ft)	3/5	4/5

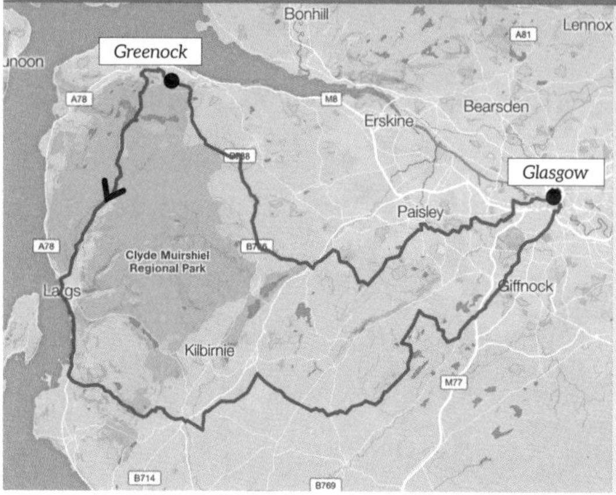

Glasgow, a mix of Victorian and contemporary architecture in perpetual effervescence, will host the inaugural multidiscipline UCI World Championships (road, track, MTB, and BMX) in 2023. We suggest that they include this loop west of the city around Clyde Muirshiel Regional Park, a stunning landscape of moorland and lakes. It is a long ride, but you can always hop on a train at Greenock, Largs, or Darly. The wall of Gleniffer (1.3 km/0.8 mi at 8%), the climb at Loch Thom, close to the Hill of Stake (522 m/1,713 ft), and finally Fairlie Moor (3 km/2 mi at 8%) add some spice.

KENDAL
DISCOVER THE LAKES

Very hilly / Intermediate
Map strava.com/routes/22084523
Test yourself km 13 (mi 8) strava.com/segments/1590025
Test yourself km 44 (mi 27) strava.com/segments/3765917

The Lakes, or Lake District, in Cumbria is among the favorite destinations for British people seeking a getaway in the great outdoors. This loop in the southern part—barely 70 km (43 mi) long—heads out from Kendal through stunning scenery of lakes and hills.

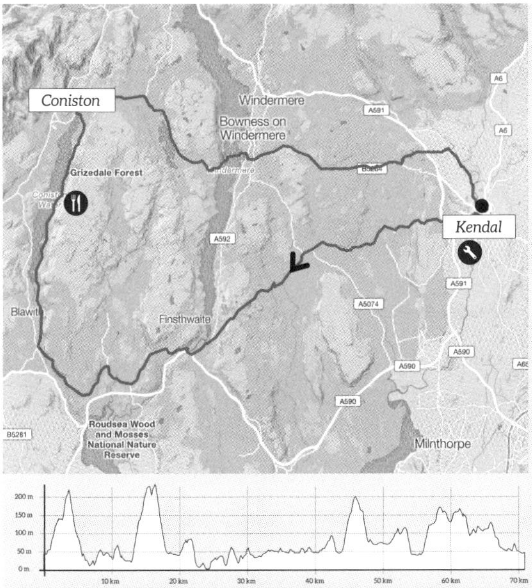

When you return from this ride through the Lake District, you will most likely want to come back and explore further west around Scafell Pike, the highest mountain in England at 978 m (3,209 ft). You will get a good view of the impressive Southern Fells surrounding it as you cycle along Coniston Water. Our route takes in deep valleys—their schist slopes covered with heather, ferns, and pine plantations. As you leave Kendal, you will find the road kicks up to a gradient of 10%. Gummer's How (km 13/mi 8) is a 2.3 km (1.4 mi) drag at 7%. Skirt the southern tip of Windermere to reach the eastern shore of Coniston. After the 2.5 km (1.5 mi) climb of Hawkshead Hill (7% average gradient), you reach a wild paradise, home of the Herdwick sheep, which is born black before graying. Stop and look back toward Scafell Pike before cycling back to Windermere and taking the ferry (km 54/mi 33.5) across the water.

Distance	E+	Difficulty	Appeal
71 km (44 mi)	1,400 m (4,595 ft)	3/5	4/5

Known as "Auld Grey Town," Kendal (pop. 30,000) is only 1h20 to 2h by train from Manchester or 1h30 by car (120 km/74.5 mi). London is 3h15 by train (Euston) or 5h by car (430 km). Carlisle (to the north) is 1h15 by train or 1h by car (80 km/50 mi).

The Terrace Coffee House (km 40/mi 25) is the perfect place to sit and ponder a future adventure expedition to Scafell Pike.

Coach House East of Lake
Coniston LA21 8AD
brantwood.org.uk/theterrace

Brucie's Bike Shop has been well established in Kendal for nearly forty years. Brucie even has his own bike brand, Brevatto, as well as a vintage corner.

9 Kirkland
Kendal LA9 5AF
bruciesbikeshop.webs.com

DALMALLY
HARRY POTTER COUNTRY

Hilly / Advanced

Map strava.com/routes/22129297

Test yourself km 42 (mi 26) strava.com/segments/1716936

Test yourself km 92 (mi 57) strava.com/segments/682682

The highlight of this long trek through the magnificent Highlands of Scotland is the rough moorland of Glencoe Valley. The mystic feel is accentuated by the shapes of the Munros: the name given to Scottish mountains over 3,000 feet (914.4 m) high. Welcome to Harry Potter country!

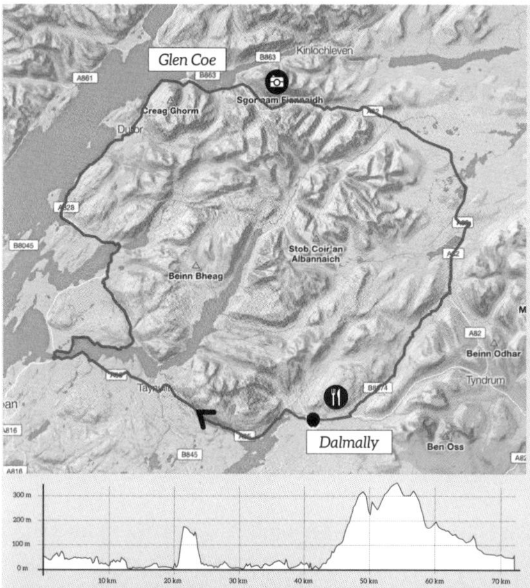

A loch refers to a stretch of water in Scotland, whether a freshwater lake, an inlet, an estuary, or a bay. This Highland route, which starts in Dalmally, with its delightful train station built of gray stone, heads out past Kilchurn Castle and passes loch after loch: Awe, Etive, Creran, Linnhe, and Tulla on the way back. You are never far from water, crossing it several times, such as at Connel (km 31/mi 19), then at Creagan (km 52/mi 32). The waypoints (Taynuilt, Appin, Ballachulish, Glencoe) are just tiny villages lost amid wooded glens, heather-clad hills, and waterfalls. In some places, you climb between two lochs, such as at Glen Salach (km 42/mi 26): 1.4 km (1 mi) at an average gradient of 9%. The climb to Glencoe Valley, after nearly 36 km (22 mi) of cycle path from Barcaldine, is gentler. One of the most beautiful parts of the Highlands, it was featured in the movie adaptation of *Harry Potter*.

Distance	E+	Difficulty	Appeal
144 km (89 mi)	1,500 m (4,920 ft)	3/5	4/5

For the Highlands, specifically Dalmally (pop. 200), Glasgow Airport is best: 2h30 by train or 1h45 by car (280 km/174 mi). Edinburgh is 2h20 by car, but 8h by train via Glasgow. The same goes for Inverness: 3h by car (200 km/125 mi).

The recently refurbished Ben Cruachan Inn is the ideal spot to relax in Dalmally, with stunning views over the loch and sixty Scotch whiskies to choose from.

Loch Awe
Dalmally PA33 1AQ
bencruachaninn.com

Glen Coe Valley offers a succession of unique landscapes. These include the ocher hues of Signal Rock (km 89/mi 55), the view of the summits of the Three Sisters after Loch Achtriochtan (km 93/mi 58), and the Meeting of the Three Waters, located 2 km (1.25 mi) further on.

The Three Sisters above Glen Coe in Scotland, United Kingdom.

SEASCALE

STRANGELY STEEP

Very hilly / Advanced — *Map* *strava.com/routes/22267092*

Distance	E+	Difficulty	Appeal
85 km (53 mi)	1,800 m (5,900 ft)	4/5	5/5

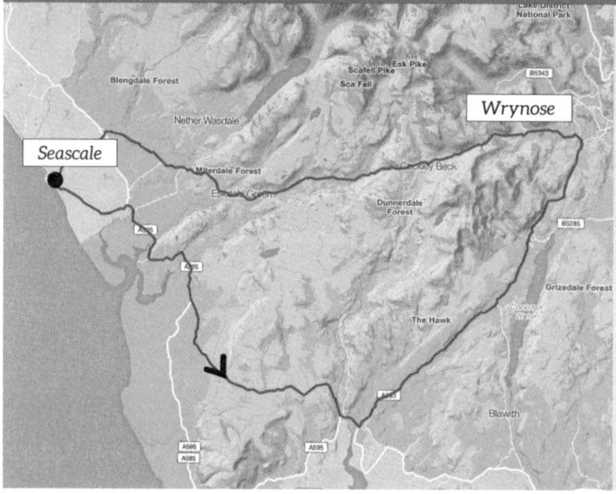

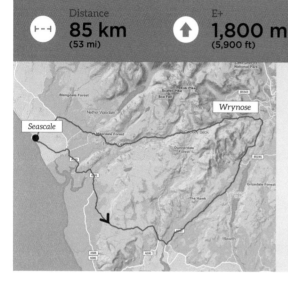

This loop through the southwest Lake District from the coastal town of Seascale includes one of the weirdest roads in the British Isles. Hardknott Pass (km 23/mi 14) is a spectacularly steep section of road that snakes gently upward for 2.4 km (1.5 mi) at an average gradient of 14%, with the first 0.5 km (0.3 mi) at 17%. On the bends, the gradient jumps as high as 33%. The madness continues soon after with Wrynose Pass: 1 km (0.6 mi) at 11.5%. Further on, at km 60 (mi 37), the first 2 km (1.25 mi) of Corney Fell have gradients of between 8% and 13%. The scenery is equally astounding.

PENRITH

THE BRITISH VENTOUX

Low mountain / Expert — *Map* *strava.com/routes/22266141*

Distance	E+	Difficulty	Appeal
143 km (89 mi)	2,500 m (8,200 ft)	5/5	5/5

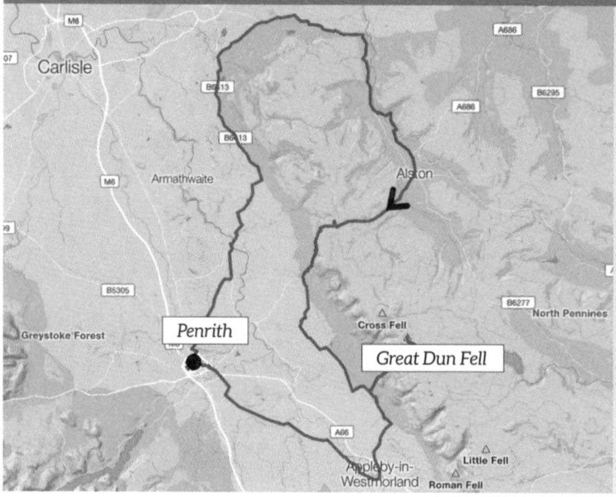

Riding out of Penrith, a peaceful town nestling between the Lake District and the low mountains of the Pennines, you would never imagine what lies ahead: Great Dun Fell (km 103/mi 64). Local cyclists compare it to Mont Ventoux. The beautifully surfaced road climbs through a barren landscape up the slope to the white dome of the radar station at the top (848 m/2,782 ft), used for air traffic control. The climb is 7.3 km (4.5 mi) long with an E+ of 600 m (2,000 ft) and with a 3 km (2 mi) stretch at 11% (18% in the middle). The views are, of course, extraordinary.

BELFAST
ROUND THE ARDS PENINSULA

- *Fairly flat / Advanced*
- *Map strava.com/routes/22496859*
- *Test yourself km 47 (mi 29) strava.com/segments/1158299*
- *Test yourself km 62 (mi 38) strava.com/segments/4115329*

There are barely any folds in the landscape, the coast is as flat as a pancake, and the tides pull the sea a long way out. Welcome to the peaceful Ards Peninsula on Northern Ireland's east coast. From Belfast, it is a lovely day's ride to tour it, as long as the weather is favorable.

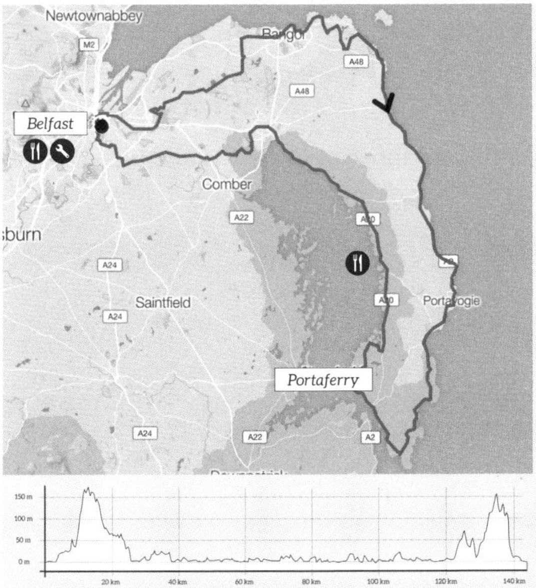

The *Titanic*, which sank in the North Atlantic in 1912, was built here. The start of our long route passes the futuristic Titanic Belfast museum on the site of the former shipyards. We soon overlook the city from Stormont Castle, the seat of the Northern Ireland Executive: 2.5 km (1.5 mi) at 6%. The rest of the route around the Ards Peninsula, which separates Strangford Lough from the North Channel (opposite Scotland) is pretty flat: a succession of little sheltered ports, beaches, and rocks. We ride past some rich heritage, including the white lighthouse at Donaghadee, the Italian-style mansion house of Ballywalter Park, Kirkistown Motor Racing Circuit, and Greyabbey. You can cut short the route at Ballywalter (92 km/57 mi from the end). The 41 m (135 ft) high Scrabo Tower above Newtownards is visible from far off, only 20 km (12 mi) from the green hills and welcoming pubs of Belfast.

Distance	E+	Difficulty	Appeal
143 km (89 mi)	1,200 m (3,940 ft)	4/5	3/5

Belfast Airport is 21 km (13 mi) outside the city: 1h30 by train or 30 minutes by car. Londonderry is 2h40 by train or 1h30 by car (120 km/75 mi). Dublin is 4h by train or 2h10 by car (170 m/105 mi).

Less than 2 km (1.25 mi) from Belfast Lanyon Place Train Station, Bicycle Coffee Shop has a lovely atmosphere. Customized bikes, garage, and yoga sessions. Retailer of Trek.

143 North Street
Belfast
bicyclecoffeeshop.com

A loop of nearly 150 km (93 mi) requires a feed stop. Saltwater Brig (km 102/mi 63) is the perfect Irish restaurant, with little tables in the garden overlooking Strangford Lough.

43 Rowreagh Road, Kircubbin
Newtownards
saltwaterbrig.com

LARNE

THE GLENS OF ANTRIM

Hilly / Intermediate

Map strava.com/routes/22495885

Distance
92 km
(57 mi)

E+
1,150 m
(3,770 ft)

Difficulty
2/5

Appeal
4/5

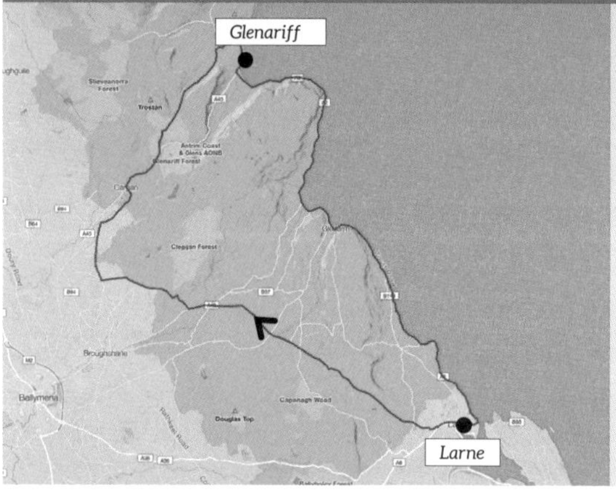

This loop between land and sea, past the volcanic landscape of the Sallagh Braes, and through the stunning glens of Antrim starts and ends in the port of Larne on the coast of the North Channel, close to Belfast (1h45 by train). After 40 km (25 mi) over bare hills at altitudes of between 200 m (6,500 ft) and 350 m (1,150 ft), we descend toward the sea at Cushendall via Glenballyeamon, the sixth of the Nine Glens of Antrim. On the way back to Larne, the coast road passes three others: Glenariffe, Glencoy, and Glenarm. Forest, sheer cliffs, and beaches.

POYNTZPASS

HAUNTED FOREST

Hilly / Advanced

Map strava.com/routes/22772047

Distance
111 km
(69 mi)

E+
1,550 m
(5,080 ft)

Difficulty
3/5

Appeal
4/5

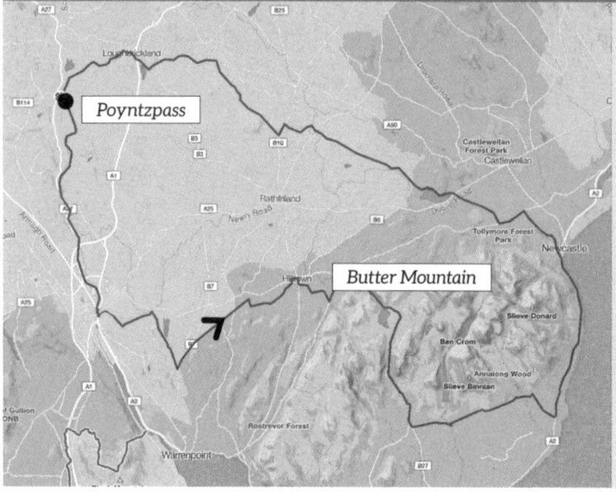

Lovers of *Games of Thrones* will be more than happy with this loop through the Mourne Mountains, starting from the little station of Poyntzpass (2h by train from Belfast or Dublin). The road up Butter Mountain, which juts from the moorland above Tollymore Forest Park (location of the Haunted Forest in Westeros), rises to 407 m (1,335 ft): 6 km (3.5 mi) at 5%. Two more *GoT* locations lie 20 km (12 mi) northeast of the pretty seaside resort of Newcastle (km 70/mi 43): Inch Abbey and, 13 km (8 mi) further on, Ward Castle (Winterfell). They will have to wait for another ride.

PORTRUSH
RIDE OF THRONES

- *Very hilly / Advanced*
- *Map strava.com/routes/22504477*
- *Test yourself km 26 (mi 16) strava.com/segments/4701301*
- *Test yourself km 64 (mi 40) strava.com/segments/827699*

With stunning scenery and remarkable sites, the coast of Northern Ireland is prime cycling territory. Fans of the series *Game of Thrones* will recognize some of them in the course of this 110 km (68 mi) loop.

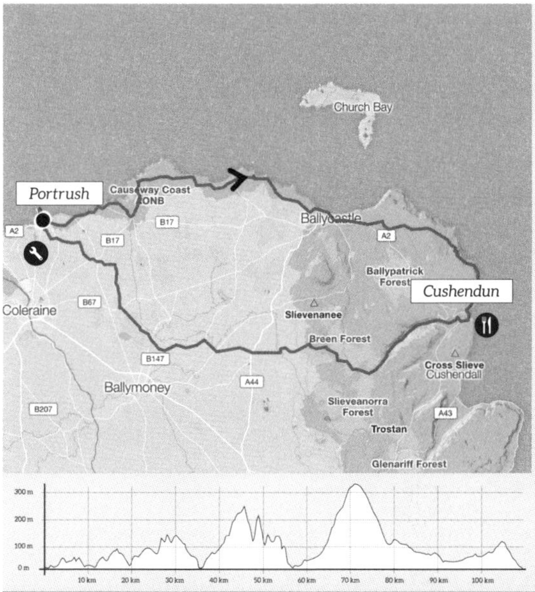

Portrush is the ideal starting point for a trek along the Northern Irish coast and into the hinterland. It only takes 15 km (9 mi) to reach the surreal Giant's Causeway, a volcanic carpet of 40,000 vertical hexagonal basalt columns on the North Channel, the gateway to the Irish Sea. One wonders why the site never appeared in *Game of Thrones*, whose fans love coming to this area to see the locations where much of the TV series was filmed: Ballintoy (km 25/mi 15), Cushendun Caves (km 57/mi 35), the Dark Hedges avenue of beech trees (close to km 87/mi 54), and the beaches of Portstewart and Downhill on the way back. From the magical cliffs of Torr Head (km 46/mi 29), you can contemplate the magical view across to the Mull of Kintyre in Scotland, immortalized by Paul McCartney's song—the melody of which will give you "Wings" as you tackle the long climb after Cushendun (from km 60/mi 37).

Distance	E+	Difficulty	Appeal
110 km (68 mi)	1,550 m (5,080 ft)	3/5	4/5

Portrush (pop. 6,500) is 1h40 by train or 1h by car (80 km/50 mi) from Belfast Airport (to the south). Closer to the west, Derry Airport is 1h25 by train or 50 minutes by car (45 km/28 mi), but it only has domestic flights.

At Cushendun (km 57/mi 35), enjoy coffee and cake at The Corner House, which is owned by the National Trust, the UK environmental and heritage conservation charity.

1 Main Street
Cushendun, Ballymena
nationaltrust.org.uk

Velo Culture (close to km 5/mi 3) is a certified Shimano Center and a retailer of Trek, Cube, and Cervelo brands, among others.

220 Ballybogey Road
Portrush, Co. Antrim
velo-culture.com

WESTPORT
GATEWAY TO CONNEMARA

Hilly / Intermediate
Map strava.com/routes/22508989
Test yourself km 37 (mi 23) strava.com/segments/2075403
Test yourself km 78 (mi 48) strava.com/segments/728978

The infinite landscapes of peatland, lakes, and gently rolling mountains in Connemara on Ireland's Atlantic Coast are beautiful enough to knock you off your bike. Here, they raise Scottish Blackface sheep, which have horns like upside-down handlebars. A good omen.

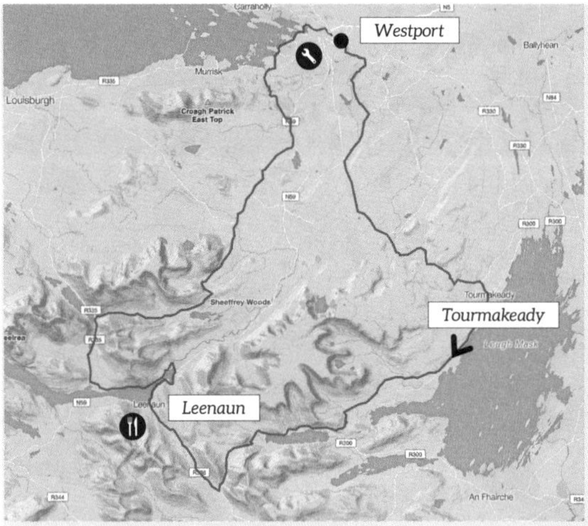

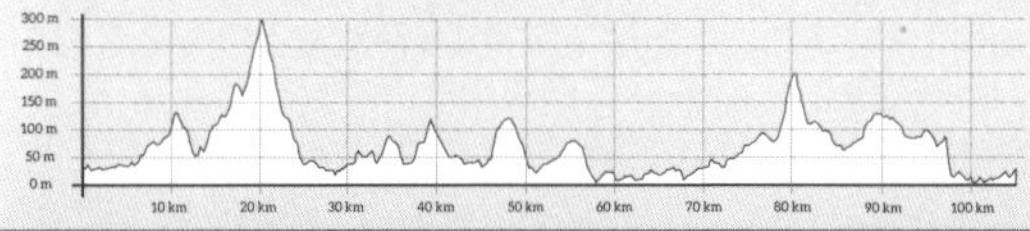

If the little fishing town of Westport is so popular in Ireland, it is not for its Georgian architecture or its ideal location as a base camp for wonderful cycling expeditions. No, it is because of the annual pilgrimage to the nearby mountain of Croagh Patrick. You will relish the warm welcome that the town extends to visitors when you return from this Connemara outing, which will leave you only wanting to return to explore the peninsulas and islands further south. This 105 km (65 mi) introductory loop is spiced up by two climbs that, though short (2 km/1.25 mi), are pretty intense (7% and 6%): Drimcogy at km 20 (mi 12), and Sheeffry Pass at km 78 (mi 48). Between the two, a series of bumps and folds lead to Killary Harbour fjord through moorland gleaming with color. In 1951, John Ford shot *The Quiet Man* in this county of Mayo. Today, it is just as perfect for cycling.

Distance
105 km
(65 mi)

E+
1,350 m
(4,430 ft)

Difficulty
3/5

Appeal
4/5

Westport (pop. 6,000) is 4h by train, but 2h by car (170 km/105 mi) from the international airport at Shannon to the south. To the east, Dublin is 3h by train or 3h20 by car (280 km/175 mi). To the south, Cork is 5h30 by train or 3h20 by car (280 km/175 mi).

The Purple Door Cafe at the eastern end of Killary Harbour fjord (km 57/mi 35) is the perfect point to stop for an Irish breakfast, coffee, donuts, or a freshly baked pie.

Leenaun
co. Galway
the-purple-door-cafe.business.site

Westport has its perfect Bike Shop. It sells Scott, Trek, Cannondale, and Lapierre bikes, and also offers road-bike rentals and indoor sessions when it rains.

Newport Road, Carrowbeg
Westport, Co. Mayo
westportbikeshop.ie

Lough Mask in Connemara, Ireland.

KILLARNEY
FANTASTIC KERRY

Hilly / Intermediate
Map strava.com/routes/22509378
Test yourself km 17 (mi 11) strava.com/segments/1537541
Test yourself km 37 (mi 23) strava.com/segments/685993

Wild, enchanting Kerry—from the lakes of Killarney to the Atlantic coast—is one of the most fascinating regions in Ireland. Before attempting the epic and very touristy Ring of Kerry (179 km/111 mi), try this more modest 60 km (37 mi) loop, which has much to delight you.

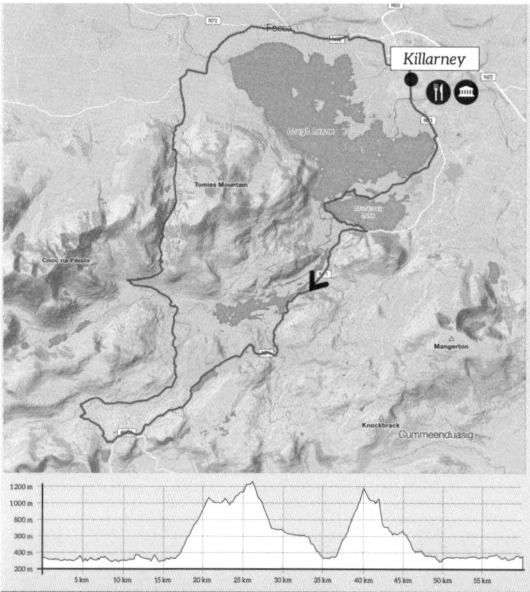

Killarney is Ireland's second city (after Dublin) in terms of visitor accommodation capacity. This is not surprising, as County Kerry's stunning landscape of moorland, expanses of water, and rocky outcrops exerts a real magnetism. From Muckross (km 5/mi 3), you will ride past an exceptional Tudor-style mansion house and a sumptuous fifteenth-century abbey. The nature is overwhelming. The first climb is up to Ladies View (3.5 km/2 mi at 5%), where there is a breathtaking panorama over the Killarney Lakes. The second, of similar style, leads to the Gap of Dunloe, a narrow pass between Tomies Mountain and Carrauntoohil, the highest mountain on the island of Ireland. You will be sorely tempted to have a go at the Ring of Kerry in its entirety (179 km/111 mi) another day via Kenmare, Sneem, Waterville, Cahersiveen, Killorglin, and, if you wish, Valentia Island, the most westerly inhabited place in the British Isles.

Distance	E+	Difficulty	Appeal
60 km (37 mi)	**750 m** (2,460 ft)	**3/5**	**4/5**

Killarney is only 20 minutes by bus (20 km/12 mi) from Kerry Airport, which has connections to Dublin, London, and Berlin. To the north, Shannon Airport is 3h by train or 2h10 by car (140 km/85 mi). To the northeast, Dublin is 3h20 by train or 4h by car. To the east, Cork is 2h by train or 1h20 by car (90 km/55 mi).

Close to the train station, Murphy's is one of the most popular pubs in Killarney, with a wide range of beers. Try its Irish stew or beef in Guinness.

18 College Street
Killarney, Co. Kerry
murphysofkillarney.com

Fitzgerald Stadium (capacity: 38,000) is the mecca of the very popular Irish sport of Gaelic football. The Killarney team, Kerry GAA, is a legend in Ireland.

Upper Lewis Road, Moyeightragh
Killarney, Co. Kerry
kerrygaa.ie

WATERFORD
WITH MR. KELLY

Hilly / Intermediate

Map strava.com/routes/22748229

Distance	E+	Difficulty	Appeal
111 km (69 mi)	1,350 m (4,430 ft)	3/5	4/5

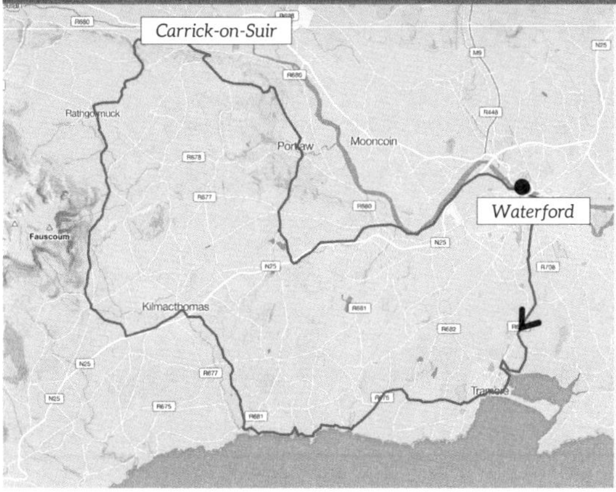

You cannot mention Ireland and cycling in the same breath without a nod to Sean Kelly, a legend of the 1980s. We depart his birthplace of Waterford (3h30 by train from Dublin) for the coast, then the foothills of the Comeragh Mountains and, if you wish, the Mahon Falls near km 50 (mi 30). Carrick-on-Suir is where he won his first race, commemorated by a plaque on Sean Kelly Square. Back in Waterford, the oldest city in Ireland (founded by Vikings in the tenth century), pop into Walsh for a *blaa* (white bread bun) served straight from the oven, filled with cheddar and spiced beef.

DUBLIN
ROCHE AND ROCKS

Very hilly / Advanced

Map strava.com/routes/22528376

Distance	E+	Difficulty	Appeal
141 km (88 mi)	2,100 m (6,890 ft)	4/5	5/5

This loop through the Wicklow Mountains, which rise to nearly 1,000 m (3,280 ft) above Poulaphouca Reservoir, celebrates renowned cyclist and national hero, Stephen Roche. The road up the Wicklow Gap is a 3 km (2 mi) slog at 5%, up to 478 m (1,558 ft). At the bottom of the descent after Glendalough, you can turn left toward the Sally Gap (503 m/1,650 ft). Return to Dublin along the coast, past the affluent resort of Killiney. In Dundrum, pop into Joe Daly, a superb store that was Roche's first sponsor in the late 1970s, before enjoying a pint of Guinness at the Harbourmaster by the waterside, near Connolly Station.

DOLGELLAU
BEWITCHING SNOWDONIA

Very hilly / Advanced
Map strava.com/routes/21472272
Test yourself km 24 (mi 15) strava.com/segments/6866164
Test yourself km 25 (mi 15) strava.com/segments/6670984

Snowdonia National Park in Wales is a cycling paradise. This route explores the southern part of it. The region is a concentration of incredible landscapes with lakes, forests, and glacial valleys. There are challenging climbs and staggering views.

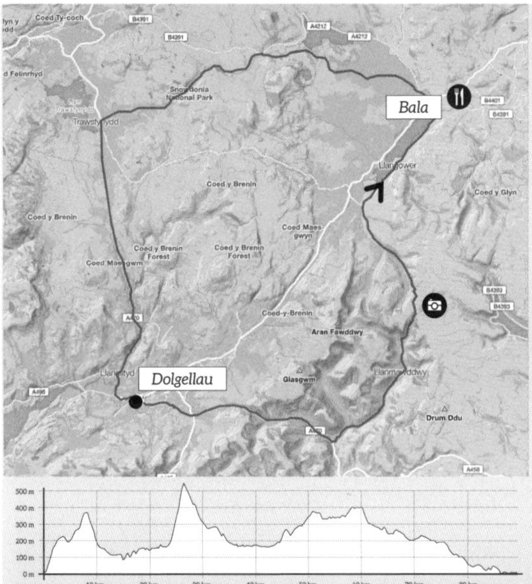

Snowdonia—named for Mount Snowdon, which rises to 1,085 m (3,560 ft)—is wonderful for cycling, with a hundred peaks over 600 m (1,968 ft) and wild natural scenery, as well as beautiful high-mountain flora, including a lily that otherwise is only found in the Alps and the Rockies. Starting in Dolgellau, this demanding route is inspired by the Cambrian Coast Sportive, an annual mass participation event. There is no shortage of climbs, starting with a 2 km (1.25 mi) stretch at an average gradient of 8.5% before the Dinas Mawddwy Pass. At km 26 (mi 16), Bwlch y Groes (also known as Hellfire Pass) is the highest surfaced road in Wales. This brutal climb ascends 360 m (1,180 ft) in less than 3 km (2 mi) at an average gradient of 13.5%, with one particular switchback at 25%. No less bewitching is the ride back via the placid lakes of Tegid and Celyn, around Bala, then the extraordinary Penllyn Forest.

Distance	E+	Difficulty	Appeal
89 km (55 mi)	1,650 m (5,415 ft)	4/5	5/5

Situated 200 km (124 mi) north of Cardiff, Dolgellau is easier to reach from Birmingham: 3h by train + a bus from Machynlleth, or 2h10 by car (160 km/100 mi). From London, allow 6h by train + bus, or 4h30 by car (350 km/217 mi).

If you fancy a coffee, a beer, or even a lobster, pop in to the typically Welsh and very welcoming Plas Yn Dre in Bala (km 43/mi 27).

23 High Street
Bala LL23 7LU
plasyndre.co.uk

Take the time to stop at km 26 (mi 16), at an altitude of 545 m (1,788 ft), and survey the splendid panorama with the Dyfi Valley to the south and the peaks of Cadair Idris (near Dolgellau) and Aran Fawddwy (to the west).

visitmidwales.co.uk

MACHYNLLETH
WELSH WHIRL

- *Hilly / Intermediate*
- *Map strava.com/routes/21987669*
- *Test yourself km 12 (mi 7) strava.com/segments/16406663*
- *Test yourself km 46 (mi 29) strava.com/segments/964374*

The Cambrian Coast Sportive is *the* Welsh cycling event. Riders head out from the seaside town of Tywyn toward Snowdonia National Park. Between the two, a shortish loop from Machynlleth—or "Mach" as it is known around here—provides a glimpse of the magical beauty of North Wales.

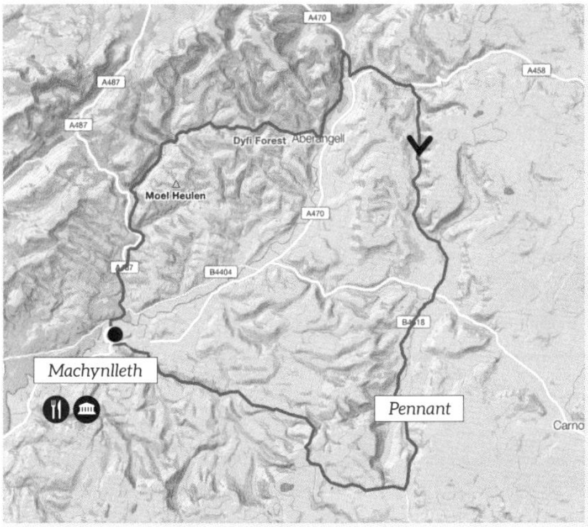

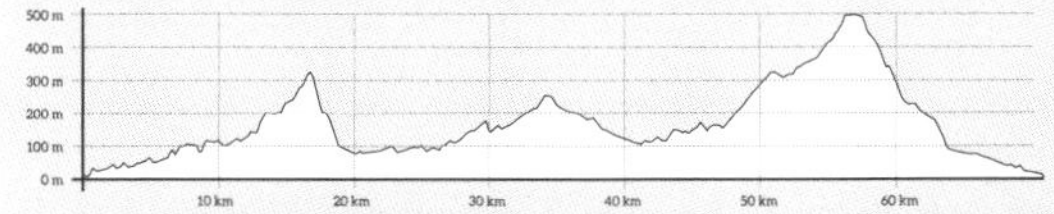

Large village or small town? What is certain is that the two thousand inhabitants of "Mach" breathe free and easy the clean air of the Powys hills as soon as they step outside. Our route heads north past the picturesque cottages of Corris (direction: Snowdonia), although we are happy just to knock at its door with a climb through Dyfi Forest: 5 km (3 mi), with the first and last kilometers at an average gradient of 7%. On the descent, we pick up the course of the River Dyfi again as we ride on toward a more demanding section, with stunning views over a mauve or green landscape, according to season. The Pennant climb—4 km (2.5 mi) long at a gradient of 4%—is but an appetizer for the final ascent of the day, nicknamed "the Mach" by local cyclists: 5 km (3 mi) at 9%, up to an altitude of 500 m (1,640 ft). The plunging descent through the Dylife Gorge is pure ecstasy. A refreshing ride for both mind and body.

Distance	E+	Difficulty	Appeal
69 km (43 mi)	1,400 m (4,595 ft)	3/5	3/5

Machynlleth lies 180 km (112 mi) north of Cardiff. To get there from anywhere in the UK, you pretty much have to go via Birmingham. Allow 2h40 by train, 2h by car (160 km/100 mi). London is 4h by train or car (380 km/236 mi). Cardiff is 5h by train or 2h30 by car.

When you return to "Mach," debrief the ride on the small terrace of Y LLew Coch (The Red Lion, the symbol of Wales) while quaffing a local ale.

11 Heol Maengwyn
Machynlleth, Powys
yllewcoch-mach.com

Like New York City, Machynlleth has its own MoMA, a contemporary art gallery housed in a former chapel. Striking collections and exhibitions.

The Tabernacle, Penrallt Street
Machynlleth SY20 8AJ
moma.machynlleth.org.uk

ABERGAVENNY
THE BLACK MOUNTAINS

Very hilly / Advanced — Map *strava.com/routes/22775348*

Distance	E+	Difficulty	Appeal
95 km (59 mi)	1,800 m (5,905 ft)	4/5	4/5

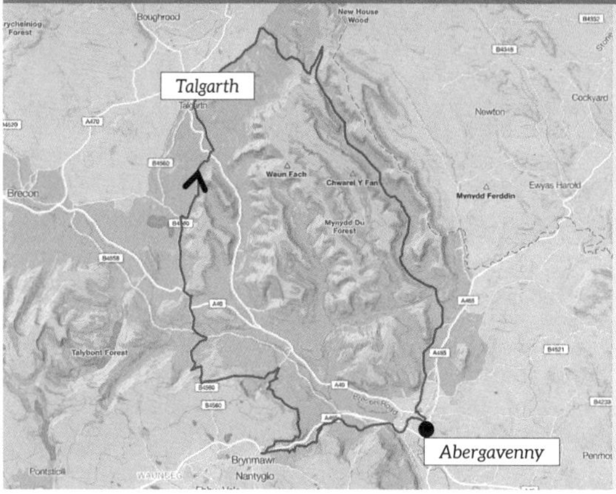

Wales is certainly not flat. The mountains of the Brecon Beacons rise to the north of Cardiff and Newport, whereas the Black Mountains run along the English border. From Abergavenny (40 minutes by train from Cardiff), there is plenty of choice as soon as you leave the Usk Valley after Llangattock, having reached Brynmawr via a cycle path. On the way back, we climb the Gospel Pass (548 m/1,800 ft) between forest, lakes, and peat land—6 km (4 mi) at 7%—passing close to the Black Mountain (703 m/2,308 ft) before a sumptuous descent to Abergavenny via the Honddu Valley.

TYWYN
SOUTH SNOWDONIA

Very hilly / Advanced — Map *strava.com/routes/21986163*

Distance	E+	Difficulty	Appeal
98 km (61 mi)	1,700 m (5,600 ft)	3/5	4/5

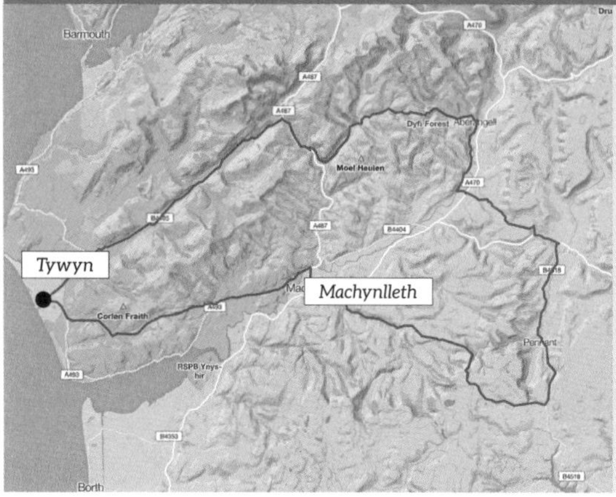

This 95 km (59 mi) loop from the coastal resort of Tywyn, a staging post on the popular Cambrian Coast Sportive, is cycling heaven. We pass through the south of Snowdonia National Park and tackle the long climb up to Cadair Viewpoint, located southeast of Machynlleth, at 500 m (1,640 ft). It is the most difficult ascent on our route: the last 5 km (3 mi) are at 8%. The return via Aberangell leads to the Dyfi Forest wall (km 62/mi 38): 2 km (1.25 mi) at 12%. We ride between lakes, down narrow valleys, through thick forests, and over low mountains with panoramic views aplenty.

BRISTOL
POP CYCLING

- *Hilly / Intermediate*
- *Map strava.com/routes/22147577*
- *Test yourself km 5 (mi 3) strava.com/segments/17423919*
- *Test yourself km 97 (mi 60) strava.com/segments/12473551*

Bristol is an exciting, multicultural city, and the cradle of trip-hop and a host of musicians and artists, including Portishead, Bansky, Massive Attack, and Tricky. The surrounding undulating countryside is perfect for exploring by bike, from Bath down to Somerset via the Severn Estuary.

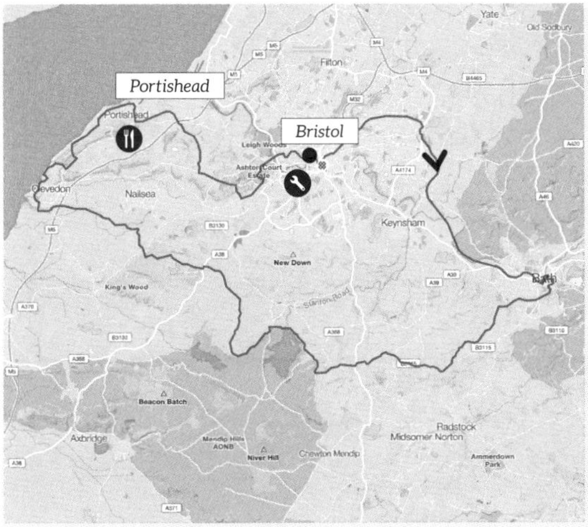

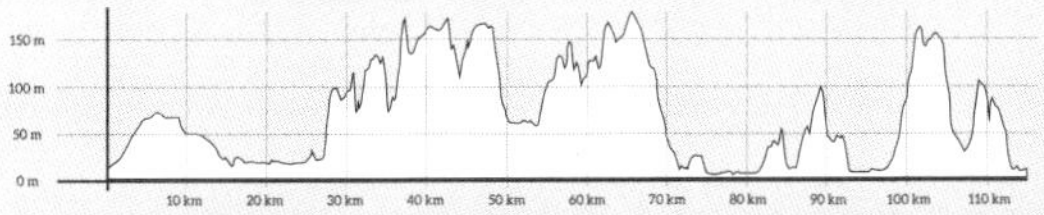

Bristol has a harbor, street art, colorful houses, music, and the audacious Clifton Suspension Bridge, hanging 75 m (245 ft) above the River Avon, over which we will cycle at the end of 115 km (72 mi) of happy pedaling. You can ride all the way to Bath along a thirty-year-old cycle path that is more than 20 km (12.5 mi) long and is laid on a former railway line. There is a taste of the Somerset Hills as you hit the 1 km (0.6 mi) long Priston climb at km 36 (mi 22), with a gradient of 9%. The rolling wooded landscape is beautiful as you pass Clutton, then on to Chew Valley Lake and the airport at km 66 (mi 41). Then, a gentle descent toward the Severn Estuary and Clevedon, with its pier pointing out toward Cardiff. Next is Portishead, which inspired the eponymous band. The final 10 km (6 mi) are not easy: the route climbs after Portbury and toward Ashton Court. More than a ride, a pretty voyage.

Distance	E+	Difficulty	Appeal
115 km (71 mi)	1,400 m (4,595 ft)	3/5	4/5

In high season, Bristol Airport is well served from all over Europe. From there, it is a 20-minute bus journey to the train station. Birmingham is the closest large city: 1h30 by train, 2h by car (160 km/100 mi). London is 1h45 by train (London Paddington) or 3h by car (200 km/125 mi).

Got a bit of an appetite or a big thirst? Stop at the Windmill Inn (km 92/mi 57), where for each pint of Seafarers sold, a few pence are donated to the local lifeboat crew.

58 Nore Rd, Portishead
Bristol BS20 6JZ
thewindmillinn.org

There is no shortage of good specialist bike stores in Bristol. Trek Bicycle Bristol (not far from the university) will not disappoint, offering brands such as Trek, Genesis, and Orbea.

Embassy House, Queen's Avenue
Bristol BS8 1SB
www.trekbikes.com

HAYLE
LAND'S END

Hilly / Intermediate
Map strava.com/routes/22115224
Test yourself km 13 (mi 8) strava.com/segments/1077299
Test yourself km 32 (mi 20) strava.com/segments/3650339

Cornwall boasts one hundred days of sun a year, and a stunning landscape of cliffs, moors, and beaches reminiscent of Mediterranean creeks. Then there is Land's End—the most westerly point of mainland England—where jagged rocks jut out into the Atlantic.

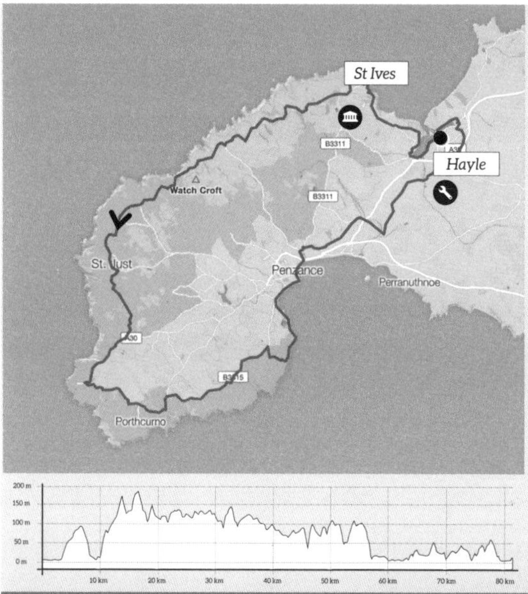

Land's End is very far from everything, jutting out into the vastness of the Atlantic Ocean. The coastline of Cornwall, at England's southwest tip, is constantly exposed to unpredictable weather. What of it? Our route heads westward from Hayle in a loop around the coast with much surprising beauty on the way. The fine sandy beaches are very popular, particularly with surfers. The cliff-top road—150 m (500 ft) above the sea—begins at Saint Ives Bay and offers fabulous views over the ocean, wild moorland, rich wooded countryside, and rolling hills. It even gets pretty steep in places, such as around Penbeagle, St Just (400 m/440 yards at an average gradient of 14%), or Treen. Make sure that you stop to explore the extraordinary limestone promontory of Land's End, close to km 41 (mi 25), and, a little further on, the beach and turquoise waters of Pedn Vounder, a foretaste of the English Riviera.

Distance	E+	Difficulty	Appeal
82 km (51 mi)	1,250 m (4,100 ft)	2/5	3/5

Land's End Airport (km 35/ mi 22) is connected to Bristol, Southampton, and the Isles of Scilly. Hayle (pop. 9,000) is 1h50 by train from Plymouth or 1h40 by car (120 km/75 mi). The train from London (Paddington) takes 5h30; the same by car (500 km/310 mi).

With its glorious bay, Saint Ives has always attracted artists. London's Tate Modern has a fine outpost here, including a cafe with a sea view.

Porthmeor Beach
Saint Ives TR26 1TG
tate.org.uk

Less than 100 meters/yards behind the train station, Hayle Cycles is the go-to bike store and workshop. Merida vendor. Bicycle rental. Purchase/sale of secondhand bikes.

6 Penpol Terrace
Hayle TR27 4BQ
haylecycles.com

PLYMOUTH

MAGICAL DARTMOOR

- *Hilly / Intermediate*
- *Map strava.com/routes/22143943*
- *Test yourself km 15 (mi 9) strava.com/segments/2137090*
- *Test yourself km 31 (mi 19) strava.com/routes/22143943*

The United Kingdom has a surprising range of cycling spots. You would never imagine that the historic naval port of Plymouth would be the starting point for a short but thrilling exploration of the fascinating landscape and enthralling rock formations of Dartmoor.

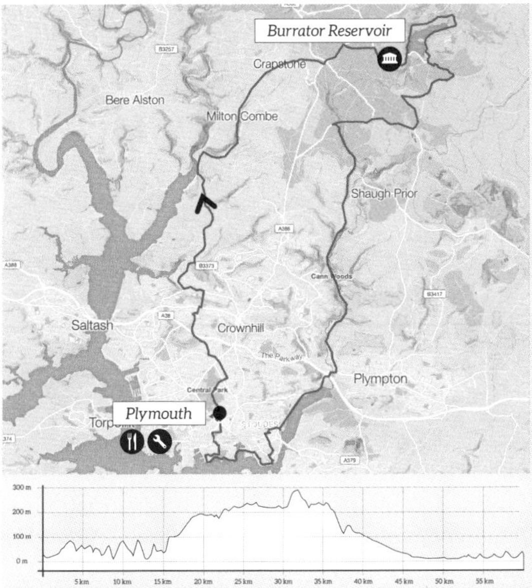

There is plenty to sink your teeth into on the ride north out of Plymouth, starting with five steep little climbs that will get your thighs and lungs burning before you reach the Tamar River. From Milton Combe (km 15/mi 9), there is a long drag up to Yelverton, gateway to Dartmoor National Park, a wild expanse of moorland that is the pride of Devon. After circling Burrator Reservoir, you climb to nearly 300 m (980 ft). You could go much further, through scenery marked by a harsh climate, in search of spectacular rock formations ("tors"), babbling brooks, old stones, ponies, and sheep. This 60 km (37 mi) route provides just a glimpse of Dartmoor's wonder. The return to Plymouth—along the River Plym, of course—passes the memorial to the Mayflower, the old port (Barbican), Plymouth Hoe Park, and wide Armada Way. A day of geography, geology, and history.

Distance	E+	Difficulty	Appeal
59 km (37 mi)	1,050 m (3,445 ft)	2/5	4/5

Exeter Airport is the nearest airport with European connections: 1h30 by train and 1h by car (90 km/55 mi). Southampton is further: 3h by car (250 km/155 mi). Plymouth is 4h by train from London (via Bristol) and 4h by car (360 km/220 mi).

With a slightly crazy atmosphere, Rockets & Rascals (in the Barbican district) is a very welcoming bike cafe, perfect for either a repair or a snack.

7 Parade, Plymouth PL1 2JL
shredordead.uk

Pause for a moment at the dam of Burrator Reservoir (km 24/mi 15), where you will get the most beautiful view of this artificial lake surrounded by thick forest. It's the gateway to Dartmoor. The reflections on the water and the colors are amazing.

facebook.com/burratorreservoir/

FISHBOURNE

SWEET ISLE OF WIGHT

Hilly / Intermediate

Map strava.com/routes/22759177

Distance	E+	Difficulty	Appeal
89 km (55 mi)	1,350 m (4,430 ft)	3/5	4/5

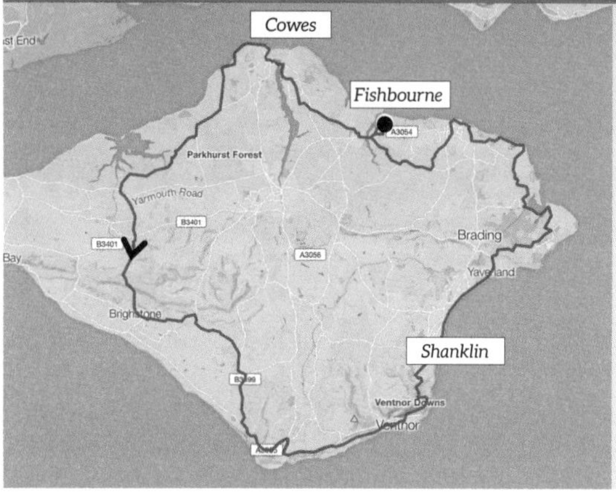

The Isle of Wight presents a staggering contrast in landscape between the north and the south. Having reached Fishbourne by ferry from Portsmouth (45 minutes), we set off west to east. After Osborne House (a former favorite residence of Queen Victoria), it is pleasant Cowes before we cross the River Medina via the chain ferry. The beautiful wooded countryside, dotted with thatched roofs, gives way to the massive cliffs of the south, then the old fishing village of Shanklin. Riding north again, we pass vineyards on our way to Ryde and its pretty beach. Yes, the Isle of Wight is mighty fine to ride.

BRIGHTON

CLIFFS AND THE SOUTH DOWNS

Hilly / Advanced

Map strava.com/routes/22759935

Distance	E+	Difficulty	Appeal
124 km (77 mi)	1,550 m (5,085 ft)	3/5	4/5

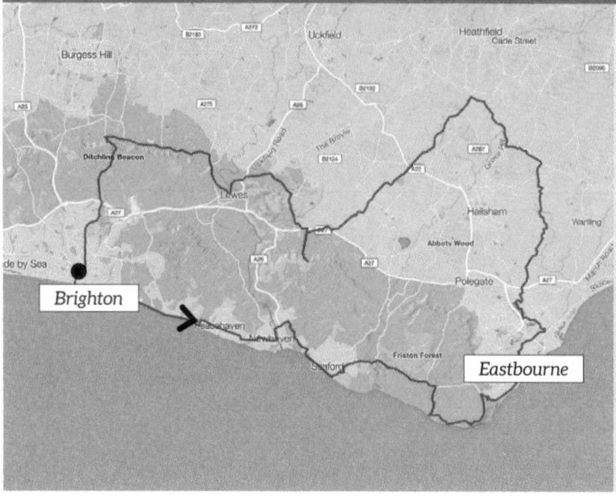

This loop through East Sussex encapsulates the appeal of cycling in England, exploring the Sunshine Coast and the South Downs in a perfect mix of sea and countryside. We ride out from Brighton up the Channel coast past Newhaven, then along the cliffs of Beachy Head with their red-and-white lighthouse and the sublime Seven Sisters, to Eastbourne, where we curve inland. The wall of Firle Beacon (1.5 km/1 mi at 10%) at km 90 (mi 55) and the classic Ditchling Beacon spice things up, not to mention Butts Brow (1 km/0.6 mi at 13%) and Bo Peep Lane, which has passages at 20%.

FRANCE

NORMANDY & BRITTANY

PARIS & LOIRE VALLEY

VOSGES

JURA

THE MASSIF CENTRAL

FRENCH ALPS

PROVENCE & CORSICA

PYRENEES

BOULOGNE-SUR-MER

THE TWO CAPES

Hilly / Intermediate

Map strava.com/routes/16760368

Test yourself km 19 (mi 12) strava.com/segments/14694704

Test yourself km 35 (mi 22) strava.com/segments/1192415

The Hauts de France region contains an unusual maritime environment that you would never believe existed until you saw it for yourself. The Boulogne cliffs are every inch the equal of those of Normandy. When the mist lifts, you can glimpse the white cliffs of Britain.

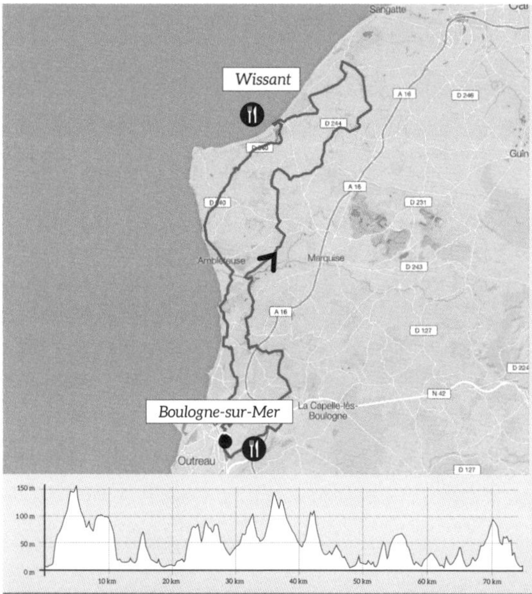

The northernmost part of this route is less than 10 km (6 mi) from the Eurotunnel Calais Terminal. The surroundings give few hints as to the delights in store on the Route des Deux Caps (Blanc Nez and Gris Nez): ever-shifting light, magnificent little valleys, the foam-flecked English Channel, and impressive cliffs. Be warned: It is very up-and-down with 1,300 m (4,265 ft) of elevation gain, and pretty tough when the wind and rain get going. Mont Lambert, just above Boulogne, will already put you in your place: 3 km (2 mi) at an average gradient of 5%. Then we roll toward Calais across the superb wooded countryside. Just before Escalles (km 40/mi 25), the route heads straight for Cap Blanc Nez before veering to follow the coast toward Cap Gris Nez. Enjoy the views and the sections through the resorts of Wissant and Wimereux. Finish with a sprint through Boulogne's upper town.

Distance	E+	Difficulty	Appeal
84 km (52 mi)	1,300 m (4,265 ft)	3/5	4/5

Boulogne-sur-Mer (pop. 42,000) is 2h30 by train from Paris, or 3h by car (280 km/175 mi). Lille is 1h20 by train or 1h40 by car (150 km/93 mi). London (Saint Pancras) is 2h by train via Calais.

In Tardinghen (km 52/mi 32), stop at the Ferme de la Belle Dalle Brewery to sample the artisanal beer "2 Caps."

1453 Route d'Ausques
62179 Tardinghen
2caps.fr

Start or end your ride with a specialty coffee at Kawa Coffee House, which is just a short walk from the fortified old town in the center of Boulogne.

4 Rue des Religieuses Anglaises
62200 Boulogne-sur-Mer
facebook.com/KawaCoffeeHouse

LE HAVRE
ALABASTER CLIFFS

- *Very hilly / Advanced*
- *Map strava.com/routes/17060232*
- *Test yourself km 41 (mi 25) strava.com/segments/3930300*
- *Test yourself km 73 (mi 45) strava.com/segments/19826510*

From the port city of Le Havre to Fécamp via Étretat, Yport, Les Petites Dalles, and Les Grandes Dalles, we follow the cliffs of Upper Normandy, emblems of France's Channel coast. Sea, salt, and sinew.

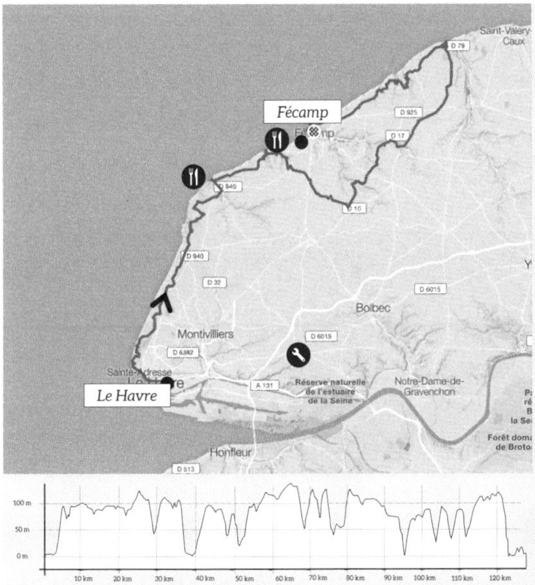

Prepare yourself for a demanding ride. Not only is it long, but the many climbs—short but tough—take their toll. Between the outskirts of Le Havre and the heights of Cap Fagnet—with its superb view over Fécamp and its stony beach, and line of cliffs—there are no fewer than fourteen ramps of at least 800 m (2,620 ft). We start with a couple of switchbacks up to the clifftops above Le Havre at a gradient of 15%. Then it's Octeville, Cauville, and Étretat. Step off the bike to go and see the geological curiosity of the Aiguille Creuse from the cliff at Amont. Then on, via Bénouville and Vaucottes, to the hilly Pays de Caux: Bec de Mortagne, Valmont, and Theuville-aux-Maillots. At Veulettes-sur-Mer, we hit the coast again before heading on to the hidden beaches of Les Petites Dalles, Les Grandes Dalles, and Saint-Pierre-en-Port. You'll have to climb back up, but that's fine; the Alabaster Coast makes you stronger.

Distance	E+	Difficulty	Appeal
128 km (80 mi)	1,350 m (4,450 ft)	3/5	4/5

Le Havre (pop. 170,000) is 2h25 from Paris by train (via Rouen) or 2h30 by car (200 km/125 mi). Lille is 4h by train via Paris (Saint-Lazare) or 3h15 by car (320 km/200 mi). It takes 45 minutes to return to Le Havre from Fécamp (six trains a day). Fécamp to Paris is 2h45 by train via Rouen.

At Étretat (km 39/mi 24), stop for a coffee on the casino terrace. It is worth it for the 180-degree view over the bay and the Aiguille Creuse.

1 Rue Adolphe Boissaye
76790 Étretat
joa.fr

Le Reidroc brasserie on the Fécamp seafront serves good food all day on its terrace. It is the perfect place to unwind after a long ride.

67 Boulevard Albert Ier
76400 Fécamp
restaurant-brasserie-fecamp.fr

ROUEN
THE SEINE BENDS

Hilly / Advanced | Map strava.com/routes/16793781

Distance	E+	Difficulty	Appeal
108 km (67 mi)	1,200 m (3,935 ft)	3/5	4/5

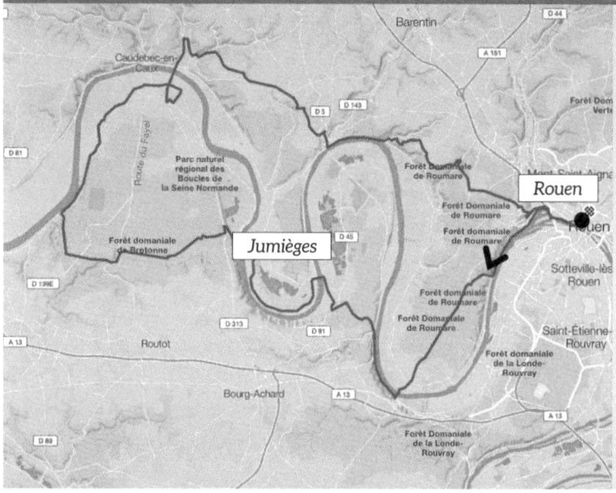

Back in the day, cycling champs used to race a French classic in the Paris area appropriately called the Boucles de la Seine (Seine Bends). We are doing something similar, but to the west of Rouen, 100 km (62 mi) northwest of Paris. Up and down we go, and across the river too: three ferry rides at Sahurs, Yville, and Jumièges. The appeal of this ride is enhanced by the Côte de Dieppedalle, Jumièges Abbey, and the Brotonne and Roumare Forests. Return to the beautiful city of Rouen and its cobbled streets, half-timbered houses, Gros-Horloge, and Guidoline, a bike workshop and cafe.

LA FERTÉ-BERNARD
PERCHE PLEASURES

Hilly / Advanced | Map strava.com/routes/17028613

Distance	E+	Difficulty	Appeal
95 km (59 mi)	1,150 m (3,770 ft)	3/5	4/5

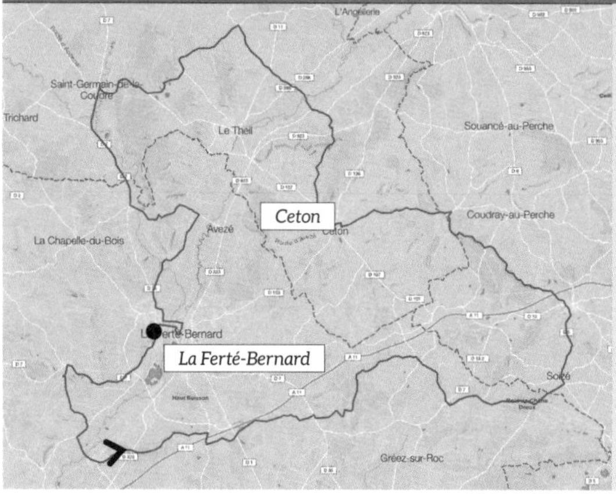

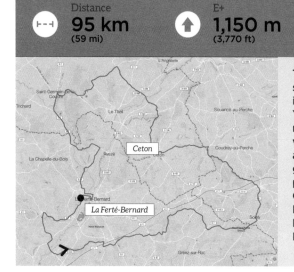

The Perche hills, located 150 km (93 mi) southwest of Paris (1h30 by train), offer some interesting contours on fairly quiet roads. You need to be strategic as you negotiate ridgelines and plateaus exposed to the westerly wind. Many of the numerous ramps are 1.5 km (1 mi) to 2 km (1.25 mi) long at gradients of between 4% and 6%—perfect preparation for a future trip to the mountains. One such is Mont Chauvel (km 22/mi 14). From Authon-du-Perche, we reach the Orne River and the Huisne Valley. Watch out for La Durandière, located 10 km (6 mi) from the end.

SAINT-MALO
REALM OF THE BADGER

- *Very hilly / Advanced*
- *Map strava.com/routes/16810219*
- *Test yourself km 15 (mi 9) strava.com/segments/7267597*
- *Test yourself km 86 (mi 53) strava.com/segments/3585880*

The most easily accessible of Brittany's coasts is a joy to explore. Saint-Malo has the sand of the Emerald Coast, the charm of the ports strung along the Rance estuary, and Dinan old town. If you are lucky, you might even catch a glimpse of The Badger himself—Bernard Hinault—on his bike.

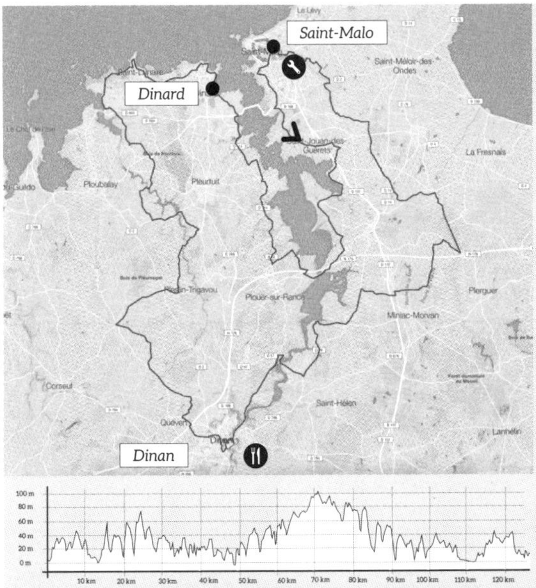

Every two years, Bernard Hinault organizes a merry vintage ride that starts in Dinan, with his family and friends. He calls it the Tour de Rance—a nod to his own victorious record. Our route, a kind of plus-size Tour de Rance, takes in more of the coast. At 130 km (80 mi) long, with 1,500 m (5,000 ft) of elevation gain, we are either climbing or descending as we progress around this triangle formed by Saint-Malo, Saint-Briac-sur-Mer, and Dinan through the wonderful scenery of coastal Ille-et-Vilaine. You can, of course, adapt it to suit your own interests. There is something for everyone in Saint-Malo, our starting point, with its ramparts and marina, chic beaches of the Emerald Coast, medieval streets of Dinan, and the charming Rance estuary, dotted with little ports and secret moorings. This is indeed a champion's realm to be explored in all its glorious detail.

Distance	E+	Difficulty	Appeal
130 km (81 mi)	1,500 m (4,920 ft)	4/5	4/5

Saint-Malo (pop. 46,000) is close to Rennes, the gateway to Brittany: 1h by train, 55 minutes by car (70 km/45 mi). Paris is 3h by train or 4h30 by car (420 km/260 mi). Nantes is 2h20 by train or 2h5 by car (180 km/112 mi).

Alex Hinault Cycles in Saint-Malo is run by the son of Bernard Hinault, who comes to lend a hand in the workshop from time to time.

Avenue de Launay Breton
35400 Saint-Malo
alexhinaultsaintmalocycles.fr

At the far end of Dinan port (km 85/mi 53), Les Rossignols is the perfect spot to recharge your batteries as you sit in a deck chair overlooking the Rance River.

Les Rossignols Taden
22100 Taden
facebook.com/Le-Rossignol-Taden

CHERBOURG
NORMAN IRELAND

Very hilly / Advanced · *Map* strava.com/routes/16798386

Distance	E+	Difficulty	Appeal
103 km (64 mi)	1,566 m (5,140 ft)	3/5	4/5

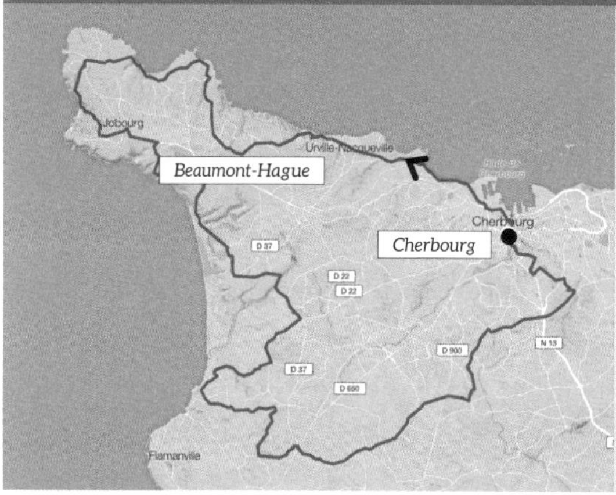

This triangular route on the "nuclear" Cotentin Peninsula (home to Flamanville Nuclear Power Plant, La Hague Nuclear Waste Recycling and Processing Plant, and the Cherbourg Naval Base) might raise some eyebrows, but do not worry. It is quite safe. In fact, the wild natural landscape is stunningly beautiful, like a "mini Ireland." The ride out along the north coast, then down the west side of Cap Cotentin, offers some wonderfully contrasting plays of light. At the coast by Auderville (km 32/mi 20), you can watch one of the most powerful sea currents in the world flow through the Alderney Race.

QUIMPER
THE SOLAR WIND

Hilly / Advanced · *Map* strava.com/routes/16817763

Distance	E+	Difficulty	Appeal
141 km (87 mi)	1,400 m (4,595 ft)	4/5	4/5

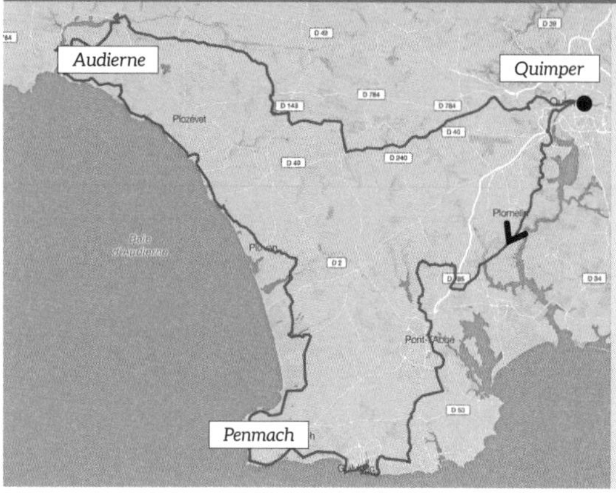

The distance (141 km/87 mi) is long, but we start and end at the nearest train station to the Pays Bigouden: Quimper (2h from Rennes). The charm of this ride to the end of Brittany is well worth the effort. It includes more than 50 km (30 mi) of scenic coastline—from the port of Guilvinec to Audierne Bay through the most beautiful surfing spots in Brittany and down a narrow road with an evocative name, Le Vent Solaire (The Solar Wind). We ride toward the Pointe du Raz, with several bumps around Penhors, Pors-Poulhan, and Mesperleuc. This coast, which faces due west, evokes the beauty of Ireland.

BREST
BRETON ADVENTURE

Hilly / Advanced
Map strava.com/routes/22380003
Test yourself km 25 (mi 16) strava.com/segments/7204106
Test yourself km 118 (mi 73) strava.com/segments/15701734

"Gravel" riding may be having a moment, but the Tro Bro Leon, a race over the rough trails of western Brittany, has been going since the 1980s. These trails are called *ribinoù* in Breton. We tackle them on a route—starting and ending in Brest—that is like a mini Paris-Roubaix.

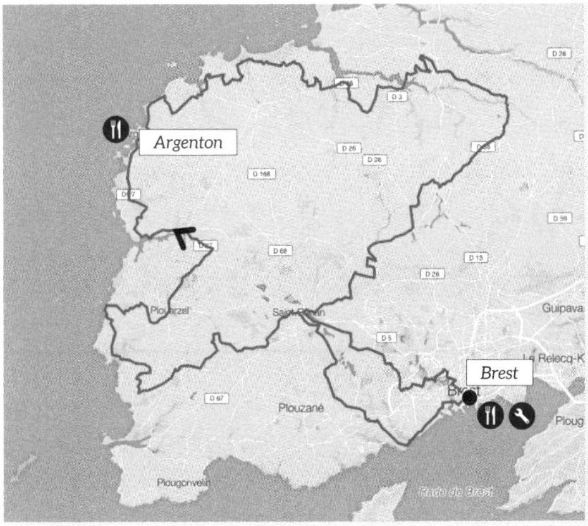

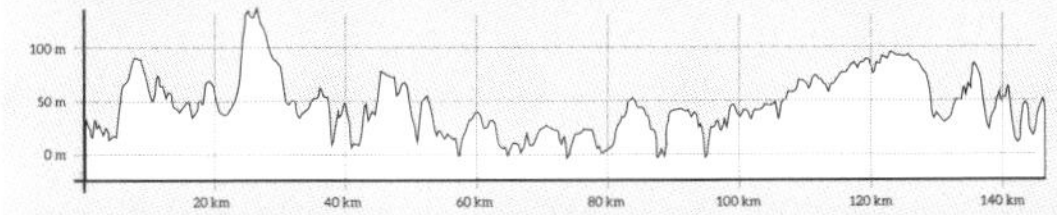

Prepare to be shaken, covered in dust or slathered in mud, and have your cycling skills (and machine) sorely tested, here at the tip of Brittany. The coastal section explores a number of *abers*—long sea inlets, similar to fjords, but without the mountains. Each year, a rather unusual race is held here, the Tro Bro Leon, whose sections of *ribinoù* (trails of earth and crushed stone with a strip of grass down the middle) mirror the cobbled sections of the "Hell of the North." Our route includes a good dozen *ribinoù* from Saint-Renan (km 18/mi 11) to Milizac (km 121/mi 75). The rocky coast of the Atlantic Ocean is a lovely surprise whenever you see it. Aber Ildut and Aber Benoît are beautifully peaceful. You could continue up past Lannilis (epicenter of the Tro Bro Leon) for yet more epic sequences, but the *ribinoù* are quite athletically demanding. A plate of crepes upon arrival will be well earned as is.

Distance	E+	Difficulty	Appeal
147 km (91 mi)	1,450 m (4,750 ft)	3/5	4/5

Brest Bretagne Airport is served by many European destinations in summer. It takes 20 minutes by bus to reach Brest (pop. 140,000). Rennes is 2h by train or 2h30 by car (250 km/155 mi). Paris is 3h50 by train or 6h by car (600 km/370 mi).

Fleur des Thés is an unfussy teashop housed in a former fishing boat in Argenton port (km 65/mi 40). It is the perfect spot for a snack just before the halfway point.

Route de la Cale
29840 Argenton
facebook.com/Fleurdesthes

Raleigh Coffee Bike is a bike cafe and concept store on Brest's Moulin Blanc marina. Éric handles the bikes, and Virginie prepares the coffee and crepes.

280 Rue Alain Colas
29200 Brest
facebook.com/raleighbrest

VANNES
AROUND THE GLITTERING GULF

Fairly flat / Intermediate
Map strava.com/routes/16839389
Test yourself km 51 (mi 32) strava.com/segments/7966227
Test yourself km 58 (mi 36) strava.com/segments/6039904

David Lappartient, president of the Union Cycliste Internationale and mayor of Sarzeau (km 21/ mi 13), will not disagree with us that this loop around the beautiful Gulf of Morbihan is a fantastic idea. Take good note of the boat times and ride a gravel bike if you can.

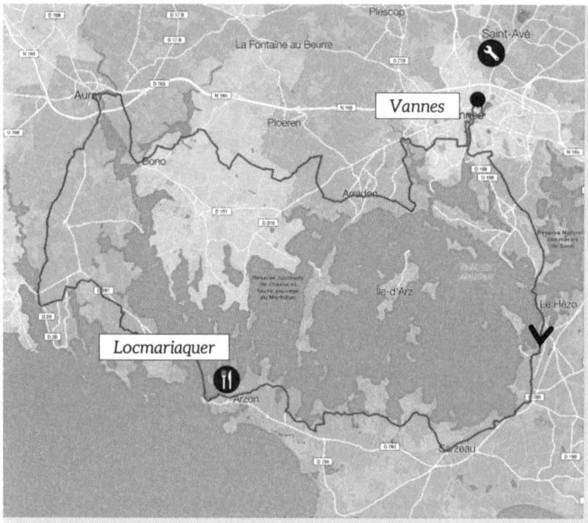

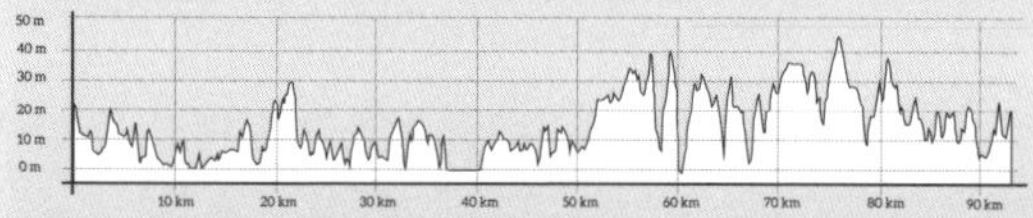

This stunning loop around the Gulf of Morbihan, with its unique light and vistas, should only be attempted from May to October. This has nothing to do with the weather, which defies common preconceptions here on the Côte du Morbihan. Rather, it is just that you will need to use the services of little ferry boats in two places: Montsarrac (km 12/mi 7.5) and Port-Navalo (km 37/mi 23); they are less reliable between November and April. This ride is an absolute delight—from the wildlife reserve of the Marais de Séné to the ramparts of pretty Vannes on the way back, not forgetting the Rhuys Peninsula and the inlets formed by the Auray and Bono rivers. As you glide around a cove, admire the splendor of the Île d'Arz archipelago of nine islands and the Île-aux-Moines. Round off this sublime coastal wander with a few ramps in the Forêt d'Arradon.

Distance	E+	Difficulty	Appeal
93 km (58 mi)	800 m (2,625 ft)	3/5	4/5

Vannes (pop. 55,000) lies equidistant (115 km/71.5 mi) between Rennes and Nantes: 1h20 by car from each, 1h10 by train from Rennes, 1h30 by train from Nantes. Paris is 2h50 by high-speed train or 4h45 by car (460 km/285 mi).

In 2006, Denoël Chedaleux opened his store and workshop Veloland. It is located 2 km (1.25 mi) from Vannes Station. Retailer of Pinarello, BMC, and Focus.

36 Rue Ampère
56890 Saint-Avé
cycles-chedaleux.fr

While you wait for the ferry to Locmariaquer, take a seat on the pretty wooden terrace of Le P'tit Zèph for a coffee, a snack, or even some oysters.

1 Rue du Phare
56640 Arzon
bar-ptitzeph.fr

NANTES
A TASTE OF BRITTANY

Fairly flat / Intermediate *Map* strava.com/routes/16372959

Distance	E+	Difficulty	Appeal
115 km (72 mi)	600 m (1,970 ft)	2/5	3/5

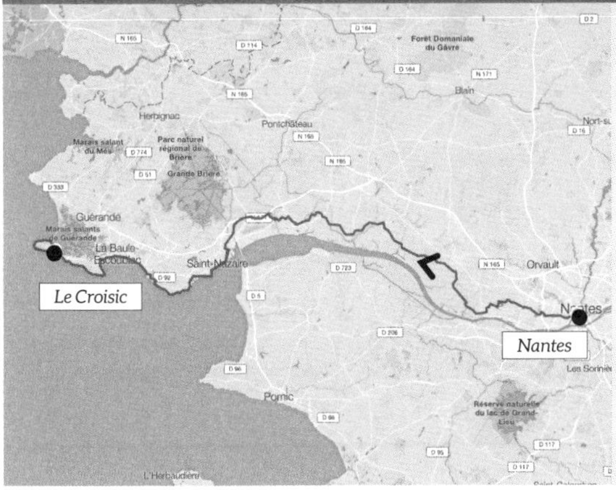

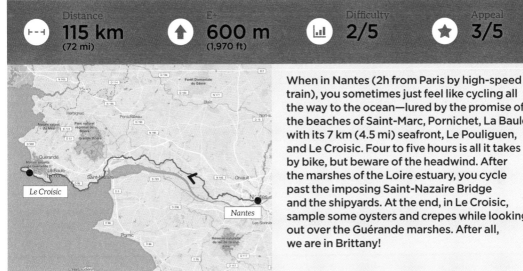

When in Nantes (2h from Paris by high-speed train), you sometimes just feel like cycling all the way to the ocean—lured by the promise of the beaches of Saint-Marc, Pornichet, La Baule with its 7 km (4.5 mi) seafront, Le Pouliguen, and Le Croisic. Four to five hours is all it takes by bike, but beware of the headwind. After the marshes of the Loire estuary, you cycle past the imposing Saint-Nazaire Bridge and the shipyards. At the end, in Le Croisic, sample some oysters and crepes while looking out over the Guérande marshes. After all, we are in Brittany!

LA ROCHELLE
IMMERSION IN RÉ

Fairly flat / Intermediate *Map* strava.com/routes/16876890

Distance	E+	Difficulty	Appeal
100 km (62 mi)	150 m (500 ft)	2/5	4/5

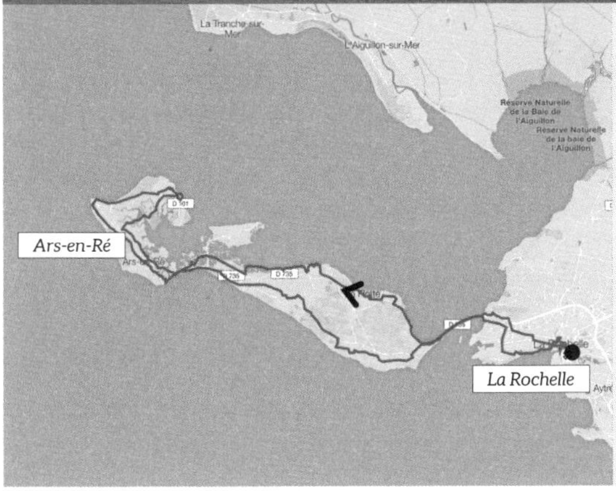

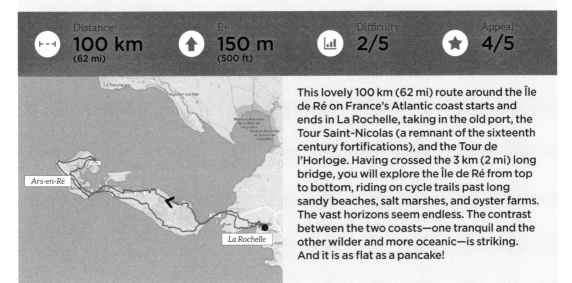

This lovely 100 km (62 mi) route around the Île de Ré on France's Atlantic coast starts and ends in La Rochelle, taking in the old port, the Tour Saint-Nicolas (a remnant of the sixteenth century fortifications), and the Tour de l'Horloge. Having crossed the 3 km (2 mi) long bridge, you will explore the Île de Ré from top to bottom, riding on cycle trails past long sandy beaches, salt marshes, and oyster farms. The vast horizons seem endless. The contrast between the two coasts—one tranquil and the other wilder and more oceanic—is striking. And it is as flat as a pancake!

CHÂTEAUROUX
THE BRENNE PONDS

- *Fairly flat / Intermediate*
- *Map strava.com/routes/22601039*
- *Test yourself km 45 (mi 28) strava.com/segments/7173282*
- *Test yourself km 57 (mi 35) strava.com/segments/11342335*

This is a beautiful route through the middle of France, between Champagne Berrichonne, the Creuse Valley, and Brenne Natural Regional Park. Take advantage of the quiet and relatively flat roads to ramp up the speed.

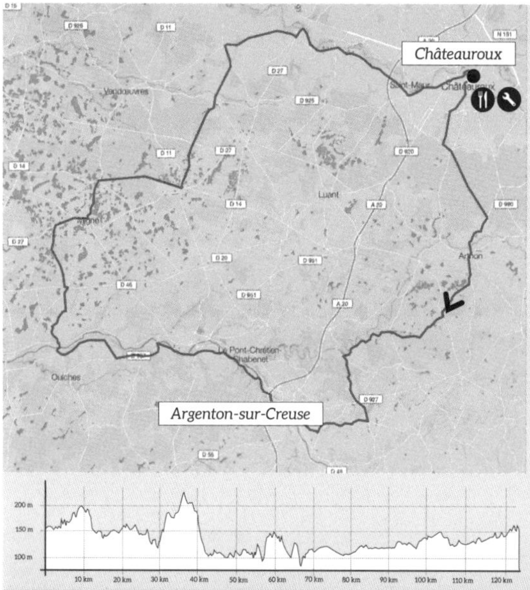

Châteauroux (birthplace of the actor Gérard Depardieu), the valleys of the Bouzanne and the Creuse, and the numerous ponds of Brenne. The air is fresh and clean here in the fairly flat center of France: less than 1,000 m (3,280 ft) of elevation gain in the course of a good 120 km (75 mi). The highest point is 220 m (722 ft) at the Argenton-sur-Creuse Airfield. You should be able to maintain a fairly fast average speed as long as the wind is not blowing too hard from the northwest as you cycle back up through the Brenne Natural Regional Park. In the twelfth century, the monks began to drain and manage the marshes here, forming a web of ponds and lakes (nearly 3,300 at the last count). Our route crosses woods, moors, meadows, and stretches of gorse, broom, and water lilies. At km 43 (mi 27), we pass through the pretty Venice-like Argenton-sur-Creuse before the pleasant Thenay-Le Blanc greenway.

Distance	E+	Difficulty	Appeal
124 km (77 mi)	900 m (2,950 ft)	2/5	3/5

Châteauroux (pop. 44,000) is 2h20 from Paris by train or 3h by car (280 km/175 mi). Bordeaux is 5h by train (via Tours) or 4h by car (330 km/205 mi). Nantes is 5h by train (via Vierzon) or 3h40 by car (320 km/200 mi).

Produits de saison et locaux pour le sucré comme le salé, l'enseigne Castel Praliné s'est installée à Châteauroux récemment. Le lieu où reprendre des forces après ce long ride.

121 Grande rue
36000 Châteauroux
castelpraline.com

Charmante cité de 5 000 habitants, Argenton-sur-Creuse (km 44 / mi 27) est surnommée la « Venise du Berry ». Elle vit au rythme de sa rivière entre ruelles d'autrefois, vieux moulins à roue, maisons à galeries de bois...

berryprovince.com

PARIS
GOOD OLE CHEVREUSE

- *Quite hilly / Intermediate*
- *Map strava.com/routes/16200126*
- *Test yourself km 42 (mi 26) strava.com/segments/4601466*
- *Test yourself km 50 (mi 31) strava.com/segments/810063*

The Vallée de Chevreuse has long been a firm favorite of Paris cyclists in search of greenery and fresh air, as well as featuring in the Grand Prix des Nations, Bordeaux-Paris, and the final time trial of the Tour de France.

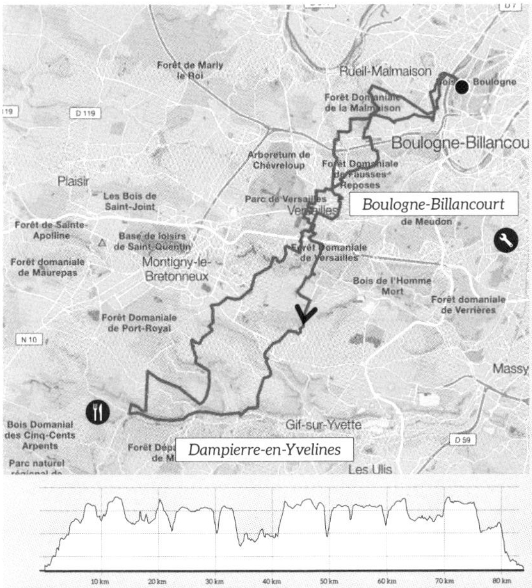

The Vallée de Chevreuse is a must for any Paris cyclist, particularly those living in the west of the capital. You will rarely find yourself alone when out for a ride. It has also played a key role in competitive cycling (the valley is peppered with tough little climbs), although encroaching urbanization has put a stop to much of that. Longchamp Racecourse (Bois de Boulogne) is the perfect starting point, followed by the climb to Saint-Cloud, then Haras Lupin, Château de Versailles, and the Buc Aqueduct. Swing round Toussus-le-Noble Airport and descend into the valley via Châteaufort—not forgetting to salute the stele to Jacques Anquetil, who forged his victories in the Grand Prix des Nations here. The climbs of Magny-les-Hameaux (1 km/0.6 mi long), 17 Tournants (1.3 km/0.8 mi long), and Romainville (1 km/0.6 mi long) are no mountains, but they do have gradients of around 6%.

Distance	E+	Difficulty	Appeal
84 km (52 mi)	900 m (3,000)	3/5	4/5

Paris is obviously very well connected internationally via its main airports of Charles de Gaulle (north) and Orly (south). High-speed trains run from London, Amsterdam, Brussels, Cologne, Lausanne, Geneva, Milan, and all major French cities.

On the city's edge, at Paris Bike Company, Sam, an American Francophile cyclist, rents out carbon-fiber bikes and leads tours through the Vallée de Chevreuse.

29 Rue Victor Hugo
92240 Malakoff
parisbikeco.com

At the foot of the 17 Tournants climb (km 41/mi 25), Le P'tit Chalet is ideal for a quick espresso or a crepe break. Its terrace can seat a whole peloton.

8 Grande Rue
78720 Dampierre-en-Yvelines
facebook.com /Le-Ptit-Chalet-Dampierre-en-Yvelines

PARIS
CITY OF LOVE

Fairly flat / Intermediate

Map strava.com/routes/16178394

Distance **61 km** (38 mi)

E+ **350 m** (1,150 ft)

Difficulty **2/5**

Appeal **3/5**

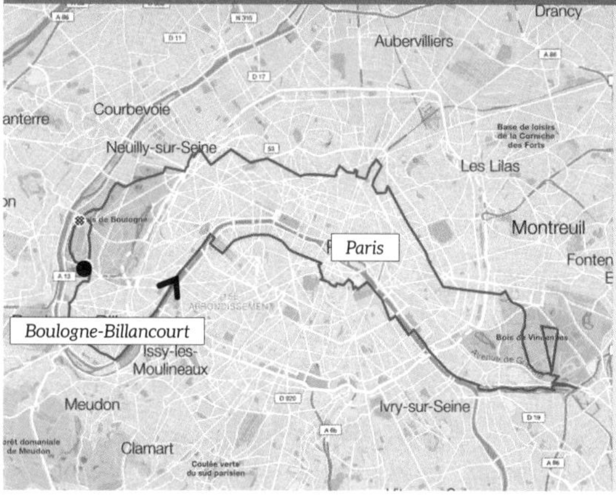

Although visiting cyclists will enjoy discovering the capital's two traditional training circuits of Longchamp and the Polygone at opposite ends of the city, it is well worth cycling around Paris itself, which recently renovated its network of cycle paths. This route from the Bois de Boulogne to the Bois de Vincennes and back passes along the Seine and close to the Eiffel Tower and Saint-Germain-des-Prés. It also takes in the Place de la Nation and the Canal Saint-Martin. You can veer off and climb Belleville and Montmartre, explore the cycle paths from Bastille to the Arc de Triomphe, and travel from Nation to Saint-Lazare.

PARIS
COLORFUL GIVERNY

Hilly / Intermediate

Map strava.com/routes/16201613

Distance **94 km** (58 mi)

E+ **950 m** (3,115 ft)

Difficulty **3/5**

Appeal **4/5**

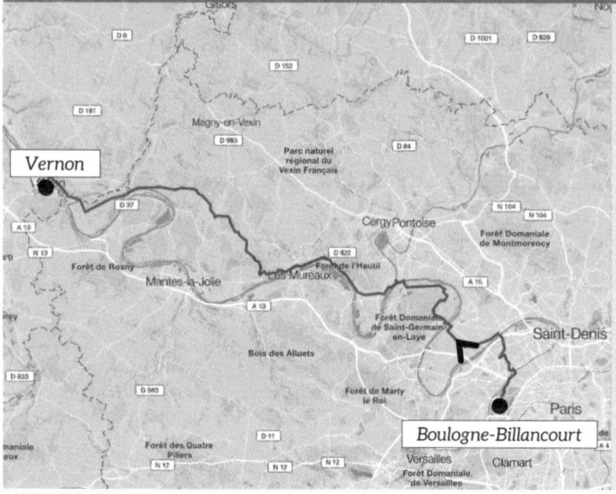

This route roughly follows the meanders of the Seine from Paris to Vernon (Normandy) by way of the gorgeous Vexin Plateau. It is a contemplative, pretty 100 km (60 mi) ride with rolling contours to the house and garden of the Impressionist painter Claude Monet. We start by crossing a series of bridges over the Seine: Courbevoie, Colombes, Sartrouville, and Conflans. At Andrésy, we enter the Vexin, which is as beautiful as a Monet painting with lovely light. The ridgeline of the limestone Coteaux de la Seine leads us to Giverny and Vernon. Return to Paris by train in 1h30.

ÉPERNAY
TOTAL CHAMPAGNE

- *Very hilly / Advanced*
- *Map strava.com/routes/16982747*
- *Test yourself km 105 (mi 65) strava.com/segments/822532*
- *Test yourself km 115 (mi 71) strava.com/segments/1397380*

This is a sublime yet testing route through the most sparkling of French vineyards. Starting and ending in Épernay, it is a full day's ride. To unwind afterward, we suggest a visit to Castelnau Champagne, official supplier of the Tour de France, in Reims.

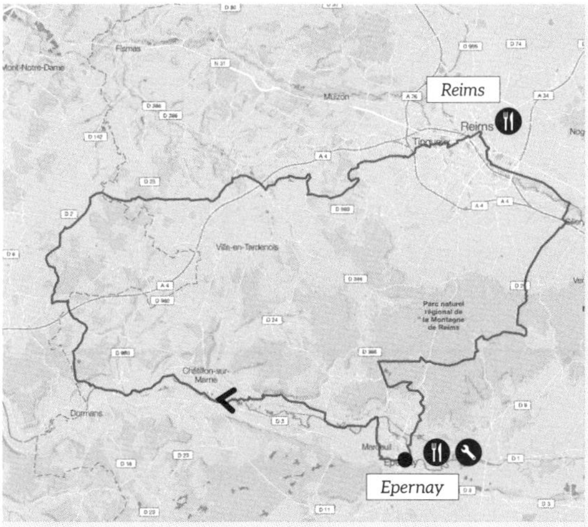

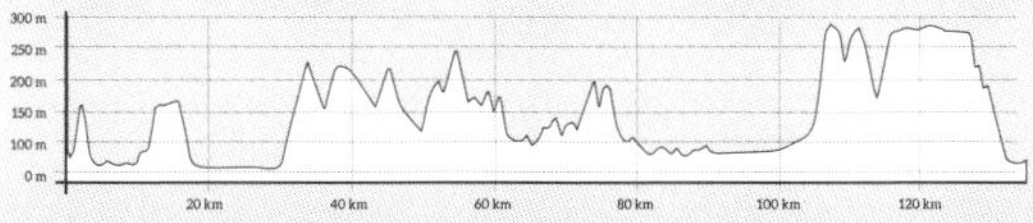

Whether you complete this long and difficult route in one or two stages, or even shortened (via the D24 at km 21/mi 13 and the D951 at km 91/mi 57), the champagne will be richly deserved. We set out from Épernay for 135 km (84 mi) in the saddle, with a total elevation gain of 1,600 m (5,250 ft). At km 30 (mi 19), we leave the Marne river and begin to climb one hill after another: Vincelles, Champvoisy, Cierges, Coulonges-Cohan, and, a little further on, Coulommes-la-Montagne, as we head for Reims and its magnificent cathedral. We leave the city on a greenway beside the Canal de l'Aisne à la Marne before turning off toward the Montagne de Reims (max. altitude: 282 m/925 ft). The Ville-en-Selve climb is tricky, as is the section after Germaine: 2 km (1.25 mi) at a gradient of 7% to 8%. But the oak forest is very pleasant indeed. On the long descent, there are superb views over the Marne Valley. Cheers!

Distance	E+	Difficulty	Appeal
135 km (84 mi)	1,600 m (5,249 ft)	4/5	4/5

Épernay (pop. 23,000) is 1h20 from Paris by train (via TGV Reims) or 1h45 by car (150 km/95 mi). Strasbourg is 2h30 by train (via Reims too) or 3h40 by car. Lille is 2h30 by car (230 km/145 mi), or 3h by train via Paris. Reims is 40 minutes by train from Épernay.

Stop at L'Opéra patisserie, close to Reims cathedral at km 88 (mi 55), for a sugar hit before tackling the "Montagne." Champagne brunch on Sundays!

4 Cours Jean-Baptiste Langlet
51100 Reims
patisserie-lopera.com

L'Alternative du Cycle, in Épernay, is a uniquely beautiful bike cafe. Excellent coffee. Retailer of Scott bikes.

49 Rue Henri Martin
51200 Épernay
lalternativeducycle.com

VALENCIENNES
COBBLED HELL

Hilly / Advanced
Map strava.com/routes/16318916

Test yourself km 13 (mi 8) strava.com/segments/7006059
Test yourself km 92 (mi 57) strava.com/segments/7010133

You will be shaken like never before. Hands blistered, backside on fire. Riding the cobbled sections of the "Hell of the North" is a unique experience: exhilarating, excruciating, enriching, and exhausting. Every cyclist should attempt it at least once.

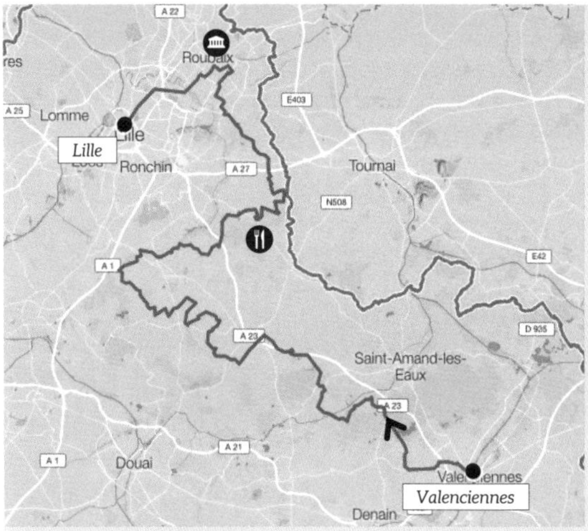

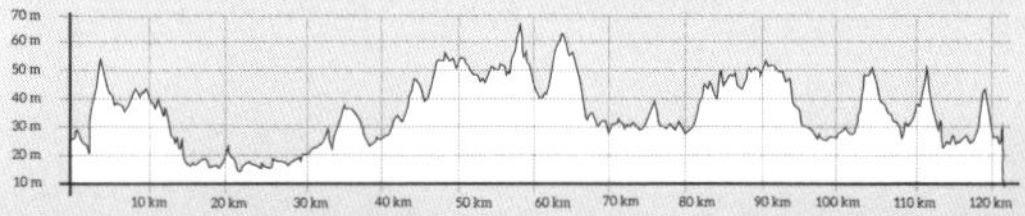

Admit that you've thought about it: hurling yourself into the magma of the Trench of Arenberg, or hitting the Bersée sector full gas, as you play at being a Paris–Roubaix champion. Well, it is possible, but do not kid yourself that you will simply be rolling for 120 km (75 mi) from Valenciennes to Lille (return by train, running every 30 minutes). Until your front wheel strikes the first cobblestone, you will have only the faintest idea of how rough and irregular the cobbled stretches of the Hell of the North truly are. The trick is to hit each section at no less than 35 km/h (22 mph) and then maintain your speed for as long as possible. The apocalyptic Arenberg (2.3 km/1.4 mi long) starts at km 12 (mi 7.5), followed by Sars-et-Rosières, Bersée, Mons-en-Pévèle, Ennevelin, Templeuve, Cysoing, and Camphin-en-Pévèle. If the Roubaix Velodrome (km 107/mi 66) is open, pop in for a quick lap.

Distance	E+	Difficulty	Appeal
121 km (75 mi)	350 m (1,150 ft)	4/5	5/5

Valenciennes (pop. 45,000) lies 50 km (31 mi) southeast of Lille—40 minutes by car and 55 minutes by train (running every 30 minutes). Paris is 2h15 by high-speed train via Lille, and the same by car (210 km/130 mi).

Fuel up with a pear and chocolate tart at the Patrick Alvin Bakery (km 82/mi 51) just before the Duclos-Lassalle sector.

62 Avenue René Ladreyt
59830 Cysoing
facebook.com/Boulangerie-Pâtisserie-Patrick-Alvin

Complete your visit to Lille with an introductory session on the track of the new Jean-Stablinksi Indoor Velodrome next to the outdoor one at the Parc des Sports.

59 Rue Alexandre Fleming
59100 Roubaix
stabvelodromeroubaix.fr

The cobbled way of
the Trench of Arenberg, France

LURE
LES BELLES FILLES

- *Low mountain / Advanced*
- *Map strava.com/routes/16909511*
- *Test yourself km 55 (mi 34) strava.com/segments/1777201*
- *Test yourself km 75 (mi 46) strava.com/segments/1539752*

This route on the edge of the Vosges takes us up to La Planche des Belles Filles, a star climb of contemporary Tours de France. It was recommended by the champion Thibaut Pinot, 018 Giro di Lombardia winner, who lives in Mélisey (km 13/mi 8). strava.com/pros/1603067

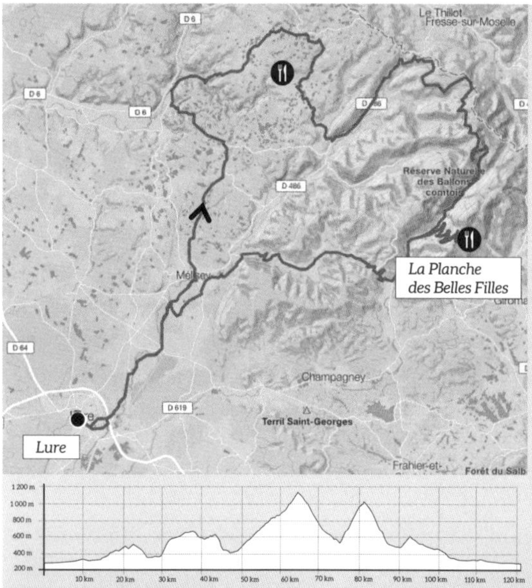

The Tour de France recently featured the sublime landscape of the Plateau des 1000 Étangs and the Ballons Comtois nature reserve, but Thibaut Pinot is fortunate enough to have the enchanting setting of the Vosges Saônoises as his regular training area. Thibaut's route takes us from his village of Mélisey to the hidden splendors of the Haute-Saône. The first 47 km (30 mi), as far as Servance, take us through the perfectly tranquil landscape of the "1,000 Ponds,". We then enter a forested area on the way to the Ballon de Servance: the final 2 km (1.25 mi) are at a gradient of 8%. Then comes the test of La Planche des Belles Filles, which has had a starring role in the Tour de France since 2012: 5.5 km (3.5 mi) at an average gradient of 8%, with sections at 14% and 12%. The final kilometer (0.6 mi) is terrifying. Return via the little Col de la Chevestraye.

Distance	E+	Difficulty	Appeal
121 km (75 mi)	2,200 m (7,200 ft)	5/5	5/5

Lure (pop. 8,000) is 3h45 from Paris by train or 4h30 by car (400 km/250 mi). Strasbourg is 2h15 by train via Mulhouse or 2h by car (200 km/125 mi). Basel (Switzerland) is 2h by train via Mulhouse or 1h20 by car (120 km/75 mi).

It is a long ride, so turn left at km 42 (mi 26) and head to the Auberge des 1000 Étangs for some fresh local produce, including frogs, crawfish, and eels.

Goutte Géhant
70440 Servance
aubergedesmilleetangs.fr

After so much effort, it would be a shame not to enjoy a slice of blueberry tart at the mountaintop Resto de La Planche des Belles Filles (km 81/mi 50).

Station de la Planche des Belles Filles
70290 Plancher-les-Mines
resto-pdbf.fr

STRASBOURG
ALSACE WINE ROUTE

- *Low mountain / Intermediate*
- *Map strava.com/routes/16387259*
- *Test yourself km 16 (mi 10) strava.com/segments/7087244*
- *Test yourself km 46 (mi 28) strava.com/segments/7374245*

The Alsace Wine Route, close to the German border, is a classic French tourist destination. It is also a magnificent (and not very challenging) cycling route from Strasbourg to Colmar, returning by train. Leave the winery tours for another time.

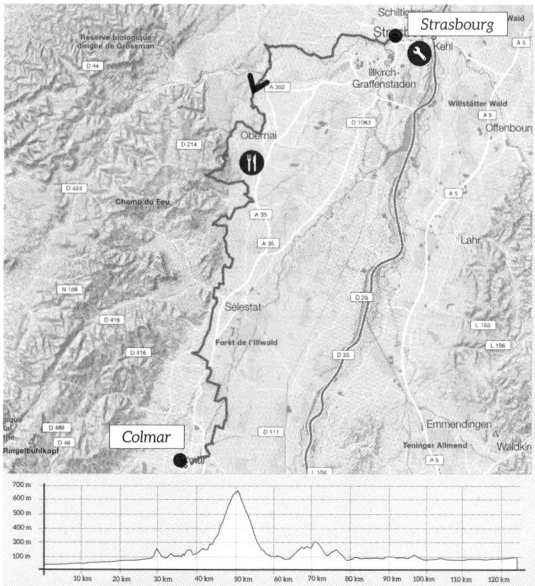

Grand cru, late harvest, biodynamic: the terminology is enough to make your head spin before you even start pedaling. This 123 km (77 mi) route from Strasbourg to Colmar along the magnificent Route des Vins d'Alsace has only one real difficulty in the middle. From km 25 (mi 15.5), the route skirts the Vosges mountains without leaving the vineyards, except for the wooded slopes of Mont Sainte-Odile. The foot of the climb at km 46 (mi 29) requires some effort, with 2.5 km (1.5 mi) at a gradient of 8%. The 6 km (4 mi) that follow, up to 761 m (2,497 ft), are easier. At km 100 (mi 62), you will pass close to two villages that are closely associated with the history of Alsatian winemaking: Ribeauvillé and Riquewihr. Apart from the luscious vineyards, you will appreciate the sumptuous hills, the half-timbered houses blooming with flowers, and the magical light of this striking and beautiful part of Alsace.

Distance	E+	Difficulty	Appeal
123 km (76 mi)	1,260 m (4,130 ft)	3/5	5/5

Strasbourg is 1h45 from Paris by high-speed train, 3h by regular train, or 5h by car (500 km/310 mi). Munich is 4h30 by train via Stuttgart, or 4h30 by car (380 km/236 mi). To the south, Zurich is 2h30 by train (via Basel) or by car (220 km/137 mi).

Savory or sweet? Pretzel or cake? After Mont Sainte-Odile, take a welcome break at Pâtisserie Le Piémont in Barr (km 58/mi 36).

32 Grande-rue
67140 Barr
lepiemont.fr

Like most bike stores in Strasbourg, Bike Avenue is more focused on urban mobility. Repairs and service available.

33 Avenue des Vosges
67000 Strasbourg
cycl-ollier-veloplus-bike-avenue.fr

MONTBARD
LAND OF THE GAULS

Hilly / Advanced *Map* strava.com/routes/17099514

Distance	E+	Difficulty	Appeal
105 km (65 mi)	1,600 m (5,250 ft)	3/5	4/5

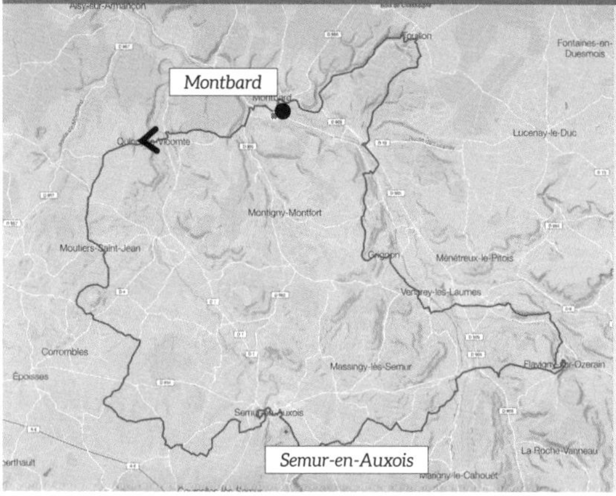

This 105 km (65 mi) route through the Auxois valleys and along the Canal de Bourgogne is packed with many sites of historical and archaeological significance, and visual stimulation galore. The varied terrain suits a range of cycling styles. After the climb to Alise-Sainte-Reine (km 70/mi 44), we reach the site of the Battle of Alesia (52 BC), a major engagement in the Gallic Wars. Before that, we pass by Époisses (famous for its cheese and castle) and through medieval Semur, while the final stretch takes in the Cistercian Fontenay Abbey. You will not be bored.

THANN
THE BALLON D'ALSACE

Low mountain / Advanced *Map* strava.com/routes/16705843

Distance	E+	Difficulty	Appeal
91 km (56 mi)	1,850 m (6,100 ft)	4/5	4/5

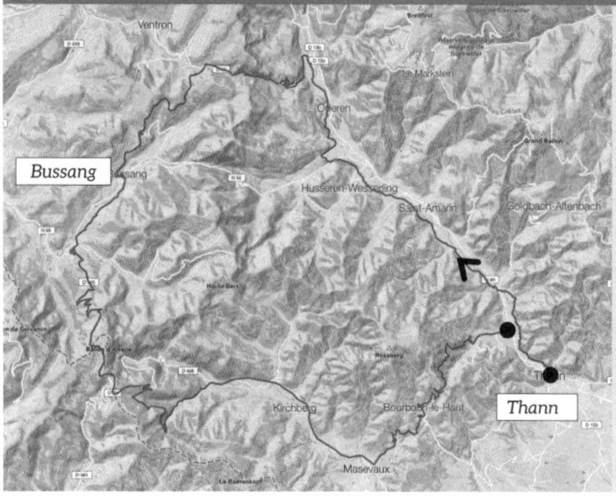

The noble Ballon d'Alsace, the most venerable mountain climb in France, begins in Saint-Maurice-sur-Moselle (km 42/mi 26): 8 km (5 mi) at a fairly regular gradient of around 6% on a beautiful road surface, with the final kilometer (0.6 mi) at 8%. There are higher summits in the Vosges, but the Ballon d'Alsace remains *the* emblematic climb. From the top, there are views as far as the eye can see. Most important, it was the first-ever official mountain climb in the Tour de France in 1905. The Col d'Oderen and the Col du Hundsruck add some spice to this Vosgian escapade.

MÂCON
GRAPES AND GRADIENTS

Very hilly / Advanced   Map strava.com/routes/17053374

Distance	E+	Difficulty	Appeal
135 km (84 mi)	1,900 m (6,230 ft)	5/5	4/5

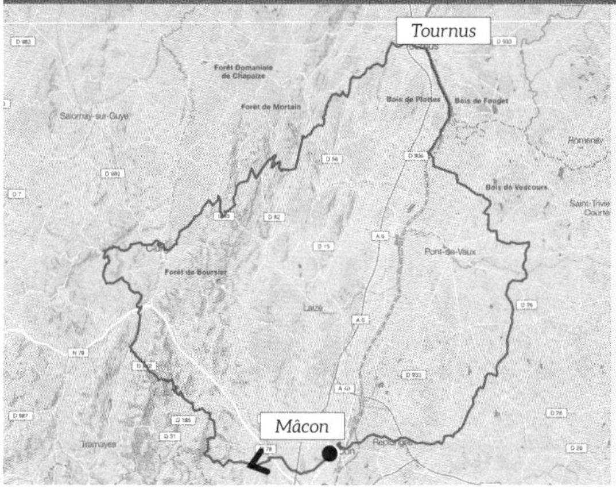

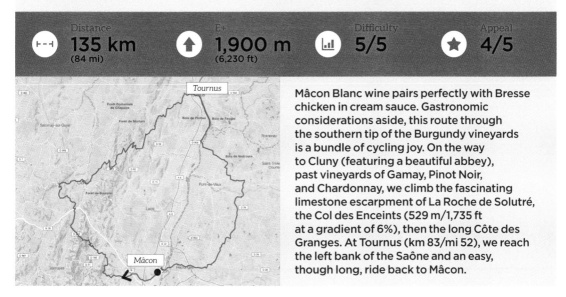

Mâcon Blanc wine pairs perfectly with Bresse chicken in cream sauce. Gastronomic considerations aside, this route through the southern tip of the Burgundy vineyards is a bundle of cycling joy. On the way to Cluny (featuring a beautiful abbey), past vineyards of Gamay, Pinot Noir, and Chardonnay, we climb the fascinating limestone escarpment of La Roche de Solutré, the Col des Enceints (529 m/1,735 ft at a gradient of 6%), then the long Côte des Granges. At Tournus (km 83/mi 52), we reach the left bank of the Saône and an easy, though long, ride back to Mâcon.

BELLEGARDE-SUR-VALSERINE
THE LORD OF THE JURA

High mountain / Advanced   Map strava.com/routes/16630755

Distance	E+	Difficulty	Appeal
76 km (47 mi)	1,900 (6,235 ft)	4/5	4/5

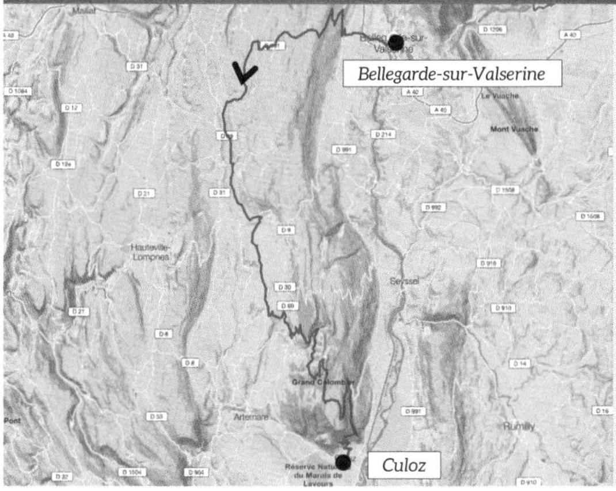

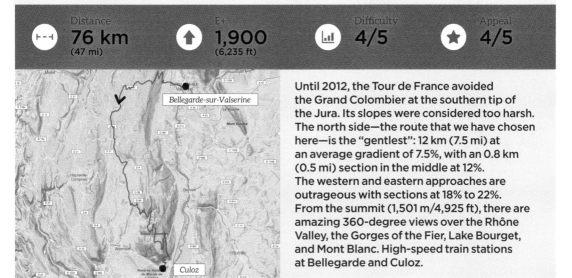

Until 2012, the Tour de France avoided the Grand Colombier at the southern tip of the Jura. Its slopes were considered too harsh. The north side—the route that we have chosen here—is the "gentlest": 12 km (7.5 mi) at an average gradient of 7.5%, with an 0.8 km (0.5 mi) section in the middle at 12%. The western and eastern approaches are outrageous with sections at 18% to 22%. From the summit (1,501 m/4,925 ft), there are amazing 360-degree views over the Rhône Valley, the Gorges of the Fier, Lake Bourget, and Mont Blanc. High-speed train stations at Bellegarde and Culoz.

Morning light over Les Ballons in the Vosges, France.

SAINT-ÉTIENNE
HEROES OF THE PILAT

Low mountain / Advanced
Map strava.com/routes/16299665
Test yourself km 10 (mi 6) strava.com/segments/697449
Test yourself km 62 (mi 39) strava.com/segments/1151695

This route from Saint-Étienne to Vienne (return by train) is the best way to explore the Pilat in the eastern Massif Central. These wooded low mountains—highly popular for outdoor activities in both summer and winter—feature heavily in cycling's history.

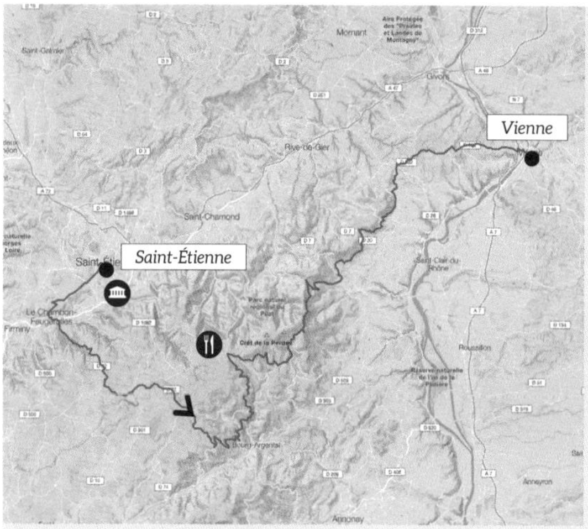

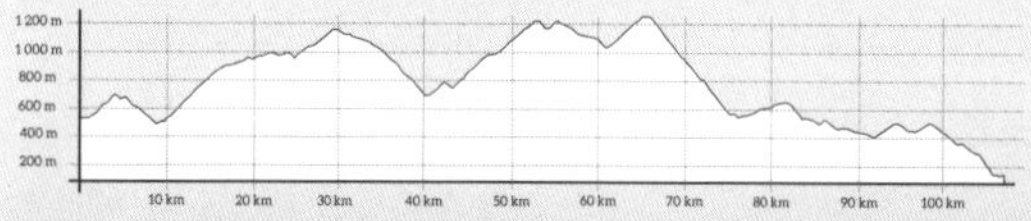

A ride through the Pilat Massif is a fine lesson both in geography and the history of cycling. At km 29 (mi 18), we skirt the Col de la République at 1,145 m (3,756 ft), which was the first climb over 1,000 m (3,280 ft) crossed by the very first Tour de France in 1903. It remains very popular with touring cyclists. Then, we veer northeast to the Col de La Croix de Chaubouret (1,201 m/3,940 ft). The climb is 9 km (5.5 mi) long with an average gradient of 5%. This is followed by the Col de l'Oeillon (1,235 m/4,050 ft), a climb of 3.7 km (2.3 mi) at 6%. We are close to the highest point in the Pilat, the Crêt de la Perdrix (1,431 m/4,695 ft). When you start the 10 km (6 mi) descent toward Pélussin down slopes that, although shaded, are much steeper, you understand why l'Oeillon remains a painful memory for so many Tour champions. The little cols of Pavezin and La Croix-Régis take us gently down to Vienne.

Distance	E+	Difficulty	Appeal
113 km (70 mi)	2,200 m (7,220 ft)	4/5	4/5

Saint-Étienne (pop. 170,000) is 65 km (40 mi) southwest of Lyon: 45 minutes by train or 1h by car. Geneva is 3h40 by train or 2h20 by car (210 km/130 mi). Paris is 3h by high-speed train or 5h by car (530 km/330 mi).

Le Chaubouret (km 53/mi 33) is the perfect place for lunch. Everything on the menu (meat, pasta, quenelles, cheese) is from the region.

La Croix-de-Chaubouret
42660 Le Bessat
hotelrest-lechaubouret.com

For a long time, Saint-Étienne was the capital of the French bicycle industry. The Museum of Art and Industry has a permanent bicycle exhibition.

2 Place Louis Comte
42000 Saint-Étienne
mai.saint-etienne.fr

LIMOGES
POULIDORISSIMO!

- *Very hilly / Advanced*
- *Map strava.com/routes/22603350*
- *Test yourself km 48 (mi 30) strava.com/segments/15868621*
- *Test yourself km 61 (mi 38) strava.com/segments/5226967*

Raymond Poulidor, the most popular French cyclist ever, died in 2019 at the age of 83. This route through the western foothills of the Massif Central in his home region of Limousin is both a beautiful homage to him and a lesson in the punchy style of riding that he pioneered.

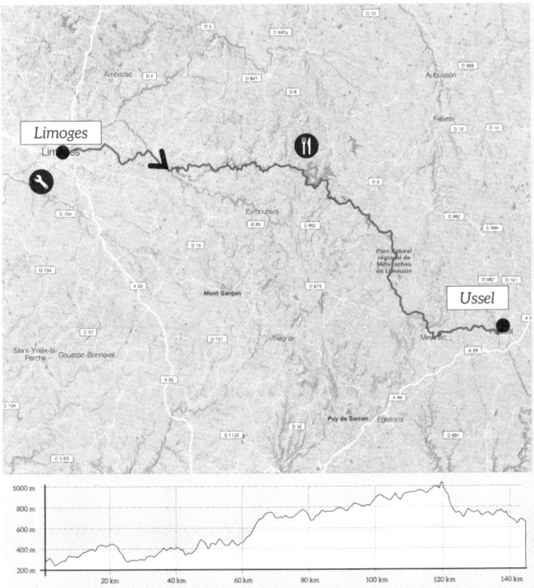

Limoges is the perfect starting point for this long pilgrimage to Ussel in honor of the memory of Raymond Poulidor, a son of this region. We roll through the Vienne Valley to the village of Saint-Léonard-de-Noblat (where Poulidor lived), then through the Mauldre Valley to Peyrat-le-Château, the lakes of Vassivière and Chammet, and the Plateau des Millevaches. It is a craggy, wooded route that opens out onto the heights of the "Limousin Mountains," an area of peat bogs and rivers. The highest point is the top of Mont Bessou, at nearly 1,000 m (3,280 ft), where there is a viewing tower from which you can make out Puy-de-Dôme, located 60 km (37 mi) away. Your heart and thighs will be pumping, even though the longest ramp—7 km (4.5 mi) up to Vassivière—has an average gradient of only 4%. And it does not let up all the way to Ussel, at an altitude of around 600 m (2,000 ft). Poulidor must have loved these roads.

Distance	E+	Difficulty	Appeal
145 km (90 mi)	2,550 m (8,370 ft)	4/5	4/5

Limoges (pop. 133,000) is 3h30 from Paris by train or 4h15 by car (400 km/250 mi). Bordeaux is 2h50 by train or 2h40 by car (230 km/143 mi). Return from Ussel: 2h by train. Other train stations on the route: Saint-Léonard-de-Noblat, Saint-Denis-des-Murs, and Meymac.

Vassivière Lake (km 66/mi 41) is a very attractive spot for lunch. L'Escale brasserie serves food all day on its terrace.

Chemin de l'Escale, Auphelle
87470 Peyrat-le-Château
escale-vassiviere.com

Vélociste (marque 3T notamment), atelier, café-vélo, espace de co-working, La Cyclisterie est le lieu de convergence de la communauté pédalante de Limoges.

9 rue Élie Berthet
87000 Limoges
lacyclisterie.fr

BORDEAUX
WINING AND BIKING

Fairly flat / Intermediate

Map strava.com/routes/16363513

Test yourself km 5 (mi 3) strava.com/segments/2421097

Test yourself km 77 (mi 48) strava.com/segments/10983050

This route is the perfect blend of wine and cycling, from Libourne to the vineyards of Saint-Émilion via the sweeping bends of the Dordogne and the Roger Lapébie bike path, named after the only Bordeaux citizen (by adoption) to have won the Tour de France (in 1937).

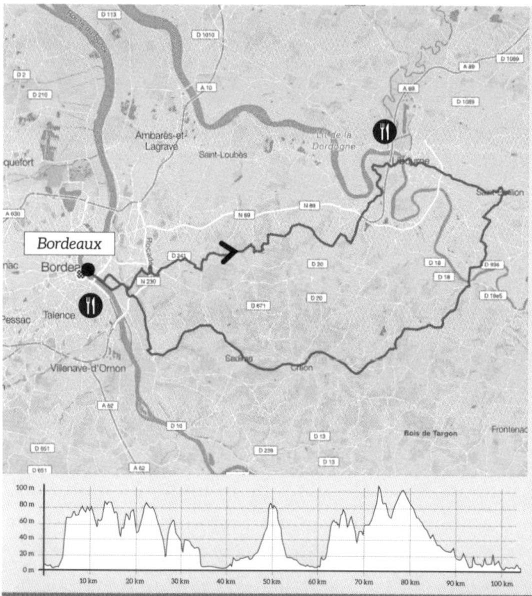

Roger Lapébie, that great champion of the interwar years, would certainly have shared his outings on Strava. He was so curious, so methodical. In 1937, he won the first Tour de France in which the derailleur was permitted, partly because he mastered it better than his rivals. For that alone, it is moving to ride for nearly 30 km (18 mi) along the greenway that bears his name—from the slopes of the Entre-Deux-Mers back along the right bank of the Garonne river. It is even more beautiful, given the landscape through which we have already cycled: the Entre-Deux-Mers on the way out of Bordeaux, the Dordogne at Libourne, and finally Saint-Émilion, with its vineyards stretching as far as the eye can see and its châteaux (Pas de l'Âne, Ambe Tour Pourret, Guadet, Villemaurine, La Gaffelière, Saint-Georges, and more). Stop to sample a fine vintage or two—in moderation, of course.

Distance	E+	Difficulty	Appeal
107 km (66 mi)	700 m (2,300 ft)	3/5	3/5

Bordeaux-Mérignac Airport serves many European cities. The high-speed train from Paris takes 2h35, whereas Nantes is 3h45 by regular train. By road, allow 3h20 from Nantes (350 km/220 km), 3h30 from Bilbao (330 km/205 mi), and 5h45 from Paris (600 km/370 mi).

Bordeaux has its own bike cafe, Musette, close to Saint-Jean Station. The staff speak English, serve delicious cakes, and sell Genesis and Brother bikes.

72 Cours de la Somme
33800 Bordeaux
musettebordeaux.com

For a coffee and something sweet, drop in to the cozy Feuillette bakery and teashop in Libourne, close to km 44 (mi 27). Rustic vibes and a roaring fire.

95 Avenue du général de Gaulle
33500 Libourne
feuillette.fr

CLERMONT-FERRAND
VOLCANO PARK

Low mountain / Advanced — Map strava.com/routes/16688679

Distance	E+	Difficulty	Appeal
100 km (62 mi)	2,250 m (7,380 ft)	4/5	4/5

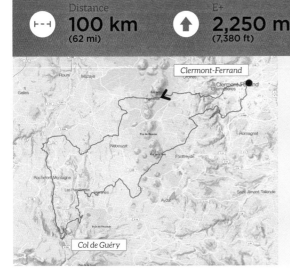

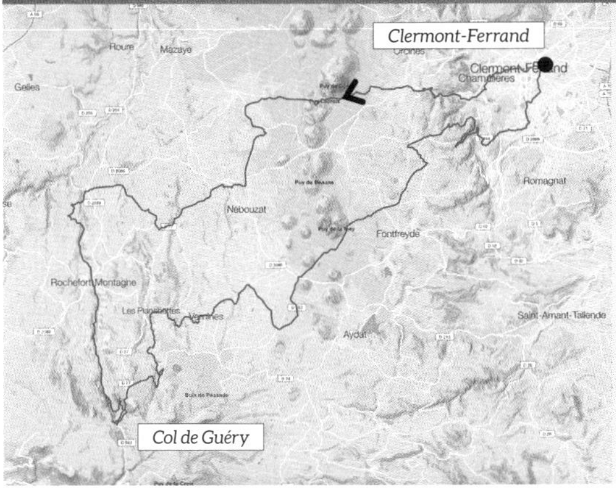

The winding ascent of Puy de Dôme, once feared by many a champion, is now only accessible to cyclists once a year (in June) via the service road for the rack and pinion railway. There are many other superb roads through the Parc des Volcans (west of Clermont-Ferrand), such as the Col de Ceyssat and the Col de Guéry (1,268 m/4,160 ft). On the way back, stop to check out the old Charade motor racing track (km 86/mi 54), or be tempted by a new pair of wheels at Cycles Victoire (km 97/mi 60), a young, hip bicycle manufacturer.

AURILLAC
CANTAL PEAKS

Low mountain / Advanced — Map strava.com/routes/16691317

Distance	E+	Difficulty	Appeal
106 km (66 mi)	2,500 m (8,200 ft)	4/5	4/5

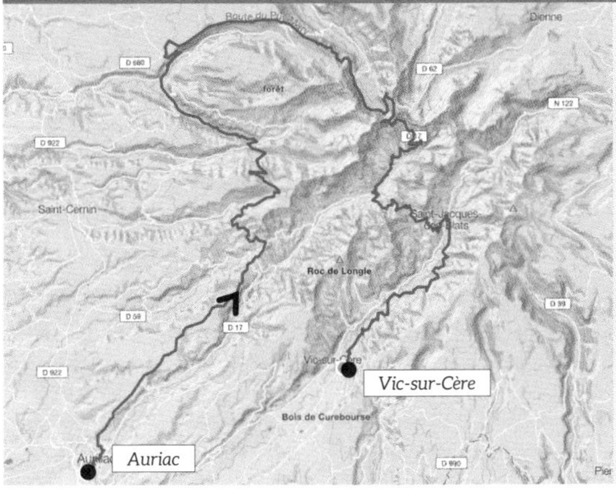

Puy Mary, in the heart of the magnificent Mounts of Cantal, is the most visited site in the Massif Central. From the top at 1,787 m (5,862 ft), there are breathtaking views on all sides. The ascent of Pas de Peyrol (200 m/650 m below the summit of Puy Mary) is a regular 6% to 7%, but over 11 km (7 mi). Since leaving Vic-sur-Cère, you will have already climbed the Côte de Thiézac and the Col du Perthus: 5,700 m (3.5 mi) at 5%. After Salers, which is renowned for its cheese and red-coated cattle, comes the Route des Crêtes before Aurillac (2h40 by train from Clermont-Ferrand).

BRIOUDE
CLIMBERS' ROADS

- *Very hilly / Advanced*
- *Map strava.com/routes/16842955*
- *Test yourself km 42 (mi 26) strava.com/segments/6619421*
- *Test yourself km 78 (mi 49) strava.com/segments/3584393*

This route in the eastern Massif Central is inspired by Romain Bardet, who was born in Brioude. This top French cyclist, 2019 Tour de France dot polka jersey, has helped to design six routes around his hometown. strava.com/pros/1630132

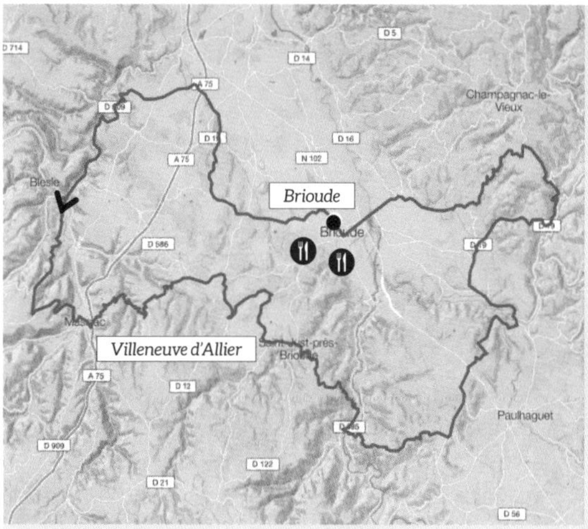

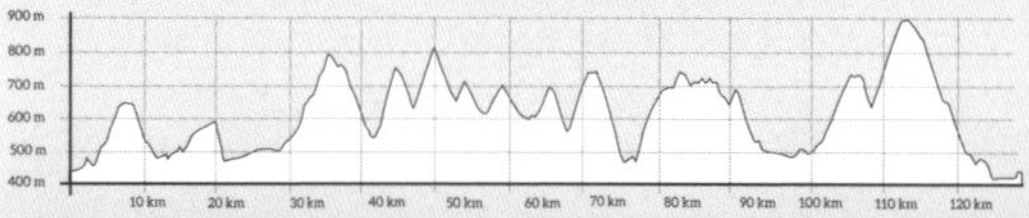

If you dream of swiping KOMs on the home turf of a famous Tour de France climber, this is the place to do it. You will need to dissect the route and target your objectives as you follow in the pedal strokes of Romain Bardet, who inspired this XXL route across the rugged terrain of the Haute-Loire around his hometown of Brioude. Within a 20 km (12.5 mi) radius of Brioude, you will tackle a dozen climbs with altitudes of between 500 m (1,640 ft) and 900 m (2,950 ft), and a total of 35 km (22 mi) of climbing and 2,700 m (8,858 ft) of elevation gain. In 2018, Brioude municipality designed six routes, all marked with "R.B." signs, to promote the locality as a cycling destination. The easiest is only 12 km (7.5 mi) long. This one, "Sur les routes de Romain," is the toughest. As you haul yourself around the course, you will understand how this local boy became one of France's best cyclists.

Distance	E+	Difficulty	Appeal
130 km (81 mi)	2,700 m (8,860 ft)	4/5	4/5

Brioude (pop. 6,700) is 1h10 by train or 1h by car (70 km/44 mi) from Clermont-Ferrand to the north. To the east, Lyon is 4h by train or 2h30 by car (230 km/143 mi) via Clermont-Ferrand. To the south, Montpellier is 5h30 by train or 3h by car (280 km/175 mi).

Fancy a nice espresso before the start 100 meters/yards from the Basilique Saint-Julien? Via della Rosa is a pleasant tea shop in the center.

2 Rue Saint-Geneix
43100 Brioude
viadellarosa.free.fr

Lard dans l'assiette is the perfect spot to celebrate a long day on the bike, with copious portions of delicious traditional Auvergne cuisine.

27 rue du 4 septembre
43100 Brioude

ROMANS-SUR-ISÈRE
DRÔME CIRCUIT

- *Low mountain / Advanced*
- *Map strava.com/routes/22635101*
- *Test yourself km 39 (mi 24) strava.com/segments/9010488*
- *Test yourself km 58 (mi 36) strava.com/segments/20324697*

Once the capital of luxury footwear, Romans-sur-Isère enjoys an ideal location between the Rhône Valley and the Vercors Massif. This route was inspired by Pierre Latour one of the best 2020s French pro cyclists. strava.com/pros/7347052

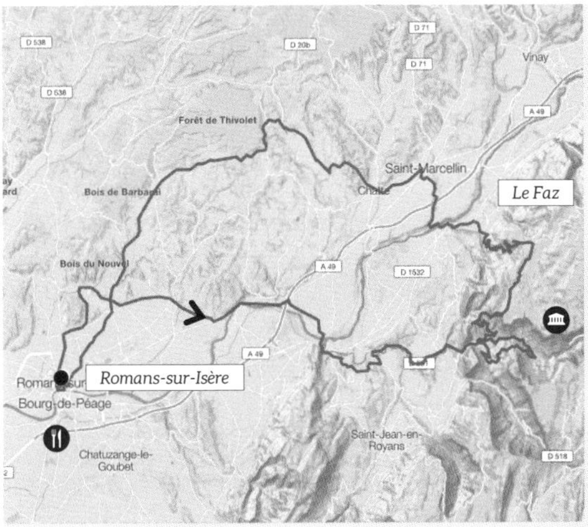

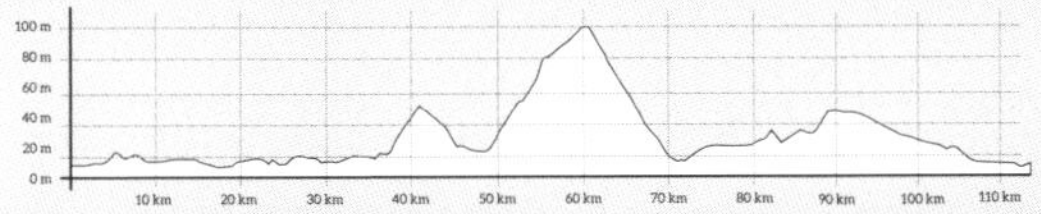

This route has plenty to offer: the aqueduct of Saint-Nazaire-en-Royans majestically spans the Isère at km 25 (mi 15.5), then the abrupt wall of the Vercors soon appears before we even reach the curious hanging houses of Pont-en-Royans and the Côte de Chatelus—3.5 km (2 mi) at a gradient of nearly 8%. Soon, we hit the Col des Toutes Aures: 12 km (7.5 mi) of climbing, with an E+ of 750 m (2,460 ft), and a long kilometer (0.6 mi) at over 10% before Presles. The limestone wall on the right retains the heat, so you will appreciate the shade of the two short tunnels. The gradient is kinder between Presles and Le Faz, the highest point of the route, at 1,000 m (3,280 ft). At km 89 (mi 55), visit the sumptuous abbey in the beautiful medieval village of Saint-Antoine. Once back in Romans, do not miss the old bridge linking the town to Bourg-de-Péage, the Shoe Museum, and the collegiate church of Saint-Barnard.

Distance	E+	Difficulty	Appeal
114 km (71 mi)	1,900 m (6,250 ft)	3/5	4/5

Romans-sur-Isère (pop. 33,000) is close to Valence, the prefecture of the Drôme: 40 minutes by train or 30 minutes by car (25 km/15 mi). Lyon is 1h30 by train or by car (105 km/65 mi). Marseille is 2h by train or 3h by car (240 km/150 mi).

It is a longish ride, so fill your pockets at Guillet, a pastry and chocolate store, before setting off. You will not be disappointed.

78, Place Jean Jaurès
26100 Romans-sur-Isère
guillet.com

The Caves of Choranche (km 46/mi 28) are among the most impressive in France, with chambers 15 m (50 ft) high full of magnificent stalactites. Guaranteed coolness in the summer heat.

visites-nature-vercors.com

ANNECY
OVERLOOKING THE LAKE

High mountain / Advanced
Map strava.com/routes/16404235
Test yourself km 10 (mi 6) strava.com/segments/3977368
Test yourself km 56 (mi 35) strava.com/segments/14793019

A town of canals surrounded by mountains, Annecy is nicknamed the "Venice of the Alps." This route overlooking the superb lake provides some extraordinary views, as well as the chance to visit the fine medieval castle of Menthon-Saint-Bernard.

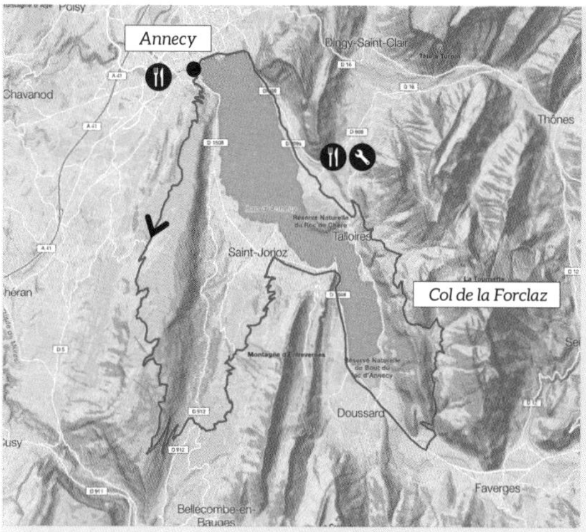

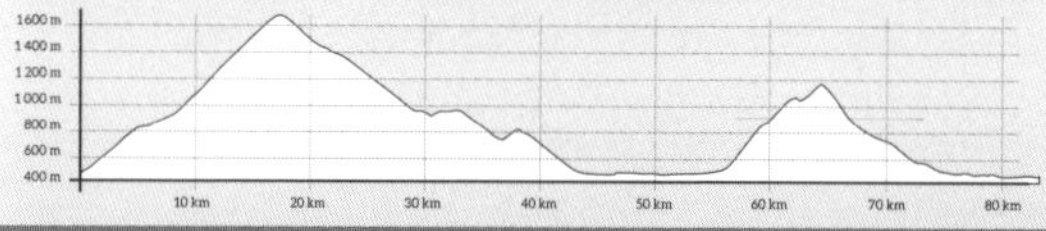

Make the most of beautiful Lac d'Annecy (jewel of Haute-Savoie) by riding this 85 km (53 mi) extended loop around its shore. Take to the heights and vanquish two obstacles overlooking the 27 km² (10.5 sq mi) body of water: the ascent of Semnoz, which lies at 1,200 m (3,937 ft) and the Col de la Forclaz de Montmin at 1,150 m (3,773 ft). Although relatively low, these two summits offer amazing views of the turquoise waters of the lake. The Semnoz climb, which starts as soon as you leave Annecy, stretches for 16 km (10 mi) and alternates gentle slopes with more brutal gradients, in the shelter of the Bauges forest. The descent is via the pleasant road off the Col de Leschaux. The southeast tip of the route (km 56/mi 39) marks the foot of the Col de la Forclaz de Montmin. This second climb is shorter (8 km/5 mi) but more demanding, with an average gradient of 8%.

Distance	E+	Difficulty	Appeal
85 km (53 mi)	2 200 m (7,218 ft)	3/5	5/5

Annecy (pop. 130,000), the Prefecture of the Haute-Savoie department, is 3h40 from Paris by high-speed train, or 5h30 (550 km/340 mi) by car. From Marseille, it takes 4h45 by train or 4h by car (430 km/270 mi). From Milan, it takes 5h by train or 4h30 by car (400 km/250 mi).

The pastry chef Philippe Rigollot is a local figure. Treat yourself to his special breakfast before you head off—having stuffed your pockets with his homemade cereal bars.

Place Georges Volland
74000 Annecy,
Francephilipperigollot.com

After conquering the Forclaz, freewheel down to Base Camp Bike (km 73/mi 45), a friendly, English speaking joint serving excellent coffee and snacks, with road-bike rental.

21 Rue Noblemaire
74290 Talloires-Montmin, France
base-camp.bike

MOÛTIERS
NEW STAR

- *High mountain / Expert*
- *Map strava.com/routes/21287772*
- *Test yourself km 12 (mi 7) strava.com/segments/10394407*
- *Test yourself km 37 (mi 23) strava.com/segments/21256356*

The Col de la Loze in the heart of the Tarentaise massif is a major novelty so attractive that it features in the 2020 Tour de France as the highest point in the race. The final 7 km (4.5 mi) of the climb to 2,304 m (7,559 ft) are on a spanking new cycle path opened in 2019.

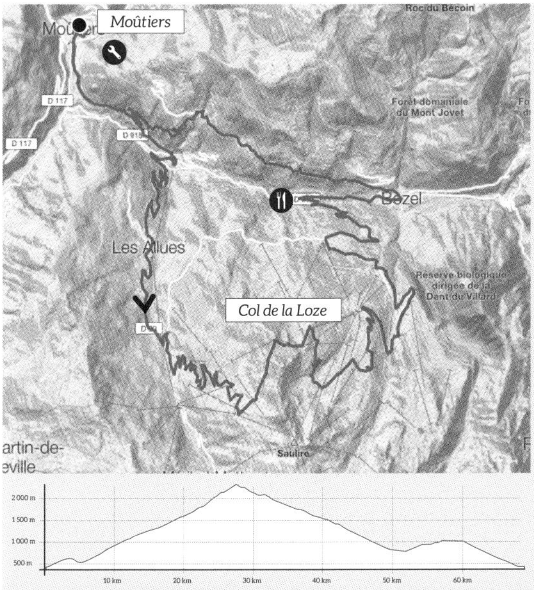

The brand new Col de la Loze cycle path was, until 2019, merely a track for the snow tamping machines of the resorts of Courchevel and Méribel. Freshly surfaced just for cyclists, it is closed to motor traffic—a first in France! Not being ones to miss an opportunity, the organizers of the 2020 Tour de France stuck it into the itinerary—and with a summit finish, no less! But as lovely as it is, this is no picnic for the average pedal-pusher: 22 km (13.5 mi) at an average gradient of 8% from Brides-les-Bains, with an E+ of nearly 1,700 m (5,577 ft), comparable to that of Mont Ventoux. The last 7 km (4.5 mi) are the hardest, at an average gradient of between 8% to more than 11%, with irregular—sometimes terrifying—ramps. Interestingly, the road follows the lines of the famous ski runs of Méribel: Rhodos, Adret, Saulire, and Dent de Burgin. Start and end in Moûtiers; descend via Courchevel.

Distance	E+	Difficulty	Appeal
71 km (44 mi)	2,500 m (8,200 ft)	4/5	5/5

Outside of the winter season, Moûtiers (pop. 3,500) is 3h by train from Lyon, 4h30 from Paris, and 5h from Marseille. By car, allow 2h from Lyon (180 km/112 mi), 4h from Marseille (420 km/260 mi) and Milan (350 km/217 mi), and 6h30 from Paris (650 km/400 mi).

La performance accomplie de l'ascension du col de la Loze vaut bien une célébration. Stop chez Maxime et sa brasserie (artisanale) de l'Antidote à Bozel, km 53 (mi 33). Pour une ale, une ambrée, une épicée, comme on veut.

719 rue Émile Machet
73350 Bozel
shop.easybeer.fr

Mout'N Bike (300 meters/yards from Moûtiers train station) specializes in everything to do with road bikes, including rentals.

328 Avenue de la Libération
73600 Moutiers
moutnbike.fr

SAINT-JEAN-DE-MAURIENNE
VANOISE SWITCHBACKS

High mountain / Advanced

Map strava.com/routes/16445085

Test yourself km 34 (mi 21) strava.com/segments/683404

Test yourself km 38 (mi 24) strava.com/segments/9258446

The Maurienne Valley is surrounded by legendary passes: Galibier, La Croix-de-Fer, and La Madeleine. But there are other climbs too, such as the Lacets de Montvernier, a narrow road twisting up a mountain flank, which was unveiled in the 2015 Tour de France.

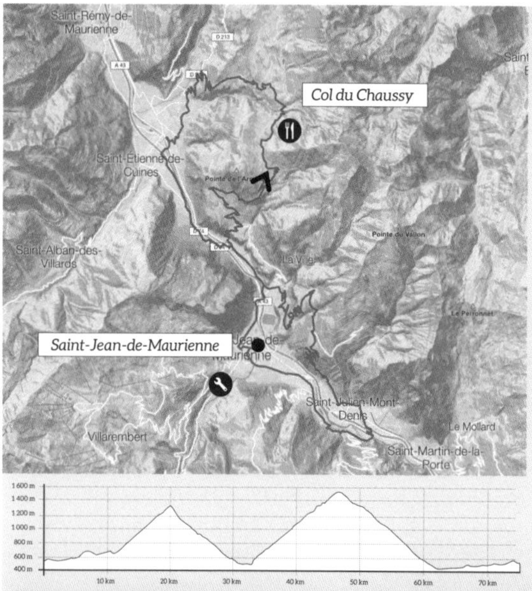

"The largest cycling area in the world" is the motto adopted by the Maurienne Valley to promote summer cycle tourism. This route, which starts in Saint-Jean-de-Maurienne, provides a glimpse of the rich cycling terrain in southern Savoie. It takes us away from the Croix de Fer (a classic climb of the Tour de France) toward the beauties of the Vanoise massif. Montdenis is the first ascent of the day in the southern section of the ride: 11 km (7 mi) long at an average gradient of 7% all the way up to 1,419 m (4,655 ft). Then, we head north for the eighteen very tight switchbacks of Montvernler, which cling closely packed together to the mountain above Pontamafrey-Montpascal. They serve merely as a running board for the Col de Chaussy: 14 km (9 mi) long at 7%, up to 1,533 m (5,029 ft), with sections at 11%. The descent off it joins that of the Col de la Madeleine. La Maurienne is full of surprises.

Distance	E+	Difficulty	Appeal
75 km (47 mi)	2,150 m (7,050 ft)	4/5	4/5

Saint-Jean-de-Maurienne (pop. 8,000) is near to Italy via the Fréjus Road Tunnel: 3h50 by train from Milan, or 3h15 by car (270 km/168 mi). Marseille is 4h by car (420 km/260 mi), but 6h by train. Paris is 5h30 by train or 6h20 by car (640 km/398 mi).

L'Auberge du col de Chaussy (km 47/mi 29) is ideal for refueling at the summit of the second climb. Spoil yourself with Fred and Babette's cooking.

Col de Chaussy
73300 Pontamafrey-Montpascal

DVélos sells bikes (Pinarello, Specialized, Cannondale, Lapierre), repairs and rents them, and organizes outings. It holds a "Qualité Cyclo Maurienne" label.

434 Avenue du Mont Cenis
73300 Saint-Jean-de-Maurienne
dvelos.com

BRIANÇON
THE MAGICAL IZOARD

- *High mountain / Advanced*
- *Map strava.com/routes/16465866*
- *Test yourself km 21 (mi 13) strava.com/segments/5104694*
- *Test yourself km 65 (mi 40) strava.com/segments/4751829*

The desolate landscape of the Casse Déserte (part of Tour de France legend) is reason enough to climb the Izoard. The final 2 km (1.25 mi)—above 2,200 m (7,218 ft)—traverse a crater that is almost lunar, with rocky pinnacles formed from a type of limestone called *cargneule.*

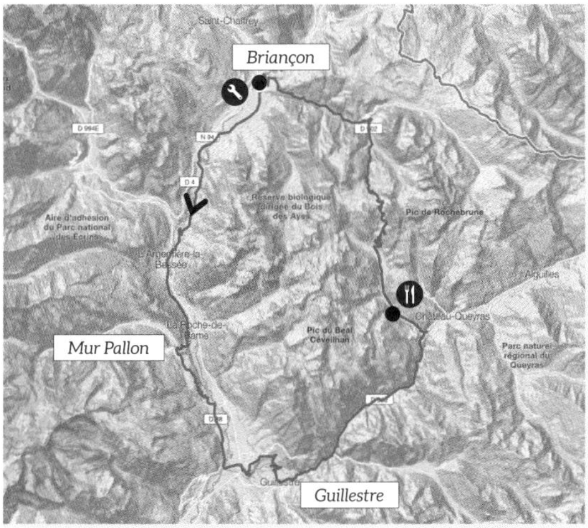

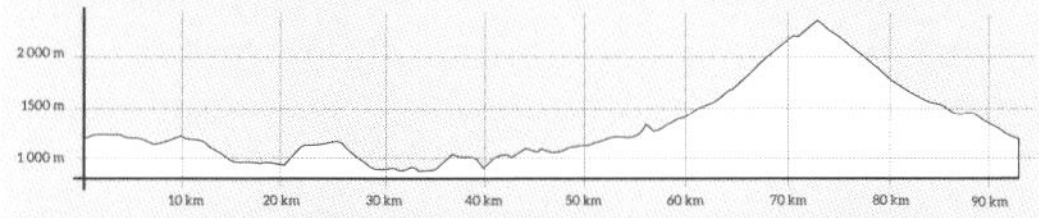

This place is legendary. In 2017, the Tour de France celebrated the centenary of its first crossing of the Col d'Izoard by a sumptuous stage finish at its summit. From Briançon, you skirt the mountain by the west, through the Durance Valley to avoid the traffic on the N94. If you feel that you have the legs, tackle the brutal Mur Pallon and the Corniche du fort de Mont-Dauphin. Past Guillestre, the gorges of Guil and La Combe du Queyras lead to Arvieux, the real start of the southern slope of the Izoard. The climb is 13 km (8 mi) long, with an average gradient of 6.9%, but never less than 8% once you reach the switchbacks just after Brunissard—except for the short freewheeling section at the entrance to the Casse Déserte, which feels like a movie set as you ride in. Then as you dip down toward Cervières and Briançon, your life will feel forever changed.

Distance	E+	Difficulty	Appeal
93 km (58 mi)	2,300 m (7,550 ft)	4/5	5/5

Briançon (pop. 12,000) is 3h by car from Lyon (230 km/143 mi), Marseille (260 km/161 mi), and Milan (250 km/155 mi). Or take the high-speed train to Oulx (Italy), followed by a 1h45 bus journey to Briançon: 2h35 from Milan, 3h from Lyon.

Avoid getting the munchies on the Izoard by stopping at the hotel-restaurant La Casse Déserte (km 62/mi 38). Excellent Queyras food.

3706 Route de l'Izoard
05350 Arvieux
facebook.com/leBistrotdelaCasseDeserte

Mountain Cycles sells Specialized and BMC equipment, and has an efficient repair service. Located on the N94, 500 m (0.3 mi) from the station.

342 Rue du Marechal de Lattre de Tassigny
05100 Briançon
mountain-cycles.fr

LE BOURG-D'OISANS
ALTERNATIVE ALPE-D'HUEZ

- *High mountain / Expert*
- *Map strava.com/routes/16445219*
- *Test yourself km 25 (mi 16) strava.com/segments/3940790*
- *Test yourself km 37 (mi 23) strava.com/segments/674677*

The twenty-one switchbacks of the climb to L'Alpe-d'Huez (that legend of modern Tours de France) are famous the world over. Every cyclist should tackle them at least once in their life. But there are some more original approaches if you set out from Le Bourg-d'Oisans.

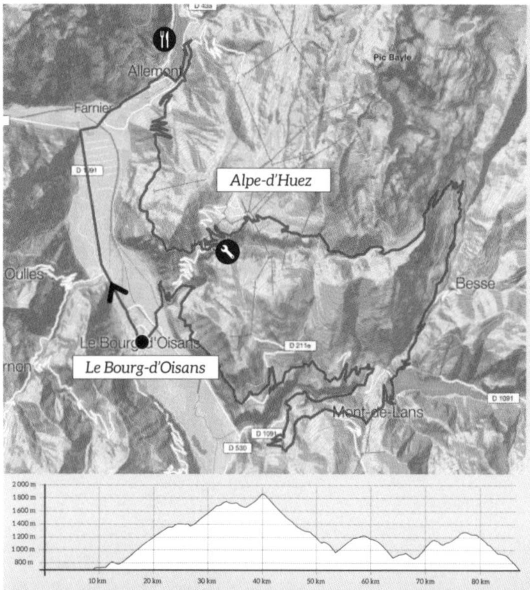

Legends become even finer when considered from a different angle. Leaving Le Bourg-d'Oisans by the northwest, our alternative adventure around L'Alpe-d'Huez starts to gain altitude around km 10 (mi 6), above Lac du Verney. There are a few nasty switchbacks on the way up to Villard-Reculas (1,444 m/4,737 ft). At Huez (km 27/mi 17), we follow the Tour de France route for barely 1 km (0.6 mi) before entering the resort from "below" and turning onto the Route du Col de Sarenne. We descend at first for 3 km (2 mi) before kicking up suddenly for a similar distance, at an average gradient of 8%, until the summit at 1,999 m (6,558 ft). Then it's 13 km (8 mi) of well-earned downhill to Lac Chambon before the return to Le Bourg-d'Oisans via the mountainside Route du Grand Rocher, the Gorges de l'Infernet, and the Balcons d'Auris, overlooking Écrins National Park. Demanding yet sublime.

Distance	E+	Difficulty	Appeal
88 km (55 mi)	2,600 m (8,530 ft)	4/5	4/5

Le Bourg-d'Oisans (pop. 3,300) is 1h15 by bus from Grenoble Train Station (50 km/30 mi). By car, allow 2h from Lyon (160 km/100 mi), 4h20 from Milan (310 km/193 mi), and 6h15 from Paris (620 km/385 mi).

Cyclists are pampered in the Oisans region. At Allemond (km 10/mi 6), La Douce Montagne offers bike parking and a pasta buffet every afternoon in summer.

450 Route des Fonderies Royales
38114 Allemond
ladoucemontagne.com

Oli and Kat, a Brit and an Australian, opened Cycle Huez in 2011. It is the perfect bike store, offering repairs, rentals, and retail. And they speak English, of course!

Place Joseph Paganon,
L'Alpe-d'Huez, 38750 Huez
cyclehuez.com

Col de Sarenne, above L'Alpe-d'Huez in the Alps, France.

EMBRUN
GRAVEL ORIGINS

High mountain / Expert
Map strava.com/routes/22465668
Test yourself km 54 (mi 34) strava.com/segments/15930340
Test yourself km 64 (mi 40) strava.com/segments/8330604

Climbing the Col du Parpaillon is a unique Alpine experience. This sublime mountain road above Embrun rises to 2,643 m (8,671 ft), although it becomes a trail from 1,860 m (6,102 ft). Few realize that the Parpaillon was the first real "gravel" challenge.

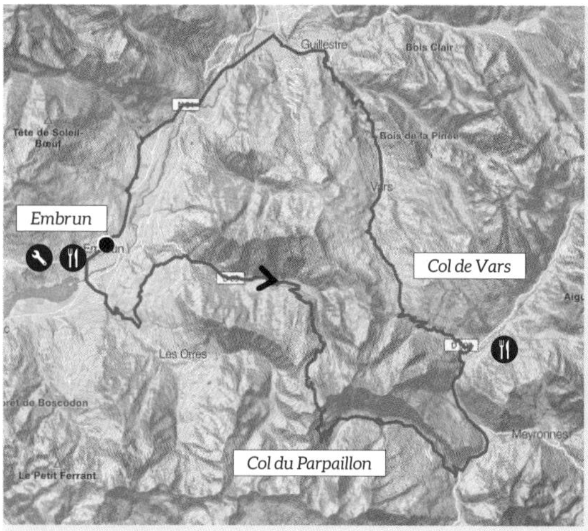

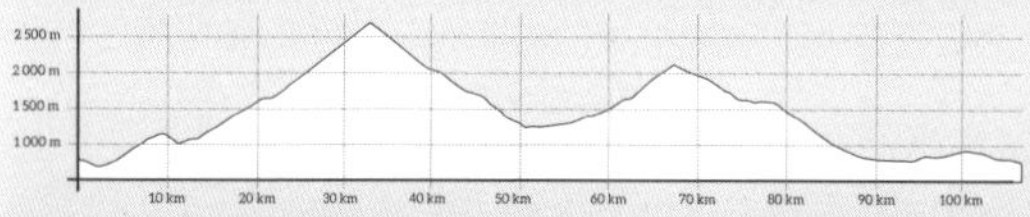

The Col du Parpaillon has never appeared in the Tour de France, although some might say that a "gravel" stage would be an excellent idea. You can get a sense of the climb from the deliciously vintage and somewhat surreal film *Parpaillon: À la recherché de l'homme à la pompe d'Ursus* (1993), available on YouTube. Climbing from the Embrun side, the first ramp is a surfaced road of 8 km (5 mi) at a gradient of over 7%. At the "Cabane des Espagnols," you turn onto a stony trail that climbs for another 8 km (5 mi) at gradients of between 9% and 10%—never less! The vast landscape, composed of scree and short grass, is stunning. You might even spot a marmot. At the summit, an unlit tunnel 0.5 km (0.3 mi) long only adds to the mystical atmosphere of a cycling adventure unlike no other. The 12 km (7.5 mi) "gravel" descent to the Ubaye River and the rather busier Col de Vars seems almost banal.

Distance **108 km** (67 mi)

E+ **3,200 m** (10,500 ft)

Difficulty **5/5**

Appeal **5/5**

Embrun (pop. 6,000) is accessible from the Rhône Valley in 3h30 by train from Valence or 3h20 by car (200 km/125 mi). To the north, Briançon is 1h10 by train or 55 minutes by car (50 km/30 mi). Marseille is 6h by train, but only 2h30 by car (220 km/137 mi).

At La Souste, an inn and grocery shop in Saint-Paul (km 60/mi 37), they serve good local food and are used to seeing cyclists and other athletes.

Le Village
04530 Saint-Paul-sur-Ubaye
gitelasouste.com

Le Tandem is an ideal base camp in Embrun. It offers original home cooking, organic fruit juices and beers, and a bike workshop.

22 Rue de la Liberté
05200 Embrun
facebook.com/letandembistrotvelo

MONT-DAUPHIN - GUILLESTRE
ROOF OF THE QUEYRAS

- *High mountain / Expert*
- *Map strava.com/routes/22470671*
- *Test yourself km 12 (mi 7) strava.com/segments/1177908*
- *Test yourself km 42 (mi 26) strava.com/segments/8211275*

On the border between France and Italy, southwest of Turin, Col Agnel rises to 2,744 m (9,003 ft), and is the third-highest paved road in the Alps. This route climbs it from the French side through the unusual landscapes of the extraordinary Queyras Massif.

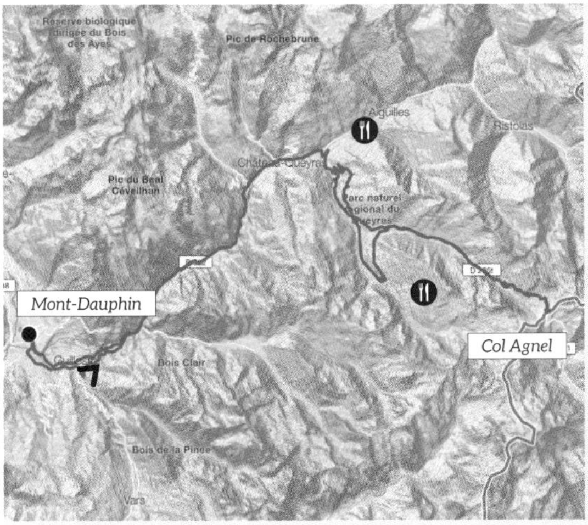

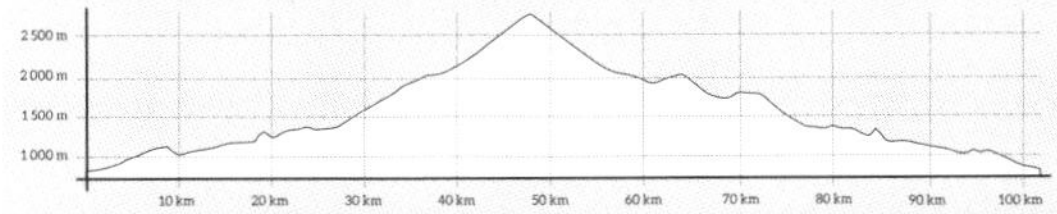

The Col Agnel is only 20 m (65 ft) lower than the Iseran (France), and 13 m (42 ft) lower than the Stelvio (Italy). Despite being a brilliant third, it is unforgettable. The ascent is long, but there are extraordinary views of the Barre des Écrins, Mont Pelvoux, Pain de Sucre, Pic d'Asti, and Monte Viso. The Queyras valley, below and above 2,000 m (6,560 ft), is stunning with its landscape of shiny schist rock—once you have climbed past the limestone and dolomite ridges. Total effort is required, for there is an average gradient of 6.5% over 21 km (13 mi) after the Guil gorges with the final, irregular 5 km (3 mi) averaging 8.8%, and ramps of between 10% and 12%—not to mention the increasingly thin air above 2,300 m (7,500 ft). The descent takes a little detour via Saint-Véran (the highest village in Europe) and its famous sundials. This is where the southern Alps really start.

Distance	E+	Difficulty	Appeal
101 km (63 mi)	2,600 m (8,550 ft)	4/5	5/5

Montdauphin-Guillestre is 3h40 by train or 3h30 by car (240 km/150 mi) from Valence and the Rhône Valley. Briançon is 30 minutes by train or 40 minutes by car (35 km/22 mi). Grenoble is 2h40 by car (150 km/93 mi).

Without a doubt, Saint-Véran (km 63/mi 40) is the best place to stop. You will find a warm welcome and delicious mountain food at La Fougagno.

Le Chatelet
05350 Saint-Véran
facebook.com/restaurantlafougagno

A little lower, at km 76 (mi 47), you can procure cold cuts, local cheeses, and Queyras jam tarts at the Maison de l'Artisanat.

05350 Château-Ville-Vieille
artisanat-queyras.fr

CASTELLANE
THRILLS IN THE GRAND CANYON

- *Low mountain / Expert*
- *Map strava.com/routes/16494816*
- *Test yourself km 24 (mi 15) strava.com/segments/11852196*
- *Test yourself km 100 (mi 62) strava.com/segments/678054*

Stop dreaming about the Grand Canyon in Colorado. You can't even get near it on a bicycle. Go instead to the one in Verdon, south of the French Alps. Thrills and hard pedaling guaranteed. Get ready for an extraordinary day.

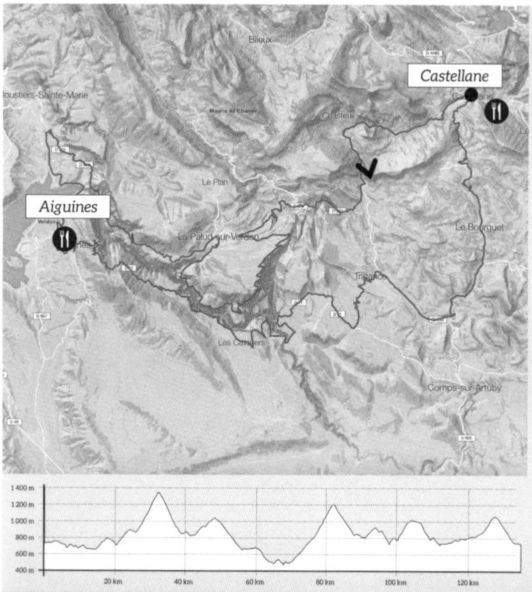

We ride out from the superb village of Castellane, under its impressive limestone Roc. Awaiting us down the road is the stunning Grand Canyon du Verdon. This is a mountainous route with some stiff climbing along the Route des Crêtes from km 26 (mi 16) up to 1,350 m (4,430 ft) over 6 km (3.7 mi) at a gradient of 8%. As you climb over La Palud, the panorama unfolds like in an IMAX film. We are 500 m (1,600 ft) above the turquoise water snaking through the sheer canyon of the Verdon Gorge, a uniquely thrilling place. A gentle 20 km (12.5 mi) descent leads to Pont du Galetas, where the canyon opens out into Lac de Sainte-Croix. The Col d'Illoire leads to the Cirque de Vaumale on the south side—an elevation gain of 650 m (2,130. ft) with a few terrifying sections. The road back to Castellane has some tricky parts around Saint-Maymes and Le Petit Robion. You will return exhausted but blissful.

Distance	E+	Difficulty	Appeal
134 km (83 mi)	2,800 m (9,200 ft)	5/5	5/5

Castellane is quite remote. The nearest high-speed train stations are in Marseille (3h by bus) or Aix-en-Provence (4h by bus, via Digne). The nearest local train stations are Saint-André-les-Alpes or Barrême. Nice is 2h by car (110 km/68 mi), and Marseille is 2h45 (180 km/112 mi).

Panisse, *fougasse*, almond specialties, quince paste: you can find all sorts of good things to stick in your pockets at Boulangerie Collomp in Castellane.

5 Rue du Lieutenant Blondeau
04120 Castellane

À Chabassole Beach (km 69 / mi 43), ne pas hésiter à quitter le tracé pour un ravitaillement-snack (à 2 km / to 1 mi) au bar du Surf Center, en compagnie d'amoureux du paddle.

Plage de Margaridon
83630 Les Salles-sur-Verdon
surfcenter.fr

ORANGE
THE GIANT OF PROVENCE

- *High mountain / Advanced*
- *Map strava.com/routes/16969121*
- *Test yourself km 25 (mi 16) strava.com/segments/5104932*
- *Test yourself km 39 (mi 24) strava.com/segments/16098831*

This place has seen some legendary episodes of the Tour de France, both tragical (the death of Tom Simpson in 1967) and comical (Chris Froome running up the slope in 2016). Mont Ventoux looks like nothing else. A cyclist hasn't lived if they haven't climbed it at least once.

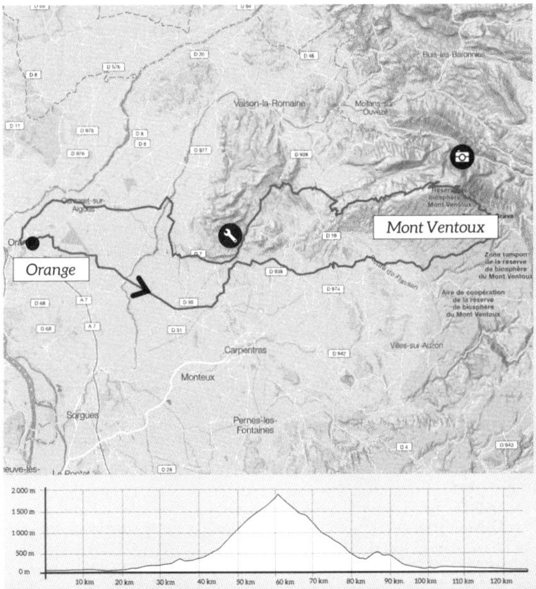

Orange is where our adventure starts and ends. Orange has a Roman theater, the atmosphere of which evokes the mystical, legendary Mont Ventoux—a stage on which every cyclist dreams of performing. The approach is a gentle slope, commencing in Aubignan (km 22/mi 14) to beyond Bédoin. The many Strava segments proposing a full climb of Mont Ventoux suggest a total distance of 21.5 km (13.5 mi). It is in fact 15 km (9.5 mi), and begins properly at the Saint-Estève switchback. From there on, it is hell: 9 km (5.5 mi) through the forest at gradients of between 9% and 11%, with not the slightest respite. After Chalet Reynard, there are 6 km (4 mi) more at over 7% amid a landscape of bare scree, sometimes straight into the wind. The final kilometer (0.6 mi) up to the TV tower (1,901 m/6,236 ft) is horrendous. We return via Malaucène, Suzette, and Beaumes-de-Venise.

Distance	E+	Difficulty	Appeal
125 km (78 mi)	2,450 m (8,040 ft)	5/5	5/5

Orange (pop. 30,000) is 2h30 by train from Marseille Airport, or 1h by car (100 km/62 mi). Lyon is 1h25 by direct high-speed train or 2h by car (220 km/137 mi). Paris is 3h30 by train or 7h by car (700 km/435 mi).

L'Étape du Ventoux is the go-to bike store at the foot of the "Giant of Provence." Retailer of Bianchi, KTM, and Time. Also rentals.

70 Avenue Raspail
84190 Beaumes-de-Venise
letapeduventoux.fr

After 6 km (4 mi) of descent, enjoy the views over the Baronnies Massif, with the Vercors and Écrins natural parks behind, at Chalet Liotard.

Station du Mont Serein
84340 Beaumont-du-Ventoux
chaletliotard.fr

NICE
THE CYCLISTS' MADONNA

Low mountain / Advanced
Map strava.com/routes/17233031
Test yourself km 18 (mi 11) strava.com/segments/2549247
Test yourself km 38 (mi 24) strava.com/segments/665117

The Madone d'Utelle enjoys a fine reputation, even beyond the French Riviera. Like Lance Armstrong before, today's champions still use it as a training climb. Strava did not exist then, but if it had existed, Lance's times would have been studied closely.

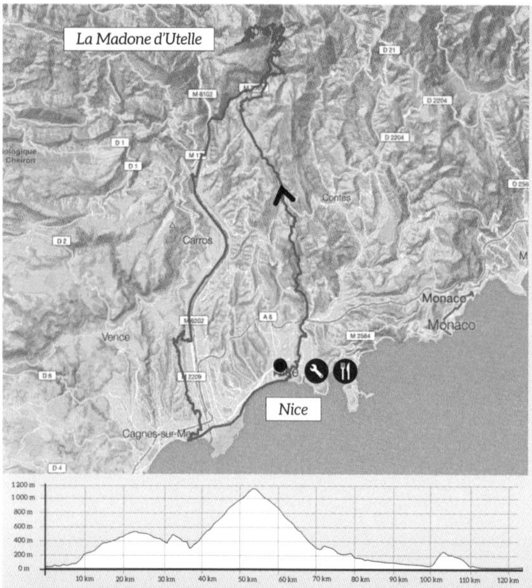

The Madone d'Utelle is an astonishing mountain. There has been a shrine at the summit (1,174 m/3,850 ft) since the ninth century. A rough trail continues for several hundred meters/yards along the rocky ridge to a TV antenna and an orientation table indicating the Mercantour National Park to the north and the Mediterranean to the south. The climb started to attract cyclists after Tony Rominger, and then Lance Armstrong, came here to check their form against the clock. It has been popular ever since. From Nice, you can reach the foot of this stiff, dead-end climb via the corniche overlooking the Vésubie Valley after Levens. The climb, which is 16 km (10 mi) long with an average gradient of 5.3%, starts at Saint-Jean-la-Rivière with 2 km (1.25 mi) at 9% through olive groves, then through forest after Utelle, before finishing above the treeline. Follow the Vésubie and Var rivers back to Nice.

Distance
124 km
(77 mi)

E+
1,900 m
(6,250 ft)

Difficulty
4/5

Appeal
4/5

Nice Airport is very well served internationally. Marseille is 2h40 from Nice by train or 2h20 by car (200 km/125 mi). Lyon is 4h30 by train or 4h45 by car. Milan is 6h by train via Genoa or 3h45 by car (320 km/200 mi).

Pan bagnat is a local specialty that is essentially a salad nicoise in a round bun. Lou Balico's was voted the best in town by the readers of *Nice-Matin* newspaper in 2018.

20 Avenue Saint-Jean-Baptiste
06000 Nice
loubalico.com

By Nice's old port, Café du Cycliste is not just a friendly cafe. It is also a great road bike store and a chic, fun, and original textile brand.

16 Quai des Docks
06300 Nice
cafeducycliste.com

PORTO-VECCHIO
AIGUILLES DE BAVELLA

Low mountain / Advanced · Map strava.com/routes/17375542

Distance	E+	Difficulty	Appeal
126 km (78 mi)	2,400 m (7,875 ft)	4/5	4/5

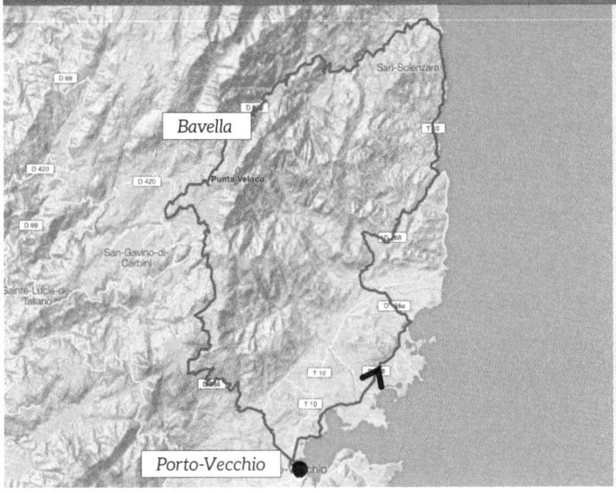

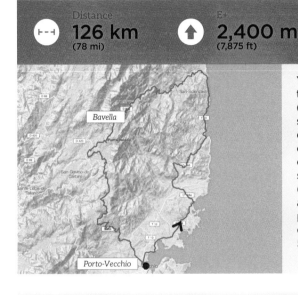

You only have to look at the profile of this loop through southern Corsica, from Porto-Vecchio (airport at nearby Figari), to understand the sporting appeal. Another reason is the extraordinary sight of Bavella's seven spikes of red granite, north of Lake Ospédale. But the climb up to the pass (1,218 m/4,000 ft) in the shadow of Punta di a Vacca is hellish: 8 km (5 mi) at an average gradient of 8.7%. But what a view! It takes at least four hours to get there, partly along the coast (Pinarellu, Conca, Cala d'Oru), then ascending the Col de Larone: 5.5 km (3.5 mi) at 8%.

BASTIA
CAP CORSE

Low mountain / Advanced · Map strava.com/routes/17348789

Distance	E+	Difficulty	Appeal
121 km (75 mi)	1,850 m (6,050 ft)	4/5	4/5

This loop around Cap Corse, which evokes the popular Cape Town Cycle Tour in South Africa, includes more than 60 km (40 mi) of the Mediterranean coast, with long beaches on the east side and a wild and ragged coast on the west. The mountain climbs in the hinterland are relatively easy except for the last, the Col de Teghime, a merciless 6 km (3.7 mi) through the forest at gradients of 7% to 8%. At km 83 (mi 52), the stunning view over the black sandy beach of Nonza makes you realize why Corsica has been nicknamed the "Isle of Beauty." Nearest airport: Bastia.

AJACCIO
THE TREASURES OF PIANA

Low mountain / Expert
Map strava.com/routes/17334269
Test yourself km 16 (mi 10) strava.com/segments/1047381
Test yourself km 67 (mi 60) strava.com/segments/1127052

The worldwide television coverage of the Tour de France threw the spotlight on the rocky inlets (calanques) of Piana during the Tour's first visit to Corsica in 2013. Since then, what cyclist has not sworn to come here? From Ajaccio, it is possible, though difficult, and not advisable when it's hot.

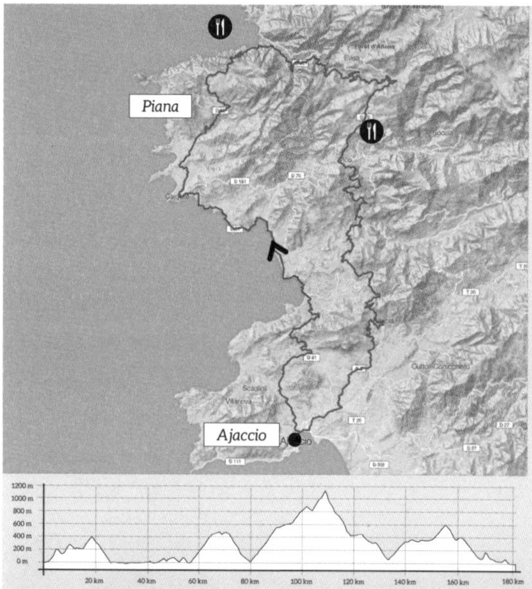

Let's be frank: this unique and magical ride is 181 km (113 mi) with a total elevation gain worthy of a Tour de France mountain stage. The surreal Piana calanques form one of the most stunning natural sites in Europe. Ajaccio is a great place to start, since it is not that far. First you climb the three little peaks of the Col de Bastiano, on the way out of town, before dropping down toward the Gulf of Sagone, followed by the Cargèse promontory.
The 10 km (6 mi) undulating climb to the magnificent village of Piana (km 68/mi 42) has a fearsome reputation with local cyclists. Stop to take in the breathtaking beauty, before the long descent to the Gulf of Porto, Piana and the ocher rocks of the calanques thrusting out of the bright blue sea. Ahead lies the long climb to the Col de Sévi at 1,102 m (3,612 ft) and the massif of Monte Redondo, via the Gorges de la Spelunca. Folly indeed.

Distance **181 km** (112 mi)

E+ **3,600 m** (11,811 ft)

Difficulty **5/5**

Appeal **5/5**

Ajaccio-Napoléon Bonaparte Airport is served by many European destinations from April to October. By ferry, 6h from Toulon, 7h30 from Nice, 11h from Marseille. Bastia is 4h from Ajaccio by train, 3h by road (150 km).

Time for a hearty meal after the big climb. Turn off into Vico at km 116 (mi 72) and head to A Piazza where they might be serving pastizzu di macaroni (the local version of mac 'n' cheese).

Place Casanelli d'Istria
20160 Vico
a-piazza.business.site

On the descent from the village, stop at Les Roches Bleues at km 75 (mi 46.6), a bar overlooking the Calanques de Piana. Friendly welcome, stunning views.

Lieu-dit Les Calanches
20115 Piana
facebook/chaletlesrochesbleues

Above the Calanques de Piana in Corsica, France.

HYÈRES
CHESTNUTS AND GRAPES

⊕ *Very hilly / Advanced* ⊕ *Map strava.com/routes/17312829*

Distance	E+	Difficulty	Appeal
121 km (75 mi)	1,550 m (5,085 ft)	3/5	4/5

This loop to the west of the Massif des Maures, where seven times King of the Mountains winner Richard Virenque cut his teeth, combines sporting appeal with good living. The popular Col de Babaou (4 km/2.5 mi at an average gradient of 5%), followed by the Col des Fourches (altitude: 535 m/1,755 ft) are a workout for your calves. Between the two lies Collobrières, a village renowned for its chestnut festival. Further on in Pierrefeu, they make delicious rosé wine. In Hyères, check out the Vélodrome Toulon-Provence-Méditerranée and its wooden track.

CANNES
MAGICAL ESTEREL

⊕ *Hilly / Intermediate* ⊕ *Map strava.com/routes/17295809*

Distance	E+	Difficulty	Appeal
62 km (39 mi)	900 m (2,950 ft)	3/5	5/5

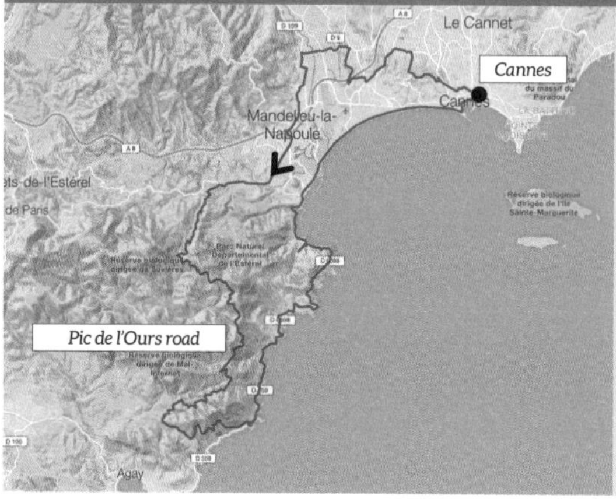

This is one of the most beautiful cycling routes on the French Riviera, starting and ending in Cannes (50 minutes by train from Nice airport). Try to avoid the summer months when the roads are very busy. The route offers two magical worlds: the forested Massif de l'Esterel, where you have the option of climbing the Pic de l'Ours (km 27/mi 17) to see an extraordinary view from its summit at 492 m (1,614 ft), and the coastal scenery of reddish brown rocks, creeks, and idyllic beaches. The final stretch takes you past the yachts in Cannes marina.

MARSEILLE
CALANQUES & CLIFFS

- *Very hilly / Advanced*
- *Map strava.com/routes/16211394*
- *Test yourself km 6 (mi 4) strava.com/segments/1072758*
- *Test yourself km 22 (mi 14) strava.com/segments/4866926*

Leave Marseille via the road to the Col de la Gineste one fine morning, as the sun rises dead ahead with the sparkling water of the *calanques* on your right, climbing ever higher, above Cassis, then back through the interior.

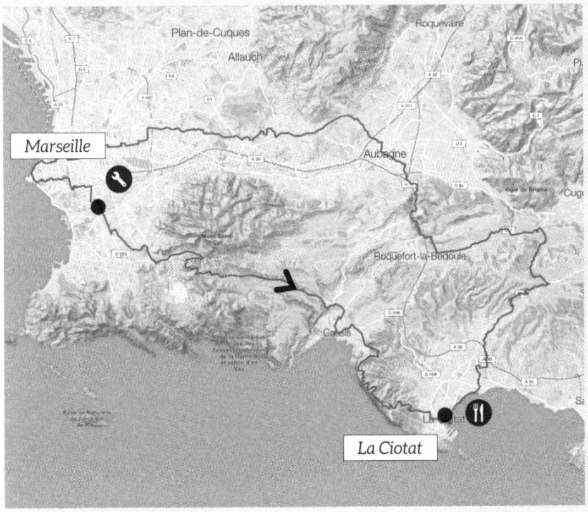

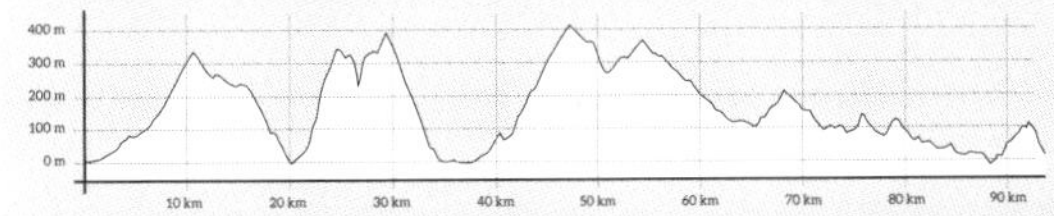

The road to the Col de la Gineste is a classic ride out from Marseille. At 4.8 km (3 mi) long at an average gradient of 4.8%, it's up to you how hard you want to push it. To your right lies one of the wonders of France: the Calanques National Park, with numerous little roads heading down to the rocky inlets. But our goal lies ahead: the descent to Cassis, then the climb to the Route des Crêtes. This is something else: 3 km (1.8 mi) of steep ascent, at an average gradient of close to 10%. Up top is a marvelous, undulating road along the side of the slope, nearly 400 m (1,300 ft) above the Mediterranean, before a wall with an average gradient of 10%. Descend to La Ciotat, then curve back inland to Le Grand Caunet (5 km/3 mi at 5.5% on this side), the Montée des Bastides, and finally the tricky Eulalie climb on the way out of Aubagne. Finally, a tour through Marseille, finishing with a kick up the steep Rue du Bois Sacré.

Distance	E+	Difficulty	Appeal
95 km (59 mi)	1,850 m (6,100 ft)	4/5	4/5

Marseille is very well connected to the rest of Europe through its airport (55 minutes by train from the city center). Paris is 3h20 by train, Lyon is 1h50, Nice is 2h40, and Perpignan is 4h. Lyon is 3h10 by car (320 km/200 mi), and Nice is 2h20 (200 km/125 mi).

Located between Orange Vélodrome and Hôpital de La Timone, CycleXperts fixes all mechanical issues. Large space. Retailer of Cannondale and Cube.

17 Rue Jean-Eugène Paillas
13010 Marseille
cyclexperts.com

If the Route des Crêtes has eaten into your reserves, step off the bike at km 36 (mi 22) for a refuel at Maison Sordillon in La Ciotat: pancakes, snacks, and coffee on a terrace.

632 Avenue Fernand Gassion
13600 La Ciotat
facebook.com/ MaisonSordillon BoulangeriePatisserieLaCiotat

NÎMES
BEACHES OF THE LANGUEDOC

- *Fairly flat / Advanced*
- *Map strava.com/routes/22614134*
- *Test yourself km 47 (mi 29) strava.com/segments/9898655*
- *Test yourself km 130 (mi 81) strava.com/segments/6763802*

France's Mediterranean coast extends way beyond Nice, Cannes, and the Riviera. This long loop starting and ending in Nîmes is a voyage of discovery of other landscapes and riches in the Languedoc—from the Camargue salt flats to Montpellier by way of historic Aigues-Mortes.

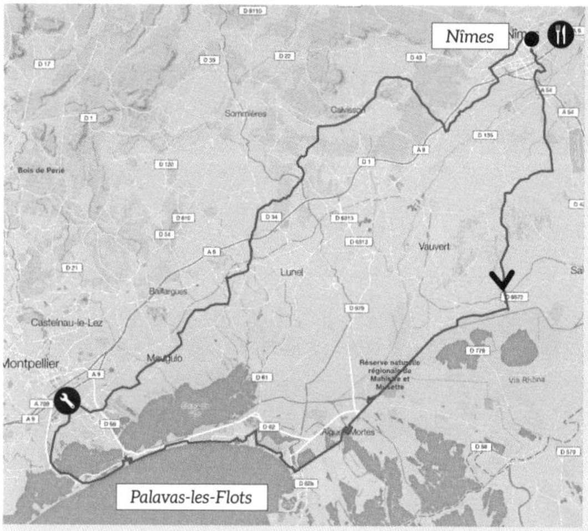

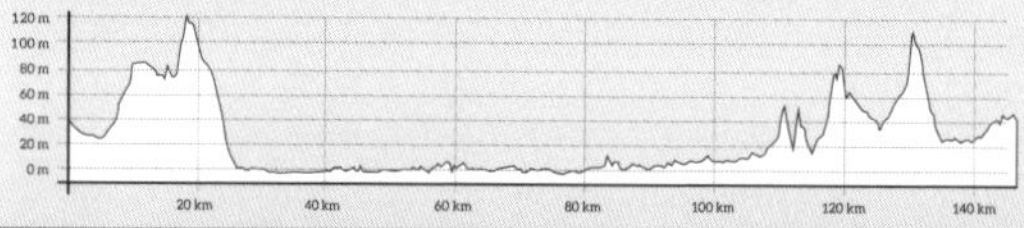

The only bumps on this long route are the "rollercoasters" of the initial and final sections. But you will not be bored—not in the Camargue, with its salt flats and the jewel that is Aigues-Mortes (km 44/mi 27). The ramparts and towers of the former royal port built by Saint-Louis (King Louis IX) are a marvel to behold. We then head west, along the gulf, on long stretches of cycle paths, having previously followed a section of the Via Rhona cycling route. Riding between sea and ponds, we pass the popular resorts of Le Grau-du-Roi, La Grande-Motte, and Palavas-les-Flots (km 75/mi 47), where we turn inland, skirting Montpellier by the south, back to Nîmes, passing the famous Roman amphitheater. You can do a shorter version of the route by turning around at Aigues-Mortes and coming back via Marsillargues, Vergèze, and Bernis: 92 km (57 mi) with an elevation gain of 330 m (1,080 ft).

Distance
147 km
(91 mi)

E+
700 m
(2,300 ft)

Difficulty
3/5

Appeal
3/5

Nîmes (pop. 150,000) is only 1h by train from Montpellier Airport, 35 minutes from Montpellier train station, or 45 minutes by car (50 km/31 mi). Marseille Airport is 1h by train or 1h15 by car (100 km/62 mi). Lyon is 1h30 by high-speed train or 2h40 by car (250 km/155 mi).

In Nîmes, Carré Jazz is a wine bar with a lovely ambiance that serves tapas. Its terrace looks out on the Roman temple called Maison Carrée (Square House).

25 Place de la Maison Carrée
30000 Nîmes
carrejazz.fr

Right by Montpellier Airport, Cyrpeo (km 86/mi 53) is a well-regarded bike shop and travel agency. Retailer of Scott, Giant, Trek, and Cannondale.

427 Rue Hélène Boucher
34130 Mauguio
cyrpeo.fr

CASTRES
DARK MOUNTAINS

Low mountain / Expert — *Map* strava.com/routes/16975676

Distance	E+	Difficulty	Appeal
124 km (77 mi)	2,650 m (8,695 ft)	4/5	4/5

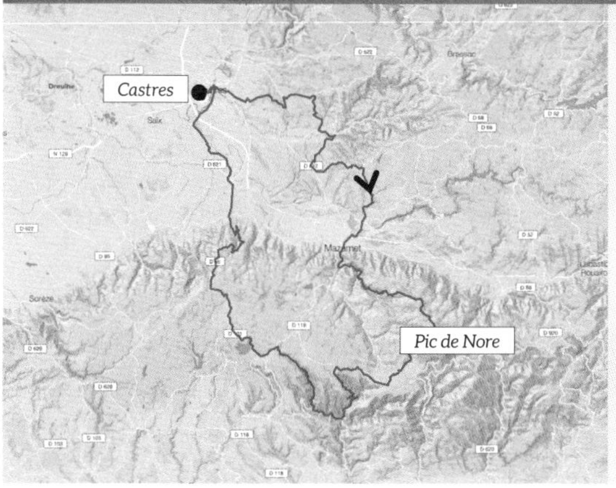

Castres and Mazamet, located 80 km (50 mi) west of Toulouse (1h30 by train), are the base camps for a singular destination, La Montagne Noire, in the southwest Massif Central.
Our route climbs to the Pic de Nore at 1,211 m (3,973 ft): 12 km (7.5 mi) at an average gradient of 6.5%, but with steeper inclines above Les Yès, such as the 1 km (0.6 mi) long "Raidard des Sapins." Sometimes the *autan* wind blows, earning the peak the nickname of "Petit Ventoux." We are in the home territory of Laurent Jalabert, a former cycling champion and ever-inspiring athlete worth following on strava/athletes/1682310.

MILLAU
THE TWO CAUSSES

Low mountain / Advanced — *Map* strava.com/routes/16664329

Distance	E+	Difficulty	Appeal
100 km (62 mi)	1,500 m (4,900 ft)	4/5	5/5

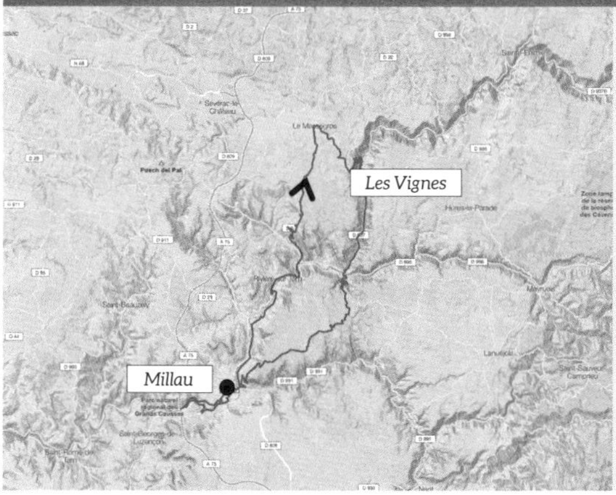

This route through Aveyron and Lozère is one of those you never forget: the astonishing Tarn gorges, the endless horizons of the Causse de Sauveterre and the Causse Noir, and the Millau Viaduct. Quiet roads run through valleys by the magnificent Tarn River or up to the heights, 500 m (1,640 ft) above, leading to extraordinary views. At km 42 (mi 26), we pass very close to the aptly named Point Sublime. On the way back, we pass the exceptional boulder field of the Chaos de Montpellier-le-Vieux before glimpsing the breathtaking Millau Viaduct. 3h by train from Montpellier.

MONTRÉJEAU
BALÈS CHALLENGE

- *High mountain / Advanced*
- *Map strava.com/routes/22476190*
- *Test yourself km 32 (mi 20) strava.com/segments/7709861*
- *Test yourself km 47 (mi 29) strava.com/segments/11839650*

Rising to 1,755 m (5,758 ft), the Port de Balès is a discovery of twenty-first century Tour de France, quickly becoming an established Pyrenean climb to rival such honored alumni as the Aubisque and the Tourmalet. The final 10 km (6 mi) through a desert environment are hard.

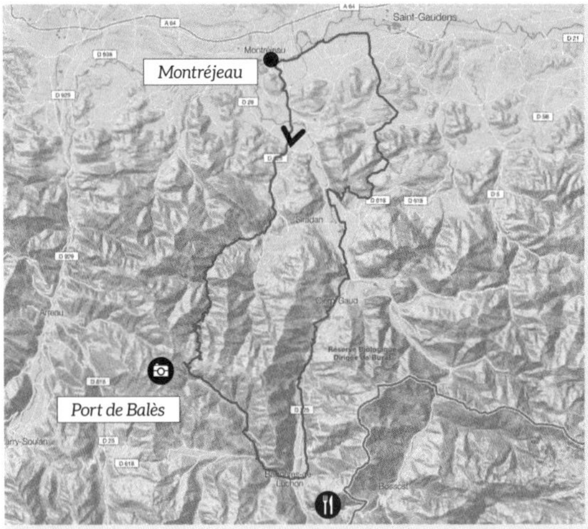

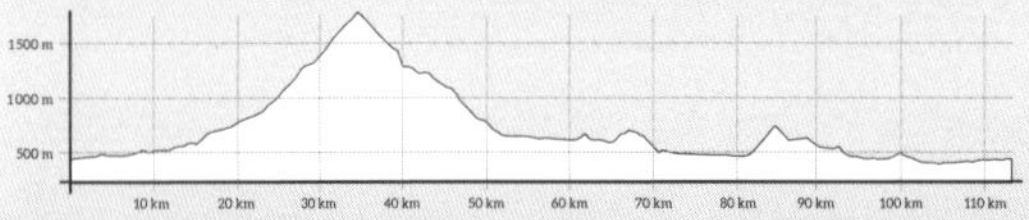

In the early 2000s, the road up the Port de Balès did not exist. It was just a track used by herds of sheep from the valley below. Since then, the champions of the Tour de France have made it a cycling destination worthy of its more prestigious Pyrenean neighbors. This route, via Mauléon-Barousse and the Oueil Valley, is tough. Three-quarters of its total elevation gain come in the final 10 km (6 mi) beyond Ferrère. As the low vegetation thins to scraggy slopes, the road climbs mercilessly at gradients of between 9% and 11%—harsher than the neighboring Tourmalet. The descent to the road up the Col de Peyresourde—13 km (8 mi) lower—is brutal and on the edge of the precipice, so be careful. Take a well-earned rest in Bagnères-de-Luchon before returning to Montréjeau via the "little" Mont de Galié (km 82/mi 8), a climb of 3 km (2 mi) at an average gradient of 9%.

Distance	E+	Difficulty	Appeal
114 km (71 mi)	2,100 m (6,900 ft)	4/5	4/5

Montréjeau is a small town (pop. 3,000) in the Haute-Garonne with a strategically placed train station. Toulouse is 1h50 by train or 1h10 by car (110 km/68 mi). Pau is 2h30 by train or 1h5 by car (100 km/62 mi). Bordeaux is 4h30 by train or 3h by car (310 km/193 mi).

Bagnères-de-Luchon is a key staging post for the Tour de France. Its management used to stay at the Hôtel d'Étigny, which has a very pleasant garden that is perfect for coffee.

3 Avenue Paul Bonnemaison
31110 Bagnères-de-Luchon
hotel-etigny.com

At the top of the Port de Balès, you will not find a cafe nor a mountain hut, but a superb view over the Oueil Valley, the summits of the Col de Peyresourde and Mont Né (2,147 m/7,044 ft), and, further away, the Pic de Maupas and the Maladeta (Spain).

LOURDES
TOURMALET DETOUR

- *High mountain / Expert*
- *Map strava.com/routes/16544366*
- *Test yourself km 8 (mi 5) strava.com/segments/652886*
- *Test yourself km 68 (mi 42) strava.com/segments/15519278*

The Col du Tourmalet is *the* giant of the Pyrenees—the one that every cyclist should climb at least once. Our route tackles it from the east (the "La Mongie" side) via a very tough route. Try it again two days later from the west, and you will have earned yourself the title of *Tourmaliste.*

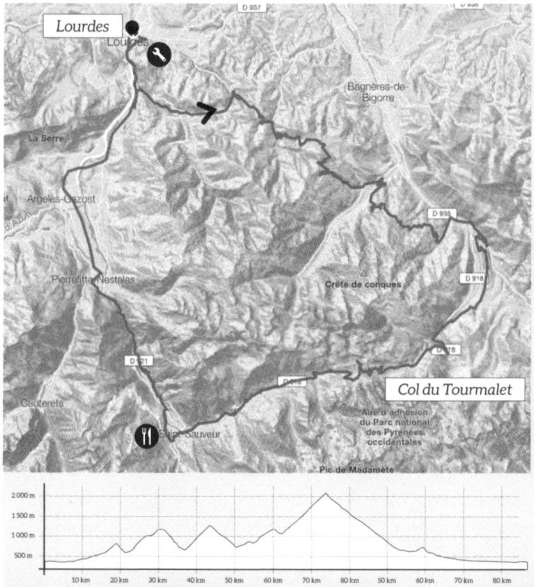

The Tourmalet may well be lower than its Alpine cousin, the Galibier, but aficionados of the Pyrenees do not give a hoot. This mountain has been a legend for more than a century, with the Tour de France rarely neglecting to climb it, from one side or the other. As a warm-up, we offer you the Col du Couret (1,199 m/3,933 ft)—the start and final stretches are at 10%—and the Col de la Courade (1,315 m/4,315 ft): 9 km (5.5 mi) at 8%, with the final section at 11%. We tackle the Tourmalet from the east: 17 km (10.5 mi) at an average gradient of 7.4%, with nearly 1,300 m (4,265 ft) of elevation gain, sections at between 9% and 10% before and through La Mongie, and with the last 6 km (3.7 mi) at 8.6%. This "ultra" route over back roads, tracks, and hidden forest trails overlooking the Adour Valley is to be relished before returning exhausted—but happy—to Lourdes along the Gave de Pau river.

Distance	E+	Difficulty	Appeal
128 km (80 mi)	3,550 m (11,600 ft)	5/5	5/5

As a pilgrimage destination, Lourdes is well served by the airports of Tarbes (15 km/9 mi) and Pau (55 km/34 mi). Toulouse is 2h15 by train and 2h by car (185 km/115 mi) from Lourdes. Bordeaux is 2h30 by train and 2h45 by car (250 km/155 mi).

Hubert Arbès, a former teammate of Bernard Hinault, is the man behind the only worthwhile bike store in Lourdes. Retailer of Cipollini bikes, among others.

10 Avenue François Abadie
65100 Lourdes
cycles-arbes.com

In Sassis, near Luz-Saint-Sauveur (km 94/mi 58.5), the Brasserie du Pays Toy brews several beers named after famous cycling climbs, including Tourmalet, Aubisque, Hautacam, and Luz Ardiden.

Le Village
65120 Sassis
brasserie-paystoy.com

SAINT-JEAN-PIED-DE-PORT
THE MYSTERIES OF IRATI

- *Low mountain / Expert*
- *Map strava.com/routes/22613998*
- *Test yourself km 12 (mi 7) strava.com/segments/6431013*
- *Test yourself km 39 (mi 24) strava.com/segments/6422424*

As you ride east into the Pyrenees, the French Basque Country reveals a world of wild mountains that are full of mystery and tough to climb—far from the glamour of Biarritz and its surfers. Welcome to the magnificent Irati Forest!

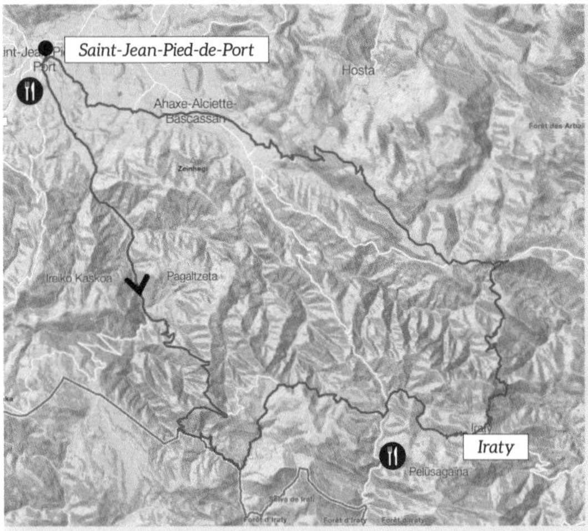

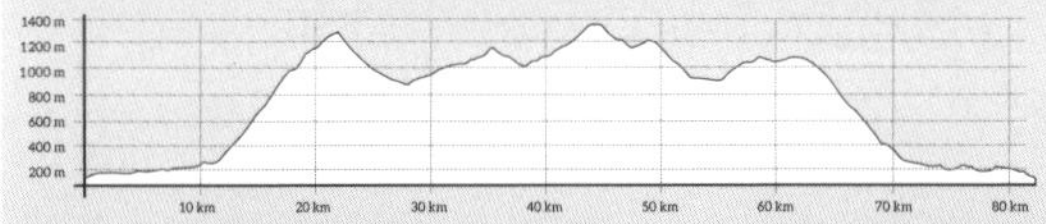

Deep in the Basque Country is a place of absolute calm. There are only a few chalets used as bases for cross-country skiing in winter, by shepherds and their sheep in summer, and by hunters of wood pigeon in the fall—and a few cyclists, who sometimes regret having left Saint-Jean-Pied-de-Port to tackle the Col d'Arthaburu: more than 10 km (6 mi) at a gradient of 10% if you extend via the Errozaté ramp (km 22/mi 14), with sections at 15%. This is the edge of the Irati, the largest beech forest in Europe, comprising 17,000 ha (42,000 acres) across Lower Navarre, Soule, and the Spanish border. The following 40 km (25 mi) are a delight, as we ride between 900 m (3,000 ft) and 1,330 m (4,400 ft)—altitude of the chalets of Irati (km 45/mi 28)—on a road that was surfaced barely fifty years ago. Around you is the enigmatic Okabé mountain, with its curious stone circles, at km 35 (mi 22).

Distance	E+	Difficulty	Appeal
83 km (52 mi)	2,350 m (7,710 ft)	4/5	5/5

Saint-Jean-Pied-de-Port (pop. 1,600) is 1h5 by train from Bayonne (to the northwest) or 1h by car (60 km/37 mi). To the northeast, Pau is 3h by train (via Bayonne) or 1h30 by car (100 km/62 mi). To the north, Bordeaux is 3h10 by train or 2h45 by car (240 km/150 mi).

Two options for some Ossau-Iraty cheese tasting are located at km 38 (mi 24): Artizarra or, close by, the more rustic but equally welcoming Kayolar ("Cabin").

Iraty Sorho
64220 Mendive
patisserie-artizarra-barbier-millox.fr

Upon your return, visit Barbier-Millox and try some traditional *gâteau basque* with either the classic filling of pastry cream or black cherry jam.

17 Rue d'Espagne
64220 Saint-Jean-Pied-de-Port
facebook.com/artizarra

IBERIAN PENINSULA

BASQUE COUNTRY & ASTURIAS

GALICIA

DOURO & ALGARVE

MADEIRA, THE AZORES, & TENERIFE

ANDALUSIA

MADRID

CATALONIA & ANDORRA

MALLORCA

SAN SEBASTIÁN
GIPUZKOA BEAUTY

Very hilly / Advanced
Map strava.com/routes/22561124
Test yourself km 32 (mi 20) strava.com/segments/2419409
Test yourself km 52 (mi 32) strava.com/segments/5297423

The Clásica de San Sebastián, which takes place each summer just after the Tour de France, is a highlight of the Union Cycliste Internationale (UCI) World Tour. Our route reflects the contrasts between the vacation feel of La Concha to the industrial valleys of Spain's Basque Country.

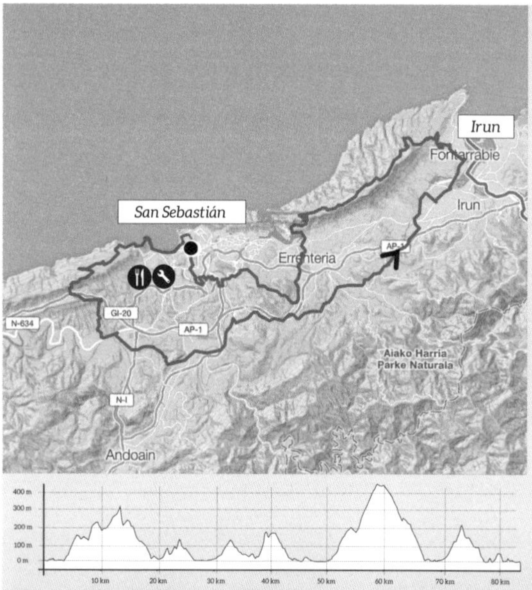

San Sebastián is a magnificent city of 200,000 people, and an elegant seaside resort of fancy buildings beneath hills that plunge into the ocean. We start by cycling through the old town along the emblematic beach of La Concha, then up Monte Igueldo for a panorama of the city. Then, we are off to ride the winding roads of the province of Gipuzkoa to explore a steeply contoured industrial Basque Country. Mendizorrotz (km 13/mi 8), Alto de Perurena (km 32/mi 20), and the wall of Oyarzun (km 38/mi 24)—1,500 m/4,920 ft at 11%—are all ramps that feature in the Clásica de San Sebastián. We flirt with the French border as we approach the deciding climb of the race, Jaizkibel: 8 km (5 mi) at 5.5%, but there are 0.7 km (0.4 mi) at 13% near the start, and the final 4 km (2.5 mi) are quite nasty. The descent allows us to admire San Sebastián from above as we return to enjoy its merry nocturnal buzz.

Distance	E+	Difficulty	Appeal
77 km (78 mi)	1,700 m (5,600 ft)	3/5	4/5

San Sebastián Airport is connected to Madrid, London, and Barcelona. It is 50 minutes from town by train or 25 minutes by car. It is also possible to fly to Biarritz (1h45 by train or 50 minutes by car) or Bilbao (2h30 or 1h15). Madrid is 5h30 by train or 4h30 by car (450 km/280 mi).

The terrace of the huge, elegant Hotel de Londres y de Inglaterra at the top of La Concha beach, offering the finest view over the bay, is the ideal spot for a snack and a coffee when you return.

Zubieta Calea 2
20007 San Sebastián
hlondres.com

Near Zurriola beach is the trendy and spacious Basque Country Cycling, which is also an agency (called Kili) that offers combined cycling, food, and wine experiences.

Calle Jose Miguel Barandiaran 24
20013 San Sebastián
basquecountrycycling.com

PAMPELONA
AT THE COURT OF "BIG MIG"

- *Low mountain / Advanced*
- *Map strava.com/routes/22565321*
- *Test yourself km 69 (mi 43) strava.com/segments/15036021*
- *Test yourself km 80 (mi 50) strava.com/segments/2893263*

Pamplona nourishes the tradition of its festival of San Fermín and two legends: the writer Ernest Hemingway, who fell in love with the city in the 1920s, and local boy Miguel Induráin, a five-time winner of the Tour de France. We cycle the roads of the latter to finish with the former.

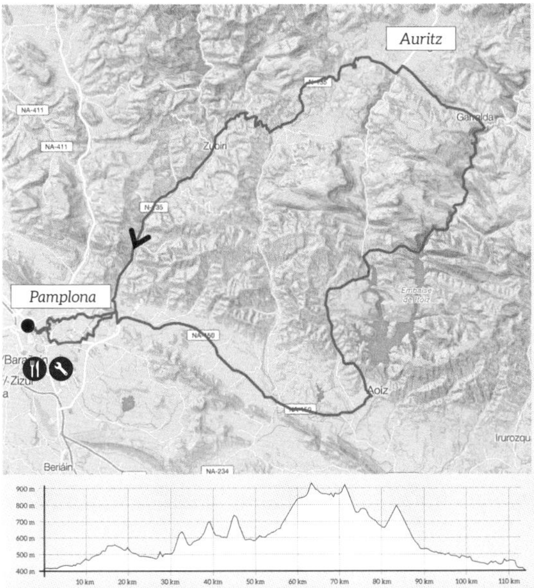

There are nearly fifty fake Miguel Induráins on Strava. The sprightly 55-year-old, who held the final yellow jersey five times between 1991 and 1995, will continue to draw the envy of many cyclists on certain segments in his native Navarre. Our route is inspired by his favorite routes and the annual sportive that bears his name. It passes through the eastern valleys of the province in the foothills of the Pyrenees. The villages are charming, and the verdant contours increasingly bolder. There are several little kickers with wearing surfaces, such as at Olaberri (km 33/mi 21) or Lakabe (km 45/mi 28). The highest point (950 m/3,120 ft) is only 5 km (3 mi) from Roncesvalles, which is close to where the Frankish military leader Roland met his death in 778. On the way back, we bypass Villava where Induráin grew up. With its arena, Monument to the Encierro (Bull Run), Hotel La Perla, and the huge Portal de Francia, Pamplona old town calls.

Distance	E+	Difficulty	Appeal
112 km (70 mi)	1,700 m (5,580 ft)	3/5	4/5

Pamplona is accessible from Madrid and Frankfurt via its airport, located 8 km (5 mi) from town. Also check flights to San Sebastian and Zaragoza, which, respectively, are 1h15 and 1h50 by car, and 3h and 2h by train. Madrid is 3h30 by train or 4h by car (400 km/250 mi).

When you return, celebrate the spirit of Pamplona at Café Iruña, where Hemingway used to write. Pinchos (little open sandwiches) and Galician beer? Or hot chocolate and churros?

Plaza del Castillo 44
31001, Pamplona, Navarre
cafeiruna.com

At Ciclos Martin in Pamplona, you might run into Prudencio Induráin (brother of the more famous Miguel), a Strava member who also represents the Navarre bike brand Conor and knows his region by heart.

Calle Esquiroz 20bis
31007 Pamplona, Navarre
ciclosmartin.com

BILBAO
GREEN BISCAY

Very hilly / Advanced

Map strava.com/routes/22838088

Distance	E+	Difficulty	Appeal
113 km (70 mi)	2,050 m (6,725 ft)	3/5	4/5

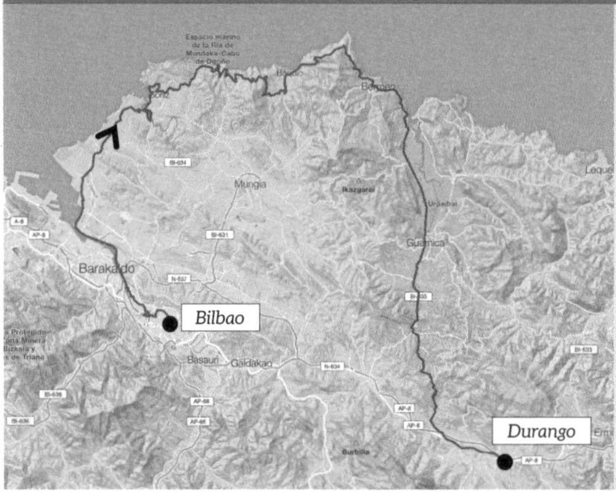

This 104 km (65 mi) ride through Biscay—from Bilbao (with its Guggenheim Museum) to Durango (return by train in 40 minutes)—runs along the jagged coast of the Bay of Biscay before heading into the interior of the verdant Basque Country. After Bilbao, there is a succession of fishing villages, cliffs, panoramic roads, and superb beaches in Gorliz, Armintza, Bakio, and Sukarrieta (with its biosphere). At Guernica, we remember the Nazi bombing of 1937 that destroyed the town. Here in the playground of the Basque climbers, there is no shortage of gradients around Jata, San Palaio, and Muniketa.

MARCILLA
PYRENEAN FAR WEST

Hilly / Advanced

Map strava.com/routes/22828163

Distance	E+	Difficulty	Appeal
125 km (78 mi)	1,100 m (3,610 ft)	3/5	4/5

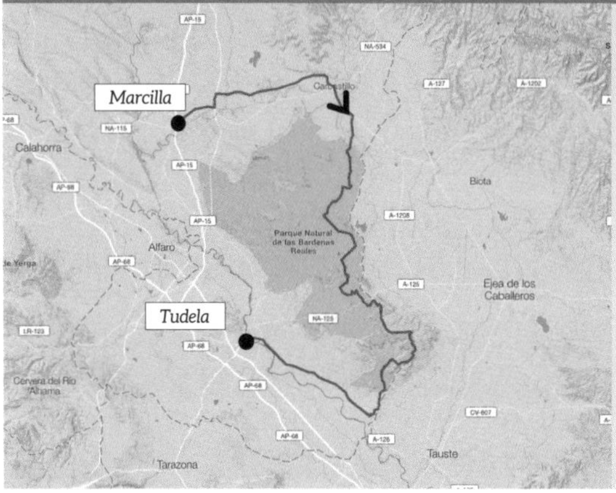

At the center of a quadrilateral formed by Pamplona, Logroño, Zaragoza, and Huesca, this atypical route from Marcilla to Tudela (return by train in 2h30) includes nearly 70 km (44 mi) of trails. It is recommended by the Bardenas Reales Natural Park in Navarre, which is on the border with Aragon. The landscape of this magnificent gravel adventure consists of ocher hills that look sublime when the sun is low in the sky, ravines, and surprising rock formations. We are at the foot of the Pyrenees, yet you would think you were in Arizona. We climb to 650 m (2,135 ft) and the imposing Punta Negra cliff. Unreal. Bring enough water.

OVIEDO

THE BEAST OF ASTURIAS

- *High mountain / Expert*
- *Map strava.com/routes/21902979*
- *Test yourself km 38 (mi 24) strava.com/segments/3583493*
- *Test yourself km 45 (mi 28) strava.com/segments/5310841*

Mortirolo, Zoncolan, Kitzbüheler Horn: a clutch of merciless climbs vie for the title of "hardest in the Alps." But the Alto de l'Angliru, south of Oviedo, would be a serious challenger for "hardest in Europe." It is a victory just to reach the top without stopping.

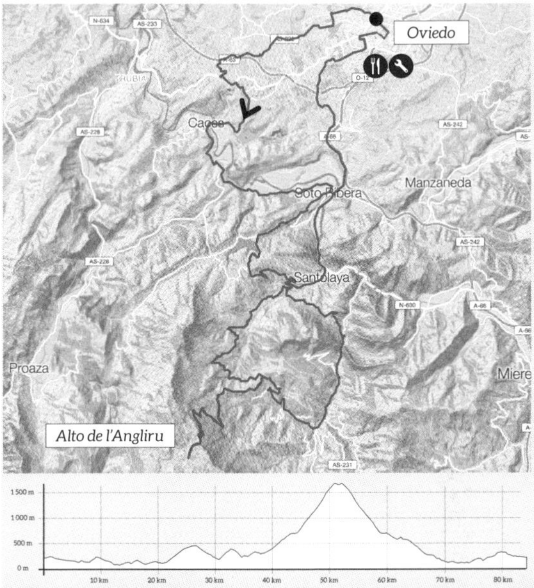

L'Angliru: Mention the name in Oviedo, and they will look at you in amazement, even though you will not be the first to ride 40 km (25 mi) out of town through the lush Asturias countryside to your reckoning with the horror that is the former mule track, which was surfaced in 1999 for its inclusion in the Vuelta a España! Sure, why not check it out? But climb it? Really?! The approach from La Vega is fine; however, there are no words to describe the final 7 km (4.5 mi), which has an average gradient of 12%, with one particular 1 km (0.6 mi) stretch at 17.5% two-thirds of the way into this insane section. There are other gradients that you will never forget: 22% at Curves de Las Cabanes, 20% on the Los Picones bend, 21% on the Los Cabayos switchback, and 23.5% at La Cueña Les Cabres. Then two more sections at 20% and over, before the summit, at 1,570 m (5,150 ft). Still feel like you can slay the Beast of Asturias?

Distance
84 km
(52 mi)

E+
2,500 m
(8,200 mi)

Difficulty
5/5

Appeal
5/5

Asturias Airport is 1h30 by train from Oviedo and 35 minutes by car (50 km/30 mi). Better connected is Santiago de Compostela Airport, which is 3h by car (300 km/185 mi). Madrid is 4h20 by train, and Bilbao is 2h50 (280 km/175 mi) by car.

At La Finca, celebrate with some Asturian cider, poured in the traditional *escanciado* way: bottle held very high and glass very low to oxygenate the beverage.

Calle Gascona 4
33001 Oviedo, Asturias
sidrerialafinca.es

Just 1 km (0.5 mi) from the station, Carma Bike caters to every need: sale of new and secondhand bikes (Wilier, KTM, Felt), rental of road bikes, and workshop.

Calle Ángel Muñiz Toca, 12 bajo
33006 Oviedo, Asturias
carmabike.es

ESPINOSA DE LOS MONTEROS
TOUGH PICÓN BLANCO

Low mountain / Advanced *Map* strava.com/routes/22371684

Distance	E+	Difficulty	Appeal
108 km (67 mi)	2,450 m (8,040 ft)	4/5	4/5

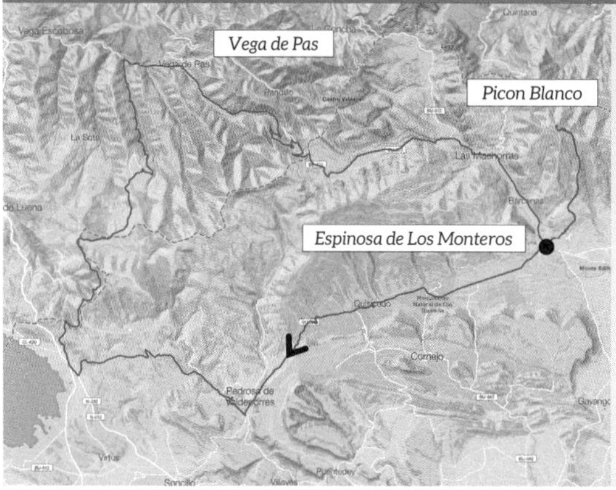

Picón Blanco is the most demanding climb in the mountainous north of Burgos province in Castile and León. Its narrow road clings to the sheer face of the mountain, and the final sections are pretty hostile. At the summit (1,512 m/4,960 ft) is an abandoned military base. The climb from Espinosa de Los Monteros is 8.5 km (5.3 mi) long at an average gradient of more than 9%, with numerous passages at gradients of 14% to 17%. We take the Las Estacas de Trueba Pass (1,166 m/3,825 ft) from the Cantabrian side. Reinosa, which is located west of Ebro Reservoir, is easier to get to, but it is 140 km (85 mi) from Picón Blanco.

VILLAMAYOR
LEGENDARY COVADONGA

High mountain / Expert *Map* strava.com/routes/22372546

Distance	E+	Difficulty	Appeal
109 km (68 mi)	2,400 m (7,900 ft)	4/5	5/5

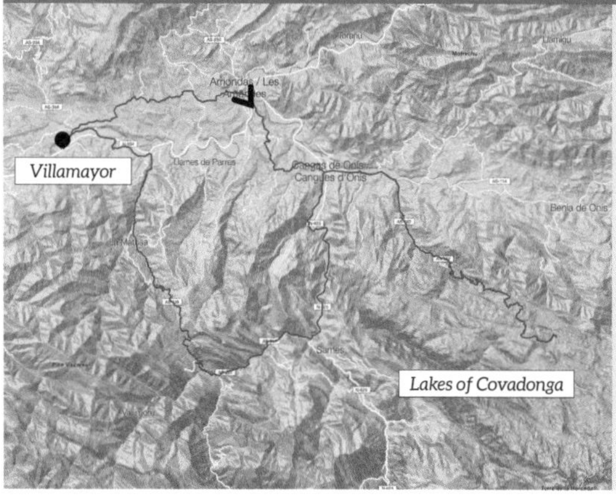

Asturias, located east of Gijón and Oviedo, is a marvelous region for cycling that enjoys a well-established prestige owing to the legendary ascent to the lakes of Covadonga in the wild landscape of the Picos de Europa National Park. The steep, tortuous road that leads to the glacial lakes of Enol and Ercina at more than 1,100 m (3,610 ft) has been a classic of the Vuelta a España since the 1980s. At 12.6 km (7.8 mi) long, the climb has an average gradient of 7.3%, although the segment known as La Huesera shoots up to 15% for 0.8 km (0.5 mi). It is a real challenge to reach the lakes without stopping.

SANTIAGO DE COMPOSTELA
BEYOND THE CAMINO

Very hilly / Advanced — *Map strava.com/routes/22851348*

Distance	E+	Difficulty	Appeal
101 km (63 mi)	2,000 m (6,560 ft)	3/5	4/5

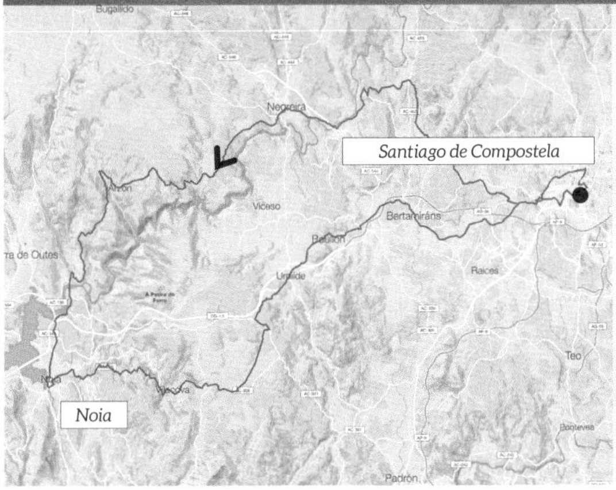

The many pilgrims' ways that comprise the Camino de Santiago converge on Santiago de Compostela in the heart of the Galician hills—from the east mainly, but also from the north and south. We set our bearings west, away from religious fervor and tourist hordes, to the Ría de Muros et Noia, a sea inlet below Cape Finisterre. We start at Praza do Obradoiro, Santiago's main square, witnessing the wide grins of those who have completed the Camino before 45 km (28 mi) of proper effort via the fortress at Negreira and the Tambre gorges. After a break in Noia, return over the heights of Villacova.

PONTECESURES
PILGRIM'S MOUNT

Hilly / Intermediate — *Map strava.com/routes/22868616*

Distance	E+	Difficulty	Appeal
84 km (52 mi)	1,550 m (3,775 ft)	3/5	4/5

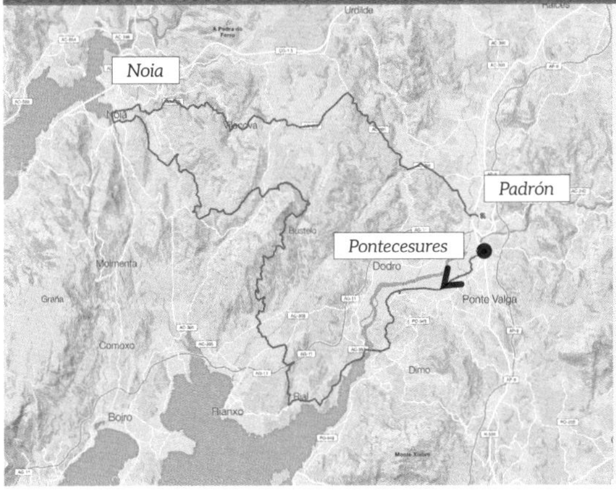

This loop southwest of Santiago de Compostela begins in Pontecesures and ends in Padrón. The towns are only 3 km (2 mi) apart, but we advise taking the train for 15 minutes rather than riding through the motor traffic. Between the inlets of Ría de Arousa and Ría de Muros y Noia, which provide a dose of sea air, we climb the 11 km (7 mi) of Pico Muralla in three tricky stages up to 530 m (1,740 ft) to wind turbines at the top. The mountain is both a key ascent for cyclists in Galicia and a destination for pilgrims from Vigo and Portugal. After you enjoy a coffee under the arcades of Noia, return via the heights of Villacova.

GUIMARAES
THE BIRTHPLACE OF PORTUGAL

Very hilly / Advanced

Map strava.com/routes/22312377

Test yourself km 21 (mi 13) strava.com/segments/5042862

Test yourself km 89 (mi 55) strava.com/segments/1611090

"Aqui nasceu Portugal" (Portugal Was Born Here). The slogan, which dates from the Middle Ages, is writ large on a wall of Largo do Toural, a superb square in Guimarães. To the east lie the seductive low mountains of Lameira, which are ripe for exploration.

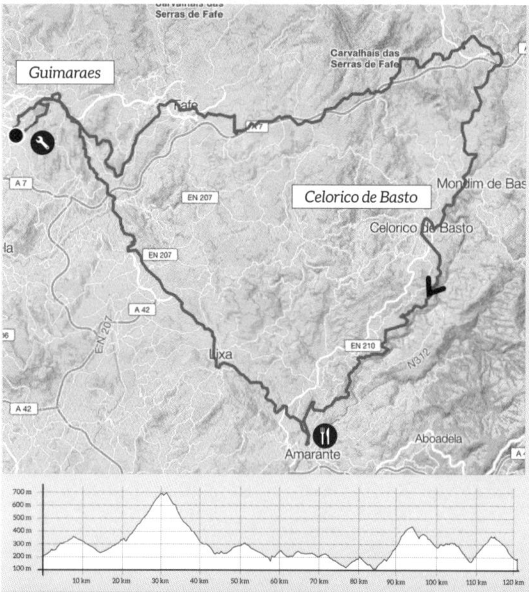

Porto, Braga, Vila Real: there is no lack of beautiful towns around Guimarães. It brims with historical landmarks, which we see in the final kilometers of our route, including a medieval castle, the Palace of the Dukes of Braganza, and the timeworn paving slabs of Rua de Santa Maria. On the way there, we ride along winding roads—sometimes cobbled (quite prettily)—with little respite except for the more than 50 km (30 mi) of cycle path (what could be more contemporary?) to Fafe and then from Arco de Baúlhe to Amarante. Between the two lies the Serra da Lameira: 8 km (5 mi) of climbing at a gradient of 4% to reach an altitude of more than 700 m (2,295 ft). From Amarante, with its mix of Roman and Renaissance styles, we climb again to Lixa: 6 km (4 mi) at 5%. At km 111 (mi 69), the bravest will defy the wall of the Sanctuary of Lapinha or the slope of Mont Penha, located 200 m (655 ft) above stunning Guimarães.

Distance	E+	Difficulty	Appeal
122 km (76 mi)	1,650 m (5,400 ft)	3/5	4/5

Guimarães is 55 minutes by train or 45 minutes by car (55 km/34 mi) from the nearest international airport at Porto: 25 to 40 minutes by shuttle bus or metro from Porto's São Bento railway station. Lisbon is 4h by train or 3h40 by car (370 km/230 mi).

At Amarante (km 85/mi 53), ride to Confeitaria da Ponte. Fabulous foguetes (deep fried pastries with a sweet filling) and toucinho da céu (almond cake).

Rua 31 de Janeiro 186
4600-043 Amarante
confeitariadaponte.pt

Like Bike is the place to go in Guimarães for a warm welcome and attentive service. Retailer of Specialized

Rua dos Cutileiros 2918
4835-044 Guimarães
likebike.pt

PESO DA RÉGUA

VINEYARDS OF PORTO

Hilly / Intermediate *Map strava.com/routes/22538519*

Distance	E+	Difficulty	Appeal
69 km (43 mi)	1,600 m (5,250 ft)	2/5	4/5

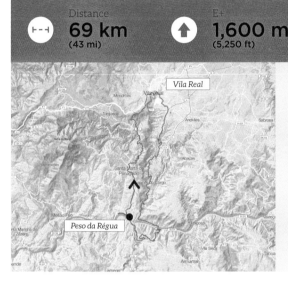

Once upon a time, wine barrels would be shipped down the Douro River from Peso da Régua to Porto on flat-bottomed boats called rabelos. In Peso, you should visit the Douro Museum and taste a few vintage wines once you return from exploring the steep yet striking Corgo Valley to the north of the town. The terraced vineyards of the Porto appellation are the jewel of northern Portugal with its landscapes, the impressive Corgo Viaduct, and superb Vila Real, from where the Vila Velha viewpoint looks over the whole valley. The final climb includes a tough 4 km (2.5 mi) at 9% up to the chapel of Santa Eufemia.

PINHAO

MAGICAL DOURO

Very hilly / Advanced *Map strava.com/routes/22538968*

Distance	E+	Difficulty	Appeal
89 km (55 mi)	2,050 m (6,725 ft)	3/5	4/5

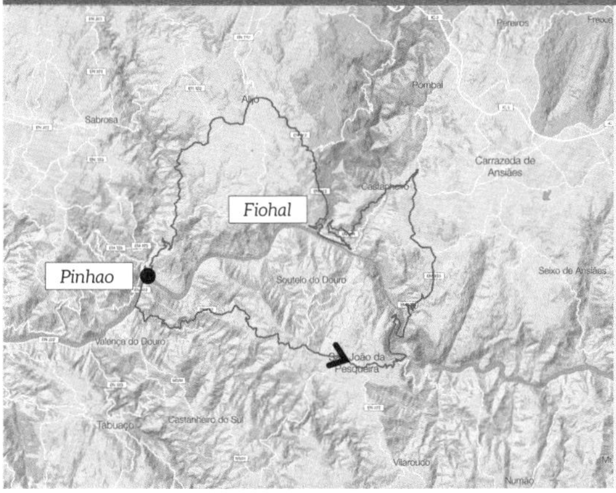

Three long ascents up to between 600 m (1,970 ft) and 700 m (2,300 ft) punctuate this route through the soaring slopes of the Cima Corgo, the largest wine-growing area in the valley of the Upper Douro. Heading out of Pinhão, you will find challenging gradients (especially after the Valeira Dam at km 30/ mi 19), dizzying descents, and sections along ridgelines. Douro, the oldest appellation in the world (dating from the eighteenth century), is made from grapes grown on terraces in a soil of light schist that contrasts with the color of the vines and the river water. The scenery is magical and a must for any cyclist visiting Portugal.

COVILHA
FIVE STARS

⊕ *Low mountain / Expert*
⊕ *Map strava.com/routes/22525831*

⊕ *Test yourself km 39 (mi 24) strava.com/segments/7549650*
⊕ *Test yourself km 80 (mi 50) strava.com/segments/755462*

Serra da Estrela is not the kind of mountain range that you expect to find in Portugal. Situated right in the middle of the country, it is one of the most beautiful cycling experiences (at up to nearly 2,000 m/6,560 ft) that you could have in Europe. It is a five-star ride in every way.

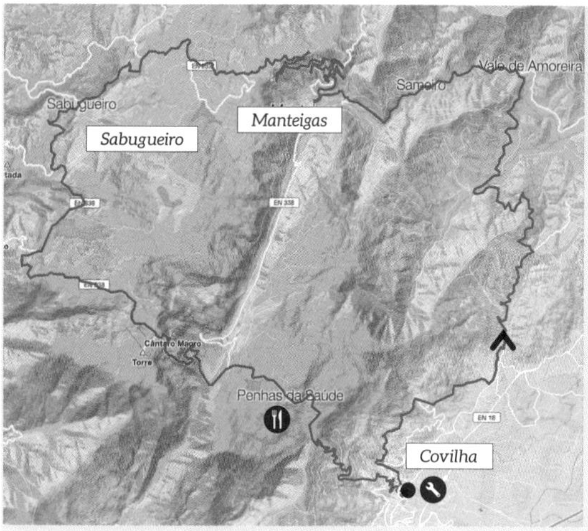

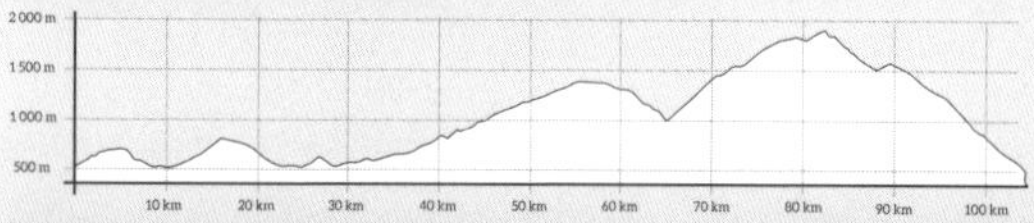

The "Star Mountain Range" is the highest in mainland Portugal, even if you have to add the 7 m (23 ft) of the observation tower at Torre to attain the 2,000 m (6,562 ft) of its highest point. This granite mass has some surprising alpine scenery. Above Sabugueiro (km 64/mi 40), we climb the switchbacks of the quiet EN339 road between rosemary shrubs and juniper bushes before reaching rockier surroundings. The ascent is worthy of an alpine pass: 8 km (5 mi) at 6.7% to start, then 6 km (4 mi) at 5% to finish. The 0.8 km (0.5 mi) up to the observatory, which is not part of our route, is at 7%. With strange hues and light, the views are stunning across a surprisingly varied landscape of schist, streams, and glacial valleys. In winter, temperatures on the descent drop below freezing at Penhas da Saúde (1,500 m/4,920 ft), the only ski resort in the country. You might even wonder if you are still in Portugal.

Distance	E+	Difficulty	Appeal
104 km (65 mi)	2,850 m (9,350 ft)	4/5	5/5

Covilhã (pop. 50,000) is 3h40 by train from Lisbon to the south or 2h45 by car (280 km/175 mi). To the northwest, Porto is 6h30 by train and 2h30 by car (250 km/155 mi). To the east, Salamanca in Spain is 2h by car (200 km/125 mi).

Penhas da Saúde ski resort (km 91/mi 56) is a great place to stop for lunch in Varanda da Estrela. It serves a fantastic local ewe's cheese.

Penhas da Saúde
6215 Covilhã
facebook.com/varandadaestrela

Located 0.5 km (0.3 mi) from the train station, CR Bike Studio is the ideal place for purchasing or repairing road gear. Retailer of Specialized and Focus.

Avenida da Anil
6200-502 Covilhã
facebook.com/CrBikeStudio

The road up to the top of the Serra de Estrela, Portugal.

NAZARÉ
PILGRIM ROUTES

Very hilly / Advanced
Map strava.com/routes/22208599
Test yourself km 23 (mi 14) strava.com/segments/4915812
Test yourself km 45 (mi 28) strava.com/segments/723198

Riding this testing route past sanctuaries and monasteries, you will understand why the surfers of Nazaré have no fear of the ocean waves, which can reach heights of 20 m (65 ft). No doubt, they feel that they are protected by the omnipresent Virgin.

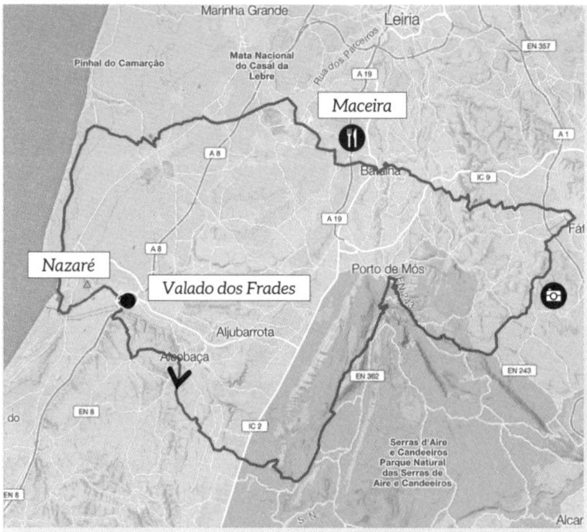

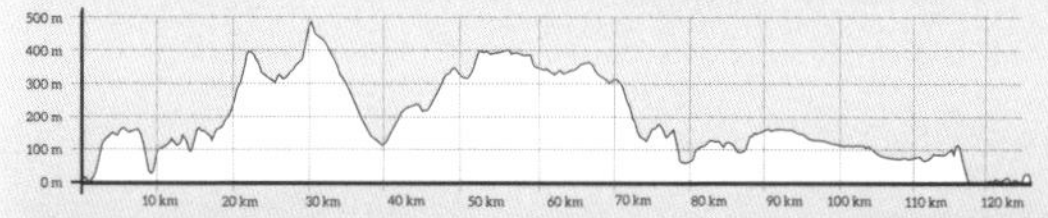

This is the real Portugal: simple, very religious, and no tourist nonsense. Through the green and fertile Serras de Aire e Candeeiros mountains runs a network of pilgrim routes leading to sites of great significance to Catholics. Our route starts and ends in Nazaré, in front of the Sanctuary of Our Lady that memorializes a miracle from the Middle Ages involving the intercession of the Virgin Mary. At km 12 (mi 7.5), we pass the imposing walls of the Alcobaça Monastery. Later, at km 86 (mi 53), we will see the Batalha Monastery too. At km 45 (mi 28) is the Castle of Mós, which was recaptured from the Moors in the eleventh century, and at km 68 (mi 42), Fátima, with its Chapel of the Apparitions and sanctuary. The course is never flat, with several 2 to 3 km (1.25 to 2 mi) ramps around São Mamede. The landscape is stunning, crisscrossed by *choucos*—little stone walls separating different plots of land.

Distance	E+	Difficulty	Appeal
130 km (81 mi)	1,850 m (6,070 ft)	3/5	3/5

Nazaré can be reached by train via Valado dos Frades Station, 5 km (3 mi) away (10 minutes by bus). Valado is 3h30 by train from Lisbon to the south, or 3h45 from Porto to the north. By car, allow 1h30 from Lisbon (125 km/78 mi) and 2h from Porto (220 km/136 mi).

Fancy something sweet 40 km (25 mi) from the finish? A Barroquinha in Maceira is the place for a good coffee and typical Portuguese treats.

Rua de Leiria 1
2405-033 Maceira
facebook.com/Café-A-Barroquinha

At km 56 (mi 35), the route runs close to the spectacular Mira de Aire Caves. The caves stretch for 11 km (7 mi), but only 600 m (2,000 ft) are open to visit. Appreciate limestone formations 150 million years old, and a lake fed by illuminated cascades.

grutasmiradaire.com

TORRES VEDRAS
IN MEMORY OF A CHAMPION

- *Low mountain / Intermediate*
- *Map strava.com/routes/22203981*
- *Test yourself km 37 (mi 23) strava.com/segments/7241112*
- *Test yourself km 46 (mi 29) strava.com/segments/4114310*

Joaquim Agostinho was a muscular, rustic champion, who was a valiant challenger of Merckx and Hinault. He died in 1984, aged 41, after a crash during the Tour of the Algarve. This route, which starts and ends in his birthplace, Torres Vedras, is a vibrant homage to a Portuguese legend.

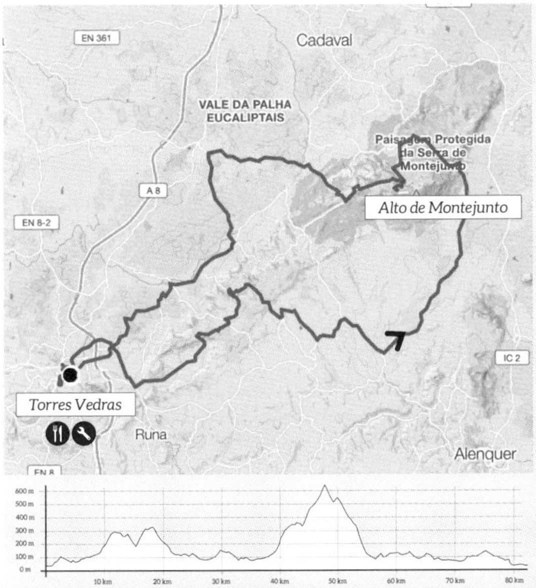

Nearly forty years after his death, the much-lamented Joaquim Agostinho still embodies the spirit of Portuguese cycling. In his birthplace of Torres Vedras, a memorial to him stands in Várzea Park (km 82/mi 50), less than 1 km (0.6 mi) from the station. Riding the roads on which he forged his career is like cycling through history. The lush Serra de Montejunto is both a magnificent place to pay homage to him and a real test. The road up to the TV antennas (at 642 m/2,100 ft) climbs for 12 km (7.5 mi). The final 4 km (2.5 mi) are harsh at average gradients of between 9% and 11%. Just before the summit, you should pause a moment at the Salvé-Rainha viewpoint for a superb panorama over the hills as far as the ocean. You might even glimpse a Bonelli's eagle soaring above the oak trees, eucalyptuses, and cypresses. Agostinho was more of a buffalo—a champion who will be long remembered.

Distance	E+	Difficulty	Appeal
83 km (52 mi)	1,700 m (5,575 ft)	3/5	4/5

Torres Vedras (pop. 80,000) lies 50 km (30 mi) north of Lisbon: 50 minutes by car, 2h by train or 2h30 by bus. Coimbra, 180 km (112 mi) to the north, is 2h by train. Porto, 280 km (175 mi) to the north, is 2h30 by car.panorama over

Torres Vedras is also famous for *pastel de feijao*, a tart filled with a creamy paste of beans and ground almonds. Casa Benjamim is the place to sample it.

Rua Almirante Gago Coutinho 2B
2560-303 Torres Vedras
facebook.com/casabenjamim

Westbike is not just a top bike store and workshop, but also a meeting point for all serious cyclists in Torres Vedras. Retailer of Specialized and Orbea.

Avenida General Humberto Delgado 24B
2560-272 Torres Vedras
facebook.com/westbike.pt

LISBON
LISBOAN BEAUTIES

- *Hilly / Intermediate*
- *Map strava.com/routes/22208402*
- *Test yourself km 37 (mi 23) strava.com/segments/6525830*
- *Test yourself km 44 (mi 27) strava.com/segments/17067659*

What a joy it is to cycle out of Portugal's bustling capital along the coast before returning via Sintra-Cascais Natural Park. But watch out for streetcars, and not just because of the rails! This means of transportation, which is painted yellow, is king in Lisbon, and cyclists must give way.

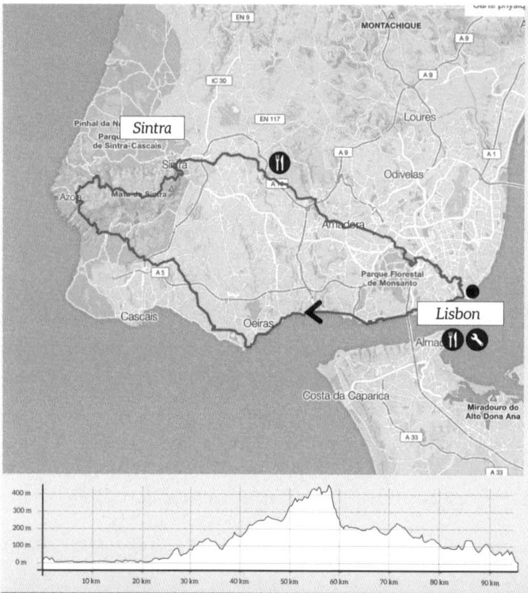

This bumpy route heads out toward the ocean before turning to climb to 450 m (1,480 ft) above Sintra. A minimum level of fitness is required, although Lisbon and the extraordinary natural scenery to the west will make you forget your aching legs. We leave the city via the Alfama neighborhood and Sé Cathedral along a cycle path, past the Jerónimos Monastery and the Belém Tower. At km 25 (mi 16), resist the tempting beaches of Estoril and Cascais and choose instead Sintra-Cascais Natural Park. The luxuriant woods and gardens are enthralling. You might well feel like pushing on to Cape Roca from km 46 (mi 29). There is no lack of flamboyant architecture around Sintra: National Palace, Pena Palace, Castle of the Moors, and Amadora. The return to Lisbon is superb: Monsanto Forest Park and the old neighborhoods of Anjos, Socorro, and Alfama (with its narrow cobbled streets).

Distance	E+	Difficulty	Appeal
96 km (60 mi)	1,350 m (4,450 ft)	3/5	4/5

Santa Apolónia train station in Lisbon is 8 km/5 mi from Humberto Delgado Airport: 16 minutes by car or 40 minutes by bus then train. To the north, Porto is 2h50 by train or 3h by car (300 km/187 mi). To the south, Faro is 3h by train or 2h30 by car (280 km/174 mi).

On the other side of the city, near Lisbon Oriente Station and Vasco da Gama Bridge, is Grupeto, a perfect bike cafe. It offers a small workshop and tasty all-day menu.

Passeio Adamastor Loja 11
1990-008 Lisbon, Portugal
grupetobikeshopcafe.com

After the wonders of Sintra-Cascais Natural Park, stop for a break at Cafe Saudade (km 68/mi 42) for a coffee and a travesseiro de Sintra (pastry with egg custard and almond).

Avenida Dr. Miguel Bombarda 6
2710-590 Sintra, Portugal
facebook.com/CafeSaudade

SANTA CLARA-SABÓIA

TERRACES OF MONCHIQUE

Low mountain / Intermediate

Map strava.com/routes/22533420

Distance	E+	Difficulty	Appeal
110 km (68 mi)	1,950 m (6,400 ft)	3/5	4/5

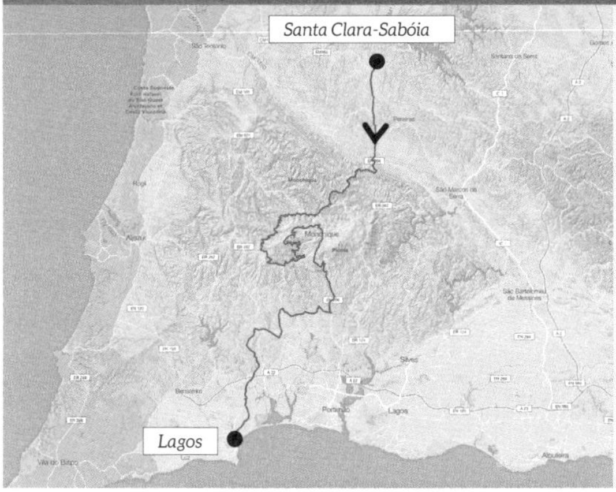

This route from Santa Clara-Sabóia in the heart of the Algarve to the languid coast at Lagos (2h30 to return by train) is a fine exploration of the Serra de Monchique through some of the most beautiful landscapes in Portugal. From the lookout at the top of Foia (902 m/2,959 ft), the panoramas evoke Tuscany and its terraces. Eucalyptus, cork, and pine trees stretch to the horizon. Then, we descend to the white-walled village of Monchique and the Roman baths at Caldas (where you should refill your water bottle) before rolling on to Lagos and its superb rocks. What a sumptuous ride!

FARO

ALGARVE AND THE CALDEIRÃO

Hilly / Intermediate

Map strava.com/routes/22821252

Distance	E+	Difficulty	Appeal
95 km (59 mi)	1,350 m (4,430 ft)	3/5	3/5

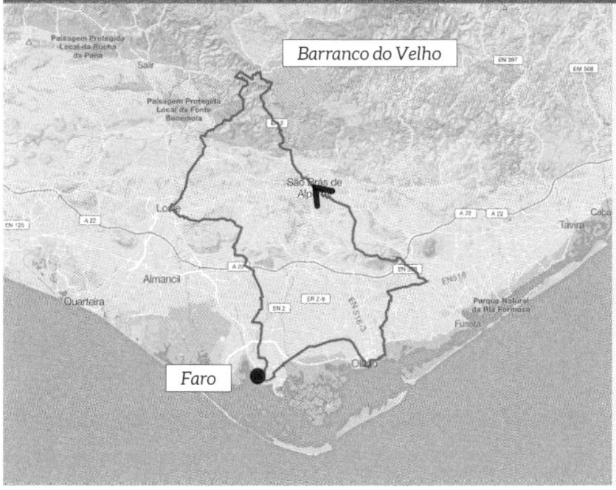

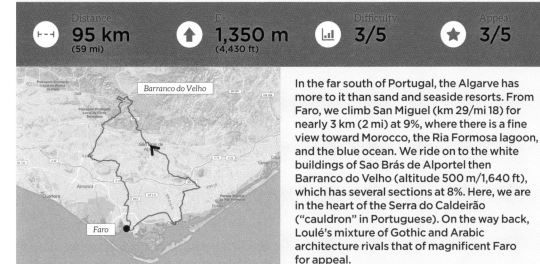

In the far south of Portugal, the Algarve has more to it than sand and seaside resorts. From Faro, we climb San Miguel (km 29/mi 18) for nearly 3 km (2 mi) at 9%, where there is a fine view toward Morocco, the Ria Formosa lagoon, and the blue ocean. We ride on to the white buildings of Sao Brás de Alportel then Barranco do Velho (altitude 500 m/1,640 ft), which has several sections at 8%. Here, we are in the heart of the Serra do Caldeirão ("cauldron" in Portuguese). On the way back, Loulé's mixture of Gothic and Arabic architecture rivals that of magnificent Faro for appeal.

FUNCHAL
FANCY FOOTWORK IN MADEIRA

Low mountain / Advanced   Map strava.com/routes/22797323

Distance	E+	Difficulty	Appeal
69 km (43 mi)	2,000 m (6,650 ft)	4/5	4/5

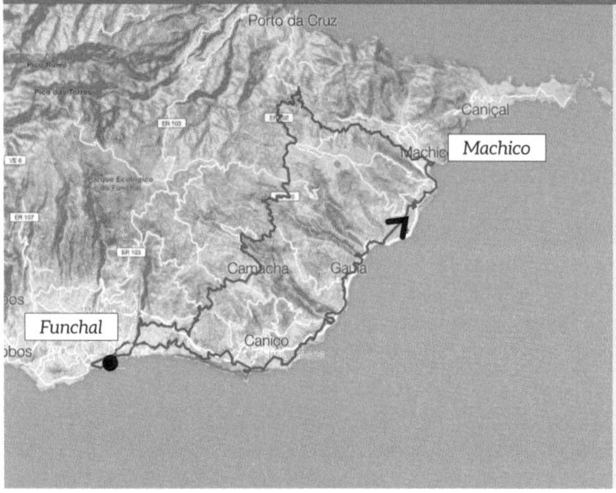

You will need to do some nifty pedaling on this route, which starts in the town where star soccer player Cristiano Ronaldo was born, to confront some scary slopes. Madeira is small (60 km/37 mi by 23 km/14 mi), but the highest point (the peak of an extinct volcano) rises to 1,800 m (5,905 ft). We ride out along a jagged coast with red rocks and the splendid Garajau Cliff (7 km/4.5 mi at 10%) before turning inland to climb up above Santo António da Serra via fabulous viewpoints. Back in Funchal (take care on the descent), relax with a glass of Madeira wine on the rooftop of the CR7 hotel.

PONTA DELGADA
VOLCANIC AZORES

Low mountain / Advanced   Map strava.com/routes/22798601

Distance	E+	Difficulty	Appeal
109 km (68 mi)	2,150 m (7,000 ft)	4/5	4/5

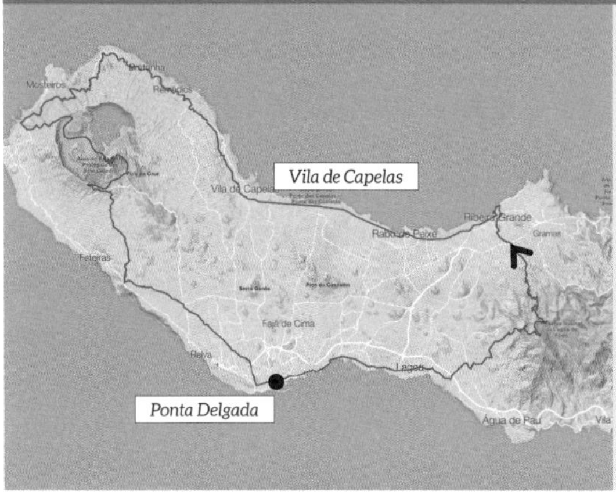

This loop around São Miguel, the largest island in the Azores and the westernmost route in our European Atlas, can be split in two if you like. The volcanic structure of the archipelago is uncompromising as we ride between fumaroles, lakes, red rocks, and forests of bay trees. The climb to Fogo Lake sets the tone: 8 km (5 mi) at 10%. The island is stunningly beautiful: the 38-degree water of Caldeira Velha, the viewpoint of Pedras Negras ("black rocks") on the curious Elephant Trunk cliff, natural bathing pools, King's View on Sete Cidades Lake, and, of course, the ocean.

TENERIFE
KOM BOSSES

High mountain / Expert

Map strava.com/routes/22804276

Distance	E+	Difficulty	Appeal
133 km (83 mi)	3,250 m (10,665 ft)	5/5	5/5

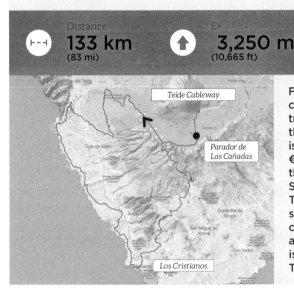

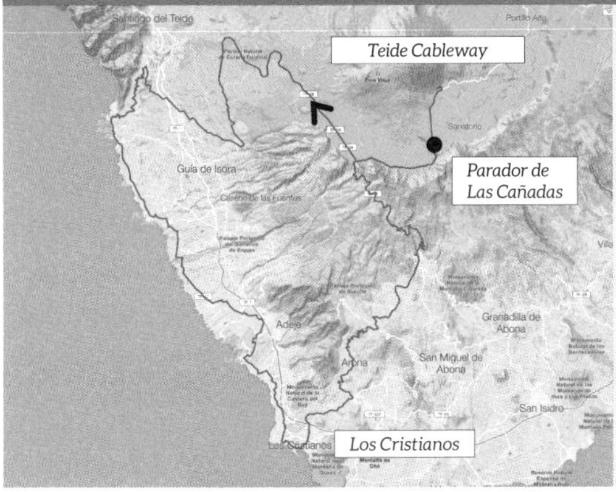

From Chris Froome to Wout Van Aert, numerous champions have undertaken high-altitude training on Tenerife in the Canary Islands, where the climate is pleasantly warm. Their base camp is the Parador de las Cañadas del Teide (from €100/$110) at more than 2,000 m (6,560 ft) on the slopes of Mount Teide, the highest point in Spain (3,718 m/12,198 ft).
The champs often cycle down to the black sandy beaches of the west coast before climbing back via Arona and Vilaflor. The ascent is 30 km (19 mi) long and as hard as it is sublime. Forget about KOMs round here! They are all held by top pros.

TENERIFE
CANARIES WARM-UP

Low mountain / Advanced

Map strava.com/routes/22804711

Distance	E+	Difficulty	Appeal
81 km (50 mi)	2,000 m (6,650 ft)	4/5	4/5

Before attempting to defy Mount Teide, first get to grips with the omnipresent mountain terrain here on Tenerife. We depart Santa Cruz from the fountain on Plaza de España in the direction of the attractive slopes of northeastern Tenerife: 8.6 km (5.5 mi) at 7% toward La Esperanza, then 11 km (7 mi) at 5% from Tegueste, and finally 3 km (2 mi) at 8% (400 m/1,315 ft at 20% at the foot) to reach the extraordinary viewpoint at Pico del Inglés. The descent through the laurel forest of Anaga Rural Park reveals incredible panoramas.
Do not be alarmed by the short stretch along the San Andrés Highway; that is normal here.

JEREZ DE LA FRONTERA
A DAY OUT TO ARCOS

- *Fairly flat / Intermediate*
- *Map strava.com/routes/21916084*
- *Test yourself km 29 (mi 18) strava.com/segments/8005368*
- *Test yourself km 79 (mi 49) strava.com/segments/8667405*

In the case of this route, it is less about the journey than the destinations: Arcos de la Frontera (midway) and Jerez de la Frontera on return. Here in the south of Andalusia, at the bottom of Spain/Europe, you will have trouble picking your favorite of these two towns.

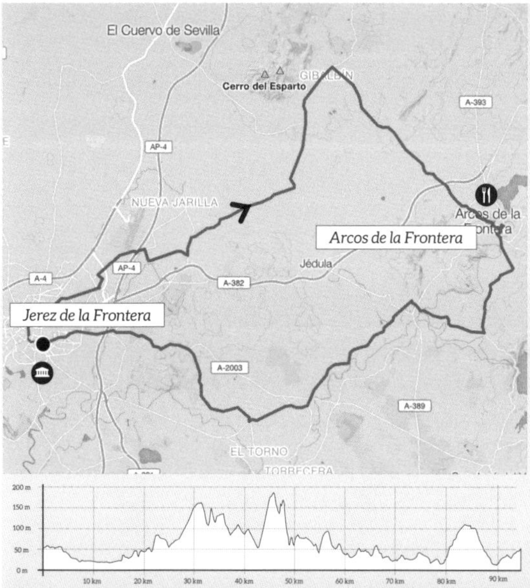

From a physical point of view, these roads through the Province of Cádiz are pleasant (cycle paths on the way out of Jerez) but not that challenging, except for the heat (do take frequent breaks) and the short climb of La Arquera just before Arcos de la Frontera. No matter, this route is designed to afford the opportunity to explore the two towns in question. Jerez, which is easily accessible from its international airport merits a whole day on its own without the bike. And Arcos de la Frontera deserves a good, long stop to have a relaxed look around. Our route takes in the most beautiful parts of the old town sitting on its sandstone ridge amid the white houses of the residential streets, full of history and Moorish influence. Step off the bike to enjoy the views from the Balcón de la Peña Nueva and the Mirador de Abades. Then follow the tranquil course of the Guadalete River back to Jerez.

Distance	E+	Difficulty	Appeal
95 km (59 mi)	950 m (3,115 ft)	2/5	3/5

There are flights to Jerez Airport (10 minutes by train from Jerez) from across the continent. Cádiz is 30 minutes from Jerez by train, Seville is 1h, and Madrid is 3h30. By car: 35 minutes from Cádiz (25 km/15 mi), 1h10 from Seville (90 km/55 mi), 6h from Madrid (620 km/385 mi).

In Arcos (km 47/mi 29), enjoy a coffee on the sublime terrace of the Paradores hotel, which was formerly the mayor's residence.

Plaza del Cabildo
11630 Arcos de la Frontera, Cádiz
parador.es

There is no excuse to miss the splendors of Jerez de la Frontera. You should spend a whole day exploring the Alcázar, its gardens, and medieval mosque; its School of Equestrian Art; San Salvador Cathedral; and the sherry producers.

andalucia.org

RONDA
VILLAGES OF WHITE

- *Low mountain / Advanced*
- *Map strava.com/routes/21918167*
- *Test yourself km 57 (mi 35) strava.com/segments/6713172*
- *Test yourself km 71 (mi 44) strava.com/segments/6652458*

The white-walled villages so typical of Spain are even more stunning in the south of Andalusia. This route, which starts and ends in Ronda (a magnificent town between Malaga and Cádiz), shows off some of the most attractive villages.

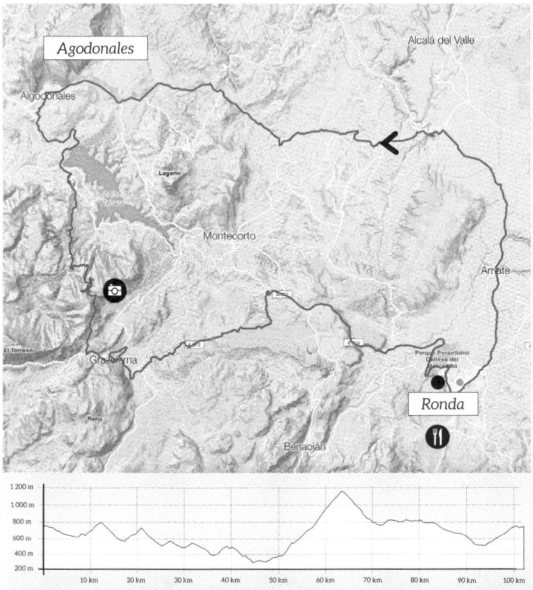

Andalusian villages are white in order to protect from the sultry summers. Remember this before riding off down these roads, which are pleasantly warm on winter afternoons, but burning hot in summer. Our route starts and ends in the superb town of Ronda by way of a tour around Lake Zahara. The radiance of the villages nestling in the little valleys is perhaps best appreciated from above. Arriate, Setenil de las Bodegas, Algodonales, or Grazalema —it is impossible to determine which of them is the most beautiful. The enchantment continues at the peak of Puerto de Las Palomas, a wide road, foreshortened view back down the switchbacks, 13 km (8 mi) at 7%, with the final 1 km (0.6 mi) at 14%. We end with a little exploration of Ronda, where you can veer off onto the little cobbled trail down to the foot of the breathtaking Puente Novo, which connects the old and new towns.

Distance	E+	Difficulty	Appeal
102 km (63 mi)	2,200 m (7,220 ft)	3/5	5/5

Trains to Ronda connect through Antequera, 90 km (55 mi). Grenada, Cordoba, and Malaga are 2h away, Seville is 3h, and Madrid is 4h (via Seville). By car, Marbella is 1h15 (65 km/40 mi), Malaga is 1h30 (100 km/60 mi), Seville is 1h45 (130 km/80 mi), and Madrid is 6h (600 km/370 mi).

The well-named La Bicicleta, 300 meters/yards from the station, is not a bike cafe (yet). Still, it is perfect for a bite before riding off or when you return.

Calle Naranja 50
29400 Ronda, Malaga
la-bicicleta-cafe-ronda.negocio.site

Step off the bike at the summit of Puerto de Las Palomas (km 63/mi 39) to take in the view. On one side, the forested slopes of the Sierra de Grazalema Natural Park. On the other, the turquoise waters of Lake Zahara.

andaluciarustica.com

ALBACETE
DON QUIXOTE COUNTRY

Fairly flat / Advanced

Map strava.com/routes/22717793

Distance	E+	Difficulty	Appeal
236 km (147 mi)	1,150 m (3,800 ft)	3/5	4/5

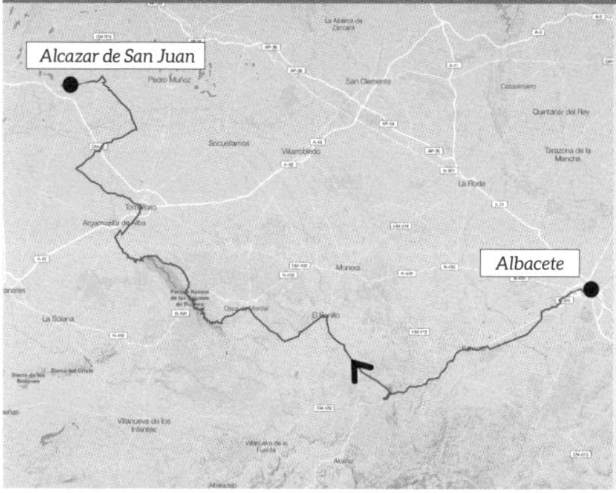

No one can claim to love Spain if they have not heard of Don Quixote de la Mancha, the main character in Cervantes's eponymous novel, published in the early seventeenth century. This route follows in his footsteps from Albacete to Alcázar de San Juan (1h10 by train) by way of the famous windmills of Campo de Criptana. It is certainly a long ride, but the adventure is nourished by the Sierra de Alcaraz greenway, Ossa de Montiel, the Ruidera Lakes, and the endless horizons of Castilla-La Mancha, dotted with wind turbines that Don Quixote would have surely wished to fight.

SEGOVIA
ADVENTURE IN MESETA

Hilly / Intermediate

Map strava.com/routes/22734214

Distance	E+	Difficulty	Appeal
116 km (72 mi)	1,300 m (4,265 ft)	3/5	3/5

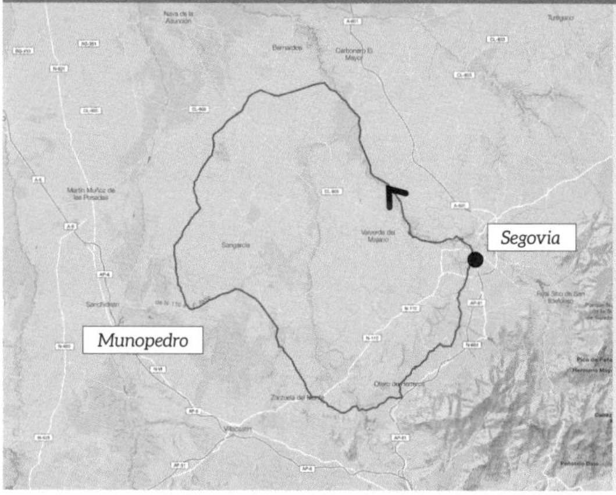

West of Segovia, the arid plains of Meseta stretch into the distance between 800 m (2,625 ft) and 1,000 m (3,280 ft) of altitude. The Eresma Valley Greenway, which requires suitable tires, is the prelude to the Monastery of Our Lady of Soterraña (km 40/mi 25) and Hoyuelos, where they filmed that masterpiece of Spanish cinema *The Spirit of the Beehive* (1973). Villages with Romanesque churches dot the horizon. At km 107 (mi 67) is the Royal Palace of Riofrío. In Segovia, apart from the Roman Aqueduct, do not miss the splendid views over the town and Alcázar Castle from Queen Victoria Eugenia Square.

SEGOVIA
PEARL OF THE GUADARRAMA

- *High mountain / Advanced*
- *Map strava.com/routes/22692708*
- *Test yourself km 21 (mi 13) strava.com/segments/2092027*
- *Test yourself km 28 (mi 17) strava.com/segments/18201386*

The Sierra Guadarrama, located northwest of Madrid, is one of the "local" mountain ranges of the Spanish capital. It is known for its beef, ski runs, and cycling spots—one of which is the surprising and quite challenging Bola del Mundo.

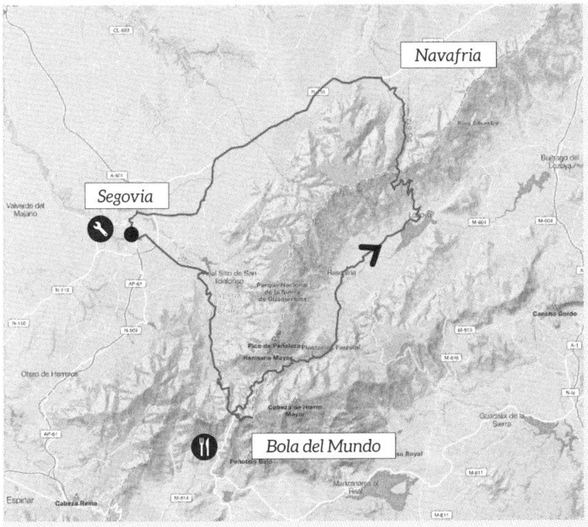

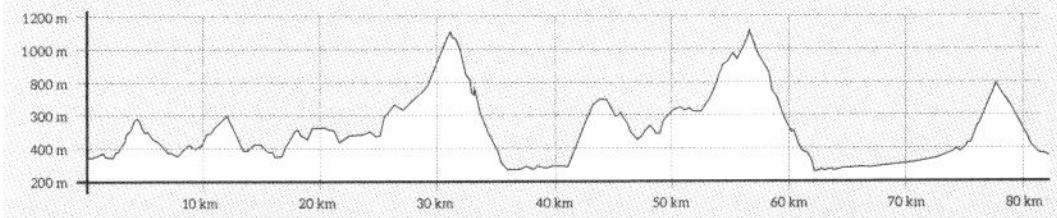

Segovia is the hometown of Pedro Delgado and the ideal start for a wonderful high-mountain route through the Sierra de Guadarrama. The sequence of seven bends (km 21/mi 13) announces the slopes of the Navacerrada Pass (1,858 m/6,096 ft). The road is wide with a perfect surface. The final 6 km (4 mi) are at 7%, with the Siete Picos arrayed to the right. The challenge comes near the top with the improbable ramp of the Bola del Mundo: 3.3 km (2 mi) of poorly laid road with 400 m (1,315 ft) of E+ and an average gradient of 12% (some sections are at 16% to 20%). Alberto Contador attempted the km 28 (mi 17.5) segment in 2019: he recommends a 34 x 30 gear ratio. Here at 2,253 m (7,390 ft), there are sublime views over the peaks in the Guadarrama. Return via the Navafria Pass at 1,778 m (5,835 ft) and a pleasant 40 km (25 mi) back to the Aqueduct of Segovia.

Distance	E+	Difficulty	Appeal
123 km (76 mi)	2,450 m (8,040 ft)	4/5	4/5

Madrid Chamartín Train Station is 1h45 by train from Segovia. From Madrid-Barajas Airport, take metro line 8 to Chamartín Train Station. Segovia is 1h20 by car from Madrid (105 km/65 mi) or 2h by bus.

The Ciclolodge (hotel, restaurant, spa) is the ideal spot for a halfway break after tackling the Bola del Mundo. It would also make an excellent base camp for future adventures.

Camino de las Quattro Calles, 4
28742 Lozoya
ciclolodge.com

Located 100 meters/yards from Segovia train station, CycloSanz provides an impeccable repair service. It is mainly for mountain bikes, but it also offers road-bike expertise and equipment.

Avenida del Obispo Quesada 24
40006 Segovia
facebook.com/cyclosanz

COLLADO VILLALBA

A MOUNTAIN BY MADRID

High mountain / Advanced — *Map* *strava.com/routes/22939053*

Distance	E+	Difficulty	Appeal
110 km (68 mi)	1,950 m (6,400 ft)	3/5	4/5

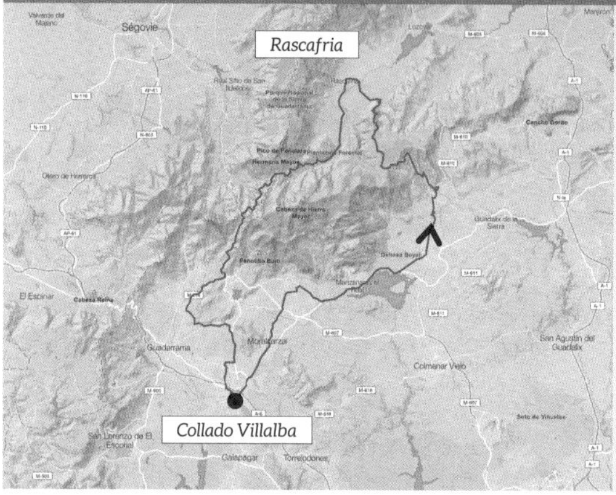

The Sierra de Guadarrama is a tempting excursion from Madrid. Closer to Segovia but no less attractive is the Cuenca Alta Manzanares Regional Park. From Collado Villalba (40 minutes by train from Madrid Príncipe Pío), we ride to Manzanares El Real—at more than 900 m (2,950 ft)—with its medieval castle and Santillana Lake before reaching Miraflores de la Sierra and the Morcuera Pass (9 km/5.5 mi at 7%). After Rascafría, between the Cobos Pass (final 6 km/3.5 mi at 6%) and the Navacerrada Pass, we cycle across a plateau at more than 1,800 m (5,900 ft) with superb views.

MADRID

THE ROYAL HILLS

Hilly / Intermediate — *Map* *strava.com/routes/22936428*

Distance	E+	Difficulty	Appeal
44 km (27 mi)	400 m (1,300 ft)	2/5	3/5

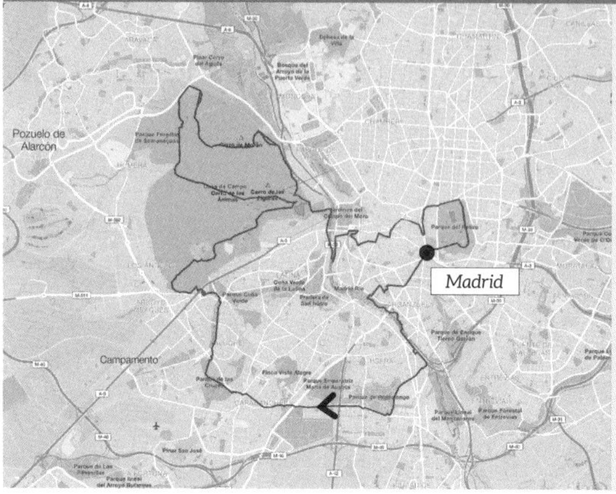

It is never easy to escape the heaving masses of an urban area of six million people, yet this escapade, which starts from Madrid Atocha railway station and heads out through southwest Madrid via parks, gardens, and cycle paths, is a delight. The succession of parks (Pradolongo, Las Cruces, and Aluche) are like a string of welcoming islands. Next, we enter the 1,500 ha (3,710 acre) hilly Casa de Campo (including the famous Cerro Garabitas) for a very pleasant workout before returning via the Prado Museum and El Retiro Park. La Bicicleta Café, located in the Malasaña neighborhood, is the perfect place for a break.

ANDORRA LA VELLA
THE PRINCELY MOUNTAIN

- *High mountain / Expert*
- *Map strava.com/routes/21478294*
- *Test yourself km 15 (mi 9) strava.com/segments/9656430*
- *Test yourself km 47 (mi 29) strava.com/segments/1708707*

The roads of Andorra are a glory of the Pyrenees, frequented by numerous cycling champions all year round. Several harsh yet beautiful mountain stages of the 2018 and 2019 Vuelta a España were raced here. This route reproduces the spirit of those stages.

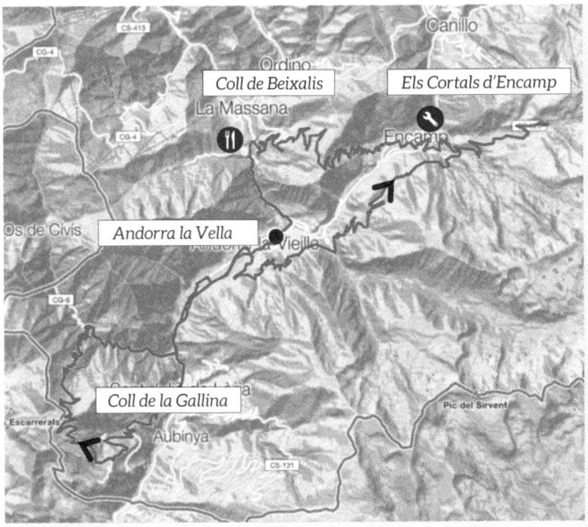

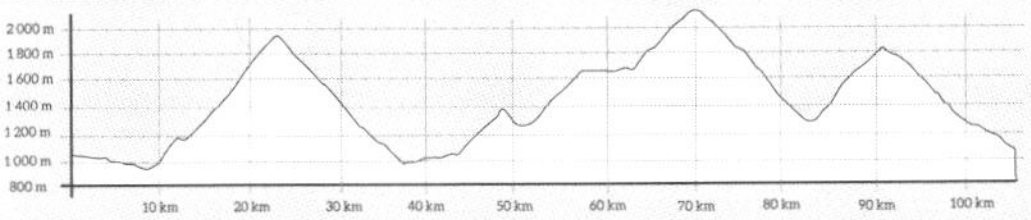

Andorra, in the heart of the gray-green Pyrenees, boasts some audacious challenges. This one, a homage to several stages in the 2018 and 2019 Vuelta, may be less than 100 km (62 mi) long, but with 3,200 m (10,500 ft) of climbing, it is for serious mountaineers only—although its three distinct sections may be tackled separately. The first, to the southwest, is one big warm-up, as we climb the Coll de la Gallina: 12 km (7.5 mi) at a gradient of more than 8% through a succession of switchbacks. The second is in three parts: 4 km (2.5 mi) to the Alto de la Comella, then 4 km (2.5 mi) at 9% to Lake Engolasters, before a flat gravel section, and the final push to the majestic Els Cortals d'Encamp (2,095 m/6,873 ft). The third, to the north, is an ascent of the Col de Beixalis: 6 km (3.7 mi) at 9%.

Distance	E+	Difficulty	Appeal
88 km (55 mi)	2,950 m (9,700 ft)	5/5	5/5

Andorra can be reached only by road. From France: via El Pas de la Casa (toll tunnel) or Port d'Envalira. From Spain: via La Seu d'Urgell. The nearest airports are Barcelona and Toulouse, 200 km (125 mi) away, and between 2h30 and 3h by bus or car.

In La Massana (2 km/1.25 mi from km 85/mi 53), drop by the Commencal Spot bike cafe, which caters mainly to mountain bikers. It has live gigs and DJs on weekends.

Avenida del Ravell, CG-4
AD400 La Massana
spot.commencal.com

The cyclist-friendly Mountain Hostel Tarter offers accommodation, a spa, food, and a bike workshop. Turn off to El Tarter at km 67 (mi 42).

Sant Pere del Tarter
AD100 Canillo
mountainhosteltarter.com

GIRONA
THE TER VALLEY

- *Low mountain / Intermediate*
- *Map strava.com/routes/22381123*
- *Test yourself km 18 (mi 11) strava.com/segments/15939443*
- *Test yourself km 54 (mi 34) strava.com/segments/3704488*

Lance Armstrong made Girona his European base in the 2000s. Since then, the town has become a cosmopolitan destination for cyclists with much related Strava activity. Life is sweet 100 km (60 mi) north of Barcelona. The terrain is well suited to enthusiastic outings on the bike.

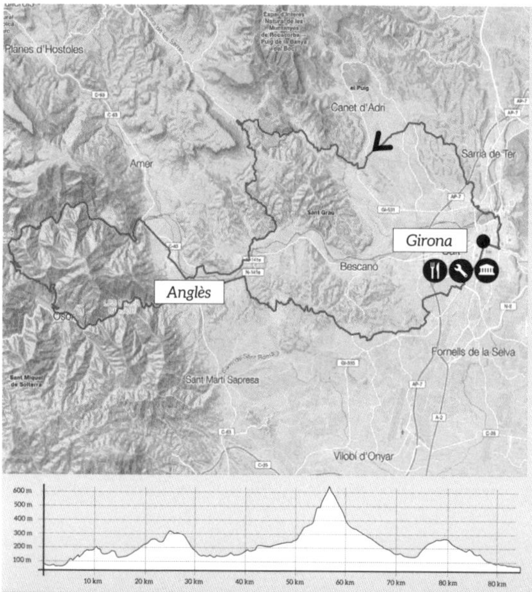

Between France (the border is 60 km/37 mi to the north) and Barcelona, and only a short distance inland, Girona has become home over the past twenty years to a cyclist diaspora that appreciates the good living and the quality of roads and contours here in the hinterland. To the north, we are very close to the foothills of the Pyrenees. Our route heads west from Girona into the Guilleries and Savassona massifs, a spectacular area of ridges and depressions. You get a good idea of the terrain when you reach Susqueda Reservoir (km 52/mi 32), after riding through the Ter Valley. The winding road up the Nafre Pass is in two stages of 3 km (2 mi) each, the first at a gradient of 6% and the second at a more demanding 8%, topping out at 615 m (2,018 ft). The descent back to the Ter Valley via Osor, with its old mines, is a delight, and the return to Girona on a cycle path with greenery all around is very pleasant indeed.

Distance	E+	Difficulty	Appeal
95 km (59 mi)	1,200 m (3,900 ft)	3/5	4/5

Barcelona Airport, which is connected to the whole of Europe, is 1h15 by train or 1h20 by car (105 km/65 mi) from Girona. Barcelona Sants train station is 40 minutes from Girona. Montpellier (France) is 5h by train or 2h30 by car (250 km/155 mi).

In Girona, La Fábrica is a fantastic cyclist base camp and sumptuous bike cafe that was established by Amber and Christian (a Canadian former pro).

Carrer de la Llebre 3
17004 Girona
lafabricagirona.com

Girona is worth exploring for a few hours on foot—not least because you might run into a Tour de France cyclist in the narrow streets. Do not miss the medieval architecture of its ramparts, the Jewish quarter, the cathedral, and the bridge (built by Gustave Eiffel) over the Onyar River.

FIGUERAS
IN DALÍ'S WHEEL

Hilly / Intermediate — *Map strava.com/routes/22811591*

Distance	E+	Difficulty	Appeal
98 km (61 mi)	1,400 m (4,600 ft)	3/5	4/5

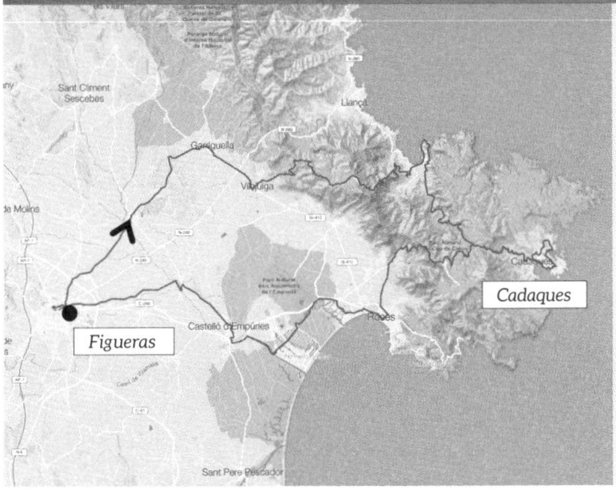

Setting out from Figueras (1h15 by train from Barcelona), where Salvador Dalí was born and died, this route celebrates the most exuberant of Catalan artists. From his House Museum in the little seaside village of Cadaques to his Theatre Museum in Figueras, Dalí is omnipresent. Among other intense moments are the ascent to the Monastery of Sant Pere de Rodes (6 km/4 mi at 9%), the descent to El Port de La Selva, the beach at Roses, and the historic center of Castelló d'Empúries. The climbs of Sa Perafita and Puig Vidriera are short but demanding all the same.

GIRONA
OBJECTIVE ROCACORBA

Low mountain / Advanced — *Map strava.com/routes/22819574*

Distance	E+	Difficulty	Appeal
111 km (69 mi)	2,000 m (6,650 ft)	4/5	4/5

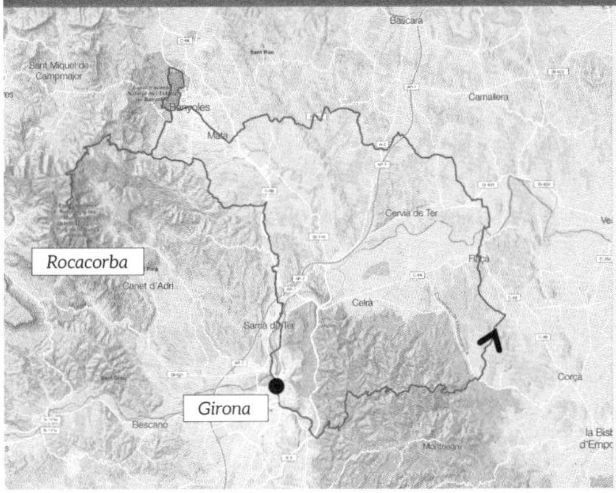

David Millar was one of the first—even before Lance Armstrong—to put Girona on the map as a Mediterranean base camp for British cyclists. He also popularized the ascent of Rocacorba. Surfaced in the early 2000s, the road climbs to the south of Lake of Banyoles for 9 km (5.5 mi), with the final 6 km (4 mi) at an average gradient of 9% and some sections at 15%. There is nothing at the top (961 m/3,153 ft) except for a tumbledown sanctuary and an incredible view south down the Costa Brava. Millar can still be followed at strava.com/athletes/13347173.

BARCELONA
A MOUNTAIN IN THE CITY

- *Low mountain / Advanced*
- *Map strava.com/routes/21509770*
- *Test yourself km 8 (mi 5) strava.com/segments/19786502*
- *Test yourself km 105 (mi 65) strava.com/segments/19574242*

Spain's Mediterranean coast has many fabulous cycling spots, one of which is the Serra de Collserola, the largest metropolitan park in the world, just a short ride from the center of Barcelona, the city of Gaudí, Miró, and Lionel Messi.

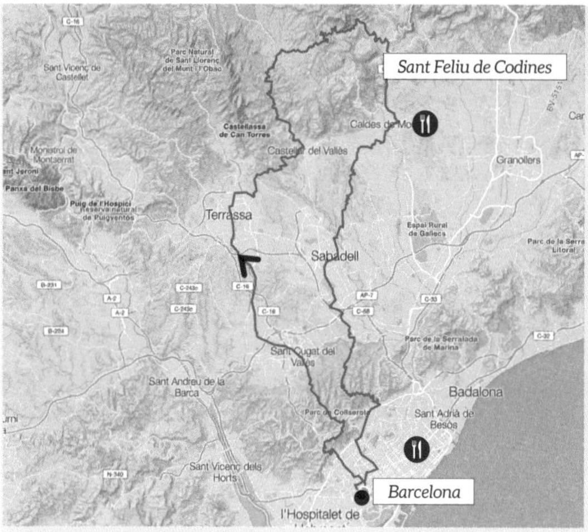

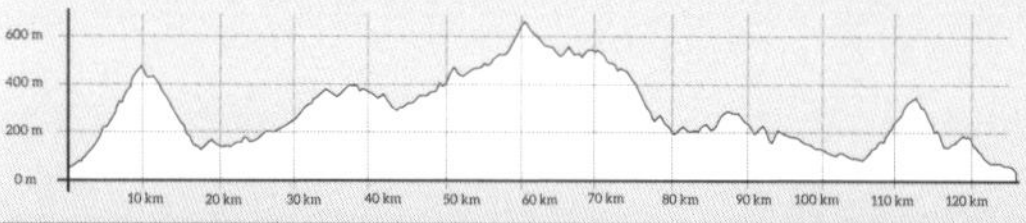

At nearly 130 km (80 mi), this route might seem long, but it is pure joy once you leave the city behind. Starting from Sants train station, you soon reach the Serra de Collserola via the Corts and Sarrià neighborhoods. The greenery commences with the ascent of Tibidabo at close to 500 m (1,640 ft), from where you can enjoy a panoramic view over the city as well as check out the TV tower, amusement park, and cathedral. Head on to Sant Cugat, then along the Palau river and through Terrassa (km 33/ mi 20) to the spectacular scenery of Sant Llorenç del Munt natural park and the renowned rock-climbing site of La Castellassa de Can Torres. Following 15 km (9 mi) of relatively easy climbing, you reach the highest point on the bike, after Sant Llorenç Savall, at 650 m (2,132 ft). The return via Sabadell is pleasantly easy, although beware of the climb at Montflorit after km 100 (mi 62). Back in Barcelona again!

Distance	E+	Difficulty	Appeal
126 km (78 mi)	**2,000 m** (6,650 ft)	**3/5**	**4/5**

Barcelona is one of the most popular destinations in Europe, with flights from all over the continent. Perpignan is 1h10 by high-speed train, and Madrid is 2h30. By road, allow 2h15 from Perpignan (200 km/ 125 mi), 4h from Valencia (350 km/220 mi), and 6h from Madrid (600 km/370 mi).

If the day is dragging on, you will appreciate the terrace of the El Remei (km 79/mi 49) on the way in to Caldes de Montbui. Delicious Catalan cuisine.

Passeig del Remei 78
08140 Caldes de Montbui, Barcelona
restaurantelremei.es

A stop at Bicioci Bike Café in the Gràcia neighborhood is a must. It offers vintage wooden decor, bike culture, top coffee, excellent pizzas, and smoothies.

Carrer de Venus 1
08012 Barcelona
facebook.com/biciocibikecafe/

SA POBLA
FORMENTOR CHALLENGE

Very hilly / Advanced

Map strava.com/routes/22810891

Distance	E+	Difficulty	Appeal
90 km (56 mi)	1,400 m (6,600 ft)	3/5	4/5

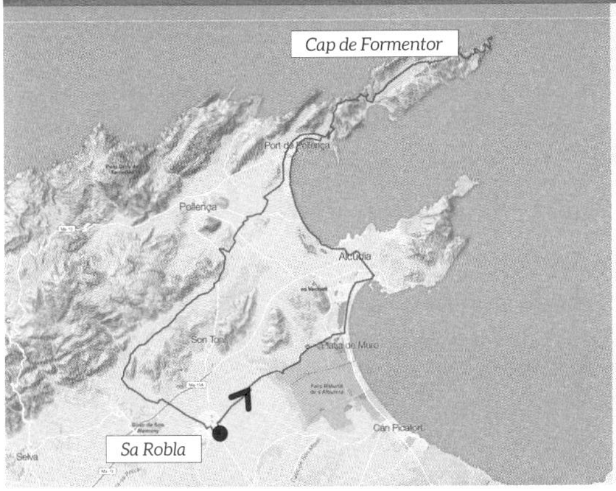

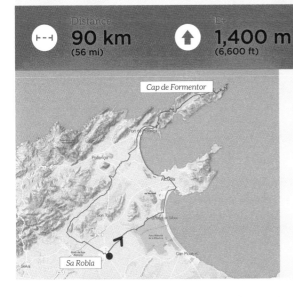

Before you think about exploring the slopes of the Serra de Tramuntana, start your Mallorca trip with a ride out to Cap de Formentor on fantastically panoramic roads. Starting from Sa Pobla Train Station (50 minutes by train from Palma), there are a few stiff ramps of 1 km (0.6 mi) to 3 km (2 mi). It is worth working up a sweat to see the emblematic white lighthouse dominating the blue horizon at the island's northern tip, located 150 km (93 mi) from Barcelona. The road surface is perfect, and the switchbacks are a poetry of curves. On the way back, prolong the pleasure with a dip in the sea or a coffee at Pollença Bay.

PALMA DE MALLORCA
SOUTH TRAMUNTANA

Very hilly / Intermediate

Map strava.com/routes/22807218

Distance	E+	Difficulty	Appeal
91 km (56 mi)	1,500 m (5,100 ft)	3/5	4/5

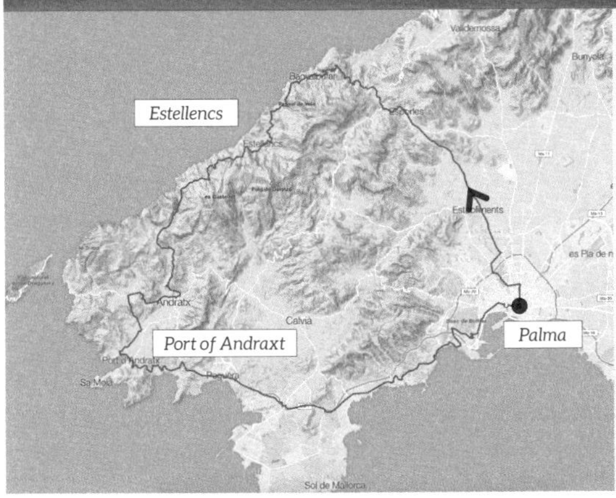

The hills of the southern Serra de Tramuntana never rise above 400 m (1,315 ft) over the Mediterranean on Mallorca's west coast. The views from the road between Banyalbufar and the edge of Cap de sa Mola via the cliffside village of Estellencs are nevertheless astounding. The first part of this route, which begins at Plaza Major in Palma and returns to the cathedral, is a tough challenge. After Andratx (km 50/mi 31), you can, if you wish, push on to Sant Elm, which is opposite the imposing island of Sa Dragonera. Beyond its sporting appeal, Mallorca is as much a balm for the soul and feast for the eyes.

PALMA DE MALLORCA
ISLAND FANTASY

- *Low mountain / Advanced*
- *Map strava.com/routes/22551834*
- *Test yourself km 33 (mi 21) strava.com/segments/14529574*
- *Test yourself km 69 (mi 43) strava.com/segments/12878849*

Sa Calobra is perhaps the most coveted KOM/QOM in the world. On Mallorca, you will never ride alone, and every bunch of riders will seem very cosmopolitan. This magical route starts at the beach and climbs Sa Calobra, the ultimate fantasy.

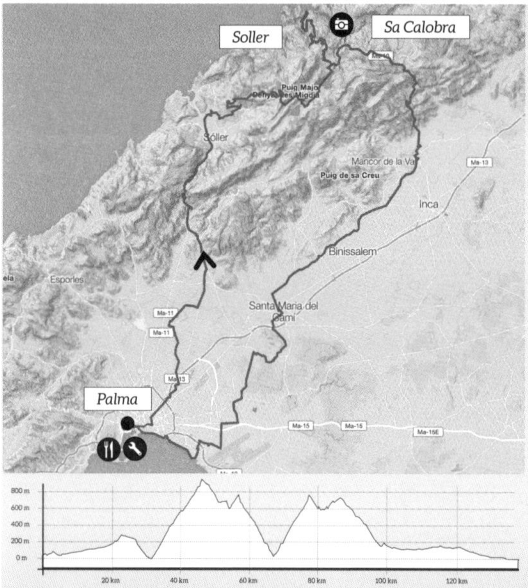

The length and difficulty of this route through northwest Mallorca, which starts at The Workshop bike cafe in Palma, is striking. We descend Sa Calobra right down to the sea before climbing back the way we came, which is the only road in and out. The Coll deis Reis ascent rises 700 m (2,300 ft) in less than 10 km (6 mi) of magical road twisting and turning dementedly between almond trees and strawberry trees, then through the rocks and above steep drops, with some sections at gradients of 12%. Then, there is the wind, which sometimes blows strongly from the mainland here in the Serra de Tramuntana. Before the summit, one particular bend turns 270 degrees to climb over itself. There are so many cyclists that safety is not even a concern. You will have climbed the Puig Major first, of course: 15 km (9 mi) at a gradient of 6%. Leave something in the tank for Sa Calobra.

Distance	E+	Difficulty	Appeal
150 km (93 mi)	2,750 m (9,000 ft)	4/5	5/5

Palma de Mallorca Airport has connections to the major European hubs. From the airport, it takes 40 minutes by bus or 15 minutes by car (12 km/7.5 mi) to get to Palma port. The century-old train to Sóller can get to 30 km (19 mi) from Sa Calobra, but you cannot take a bike with you.

Majorca's popularity with cyclists led Rapha to open one of their superb clubhouses here, close to the port and the cathedral. Screenings, talks, exhibitions, and excellent coffee.

Plaça del Rosari 1
07001 Palma, Balearic Islands
rapha.cc

There is no shortage of extraordinary views on the Sa Calobra road. The most fascinating is at the 270-degree bend before the summit. Other spots include the reservoirs on Puig Major and at Entreforc (km 89/mi 55), just before the famous restaurant Escorca, a perfect place for lunch.

There are many short, pleasant tunnels in Mallorca, Spain.

SEGORBE
VALENCIAN ACCENT

Low mountain / Intermediate
Map strava.com/routes/22901838
Test yourself km 13 (mi 8) strava.com/segments/6177547
Test yourself km 57 (mi 35) strava.com/segments/6407747

There are many wonderful cycle routes in the north of the Spanish Levant, especially around magnificent Valencia. We head a little off the beaten track, riding out of Segorbe and through the amazing Serra d'Espadà Natural Park.

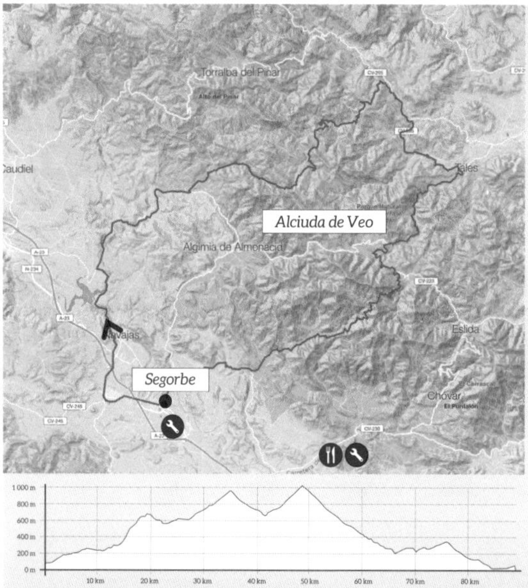

From Valencia, you have the choice of the lagoons of Albufeira to the south and the two massifs of Calderona and Andilla to the north; we reach them by cycling through the orange fields toward (distant) Barcelona. Starting in Sagunto or Castellón de la Plana reduces the distance and even allows you to tackle the crazy ascent of the Mas de la Costa.
This loop around Segorbe, located in the low mountains of Espada, is another option where you have to dig deep, surrounded by 1,000 m (3,280 ft) high cliffs and dense vegetation.
In addition to the two straight climbs at km 22 (mi 14) and km 57 (mi 35), there are old remote villages such as Veo, Aín, and Almedíjar to enjoy in the second part of the route.
A total immersion in authentic Spain.

Distance	E+	Difficulty	Appeal
76 km (47 mi)	1,600 m (5,250 ft)	3/5	4/5

Segorbe (pop. 9,000) is 85 km (53 mi) north of Valencia: 1h30 by train or 1h by car. Barcelona is 5h by train or 3h30 by car (350 km/220 mi). Madrid is 5h by train or 4h by car (400 km/250 mi).

If you pass by Valencia, drop by Dandy Horse bike cafe, located close to Mestalla Stadium, for a very merry atmosphere.

Carrer d'Antoni Suárez 34
46021 Valencia
facebook.com/dandyhorsecafe

Cicloespai is a bike store and workshop that is warmly recommended by local cyclists in Segorbe. Retailer of Specialized.

Av. España 99
12400 Segorbe
cicloespai.com

CALPE
THE ROCKS OF MARINA ALTA

- *Hilly / Intermediate*
- *Map strava.com/routes/21340260*
- *Test yourself km 23 (mi 14) strava.com/routes/21340260*
- *Test yourself km 39 (mi 24) strava.com/segments/4887151*

Penyal d'Ifac—commonly called Calpe Rock—rises 322 m (1,089 ft) above the Mediterranean, and is a beacon on the Dénia Peninsula for thousands of cyclists of all nationalities. The balmy climate makes the roads of Marina Alta very popular in winter.

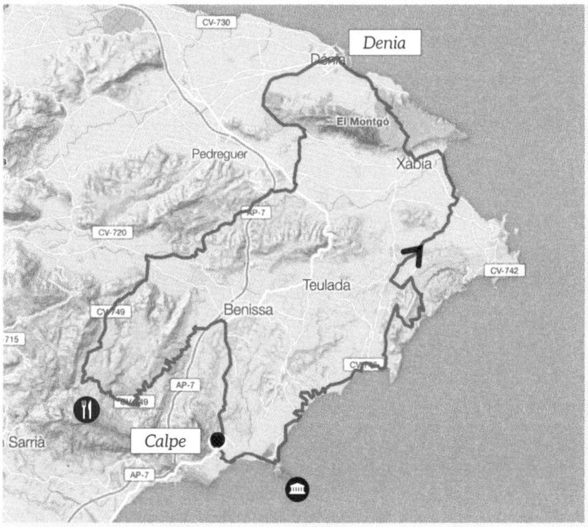

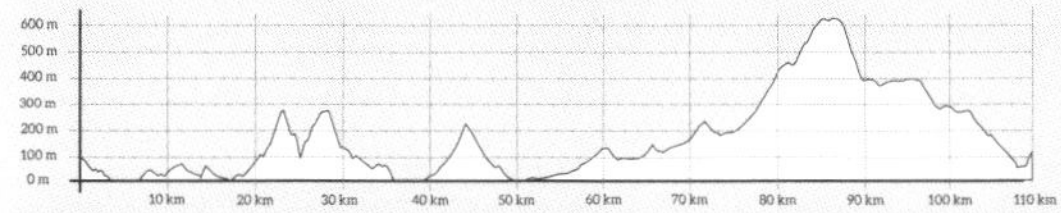

At this point halfway between Valencia and Alicante, the Costa Blanca sticks out into the Mediterranean as if to defy the island of Ibiza. You cannot miss either the Penyal d'Ifac (Calpe Rock) or the Montgo, a mass of limestone that dominates Dénia. This looping route travels up the coast and back down through the hinterland. La Cumbre del Sol proffers two aggressive climbs of 2 km (1.25 mi) each, at a gradient of 10%. Between the two, we plunge back down to the turquoise sea. Further on, before Dénia, we traverse the lower slopes of the Montgo, 3 km (2 mi) at a gradient of 7%. Next, there is something for everyone, with the Gorgos gorges and the barren Sierra de Bernia: from Jalon, the 12 km (7.5 mi) of this pass, at 620 m (2,034 ft), are quite splendid, with a perfect road cutting through the rocky landscape. Once you have explored Calpe and Dénia by bike, you will want to return for more.

Distance	E+	Difficulty	Appeal
106 km (66 mi)	1,700 m (5,600 ft)	3/5	4/5

You can reach Calpe from Benidorm or Dénia by the recently constructed streetcar line (our route starts at its station). Alicante Airport is 1h30 by bus or 1h by car (80 km/50 mi). Valencia Airport is also 1h30 by bus or car (120 km/75 mi).

After the pass at km 90 (mi 56), the Casa Rural El Peon de Pinos serves refreshing draft beer and delicious meat, fish, and seafood dishes on a perfect mountain terrace.

Partida Pinos, 9
03720 Benissa
benissa.net

The ancient Roman baths Els Banys de la Reina (km 4/ mi 2.5) are a feat of geology and human ingenuity. Seawater flows into the large pool covering 165 m² (1,776 sq ft) via four channels hewn from the rock. Ideal for a paddle when you return from your ride.

calpe.es

BENIDORM
DAYTIME TEMPTATIONS

Low mountain / Intermediate
Map strava.com/routes/21333803
Test yourself km 32 (mi 20) strava.com/segments/3472549
Test yourself km 79 (mi 49) strava.com/segments/4051763

How can one escape Benidorm, with its mass tourism, chaotic urban planning, ugly skyscrapers, and rowdy nightlife? The answer lies in the year-round balmy weather and the superb roads of the Marina Baixa.

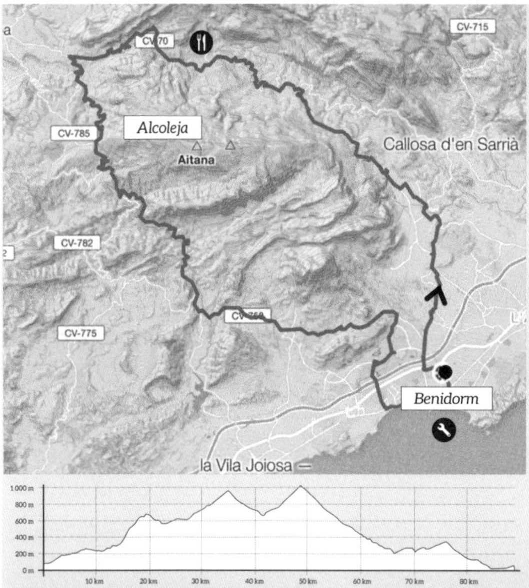

The packed beaches of the Costa Blanca are a world away—but only an hour by bike over perfect roads—from beautiful, wild mountains. The route out of Benidorm climbs north, with a kick-up beyond La Nucia. At nearly 600 m (2,000 ft), you will pass Guadalest, with its castle and lake, before tackling the gentle slope of the Puerto de Confrides: 10 km (6 mi) at an average gradient of 4%. Just before the summit, there is a fine view across to the spectacular site of El Pla de la Casa and its peak of 1,380 m (4,527 ft). Then you turn south to return to Benidorm via a section of the course of the 1992 World Championship (featuring Bugno and Jalabert) above Finestrat (km 71/mi 44). On the way, you will pass through Alcoleja and climb the winding road of the Puerto de Tudons against a rocky backdrop. At the highest point (1,028 m/639 ft), you can look down to Safari Aitana, a wildlife adventure park.

Distance
98 km
(61 mi)

E+
1,900 m
(6,250 ft)

Difficulty
3/5

Appeal
4/5

From Alicante Airport, allow 1h by bus (numerous shuttles) or car (60 km/37 mi). From Valencia, it takes 2h by bus or 1h40 by car (160 km/100 mi). From Madrid, it takes 2h30 by high-speed train to Alicante + 1h by bus, or 4h30 by car (460 km/285 mi).

At the start of the climb, stop at El Pirineo (km 30/mi 19) in Confrides for the simple pleasure of a coffee with a mountain view.

Carrer San Antoni 52
03517 Confrides
elpirineoconfrides.com

Situated between the station and the Balcon del Mediterraneo, Bicimarket is Benidorm's preeminent bike shop. Retailer of Merida, BH, KTM, Basso, and Wilier.

Calle del Pino 5
03501 Benidorm
bicimarket.com

ALICANTE

BACK ROADS OF ALCOIÀ

- *Low mountain / Intermediate*
- *Map strava.com/routes/21341114*
- *Test yourself km 28 (mi 17) strava.com/segments/1493277*
- *Test yourself km 70 (mi 43) strava.com/segments/1089236*

Alicante is the capital of the Costa Blanca. The roads of the interior through the low mountains of the Alcoià in the south of the Valencian Community are much more interesting than the roads on the coast. Avoid the heat of summer, if you can.

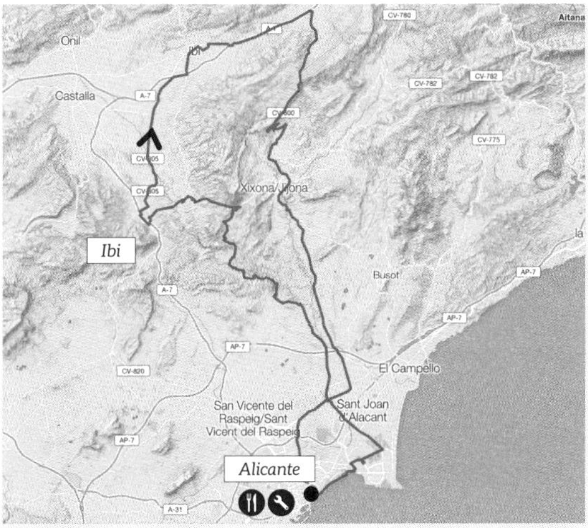

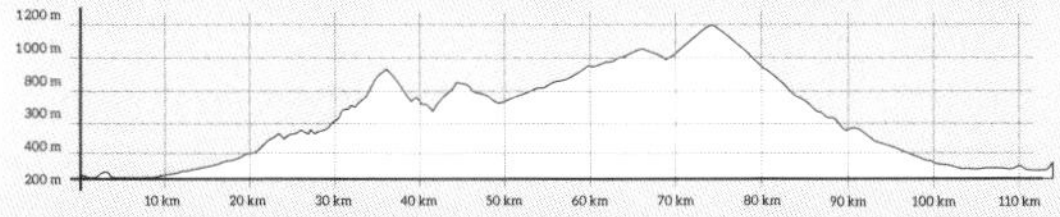

There is no shortage of viewpoints along this route, which starts in Alicante. You can see the nearby slopes from just behind the rows of tourist apartments on the Costa Blanca. At km 31 (mi 19), you will pass very close to the Pantano de Tibi, a medieval masonry dam with an impressive spillway. At km 40 (mi 25) is the lovely little town of Tibi, with its Moorish castle perched on a rocky outcrop. Continue through the foothills of the Serra del Maigmó, amid pines and holly oaks, with a stiff little climb at km 42 (mi 26). The highest point is the Puerto de la Carrasqueta at 1,020 m (3,346 ft), with a beautiful descent through switchbacks down to Xixona. The contemplative scenery is the real draw, but there is also a pleasant 1.5 km (1 mi) greenway after Ibi (km 60/mi 37). Finish with a short climb up to the old fortress of Santa Barbara with a view over the sea on one side and Alicante on the other.

Distance	E+	Difficulty	Appeal
115 km (71 mi)	2,000 m (6,560 ft)	3/5	4/5

There are flights to Alicante-Elche Airport (10 km/6 mi SE of the city) from all over Europe. Alicante is 2h30 from Madrid by high-speed train and 1h40 from Valencia by regular train. By car, allow 4h from Madrid (400 km/249 mi), and 2h from Valencia (200 km/124 mi).

Mas de Roc (km 70/mi 43) is a family cooperative where you can fill your pockets with seasonal, sun-kissed, pesticide-free fruit for the last two hours of riding.

Diseminado Sector 1, La Sargua
03100 Alicante
masderoc.com

Even if you are not riding a Specialized bike, Master Bike is *the* bike store and repair outlet in Alicante. It is only a 7-minute ride or 20-minute walk from the station, toward Elche.

Carrer Club de Futbol Hercules 7
03008 Alicante
masterbike.es

GRANADA
ANDALUSIAN SNOW

High mountain / Advanced — *Map strava.com/routes/22831119*

Distance	E+	Difficulty	Appeal
89 km (5 mi)	2,300 m (7,750 ft)	4/5	5/5

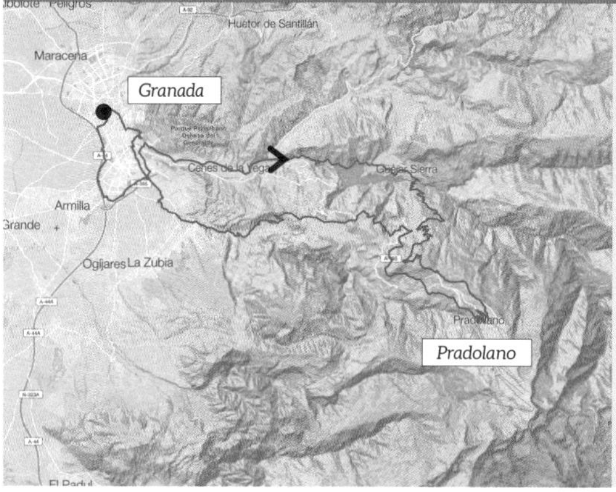

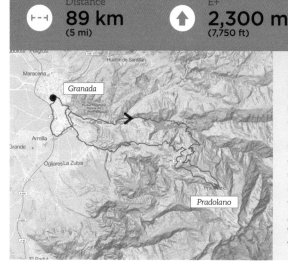

The conquest of the Sierra Nevada, which seems to protect Granada from its almost endless snows, is a must in Andalusia. It is, however, not within everyone's grasp. This climb up to Pradollano ski resort at 2,400 m (7,875 ft) is 17 km (11 mi) long with an E+ of 1,400 m (4,595 ft), and a gradient of 10% over the first 4 km (2.5 mi). As a prelude, we pass the villages of Cenes de La Vega, Los Pinillos, Güéjar Sierra, and Canales Reservoir. We return via Monachil before the splendors of Granada: Alhambra, Generalife park (cross it on a gravel trail if you like), Granada Cathedral, and the Albaicín neighborhood.

GERGAL
CELESTIAL ASCENT

High mountain / Intermediate — *Map strava.com/routes/22856112*

Distance	E+	Difficulty	Appeal
60 km (37 mi)	1,600 m (5,250 ft)	3/5	4/5

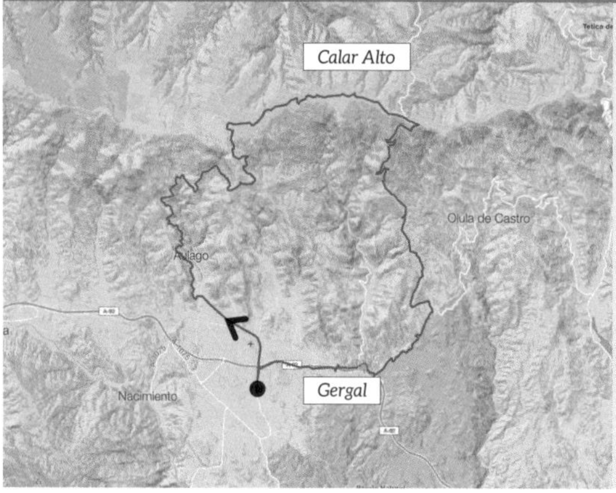

Spain is full of cycling surprises, and this celestial climb through the Sierra de Los Filabres to the Calar Alto Observatory (2,168 m/7,113 ft) is one of the best. We are 50 km (30 mi) north of Almería on the other side of the Tabernas Desert, where Sergio Leone filmed his most famous westerns. The slope is kind and the road surface impeccable as it snakes through a barren landscape with zero shade above 1,500 m (4,920 ft). From Gérgal, there are other unforgettable options such as Alto de Velefique to the northeast. Its succession of switchbacks evokes the Stelvio in Italy.

ITALY

SARDINIA & SICILY

NAPLES & ROME

EMILIA-ROMAGNA

TUSCANY

LIGURIA

PIEDMONT

LOMBARDY

DOLOMITES

CARBONIA
SARDINIAN DEMONSTRATION

- *Low mountain / Intermediate*
- *Map strava.com/routes/22527081*
- *Test yourself km 25 (mi 16) strava.com/segments/6982953*
- *Test yourself km 69 (mi 43) strava.com/segments/6858785*

Each Sardinian route is a wonderful Mediterranean voyage, as long as you avoid the busier roads during the summer season. This route between sea and low mountain, which starts and ends in Carbonia in the southeast of the island, is one of the most beautiful.

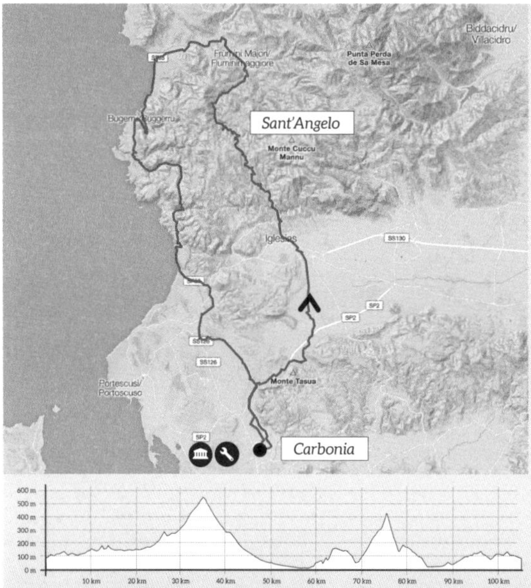

Sardinia lives off tourism, but the island also relies on the extraction of minerals. The Serbariu mine, located in Carbonia, is now a museum. At km 82 (mi 50), we pass the Nebida lead and zinc washing station. Between the two are some superb low mountains covered in eucalyptus and oak, such as around Monte Segarino (636 m/2,085 ft), with breathtaking views down. The final 7 km (4.5 mi) to Sant'Angelo at 555 m (1,820 ft), close to the ancient Temple of Antas (km 39/mi 24), have a gradient of 5%. Closer to the coast, between beaches, slipways, dreamy creeks, and unusual rock formations, such as the Masua Sugarloaf, the Montecani pass (440 m/1,445 ft) stretches for 7 km (4.5 mi) at 6%. On either side are the heavenly destinations of Buggerru, which can also be reached by a shortcut from Sant'Angelo on a gravel road, and Masua.

Distance	E+	Difficulty	Appeal
105 km (65 mi)	1,650 m (5,415 ft)	3/5	4/5

Carbonia (pop. 28,000) lies 50 km (30 mi) west of Cagliari in the south of Sardinia. The town is 1h25 by train or 55 minutes by car (65 km/40 mi) from Cagliari Airport. Cagliari is 2h by train or 1h by car (75 km/47 mi). To the north, Sassari is 4h30 by train or 2h40 by car (240 km/150 mi).

The Museo del Carbone has nothing to do with your bike's composite frame. Carbonia ("coal" in Italian) was named in honor of the mine whose workers it was built to house.

Grande Miniera di Serbariu
09013 Carbonia
museodelcarbone.it

Newgreenstore is *the* Carbonia cycling address, located 15 minutes south of the city. It offers irreproachable workshop service. Retailer of Cannondale.

SS126 km 12, 070,
09013 Carbonia
newgreenstore.it

PORTO TORRES
STONES AND SEA

Hilly / Advanced

Map strava.com/routes/22544531

Distance	E+	Difficulty	Appeal
124 km (77 mi)	1,600 m (5,250 ft)	3/5	3/5

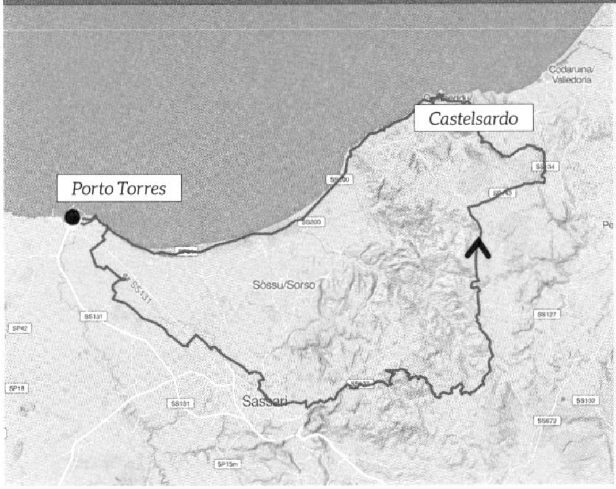

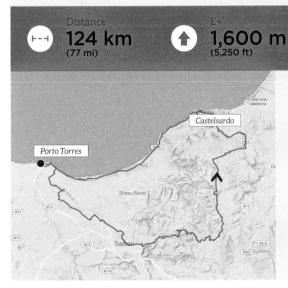

This loop in northwestern Sardinia has no shortage of appeal: the splendors of the north coast between Porto Torres and Punta Tramontana, the irresistible charm of Sassari, the beautiful mountaintop villages of Osilo and Nulvi, and picturesque Castelsardo overlooking the Mediterranean. Approach it seriously though, because the slopes steepen sharply on the way out of Sassari and as you near Monte Tuffudesu (766 m/2,513 ft). It is a superb, wild, and intense ride. Marked by the island's tumultuous history, Castelsardo deserves more than a brief stop. Do not miss the striking Elephant Rock (km 83/mi 52).

OZIERI-CHILIVANI
PREHISTORIC RIDE

Low mountain / Advanced

Map strava.com/routes/22518767

Distance	E+	Difficulty	Appeal
97 km (60 mi)	1,900 m (6,235 ft)	3/5	4/5

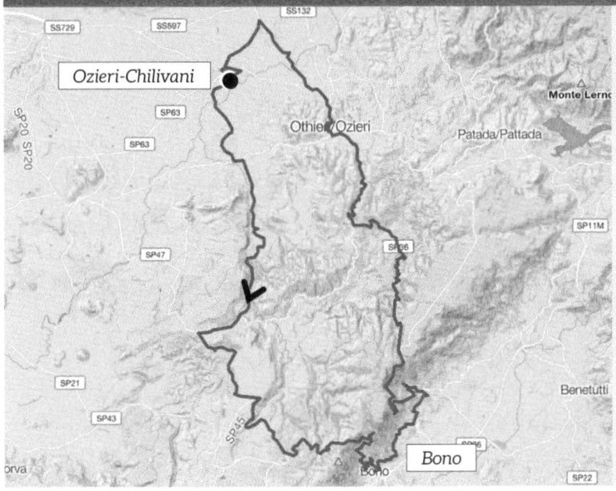

A little planning to avoid the tourist hordes is necessary before any Sardinian escapade. Leave Olbia and the spectacular Costa Smeralda in the northeast and head for the more authentic interior. The appeal of the prehistoric Ozieri culture is worth as much as a Mediterranean landscape. At km 81 (mi 50), we pass very close to its heart, the Cave of San Michele. Before that, you will have climbed to 1,040 m (3,415 ft) close to Monte Rasu, and then to 980 m (3,215 ft) after Bultei. The roads are winding and panoramic above sheer drops. We are only 1h30 by train from Sassari and 3h from Cagliari.

PALERMO
SICILIAN SOUL

Hilly / Intermediate

Map strava.com/routes/22785305

Distance **80 km** (50 mi)

E+ **1,350 m** (4,450 ft)

Difficulty **3/5**

Appeal **4/5**

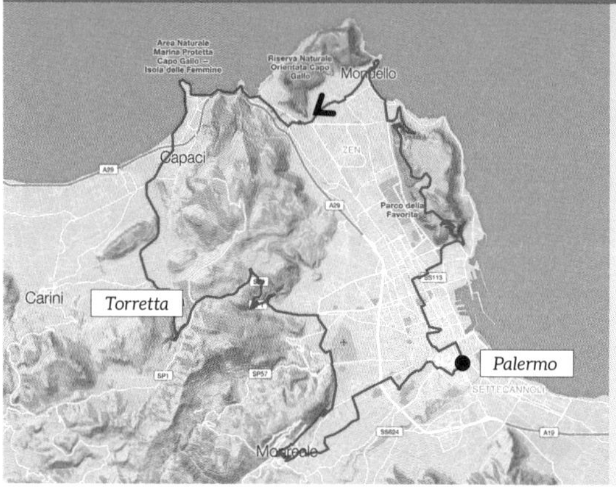

This loop around Palermo, the cradle of the Sicilian soul, takes in this superb, intriguing city, the sea, and hills up to an altitude of nearly 600 m (1,960 ft). Piazza Quattro Canti, the cathedral, and the Norman Palace compose a splendid appetizer. Things get physical with the climbs of Monte Pellegrino (1.5 km/1 mi at 10%) up to the sanctuary of Santa Rosalia, Bellolampo (6 km/3.7 mi at 4%, then 4 km/2.5 mi at 6%), and Monreale with its Byzantine cathedral. It is also pleasant to ride the route in the opposite direction. Back in town, enjoy a coffee with *cassata* (sponge cake layered with ricotta and candied fruit).

SYRACUSE
OUT OF TIME

Very hilly / Advanced

Map strava.com/routes/21555605

Distance **144 km** (89 mi)

E+ **2,100 m** (6,890 ft)

Difficulty **3/5**

Appeal **4/5**

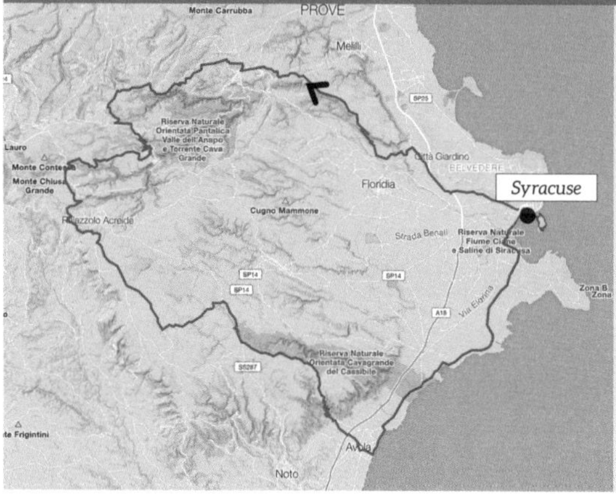

Cicero said of Syracuse that it was the most beautiful Greek city in Antiquity. As you pass the archaeological park on the way out of town and the ancient city on the little island of Ortigia when you return, you will surely see that he was right. This route through the hinterlands of southeast Sicily offers choice cycling territory with peaks of 500 m (1,640 ft) to 800 m (2,625 ft) between villages, remote valleys, and nature reserves. The Necropolis of Pantalica, the gorges of Cassibile (where you will ache to take a dip), and the views on the descent to the Mediterranean and Avola make this route very special indeed.

CALATABIANO
ETNA IN CLOSE-UP

- *Low mountain / Advanced*
- *Map strava.com/routes/21551953*
- *Test yourself km 13 (mi 8) strava.com/segments/7309807*
- *Test yourself km 27 (mi 17) strava.com/segments/7686919*

Mount Etna, on the island of Sicily, is both feared and respected. People ski on its slopes; however, it remains an active volcano under constant surveillance. The highest point of this route lies just east of the famous summit, which rises to 3,326 m (10,912 ft).

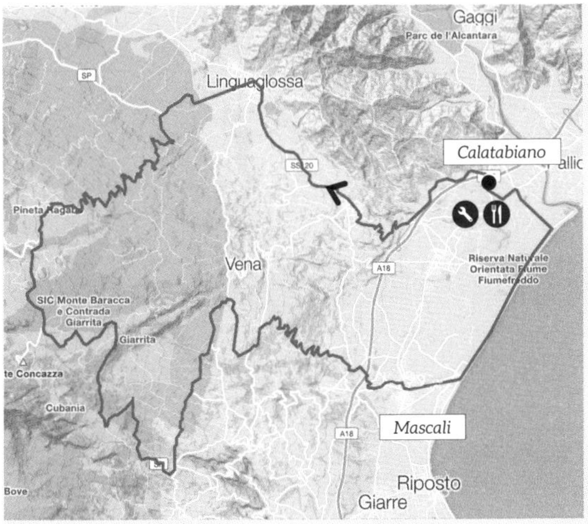

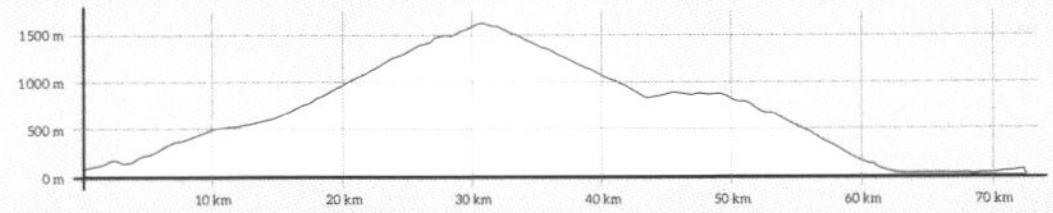

Before attempting a complete circuit of Etna, whet your appetite with this loop to the east of the volcano, starting from Calatabiano train station. It is an attractive profile and not too long. The first 24 km (15 mi) ascend to 1,632 m (5,354 ft). After Linguaglossa (km 15/mi 9), you enter the forest at a steady gradient of between 6% and 7%. Above 1,000 m (3,280 ft), the sultry Sicilian climate gives way to a milder atmosphere, although you should avoid very hot days. You will finally see a volcanic landscape on the approach to Monte Baracca. At km 32 (mi 20), you can veer right and explore the promontory of Monte Concazza (elevation gain 135 m/443 ft), with its vitreous rocks, lava solidified by lightning, and marvelous views. Etna's cone seems within your grasp. Then, it is a fast descent as far as Fornazzo (km 43/ mi 27). The final run-in is a lovely ride along Marina di Cottone beach.

Distance	E+	Difficulty	Appeal
73 km (45 mi)	1,800 m (5,905 ft)	3/5	4/5

Calatabiano lies on Sicily's Ionian Coast between Catania and Messina. It is 40 minutes by train and car from the former (40 km/25 mi), and 1h20 by train and 50 minutes by car from the latter (60 km/37 mi). Served by Catania-Fontanarossa Airport.

If the ride has given you an appetite, head to La Tana Dell'Orso di Spinella Giuseppe and sample its succulent mix of family dishes and creative recipes.

Piazza Vittorio Emanuele, 20
95011 Calatabiano
la-tana-dellorso-di-spinella-giuseppe.business.site

New Bike Revolution is the go-to address for cyclists in Calatabiano. It has a workshop, sells Italian brands, and organizes outings around Etna.

Via Savona 10
95011 Calatabiano
newbikerevolution.it

MESSINA
IN THE SHARK'S WHEEL

- *Very hilly / Advanced*
- *Map strava.com/routes/22487026*
- *Test yourself km 35 (mi 22) strava.com/segments/2308952*
- *Test yourself km 62 (mi 38) strava.com/segments/7120978*

Vincenzo Nibali, the modern *campionissimo* (champion), is one of the most popular cyclists on Strava (more than 100 000 followers in 2022). When he returns home to Sicily, the "Shark of Messina" likes to alternate between coast and (hilly) hinterland. strava.com/pros/8842341

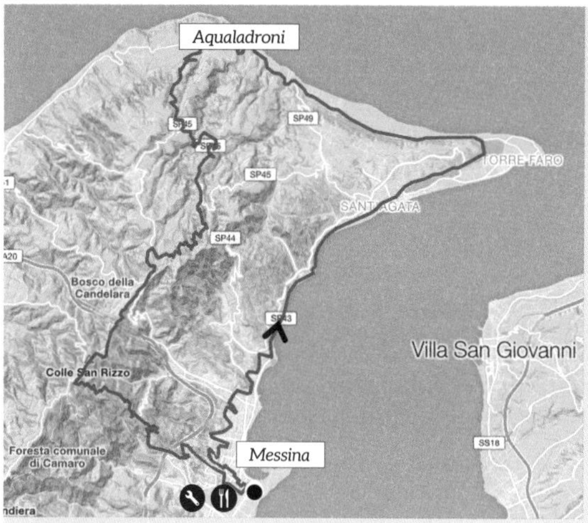

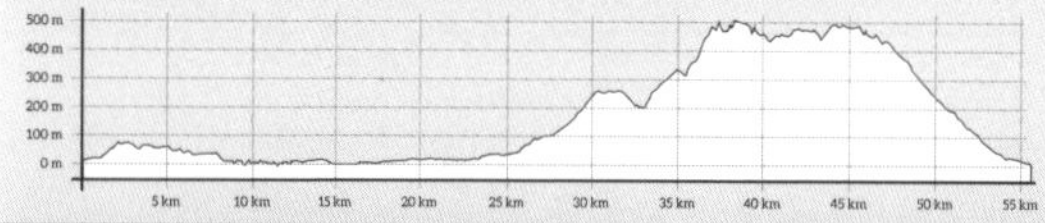

Born in Messina, Nibali shares his routes and photos on Strava, alternating the seaside with the steep foothills of the Peloritani mountains. Starting and ending in Messina, this route is a mix of his favorite rides via fine sandy beaches and marinas, the former electricity pylon at Torre Faro—from where the mainland seems so close (barely 3 km/2 mi)—and old villages. We never ascend higher than 500 m (1,640 ft), but the climbs are not short: more than 3 km (2 mi) at 9% near Marotta, nearly 7 km (4.5 mi) to reach Castanea, and 4 km (2.5 mi) at 7% before San Rizzo. There are some amazing views from these slopes. After the 10 km (6 mi) descent back to Messina, there is a little kick up to Monte Piselli, 140 m (460 ft) above the water, with a sumptuous panorama over the city, the strait, and Calabria. There are plenty of KOMs to chase along the way, although guess who holds them all?

Distance	E+	Difficulty	Appeal
56 km (34 mi)	**750 m** (2,500 ft)	**3/5**	**4/5**

Messina is served by the airports of Catania, which is 3h by train or 1h20 by car (110 km/68 mi), and Palermo, which is 5h by train or 2h40 by car (250 km/155 mi). By ferry: 20 minutes from Reggio di Calabria, and 9h from Salerno.

At the peak of San Rizzo, Don Minico (km 71/mi 44) makes possibly the best sandwich in the world, with house-baked bread and local olive oil, herbs, ham, and cheese.

Colle San Rizzo
98152 Messina
donminico.com

Although it is not necessarily the ideal workshop if you have a serious problem, Bici Messina, located near Piazza del Popolo, is one elegant bike store.

Via Francesco Faranda, 9
98123 Messina
bicimessina.it

TARANTO
PUGLIA IN BLUE AND WHITE

- *Hilly / Intermediate*
- *Map strava.com/routes/21804798*
- *Test yourself km 32 (mi 20) strava.com/segments/17565208*
- *Test yourself km 40 (mi 25) strava.com/segments/5598322*

A blessed region that encourages *farniente* (doing nothing) can turn into a cyclist's paradise. There is not a mountain on the Puglian horizon between the Gulf of Taranto and the beaches of Monopoli—only hills, sky and sea.

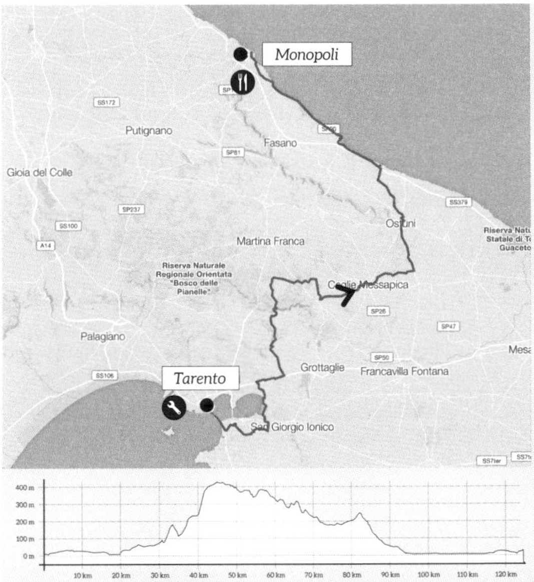

Puglia forms the heel and spur of the Italian "boot." This route from Taranto to Monopoli joins two seas—the Ionian and the Adriatic—and two sublime towns at the top of the heel. You should absolutely make the time to explore both of them, and also return to the hilltop town of Ostuni (km 83/mi 52) for a glass of local wine on Piazza della Libertà. The route is a fair length (125 km/78 mi), and there is a little climbing too, such as Spaccamonti (km 40/mi 25): 2.5 km (1.5 mi) at a gradient of 7%. The rest is a dream: Taranto harbor, Mar Piccolo, the wild landscape with occasional vineyards and olive plantations, the ducal palace at Ceglie Messapica, Ostuni (of course!), and the final 30 km (18 mi) beside the Adriatic between dunes, rocks, and beaches of the Dune Costiere, with stretches of the old Appian Way and Monopoli with its port, old town, and white walls.

Distance	E+	Difficulty	Appeal
125 km (78 mi)	2,100 m (6,900 ft)	3/5	4/5

Taranto (pop. 200,000) is served by Bari Airport: 2h by train or 1h10 by car (100 km/62 mi). Possible low cost flights to Brindisi Airport: 1h10 by train or 1h by car (70 km/45 mi). Naples is 4h10 by train or 3h40 by car (300 km/185 mi).

In the evening, lose yourself in Monopoli's narrow streets before settling at the no-frills Il Guazzetto, which is a short stroll from the port, where Mario and Francesco serve wonderful seafood.

Via dell'Erba, 39
70043 Monopoli
ristoranteilguazzetto.it

Whatever you want to buy a bike, get yours adjusted, or simply chat cycling, drop in to friendly and trendy MF Cycling, corso Italia, close to km 5 (mi 3).

Corso Italia, 316
74121 Taranto
mf-cycling.business.site

POMPEII
MAGICAL AMALFI

Low mountain / Advanced
Map strava.com/routes/21654144
Test yourself km 15 (mi 9) strava.com/segments/714439
Test yourself km 53 (mi 33) strava.com/segments/4269542

To the south of Naples, the Amalfi Coast is one of the most sublime parts of Italy. The combination of divine views and picturesque villages make it unique. You need to be in fine physical condition to cycle here (whether in spring or even winter), but it is hugely enjoyable.

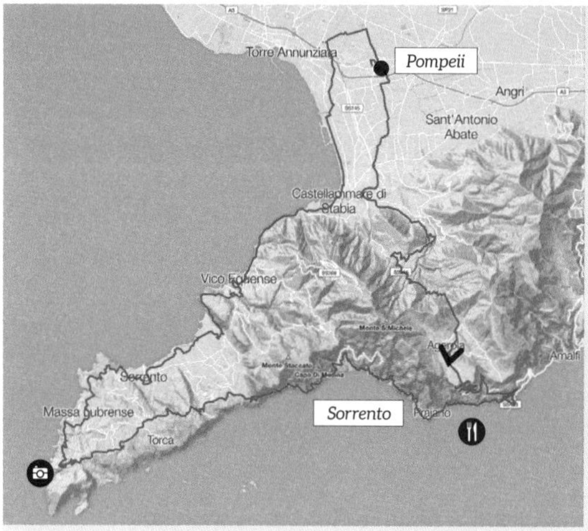

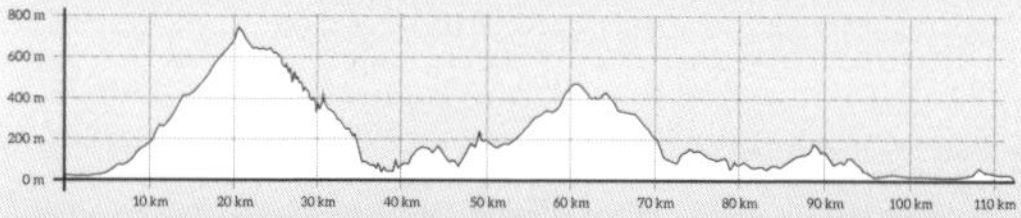

Although challenging, the Amalfi Coast is a cyclist's paradise. Avoid the high season because tourists flock here each summer from all over the world (narrow roads, many buses). Our route around the Sorrento Peninsula rolls east to west. The first major test comes on the road to Agerola, not long after leaving Pompeii: 13 km (8 mi) of irregular climbing up to nearly 800 m (2,600 ft), with several sections at an average gradient of 15%. We then descend toward Conca dei Marini (km 36/mi 22) and into enchantment. This is the Amalfi Coast, with its rocky cliffs, low mountains, spectacular scenery, and charming villages. We pass Praiano, Positano, and San Pietro before returning via the Bay of Naples. As beautiful a ride as it is, you will expend considerable effort over a dozen climbs—some of them quite short, but with a total elevation gain of more than 3,000 m (9,800 ft).

Distance	E+	Difficulty	Appeal
112 km (70 mi)	3,300 m (10,830 ft)	4/5	5/5

Pompeii is 1h30 by train from Naples Airport, and 30 minutes by train from Naples Centrale station. Alternatively, pick up the route at Amalfi (not too far from km 34/mi 21), after taking the ferry from Salerno (50 minutes, €15/$17). It is a wonderful way of seeing the coast.

At the edge of Praiano (km 39/mi 24), walk down the slipway to Trattoria Da Armandino for an espresso or one of its astounding seafood dishes.

Via Marina di Praia 1
84010 Praiano SA

In Termini (km 68/mi 42), wander down to Mitigliano Beach for an extraordinary view of Capri, which is less than 10 km (6 mi) away. Sure, you will have added 300 m (980 ft) of climbing to get back up to the road, but you will not be disappointed.

One of the numerous tunnels on the Amalfi Coast, Italy.

NAPLES
MARRIAGE ITALIAN STYLE

Hilly / Intermediate

Map strava.com/routes/21748004

Test yourself km 24 (mi 15) strava.com/segments/11574568

Test yourself km 64 (mi 40) strava.com/segments/1047802

Naples is a city apart. It is a noisy, frenetic, colorful place where people have their own particular interpretation of the rules of the road, so take care. This reasonably short ride gets you out of the tumult to explore amazing scenery before returning via the vestiges of a rich past.

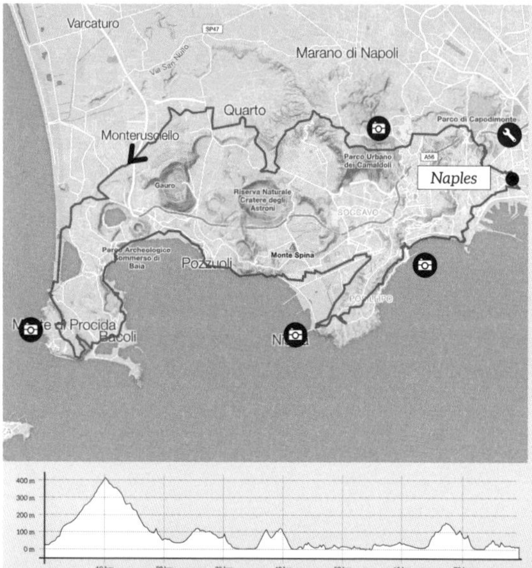

The classic film *Marriage Italian Style* (1964), starring Sophia Loren and Marcello Mastroianni, threw the spotlight on Naples. This route offers a cycling remake: a three-way marriage between the commotion of this unique city, the rich natural surroundings, and the wealth of history. From the bustling central train station, we start climbing (9 km/5.5 mi at 5%) up past Capodimonte Park and Camaldoli Park. Descending toward the Tyrrhenian coast, we pass the majestic markers of a volcanic environment: the Astroni and Barbaro craters and, further on, Monte Nuovo and Solfatara. From Bacoli on Cape Miseno (km 41/mi 25) to San Paolo Stadium (km 60/mi 37), we explore the splendors of the bay. We return to indomitable Naples via the sublime traces of the past: Royal Palace, Piazza del Plebiscito, Castel Nuovo, and the historic center.

Distance	E+	Difficulty	Appeal
80 km (50 mi)	1,250 m (4,100 ft)	3/5	5/5

Naples' metropolitan area has a population of 4.4 million. It is well connected to Europe and the rest of Italy via its airport, which is 25 minutes from the central station by bus or taxi. Rome is 1h10 by train or 2h15 by car (230 km/143 mi). Bari is 4h30 by train (via Foggia) or 2h40 by car (260 km/160 mi).

The Milano Cicli, located 100 meters/yards from Naples Central Train Station, offers impeccable workshop service and road bike rental. Retailer of Colnago, Bianchi, and Giant.

Corso Novara, 86
80143 Naples
milano-cicli.business.site

This route provides some great views. Four key spots are Hermitage of Camaldoli (km 10/mi 6), the island of Ischia seen from Monte di Procida (km 37/mi 23), the promontory of Virgiliano Park (km 64/mi 40), and the Church of Saint Anthony (km 71/mi 44).

ROME
PAPAL AND ANCIENT

⊕ *Hilly / Advanced*   ⊕ *Map strava.com/routes/21866247*

Distance	E+	Difficulty	Appeal
179 km (111 mi)	1,250 m (7,000 ft)	4/5	4/5

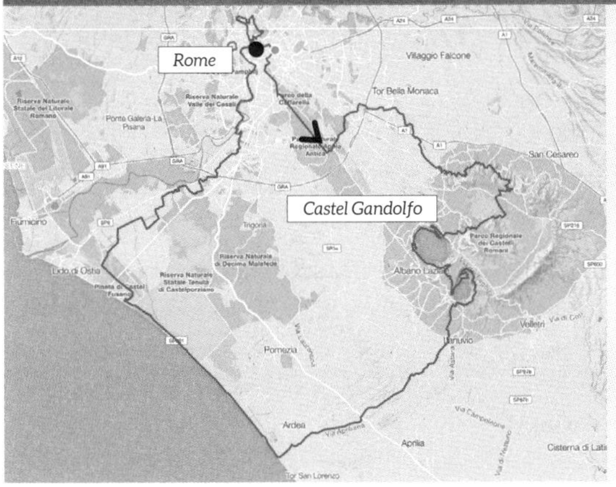

If you are going to cycle out of Rome, you might as well go big. This 179 km (111 mi) route to the south of the Eternal City can be ridden as you wish because it passes several train stations (Ciampino, Frascati, Albano Laziale, Aprilia, Anzio, Villa Bonelli, and Ostia Antica). We cycle past ancient monuments along the Via Appia, around Castelli Romani Park and its lakes, past the papal residence of Castel Gandolfo, and up several climbs (the last one being the cobbled Nemi) along a stretch of Tyrrhenian coast, then back via Ostia (and the archaeological site of Ostia Antica at km 133/ mi 83), and the banks of the Tiber.

ROME
A TRIP TO THE ISLANDS

⊕ *Hilly / Advanced*   ⊕ *Map strava.com/routes/21847512*

Map	E+	Difficulty	Appeal
169 km (105 mi)	1,950 m (6,400 ft)	3/5	4/5

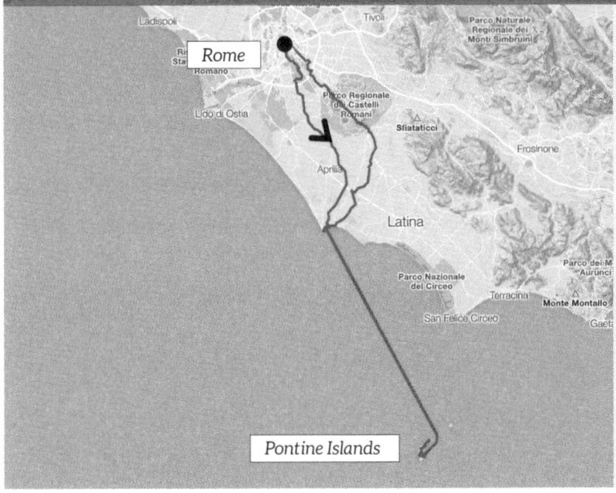

Ah, *la dolce vita*! This audacious escapade departs Roma-Termini train station for a day out in the heavenly setting of the Pontine Islands, including 169 km (105 mi) on the bike and four hours on the ferry there and back. Leave early to catch the sunrise over the Colosseum and the ancient stones of the Via Appia. Return in the early evening via Velletri (with its medieval gates, arcades, and convent), Castelli Romani Park, and Cinecittà film studios. Spend the day on the fascinating and enchanting island of Ponza, where Circe supposedly bewitched Ulysses: barely 20 km (12 mi) but worth spending hours exploring.

CHIETI
ASSAULTING THE BLOCKHAUS

- *High mountain / Advanced*
- *Map strava.com/routes/21807169*
- *Test yourself km 32 (mi 20) strava.com/segments/7930051*
- *Test yourself km 44 (mi 27) strava.com/segments/7808436*

The Madonnina del Blockhaus is the only road in the Maiella to ascend higher than 2,000 m (6,560 ft). You might spot local cyclist Giulio Ciccone, who won the 2019 Giro d'Italia mountains classification and held the Tour de France yellow jersey for two days. strava.com/pros/29028250

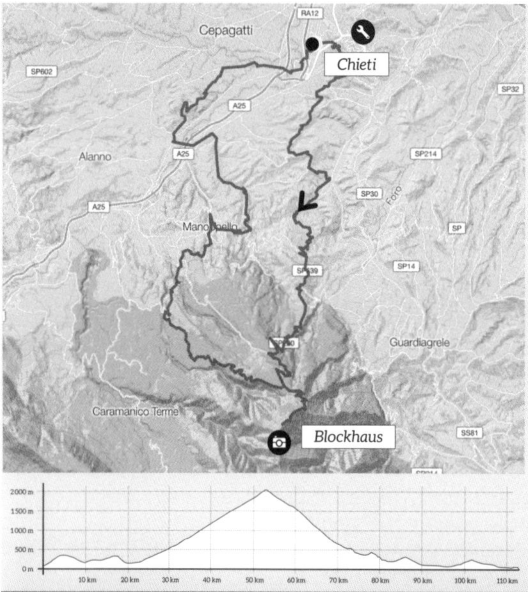

In the 1860s, the army of Victor Emmanuel II was busy fighting brigands in the Abruzzi. A small fort on one of the peaks of the Maiella was nicknamed Blockhaus, and the moniker stuck. In 1967, a 22-year-old Eddy Merckx made his mark here. After limbering over the Chieti hills, the approach to the Blockhaus is long—nearly 30 km (18 mi) with an elevation gain of 1,900 m (6,200 ft)—and comprises three stages: first, the Passo Lanciano at 1,306 m (4,285 ft): 12 km (7.5 mi) at an average gradient of 6.5%, starting at Pretoro; second, the Maielletta at 1,650 m (5,400 ft): 5 km (3 mi) at 7%, with several "escape routes"; and finally, the narrow, dead-end road up to the Blockhaus at 2,142 m (7,028 ft): 6 km (3.5 mi) at an average gradient of 9%, rising to 11% in the final section. The landscape after Lanciano is dry and rocky, with short grass burned by the sun. Around you, are the majestic summits of the Maiella.

Distance	E+	Difficulty	Appeal
113 km (70 mi)	3,050 m (10,005 ft)	4/5	4/5

Chieti (pop. 55,000) is 20 minutes by train and by car (20 km/12 mi) from Pescara, the principal urban area (and seaside resort) of the Abruzzo region. To the west, Rome is 3h by train or 2h20 by car (200 km/125 mi). To the north, Bologna is 4h by train or 3h45 by car (380 km/235 mi).

Bike Pro Chieti is the go-to sports cycling store in Chieti. Retailer of Specialized and Merida, among others. Workshop and bike fitting.

**Via Maestri Del Lavoro, 14
66100 Chieti**

After the Rifugio Bruno Pomilio, there is a viewpoint and orientation table 200 meters/yards from the summit of the Madonnina del Blockhaus (km 53/mi 33), offering stunning panoramas over the Abruzzi and the plain to the Adriatic. It is rare to have such a clear view above 2,000 m (6,500 ft).

GALLESE IN TEVERINA
SURPRISING LATIUM

- *Hilly / Intermediate*
- *Map strava.com/routes/21803936*
- *Test yourself km 53 (mi 33) strava.com/segments/9632270*
- *Test yourself km 65 (mi 40) strava.com/segments/2371060*

This fantastic route can be ridden if you are staying in Rome because we are only an hour from the Eternal City. Bracciano and Vico, the two loveliest lakes in Latium, sit amid stunning nature and towns rich in history.

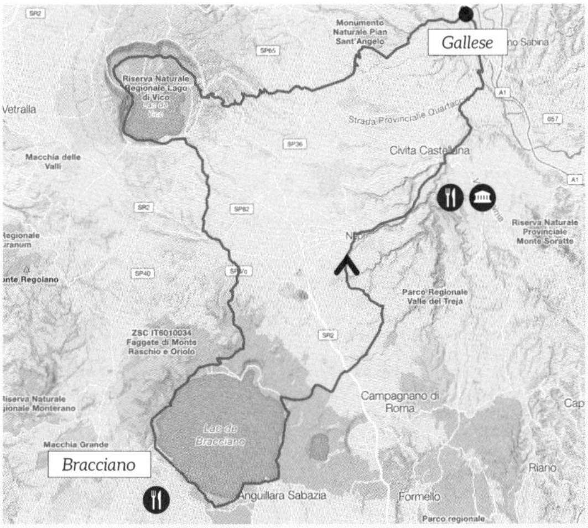

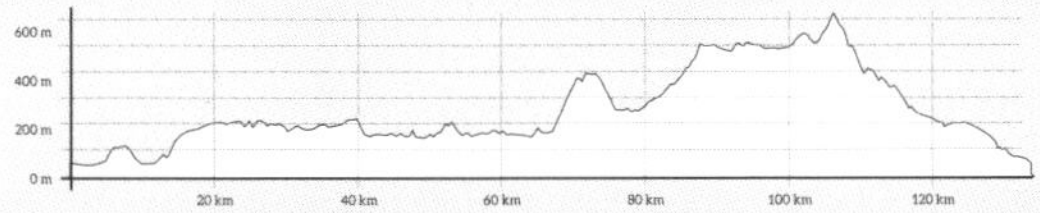

It happened north of Rome at the dawn of time. The Sabatini volcanoes created two sumptuous lakes: Bracciano and Vico. Even Hercules was involved apparently! Above Vico, Monte Cimino spewed its rocks over Monte Venere (851 m/2,790 ft), where you will find the astonishing Cave of the Devil. Stone pines now cover the slopes, and birch trees have spread along the waterside. Humans built and fought here. See the citadel of Civita Castellana (km 13/mi 8), or the military architecture of Renaissance Bracciano Castle (km 57/mi 35). The second part of the route is very hilly, with climbs of 6% to 7% from Rocca Romana above Lake Bracciano (3 km/2 mi) up to Ronciglione and Lake Vico (3 km/2 mi), then around Monte Venere (2 km/1.25 mi). The ride back includes such delights as the Villa Farnese in Caprarola, the narrow streets of Fabrica di Roma, and the Corchiano gorge.

Distance	E+	Difficulty	Appeal
134 km (83 mi)	1,750 m (5,550 ft)	3/5	3/5

To the south, Gallese (pop. 2,800) is close to Rome: 1h15 by train from Roma Termini, 50 minutes by train from Roma-Tiburtina, and another 30 minutes from Fiumicino Airport. By car, Rome is 1h20 (75 km/47 mi). Florence is 3h by train or 2h50 (220 km/135 mi) by car.

At km 13 (mi 8), turn left to visit the fifteenth century citadel of Civita Castellana and stop for an espresso in the bar of the beautiful Relais Falisco Hotel.

Via Don Giovanni Minzoni, 19
01033 Civita Castellana
relaisfalisco.it

If you would like to split the route in two, stop at the restaurant Le Papere in Bracciano (km 57/mi 35) for some local cuisine on its terrace standing on stilts above the lake.

Lungolago Giuseppe Argenti, 20
00062 Bracciano
lepapere.it

SAN PIERO IN BAGNO
TO THE SOURCE OF THE TIBER

- *Low mountain / Advanced*
- *Map strava.com/routes/21834870*
- *Test yourself km 25 (mi 16) strava.com/segments/3924180*
- *Test yourself km 88 (mi 55) strava.com/segments/2454260*

The lush Romagnol Apennines, lying between Florence and the Republic of San Marino, are not the first mountains that come to mind when you think of Italy. Explore them with this route via Monte Fumaiolo, the source of the Tiber, a river sacred to the Romans.

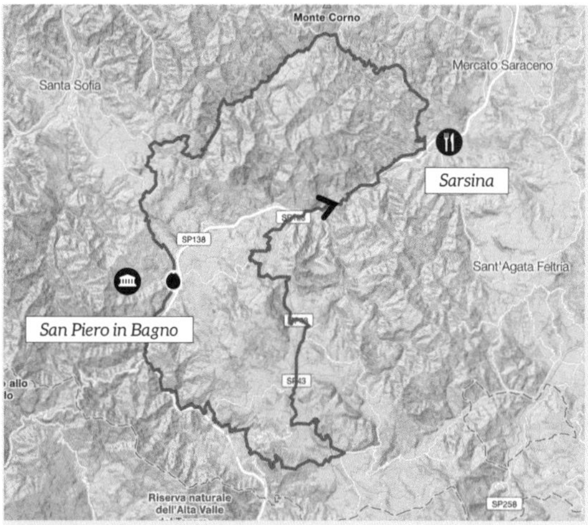

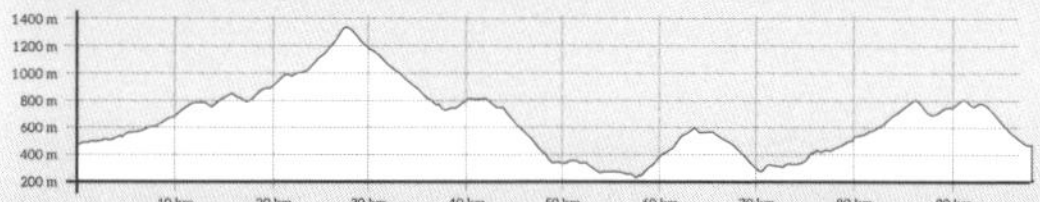

The hot springs of Bagno di Romagna (km 3/mi 2) have been renowned for millennia. At the summit of the road up Monte Fumaiolo (km 28/mi 17) is the source of the Tiber, which majestically enters Rome 200 km (125 mi) to the south. Fill your bottle at the fountain that marks the spot; the final 4 km (2.5 mi) of the climb, at an average gradient of more than 8%, will have been tough. Here in the Romagnol Apennines, the landscape comprises forests of oak, and maple; waterfalls; and rocky ground. Further on at km 63 (mi 39), we climb again, up to 600 m (1,970 ft), via a 5 km (3 mi) stretch at 7% to Monte Finocchio, and then up to more than 800 m (2,600 ft) to Spinello (km 86/mi 53) via 10 km (6 mi) at 4.5%. The route is 98 km (59 mi) long, but the total elevation gain is more than 2,500 m (8,200 ft), which gives you some idea of the terrain. It is good for forgetting everything except the essential.

Distance	E+	Difficulty	Appeal
98 km (59 mi)	2,300 m (7,550 ft)	3/5	4/5

San Piero in Bagno (pop. 3,200) is connected by train to Florence (1h30), Bologna (1h10), and Milan (2h) via Cesena (50 km/30 mi); the bus takes 1h30. By car, Florence is 2h20 (100 km/62 mi), Bologna is 1h30 (130 km/80 mi), and Milan is 3h45 (350 km/220 mi).

Born in Sarsina (km 58/mi 36), Plautus was a comic dramatist of Roman times. La Taverna di Plauto pays homage to him. Rustic decor and Romagnole cuisine.

Via Cesio Sabino, 16
47027 Sarsina
latavernadiplauto.it

The mineral-rich waters and hot springs of Bagno di Romagna are the perfect way to unwind between two rides. The three magnificent ancient spas are located 3 km (1.8 mi) from San Piero.

bagnodiromagnaterme.it

RIETI
APENNINE FJORD

Low mountain / Advanced

Map strava.com/routes/21809411

Distance	E+	Difficulty	Appeal
115 km (71 mi)	1,850 m (6,070 ft)	3/5	4/5

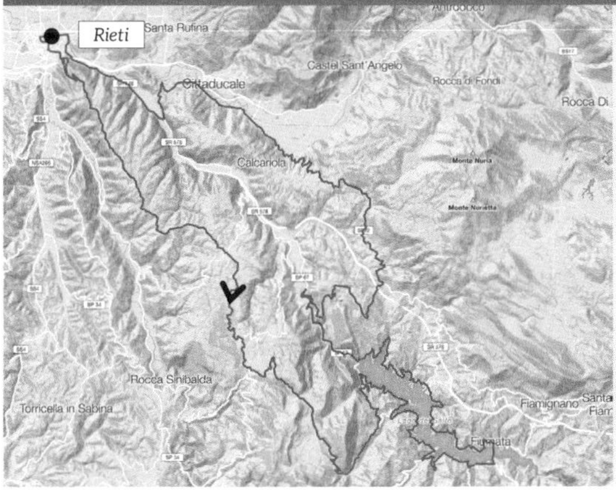

Pretty Rieti, located 80 km (50 mi) northeast of Rome (3h by train), enjoys a relative remoteness that lends itself to cycling adventures. This is not a short ride, but the tour of Lake Salto, named after the river that has its source near Avezzano, is a joy. Leaving Rieti, we hoist ourselves up to 800 m (2,600 ft) in just a few kilometers before ascending to nearly 1,100 m (3,600 ft) on Monte Valli. We are in the heart of the Apennines, yet Lake Salto (altitude 550 m/1,800 ft) evokes the Norwegian fjords. The 30 km (18 mi) stretch beside its clear waters—crossing two spectacular bridges—is stunning.

FLORENCE
LIFE IS BEAUTIFUL

Low mountain / Advanced

Map strava.com/routes/21835097

Distance	E+	Difficulty	Appeal
103 km (64 mi)	1,800 m (5,905 ft)	3/5	4/5

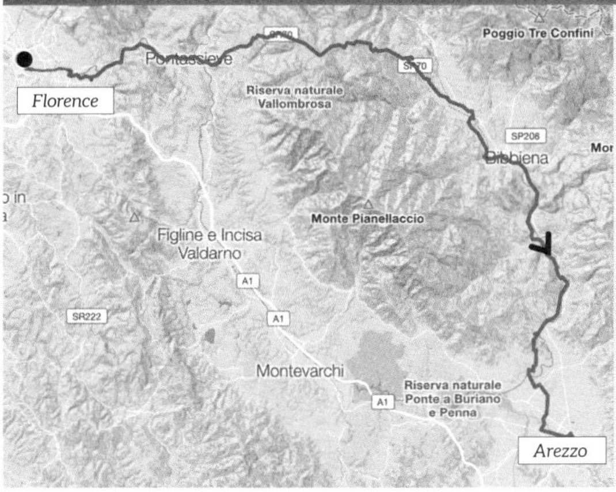

This route from Florence to Arrezo (1h to return by train or by car—80 km/50 mi) features two superb cities: Florence, of course, which we leave via the banks of the Arno, and the ancient Etruscan city of Arezzo, which provided the backdrop for Roberto Benigni's triple-Oscar-winning film, *Life Is Beautiful* (1999). We then venture into the lush green Tuscan Apennines on a long climb up to Consuma (1,060 m/3,477 ft): 13 km (8 mi) at an average gradient of 7%. Then, we pick up the course of the Arno again, passing several pretty villages with fine views over the hills of Emilia-Romagna.

SIENA
CHALKED UP

Very hilly / Advanced
Map strava.com/routes/21669495

Test yourself km 58 (mi 36) strava.com/segments/2476906
Test yourself km 114 (mi 71) strava.com/segments/3547126

The Crete Senesi is a range of hills southeast of the Tuscan city of Siena. Since 1997, cyclists have celebrated the white gravel roads of these hills with a vintage bike race (the Eroica) and, since 2007, a professional race (the Strade Bianche or White Road).

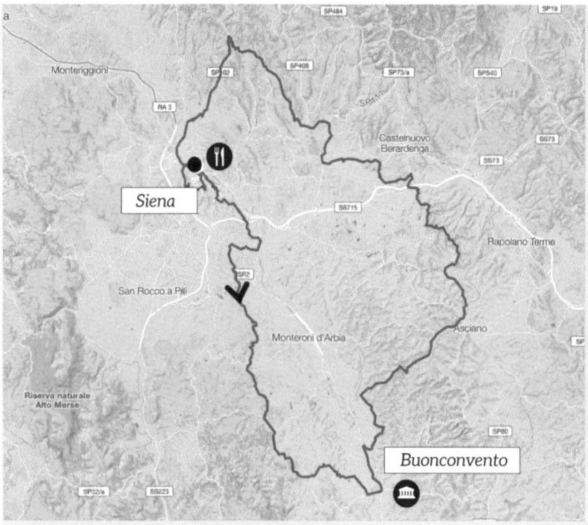

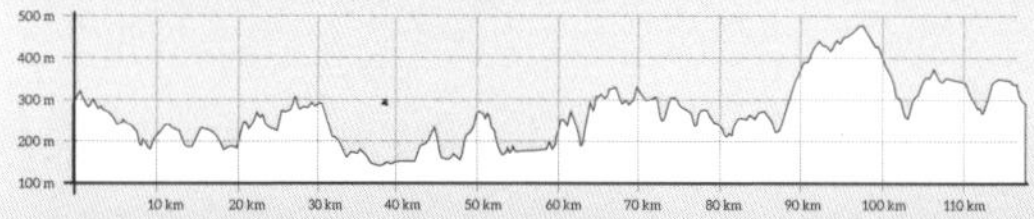

Tackling the Strade Bianche means engaging in a form of cycling that is at once deeply historic and furiously modern. The ancient white roads of Tuscany have been one of the inspirations of the recent emergence of the "gravel" trend. The choice of tire is therefore essential before setting out on this 118 km (73 mi) hilly route, 50 km (30 mi) of which are on roads of clay, tuff rock, and sand, past rows of cypresses and remote villages. There are six such sectors at the following km (mi) points: 22 (14), 32 (20), 42 (26), 59 (37), 74 (45), and 87 (54). The hills constantly rear up and down. After Pianella, we even climb 3.5 km (2 mi) at an average gradient of 7%. The return to Siena is a delight. As you roll onto the Piazza del Campo like the pros to the foot of the 102 m (335 ft) Torre del Mangia, having negotiated the Via Santa Caterina (0.7 km/0.45 mi at 10%), you will be the color of chalk, yet proud and happy.

Distance	E+	Difficulty	Appeal
118 km (73 mi)	2,150 m (7,055 ft)	3/5	4/5

The closest airport to Siena is Florence: 2h to 2h45 by train or 1h by car (80 km/50 mi). Milan is 3h30 by train or 3h55 by car (370 km/230 mi). Rome is 3h30 by train or 2h30 by car (230 km/143 mi).

Having reach the Campo, you will no doubt be hungry. Head to Trattoria Da Dino in the Onda district for the best bruschetta in town. Exceptional!

Via Casato di Sopra 71
53100 Siena
facebook.com/trattoriadino

At km 39 (mi 24), Buonconvento is worth a stop. This medieval village has retained its fourteenth-century defensive walls. Within, you will find red brick houses and mansions, and the church of Santi Pietro e Paolo.

terredisiena.it

The Strade Bianche snake across Tuscany, Italy.

FLORENCE
CHIANTI AND MAGICAL TUSCANY

- *Very hilly / Advanced*
- *Map strava.com/routes/21841998*
- *Test yourself km 41 (mi 25) strava.com/segments/2883817*
- *Test yourself km 62 (mi 39) strava.com/segments/1319941*

This route is dreamy, with lush green hills and cypresses as far as the eye can see, panoramic roads, the vineyards of Chianti, and villages of old stones and ocher roofs. We start and end in Florence, the cradle of the Renaissance.

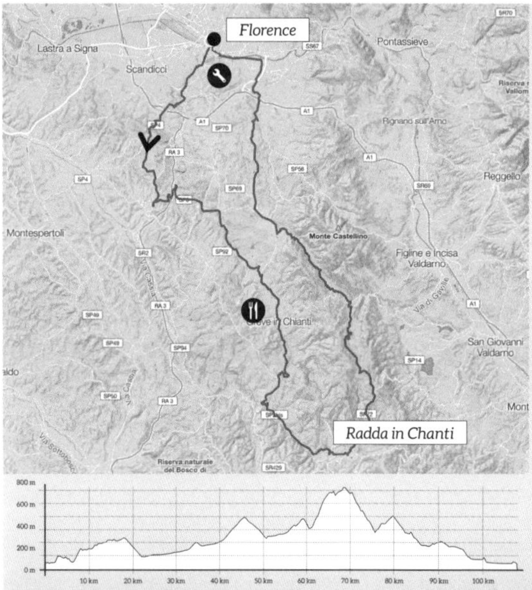

The most difficult thing about this stunning loop to the south of Florence through the Chianti countryside and its pretty villages is to remain focused on your physical effort when there is so much surrounding beauty. But the route requires it because of the wall of Le Gore at km 7/mi 4.5, Bolle della Sacci at km 33/mi 20, the Panzano climb at km 41/mi 25 (5 km/3 mi long at 4.6%), and, further on, Albola (4 km/2.5 mi long at 8%). Let your eyes feast all the same! There is the sublime Castello di Verrazzano, Greve in Chianti and its triangular Piazza Giacomo Matteotti, the stunning village of Montefioralle, Panzano and its church, medieval Radda in Chianti, Lucolena and its cobbled streets. We enter beautiful Florence on a cycle path between parks and the bank of the Arno River before passing the Basilica of the Holy Trinity, Palazzo Strozzi, and the Cathedral of Santa Maria del Fiore.

Distance	E+	Difficulty	Appeal
108 km (67 mi)	1,750 m (5,550 ft)	3/5	5/5

Florence (pop. 380,000) is well connected to the whole of Europe via its airport, located 20 minutes from Florence's central train station. Milan, Rome, and Venice are 3h by car from Florence. Pisa is easily reached from the airport: 1h by train or 1h20 by car (90 km/55 mi).

For a simple espresso and something sweet (you have ridden a fair way), stop at Pasticceria Chianti under the arcades on Piazza Matteotti in Greve (km 39/mi 24).

Piazza Giacomo Matteotti, 26
50022 Greve in Chianti
facebook.com/pasticceriachianti

Located close to the Basilica San Marco, Sergio Bianchi has his own bike brand, which he sells in his elegant, efficient, and very Italian store that is a touch retro.

Via San Gallo, 42
50129 Firenze
ciclisergiobianchi.it

GROSSETO
ANOTHER TUSCANY

Hilly / Intermediate

Map strava.com/routes/22540793

Distance	E+	Difficulty	Appeal
88 km (55 mi)	1,150 m (3,775 ft)	3/5	3/5

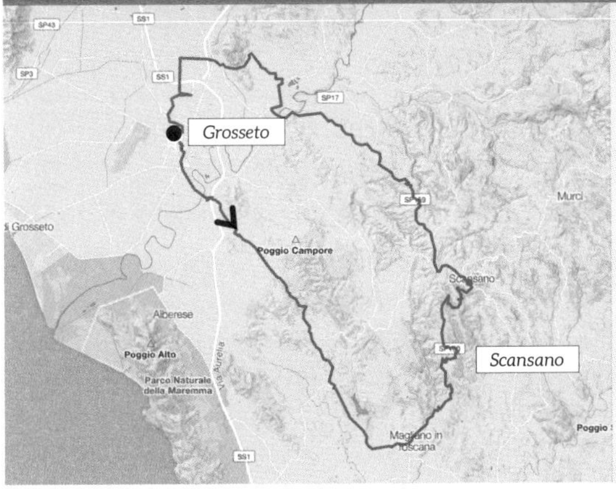

There are a thousand reasons to stop at Grosseto, the main city in the Maremma area, south of Tuscany, including the Medicean walls laid out in the shape of a star, the archaeological museum, and the cathedral. There are also the premises of Tommasini, one of Italy's preeminent bicycle manufacturers. The scenery outside the city is stunning, with the long climb through the hills to the old village of Scansano (altitude: 560 m/1,835 ft) at km 48 (mi 30), after the warm-up on Poggio Osteria (km 16/mi 10), not forgetting the ancient Etruscan city of Magliano in Toscana.

FLORENCE
A PENCHANT FOR PISA

Fairly flat / Intermediate

Map strava.com/routes/21787928

Distance	E+	Difficulty	Appeal
106 km (66 mi)	300 m (1,000 ft)	2/5	3/5

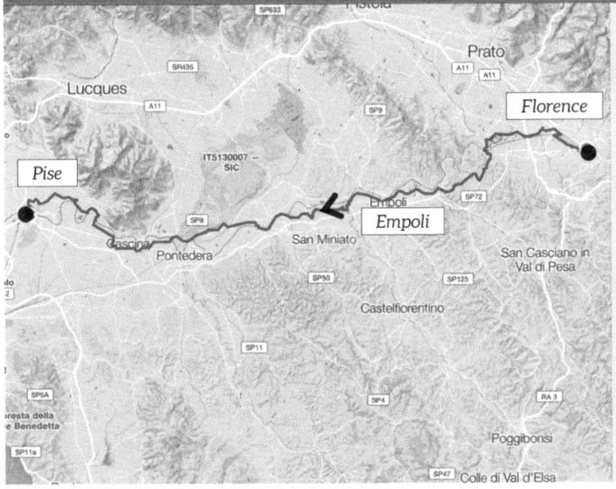

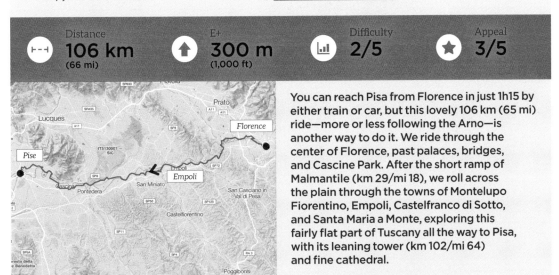

You can reach Pisa from Florence in just 1h15 by either train or car, but this lovely 106 km (65 mi) ride—more or less following the Arno—is another way to do it. We ride through the center of Florence, past palaces, bridges, and Cascine Park. After the short ramp of Malmantile (km 29/mi 18), we roll across the plain through the towns of Montelupo Fiorentino, Empoli, Castelfranco di Sotto, and Santa Maria a Monte, exploring this fairly flat part of Tuscany all the way to Pisa, with its leaning tower (km 102/mi 64) and fine cathedral.

CESENATICO
A PIRATE'S RAID

Hilly / Intermediate
Map strava.com/routes/21617731
Test yourself km 38 (mi 23) strava.com/segments/7507495
Test yourself km 46 (mi 29) strava.com/segments/8504895

The memory of Marco Pantani, the punchiest climber of modern times, who sadly died in February 2004, remains very much alive, especially here in Cesenatico, where he grew up. This route is a homage to "The Pirate."

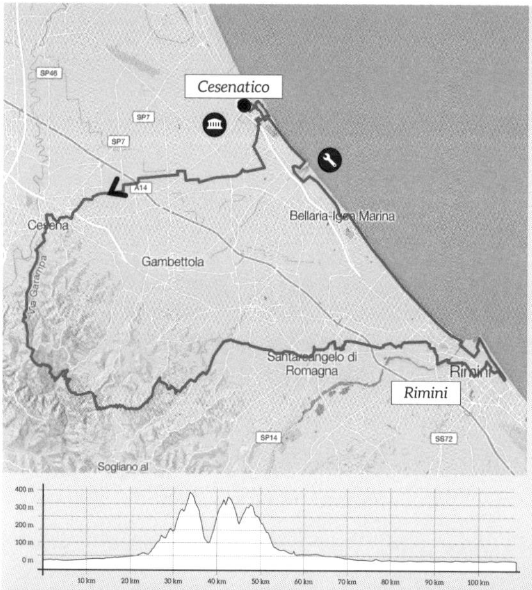

Remember "The Pirate" as you tackle this route—especially the exciting way in which he would propel his attacks in the mountains. From Cesenatico, where Pantani grew up, we ride to his birthplace of Cesena, with its lovely old town and superb Piazza del Popolo. Then, it is up into the hills where the teenage Pantani developed his highly individual style and exceptional abilities. The ascent gets pretty tough around Diolaguardia at km 34 (mi 21), with two ramps of 1.5 km (1 mi) at a gradient of 9%, followed by Monteleone: 3 km (2 mi) at 8%. We then descend back to the Adriatic and the beaches of Rimini (where the champion died) before returning along the coast to Cesenatico. Make sure that you go and see the bronze statue of Pantani on Piazza Marconi, and also try a slice of the Romagna specialty *piadine* (the "bread of the poor") in the little restaurant that belonged to Tonina, Pantani's mother, on Via Cartesio.

Distance
109 km
(68 mi)

E+
1,050 m
(3,445 ft)

Difficulty
3/5

Appeal
4/5

Cesenatico (pop. 25,000) lies 25 km (15 mi) north of Rimini. Bologna is 1h30 by train or 1h15 by car (100 km/62 mi). Milan is 3h10 by train (via Bologna and Ravenna) or 3h20 by car (320 km/200 mi). Florence is 2h30 by car (210 km/130 mi).

Cicli Nanni was established by Agostino Nanni, who saw Marco Pantani make his debut. It is a beautiful store with a workshop that offers route tips and road bike rental.

Via Pitagora, 5
47042 Villamarina
ciclinanni.com

Abutting Cesenatico station, Spazio Pantani is both a museum to the champion's glory and the headquarters of the eponymous foundation devoted to supporting all those who need help.

Via Cecchini, 2
47042 Cesenatico
pantani.it

BOLOGNA
THE HEIGHTS OF EMILIA

- *Hilly / Intermediate*
- *Map strava.com/routes/21649497*
- *Test yourself km 4 (mi 2) strava.com/segments/2447485*
- *Test yourself km 52 (mi 32) strava.com/segments/828752*

This short route through the hills south of Bologna was inspired by the Giro dell'Emilia, a lovely late-season semi-classic that serves as a warm-up for the Tour of Lombardy. Toward the end of the route, we climb to the local landmark of the Sanctuary of the Madonna di San Luca.

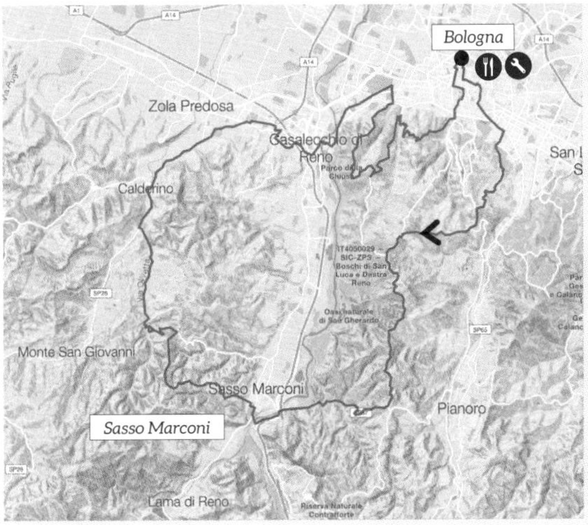

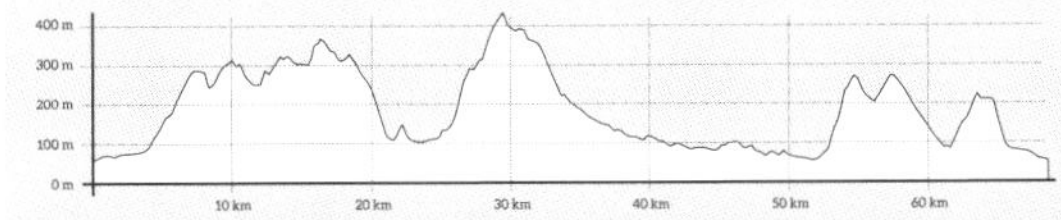

Bologna is a vibrant city that is home to the oldest university in the world. The charming hills of Emilia-Romagna are just a few pedal-turns away. To the south, they rise to more than 400 m (1,300 ft), providing breathtaking views of the city. We ride out of Bologna—although without really leaving it—via Monte Donato: 3 km (2 mi) at a gradient of 7%. We reconnect with the city again at the top of Via Castello (km 29/km 18) after Sasso Marconi (birthplace of the radio pioneer): 4 km (2.5 mi) at 8% between vineyards with the last part at 11%. We return via the hills that abut the city, starting with the climb to the Sanctuary of the Madonna de San Luca at km 55 (mi 34), riding alongside the arcade formed of 666 (!) arches: 1.8 km (1.1 mi) at 11%. Then, it is Monte Albano, followed by the Via del Genio. With its red-tiled roofs, Bologna is a city made for being admired from above—not to mention its delicious food.

Distance	E+	Difficulty	Appeal
68 km (42 mi)	1,450 m (4,760 ft)	3/5	3/5

Bologna is well connected via its airport, located 6 km (4 mi) northwest of the center. Milan is 1h by train from Bologna or 2h30 by car (200 km/125 mi). Venice is 2h by train or 1h50 by car (150 km/93 mi). Florence is 35 minutes by train or 1h30 by car (110 km/68 mi).

The very welcoming Ruote Ciclocaffè, located very close to San Vitale station, is a mix of cycling cultures: urban, fun, and sport.

Via Giuseppe Massarenti, 105
40138 Bologna
facebook.com/LeRuoteCicloCaffe

Forget bolognese sauce. Try the classic *tortellini in brodo* (pasta parcels stuffed with pork) at All'Osteria Bottega.

Via Santa Caterina 51
40123 Bologna
facebook.com/Osteria-Bottega

PARMA

FILMIC PO

Fairly flat / Intermediate   *Map strava.com/routes/21691436*

Distance **147 km** (91 mi) | E+ **350 m** (1,150 ft) | Difficulty **3/5** | Appeal **3/5**

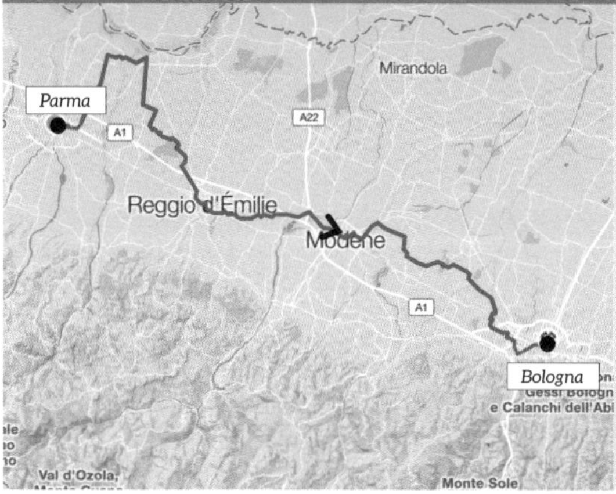

This route from Parma to Bologna (1h by train or 1h15 by car) traverses the Po Valley to the south of the river between wetlands and towns for nearly 150 km (93 mi). The only challenge is the distance, so make a detour at Reggio nell'Emilia (km 58/mi 36) to visit the the Villa d'Este, and stop in Modena (km 87/mi 54) for some ham and a glass of Lambrusco. Brescello (km 26/mi 16) is the home of Don Camillo and Peppone. Snap a selfie in front of the church, the town hall, and the statues of these famous characters who have been portrayed in so many films and TV adaptations.

MODENA

START YOUR ENGINES!

Fairly flat / Intermediate   *Map strava.com/routes/21635780*

Distance **107 km** (66 mi) | E+ **750 m** (2,460 ft) | Difficulty **3/5** | Appeal **4/5**

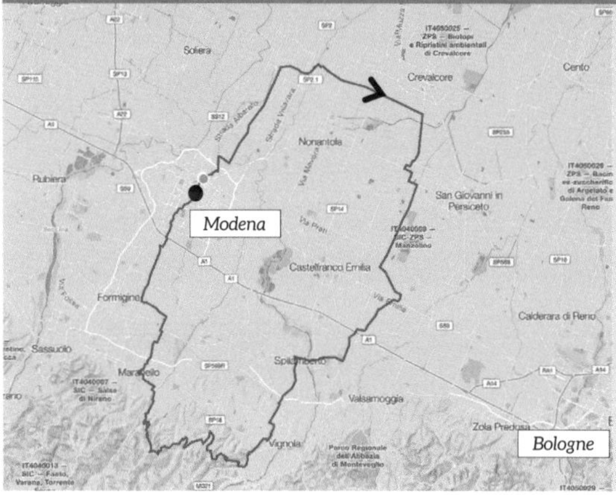

The most prestigious car manufacturers often like to use cycling imagery in their promotional materials. This loop is a celebration of Lamborghini and Ferrari, which are based between Modena and Bologna in the heart of Emilia Romagna. Bullish Lamborghini has its headquarters in Sant'Agata Bolognese (km 28/mi 17), while prancing Ferrari's stable is in Maranello (km 88/mi 55). Between the two are the foothills of the Apennines, with one big climb up to the Sanctuary of Puianello, including a 2 km (1.25 mi) section at 8%. On the descent, stop for coffee at Giallo in the Enzo Ferrari Museum.

LA SPEZIA
FABULOUS CINQUE TERRE

- *Low mountain / Expert*
- *Map strava.com/routes/21466296*
- *Test yourself km 15 (mi 9) strava.com/segments/1580944*
- *Test yourself km 48 (mi 30) strava.com/segments/2460527*

Cinque Terre is one of the most extraordinary parts of Italy, with low mountains rolling down to ocher cliffs that plunge into the Ligurian Sea, and villages painted in every color nestling in the crooks. This is extreme cycling territory, but it is so beautiful!

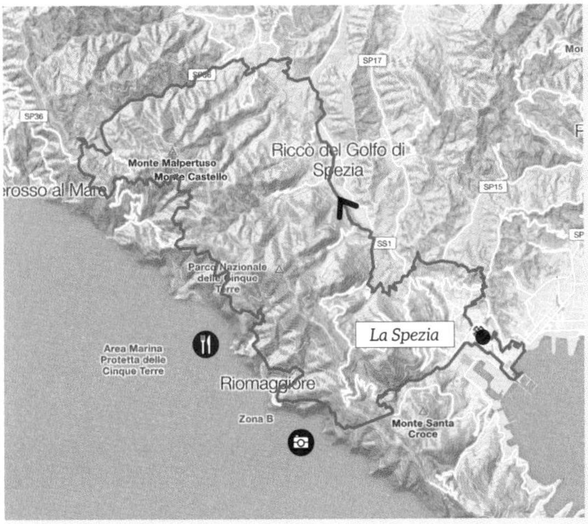

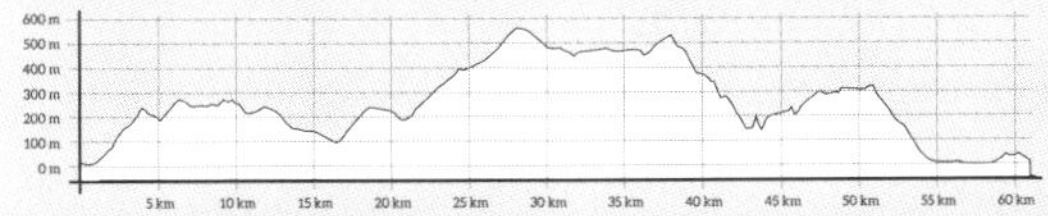

The Cinque Terre comprises five magical villages on the Ligurian Sea. Above them, agricultural terraces planted with grapevines and olive trees spread up the slopes of the fabulous low mountains. Riding from west to east, we bypass the first village, Monterosso al Mare (km 51/mi 32), to climb Colla di Gritta (5 km/3 mi at 6%), followed by its continuation, the Passo Termine (3 km/2 mi at 7%) and, further on, the Corniglia. We take in the villages of Vernazza (km 63/mi 49) and Manarola (km 76/mi 47) with their houses painted all kinds of colors, as well as Riomaggiore (km 82/mi 50), with delightful detours right down to the sea. This ride is a challenge because we climb to more than 500 m (1,640 ft) on three occasions. This route, which starts and ends in La Spezia, is a wonderful collection of difficulties with nearly 3,500 m (11,500 ft) of elevation gain. The Cinque Terre experience is unique.

Distance	E+	Difficulty	Appeal
105 km (65 mi)	2,750 m (9,000 ft)	5/5	5/5

The closest airports to La Spezia are Pisa and Genoa. The former is 1h10 by train or 1h by car (85 km/53 mi). The latter is 2h by train or 1h30 by car (110 km/68 mi). Milan is 3h10 by train (via Genoa) or 3h by car (230 km/143 mi).

Because we descend right down to Manarola at km 76 (mi 47), stop at La Cambusa for the best focaccia and farinata in the Cinque Terre.

Via Renato Birolli, 114
19017 Manarola
lecinqueterre.org

Just after Riomaggiore (km 86/mi 53), stop at the Sanctuary of Montenero. Its yellow and white bell tower stands 335 m (1,100 ft) above the sea. There is a magical view up the whole length of the Cinque Terre coast; it is a tough ride to get here.

MILAN
PRIMAVERA MIA!

- *Hilly / Advanced*
- *Map strava.com/routes/21824190*
- *Test yourself km 274 (mi 170) strava.com/segments/20417525*
- *Test yourself km 292 (mi 181) strava.com/segments/626919*

Everyone dreams of riding their Milan-San Remo in their own way: for example, 160 km (100 mi) from Genoa, picking up our route at Voltri; or 108 km (67 mi) from Savona. Our "complete" route from Milano Centrale Train Station can also be ridden in two days. *La Primavera à la carte.*

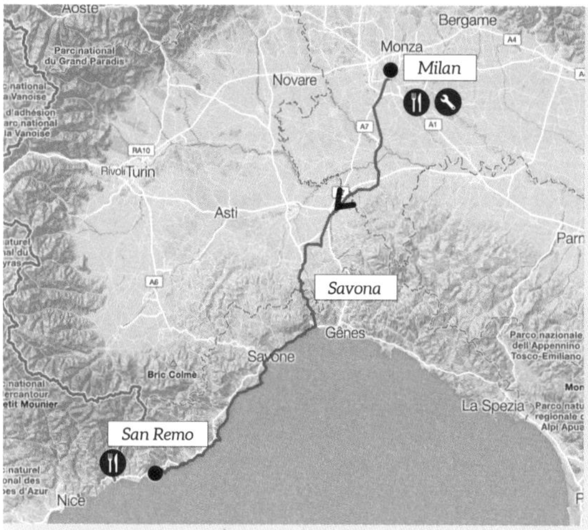

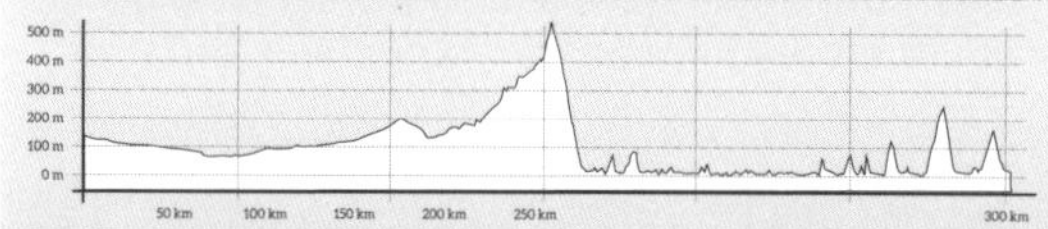

The most adventurous will head off from Milan for a 300 km (185 mi) ride. Our itinerary avoids the traffic by taking the cycle path out of the city along the Naviglio Pavese canal, passing Tortona and Novi Ligure—still marked by the legend of Fausto Coppi—before slowly approaching the Passo del Turchino. Once we hit the Riviera, we stick to the true route of the Primavera through Savona, Finale Ligure, and Alassio before rounding the famous capes: Mele, Cervo, and Berta. Then, on the way out of San Lorenzo, we climb Cipressa, which rises 240 m (787 ft) above the Mediterranean.
We are just 15 km (9 mi) from the foot of Poggio: 3.6 km (2.25 mi) with two severe 300 m (1,000 ft) ramps where the final contenders for the Milan-San Remo slug it out. You, of course, will pause at the top to take a glorious selfie in front of the famous telephone booth in the left-hand switchback.

Distance	E+	Difficulty	Appeal
302 km (188 mi)	1,800 m (5,905 ft)	4/5	4/5

Milan is very well connected to the whole of Europe via its three airports (Malpensa, Linate, and Bergamo), as well as by high-speed train from France, Turin, Bologna, Florence, Rome, and Naples. San Remo is 4h by train (via Genoa), whereas Savona is 1h40 and Genoa 1h55.

A challenge like this should ideally start at Milan's Upcycle, a bike cafe that is the perfect mix of tradition and modernity in the city's hip Città Studi quarter.

Via Andrea Maria Ampère, 59
20131 Milan
upcyclecafe.it

The nicest place to celebrate your Primavera is the terrace of Bar Portovecchio, located on a cycle path that is a short stroll from Via Roma.

Pista Ciclabile Parco Costiero 235
18038 San Remo
facebook.com/
BarPortovecchioSanremo

CUENO
ADVENTURE ON THE FAUNIERA

- *High mountain / Advanced*
- *Map* strava.com/routes/21526531
- *Test yourself km 35 (mi 22)* strava.com/segments/4952282
- *Test yourself km 51 (mi 32)* strava.com/segments/12349553

In the southern Piedmont region, the Colle Fauniera is one of the lesser known Alpine passes, yet it is the climax of the annual Fausto Coppi *gran fondo* race. It remains relatively car free, even at the height of the summer season. A challenging ride, for sure.

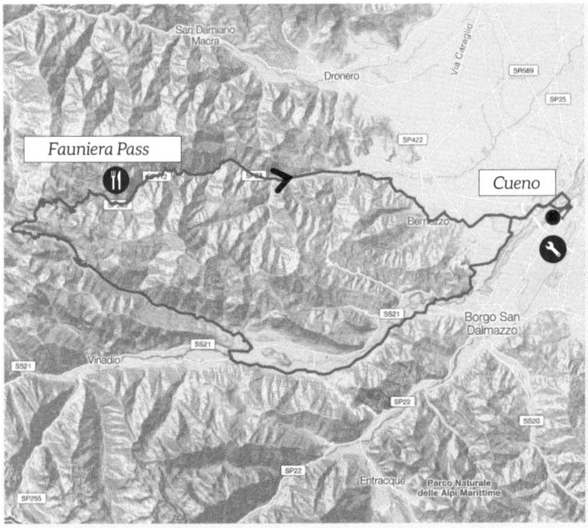

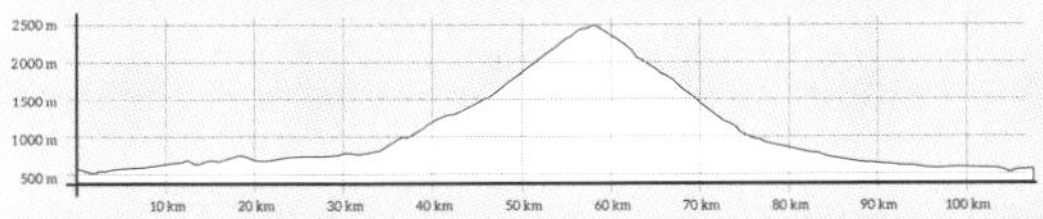

Cyclists often find the mountains rather crowded in summer. This is never the case with the Colle Fauniera, a key pass through the Piedmont Alps. The monument to Marco Pantani at the summit is a reminder that the Giro raced here in 1999. Given the pitiful state of the road (take care on the descent), which is maintained only by volunteers from the Fausto Coppi *gran fondo*, it is doubtful if the race will ever return there. The wild, arid, rocky scenery has something of the world's end about it. Setting out from Cuneo through the Stura Valley, the climb of the southern slope is hard: 25 km (15.5 mi) at an average gradient of 7%. But it is the second part of the ascent—dubbed the "Rifugio Carbonetto"—that is the toughest: only 10 km (6 mi) in which to pull yourself up from 1,500 m (4,900 ft) to 2,481 m (8,140 ft) You will feel quite fulfilled when you return to the lovely cyclists' town of Cuneo.

Distance	E+	Difficulty	Appeal
108 km (67 mi)	2,300 m (7,550 ft)	4/5	5/5

By train, Cuneo is 1h15 from Turin and 4h from Nice. By car, it is 3h from Milan (255 km/158 mi), 1h15 from Turin (100 km/62 mi), and 2h30 from Nice (130 km/80 mi). Closest international airports: Nice and Turin.

After the summit, stop at Rifugio Fauniera for a plate of perfect polenta and a splendid view. It also organizes stargazing events.

SP del Colle Fauniera
12020 Castelmagno
rifugiofauniera.it

Located close to Cuneo's historic center, the Bike Self-Maintenance Spot is an original concept: a free, self-service station with foot pump and emergency tool kit.

Via Carlo Pascal
12100 Cuneo

TURIN
ENCHANTED HILLS

Very hilly / Advanced
Map strava.com/routes/21496521
Test yourself km 23 (mi 14) strava.com/routes/21496521
Test yourself km 31 (mi 19) strava.com/segments/6587796

If Turin still conjures up images of an industrial city of the past, then this short, tight loop over the green hills of the right bank of the Po will give you a fresh perspective. Extraordinary panoramas across a splendid city and the Alps.

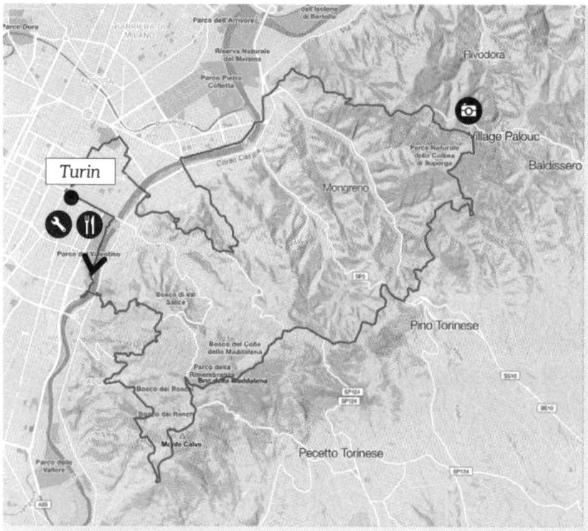

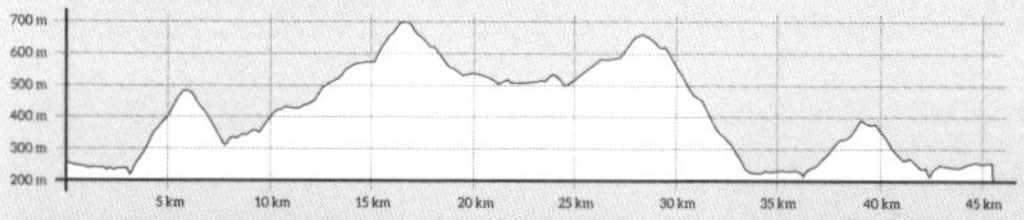

There is nothing like this short but intense route to (re)discover Turin from the hills overlooking it. Things get tough when you hit Moncalvo (7 km/4.52 mi at an average gradient of 5%), which leads to the Bric della Maddalena (km 16/ mi 10), the final 1.5 km (1 mi) of which is at a gradient of 10%. On your left is the Victory statue, standing on the first of our Turin promontories, at an altitude of 715 m (2,345 ft). A wooded section then takes us to Superga hill, where you can climb past the basilica to the right for another amazing view. But take care on the steep descent. Marco Pantani was seriously hurt in a crash here in 1995. This enjoyable route still has one more difficulty: the ascent of Val San Martino (3 km/2 mi at 10%) before you coast past the Villa della Regina (a former residence of the House of Savoy) to a final panorama across the city from Monte dei Cappuccini (a lovely little church).

Distance **47 km** (29 mi)

E+ **1,100 m** (3,600 ft)

Difficulty **3/5**

Appeal **4/5**

Turin Airport is 20 minutes by train from Porta Nuova train station—Italy's third busiest. Milan is 1h15 by train and 2h15 by car (170 km/106 mi). Genoa is 2h25 by train and 2h10 by car (170 km/106 mi). Lyon is 3h30 by car via the Mont Blanc Tunnel.

Pai Bikery is a relatively new address that distills all the current cycling trends. It is a bike cafe with a slightly vintage atmosphere that offers food, a workshop, and store.

Via Cagliari, 18
10153 Turin
paibikery.com

Of the three most popular viewpoints over Turin, the one from the square in front of the Basilica of Superga (km 29/ mi 18) is the most spectacular. On a clear day, you can see the shapes of Monte Viso, Monte Rosa, and Mont Blanc in the distance.

OULX
FASCINATING FINESTRE

- *High mountain / Expert*
- *Map* *strava.com/routes/21827711*
- *Test yourself km 37 (mi 23)* *strava.com/segments/1797766*
- *Test yourself km 64 (mi 40)* *strava.com/segments/1944771*

In the contemporary cyclist's imagination, the Finestre conjures power, fantasy, rusticity, and modernity. The Giro d'Italia has only ventured onto this Piedmont pass since 2005, when the sight of champions tackling its "off road" ramps helped trigger the "gravel" trend.

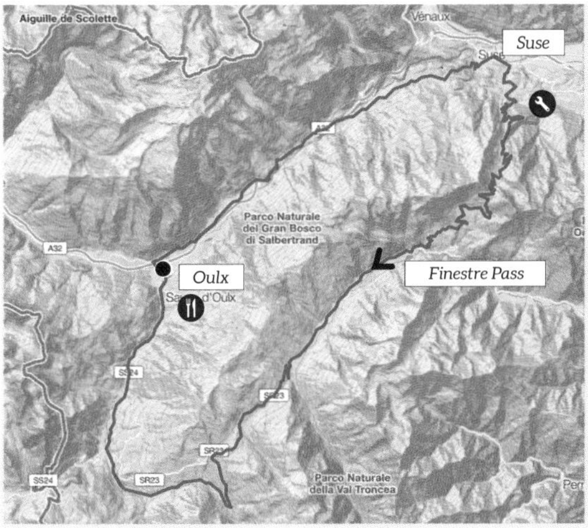

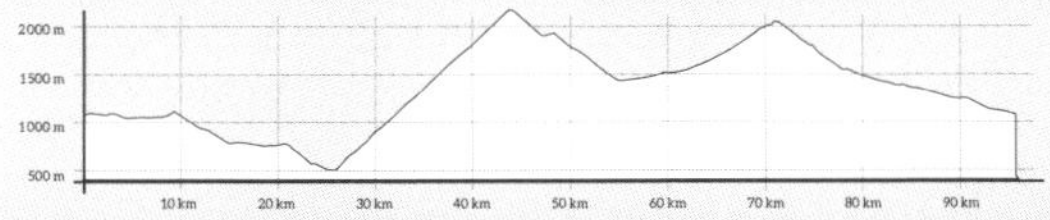

Above the Susa Valley and the castle of Countess Adelaïde is a harsh modern legend of the Giro d'Italia. The monster of the Piedmont stands at the end of 25 km (15.5 mi) of gentle descent. Pray for no headwind. The Colle delle Finestre tops out at "only" 2,178 m (7,146 ft), but it owes its fearsome reputation to an average gradient of 9.4% over 18 km (11 mi) of climbing with 55 switchbacks, and the final 7 km (4.5 mi) on a military road of earth and gravel with a gradient that never drops below 9%. The energy expenditure is considerable, but you will have the taste of adventure—not to mention some truly exceptional views over the Graian Alps. We return via the resort of Sestrières and its pass of which the final 6 km (3.8 mi) are at 6%. Then, it is only another 25 km (15.5 mi) of descent back to Oulx. This is one day on the bike that you will not soon forget .

Distance	E+	Difficulty	Appeal
96 km (60 mi)	2,500 m (8,200 ft)	5/5	5/5

Oulx (pop. 3,300) is fortunate to be on a high-speed train line: 1h10 from Turin, 2h30 from Milan, 2h50 from Lyon, and 4h50 from Paris. By car, Briançon is 35 minutes (30 km/20 mi), Turin is 1h (80 km/50 mi), and Chambéry is 1h30 via the Fréjus Road Tunnel (130 km/80 mi).

If you fancy a hearty meal after the Finestre, then Taverna d'Argalesse (km 55/mi 34) is the place. Try its house-made gnocchi and wine-stewed fruit with melted chocolate.

Via Sestriere, 4
10060 Pourrieres
dargalesse.it

In Susa (km 25/mi 15), Nonsolobici is the go-to address for road cyclists in search of repairs and a friendly chat. Passing champions often pop in.

Via Norberto Rosa, 16
10059 Susa
facebook.com/
nonsolobicisusa1994

AOSTA
ABOVE THE VALLEY

- *Low mountain / Advanced*
- *Map strava.com/routes/21500485*
- *Test yourself km 15 (mi 9) strava.com/routes/21500485*
- *Test yourself km 56 (mi 35) strava.com/segments/4114435*

This route around the heights of the Dora Baltea Valley may seem a little unambitious in light of some of the more prestigious surrounding peaks (Cervin, Mont Blanc, Grand Paradiso), but it is appealing and good preparation for future challenges.

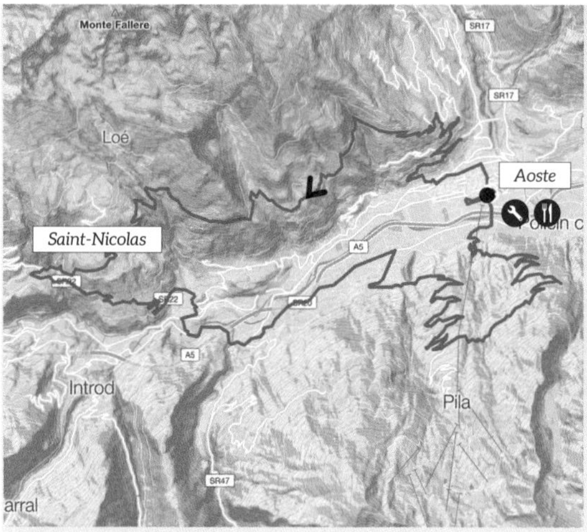

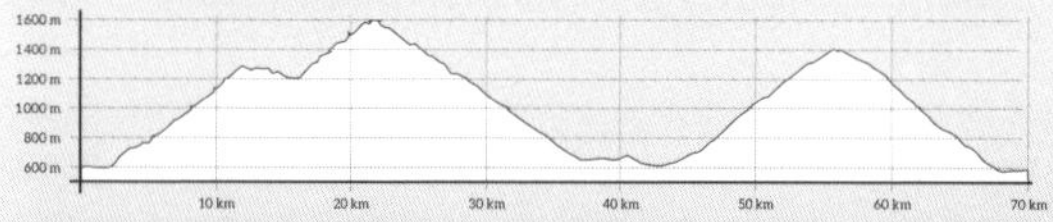

Although you can head straight for the very high mountains from the historic, bilingual Italian-French town of Aosta, why not acclimatize with this 70 km (44 mi) loop through the greenery above the Dora Baltea river, which flows from the foot of Mont Blanc? But it is not all easy pedaling, there is 25 km (15.5 mi) of climbing with average gradients of between 7% and 9%. The Salassi Trail (10 km/6 mi with 700 m/2,300 ft of climbing) will cool your ardor. Next comes 5 km (3 mi) at 9% up to Verrogne, with views across the Aosta Valley. Finally, after descending and crossing to the right bank, climb toward Pila from the south, as far as Petite Cerise: 10 km (6 mi) at a gradient of nearly 8%. If you have had enough climbing, simply turn off at Gressan onto the cycle path along the left bank back to Aosta; the total distance will be 50 km (30 mi) with an average elevation gain of 1,400 m (4,600 ft).

Distance **70 km** (44 mi)

E+ **2,200 m** (7,220 ft)

Difficulty **3/5**

Appeal **4/5**

To reach the Aosta Valley, allow 3h by car from Lyon and 2h from Geneva via the Mont Blanc Tunnel. It takes longer by train: 2h30 from Milan Centrale, with changes at Chivasso and Ivrea.

The terrace of the hotel Les Plaisirs d'Antan (km 43/mi 27) is a pleasant spot for a break before tackling the climb to Pila.

Frazione Clou 44
11020 Jovençan
lesplaisirsd'antan.com

In the center of Aosta, right next to the old town, Cicli Lucchini is the go-to place for repairs and rentals. Retailer for Specialized.

Corso Battaglione Aosta, 49/51
11100 Aosta
ciclilucchini.it

VERBANIA
PIEDMONT LAKES

Very hilly / Advanced

Map strava.com/routes/22787836

Distance **87 km** (54 mi) | E+ **1,200 m** (3,950 ft) | Difficulty **3/5** | Appeal **4/5**

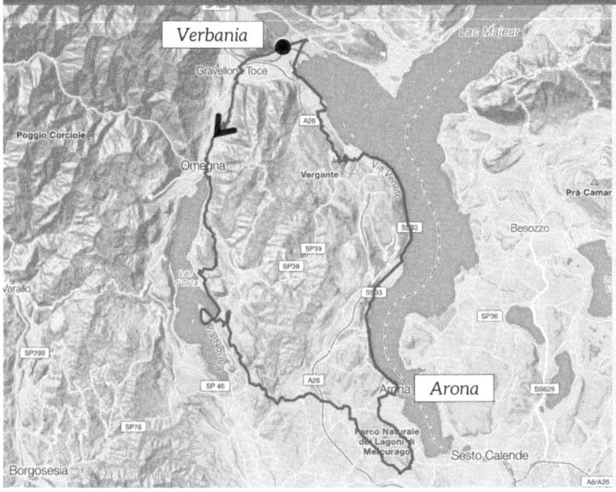

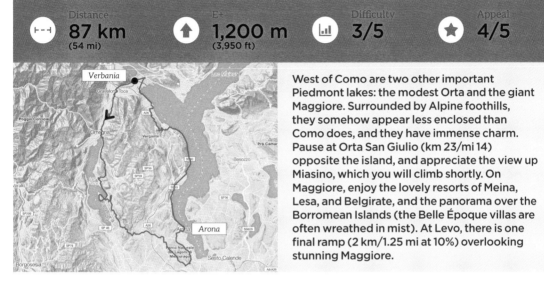

West of Como are two other important Piedmont lakes: the modest Orta and the giant Maggiore. Surrounded by Alpine foothills, they somehow appear less enclosed than Como does, and they have immense charm. Pause at Orta San Giulio (km 23/mi 14) opposite the island, and appreciate the view up Miasino, which you will climb shortly. On Maggiore, enjoy the lovely resorts of Meina, Lesa, and Belgirate, and the panorama over the Borromean Islands (the Belle Époque villas are often wreathed in mist). At Levo, there is one final ramp (2 km/1.25 mi at 10%) overlooking stunning Maggiore.

COMO
A LAKESIDE DREAM

Very hilly / Advanced

Map strava.com/routes/21588948

Distance **130 km** (81 mi) | E+ **1,000 m** (3,280 ft) | Difficulty **3/5** | Appeal **4/5**

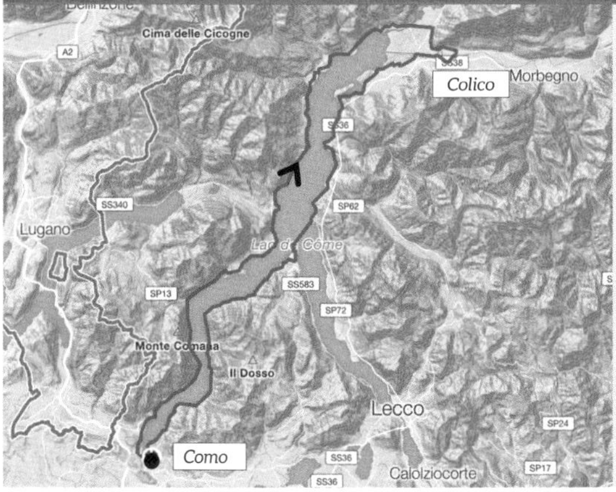

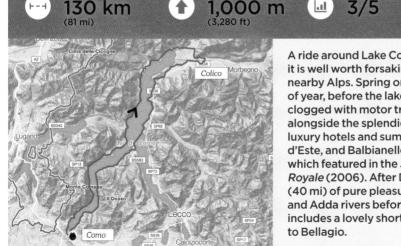

A ride around Lake Como is a delight for which it is well worth forsaking the allure of the nearby Alps. Spring or fall are the best times of year, before the lake's shores become clogged with motor traffic. The route proceeds alongside the splendid waters of the lake, past luxury hotels and sumptuous villas: Olmo, Erba, d'Este, and Balbianello at km 26 (mi 16), which featured in the James Bond film *Casino Royale* (2006). After Domaso—and 60 km (40 mi) of pure pleasure—we cross the Mera and Adda rivers before the return leg, which includes a lovely short ferry trip from Varrena to Bellagio.

VARESE
ABOVE THE LAKES

- *Low mountain / Advanced*
- *Map strava.com/routes/22473258*
- *Test yourself km 14 (mi 9) strava.com/segments/1696598*
- *Test yourself km 30 (mi 19) strava.com/segments/4565096*

This loop proves that it is not only by the waters of Lake Como where you can combine cycling and romanticism in Lombardy. We are on the roads of Ivan Basso, winner of the Giro d'Italia in 2006 and 2010, and still very active. strava.com/athletes/8754894

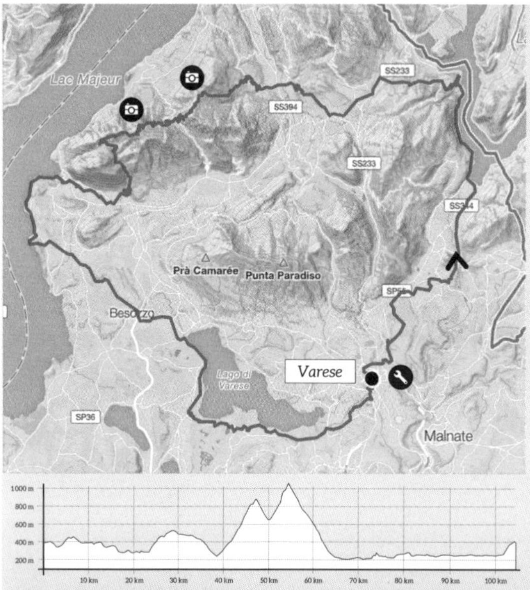

In barely 100 km (60 mi), we tour three major lakes north of Milan, exploring key sites of each: Lugano (Porto Ceresio and Brusimpiano), Maggiore (Laveno-Mombello, Quicchio and the hermitage of Santa Caterina), and Varese (Cazzago Brabia). It is a magical ride past Belle Époque villas, old houses, creeks, and little cliffs. The wooded mountain road between Lugano and the shore of Lake Maggiore is a demanding one. The ascent to the sanctuary of Ardena at km 30 (3 km/2 mi at 6%), and the passes of San Michele then Cuvignone comprise 1,100 m (3,600 ft) of elevation gain in 12 km (7.5 mi) of climbing. San Michele (880 m/2,900 ft) has one section that is 2 km (1.25 mi) long at a gradient of between 11% and 13%; the 4 km (2.5 mi) of Cuvignone (1,052 m/3,450 ft) has an average gradient of 10% with a very winding descent.

Distance	E+	Difficulty	Appeal
104 km (65 mi)	1,950 m (6,400 ft)	3/5	4/5

Varese (pop. 81,000) is very close to Milan: 1h by train (Milan Centrale) or 55 minutes by car (60 km/37 mi). To the southwest, Turin is 3h by train or 1h40 by car (150 km/93 mi). To the north, Lugano (Switzerland) is 50 minutes by train or by car (40 km/25 mi).

Only 200 meters/yards from the station, Cicli Ambrosini has been serving cyclists in Varese for more than fifty years. Retailer of Giant, Felt, De Rosa, Olmo, and Bianchi.

Piazza Madonnina in Prato, 1
21100 Varese VA
cicliambrosini.it

The views over Lake Maggiore from this route are extraordinary. At the chapel of San Michele (km 46/mi 28) turn right onto a gravel track and ride for 0.6 km (0.4 mi) to a viewpoint over Pian Nave. At km 53 (mi 33), turn right before the Cuvignone Pass and walk for two minutes to the Rifugio Grandi Adamoli.

COMO
EXPERIENCE *IL LOMBARDIA*

- *Low mountain / Expert*
- *Map strava.com/routes/21490734*
- *Test yourself km 39 (mi 24) strava.com/segments/625479*
- *Test yourself km 60 (mi 37) strava.com/segments/2543593*

After leaving Como and its sublime lake, the final 80 km (50 mi) follow the route of the magical autumnal race that is the modern Tour of Lombardy, with 3,000 m (9,840 ft) of climbing and the ascent of the hellish Muro di Sormano.

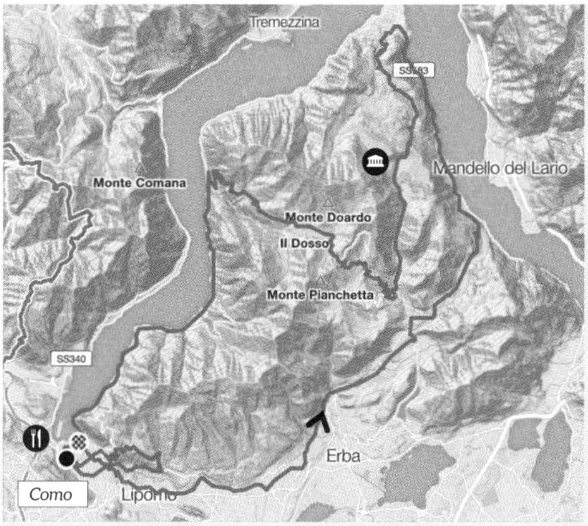

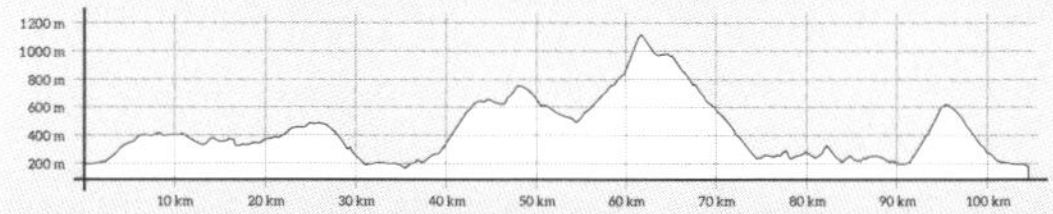

This loop between the two forks of Lake Como shows not only how tough the prestigious Tour of Lombardy is, but also how romantic.
The difficult final section is something else, particularly the Muro di Sormano, which nonprofessional cyclists will find very hard to complete without stopping. We join the course of the modern *Il Lombardia* (km 22/mi 14) before the two-stage ascent of the Madonna Del Ghisallo—4 km (2.5 mi) at an average gradient of 9%, then another 2 km (1.25 mi), also at 9%, just before the legendary cyclists' chapel. The torture that is the Muro di Sormano begins at km 55 (mi 34). The average gradient over the last 2 km (1.25 mi) is 15%, with a 400 m (437 yard) section at 20%. In 7 km (4.5 mi), we climb from 500 m (1,640 ft) to 1,128 m (3,701 ft). And there is still the tough little Civiglio climb before Como: 4 km (2.5 mi) at a gradient of 9% to 11%. Lombardy spurs are hard-earned.

Distance	E+	Difficulty	Appeal
104 km (65 mi)	2,400 m (7,900 ft)	5/5	5/5

Como is 40 minutes by train from Milan, with hourly departures. Allow 1h by car (50 km/30 mi on the A9), owing to traffic. From Lugano, to the north, it is 1h05 by train or 40 minutes by car (35 km/22 mi).

Sartoria Ciclistica, a bike cafe that opened in 2017 and is only a two-minute walk from the finish of the Tour of Lombardy, is the place to go in Como for an espresso. Try its Ghisallo Power blend.

Via Pretorio 7
22100 Como
sartoriaciclistica.cc

The Ghisallo Cycling Museum abuts the chapel (km 48/ mi 30). It is a kind of MoMA of cycling, open every day from March to November.

Via Gino Bartali 4
22030 Magreglio (CO)
museodelghisallo.it

MILAN
BEAUTIFUL MACHINES

Fairly flat / Intermediate *Map strava.com/routes/22791599*

Distance	E+	Difficulty	Appeal
77 km (48 mi)	350 m (1,150 ft)	2/5	3/5

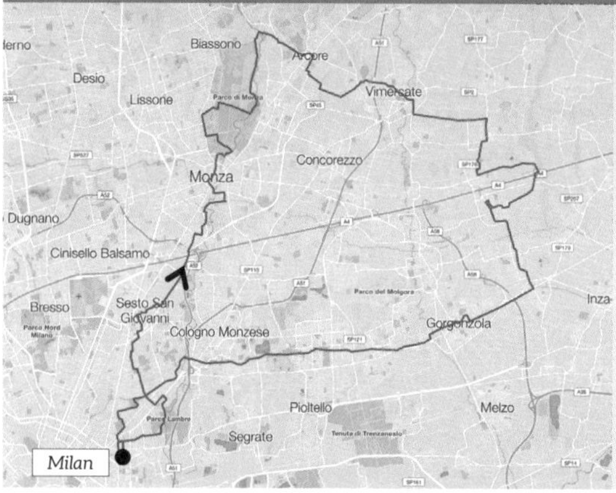

With a penchant for beautiful machines, Milan has cycling in its soul. We ride out from Upcycle Bike Cafè toward Monza via Rottole, Adriano, and Sesto San Giovanni. The F1 track at Monza is even open to cyclists some days. Otherwise, the park itself is lovely.

At Virmercate (km 37/mi 23), we pass close to the factory of the titanium frame specialists, Passoni (in the Torri Bianche district), before Cambiago (km 50/mi 31) and the premises of Ernesto Colnago, the race-bike artist.

We return via Gorgonzola (home of the famous cheese), then along the Naviglio Martesana canal for 17 km (10 mi).

MILAN
OPTION GREEN

Fairly flat / Intermediate *Map strava.com/routes/22789029*

Distance	E+	Difficulty	Appeal
80 km (50 mi)	250 m (820 ft)	2/5	3/5

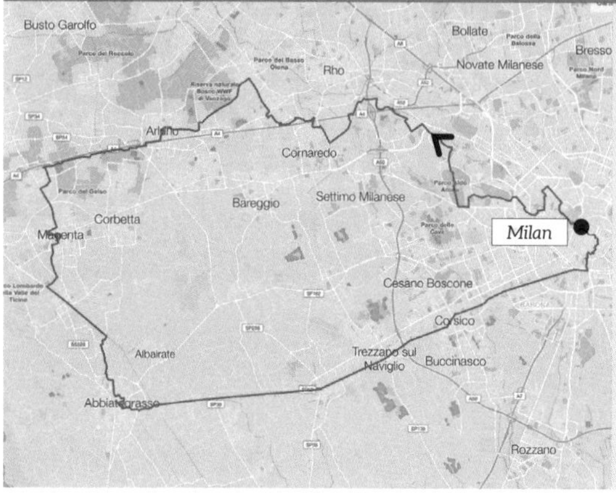

The Ticino Valley west of Milan is a lovely green alternative to the city. We ride out of Milan from Sforza Castle on the way to Magenta (km 41/mi 25), site of a major battle in the nineteenth century, passing Sempione Park, Vigorelli Velodrome, the futuristic CityLife towers, San Siro horse racing track and stadium, Boscoincittà Park, and the Arluno district with its church of Santi Pietro e Paolo, before reaching the edge of the valley.

Then, we swing south and begin to head back via Abbiategrasso with its Visconti Castle, then along the cycle path by the Naviglio Grande canal for 20 km (12 mi).

TIRANO

PILGRIMAGE TO THE MORTIROLO

- *High mountain / Expert*
- *Map strava.com/routes/21587988*
- *Test yourself km 13 (mi 8) strava.com/segments/10247952*
- *Test yourself km 19 (mi 12) strava.com/segments/5362311*

What is the toughest road climb in Europe? The debate rages hard. The Angliru (Spain), the Zoncolan (Italy), and the Kitzbüheler Horn (Austria) all have their supporters, but the Mortirolo has its fanatics. Respect to all those who reach the top without stopping.

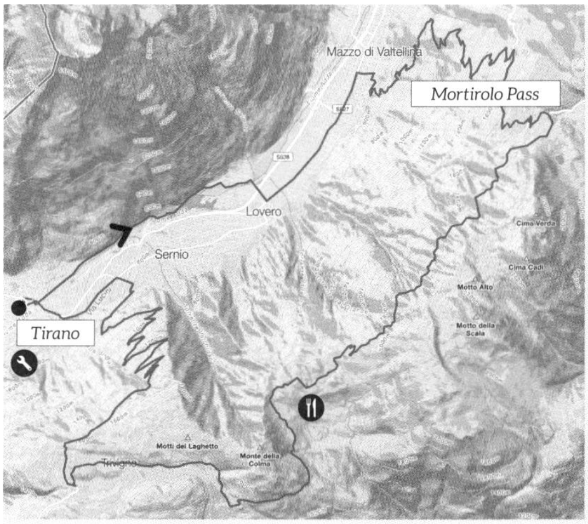

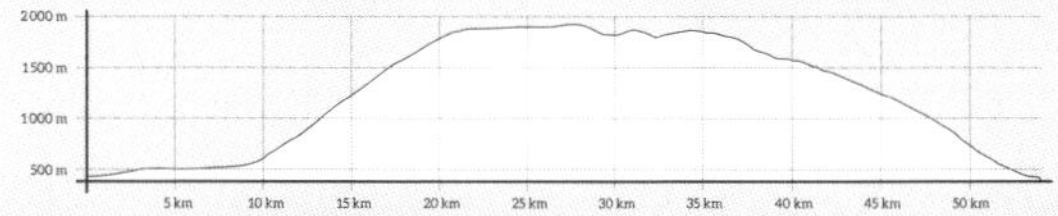

The road is actually called the Foppa Pass. "Mortirolo" is the name of a nearby mountain track, but because *morte* means "death" in Italian, the alternative name stuck. Cyclists venerate it in their own way. It is quite a feat to climb its steep slopes without stopping. Mazzo di Valtellina, between Sondrio and Bormio in northern Lombardy, is where its slopes begin to rise at an average gradient of 11% over 12 km (7.5 mi). A third of the way up the ascent, after the little church of San Matteo, you feel as if you are defying the laws of equilibrium: average gradient of 14% over nearly 2 km (1.25 mi) with four sections at 18% and, further on, eight others at 15%. Appreciate the bucolic scenery of this monster that, although it sometimes snakes across bare terrain, more often than not weaves beneath the pines. Once at the top, enjoy the 15 km (9 mi) along the ridgeline before the descent to Tirano.

Distance	E+	Difficulty	Appeal
54 km (34 mi)	1,700 m (5,580 ft)	5/5	5/5

Our short route begins at Tirano station, 40 km (25 mi) from Bormio. Milan is 2h30 by train or car (160 km/100 mi). Verona (200 km/125 mi) and Bolzano (180 km/112 mi) are both 3h by car. International airports: Milan.

Following the hellish ascent of the Mortirolo, you'll be more than deserving of a proper refuel at the Ristorante Albergo Paradiso (km 38/mi 24)—hearty local fare of course.

Trivigno
23037 Tirano
valtellina.it

Ivan and Marco (after Gotti and Pantani) were predestined to open a bike store here. Impeccable service and rental of Bianchi bikes, located only 500 meters/yards from Tirano station.

Via Trivigno, 2
23037 Tirano SO
cicliama.it

EDOLO
THE LEGENDARY GAVIA

- *High mountain / Expert*
- *Map strava.com/routes/22351218*
- *Test yourself km 58 (mi 36) strava.com/segments/5330345*
- *Test yourself km 83 (mi 52) strava.com/segments/2024641*

The Gavia Pass in Lombardy, which separates the provinces of Sondrio and Brescia, is a modern legend. In 1988, the riders in the Giro d'Italia faced a blizzard here—the likes of which have not been seen since—without the race being halted. In fine weather, it is splendid.

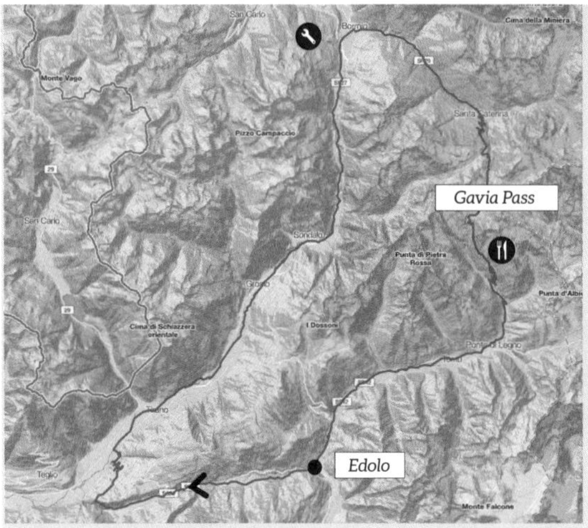

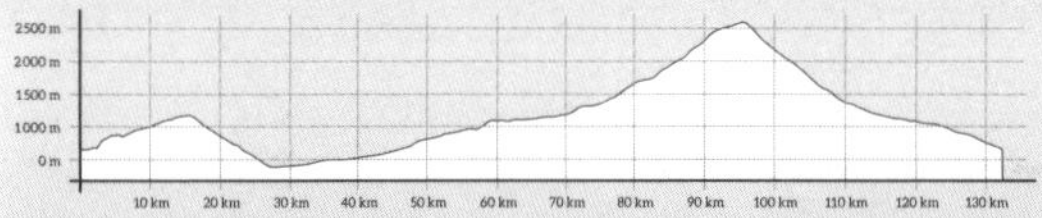

The Gavia Pass (2,652 m/8,701 ft) is the third-highest paved road in Italy, after the Stelvio and the Agnel. The narrow road, which clings to the edge of the ravine, is like no other. It offers fabulous panoramas over the Corno dei Tre Signori and the Monte Gaviola. The parapet is fragile; at points, you feel as if you are on a road in the Andes. Our route tackles the Gavia by its north face—which is barely any easier than the south face—from Bormio: 25 km (15 mi), with the second section at an average gradient of 8% between Santa Caterina (with its series of spectacular switchbacks) and km 93 (mi 58), 2 km (1.25 mi) from the top. At the summit, the very contemporary Madonna delle Vette keeps watch, alongside statues of cycling champion Fausto Coppi and sports director Vincenzo Torriani. Take care not to turn right at km 128 (mi 80) to Monno; the road leads up the Mortirolo Pass, another legendary climb!

Distance	E+	Difficulty	Appeal
133 km (83 mi)	**2,900 m** (9,500 ft)	**5/5**	**5/5**

Edolo (pop. 4,500) is 3h by train from Milan (to the southwest), or 2h30 by car (150 km/93 mi). To the southeast, Verona is 3h by train or 2h20 by car (260 km/160 mi). To the east, Bolzano is 2h30 by car (140 km/85 mi).

You must stop at the Rifugio Bonetta at the summit of the Gavia (km 96/mi 60) for a selfie, coffee, plate of polenta, or simply the view.

Col du Gavia, SP29
23030 Valfurva
passogavia.it

Being well-positioned between the Gavia, the Mortirolo, and the Stelvio, Spot-On Bike Shop (km 70/mi 44) is aptly named. Rental of Pinarello, 3T, and Cervelo.

Via Monte Cristallo, 9
23032 Bormio
spotonbormio.it

The summer colors of the Gavia Pass in Lombardy, Italy.

SPONDIGNA
THE LEGENDARY STELVIO

High mountain / Expert

Map strava.com/routes/21534692

Test yourself km 13 (mi 8) strava.com/segments/10022811

Test yourself km 27 (mi 17) strava.com/segments/7521504

At 2,757 m (9,045 ft), the Stelvio is not the highest mountain pass in Europe (the Iseran pass in France is 7 m/23 ft higher), but it is the most spectacular. Its steep slopes and sixty photogenic switchbacks make unforgettable memories for any cyclist who reaches the top.

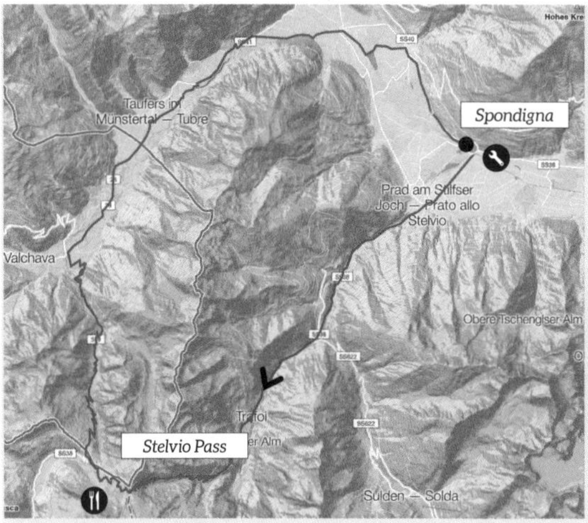

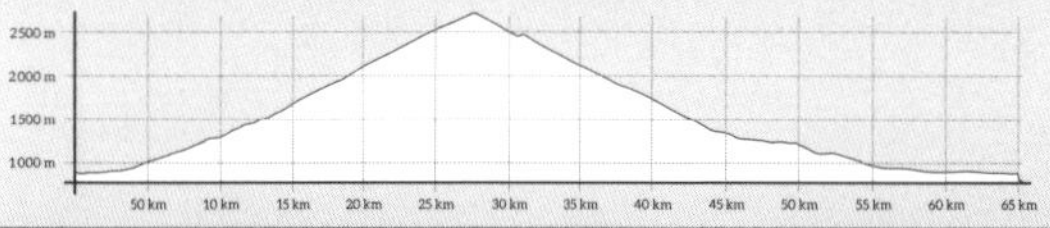

Dawn is the perfect time to ride out of Spondigna, preferably on a weekday in order to avoid the hordes of motorcyclists who drive from across Europe to enjoy the Stelvio's curves. Cycling up the north side provides a spectacle unlike no other, but it is tough: 24 km (15 mi) with 1,800 m (5,900 ft) of elevation gain. It is quite a gentle slope until Gomagoi, but then it kicks up for 17 km (10.5 mi) over irregular terrain at a gradient between 7% and 9%. Once you reach Trafoi (km 13/mi 8), the sight of the sixty switchbacks, which are numbered in reverse order (on the low roadside wall) from bend 48, will lift your spirits. The air becomes harder to breathe above 2,000 m (6,560 ft), and there is still 8 km (5 mi) to climb. Better to keep looking down at the sublime perspective of the bends passed. Take a selfie at the top and then descend, veering north into Switzerland via the Umbrail Pass and the bucolic Val Müstair.

Distance	E+	Difficulty	Appeal
65 km (40 mi)	2,000 m (6,560 ft)	5/5	5/5

Spondigna is 7h by train from Milan, and 5h by train and bus from Innsbruck. It is easier to get there by car: 4h from Milan's airports, 2h from Innsbruck Airport.

Overlooking the Stelvio's summit, Tibet Hut restaurant is a must for its unforgettable views and hearty Tyrolean cuisine.

Passo dello Stelvio
30029 Trafoi BZ
tibet-stelvio.com

Andreas Wieser had the clever idea of opening his store and workshop right next to Spondigna Station. Retailer of Stevens.

Bahnhof Spondinia, 22
39020 Schluderns BZ
ss38-bike.com

MERANO
THE BELL TOWER OF VAL VENOSTA

- *Low mountain / Expert*
- *Map strava.com/routes/21532243*
- *Test yourself km 23 (mi 14) strava.com/segments/9153105*
- *Test yourself km 64 (mi 40) strava.com/segments/7377772*

The Val Venosta, through which flows the upper part of the Adige river, is renowned for its mild climate, apples, and paragliding spots. Tinged with something mystical, the valley is well worth this long, exploratory route, if only for one surprising curiosity.

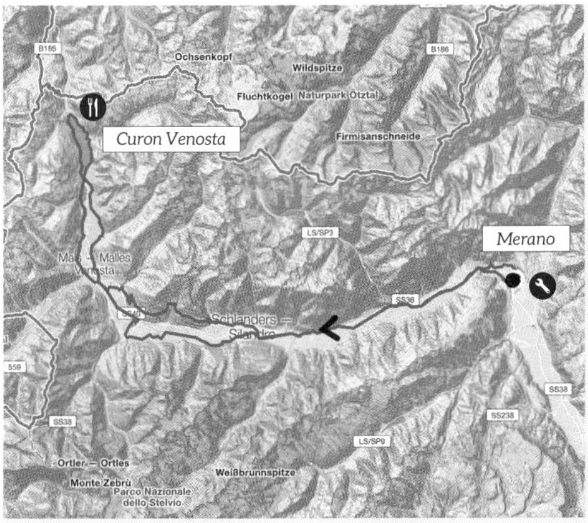

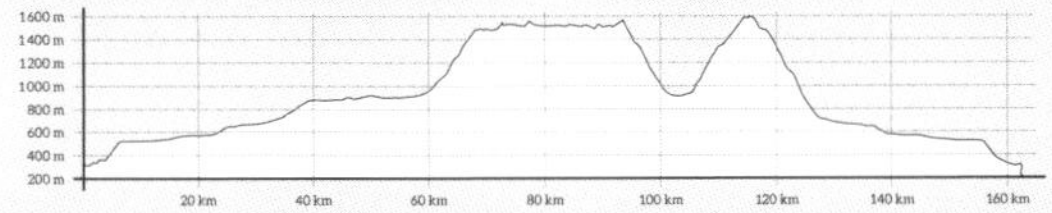

The surreal sight that awaits you at km 83 (mi 52) is itself worth this long trek from Merano toward the Swiss and Austrian borders. Rising from the waters of Lake Resia is the famous bell tower of the submerged village of Graun. The village was forever swallowed by the waters when the dam was built in 1950. This curiosity is the cherry on the cake of a magical ride in the shadow of the legendary Stelvio Pass, to your left as you reach km 50 (mi 31). But you will need to dig deep; the climb to San Valentino Lake is an 8 km (5 mi) drag at 7%, all the way to km 68 (mi 42). We are at 1,500 m (4,900 ft) as we glide along to Lake Resia, which is 8 km (5 mi) long. Pure paradise. On the return leg, the lovely Grossfeld climb (9 km/5.5 mi at 7%) to Tanas (km 116/mi 72) is a pleasant way to avoid the traffic. The South Tyrol is simply divine; the first and last 35 km (22 mi) are along a cycle path.

Distance	E+	Difficulty	Appeal
163 km (101 mi)	2,300 m (7,550 ft)	4/5	4/5

Merano is 4h by train from Milan Centrale station, and 3h30 from Innsbruck. It is shorter by car: 3h from Milan (300 km/186 mi) and 2h from Innsbruck (160 km/100 mi). Verona-Villafranca, the nearest international airport, is 3h by train and 2h by car.

Distance + altitude = hunger! Fuel up at the beautiful Mein Dörfl Hotel (km 81/mi 50) on the way out of Riesa. Terrace, delicious coffee, and amazing apple strudel.

Via Paese Vecchio, 11
39027 Resia BZ
meindoerfl.com

Only 2 km (1.25 mi) from the train station, Flarer and Co is the go-to place in Merano for road cyclists. It is a lovely store with tip-top service. Retailer of Pinarello, De Rosa, and Colnago.

Via dei Prati, 8
39012 Merano BZ
flarer.it

BOLZANO
TYROLEAN APPROACH

- *Low mountain / Intermediate*
- *Map strava.com/routes/21771825*
- *Test yourself km 19 (mi 12) strava.com/segments/15509351*
- *Test yourself km 41 (mi 25) strava.com/segments/11174174*

We are within reach of the highest and most difficult mountains in Italy. Val Gardena and the Dolomites lie to the east, and the Stelvio lies to the west, a little further away. There is no better way to prepare for them than this route heading out from Bolzano above the Valle dell'Isarco.

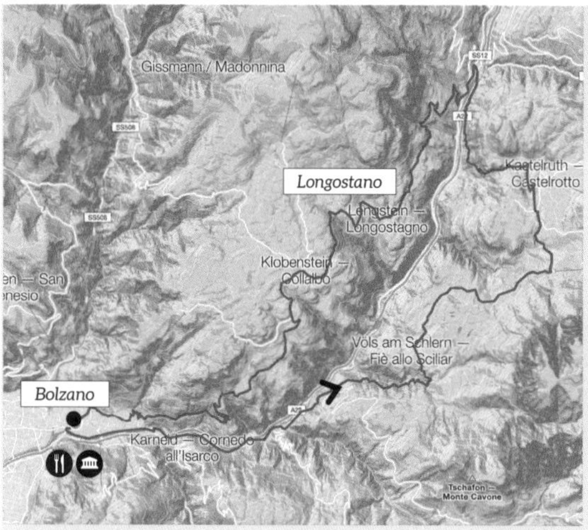

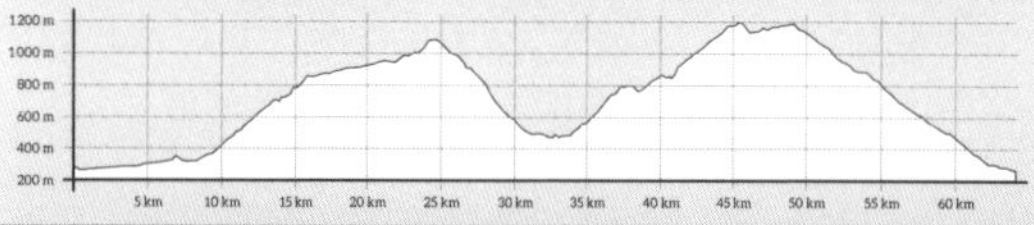

At Telfen-Lanzin (both Italian and German are used in this region), you can turn right toward Val Gardena and the more prestigious passes in the Dolomites. But not yet. This route, which starts and ends in Bolzano, is an ideal warm-up before exploring them. It takes to the slopes overlooking the Valle dell'Isarco, a tributary of the Adige. After the cycle path to Prato at km 9 (mi 5.5), we start with 5 km (3 mi) at a gradient of 7.5%, before a gentler slope as far as Lanzin at km 25 (mi 15). At Ponte Gardena, we cross back over the Isarco for the return to Bolzano. The slopes of the west bank are more jagged, such as after Colma (3 km/1.8 mi at 9%) and before Longostagno: 1 km (0.6 mi) at 13%, with a section at 20%. Variant: from Bolzano, you can stay on the cycle path all the way to Ponte Gardena, tackling only the second stretch of climbs. One way or another, you will soon feel like going higher and further.

Distance	E+	Difficulty	Appeal
64 km (40 mi)	**1,750 m** (5,750 ft)	**3/5**	**3/5**

Bolzano (pop. 107,000) can be reached from the airports of Milan, Bergamo, and Verona. Milan is 2h45 by train or 3h20 by car (280 km/175 mi). Verona is 1h30 by train or 1h45 by car (150 km/93 mi). Innsbruck (Austria) is 2h by train or 1h40 by car (120 km/75 mi).

We are in Italy, but also in South Tyrol. Nothing is tastier than Bolzano's best *apfelstrudel* with an espresso at Klaus Pasticceria, located in the town center.

Piazza Maria Delago, 1
39100 Bolzano
pasticceriaklaus.it

Pioneering Italian mountaineer Reinhold Messner established his fourth Messner Mountain Museum in the ruins of Sigmundskron Castle, located 4 km (2.5 mi) from Bolzano train station.

Via Castel Firmiano, 53
39100 Bolzano
messner-mountain-museum.it

ISEO
IDEAL LAKE

Low mountain / Advanced   Map strava.com/routes/21456165

Distance	E+	Difficulty	Appeal
100 km (62 mi)	1,550 m (5,100 ft)	4/5	4/5

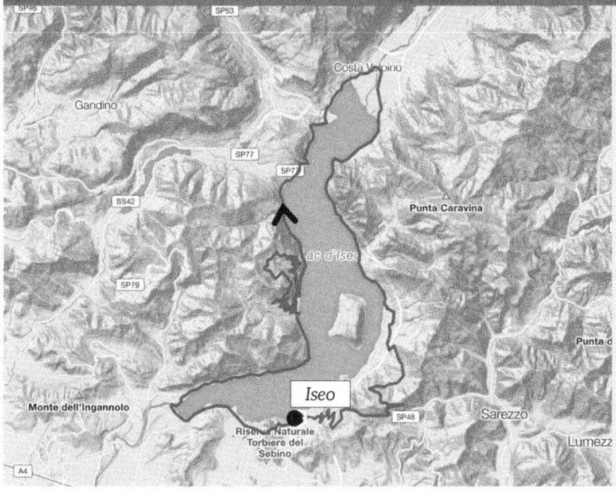

At 25 km (15.5 mi) long by 4 km (2.5 mi) wide, and sandwiched between Lakes Como and Garda, Lake Iseo looks small on the map. But it is most appealing—not least for its curious island of Monte Isola—and it is easily accessible from Bergamo and Brescia. There are beaches, rocky spurs, and olive plantations—not to mention the Roman spa at Predore, the Bogn gorges after Riva di Solto, and the charming towns of Lovere, Pisogne, and Iseo. There are also two beautiful 10 km (6 mi) climbs: one above Tavernola Bergamasca and, near the end, the more difficult Sale Marasino.

MORI
STUNNING GARDA

Low mountain / Expert   Map strava.com/routes/22786856

Distance	E+	Difficulty	Appeal
104 km (65 mi)	2,000 m (6,550 ft)	4/5	4/5

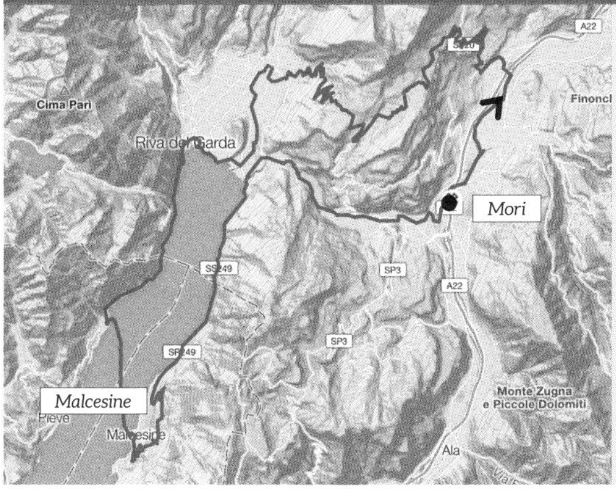

Two major elements of interest are here: stunning Lake Garda, the treasure of northern Italy, and the foothills of the Dolomites, close to Monte Stivo, which dominates the switchbacks of the Passo Bordala (1,267 m/4,157 ft), a 14 km (9 mi) long climb at an average gradient of 7%, with sections at 12% around Castellano. Aches and fatigue melt away on the descent to the lake and magnificent Riva del Garda, Limone, and Malcesine (on the opposite shore) before the final ramp of Nago-Torbole. There are many cycle paths. The ferry between Limone and Malcesine runs from March to November.

CORVARA IN BADIA
INVITATION TO THE DOLOMITES

- *High mountain / Advanced*
- *Map strava.com/routes/21786350*
- *Test yourself km 11 (mi 7) strava.com/segments/4817480*
- *Test yourself km 26 (mi 16) strava.com/segments/5220560*

Among 3,000 m (9,800 ft) peaks and renowned ski resorts, this is an ideal route with which to kick off a cycling trip to the Dolomites. There are few better warm-ups than these four mountain passes, with more than 25 km (15 mi) of climbing in a single 52 km (32 mi) loop.

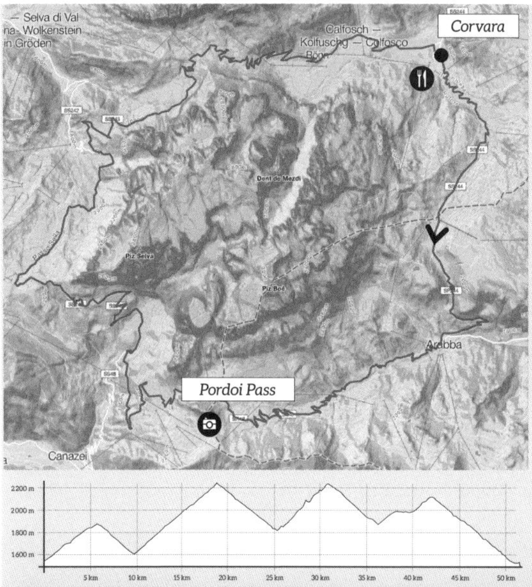

This compact yet demanding loop, which starts and ends in Corvara in Badia, is also a tour of some of the area's most well-known resorts: Alta Badia, Canazei, Sellaronda, and Val Gardena. In summer, though, the bicycle is king. The road surface is perfect, and the views are amazing. In the course of this ride, you will never descend below 1,600 m (5,200 ft), taking in four superb passes between altitudes of 1,875 m/6,152 ft (the Campolongo) and 2,239 m/7,346 ft (the Pordoi). The latter is the hardest: 9 km (5.5 mi) at an average gradient of 7.1%, with sections at 10% before the halfway point. Completing the picture are the Sella (2,218 m/7,277 ft, 5.5 km/3.5 mi at 7.2%) and the Gardena (2,136 m/7,008 ft, 6 km/3.7 mi at 4.2%). This 52 km (32 mi) ride may not look like much, but with more than 25 km (15 mi) of climbing, a total elevation gain of 1,750 m (5,740 ft), and zero flat stretches, it is no picnic.

Distance	E+	Difficulty	Appeal
52 km (32 mi)	**1,750 m** (5,740 ft)	**4/5**	**5/5**

Corvara in Badia is not the easiest Dolomite resort to reach. From Milan, it is 4h by train to Ora + 4h by bus. From Venice: 3h30 to Ora + 4h by bus. By car, Corvara is 4h30 from Milan (350 km/220 mi), 3h from Venice (180 km/112 mi), and 1h30 from Bolzano (65 km/40 mi).

Offering contemporary decor with a mountain feel and a mouthwatering menu at any time of day, the Posta Zirm Hotel is ideal when you return to Corvara.

Col Alt, 95
39033 Corvara In Badia
postazirm.com

At the summit of the Pordoi (km 19/mi 12), you will not resist the temptation of the very beautiful Hotel Col di Lana for a divine espresso and a sublime view.

Strada del Pordoi, 132
38032 Canazei
coldilana.it

CORTINA D'AMPEZZO
MAJESTIC GIAU PASS

- *High mountain / Advanced*
- *Map* *strava.com/routes/21786774*
- *Test yourself km 8 (mi 5)* *strava.com/segments/656178*
- *Test yourself km 53 (mi 33)* *strava.com/segments/5386447*

Cortina d'Ampezzo is the swankiest ski resort in Italy—the Saint-Moritz of the Dolomites. It also has a long sporting history, having hosted the 1956 Winter Olympics, which it will do again in 2026 (jointly with Milan). Cyclists also flock here to climb the magnificent Giau Pass.

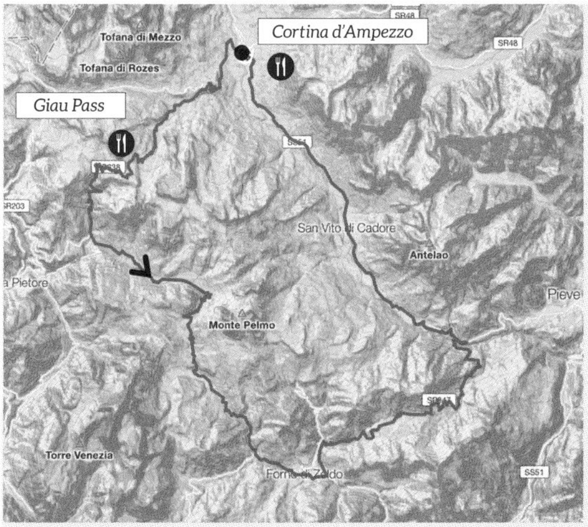

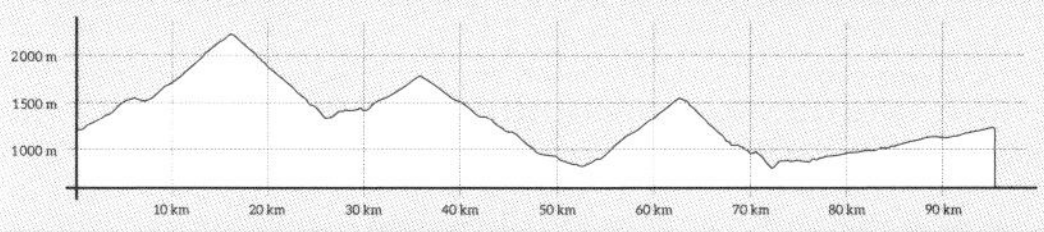

From the summit of the Giau Pass (2,236 m/7,336 ft), the impressive limestone chimneys of the Dolomites evoke the American West, with the majestic Ra Gusela and the curious Cinque Torri. First, you must vanquish one of the most feared mountain passes in the Giro d'Italia, with an initial stretch of 5 km (3 mi) at a gradient of 6%, from Cortina to Pocol, then the formidable switchbacks of the Giau: nearly 9 km (5.5 mi) with one section at 11%, halfway up the slope, after which the gradient never drops below 9%. Descend the Giau via twenty-nine switchbacks to Selva di Cadore before ascending the Staulanza (5.5 km/3.5 mi at 6%) followed by the Cibiana: 10 km (6 mi) at 7%. But watch out! Having descended the Cibiana at km 72 (mi 45), you now have 20 km (12.5 mi) of false flat to negotiate on the way back to Cortina. With 3,000 m (9,800 ft) of E+ in barely 100 km (60 mi), this is a tough ride.

Distance **96 km** (60 mi)

E+ **2,800 m** (9,200 ft)

Difficulty **5/5**

Appeal **4/5**

The closest train station to the route (at km 73/mi 45) is Calalzo di Cadore (12 km/7.5 mi by cycle path), which is 4h from Venice and 8h from Milan. By car, Cortina d'Ampezzo is 2h10 from Venice (160 km/100 mi), 4h40 from Milan (410 km/255 mi), and 2h15 from Bolzano (130 km/80 mi).

Even though the Giau lies only 16 km (10 mi) into the route, its beauty is worth a break at the summit. The terrace of the Berghotel is the perfect spot.

Passo Giau, 7
32020 Colle Santa Lucia
passogiau.it

At the end of this demanding ride, take a seat on the terrace of the Embassy, located on the very chic Corso Italia, for a restorative snack, such as *Sachertorte* (chocolate cake) or ricotta cake. Or both.

Corso Italia, 44
32043 Cortina d'Ampezzo
facebook.com/
Pasticceriaembassycortina

DOBBIACO
TRE CIME DI LAVAREDO

High mountain / Advanced
Map strava.com/routes/21667932
Test yourself km 13 (mi 8) strava.com/segments/665196
Test yourself km 23 (mi 14) strava.com/segments/5511397

Here, in the South Tyrol, there is a breathtaking sight: the three serrated fingers of the Tre Cime di Lavaredo, a rock-climber's paradise, and symbol of the Dolomites. They also have a place in cycling legend, having been featured in several memorable stages of the Giro d'Italia.

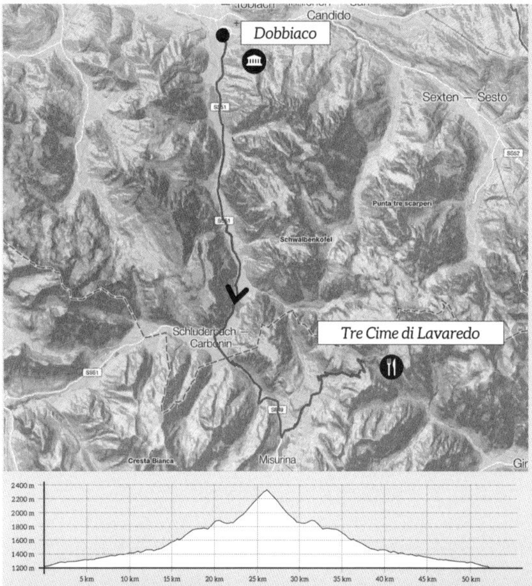

The Tre Cime di Lavaredo (Piccola, Ovest, Grande) rise to 2,999 m (9,839 ft). Their unique appearance has made them a symbol of the Dolomites—renowned for their rock-climbing sites, but also for their place in cycling history. Merckx made his mark here, and Nibali was inspired. What links these two memorable episodes of the Giro (separated by 45 years) is that it was snowing in early June—as if the difficulty of the slopes did not suffice! Our route is a return trip from Dobbiaco. The ascent up the old military road of the Tre Cime, which comes to a dead end at 2,333 m (7,654 ft), is 13 km (8 mi) long with an average gradient of 6.6%. This includes a 1 km (0.6 mi) section after the conifer forest at a gradient of over 11%, finishing with 3.3 km (2 mi) at 12%—through a rocky landscape—with one section at 19%. Epic, but what a sense of achievement when you reach the Rifugio Auronzo at the summit.

Distance	E+	Difficulty	Appeal
52 km (32 mi)	1,250 m (4,100 ft)	4/5	4/5

Dobbiaco (pop. 3,300) lies 10 km (6 mi) from the Austrian border. Innsbruck is the nearest large town: 2h35 by train, 2h by car (140 km/87 mi). Venice is 4h30 by train or 2h45 by car (190 km/118 mi). Milan is 5h20 by train or 4h40 by car (380 km/236 mi).

At the summit, grab a hot drink or a mountain snack from the Rifugio Auronzo, which offers amazing views over the Tre Cime.

32041 Auronzo di Cadore BL
rifugioauronzo.it

Before or after conquering the Tre Cime, why not hire an electrically assisted mountain bike and set out from Dobbiaco to explore other wonders of Italy's South Tyrol, such as Lake Dobbiaco, Monte Paterno, Prato Piazza, and the Fanes-Sennes-Prags Nature Park?

dobbiaco.bz

PADUA
VENETIAN PEARLS

- *Hilly / Intermediate*
- *Map strava.com/routes/21922248*
- *Test yourself km 18 (mi 11) strava.com/segments/3926760*
- *Test yourself km 62 (mi 39) strava.com/segments/7945622*

Padua is Venice's neighbor, and it can certainly rival it for architectural wonders and atmosphere, but without the crowds. It is also a city that has embraced cycling, which only adds to its charms. The surrounding region has many sporty attractions.

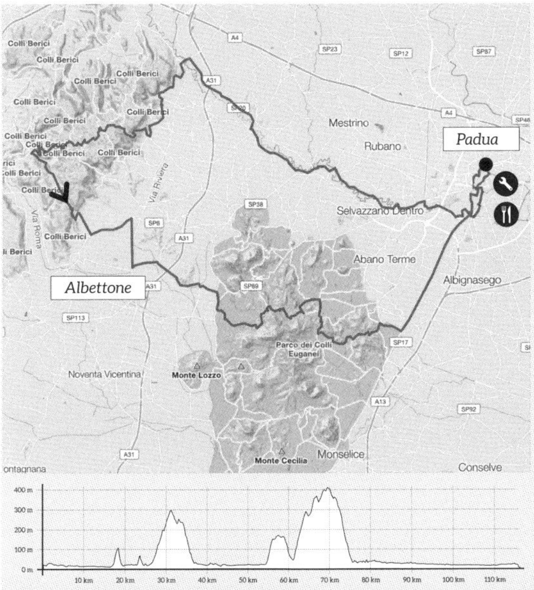

One never tires of Padua. With its maze of narrow streets winding between the towers of medieval palaces, church cupolas, and arcades of buildings laden with history, Padua is just so Italian. But before sipping a Spritz or tasting a gelato on the vast Prato della Valle, hop on the bike for an invigorating ride through the Euganean Hills to the south and the Berici Hills to the west with varied, playful terrain between portions of the Venetian Plain. The Castelnuovo climb (km 27/mi 16) is 4.3 km (2.7 mi) long at a gradient of 6%. To reach Zovencedo and then San Giovanni in Monte (km 69/mi 43) at an altitude of 400 m (1,315 ft), we climb 8 km (5 mi) at an average gradient of 5%, traversing several ramps at around 10%. The ideal season to enjoy Padua is late summer, when the week-long Padova Bike City festival celebrates local cycling culture, drawing in young people and students from the university (founded in 1222).

Distance	E+	Difficulty	Appeal
116 km (72 mi)	1,200 m (3,950 ft)	3/5	4/5

Padua (pop. 210,000) is served by high-speed train. The nearest airport is Venice, to the east: 55 minutes by train or 45 minutes by car (50 km/30 mi). To the south, Bologna is 1h by train or 1h30 by car (120 km/75 mi). To the west, Milan is 2h by train or 2h40 by car (250 km).

You will not get a quick fix at Faggin Bikes, but you absolutely must visit this Italian hand-built frame specialist (all materials), founded in Padua seventy-five years ago.

Via Jacopo Filiasi, 436
35128 Padua
fagginbikes.com

If you fancy a coffee, smoothie, cake, ice cream, or sorbet when you return, visit Gelataria Panciera at the corner of Prato della Valle. It is the perfect place.

Via Umberto I, Prato della Valle, 130
35122 Padua
pancieragelati.com

The iconic Tre Cime di Lavaredo in the Dolomites, Italy.

VITTORIO VENETO

THE TUNNELS OF SAN BOLDO

- *Low mountain / Advanced*
- *Map strava.com/routes/21684805*
- *Test yourself km 48 (mi 30) strava.com/segments/4060077*
- *Test yourself km 68 (mi 42) strava.com/segments/8432804*

This route is a loop between two sublime Venetian towns: Vittorio Veneto and Belluno (km 42/mi 26). The panoramic views over the Dolomites are breathtaking. There is a surprise too in the form of the unusual descent from the San Boldo Pass.

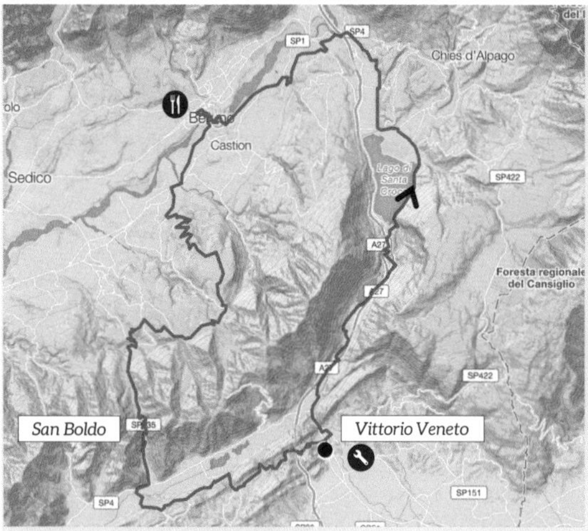

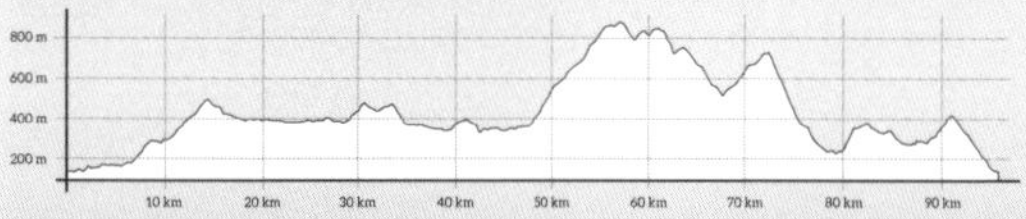

Prosecco—that sparkling wine now very much in vogue—is made using the Glera grape variety, which grows in abundance around Belluno. But do not drink too much of it before descending the little San Boldo Pass (706 m/2,316 ft) by its south slope. This road, which was built in a hundred days in 1918 by the Austro-Hungarian army (using forced local labor), is unlike any other. The first kilometer (0.6 mi) is cut into a spectacularly steep mountainside, with seven switchbacks bending through short tunnels blasted out of the very rock. Traffic is one-way (alternating) controlled by lights. It is an unusual, if not unique, road. The entirety of this route through the foothills of the Dolomites (including the Valmorel da Limana: 10 km/6 mi at 5%) is quite superb from the Lago di Santa Croce (km 15/mi 9) to the sporty final section over the climbs of Zuel and Tarzo.

Distance	E+	Difficulty	Appeal
96 km (60 mi)	1,800 m (5,900 ft)	3/5	4/5

Vittorio Veneto is close to the airports (to the south) of Treviso and Venice. The latter is 2h15 by bus or 40 minutes by car (63 km/40 mi). To the east, Udine is 1h30 by train or by car (125 km/78 mi). To the west, Milan is 3h30 by train or 3h by car (330 km/205 mi).

On the superb Piazza dei Martiri, Caffè Deon 1870 serves the best espresso in Belluno (km 40/mi 25) with a terrace that is perfect for lunch.

Piazza dei Martiri, 31
32100 Belluno
facebook.com/deonbelluno

To the south of the town, Eurovelo is Vittorio Veneto's road bike specialist. Retailer of Pinarello, Bottecchia, Trek, and Specialized. Workshop and route tips.

Via Giacomo Matteotti, 89
31029 Vittorio Veneto
eurovelo.it

CARNIA
DEFY THE ZONCOLAN

High mountain / Expert

Map strava.com/routes/21962960

Test yourself km 37 (mi 23) strava.com/segments/1635485

Test yourself km 46 (mi 29) strava.com/segments/10259994

The legend of Monte Zoncolan is a recent one. Originally a military road, this pass, which is close to Italy's borders with Austria and Slovenia, is one of the scariest monsters that twenty-first-century champions have had to face. It is a must for any serious alpine cyclist.

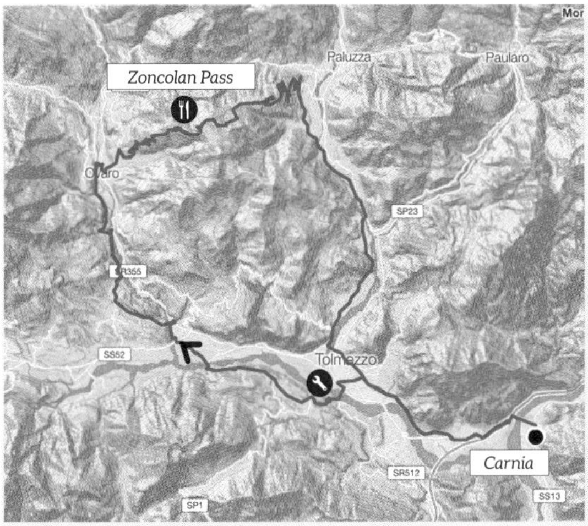

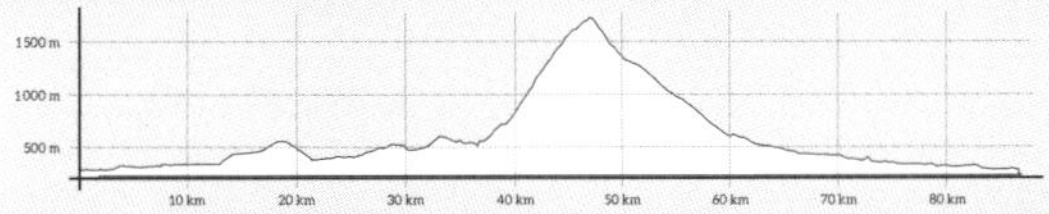

From Carnia to Ovaro (km 36/mi 22), this is a pleasant ride alongside mountain streams. Suddenly, the road twists right into a wall with no summit. The following 10 km (6 mi) soar from an altitude of barely 500 m (1,600 ft) to 1,725 m (5,660 ft). This is Monte Zoncolan. A banner warns, *"Coraggio, vi attende l'inferno"* (Hang in there, hell awaits). The Strava segments speak for themselves: the 3.4 km (2.1 mi) from Liariis ascend at a gradient of 14%; km 5 (mi 3) of the climb is at a gradient of 15.1%, the last 350 m (380 yards) at 15.2%; and from Liarris to the top—a distance of 7.5 km (4.6 mi)—the average gradient is 13.5%. It is a rare feat to reach the three short tunnels just before the bare summit without dismounting. But you are not alone in your ordeal: giant photos of legends past, such as Merckx, Hinault, and Indurain, have been placed at some of the toughest points. Once you reach Pantani, it's in the bag!

Distance	E+	Difficulty	Appeal
86 km (53 mi)	1,900 m (6,250 ft)	5/5	5/5

From Udine, you have two choices: take the train to Carnia (30 minutes), where our route begins, or the bus to Tolmezzo (50 minutes, except Sundays) and do a shorter loop of 64 km (40 mi). Trieste Airport is 30 minutes by train from Udine.

At the summit of the Zoncolan, reward yourself with platters of delicious cold cuts and local cheeses at the excellent *agriturismo* (farm-restaurant) Gortani Malga Pozof.

Localita Monte Zoncolan
33025 Ovaro
gortanifarm.it

In Tolmezzo, visit All Motorcycle and Bike at km 11 (mi 7) and km 75 (mi 47). Do not be fooled by the sign; it provides an excellent service for bicycles. Retailer of Specialized and Bottecchia.

Via Grialba, 35
33028 Tolmezzo
tuttomotoebike.it

TRIESTE
SLOVENIAN ESCAPADE

Very hilly / Advanced

Map strava.com/routes/21706858

Distance
90 km
(56 mi)

E+
1,700 m
(5,580 ft)

Difficulty
3/5

Appeal
4/5

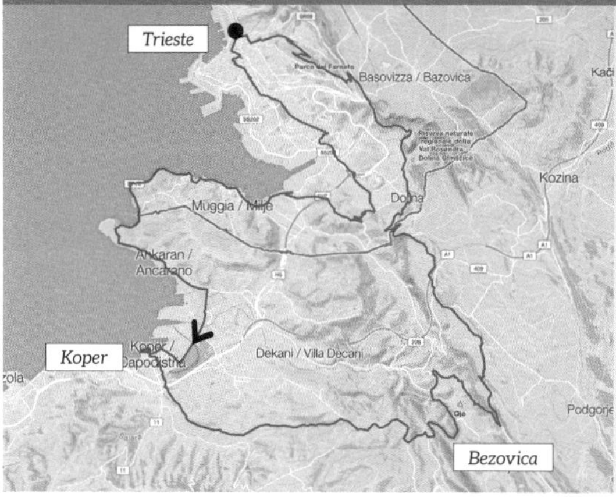

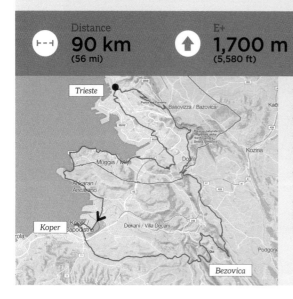

This route has the particularity of being split almost equally between Italy and Slovenia at the top of the Istria peninsula, where coastal scenery and mountainous hinterland rival each other in beauty. From cosmopolitan Trieste, we ride along the coast to Koper in Slovenia before turning inland to the wide, green Slovenian valleys for some climbing. It is superbly demanding, especially toward Potok (km 46/ mi 28), Bezovica (km 60/mi 37), and, back in Italy, Sant'Antonio in Bosco (km 78/mi 48).

TRIESTE
A TRIP TO THE STAR

Very hilly / Advanced

Map strava.com/routes/21687499

Distance
145 km
(90 mi)

E+
1,300 m
(4,250 ft)

Difficulty
4/5

Appeal
4/5

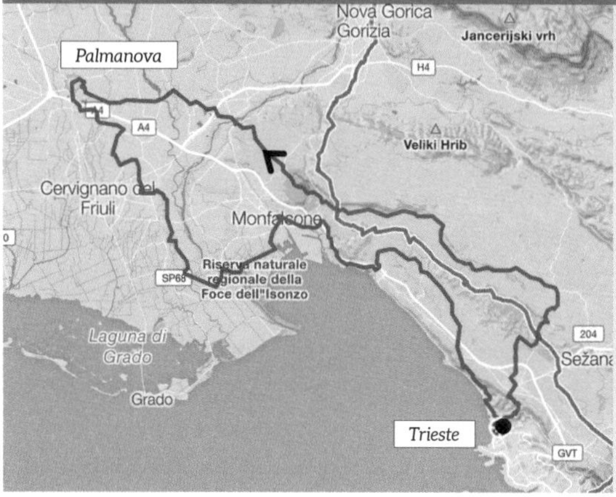

This loop, which starts and ends in Trieste, is effectively a long excursion to one of the most amazing constructions in Europe at km 70 (mi 44), the fortified Renaissance town of Palmanova, which is laid out in the shape of a nine-pointed star. To get there, ration your efforts above Trieste through Slovenia (30 km/18 mi) and toward Doberdò Lake. The return leg, via the marshland of the Isonzo estuary, is easier. There is a climb after Sistiana, but it is more than worth it for the view over the Gulf of Trieste. There are train stations at Sagrado, Palmanova, and Monfalcone.

SLOVENIA AUSTRIA SWITZERLAND

CENTRAL SLOVENIA

VIENNA

GRAZ & LINZ

SALZBURG & TYROL

GRAUBÜNDEN & TICINO

VALAIS & VAUD

ZURICH

LESCE
SLOVENIAN STEEPLES

Low mountain / Advanced
Map strava.com/routes/22437427
Test yourself km 13 (mi 8) strava.com/segments/1327144
Test yourself km 65 (mi 40) strava.com/segments/11971952

The Julian Alps promise unexpected panoramas in all seasons. On a bike, you do not have to climb very high (1,300 m/4,265 ft at the most on this route) to feel the pull of these beautiful Slovenian mountains. Still, it is best to arrive in good physical condition.

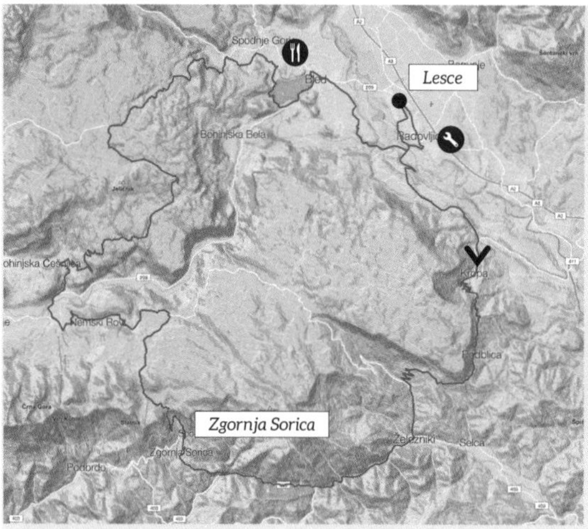

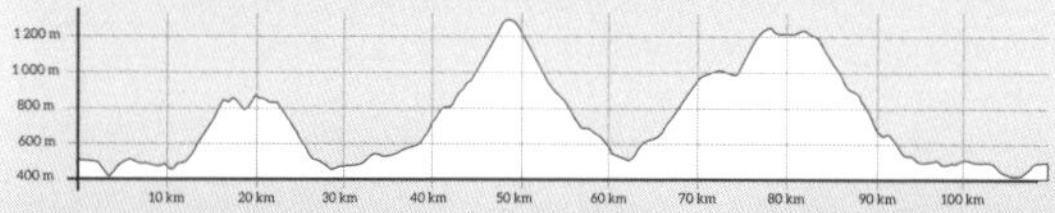

This route in the eastern Julian Alps is a gift to anyone who fancies exploring the most beautiful cycling territory in Slovenia. The shapes of high cliffs and limestone peaks emerge at more than 2,000 m (6,560 ft). At first glance, the slopes seem gentle and green, dotted with villages of dollhouse-like chalets that are recognizable from afar, thanks to their white churches with pointed steeples. However, this is a demanding route with more than 2,500 m (8,200 ft) of E+, split into three major sections. The first (4.5 km/2.8 mi at 7.3%) leads to picturesque Jamnik with its striking hilltop church. The ascent to Soriška Planina (1,286 m/4,220 ft) is the longest on our route: 10 km (6 mi) at 7%. Lastly, the Pokljuka Plateau, which we climb in two stages: 5 km (3 mi) at 7%, then 3 km (2 mi) at 8%. On the descent to the popular vacation spot of Lake Bled, the Pokljuka Gorge is worth a short detour (km 90/mi 56).

Distance	E+	Difficulty	Appeal
108 km (67 mi)	2,400 m (7,900 ft)	4/5	4/5

Lesce (pop. 3,000) lies 50 km (31 mi) northwest of Ljubljana: 40 minutes by train or 35 minutes by car. Klagenfurt Airport (Austria) is 1h30 by train or 1h by car (80 km/50 mi) via Villach. Udine (Italy) is 3h by train or 1h50 by car (170 km/105 mi).

On the shore of Lake Bled (km 96/mi 60), stop at Café Belvédère for its commanding view, art deco columns, and cream cake.

Cesta Svobode 18
4260 Bled
bled.si

In Radovljica (km 2/mi 1.25), Extreme Vital is a large bike store with an excellent workshop service. Rental of Specialized bikes.

Gorenjska cesta 41
4240 Radovljica
extremevital.com

TARVISIO
UNIQUE MANGART

- *High mountain / Advanced*
- *Map strava.com/routes/21631620*
- *Test yourself km 13 (mi 8) strava.com/segments/687457*
- *Test yourself km 17 (mi 11) strava.com/segments/7482117*

Slovenia has caused something of a surprise with its recent cycling champions. The country's mountain landscape is surprising too. Straddling the border with Italy, the Mangart is the most stunning peak in the Julian Alps. The road itself is a wonderful athletic adventure.

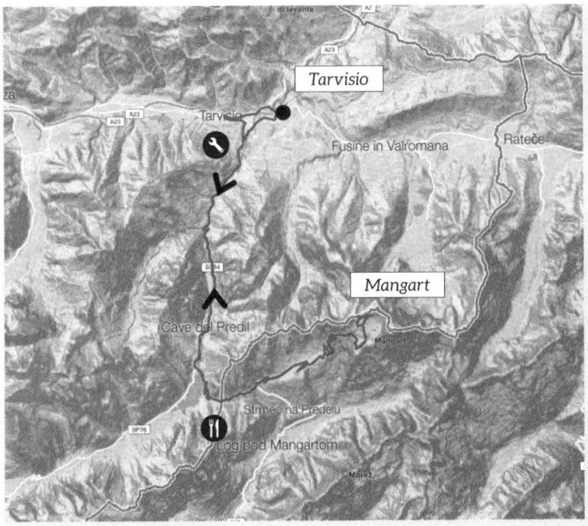

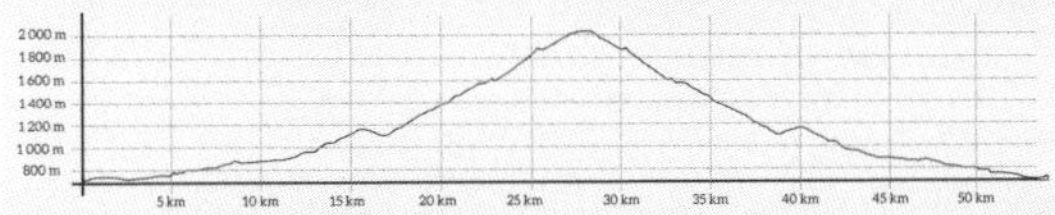

Bovec (to the south), Pontebba, and Ugovizza (on the Italian side) are other possible starting points that will extend this ride to Mangart. The approach from Tarvisio limits it to 54 km (34 mi). The Mangart is not a pass like its neighbor Vršič. A huge sugarloaf rising to 2,679 m (8,789 ft), its famous road—for which cars and motorcycles must pay a toll—ends with a 1.7 km (1 mi) circuit of the Mangart Saddle (2,050 m/6,725 ft), from where there are breathtaking 360-degree views as far as the surrounding slopes are clear. These Julian Alps are as grandiose as they are wild. To get there, you climb for 10 km (6 mi) at nearly 9% (with one passage at 15%) on a narrow road with sheer drops and tunnels blasted out of light limestone and dolomite rock. Vegetation gradually gives way to a landscape of stone and scree. The Mangart is unique.

Distance	E+	Difficulty	Appeal
54 km (34 mi)	1,550 m (5,100 ft)	4/5	5/5

Tarvisio lies in the far northeast of Friuli Venezia Giulia. This town of 5,000 inhabitants is easily reached by train: 1h from Udine and 3h from Trieste. By car, allow 1h15 from Udine (90 km/56 mi), 2h from Trieste (170 km/105 mi), and 2h30 from Venice (225 km/140 mi).

If the Mangart has given you an appetite (which is likely), Hermanov Hram Inn, located right at the border (km 40/mi 25), is the place to eat. Rustic and friendly.

Strmec na Predelu 30
5231 Log Pod Mangartom
facebook.com/HermanovHram

Located 3 km (2 mi) west from Tarvisio Boscoverde Train Station toward Camporosso, Lussari Sport provides workshop services and road-bike rental.

Via Lussari 20
33018 Tarvisio, Italy
lussari.com

TARVISIO
THE COBBLES OF VRŠIČ

- *High mountain / Advanced*
- *Map strava.com/routes/21633549*
- *Test yourself km 24 (mi 15) strava.com/segments/5367839*
- *Test yourself km 67 (mi 42) strava.com/segments/4120959*

This route starts and ends in Italy (Tarvisio), but its main attraction is Slovenian. The Vršič Pass is the highest and most beautiful pass in this part of the Alps. The *Ruska cesta* (Russian road) is demandingly steep with numbered switchbacks paved with setts.

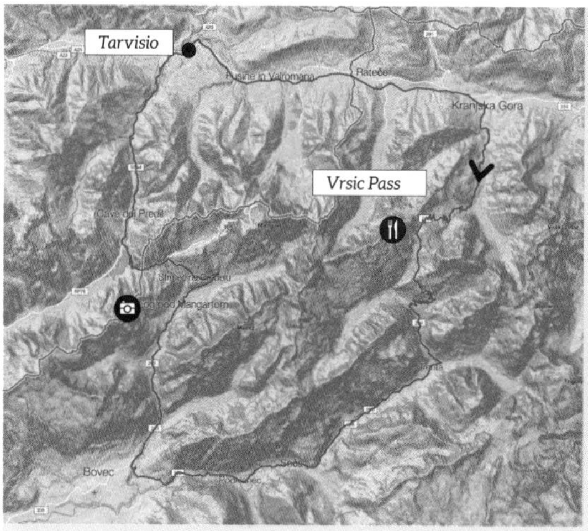

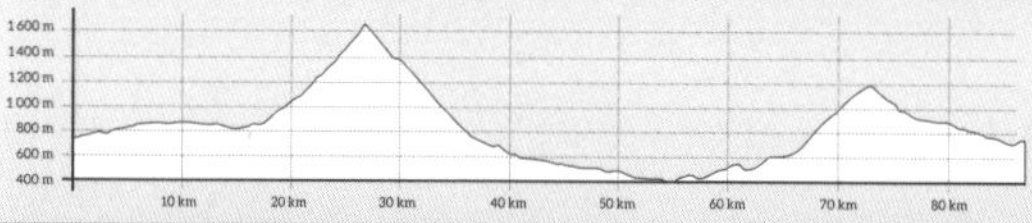

Any trip to this part of the Alps must include an attempt on the Zoncolan in the Carnic Alps (Italy), as well as a visit to the Julian Alps (Slovenia) for another wonder: the Vršič Pass. Indeed, it is hard to know which to make a priority. Vršič is unique. The road up the north slope climbs for less than 10 km (6 mi) from the ski resort of Kranska Gora. Each bend is numbered from 1 to 50 from north to south (same system on the south slope). At bend 8, an orthodox chapel commemorates the sacrifice of the Russian prisoners of war who died in an avalanche in 1916 while building this road. There are only 5 km (3 mi) to go, but at an average gradient of 11%. Bend 24 announces a short, flatter stretch before the summit at 1,611 m (5,285 ft). The descent toward Trenta and the Soča Gorges is vertiginous. Return to Italy via the Predil Pass: 6.5 km (4 mi) at 8%. You will have stars in your eyes.

Distance	E+	Difficulty	Appeal
87 km (54 mi)	1,900 m (6,250 ft)	4/5	4/5

Tarvisio (pop. 5,000) lies in the far northeast of the Friuli Venezia Giulia region. It is easily reached by train —1h from Udine and 3h from Trieste. By car, allow 1h15 from Udine (90 km/55 mi), 2h from Trieste (170 km/105 mi), and 2h30 from Venice (225 km/140 mi).

If your legs are willing, turn left at the end of Lake Predil (km 75/mi 47), and cycle 0.5 km (0.3 mi) to the fort, a relic of the terrible battles fought in the region during World War I. Stunning views over the superb lake and the surrounding mountains.

Looking out at the Vršič summit, Erjavčeva Koča serves Slovenian beer and hearty mountain fare at wooden tables on its terrace.

Vršiška cesta 90
4280 Kranjska Gora
erjavceva.business.site

Fall colors above the Vrsic Pass, Slovenia.

LJUBLJANA

« POGI » STYLE

Very hilly / Intermediate   *Map* *strava.com/routes/23305302*

Distance
90 km
(56 mi)

E+
1,250 m
(4,100 ft)

Difficulty
3/5

Appeal
4/5

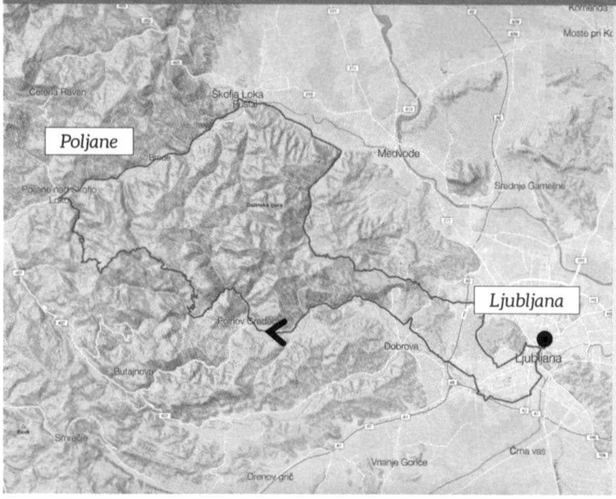

Soak up the charm of Ljubljana, and explore its rich heritage—such as the Triple Bridge (Tromostovje) and the vast Tivoli Park—before heading west through the achingly beautiful hills of the Polhograjski Dolomiti on snaking roads well pedaled by the national darling, Tadej "Pogi" Pogačar (strava.com/pros/6021015), the first Slovenian to win the Tour de France. Dig deep as you climb toward the weather station on Pasja Ravan (km 38/mi 24), and then up to Topol (km 72/mi 45), where you can veer left and haul yourself up to St. James's Parish Church, whose quintessentially Slovenian bell tower overlooks a dreamy horizon.

CELJE

RIDE IT LIKE PRIMOŽ

Low mountain / Advanced   *Map* *strava.com/routes/23279826*

Distance
85 km
(53 mi)

E+
1,800 m
(5,900 ft)

Difficulty
4/5

Appeal
4/5

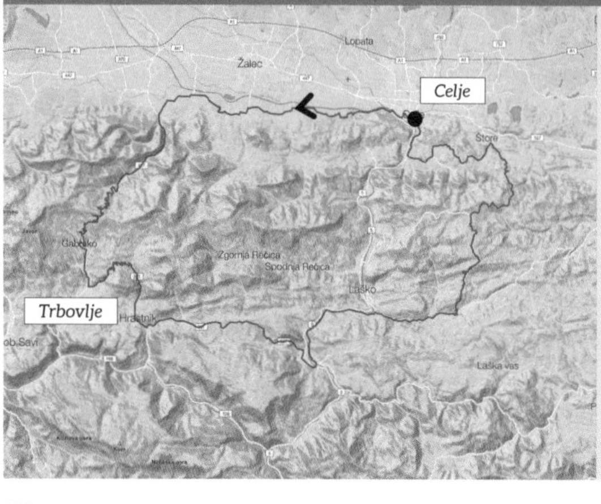

Trbovlje is famous for its 360 m (1,180 ft) power station chimney (the highest in Europe) and for being the birthplace of Primož Roglič, the first Slovenian to win a Grand Tour (the 2019 Vuelta). Unfortunately, we cannot follow him on Strava, but we can earn ourselves some climbing stripes on his roads with this ride out from Celje along the Savinja River. We climb for 6 km (3.7 mi) at 6% through the thirteen switchbacks of the Podmeja above Trbovlje, then for another 3 km (2 mi) at 7% before Boben, and for 5 km (3 mi) at 9% after Tevče. There is a wonderful view over Celje from the fourteenth-century castle.

MARIBOR
SKI OR BIKE

Low mountain / Intermediate

Map strava.com/routes/23281796

Distance	E+	Difficulty	Appeal
96 km (60 mi)	1,300 m (4,250 ft)	3/5	3/5

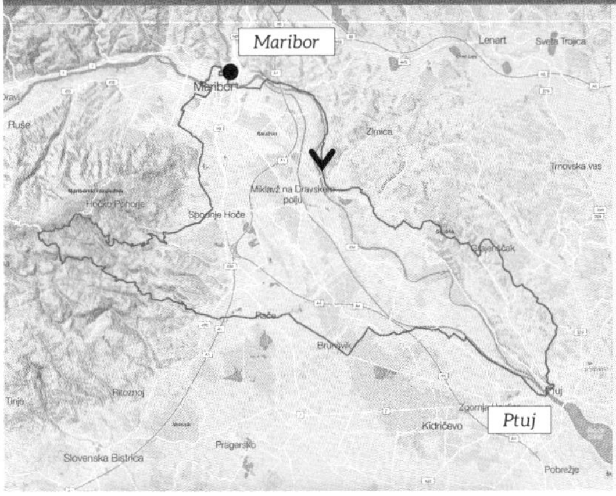

Enthusiasts of downhill skiing will recognize the name Maribor (Slovenia's second city) because the Women's World Cup is held here each year. The town itself is at less than 300 m (985 ft). The skiing takes places 1,000 m (3,280 ft) above on the slopes of Mariborsko Pohorje, which we catch a glimpse of at the end of the route. First, we ride through the Drava Valley to delightful Ptuj with its elegant castle, cobbled streets, and traces of its Roman past. No cycle trip to the Styria region would be complete without a real ascent—in this case, 12 km (7.5 mi) at 6.5% to Frajhajm, just behind Mariborsko Pohorje.

NOVO MESTO
BEAUTIFUL ŽUMBERAK

Very hilly / Advanced

Map strava.com/routes/23294426

Distance	E+	Difficulty	Appeal
96 km (60 mi)	1,850 m (6,100 ft)	3/5	4/5

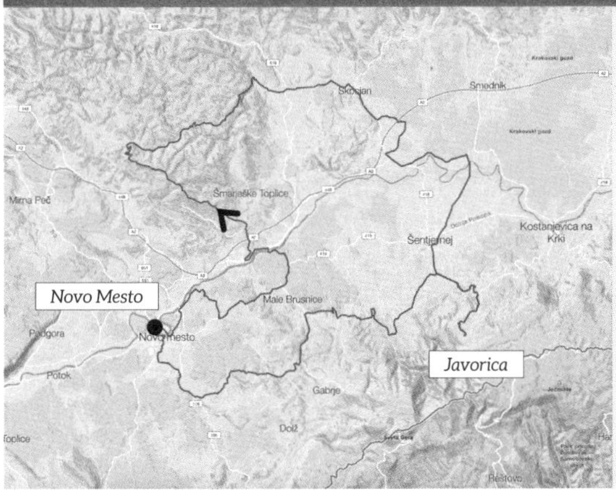

Winner of the 2010 Critérium du Dauphiné, Janez Brajkovič (strava.com/pros/109652) is a role model for up-and-coming Slovenian cyclists. Born in Metlika, he takes us on a ride through his winemaking region of Dolenjska. A climber, he proffers two fine 5 km (3 mi) ramps that rise to around 600 m (1,970 ft): on the steep slopes of Paha in the Jagodnik area, and then the more difficult Javorovica in the Žumberak Mountains, which separate Slovenia from Croatia. The old buildings of Novo Mesto—equidistant (80 km/50 mi) from Ljubljana and Zagreb—are also worth exploring.

GRAZ
SURPRISES IN STYRIA

Low mountain / Advanced
Map strava.com/routes/22150398
Test yourself km 21 (mi 13) strava.com/segments/4859128
Test yourself km 45 (mi 28) strava.com/segments/10078753

Graz is Austria's second largest city. Being very close to Slovenia and not far from Hungary and Croatia, it has retained a certain Balkan feel. The roads through the low mountains of Styria toward Vienna are also well worth exploring.

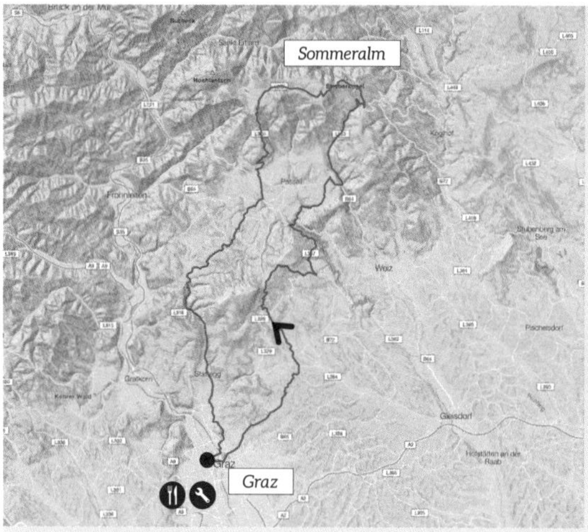

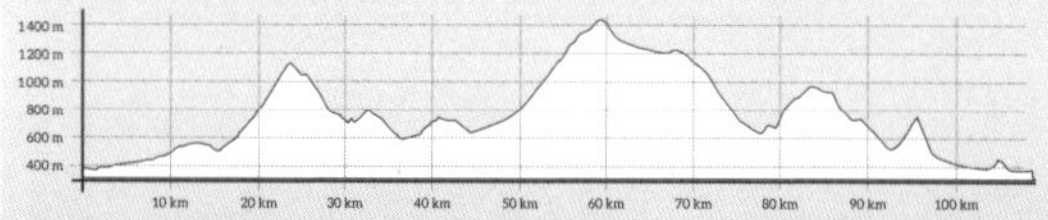

Head out of Graz via the Stadtpark at the foot of the Schlossberg for a long route north through the countryside toward the low mountains of Styria, which draw into view as you leave Sankt Radegund and climb the Schöckl: a tough 8 km (5 mi) at 8%, with the final 3 km (2 mi) at more than 10%. You will certainly feel warmed up once you reach the summit (1,445 m/4,740 ft) at km 24 (mi 15). The main course is the ascent to Sommeralm Ski Resort (1,434 m/4,705 ft) after riding through lovely Raab Gorge.
This pass may be not very well-known, but it wears you down despite the fine road surface: 10 km (6 mi) at an average gradient of 7%.
The scenery is all forest, small lakes, and gentle contours. After the long descent to Tulwitz (km 80/mi 50), we ascend to Anger (5 km/3 mi at 6%) before hitting the Leber: 2.5 km (1.5 mi) at 8%. It is not an easy day, but sublime and peaceful all the same.

Distance **123 km** (76 mi)

E+ **2,750 m** (8,000 ft)

Difficulty **4/5**

Appeal **5/5**

Graz Airport is not the best connected, but you can also fly to Klagenfurt: 2h away by train or 1h30 by car (135 km/84 mi to the east). Graz is 2h35 from Vienna by train or 2h10 by car (200 km/125 mi). Budapest is 4h by car (350 km/220 mi), and Venice is 4h30 (420 km/260 mi).

Maghanoy Bespoke Boutique is an elegant shop selling custom bikes and bags. It's also a gathering point for local riders, serving excellent coffee, and delicious pastries.

Körösistrasse 1
8010 Graz
maghanoywilson.com

Located only 100 meters/yards from the train station, RadAktiv opened in 2017. It is the most contemporary of Graz's bike stores, specializing in Trek bikes.

Annenstrasse 50
8020 Graz
radaktiv.at

VIENNA
THE SPLENDOR OF SCHÖNBRUNN

Hilly / Intermediate
Map strava.com/routes/21444801
Test yourself km 12 (mi 7) strava.com/segments/5037977
Test yourself km 30 (mi 19) strava.com/segments/9306272

This route, which sets out along the Danube, crosses the modest hills of the Viennese forests, dips into Lower Austria, and swings by Schönbrunn Palace, starting and finishing at Queen Mary's Bridge (Marienbrücke), is as delicious as a Viennese pastry.

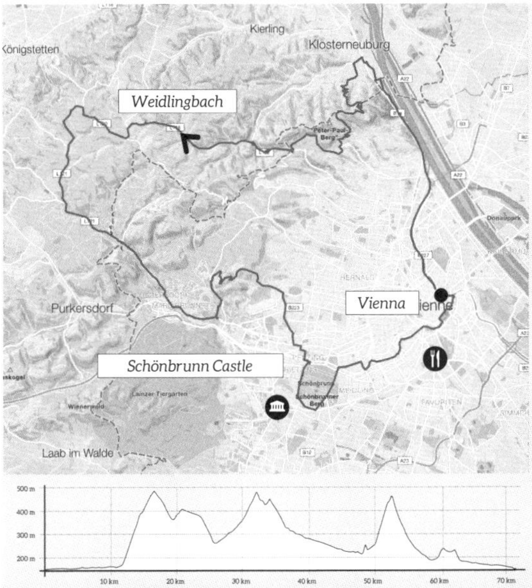

A ride out to Schönbrunn Palace is not only a trip through Austrian history, but also an opportunity to explore the forested countryside west of Vienna. Although we stay away from the Danube for most of the route, we do start out along the canal and then the river for 10 km (6 mi) before the surprising Kalhenberg: 4.5 km (2.8 mi) of snaking road at an average gradient of 6% up to a point 300 m (1,000 ft) above the Danube with a majestic view. Further on, the ramp of Steinriegl (4 km/2.5 mi at 4%) will test your legs before the descent to Mauerbach. At km 50 (mi 31), we hit Satzberg (2 km/1.25 mi long at 9%), the most demanding part of the entire route. We are not far from Hietzing, an affluent neighborhood in Vienna's 13th District, and the Schönbrunn Palace. Our route circles the gardens but do stop to go explore its imposing architecture. Return to Vienna along the Wien river.

Distance	E+	Difficulty	Appeal
71 km (44 mi)	1,000 m (3,280 ft)	3/5	4/5

Vienna is 2h40 by train from Budapest, and 4h from Prague and Munich. By car, allow 2h30 from Budapest (250 km/155 mi), 4h from Prague (330 km/205 mi), and 4h30 from Munich (400 km/250 mi).

At km 66 (mi 41), Ghisallo is the perfect bike cafe, comprising a beautiful road bike store and a Mediterranean restaurant. Retailer of Pinarello, Colnago, and Passoni.

Schönbrunnerstrasse 97
1050 Vienna
ghisallo.cc

Schönbrunn Palace is well worth a return visit. Its rococo style, neoclassical arcades, and formal gardens make it the "Austrian Versailles" so desired by Leopold 1, a key player in European history. Take the U4 subway or streetcar lines 10 or 60.

schoenbrunn.at

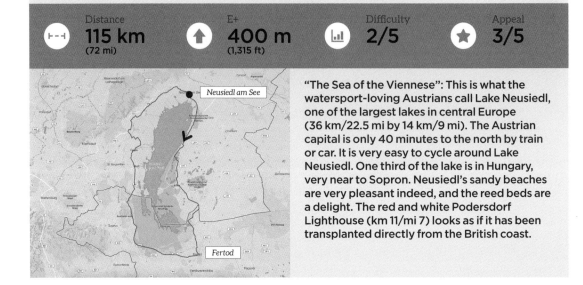

NEUSIEDL AM SEE

SEA OF THE VIENNESE

Fairly flat / Intermediate

Map strava.com/routes/22907932

Distance	E+	Difficulty	Appeal
115 km (72 mi)	400 m (1,315 ft)	2/5	3/5

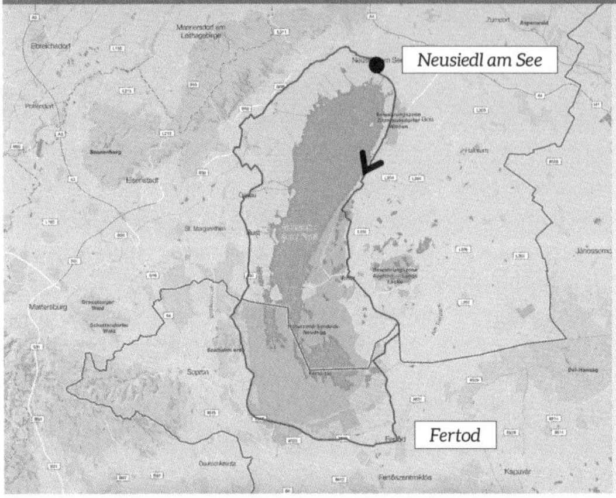

"The Sea of the Viennese": This is what the watersport-loving Austrians call Lake Neusiedl, one of the largest lakes in central Europe (36 km/22.5 mi by 14 km/9 mi). The Austrian capital is only 40 minutes to the north by train or car. It is very easy to cycle around Lake Neusiedl. One third of the lake is in Hungary, very near to Sopron. Neusiedl's sandy beaches are very pleasant indeed, and the reed beds are a delight. The red and white Podersdorf Lighthouse (km 11/mi 7) looks as if it has been transplanted directly from the British coast.

KLAGENFURT

GREEN CARINTHIA

Low mountain / Intermediate

Map strava.com/routes/23265977

Distance	E+	Difficulty	Appeal
97 km (60 mi)	1,500 m (4,920 ft)	3/5	4/5

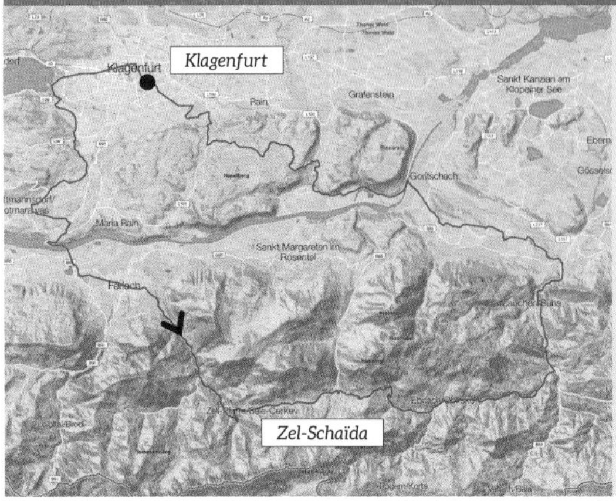

In Carinthia, you will find castles, Lake Wörth (which apparently holds the warmest waters in the Alps), signs in two languages (German and Slovenian), and, south of Klagenfurt, the Prealps straddling both banks of the sometimes-turbulent Drava river with wide valleys, villages covered in flowers, and pointed belfries amid pastureland. We climb to 1,065 m (3,495 ft) at Zell via a final ramp of 2 km (1.25 mi) at 10%. At km 70 (mi 44), we are very near the Wildensteiner Waterfall, which is one of the highest in Europe at 54 m (178 ft), before tackling 3 km (2 mi) at gradients of between 8% and 10% until Kreuth.

LINZ
BIKE THROUGH BOHEMIA

- *Low mountain / Intermediate*
- *Map strava.com/routes/21444304*
- *Test yourself km 29 (mi 18) strava.com/segments/19858412*
- *Test yourself km 90 (mi 56) strava.com/segments/4252928*

With its main square, cathedral, modern art museum, rooftop Hohenrausch exhibition, and the Danube snaking past, Linz is an astonishing city. To the north lie the gentle undulations of the Bohemian Massif, the destination for our beautiful route, up to around 800 m (2,600 ft).

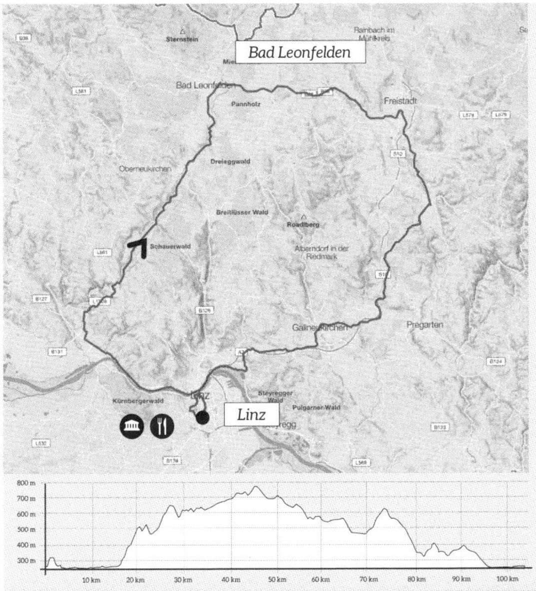

Much as you might enjoy the lovely cycle paths along the majestic Danube around Linz, it is worthwhile getting out of the city. The tempting Bohemian Massif is not far away, perfect for a nice little "seventy miler" along sinuous roads that require relatively little effort: less than 1,500 m (4,900 ft) of total elevation gain. We leave the shores of Johan Strauss's favorite river at km 15 (mi 9) for a straight climb, the hardest of the whole route: 4 km (2.5 mi) at an average gradient of 6%. Thereafter, we progress in stages. Bad Leonfelden (km 43/mi 27) is only 5 km (3 mi) from the Czech border. We reach the highest point of our route—762 m (2,000 ft)—between the forests of Pannholz and Miesenwald. At Freistadt, we turn back toward Linz before hitting the Lasberger climb—3 km (2 mi) at 5%. The final 10 km (6 mi) are a pleasant ride along the Danube.

Distance	E+	Difficulty	Appeal
111 km (69 mi)	1,850 m (6,000 ft)	3/5	4/5

Linz Airport has few regular European connections. Vienna is 1h15 by train or 2h by car (190 km/118 mi). Munich is 2h40 by car (240 km/150 mi) or 3h30 by train. Prague is 3h by car (240 km/150 mi) or 6h by train.

In the city center, you will find the best Linzer torte (shortcrust pastry, blueberry jam, latticework top), which is believed to be the oldest known cake in the world, at Jindrak Cake Shop.

Herrenstrasse 22
4020 Linz
jindrak.at

Linz has been a dedicated center of digital culture since the 1980s. Beside the Danube, the Ars Electronica Center is a museum of the future that is well worth a visit.

Ars-Electronica-Strasse 1
4040 Linz
ars.electronica.art

ATTERSEE
THE THREE LAKES

Hilly / Intermediate   Map strava.com/routes/22912422

Distance	E+	Difficulty	Appeal
116 km (72 mi)	850 m (2,790 ft)	2/5	4/5

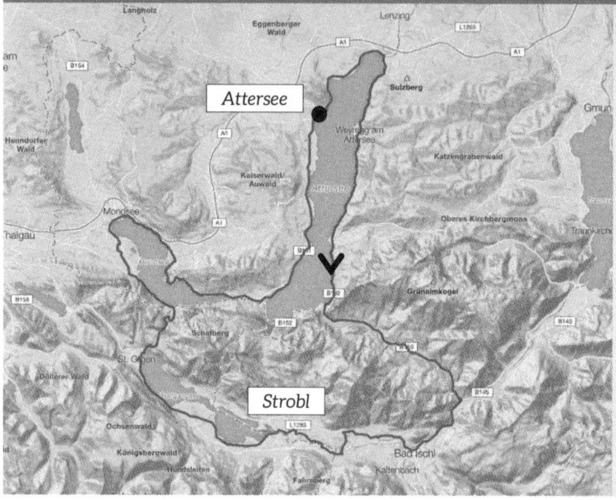

One loses count of the number of lakes east of Salzburg. Officially, there are seventy-six in the superb region of Salzkammergut alone. Setting out from Attersee, we tour three of the most majestic lakes: Attersee, Wolfgangsee, and Mondsee. Salzburg is just 30 km (19 mi) from the latter, meaning you can cycle there. Add the neighboring Traunsee lake, and you have a 130 km (81 mi) ride. The tour of the Attersee, the largest lake in Austria, is only 47 km (29 mi). Gliding past water that shifts in color from blue to green, each bend in the road brings a fresh surprise before you hit the mountain passes.

BAD GASTEIN
FABULOUS GROSSGLOCKNER

High mountain / Advanced   Map strava.com/routes/22290386

Distance	E+	Difficulty	Appeal
160 km (100 mi)	3,340 m (10,960 ft)	5/5	5/5

Everything is outsized here—from the chic resort of Bad Gastein to the 10 km (6 mi) rail tunnel from Böckstein to Mallnitz. Of course, this breathtaking adventure is the conquest of the Grossglockner, the highest road in Austria in the shadow of the highest mountain in Austria (3,798 m/12,461 ft) and the longest glacier in Austria, the Pasterze. From the Grossglockner's south side, the pass stretches from Pockhorn over 13 km (8 mi) of sublimely surfaced road at an irregular gradient: 7% average, but with four 2 km (1.25 mi) segments at more than 10%. There are sumptuous views all the way up to 2,571 m (8,435 ft).

SALZBURG
THE PEARL OF BAVARIA

- *Medium mountain / Advanced*
- *Map strava.com/routes/22262152*
- *Test yourself km 23 (mi 14) strava.com/segments/1463727*
- *Test yourself km 29 (mi 18) strava.com/segments/12145005*

Mozart was born in Salzburg, the Austrian city where classical music is celebrated like few other places. The beauty of the Bavarian Alps leads us on a cross-border loop into Germany via harsh but sublime Rossfeld Pass.

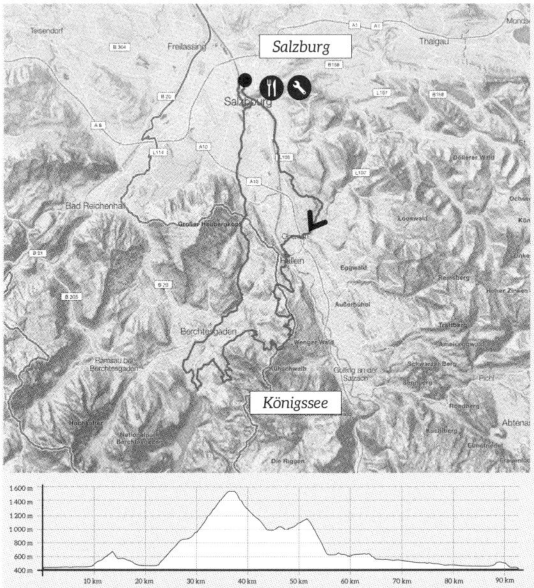

We ride south from magnificent Salzburg along the Salzach River up to the ridge that separates Austria and Germany. The ascent of the tough Rossfeld Pass awaits: a first stage of 4.2 km (2.6 mi) at 8%, then a short flat stretch before a second stage of 7 km (4.5 mi) at 9%, with the last part at 11%. The views from 1,500 m (4,920 ft) over the Dachstein glacier and the Bavarian peaks are like a picture postcard. At the bottom of the descent, we find ourselves at the crossroads of history: the museum of the Berghof (a residence of Hitler's) and the road up to the dictator's Eagle's Nest, which is closed to all motor traffic because of its narrowness and the slope (6.5 km/4 mi at 12%). It is best to head on to the waters of the Königssee, the most beautiful lake in Bavaria, before returning via Berchtesgaden. From Mönchsberg, there is a fantastic view over Salzburg, the old town and Saint Rupert's Church.

Distance	E+	Difficulty	Appeal
93 km (58 mi)	1,800 m (5,900 ft)	3/5	4/5

To the northwest, Munich is the closest big city to Salzburg: 1h30 by train or by car (150 km/93 mi). To the east, Vienna is 2h30 by train or 3h by car (300 km/185 mi). To the southwest, Innsbruck is 1h45 by train or 2h by car (200 km/125 mi).

Wander over to the Alter Markt (km 88/mi 55) to be tempted by the trays of cakes and pastries at Café Tomaselli, which has been serving treats on a terrace for 150 years.

Alter Markt 9
5020 Salzburg
tomaselli.at

In the Nonntal District of south Salzburg, M&M Bikeshop offers a prolific choice of equipment and workshop service. Retailer of Trek, Scott, and Diamant.

Michael-Pacher Strasse 19
5020 Salzburg
mm-bikeshop.com

KITZBÜHEL
THE AUSTRIAN MONSTER

- *High mountain / Advanced*
- *Map strava.com/routes/21445999*
- *Test yourself km 28 (mi 17) strava.com/segments/16640903*
- *Test yourself km 34 (mi 21) strava.com/segments/9842407*

Is the straight climb up the slopes of the terrifying Kitzbüheler Horn, in the heart of the Tyrol, the toughest cycling challenge in Europe? It may not get the media attention of the Tour de France or the Giro, but this Austrian monstrosity has got a lot going for it.

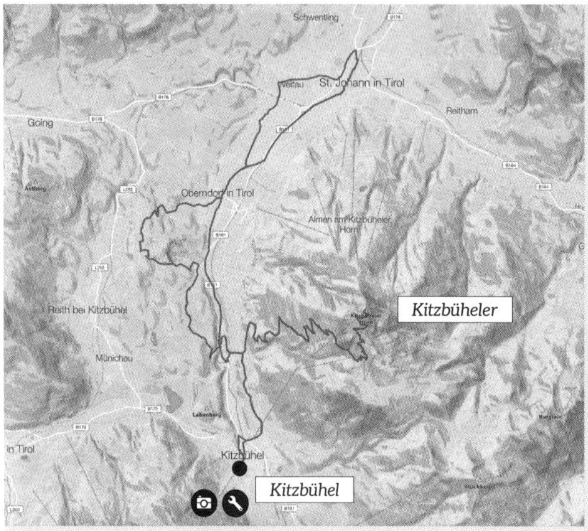

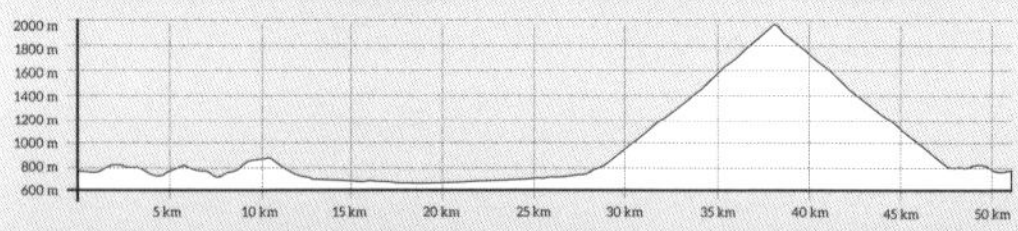

The chic resort of Kitzbühel, with its Gothic churches, sits on the western slope of the valley, overlooked by the Hahnenkamm (or *rooster's comb*), which draws the cream of the world's skiers every January to test their skills on the fearsome Streif downhill course. To the east rises the magnificent Kitzbüheler Horn, its 1,996 m (6,549 ft) summit topped by a TV tower. The road up to it is a challenge unlike few others and should be tackled after a good warm-up—in this case, via St. Johann and back. The climb itself is hell for the thighs, the heart, and the lungs because the Horn affords not the slightest respite in the course of its fifteen tight switchbacks. The official climb is only 7.8 km (4.85 mi) to the Gipfelhaus at 1,670 m (5,479 ft), but the average gradient is 12%, with the final kilometer (0.6 mi) at 17%. If you are still in the saddle, you can push on up to the TV tower: 2.2 km (1.4 mi) further at 14%.

Distance	E+	Difficulty	Appeal
50 km (31 mi)	1,450 m (4,750 ft)	4/5	5/5

In the heart of the Austrian Tyrol, Kitzbühel is 1h20 by train from Innsbruck, to the west, and 1h10 by car (90 km/55 mi). To the north, Munich is 1h30 by car (120 km/74.5 mi), and Salzburg, to the east, is 1h15 by car (80 km/50 mi).

The Gipfelhaus mountain inn marks the official end of the Kitzbühel Challenge. The road carries on up the Horn to the TV tower (1,996 m/6,549 ft). If you have the legs, the 360-degree view over the Alps is unforgettable.

Martin provides a perfect service in his Team Comp store and workshop, located less than 1 km (0.6 mi) from the train station. Retailer for BMC and Bergamont.

Sportfeld 1
6370 Kitzbühel
team-comp.at

Peaks and pastureland around Kitzbühel, Austria.

INNSBRUCK
HELL IN RAINBOW

- *Low mountain / Expert*
- *Map strava.com/routes/22292762*
- *Test yourself km 7 (mi 4) strava.com/segments/1163730*
- *Test yourself km 21 (mi 13) strava.com/segments/3806350*

Located above Innsbruck, Gramart has only appeared once on cycling's main stage—at the 2018 World Championships. Nobody who watched it can forget the sight of the greatest cyclists in the world virtually at a standstill on its hellish slope. Do you have what it takes?

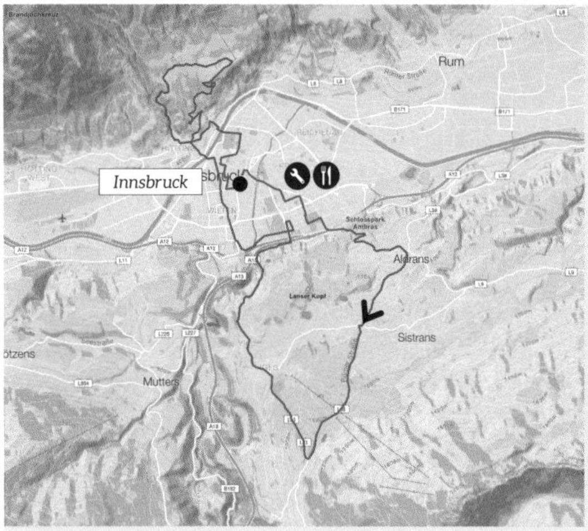

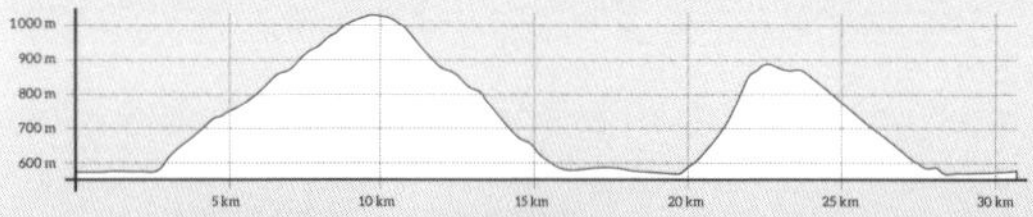

It is true that Alejandro Valverde (the eventual winner of the "rainbow" jersey) already had 250 km (155 mi) in his legs when he tackled the Gramart in the finals of the 2018 World Championships. Nevertheless, the greatest riders of their era all found themselves struggling (despite using gears designed for the likes of you and me) on a slope of barely imaginable incline: 2 km (1.25 mi) at an average gradient of 13%, but with the final 0.5 km (0.3 mi) at 19%, rising to 28% at one point. The Hell of Höttinger, as local cyclists call it (after the name of the district at its foot), lives up to its reputation. You must be in excellent condition to tackle this ascent, hence the short route distance. There is a warm-up in the shape of an initial climb above Igls, opposite Lake Lans, on the other side of the River Inn: a bracing 7 km (4.5 mi) at an average gradient of 6%. But conserve your energy for the "Hell" to come.

Distance	E+	Difficulty	Appeal
31 km (19 mi)	800 m (2,625 ft)	5/5	5/5

Outside of the winter season, Innsbruck only has connections to London, Amsterdam, and Vienna. Munich is 1h45 by train and car (160 km/100 mi). Vienna is 4h15 by train or 4h45 by car (500 km/310 mi). Milan is 5h20 by train or 4h15 by car (400 km/250 mi).

For caffeine fiends, there is just one address: Brennpunckt Coffee, the best coffee in town (roasted on site). Hearty snacks too.

Viaduktbogen 46-48
6020 Innsbruck
brennpunktcoffee.at

Go to road bike specialist Bike Point—only 500 meters/yards behind the train station—for any mechanical issues. Retailer of Specialized and Cannondale, among others.

Gumppstrasse 20
6020 Innsbruck
bike-point.at

ÖTZTAL-BAHNHOF
THE HELLISH GLACIER

High mountain / Expert *Map* *strava.com/routes/22909249*

Distance	E+	Difficulty	Appeal
104 km (65 mi)	2,150 m (7,055 ft)	5/5	5/5

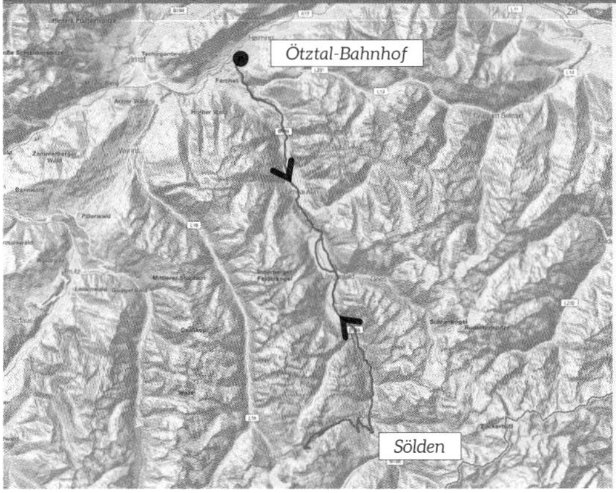

Sölden owes its worldwide reputation less to cycling than to the ski resort where Spectre (2015) was filmed and where the first races of the season of the downhill skiing World Cup are held each year on the Rettenbach glacier. Our incredible challenge is the ascent of the Ötztal Glacier Road in the shadow of Austria's second-highest peak, the Wildspitze (3,770 m/12,370 ft): 12 km (7.5 mi) at an average gradient of 10.4%, with three quarters of the climb between 10% and 12%. Only attempt the feat if you are as keen as Austrian alpine ski champion Marcel Hirscher's blades.

INNSBRUCK
TYROLEAN VALLEYS

High mountain / Advanced *Map* *strava.com/routes/22908727*

Distance	E+	Difficulty	Appeal
107 km (67 mi)	1,750 m (5,740 ft)	3/5	4/5

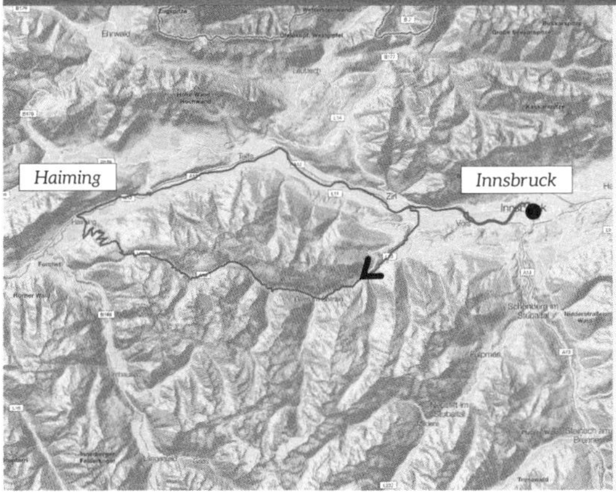

The Kühtai Saddle is a lovely pass rising to 2,017 m (6,617 ft) over 23 km (14.5 mi) at an average gradient of 6% from Kematen. At the top, the road winds its way between the ski lifts of the eponymous resort. Riding out of Innsbruck, we traverse one pass and two valleys of the kind found only in the Austrian Tyrol (the Stubai Alps, to be precise): wide, green, and at the foot of majestic peaks. Sellrain Valley is the first before we climb the Saddle, so fill your bottle with the invigorating water of the Rothenbrunn spring (km 21/mi 13). The second is the Inn Valley. There are many cycle paths—some of them on gravel.

SAINT-MORITZ
HIGH ALTITUDE LOOP

High mountain / Advanced
Map strava.com/routes/21469363
Test yourself km 33 (mi 21) strava.com/segments/4667096
Test yourself km 79 (mi 49) strava.com/segments/677009

It is rare, almost paradoxical, to climb three cols between 1,800 m (5,900 ft) and 2,300 m (7,545 ft) in a loop of barely 100 km (60 mi), with an elevation gain of less than 2,000 m (6,560 ft). But this challenge is possible if you start at the luxury resort of Saint Moritz.

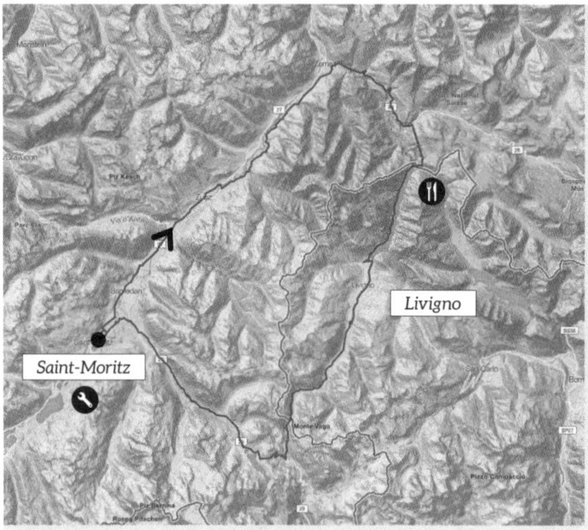

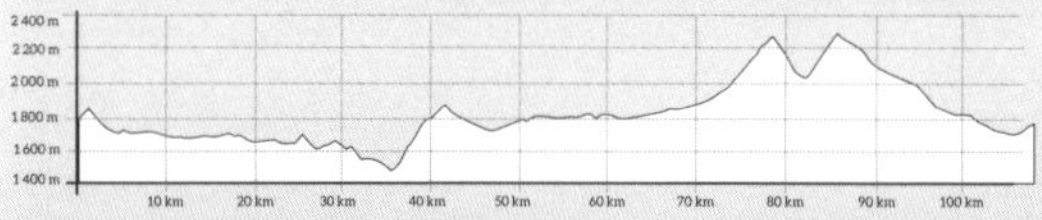

The high plains of South America and Mount Teide volcano on the Canary Islands are traditional destinations for cyclists seeking high-altitude training; however, they face some competition from this region straddling Switzerland and Italy. Leaving Saint Moritz, we are already at 1,822 m (5,977 ft), which helps. Our route heads north to the Engadin valley, where you can glimpse chamois and ibexes. Zenez is the lowest point on the route at 1,470 m (910 ft). The first stage of the Ofenpass up to Ova Spin reservoir is 6 km (4 mi) long at an average gradient of 6%. At km 45 (mi 28), you must take the shuttle bus through the Munt la Schera Tunnel (operational from June to September: €6/$7) into Italy, then cycle along Lago di Livigno and on to Livigno Pass (2,315 m/7,595 ft): 7 km (4.5 mi) long at just 5.5%, then the Bernina Pass (2,328 m/7,638 ft): 3.4 km (2.1 mi) of ascent at no more than 8%.

Distance	E+	Difficulty	Appeal
105 km (65 mi)	1,900 m (6,235 ft)	4/5	4/5

Zurich or Milan Malpensa Airports. Saint Moritz is 3h30 by train from Zurich to the northwest, and 5h from Milan Centrale to the south. By car, allow 2h40 to 3h for Zurich (200 km/125 mi), Milan (170 km/105 mi), and Innsbruck (200 km/125 mi).

At km 52 (mi 32), Ristoro Fopel is an old-style mountain inn. Perfect for a simple coffee, a plate of tagliatelle, or a cheese platter. Terrace by the lake.

Via della Val 6071
23030 Livigno SO, Italy

Less than 1 km (0.6 mi) from the station, Engadin Bikes specializes in the Giant and Liv brands. It also offers an excellent "bike doctor" service.

Via del Bagn 1
7500 Saint-Moritz
engadinbikes.com

DAVOS
SUMMIT OF SUMMITS

High mountain / Expert   Map strava.com/routes/23253715

Distance	E+	Difficulty	Appeal
117 km (73 mi)	2,800 m (9,200 ft)	4/5	4/5

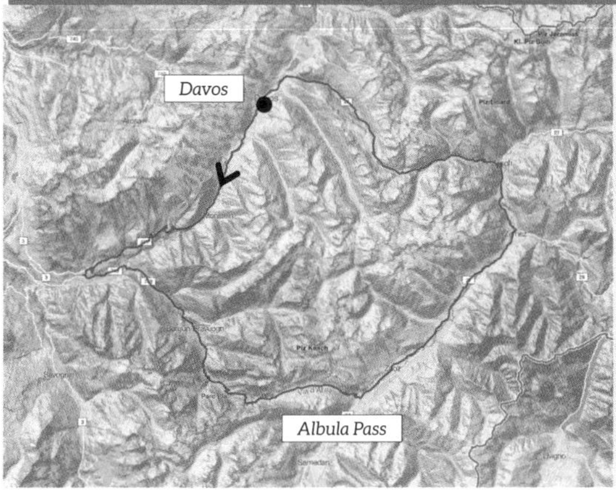

When we speak of the Davos summit, we tend to think of the annual World Economic Forum held at this Swiss ski resort. Our route, however, explores Alpine summits: two mountain passes above 2,300 m (7,545 ft), offering amazing panoramas. The Albula is a 22 km (14 mi) ascent from Filisur with an E+ of 1,300 m (4,265 ft). The 3 km (2 mi) after Bergün are at 10%, and the final 5 km (3 mi) at 8%. Cars are rare, and the road appears to flirt with the tunnels and viaducts of the Rhaetian Railway—the bright red train that serves the canton of Grisons. Finally, the Flüela Pass: 960 m (3,150 ft) of E+ from Susch.

SCHAAN-VADUZ
SECRETS OF LIECHTENSTEIN

High mountain / Advanced   Map strava.com/routes/23273994

Distance	E+	Difficulty	Appeal
68 km (42 mi)	1,800 m (5,905 ft)	4/5	4/5

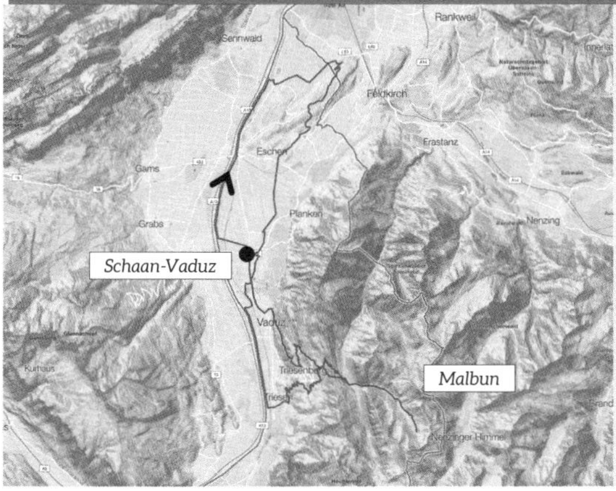

The Principality of Liechtenstein, the richest country in Europe, is modest in size: 160 km^2/62 sq mi (1/15th the size of Luxembourg), 78 km (49 mi) of borders with Switzerland and Austria, and has 38,000 inhabitants. We start at Schaan-Vaduz train station and ride up to the chic ski resort of Malbun (1,700 m/5,580 ft) by way of the cycle paths that run alongside the Rhine River on the western border, past a few vineyards. The big push comes at the end: 8 km (5 mi) at more than 11% after Triesen (km 37/mi 23), then 5 km (3 mi) at 9% from Steg to Malbun. The Austrian mountains are right before we return to Vaduz with its castle.

ANDERMATT
THE FINEST ALPINE 100 KM

- *High mountain / Expert*
- *Map strava.com/routes/21447495*
- *Test yourself km 15 (mi 9) strava.com/segments/15347304*
- *Test yourself km 51 (mi 32) strava.com/segments/4905381*

This is perhaps the finest 100 km (62 mi) Alpine ride that includes at least two major passes. Starting from Andermatt, you cross the Furka Pass, followed by the Nufenen Pass with its succession of switchbacks, and finally the Gotthard Pass via the old cobbled road. It is simply sublime.

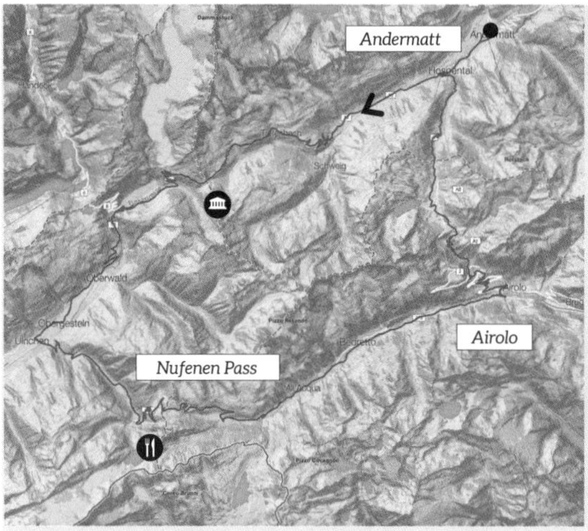

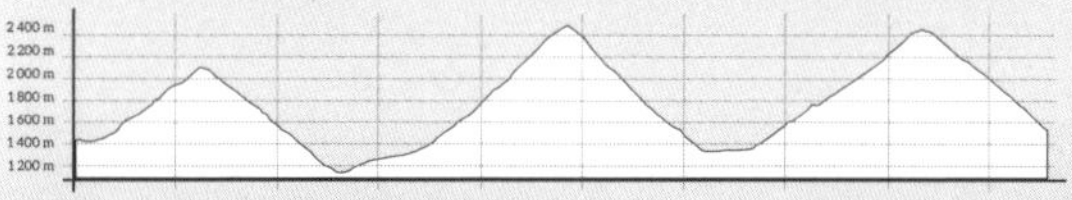

The elevation gain (3,300 m/10,800 ft) of this high-mountain challenge seems almost reasonable in light of the route itself: three Swiss passes, all more than 2,000 m (6,561 ft) high—every one of them a historic climb—but you never descend below 1,200 m (3,937 ft). First, we head up the Furka Pass (2,429 m/ 7,969 ft): 13 km (8 mi) at an average gradient of 7%, through a rocky landscape to the source of the Rhône, with surrounding peaks more than 3,500 m (11,482 ft) high. At Ulrichen, we begin the climb to the Nufenen Pass—the hardest part of this loop: a relentless 13 km (8 mi) at 8.6%, reaching 2,478 m (8,130 ft), but with an extraordinary perspective view of the switchbacks. Then descend the Ticino side toward Airolo (km 80/mi 50) before the ascent to the Gotthard Pass via the Vecchia Tremola ("old trembler")—13 km (8 mi) at 7.3% over cobbles that are nearly two hundred years old.

Distance	E+	Difficulty	Appeal
105 km (65 mi)	3,300 m (10,830 ft)	5/5	5/5

Andermatt is 2h20 by train and 1h40 by car (120 km/75 mi) from Zurich Airport, a major international hub. Allow 4h30 by train and 3h30 by car (330 km/205 mi) from Geneva Airport. Bern is 2h40 by train or 2h by car (180 km/112 mi).

Hearty mountain fare can be found at the restaurant of the Hotel Nufenen (km 56/mi 35), at an altitude of 2,478 m (8,130 ft), with fantastic views over the surrounding peaks.

3988 Obergoms VS
hotel-nufenen.ch

The iconic Belvedere Hotel (3 km/2 mi from the top of the Furka Pass) was featured in the film *Goldfinger*, but is currently closed. But you can visit its nearby ice cave, at the source of the Rhône, from June to October. Bring a jacket.

gletscher.ch

Switchbacks of the Vecchia Tremola on the south slope of the Gothard Pass, Switzerland.

INTERLAKEN
IN THE SHADOW OF THE EIGER

High mountain / Expert
Map strava.com/routes/22368410
Test yourself km 34 (mi 21) strava.com/segments/10056167
Test yourself km 47 (mi 29) strava.com/segments/1070982

The Grosse Scheidegg is not a well-known pass, but riding it is one of the most beautiful high-mountain cycling experiences that you can have in Europe. It is a tough climb, but the landscape is lovely, and the road is used almost exclusively by cyclists.

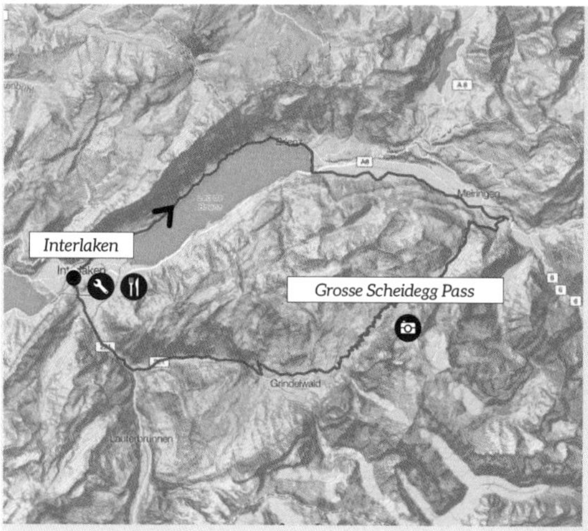

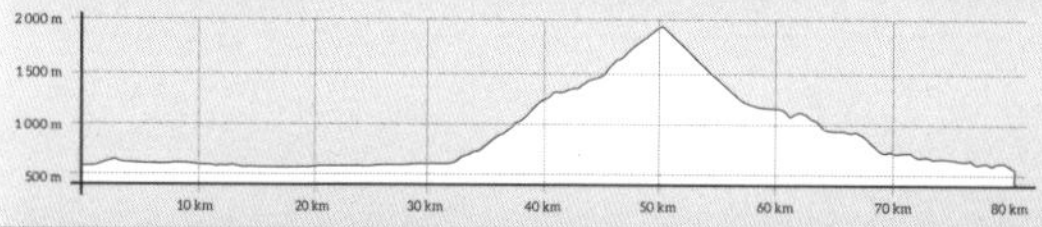

The surfacing of the Grosse Scheidegg Pass, was only completed in 1979. Since then, it has been used almost exclusively by cyclists and the yellow buses carrying hikers. Only guests staying at the Berghotel at the summit are allowed to drive up, which means that cyclists can focus fully on maximum effort: 16.4 km (10.2 mi) of ascent from Meiringen with nearly 1,300 m (4,265 ft) of E+ at an average gradient of 7.7% (with long portions at 10% to 12% toward the foot of the climb), plus a 0.5 km (0.3 mi) wall at 14% announcing the final 5 km (3 mi), which is at nearly 11%. The descent to Grindelwald—where a key scene of the James Bond film *On Her Majesty's Secret Service* (1969) was shot—is intoxicating, but take care. There is a wonderful view of the sheer north face of the Eiger (1,650 m/5,415 ft). Interlaken (pop. 5,600) is an ideal base camp, providing a key hour of warm-up beside the superb Lake Brienz.

Distance **81 km** (50 mi)

E+ **1,650 m** (5,400 ft)

Difficulty **4/5**

Appeal **5/5**

To the northwest, Bern is 1h20 by train or 1h by car (60 km/37 mi). Other Swiss airports are within close reach. To the northwest, Zurich is 2h by train or 1h45 by car (130 km/80 mi) via Lucerne. To the west, Geneva is 3h by train or 2h30 by car (220 km/137 mi).

Interlaken has its go-to spot: Vélo Café (the name speaks for itself), which has a cozy atmosphere, vintage decor, amazing bar, and snack menu.

Nionsgasse 10
3800 Interlaken
velo-cafe.ch

On the road to Grindelwald, there is no shortage of panoramas over the Eiger, Mönch and Jungfrau. From Grindelwald, you can ride the gravel climb to Kleine Scheidegg, where an extraordinary train ascends. You may not, however, bring your bike on board.

SION
CHALLENGES ABOVE THE RHÔNE

- *Low mountain / Expert*
- *Map strava.com/routes/22308384*
- *Test yourself km 16 (mi 10) strava.com/segments/9266511*
- *Test yourself km 77 (mi 48) strava.com/segments/3717520*

Valais is a pleasant, colorful canton with the burgeoning Rhône at the end of the valley, vineyards (including the popular Fendant), and the first levels of a rich mountain landscape. No big cols here, but there are short, sharp climbs to ski resorts. It is a challenge of guile and sinew.

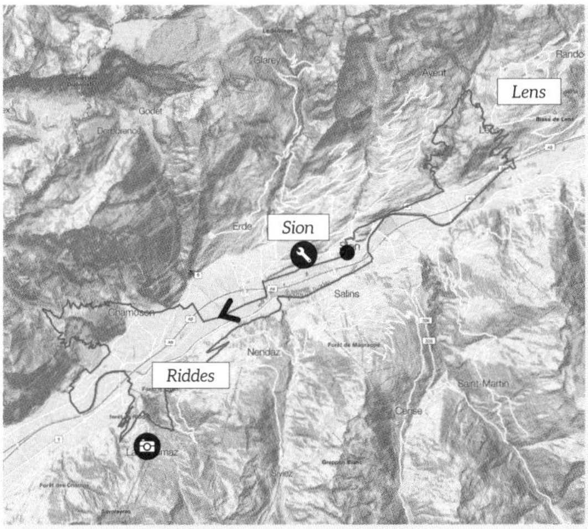

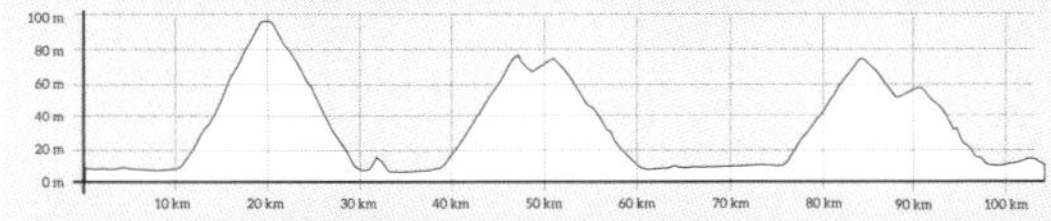

The indicated distances of the ascents are short, but they are not easy. Our route comprises three ascents of less than 10 km (6 mi). First, we climb from km 9 (mi 5.5) to Ovronnaz (also a spa resort): 9 km (5.5 mi) at an average gradient of nearly 10%. Next, we climb from Riddes Forest: km 39 (mi 24) to the charming village of Isérables: 8.4 km (5.2 mi) at nearly 9%. Finally, we climb from Granges (km 77/mi 48) to Lens: 8.3 km (5.15 mi) at 7.5%. Throughout, the road surfaces and layouts (series of multiple switchbacks) are perfect. Lower down, we pass vineyards—the pride of Valais—whereas higher up we ride between pastureland and forests of beech, ash, and Scots pine. We never climb above 1,400 m (4,595 ft), but that does not spoil the experience. At Riddes, you can continue straight on along the cycle path by the Rhône, reducing the ride to 90 km (56 mi) with 2,040 m (6,695 ft) of E+, which is already a lot.

Distance	E+	Difficulty	Appeal
105 km (65 mi)	2,550 m (8,350 ft)	4/5	4/5

Sion (pop. 35,000) is only 1h30 by train from Bern (the de facto capital) via Brig or 2h by car (160 km/100 mi). Geneva is 1h45 by train or 2h by car (160 km/100 mi). Milan (via Simplon) is 2h30 by train or 3h30 by car (250 km/155 mi).

In Riddes Forest (km 47/ mi 29), you can opt for the (tough) climb to La Croix-de-Coeur (2,171 m/7,125 ft) via La Tzoumaz: E+ of 1,000 m (3,280 ft) over 11 km (7 mi), with irregular surfacing over the final 6 km (3.7mi).

Located 0.5 km (0.3 mi) from Sion Train Station, Cycles Ferrero is a very old store that is very charming. Retailer of Giant, Felt, and Orbea.

Rue des Casernes 27
1950 Sion
cyclesferrero.com

MARTIGNY
AROUND LE CATOGNE

⊕ *High mountain / Advanced* ⊕ *Map strava.com/routes/22365265*

Distance	E+	Difficulty	Appeal
57 km (36 mi)	1,900 m (6,250 ft)	4/5	4/5

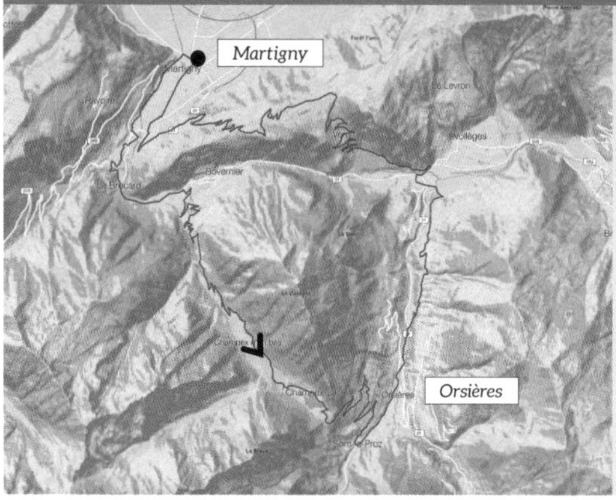

Appreciate the beauty of Le Catogne (2,598 m/8,524 ft) from every angle on this punchy route around the mountain. Setting off from Martigny, body and mind will be sorely tested as you climb 10 km (6 mi) to 1,466 m (4,810 ft) at more than 8%, before catching your breath at peaceful Lake Champex. The Col des Planches, though, is not to be outdone. As you pull yourself up its 8 km (5 mi) climb at 9%, through a landscape of trees, the valley soon becomes minuscule. Note that just before Les Rappes (km 5/mi 3), we are at the foot of the Petite Forclaz, a star difficulty in the 2020 Road World Championships.

STALDEN-SAAS
DAMS AND THE MATTERHORN

⊕ *High mountain / Expert* ⊕ *Map strava.com/routes/22350259*

Distance	E+	Difficulty	Appeal
120 km (75 mi)	2,850 m (9,350 ft)	5/5	5/5

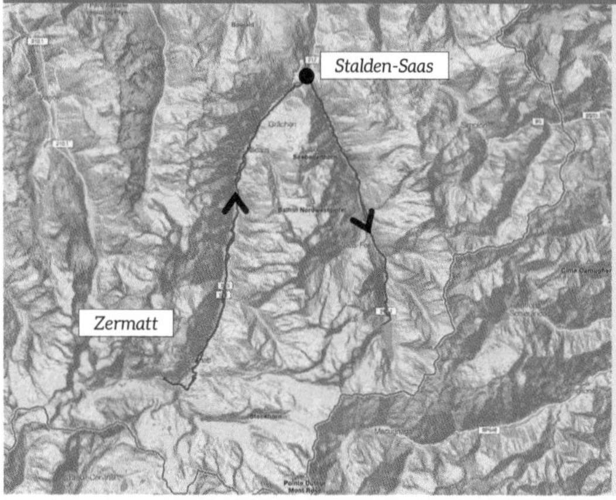

This route has a mountaineering feel, as we ride in the shadow of the Matterhorn, whose sheer faces straddle the border between Switzerland and Italy. A mecca for climbers, the mountain features in the logos of Paramount Pictures and Toblerone. Our XXL route (more than 3,000 m/9,845 ft of E+) up from Stalden-Saas may be split in two. The ascent to the Mattmark Dam in the east is 53 km (33 mi) long with an E+ of 1,600 m (5,250 ft). The climb to Zmutt Dam in the west (7 km/4.5 mi beyond Zermatt) is 70 km (44 mi) long with an E+ of 1,670 m (5,480 ft). Above you towers the wild, austere shape of the Matterhorn.

AIGLE
VAUD AND BERN

- *High mountain / Advanced*
- *Map strava.com/routes/21187230*
- *Test yourself km 62 (mi 39) strava.com/segments/832619*
- *Test yourself km 73 (mi 45) strava.com/segments/1573064*

The Bernese Alps straddle several cantons. Our route, inspired by the cycling guide and storyteller Alain Rumpf (strava.com/athletes/11794), passes mostly through the Vaud canton, with a small section through the Bern canton. Watch out for traffic in the Col des Mosses.

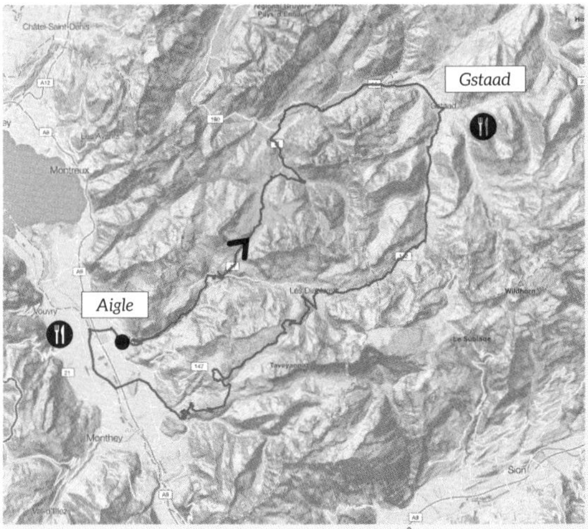

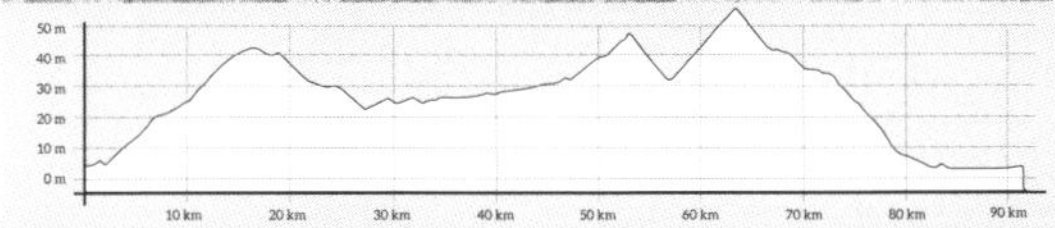

Situated in the Swiss Rhône Valley, barely 15 km (9 mi) from Lake Geneva, Aigle holds a special place in cycling as the headquarters of the Union Cycliste Internationale (UCI). Our route is a pretty alpine ride through parts of the French-speaking Vaud and German-speaking Berne cantons, via three beautifully surfaced passes: the Mosses (1,455 m/4,773 ft), the Pillon (1,546 m/5,072 ft), and the La Croix (1,778 m/5,833 ft). The elevation gain is close to 3,000 m (10,000 ft), but you can spare yourself the 600 m (1,968 ft) of the La Croix by carrying straight on at Les Diablerets (km 73/mi 45) toward Ormont-Dessous. That would be a pity though, because the third climb is the most attractive not only in terms of the cycling (8 km/5 mi of sustained gradient between 7% and 8%), but because of the fantastic view of the Dents du Midi from the summit. Better to pace yourself on the long Col des Mosses.

Distance	E+	Difficulty	Appeal
113 km (70 mi)	2,550 m (8,350 ft)	4/5	4/5

From Geneva to Aigle, 90 minutes by train and 1h20 by car (110 km/68 mi), Chamonix is 1h15 (80 km/50 mi), and Zurich is 2h30 (230 km/143 mi). Remember to buy an obligatory sticker (vignette) for the freeways: $40, valid 14 months (December to following January).

The World Cycling Centre (headquarters of the UCI) has its own cafe-restaurant, Vélodrome, open every day for both sports and leisure cyclists.

Chemin de la Mêlée 12
1860 Aigle
cmc-aigle.ch/velodrome

For a coffee or a snack en route, turn off into Gstaad (km 52/mi 32) and stop at Charly's, a cozy, friendly coffee shop amid the bustle of this luxury resort.

Promenade 76
3780 Gstaad
charlys-gstaad.ch

AIGLE
A TASTE OF GRUYÈRE

Medium mountain / Advanced — *Map strava.com/routes/22329638*

Distance	E+	Difficulty	Appeal
133 km (83 mi)	1,850 m (6,100 ft)	3/5	4/5

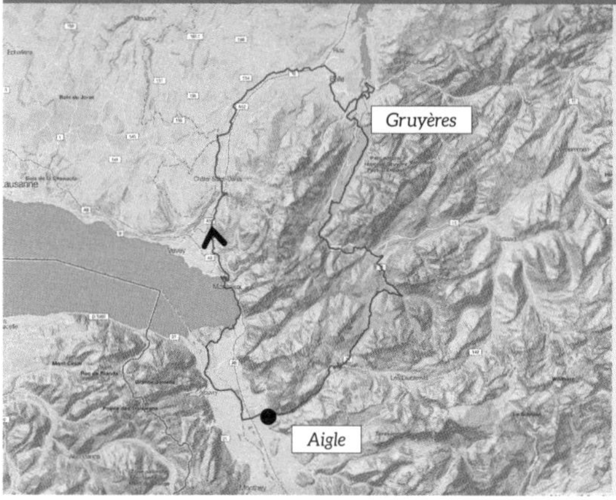

Cheese (without holes), chocolate, castles, and pleasant roads: this loop through Gruyère in the Pays-d'Enhaut District, located east of Lake Geneva, is full of promise. After leaving Aigle and hauling yourself above Montreux, you will find some superb views at Châtel-Saint-Denis. From Bulle, you glimpse what is coming next, and it is splendid: the town of Broc—home to Cailler, the Swiss chocolate pioneer; Gruyères and its castle; picturesque La Tine, and Rossinière (see the facade of the huge Grand Chalet). Then, climb the gentle 12 km (7.5 mi) of the Col des Mosses before descending back to Aigle.

LAUSANNE
ROMANESQUE JEWEL

Very hilly / Advanced — *Map strava.com/routes/22323791*

Distance	E+	Difficulty	Appeal
98 km (61 mi)	1,300 m (4,250 ft)	3/5	4/5

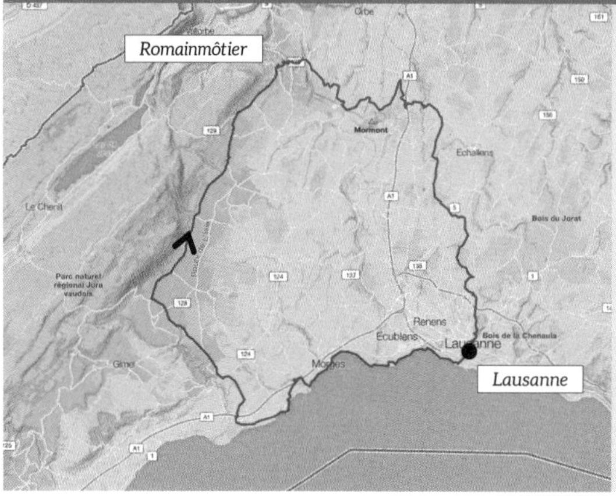

On the shores of Lake Geneva, Lausanne is the headquarters of the International Olympic Committee, which has a lovely museum. Above it, the radiant countryside of the canton of Vaud boasts a fine selection of Romanesque churches, including the marvelous former Cluniac priory of Romainmôtier (pop. 540), one of the most beautiful villages in the country. We reach this Romanesque jewel, which is constructed of yellow Vaud stone, halfway through the ride, having left the vineyards behind us and with the Jura Plateau ahead. We are not far from the Joux Lake and Valley, the cradle of Swiss watchmaking.

GENEVA
FRENCH SWITZERLAND

Low mountain / Intermediate — *Map strava.com/routes/23255037*

Distance	E+	Difficulty	Appeal
98 km (61 mi)	1,650 m (5,415 ft)	3/5	4/5

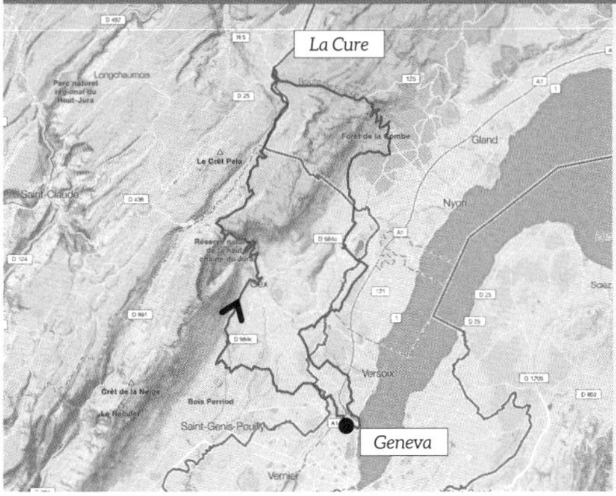

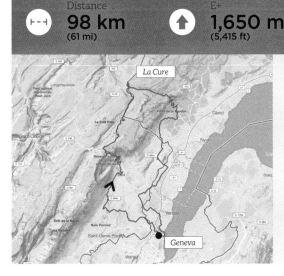

Playing with the French border is second nature in Geneva. From Velosophe Shop in Chambésy—where a house-brewed beer awaits your return—cycle out of the city, past the Ferney-Voltaire customs post, and up into the mountains of the French Jura via Gex and the Col de la Faucille—a classic climb forgotten by Tours de France: 12 km (7.5 mi) at an average gradient of 6%, and then 20 km (12.5 mi) of plateau—a paradise for cross-country skiers—to La Cure before a descent to the border through Combe Forest over the ramp of the former Bonmont Abbey and through Divonne-les-Bains. Do not forget your passport.

NEUCHÂTEL
RIDE ON TIME

Low mountain / Advanced — *Map strava.com/routes/22342092*

Distance	E+	Difficulty	Appeal
154 km (96 mi)	2,400 m (7,900 ft)	4/5	4/5

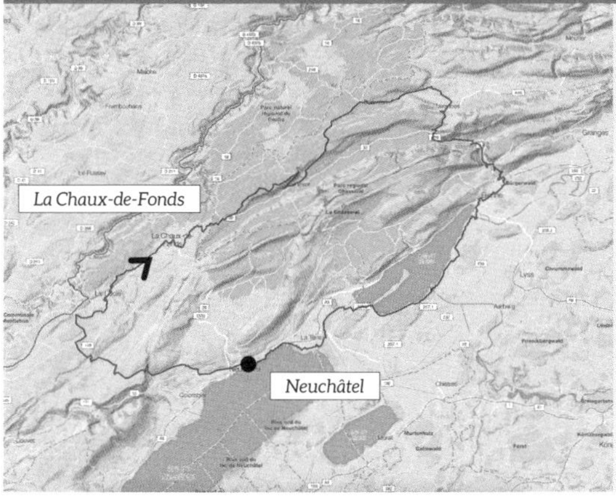

We ride out of Neuchâtel and up into the Jura Mountains via the ramps of La Tourne (9 km/5.5 mi at 6%). This is the beating heart of Swiss watchmaking. First comes Le Locle, home to Tissot (the official timekeeper of world cycling) and its museum. Next are La Chaux-de-Fonds (home to the International Museum of Horology), Saint-Imier (where Longines watches are made), and Bienne (where Omega, Rolex, and Swatch are based). There is little danger of being late, but if you are, you may take a very tempting shortcut from Saint-Imier via the pretty Chasseral Pass and avoid the tough Mont Crosin Pass (5 km/3 mi at more than 8%).

NEUCHÂTEL
A LAKE FULL OF HISTORY

- *Low mountain / Intermediate*
- *Map strava.com/routes/21446791*
- *Test yourself km 26 (mi 16) strava.com/segments/650670*
- *Test yourself km 132 (mi 82) strava.com/segments/9064452*

At 38 km (23 mi) long and 8 km (5 mi) at its widest, Lake Neuchâtel has an imposing position at the foot of the Jura Mountains. It is the largest entirely Swiss lake—Lake Geneva being shared with France, and Lake Constance with Germany and Austria.

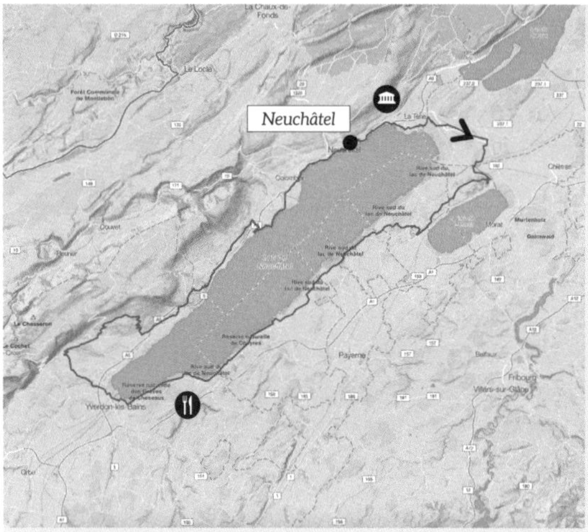

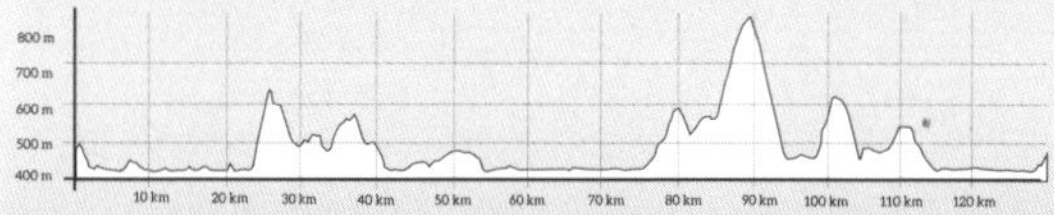

This ride around Lake Neuchâtel is long, but relatively easy. Departing in a clockwise direction (this is the land of watchmakers, after all), we climb Mont Vully (km 26/mi 16), a strategic route for more than two millennia: 2.3 km (1.4 mi) at an average gradient of nearly 10%. This provides our first panorama before we descend alongside Lake Morat, which is somewhat smaller than its neighbor. We reach the south bank of Lake Neuchâtel at Estavayer and ride along it until Yverdon-les-Bains at the western end, and the Neolithic standing stones of Clendy. From the top of the Tévenon ramp (4 km/2.5 mi at 8%), the view is stunning. Further on, at Gorgier, you can turn off the route and climb up to the Creux du Van, an amphitheater-shaped canyon, but be warned: there is an elevation gain of 1,000 m (3,200 ft), although the promise of a beer in the sunshine by Neuchâtel Castle should encourage you.

Distance	E+	Difficulty	Appeal
129 km (80 mi)	1 500 m (4,900 ft)	3/5	4/5

Neuchâtel is 1h40 by train from Basel Airport to the north, or 1h45 by car (130 km/80 mi). To the south, Geneva Airport is 2h by train, or 1h30 by car (120 km/75 mi). Bern is 50 minutes by train, and 1h by car (60 km/37 mi).

At km 68 (mi 42), Le Colvert is a perfect spot where you can feast on fresh fish from the lake. Open every day, 8 a.m. to midnight.

Avenue des Pins 34
1462 Yvonand
lecolvert.ch

Neuchâtel old town is worth exploring, with its simple, *Protestant*-influenced architecture. Visit the castle and the twelfth-century collegiate church. There is a superb view from the top of the Tour des Prisons.

j3l.ch

BERNE
EMMENTAL VALLEY

- *Low mountain / Intermediate*
- *Map strava.com/routes/21446456*
- *Test yourself km 24 (mi 15) strava.com/segments/2441197*
- *Test yourself km 41 (mi 25) strava.com/segments/696607*

The Emmental valley lies to the east of Bern—Switzerland's de facto capital. It is a landscape of meadows and pastures grazed by Simmental cattle (white and light-brown coat), which produce the famous cheese. There are also some fantastic cycling routes.

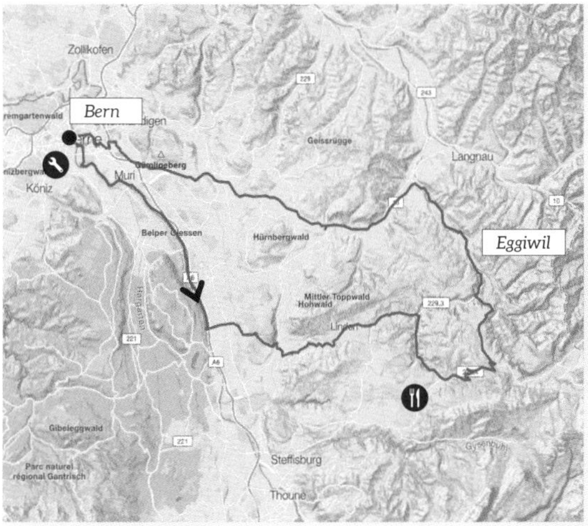

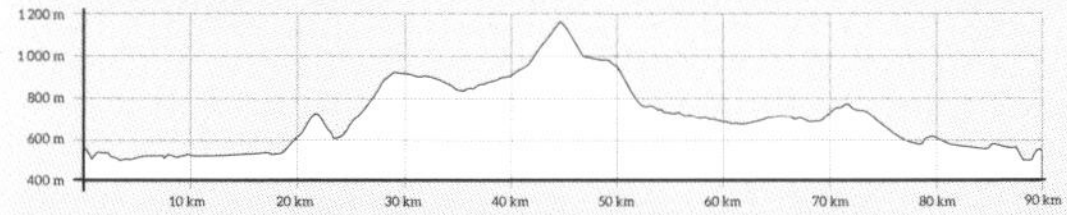

Here, in the German-speaking part of Switzerland, they are rightly proud of their local cheese, Emmental, with its fruity flavor and regular holes. Leaving behind the attractive old city of Bern, we follow the fast-flowing Aare River. At km 18 (mi 11), we reach the foothills of the Bernese Oberland, and a climb of 5 km (3 mi) at a gradient of 6.5% to the ski resort of Linden, followed by the 4.5 km (3 mi) winding Schallenberg Pass after Oberei, at a gradient of 6%. Here, we are at an altitude of 1,163 m (3,815 ft). The descent is exhilarating. At Eggiwil (km 54/mi 33), we follow the Emme River along the valley. At Grosshöchstetten (km 72/mi 45), the route becomes a kind of ode to Switzerland's most exported cheese as we return to Bern and its arcades, not far from the house where Albert Einstein once lived when he was a promising young physicist.

Distance	E+	Difficulty	Appeal
100 km (62 mi)	1,400 m (4,600 ft)	3/5	4/5

Bern is 1h15 from Zurich Airport by train and 1h30 by car (120 km/75 mi). It is 2h from Geneva Airport by train or by car (160 km/100 mi).

Step off your bike at award-winning cheese producer Hans-Rudolph Gasser in Oberei, close to km 40 (mi 25) for a snack and to taste some delicious Emmental.

Oberei 313
3618 Süderen
berg-kaeserei-oberei.ch

Located approximately 1 km (0.6 mi) south of Bern train station, Schaller is Bern's go-to bike store. It has a large showroom and was once a sponsor of the young Fabian Cancellara.

Seftigenstrasse 57
3007 Berne
schaller-radrennsport.ch

AARAU

HEAVEN IN AARGAU

Very hilly / Intermediate

Map strava.com/routes/23310795

Distance	E+	Difficulty	Appeal
77 km (48 mi)	1,400 m (4,600 ft)	3/5	4/5

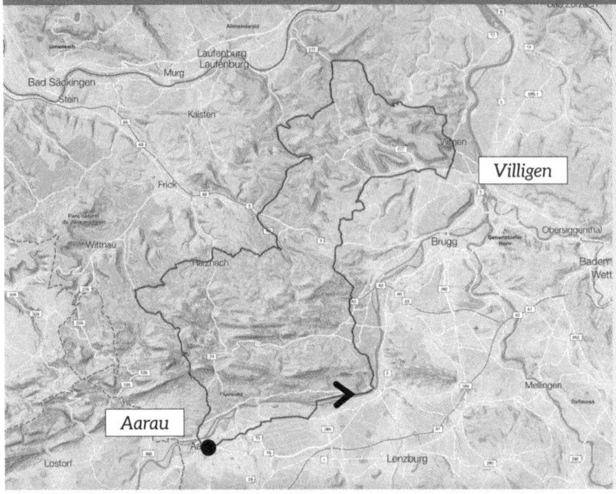

Northern Switzerland between the Rhine and the Aar rivers, Zurich, and Basel, is rather urban. The greenery of the Aargau Jura is an exception—a real paradise. The pastureland goes right up to 500 m (1,640 ft) above orchards and vineyards, and beneath pine forests and a few rocky peaks. The route gets bumpier after Schinznach, Villingen, and Oberbüren around the mountain of Cheisacher with its wooden observation tower. Having crossed the Table Jura, we climb the Benkerjoch Pass (680 m/2,230 ft) before returning to Aarau, pausing to enjoy the splendid view south over the Alps.

ZURICH

THE RHINE FALLS

Hilly / Intermediate

Map strava.com/routes/23287834

Distance	E+	Difficulty	Appeal
119 km (74 mi)	1,550 m (5,100 ft)	3/5	4/5

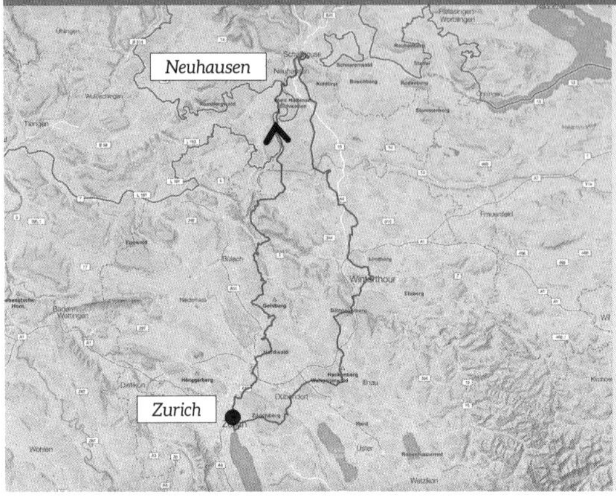

From Zurich, the most expensive city in Europe, the simple pleasure of an excursion north to the Rhine Falls is priceless. We skirt Zurich Airport and climb Büliberg mountain (590 m/1,935 ft). At Rheinau (km 47/mi 29), an abbey stands on an island in the middle of the Rhine river, where it twists into extreme meanders. The surrounding villages are divine, and there is a magical feel that turns into high drama at Neuhausen (km 52/mi 32) before the intense spectacle of the Rhine Falls. Return via Schaffhausen, Winterthur, the heights of Adlisberg, the mouth of the Limmat on the lake, and Zurich old town.

GERMANY

BLACK FOREST

BADEN-WÜRTTEMBERG

BAVARIA

SAXONY

BERLIN

FREIBURG IM BREISGAU
EXPLORE THE BLACK FOREST

- *Low mountain / Advanced*
- *Map strava.com/routes/21260987*
- *Test yourself km 16 (mi 10) strava.com/segments/12280389*
- *Test yourself km 40 (mi 25) strava.com/segments/4632481*

This route is inspired by the Strava account of Simon Geschke, the man with the most striking beard in the Tour de France peloton. The German rider has an intimate knowledge of the roads and the paths less traveled of the Black Forest. strava.com/pros/13872795

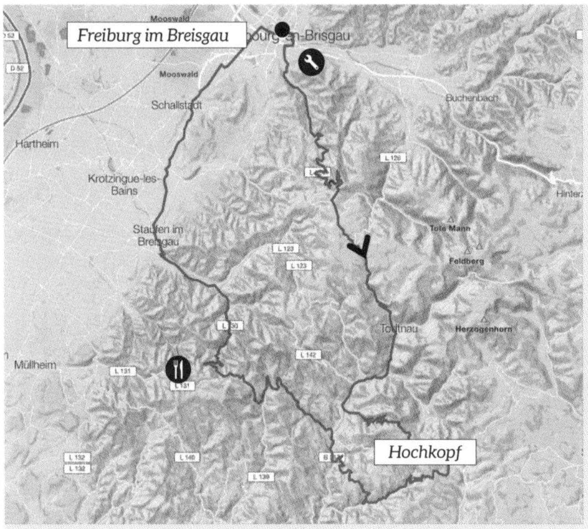

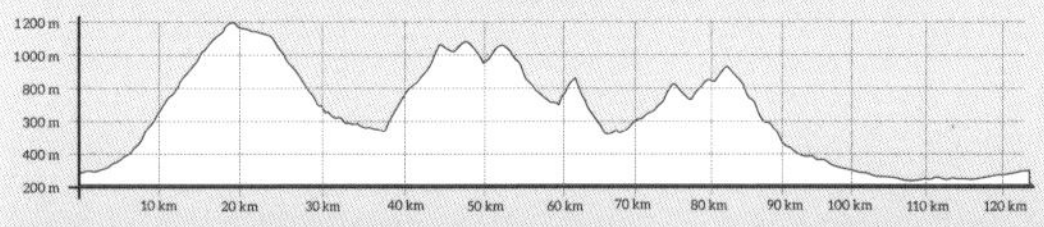

Simon Geschke serves up a superb ride through woods of spruce, fir, and beech south of the city of Freiburg im Breisgau, in this corner between France and Switzerland. It is a longish ride, but two-thirds of the climbing is concentrated in the first half. The 11.5 km (7 mi) of the Schauinsland (average gradient: 7%) are soon devoured. At km 19 (mi 12), you find yourself at the highest point of this Black Forest itinerary: 1,196 m (3,924 ft). As you ride out of Schönau (km 46/29 mi), you hit the Fuchswald with its 7 km (4.5 mi) at an average gradient of 8% (rising to 20% over the final 300 meters/yards, just before the Hochkopf ski slopes). Four more shorter climbs—from 2 km (1.25 mi) to 6 km (3.7 mi)—await before Hinterheubronn (km 85/53 mi). There, follow nearly 40 km (25 mi) of gentle descent to the Altstadt, Freiburg's old town, with its Gothic cathedral with a single spire.

Distance	E+	Difficulty	Appeal
122 km (76 mi)	2,500 m (8,200 ft)	4/5	4/5

Freiburg im Breisgau is 1h40 by train or 1h by car (90 km/55 mi) from Strasbourg, 40 minutes by train from Basel, and 2h by train from Frankfurt.

Having tackled the final climb, stop at Berggasthof Haldenhof (km 84/mi 52), a typical mountain hotel where you can eat from midday to 8 p.m., at km 84 (mi 52).

Haldenhof 1, Ortsteil Neuenweg
D-79692 Kleines Wiesental
haldenhofberggasthof schwarzwald.de

With its beautiful open workshop, Dynamo Bikes—located less than 2 km (1.25 mi) from Freiburg Train Station—is well worth a visit.

Schwarzwaldstrasse 149
79102 Freiburg im Breisgau
dynamo-bikes.de

FREIBURG IM BREISGAU
HIGHEST VILLAGE

Low mountain / Expert — *Map strava.com/routes/23412766*

Distance **107 km** (67 mi) · E+ **2,100 m** (6,900 ft) · Difficulty **4/5** · Appeal **4/5**

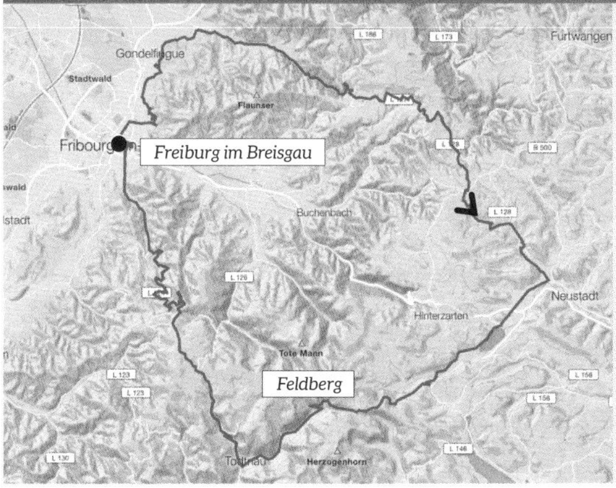

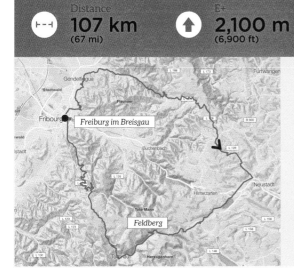

East and southeast of Freiburg im Breisgau lie some of the most impressive parts of the Black Forest. There is no shortage of climbing either. Feldberg (km 64/mi 40) is the highest village in the country (1,277 m/4,025 ft). We reach it following a 5 km (3 mi) ascent at 6% after the Titisee lake, a major summer tourism spot that is itself at 850 m (2,790 ft). Preceding it is a 23 km (14.5 mi) climb to the ski resort of Thurner (km 39/mi 24). Ration your effort. After Feldberg, there is a 6 km (3.7 mi) ascent at 8% to reach Schauinsland (the road peaks at 1,200 m/3,940 ft) before the long descent to Freiburg.

BADEN-BADEN
GRAND SPA

Low mountain / Advanced — *Map strava.com/routes/23487004*

Distance **110 km** (68 mi) · E+ **2,000 m** (6,550 ft) · Difficulty **4/5** · Appeal **4/5**

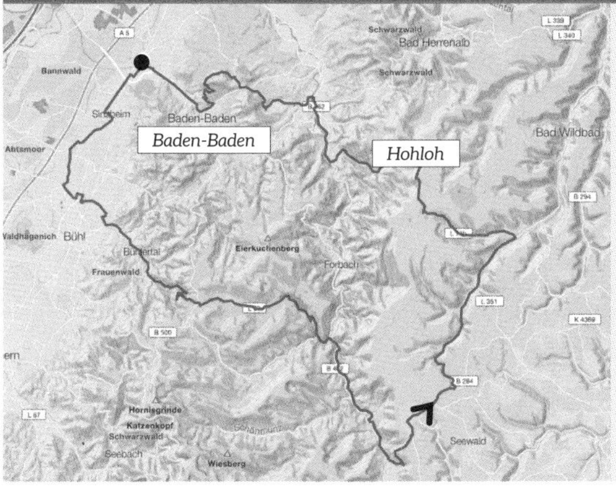

The train station of Baden-Baden lies several miles from the town center, allowing you to warm up the legs before tackling the rugged contours of this northern part of the Black Forest. Baden-Baden is one of the chicest spa towns in the world—a baroque paradise to be enjoyed at the end of the day's ride. There are three "peaks" to conquer: Mehliskopf (8 km/5 mi at 7%), the wall of Schönegründ (2.5 km/1.5 mi at 13%), and Hohloh with its watchtower—the highest point on our route (935 m/3,070 ft) through one of the most beautiful low-mountain ranges in Europe (5 km/3 mi at 6%).

The endless horizons of the Black Forest, Germany.

CONSTANCE
PLEASURES OF THE UNTERSEE

- *Low mountain / Intermediate*
- *Map strava.com/routes/22263634*
- *Test yourself km 32 (mi 20) strava.com/segments/7479660*
- *Test yourself km 63 (mi 40) strava.com/segments/3762032*

In the foothills of the Alps, Lake Constance straddles the border between Germany, Switzerland, and Austria. Fed by the Rhine, it has something of the charm of Italy, with warm temperatures and vineyards. This tour around its smaller part, the Untersee, takes in two lovely climbs.

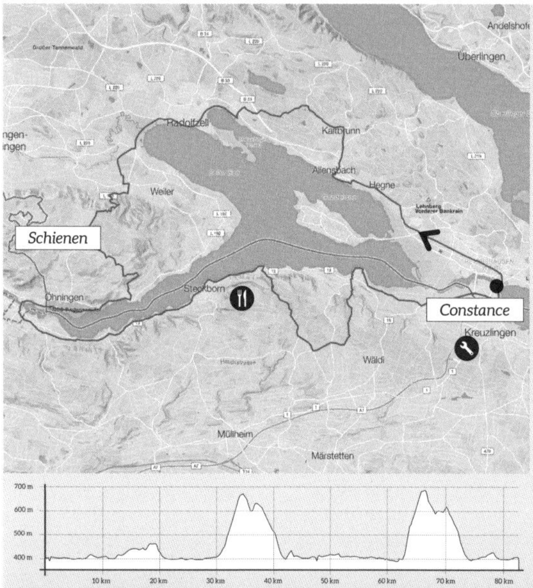

Lake Constance is Germany's top vacation spot, and one of the largest lakes in Western Europe. Its particularity is that the Obersee, its larger part, is connected to the smaller Untersee by a 4 km (2.5 mi) stretch of the Rhine. The town of Constance straddles both banks. This loop around the Untersee takes in the Radolfzeller Nature Reserve (km 24/mi 15) and rolls gently past vineyards, although it is a stiffer pedal when the foehn mountain wind is blowing. Two ascents lift you 300 m (1,000 ft) above the water: the Schiener Berg in Germany—4 km (2.5 mi) long at an average gradient of 7%, with the summit at km 35 (mi 22)—and the Berlinger Berg in Switzerland—3.5 km (2 mi) long at an average gradient of 9%, with the summit at km 66 (mi 41). After your ride, stroll through Constance and see the Romanesque cathedral with Gothic spire, and the old Paradies quarter.

Distance	E+	Difficulty	Appeal
83 km (52 mi)	950 m (3,100 ft)	3/5	4/5

Constance (pop. 80,000) is just 1h30 by train or 55 minutes by car (70 km/43.5 mi) from Zurich. Strasbourg is 3h by train via Offenburg or 2h30 by car (180 km/112 mi). Munich is 5h by train via Ulm or 3h30 by car (230 km/143 mi).

On the Swiss side, Pipo's Bar (km 63/mi 39) is a perfect spot to enjoy an espresso on a terrace looking over the lake, right at the foot of the Berlinger Berg.

Pipo's Bar
Philipp Kaster, West Point
8267 Berlingen
pipos-bar.ch

At the entrance to Altstadt (Constance's old town), Radical is a beautiful bike store with impeccable service. Retailer of BMC.

Inselgasse 13
78462 Constance
radial.de/cms-team.asp

FRIEDRICHSHAFEN
ZEPPELIN TOWN

- *Hilly / Intermediate*
- *Map strava.com/routes/22264671*
- *Test yourself km 16 (mi 10) strava.com/segments/1751951*
- *Test yourself km 34 (mi 21) strava.com/segments/6810622*

The historic town of Friedrichshafen (pop. 60,000), where Zeppelin airships were built, hosts the Eurobike trade fair each year in early summer. It is a pity that few attendees will have time to savor the delights of Lake Constance and the countryside of Baden-Württemberg.

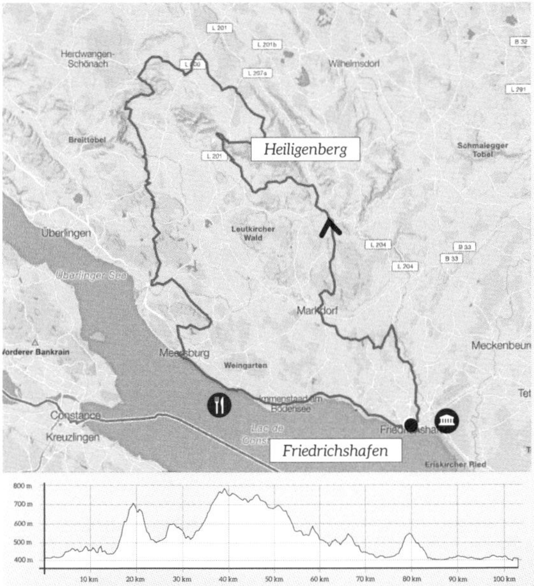

Beyond the opposite (Swiss) bank of Lake Constance, you can see the line of the Alps not too far away. Our loop on the northern side in the German state of Baden-Württemberg does not include any mountains, even though we start in Friedrichshafen, where the legendary Zeppelin airships were built, and where the cream of bicycle manufacturers gather each year for the Eurobike trade fair. The highest that we reach is 800 m (2,625 ft) above sea level. The climbing is gentle on perfect roads, past picturesque villages of low-roofed houses blooming with flowers. Away from the lake, Gehrenberg (km 16/mi 10) is a 3 km (2 mi) ascent at more than 7%, but it is the toughest part of a route, which does not ease up until after the Baitenhauser climb: 2 km/1.25 mi at 5%, with a pretty panorama over Lake Constance. The final 20 km (12.5 mi) run along the shore from Meersburg to Friedrichshafen.

Distance	E+	Difficulty	Appeal
104 km (65 mi)	1,350 m (4,450 ft)	3/5	3/5

To the north, Stuttgart is 3h50 by train or 2h40 by car (200 km/125 mi). To the east, Munich is 4h15 by train or 2h30 by car (200 km/125 mi). To the southwest, Zurich (Switzerland) is 2h by train or 2h15 by car (130 km/80 mi).

If you feel like enjoying the lake on the way back, take a seat on the charming terrace of Seeblick restaurant in the little pleasure port of Hagnau (km 88/mi 55). Open all day.

Seestrassee 11
88709 Hagnau am Bodensee
seeblick-hagnau.de

If you attend the Eurobike trade fair, spend half a day at Zeppelin Museum—the world's largest aviation collection—on Friedrichshafen Port (km 103/mi 64).

Seestrasse 22
88045 Friedrichshafen
zeppelin-museum.de

FÜSSEN
ROMANTIC ESCAPE

- *Hilly / Intermediate*
- *Map strava.com/routes/22260657*
- *Test yourself km 68 (mi 42) strava.com/segments/8083476*
- *Test yourself km 98 (mi 61) strava.com/segments/7924651*

Füssen (pop. 15,000) is the southernmost point on the Romantic Road—a route dreamt up in the 1950s to link several picturesque German towns and castles. Several pivotal scenes in *The Great Escape* (1963) were filmed here. The town is also the gateway to the Allgäu Alps.

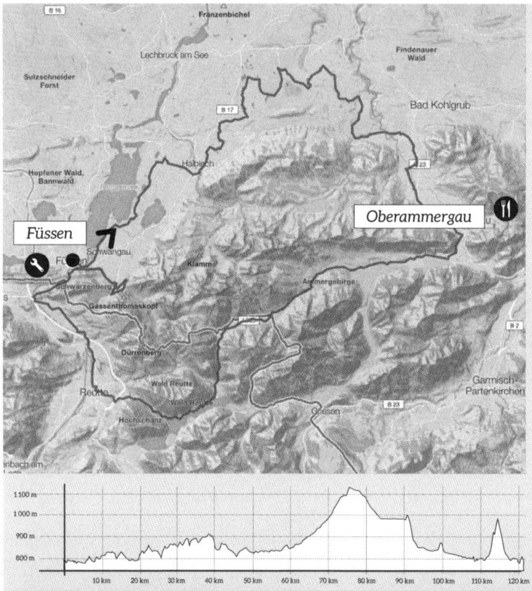

Mountain, water, forest: Everything is perfect in Allgäu. This 121 km (75 mi) route is nothing but harmony. It starts in Füssen, with its red-tiled roofs and the Lech river, which is the terminus of the Romantic Road. The Austrian border is on the way out of town. We will return from that direction. Our route never descends below 800 m (2,625 ft), but it does not climb excessively either—1,133 m (3,718 ft) at its highest point on the border. Close to Oberammergau is beautiful Ettal Abbey. The 30 km (19 mi) stretch through Austria runs alongside the Plansee (at 1,000 m/3,280 ft), a superb mountain lake, before Reutte and its hanging pedestrian bridge. We roll back to Füssen before one final steep ascent via the flamboyant castles of Hohenschwangau and Neuschwanstein. There is a stunning view of the latter from the Marienbrücke footbridge (km 114/mi 71).

Distance	E+	Difficulty	Appeal
121 km (75 mi)	1,200 m (3,950 ft)	3/5	4/5

To the northeast, Munich is 2h30 by train via Ausbourg or 1h50 by car (140 km/87 mi). To the northwest, Stuttgart is 3h40 by train or 2h30 by car (220 km/137 mi). To the south, Innsbruck (Austria) is 5h30 by train or only 1h45 by car (110 km/68 mi).

The promise of the charming Edelweiss cafe (plus a flamboyant baroque abbey) is encouragement enough to turn off the route at km 57 (mi 35) to Ettal (barely 1 km/0.6 mi).

Kaiser-Ludwig-Platz 3
82488 Ettal
edelweiss-ettal.de

Located 1 km (0.6 mi) from Füssen Train Station, CUBE Store focuses on the iconic German bicycle brand. Workshop services for all bike models.

Froschenseestrasse 45
87629 Füssen
multicycle.de

MUNICH
SISI'S PARADISE

- *Fairly flat / Intermediate*
- *Map strava.com/routes/21207149*
- *Test yourself km 13 (mi 8) strava.com/segments/2942031*
- *Test yourself km 73 (mi 45) strava.com/segments/1922007*

This ride round the translucent waters of Lake Starnberg is a classic and a favorite among the Strava community in Munich. It is 95 km (59 mi) long with stunning Alpine views, lush greenery, and a hearty dose of pure romanticism.

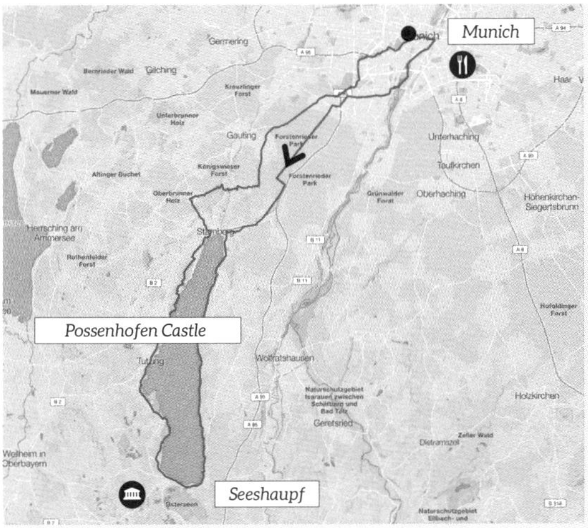

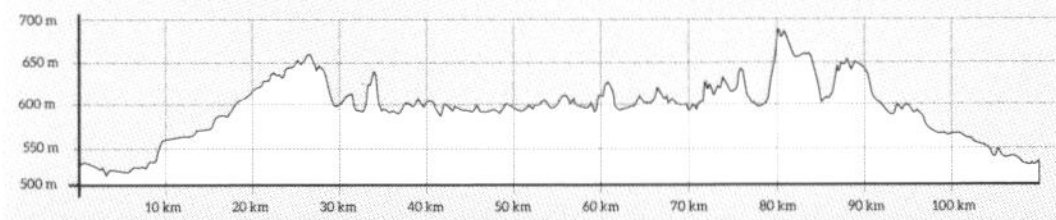

Starting at the famous Hellabrunn Zoo and Thalkirchen Metro Station, we head southwest out of Munich through the vast Forstenrieder Park on a cycle path running along Olympiastraße. At Percha (and still on a cycle path), we hit the northern end of the lake, which is 21 km (13 mi) long by 3.5 km (2.2 mi) wide. It is a popular vacation spot for Munichers. Seven grassy beaches stretch around the lake with the panorama of the Alps as a backdrop. Starnberg also has a firm place in the German imagination because of the rococo Possenhofen Castle (km 72/mi 45), where "Sisi," the future Empress Elisabeth of Austria, grew up. Enjoy a pleasant pause in "Possi" Park, a refreshing dip off the jetty opposite romantic Rose Island (where King Ludwig II of Bavaria had a little villa, which is now a museum), or a swim at Paradise Beach—Sisi's favorite, of course.

Distance	E+	Difficulty	Appeal
110 km (68 mi)	650 m (2,150 ft)	2/5	3/5

Munich is very well connected by plane, train, and bus. Forget the car in town, where only the most environmentally friendly vehicles are allowed. The route starts from Thalkirchen Metro Station on line U3. Bicycles are allowed outside of peak hours.

For breakfast on the way out or a snack when you return, Wünsche Bakery, located a stone's throw from Thalkirchen Metro Station, is ideal.

Schäftlarnstrasse 181-183
81371 Munich
backstube-wuensche.de

Stop at (or return to) the Buchheim Museum of Imagination (km 53/mi 33): an example of amazing contemporary architecture, with a diverse collection and a welcoming cafeteria.

Am Hirchgarten 1
82347 Bernried
buchheimmuseum.de

NUREMBERG
PUNCHY FRANCONIA

Hilly / Intermediate *Map strava.com/routes/22694299*

Distance	E+	Difficulty	Appeal
110 km (68 mi)	1,350 m (4,430 ft)	3/5	4/5

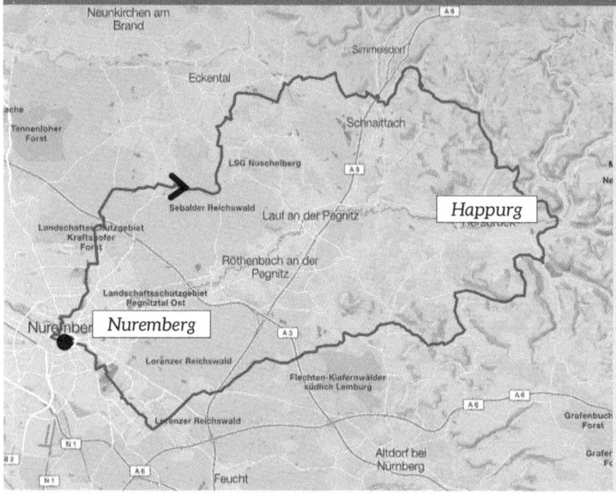

Middle Franconia in north Bavaria—the land of beer brewing and sausage with horseradish sauce—offers a terrain with ramps that climb for 200 m (655 ft) to 300 m (985 ft) and that require a punchy approach. Above the Pegnitz Valley, the Glatzenstein (km 38/mi 24) rises for 2 km (1.25 mi) at 10%. Further on, the Deckersberg serves up a good 3 km (2 mi) at more than 7%. Wooded hills alternate with fields of crops. Despite its troubled history, Nuremberg, which is 1h by train from Munich, is splendid. It has pretty cobbled streets, proud churches, ramparts so thick that they support gardens, and Kaiserburg Castle.

REGENSBURG
DANUBE AND JURA

Hilly / Intermediate *Map strava.com/routes/22693063*

Distance	E+	Difficulty	Appeal
86 km (53 mi)	850 m (2,790 ft)	2/5	3/5

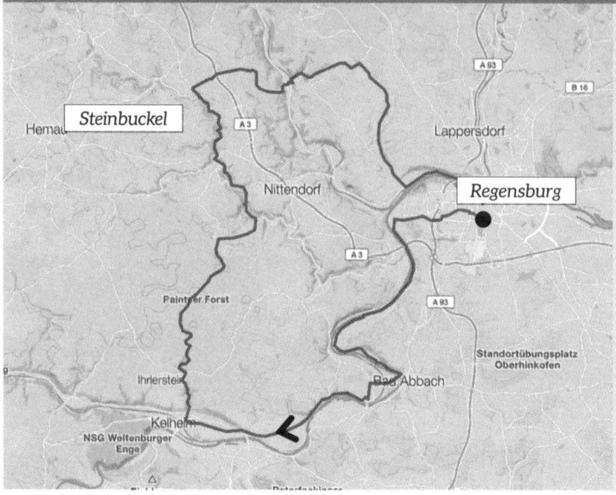

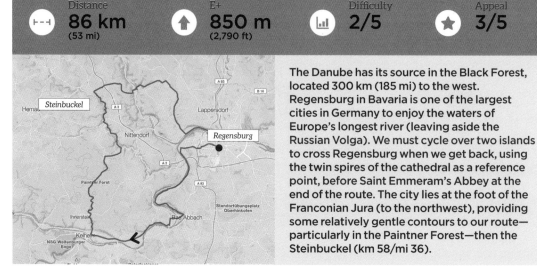

The Danube has its source in the Black Forest, located 300 km (185 mi) to the west. Regensburg in Bavaria is one of the largest cities in Germany to enjoy the waters of Europe's longest river (leaving aside the Russian Volga). We must cycle over two islands to cross Regensburg when we get back, using the twin spires of the cathedral as a reference point, before Saint Emmeram's Abbey at the end of the route. The city lies at the foot of the Franconian Jura (to the northwest), providing some relatively gentle contours to our route—particularly in the Paintner Forest—then the Steinbuckel (km 58/mi 36).

GOTHA
THE HILLS OF THURINGIA

🌐 *Hilly / Intermediate*
🌐 *Map strava.com/routes/21418782*

⊕ *Test yourself km 24 (mi 15) strava.com/segments/695315*
⊕ *Test yourself km 64 (mi 40) strava.com/segments/678259*

The Thuringian-Franconian Highlands—Germany's lungs—lie on the edge of old East Germany. These low mountains are all under 1,000 m (3,280 ft), but there is a lot of cycling around Oberhof, the German cross-country skiing capital.

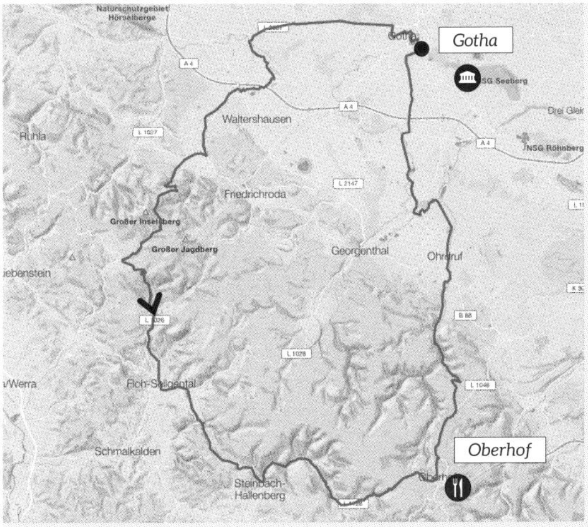

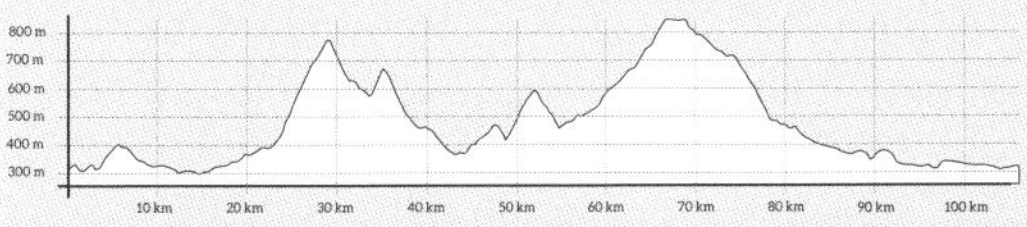

The hilliest stages of the Deutschland Tour take place in the heart of the Thuringian Highlands, guaranteeing fine media coverage. To get the most out of a ride through these parts, it is better to start in Gotha than in Erfurt, the state capital. This means that the climbing commences at km 24 (mi 15) with the ascent of the classic Grosser Inselsberg: 5 km (3 mi) at an average gradient of 6.5%. The forested slopes and the rounded summits evoke the profiles of the Vosges in France. There are some stiff climbs here—chiefly, the 1.5 km (1 mi) Brotterode at km 35 (mi 22), at an average gradient of 7%; then the 3 km (2 mi) Rotteroder Höhe at 5.5%; and, finally, the Grenzadler, 10 km (6 mi) climb at a gradient of 4%, but with the final 3 km (2 mi) being somewhat steeper. Oberhof (altitude 810 m[/2,657 ft]) is very popular in winter with devotees of biathlon. In summer, cyclists are welcomed liked royalty.

Distance	E+	Difficulty	Appeal
107 km (66 mi)	1,700 m (5,580 ft)	3/5	4/5

Gotha (pop. 45,000), the fifth largest city in the state of Thuringia, is 20 minutes from Erfurt by train or 30 minutes (30 km/18.5 mi) by car. From Leipzig, allow 1h- to 2h by train or 2h by car (180 km/112 mi). Frankfurt Airport is 2h40 by train or 2h30 by car (230 km/143 mi).

They know how to eat in Oberhof (km 69/mi 43). With the climbs behind you, sit down at Thüringer Hütte and enjoy some *Thüringer Rostbratwurst* (a local sausage).

Am Grenzadler 3
98587 Oberschönau
thueringen.info/thueringer-huette.html

Do not miss the superb seventeenth century Friedenstein Palace in Gotha. Fascinating museum and archives, and impressive fortifications.

Schlossplatz 1
99867 Gotha
stiftungfriedenstein.de

LEIPZIG
COAL LAKES

Fairly flat / Intermediate
Map strava.com/routes/22621238

Test yourself km 11 (mi 7) strava.com/segments/15610977
Test yourself km 54 (mi 33) strava.com/segments/10023082

In Leipzig, where composers Richard Wagner was born and Johann Sebastian Bach died, the sweet music of everyday sports cycling resounds. The most populous city in Saxony is resolutely green, as evidenced by this southern excursion to the former coal mines turned into lakes.

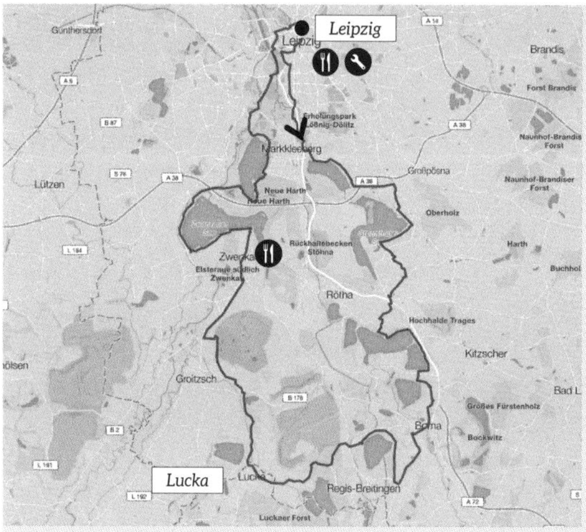

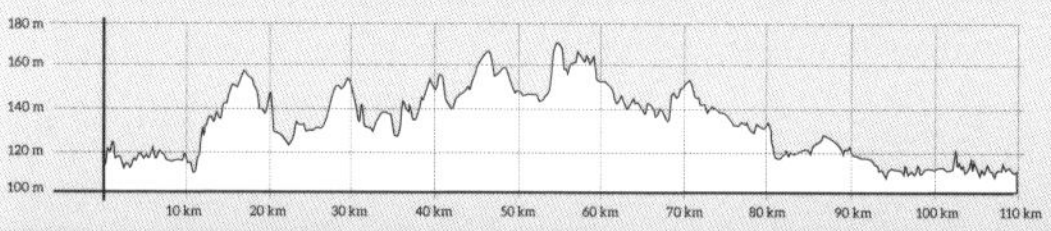

The alternative, green, university city of Leipzig, which played a key role in the development of the German railways, is a buzzy place. Bicycle culture is well established, and car drivers pay attention to bike riders even outside of the cycle paths. The green spaces seem limitless: 2,500 ha (6,180 acres) in all. Happiness is assured on condition that you accept the flat relief of the Plain of Saxony. One of the loveliest rides out from the city is a loop to the south around the artificial lakes of the reclaimed coal mines of the former East Germany. There are twenty-two in total, covering 7,000 ha (17,300 acres). We ride along the shores of the Markkleeberger, the Störmthal, the Zwenkauer, and the Cospudener lakes. On the way out of Leipzig, we pass the hip student neighborhood of Südvorstadt, as well as Connewitz, with its little courtyard gardens. We return via the former industrial area of Plagwitz, which is now full of artists' studios.

Distance
110 km
(68 mi)

E+
400 m
(1,300 ft)

Difficulty
2/5

Appeal
3/5

Leipzig/Halle Airport is 30 minutes by train, but there are few European flights. Berlin is better: 1h10 by train or 2h20 by car (190 km/120 mi). To the southwest, Frankfurt is 3h by train or 4h by car (400 km/250 mi). To the southeast, Prague is 5h by train or 3h by car (260 km/160 mi).

Located in the Neuschönefeld neighborhood, Coco No Fahrradladen is a bike cafe with a warm, friendly, and slightly weird and vintage atmosphere—a bit like the city itself. It draws real enthusiasts.

Wiebelstrasse 10
04315 Leipzig
facebook.com/cocofahrradladen

Stop at the charming Café Kandler on Markkleeberg marina (km 96/mi 60), right by the water. It serves excellent bratwurst and delicious rostis with apple compote.

Hafenstrasse 23
04416 Markkleeberg
cafekandler.de

PIRNA
SURPRISING SAXONY

Very hilly / Advanced — *Map strava.com/routes/23417134*

Distance	E+	Difficulty	Appeal
95 km (59 mi)	1,200 m (3,950 ft)	3/5	4/5

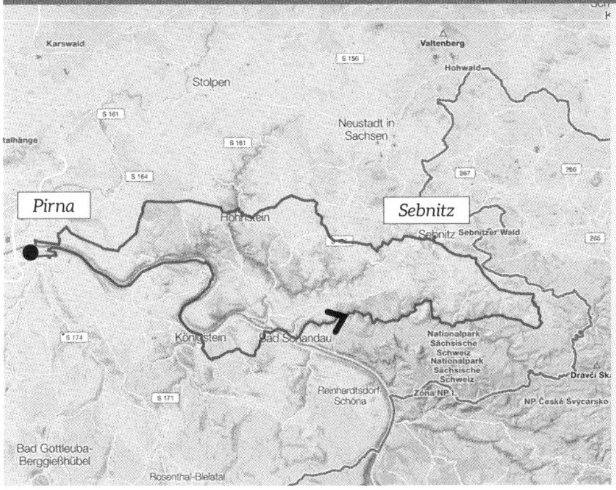

The amazing sandstone formations of Saxon Switzerland are the setting for this route southeast of Dresden between the Elbe Valley and the Czech border. No mountains here! We never climb above 400 m (1,315 ft). The rocky landscape, which is an unbelievable jumble of stone chimneys, sometimes evokes the American West. From Pirna and its castle, we ride along the Elbe to Königstein Fortress before a 2 km (1.25 mi) ascent at 10%. The climbs that follow are less brutal. If you turn left toward the Elbe at km 77 (mi 48), you are only 10 minutes from the Bastei, the most amazing rocky spectacle in Saxon Switzerland.

AUE
THE ORE MOUNTAINS

Low mountain / Advanced — *Map strava.com/routes/23482473*

Distance	E+	Difficulty	Appeal
96 km (60 mi)	2,250 m (7,380 ft)	4/5	4/5

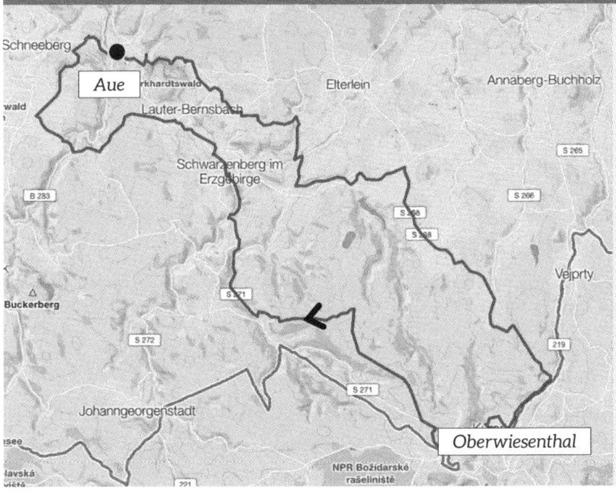

Despite global warming, the Ore Mountains remain the "Saxon Siberia," so come here between June and September, when the area becomes choice cycling terrain. The gentle curves belie the constantly changing relief. There are no long ascents here, but our route comprises more than 2,000 m (6,560 ft) of elevation gain. From the mining town of Aue (110 km/68 mi south of Leipzig), which formerly prospered thanks to silver, tin, and nickel, we climb to the former East German ski resort of Oberwiesenthal and the Fichtelberg (at 1,100 m/3,610 ft). The Czech border is right there as we straddle Saxony and Bohemia.

BERLIN
CAPITAL FORESTS

- *Fairly flat / Advanced*
- *Map strava.com/routes/22251680*
- *Test yourself km 20 (mi 12) strava.com/segments/11705452*
- *Test yourself km 115 (mi 71) strava.com/segments/8510559*

Berlin's passion for cycling comes in various forms, although there are few contours to speak of. The countryside to the north lends itself very well to two-wheeled exploration. A hybrid bike is de rigueur. Get some tips from Standert Mitte, where we begin our ride.

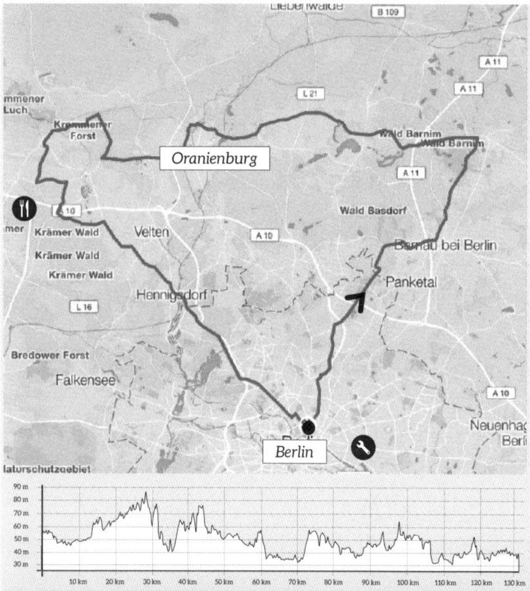

Germany is a forested country, even if we tend to imagine it as being urban and industrial. Trees cover 11 million ha (27 million acres)—one-third of Germany's surface area! Berlin is surrounded by greenery. To the north, once you leave the urban jungle of Mitte and Pankow, you ride either through or between beech forest(s)—the smooth, silvery tree trunks illuminated by shafts of sunlight that pierce the canopy. The last Ice Age left its traces here in the form of lakes and marshes. The forests of Biesenthal, Kremmen, and Krämer lend themselves to different kinds of cycling. In the course of this long, heart-shaped route, the asphalt is punctuated by gravel or cobblestone sections. We also pass sites that recall the darkest moments of history, such as the Sachsenhausen National Memorial (km 63/ mi 39) in Oranienburg, where the Nazis interned tens of thousands of mainly political prisoners.

Distance	E+	Difficulty	Appeal
132 km (82 mi)	**650 m** (2,130 ft)	**3/5**	**4/5**

Berlin is highly accessible by plane, train, and road. Bicycles are part of the culture here, whether in the parks or on public transit. You might be asked to pay a fee of around €1.50 ($1.65) to bring your bicycle on the subway.

In addition to their Performance concept store in Kreuzberg, Standert Bicycles have opened a modern and bohemian space in the Mitte neighborhood.

Invalidenstrasse 157
10115 Berlin
standert.de

If you are getting hungry with 1h30 to go, the terrace of the Gartenhaus is the place to stop. It is located only a few pedal strokes off the route at km 98 (mi 61) and offers an appetizing menu.

Hauptstrasse 95
16727 Oberkrämer
gartenhaus-schwante.de

BERLIN

TAKEOFF FOR TEMPELHOF

Fairly flat / Intermediate — *Map strava.com/routes/22551052*

Distance	E+	Difficulty	Appeal
75 km (47 mi)	350 m (1,150 ft)	2/5	3/5

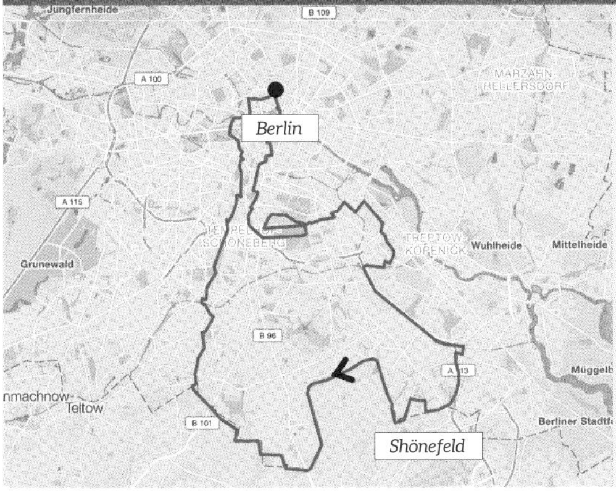

From the Standert Urban store in the north of Spandau and Mitte, this route heads south of Berlin via the old Tempelhof Airport, which closed in 2008 and has been turned into a giant park that Berliners have made into a popular cycling spot, both for sport and for recreation. You can repeat the 4 km (2.5 mi) loop ad infinitum or else continue further along Teltow Canal, for example, to chase some KOMs, or along the Berlin Wall Trail, starting in Schönefeld (km 39/mi 24) very close to the new Willy Brandt Airport, to explore this vestige of twentieth century history: the Iron Curtain made concrete.

COTTBUS

THE SORBIAN SPREE

Fairly flat / Intermediate — *Map strava.com/routes/23482159*

Distance	E+	Difficulty	Appeal
106 km (66 mi)	360 m (1,180 ft)	2/5	3/5

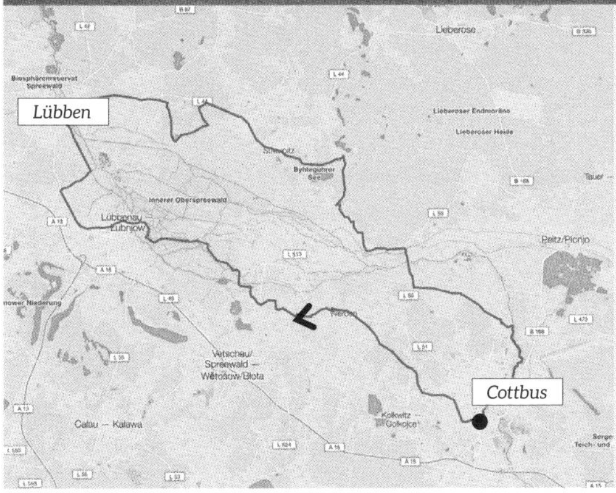

A short distance from Poland and 1h30 by train from Berlin (100 km/62 mi by car), the town of Cottbus is right next to the Spreewald Biosphere Reserve in the heart of the forest that bears the name of the major river of the former East Germany. There is not the slightest ramp here—only vast areas of marshes and no fewer than two hundred canals. There are many cycle paths, lined with alders and pines, leading to the historical village of Lehde and Lübbenau Castle. You might well feel like swapping your bike for a boat or kayak for an immersion in the culture of the Sorbs, a Slavic minority who still live here.

BERLIN
GO WEST

- *Flat / Intermediate*
- *Map strava.com/routes/21913741*
- *Test yourself km 28 (mi 17) strava.com/segments/1001152*
- *Test yourself km 33 (mi 21) strava.com/segments/1062268*

In the absence of any meaningful hills, green spaces are the key draw of Berlin—that apparently limitless megacity. Taking barely two hours, this western trek loops through Grunewald forest, the banks of the Havel, and Charlottenburg Palace. It is a delight.

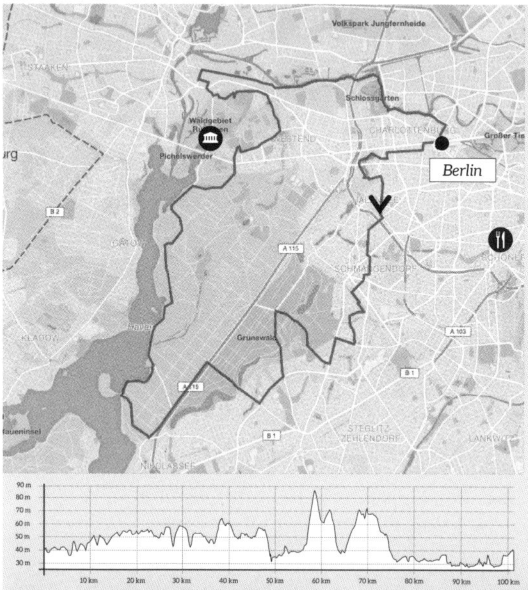

Berlin, the capital of Germany, seems made for cyclists. This 51 km (32 mi) route, which begins at buzzy Ernst-Reuter-Platz (easily accessible by public transit from across the city), is a two-hour loop covering a fair amount of greenery and providing a glimpse of Berlin's history. It avoids the main thoroughfares (such as the prestigious Kurfürstendamm) by way of side streets and parks where cycling is permitted. At km 12 (mi 7.5), you enter the vast forest of Grunewald (3,000 ha/7,400 acres), with its Scots pines and oaks. It covers half the route and incorporates several short gravel sections. Next, we ride alongside the Havel River at its widest point, before making a detour in front of the Olympic Stadium (1936 Summer Games), then the cycle path beside the Spree River. At km 47 (mi 29), we pass Charlottenburg Palace, the largest one in the city and the baroque residence of the kings of Prussia.

Distance	E+	Difficulty	Appeal
51 km (32 mi)	350 m (1,150 ft)	2/5	4/5

Berlin is highly accessible by plane, train, and road. Bicycles are part of the culture here, whether in the parks or on public transit. You might be asked to pay a fee of around €1.50 ($1.65) to bring your bicycle on the subway.

Before or after your ride, head to the Mitte district, east of the Tiergarten park, for a snack at Steel Vintage Bikes, a perfect bike cafe in every way.

Wilhelmstrasse 91, Mitte
10117 Berlin
steel-vintage.com

Check out the monumental Olympic Stadium (km 35/ mi 28), scene of Jessie Owens's triumph in the face of the Nazis, and Zinedine Zidane's headbutt in the 2006 World Cup Final.

Olympischer Platz 3
14053 Berlin
olympiastadion.berlin

BERLIN
ESCAPE TO POTSDAM

- *Fairly flat / Intermediate*
- *Map strava.com/routes/22249844*
- *Test yourself km 69 (mi 43) strava.com/segments/7676905*
- *Test yourself km 95 (mi 59) strava.com/segments/1001152*

Whether pedaling down cycle paths alongside the Havel river or rolling across the parks of greater Berlin, it is hard to imagine the complex history of Potsdam. The city was once the capital's alter ego before being literally walled off from Berlin during the Cold War.

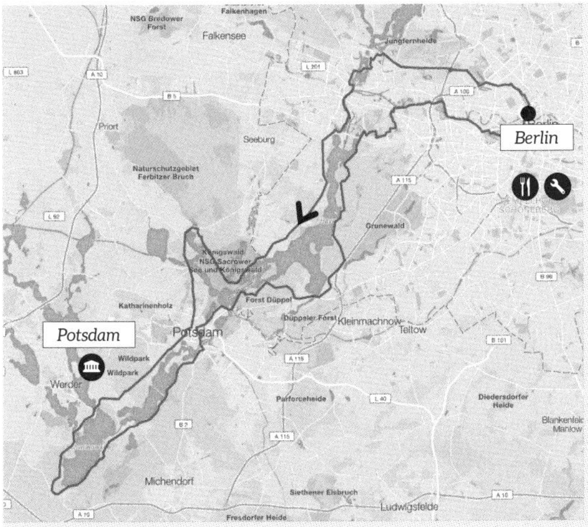

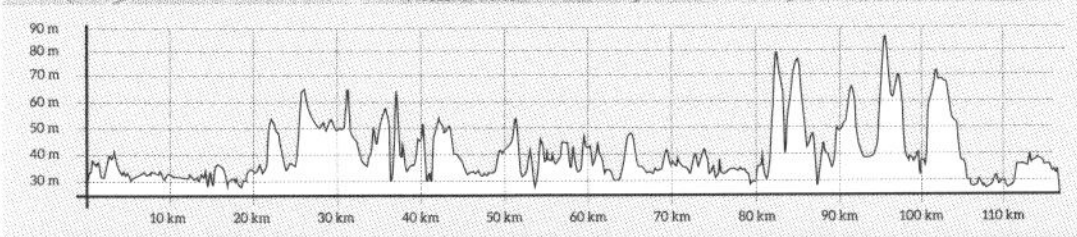

Given the fairly flat terrain and the abundance of cycle paths, the western part of greater Berlin seems limitless. Setting out from the central station, along the banks of the Spree, you can easily pedal for quite a distance on the way to glorious Potsdam and beyond. The Schifffahrt canal leads to Spandau lake, then along the right bank of the Havel, which widens to nearly 2 km (1.25 mi) at Kladow (km 28/ mi 17). You will no longer be sure if you are following the river's course or skirting the lakes of Sacrower, Lechnitz, and Templiner that it links. In Postdam, you will ride past Sanssouci Palace and Brandenburg Gate on the way out at km 45 (mi 28), then through the narrow cobbled streets on the way back at km 76 (mi 47). The left bank of the Havel is even greener with Düppel and Grunewald forests, Olympic Stadium, and Charlottenburg Palace. Cycling in Berlin is a royal treat.

Distance	E+	Difficulty	Appeal
116 km (72 mi)	550 m (1,800 ft)	3/5	4/5

Berlin is highly accessible by plane, train, and road. Bicycles are part of the culture here, whether in the parks or on public transit. You might be asked to pay a fee of around €1.50 ($1.65) to bring your bicycle on the subway.

Located 300 meters/yards south of Checkpoint Charlie, Standert Bicycles has created a sublime concept store and bike cafe in Kreuzberg.

Friedrichstrasse 23a
10969 Berlin, Germany
standert.de

Potsdam (30 minutes by train from Berlin) is known for its cobbled streets, pastel houses, and Sanssouci Palace, an eighteenth century rococo extravagance with elaborate gardens that was once considered to be the "Prussian Versailles."

potsdam-tourism.com

HEIDELBERG
STUNNING ODENWALD

Low mountain / Advanced — *Map* strava.com/routes/22962241

Distance	E+	Difficulty	Appeal
112 km (70 mi)	1,850 m (6,000 ft)	4/5	5/5

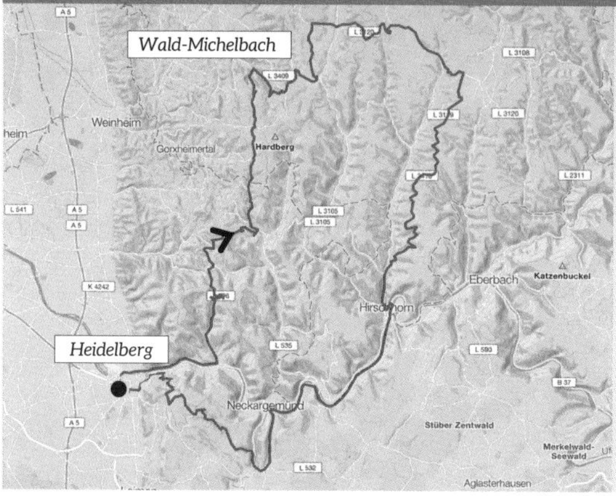

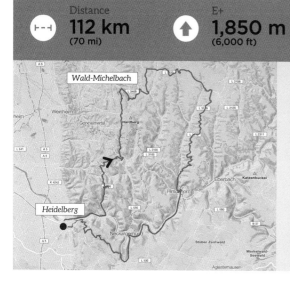

With its old bridge, colorful narrow cobbled streets, and infinitely wonderful baroque architecture, Heidelberg (1h by train from Frankfurt) is rightly considered the most romantic city in Germany. It also has tons of cycling appeal. This 112 km (70 mi) loop through the beautiful Odenwald mountains is a must—not only for the sport (there are some vicious ramps) but also for the contemplative pleasure: forests, traditional villages, the shape of the Hardberg, and the descent to fascinating Heidelberg Castle—the oldest parts of which date from the thirteenth century—overlooking the Neckar Valley.

HEIDELBERG
ABOVE THE NECKAR

Low mountain / Intermediate — *Map* strava.com/routes/23006675

Distance	E+	Difficulty	Appeal
61 km (38 mi)	1,000 m (3,300 ft)	3/5	4/5

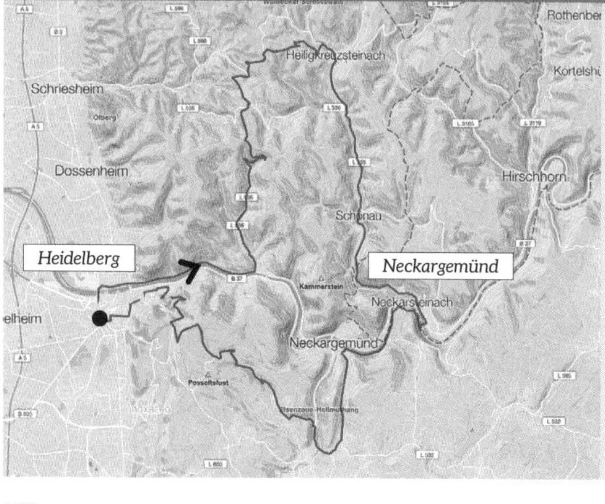

From Heidelberg, a university city with a population of 160,000, you can enjoy the nearby slopes of the Odenwald without having to worry about distance. We start by tackling the 6 km (3.7 mi) climb at 7% to the plateau of the Dossenheimer Kopf at more than 500 m (1,640 ft). You may continue to the Hardberg if you wish. The final part of the route is spiced up by the 6 km (3.7 mi) ascent of the Königstuhl at a gradient of more than 6% when climbed from the Elsenz Valley. There is also much pleasant riding to be done around the meanders of the Neckar. Of course, take the time to stroll around Heidelberg.

FRANKFURT AM MAIN
INVIGORATING TAUNUS

Low mountain / Advanced *Map strava.com/routes/23528246*

Distance	E+	Difficulty	Appeal
91 km (57 mi)	1,350 m (4,430 ft)	3/5	3/5

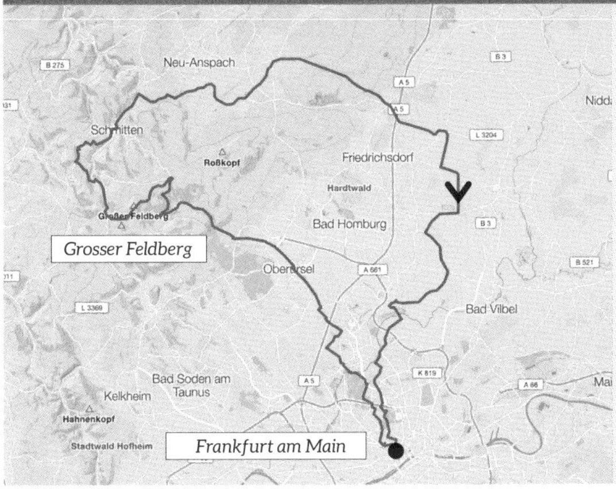

Founded by Charlemagne, Frankfurt—the city of Goethe, the famous sausage, and banking—likes to call itself "the smallest big city in the world." Do not let the skyscrapers fool you. From the right bank of the Main, it is very easy to ride out of the city on the cycle paths toward vast green spaces. The largest of these lies to the northwest: the Taunus mountains, of which Großer Feldberg is the highest. At km 31 (mi 19), climb the ramp to the right leading to the TV tower and the peak (879.5 m/2,885 ft). The view over Frankfurt is worth it. There are several little kickers on the long descent back.

DÜSSELDORF
CITIES OF THE RHINE

Fairly flat /Advanced *Map strava.com/routes/23526877*

Distance	E+	Difficulty	Appeal
128 km (80 mi)	550 m (1,805 ft)	3/5	3/5

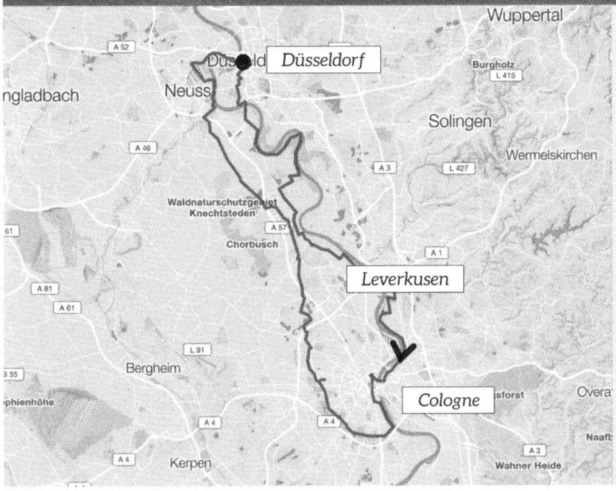

In the south of the Ruhr, Germany's industrial and heavily urbanized heart, you must play clever and fit suitable tires for a variety of surfaces, including trails and cycle paths. We ride out from the Europa bike cafe in Düsseldorf's Altstadt, heading to Cologne and its cathedral (30 minutes by train if you wish to cut the route short) by way of the very contemporary Leverkusen—two major cities on the Rhine and the two largest in North Rhine-Westphalia. Most of the route follows the left bank of the river, which we cross four times. It is inspired by the outings of Nils Politt (strava.com/pros/2592883), who is from Cologne.

MANNHEIM
CASTLE LIFE

Hilly / Advanced

Map *strava.com/routes/22943721*

Distance	E+	Difficulty	Appeal
108 km (67 mi)	850 m (2,800 ft)	3/5	4/5

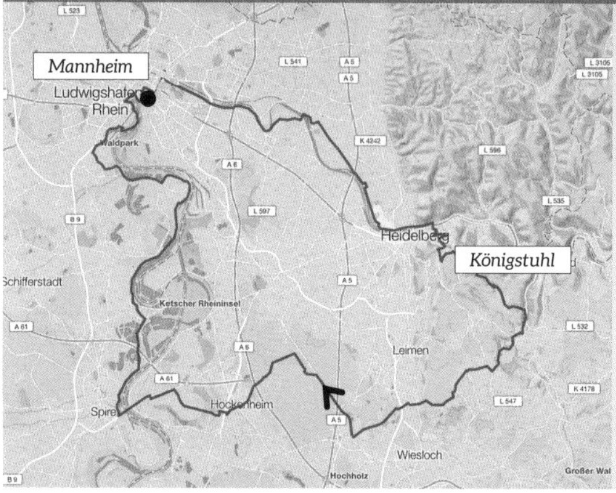

The rivers of Baden-Württemberg are pure delight. Heidelberg's old bridge (km 25/mi 16) is just below the city's sumptuous castle. Schwetzingen Palace is 10 minutes from km 80 (mi 50). At km 105 (mi 65), we enter Mannheim through the park of the impressive baroque palace, the second largest in Europe after Versailles in France. Fancy some sport? The Königstuhl climb after Heidelberg is brutal: 4.2 km (2.6 mi) at nearly 11%! At km 63 (mi 39), we pass Hockenheim motor racing circuit, which is open to cyclists once a year in May. From Speyer (km 74/mi 46), we follow the meanders of the Rhine all the way to Mannheim.

KAISERSLAUTERN
THE PALATINE FOREST

Very hilly / Advanced

Map *strava.com/routes/23492268*

Distance	E+	Difficulty	Appeal
119 km (74 mi)	1,850 m (6,000 ft)	4/5	4/5

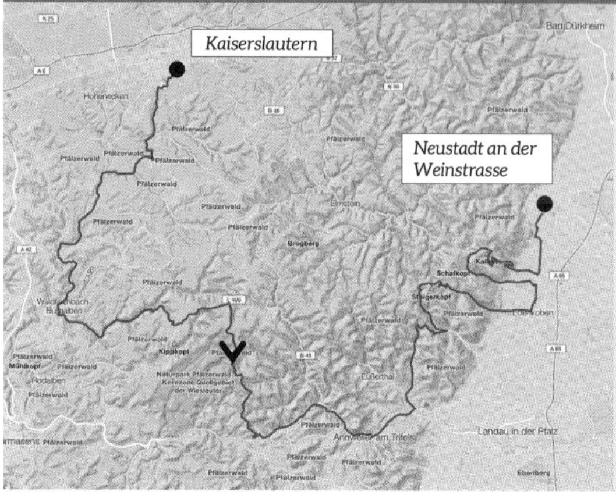

This route from Kaiserslautern (1h35 by train from Frankfurt and Stuttgart) to Neustadt an der Weinstraße explores the Palatine Forest, the largest in Germany and a natural extension of the French Vosges. You can spare yourself 20 km (12.5 mi) and 800 m (2,625 ft) of climbing by turning off at km 82 (mi 51) to cut through the impressive Haardt vineyards to Neustadt. If you are feeling bold, you can get your satisfaction on the ramps of Steigerkopf (.5 km/2.2 mi at 6%) and Kalmit (8 km/5 mi at 6%). Appreciate the sandstone cliffs, a particularity of the Palatine Forest. Return to Kaiserslautern by train in 30 minutes.

KOBLENZ
RHEINGOLD

- *Hilly / Intermediate*
- *Map strava.com/routes/22563405*
- *Test yourself km 37 (mi 23) strava.com/segments/9346926*
- *Test yourself km 74 (mi 46) strava.com/segments/5197437*

The name "Koblenz" originates from the Latin word for "confluence." This superb waterside city is where the Moselle meets the Rhine. The surrounding area boasts vineyards and the Westerwald low mountain range. There is much pleasant cycling to be done around here.

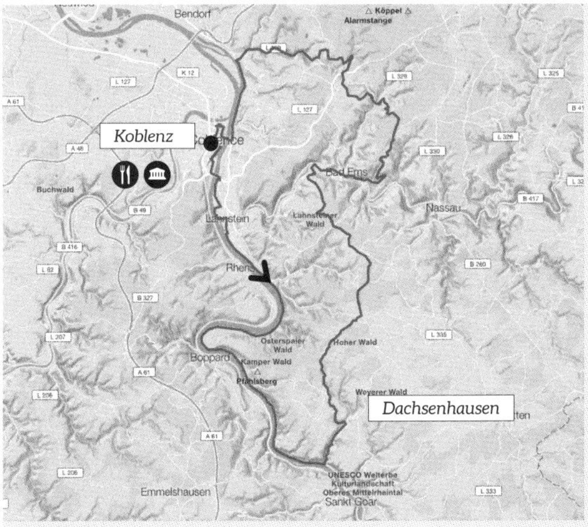

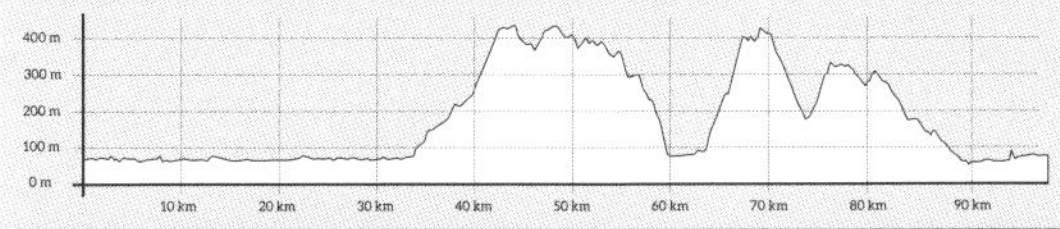

Life is sweet in Koblenz, a riverside university city in the Rhineland-Palatinate where pedestrians and cyclists have it good. They make fine wine on the surrounding hills too. We ride south out of Koblenz on a cycle path. Just after the castles of Stolzenfels and Markburg, the river bends into a beautiful meander that encloses the large winegrowing area of Bopparder Hamm, where Riesling and Pinot noir flourish. Before Saint Goar and the famous Lorelei rock, we turn and immediately start climbing above the Rhine into the Westerwald, an area of forests: around Dalheim (6 km/3.7 mi at 5%), up to Kemmenau (4 km/2.5 mi at nearly 8%), and before Eitelborn (1.5 km/1 mi also at nearly 8%). There is no time to catch your breath between hillside villages and valley floors.
The ride in to Koblenz passes Ehrenbreitstein Fortress, the Electoral Palace, the Altstadt, and Deutsches Eck, the tip of the confluence.

Distance	E+	Difficulty	Appeal
98 km (61 mi)	1,150 m (3,800 ft)	3/5	4/5

Cologne Bonn Airport is the closest to Koblenz: 1h30 by train or 1h10 by car (100 km/62 mi). There are also many European connections to Frankfurt (1h15 by train or 1h15 by car [120 km/75 mi]) and to Düsseldorf (2h10 by train or 2h by car).

Named after Koblenz's old town, the Altstadt Hotel is a little chic, but because you cycle past it (km 96/mi 60), you might as well enjoy its cafe terrace.

Jesuiten Platz 1
56068 Koblenz
altstadt-hotel-koblenz.de

The German bike manufacturer Canyon has built a strong reputation in barely twenty years. Visit their showroom and museum at its headquarters in Koblenz's Rauental neighborhood.

Karl-Tesche-Strasse 12
56073 Koblenz
canyon.com

TRIER
RIESLING SLOPES

Hilly / Intermediate

Map strava.com/routes/22692970

Distance	E+	Difficulty	Appeal
83 km (52 mi)	1,400 m (4,595 ft)	3/5	4/5

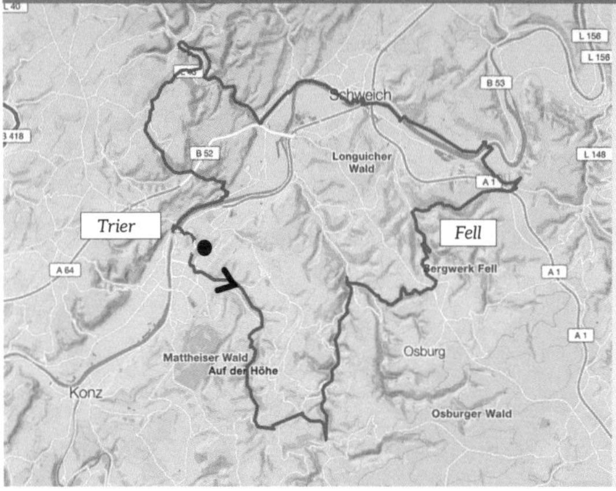

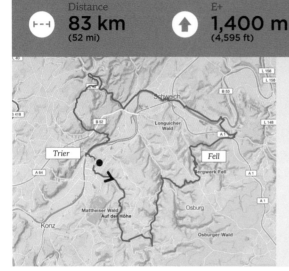

France owes the reputation of its Alsatian wines to the Riesling grape variety. In Rhineland-Palatinate, Riesling has done the same for German vintages. On the hills of the Moselle and the Ruwer rivers, the slopes are so steep that it is impossible to use mechanical equipment, particularly for harvesting. Let that serve as a warning to cyclists. Our route serves up four fine ramps of 3 km (2 mi) to 5 km (3 mi) around Waldrach, Thomm (close to the Fell Exhibition Slate Mine), and Kordel: 9% in places. The scenery is wonderful. Trier was known as the "second Rome" because of its impressive Roman ruins, which include the Porta Nigra.

KOBLENZ
THE LAHN VALLEY

Hilly / Intermediate

Map strava.com/routes/23009009

Distance	E+	Difficulty	Appeal
80 km (50 mi)	900 m (3,000 ft)	2/5	3/5

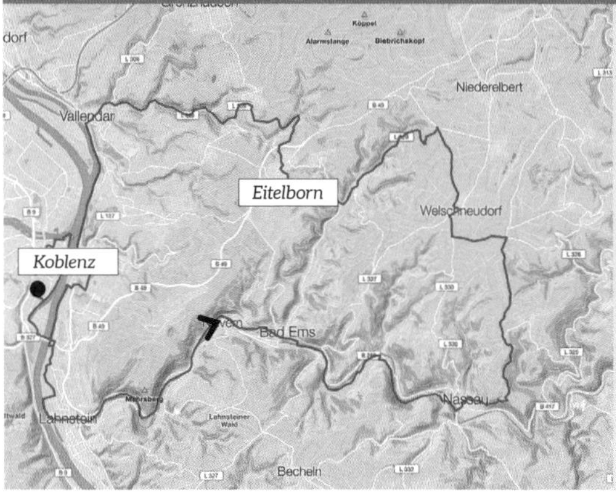

The Lahn flows into the Rhine opposite Stolzenfels Castle, located south of Koblenz. This majestic backdrop sets the tone for a route that follows the charming meanders of the river to Nassau, with its old buildings and half-timbered houses, via the jewel of a spa town that is Bad Ems. We then climb for 5 km (3 mi) at 6% in a landscape of woods and meadows, then along quiet roads through little valleys—past Arzbach and Neuhäusel—before rejoining the Rhine at Vallendar. Koblenz is so close that you might as well climb up to Fort Asterstein to admire the city.

MONREAL
FULL GAS AT THE NÜRBURGRING

Very hilly / Advanced
Map strava.com/routes/22267681
Test yourself km 55 (mi 34) strava.com/segments/8038832
Test yourself km 68 (mi 42) strava.com/segments/2091505

The Rad am Ring is a cycle racing festival held at the legendary motorsport complex, the Nürburgring, every July. The 20 km (12 mi) Nordschleife track has nearly 500 m (1,640 ft) of elevation gain, and is also open to cyclists at several other times of the year.

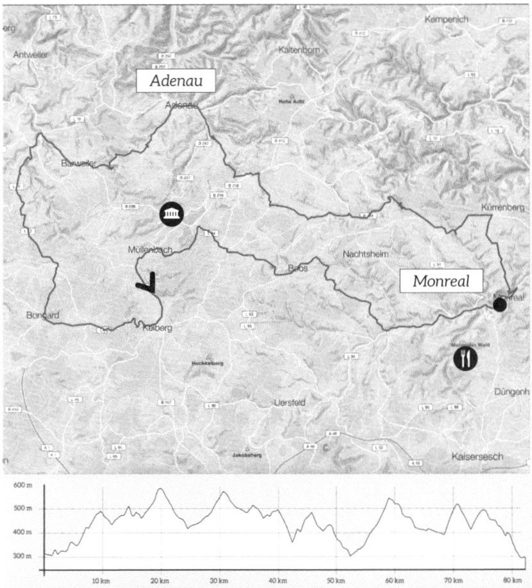

We are not in the mountains proper but, just as in the neighboring Belgian Ardennes, there is a lot of up and down to attract cyclists here in Rhineland-Palatinate. The Nürburgring motor racing track (nearly a century old) is renowned for its undulating terrain. Sadly, it is only open to cyclists a few times a year. However, this 82 km (51 mi) route around it provides an opportunity to appreciate the topography and charm of the Eifel mountains: 1,500 m (4,920 ft) of elevation gain by the end. You will pass the race track, at km 20 (mi 12) and km 59 (mi 37), at the top of the long but irregular Adenau climb, with its 7 km (4.5 mi) at an average gradient of 4%—having already tackled three similar hills near Bermel, Welcherath, and Kelberg, so it is a brisk workout for the legs. The road often passes through beech woods, with glimpses of narcissuses or orchids in the clearings, and the occasional roar of sports cars.

Distance	E+	Difficulty	Appeal
82 km (51 mi)	1,500 m (4,920 ft)	3/5	4/5

Monreal (pop. 900) lies 40 km (25 mi) west of Koblenz. It is 2h30 by train from Düsseldorf, or 1h30 by car (140 km/87 mi). Frankfurt is 3h15 by train or 1h30 by car (160 km/100 mi). Brussels is 5h by train or 2h45 by car (280 km/174 mi).

Cafe Plüsch is the perfect spot for a snack when you return to Monreal. Amazing local cakes and delicious waffles in a friendly atmosphere.

**Obertorstrasse 14,
56729 Monreal
cafe-plüsch-monreal.de**

Even if you are not a motor racing specialist, the Nürburgring has a wide range of events and activities all year round, including tours, drives around the track with a pro, lessons, sports car hire, and virtual races.

nuerburgring.de

NIDEGGEN
BETWEEN EIFEL AND RUR

Very hilly / Advanced

Map strava.com/routes/22267860

Distance	E+	Difficulty	Appeal
85 km (53 mi)	1,450 m (4,760 ft)	3/5	4/5

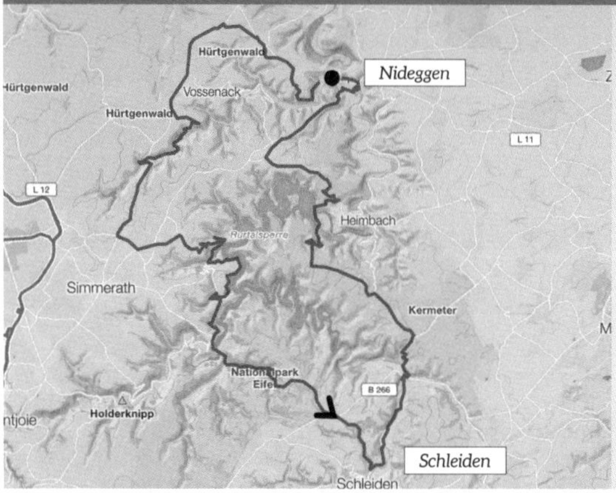

Eifel National Park (2h by train southwest of Cologne) is a popular destination in Germany despite its being rather isolated—although that is a key part of its appeal. If you can handle the very heavy motorcycle traffic in summer, you will find the roads to be magnificent, evoking the not-so-distant Belgian Ardennes. The artificial lake created by the damming of the Rur—a tributary of the Meuse—forms the epicenter of this route that flirts with its shores and surrounding hills. We climb above 500 m (1,640 ft) several times in a landscape of beech trees and juniper bushes, orchids, and wild garlic.

BRILON
HILLS OF THE SAUERLAND

Low mountain / Advanced

Map strava.com/routes/22943550

Distance	E+	Difficulty	Appeal
103 km (64 mi)	1,200 m (3,900 ft)	3/5	4/5

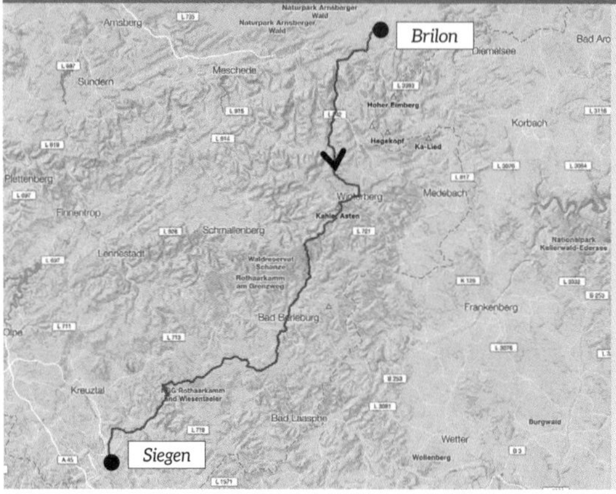

The sublimely beautiful hills of the Sauerland lie 100 km (62 mi) east of the impressive Rhine-Ruhr metropolitan region. The hills, which are easy to reach (especially from Dortmund), are very popular with hikers and skiers—especially the Kahler Asten (842 m/2,762 ft), the second-highest (by just one meter after the Langenberg), which we approach from the ski resort of Winterberg. Before you set off from Brilon, fill your water bottles with the local mineral water. This idyllic ride finishes in Siegen, which has two castles and was the birthplace of the great seventeenth-century painter Peter Paul Rubens.

Morning mist in the Eifel Hills, Germany.

HAMBURG
BANKS OF THE ELBE

Fairly flat / Intermediate

Map strava.com/routes/22628200

Test yourself km 47 (mi 29) strava.com/segments/6094496

Test yourself km 72 (mi 45) strava.com/segments/10145613

Hamburg is Germany's second-largest city and Europe's second-largest port, but it has much more to make you love it, such as its relaxed atmosphere, canals, and architecture. Cycling is also integral to Hamburg, and our route is inspired by the annual Cyclassics.

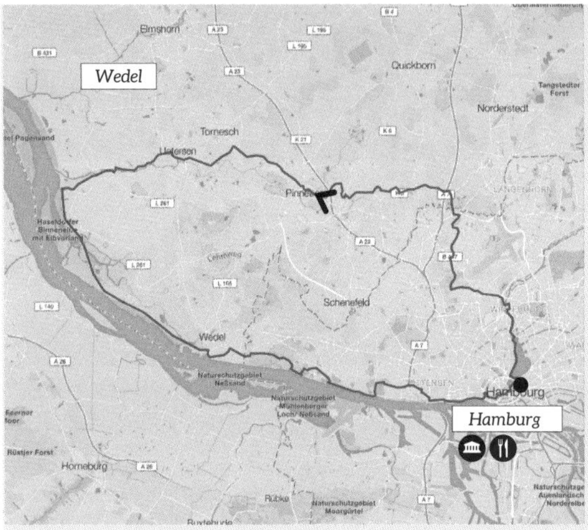

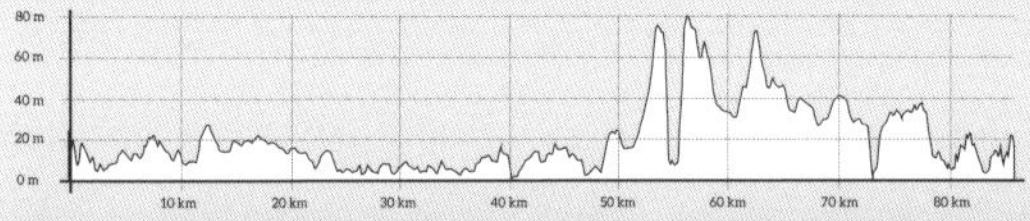

The Elbe is so wide that Hamburg has a maritime feel to it, despite being 100 km (62 mi) from the North Sea. From the central train station, we ride up the Alster River, past the reservoir with its geyser-like fountain. Greenery is everywhere as we leave the city via the Eppendorf district with its art nouveau buildings and head west into neighboring Schleswig-Holstein. The countryside is lush and smooth. Roughly halfway, we meet the banks of the Elbe River again at Wedel. It is here, between the villas of the famous Elbchaussee, that we find the few climbs of the annual Cyclassics: Wittenberg (900 m/2,995 ft at 7%), the famous Kosterberg (1.4 km/0.9 mi at a similar gradient but with one section at 16%), and Krähenberg. We reenter Hamburg via the neighborhoods of Altona, St. Pauli, and Speicherstadt, where rows of emblematic nineteenth-century warehouses line the canals.

Distance	E+	Difficulty	Appeal
91 km (57 mi)	400 m (1,300 ft)	3/5	4/5

Hamburg Airport has numerous European connections. It takes 25 minutes by train to reach Hamburg Central Station. Berlin is 1h45 by train or 3h15 by car (300 km/185 mi). Düsseldorf is 4h by train or 4h30 by car (400 km/250 mi).

On the way back, stop at the waterside terrace of Brücke 10 (km 82/mi 51) for a glass of local Holsten beer and a *fischbrötchen* (a sandwich filled with herring, onion, and horseradish).

St. Pauli-Landungsbrücken 10
20359 Hamburg
bruecke10.com

If you are a good cyclist, you surely like coffee, right? You must not neglect a visit to the Coffee Museum in Speicherstadt (km 84/mi 52), where they offer tastings.

St. Annenufer 2
20457 Hamburg
kaffeemuseum-burg.de

BERGEN
BALTIC CLIFFS

⊕ *Hilly / Intermediate* ⊕ *Map strava.com/routes/22944169*

Distance	E+	Difficulty	Appeal
104 km (65 mi)	1,050 m (3,445 ft)	2/5	3/5

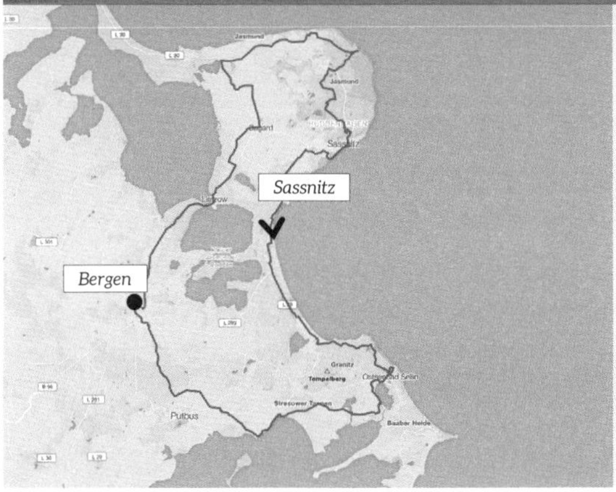

Explore the large Pomeranian island of Rügen via this coastal route. We start from Bergen (30 minutes by train from Stralsund) so as to keep the distance reasonable. The invigorating air of the Baltic Sea is not the only point of interest. Right in the north, the high limestone cliffs of Jasmund National Park, which are covered by forest, are dramatic to ride through, particularly when you reach Stubbenkammer rock (km 35/mi 22), 120 m (395 ft) above the water. The pebble beach at Sassnitz, the photogenic Sellin Pier, and Seedorf Port—all connected by cycle paths—display a number of the island's other charms.

LÜBECK
WINDOW ON THE SEA

⊕ *Fairly flat / Intermediate* ⊕ *Map strava.com/routes/23521246*

Distance	E+	Difficulty	Appeal
115 km (71 mi)	800 m (2,600 ft)	2/5	3/5

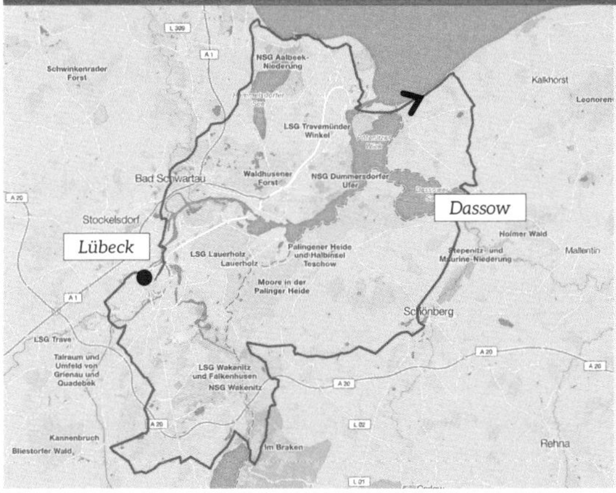

The waters of the Trave River flow around Lübeck (pop. 212,000) in wide meanders upstream of its opening to the Baltic, a wide window on the sea. We are in Schleswig-Holstein. Danish and Swedish neighbors are only a ferry ride away. Our route includes a fifteen-minute boat crossing from the hip sandy beaches and lighthouses of Travemünde to the little Priwall Peninsula. Indeed, the whole ride is an aquatic one between coastline, marshes, and lakes with barely a slope on the horizon. Explore Lübeck when you get back: Obertrave Promenade, and many Gothic and red-brick buildings.

STRALSUND
POMERANIAN ISLAND

- *Fairly flat / Intermediate*
- *Map strava.com/routes/22562870*
- *Test yourself km 24 (mi 15) strava.com/segments/14615132*
- *Test yourself km 46 (mi 28) strava.com/segments/8167712*

The Baltic island of Rügen is a vast territory devoted to arable and pastoral farming and tourism. As such, it offers something quite unexpected in Germany. The terrain is pretty flat except for the spectacular chalk cliffs along the coast, which protect you from the wind as you ride.

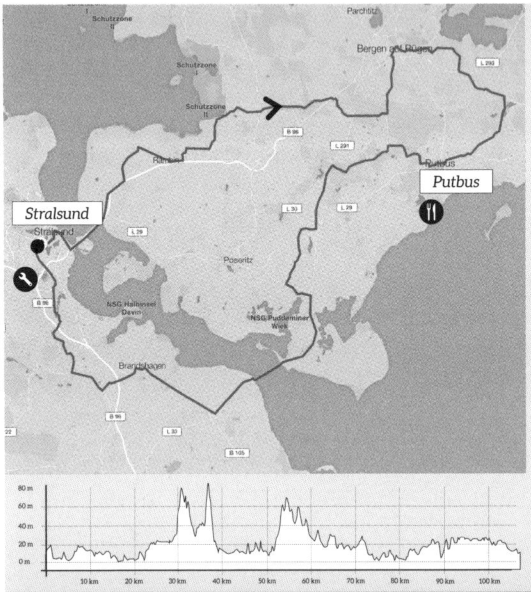

Northeast Germany is a maritime region. German Chancellor Angela Merkel is an elected representative of the state in which the island of Rügen is located. Germans flock here for the magnificent white sandy beaches and the imposing cliffs. There is a particular atmosphere once you cross Rügendamm Bridge after Stralsund, with charming towns surrounded by farmland, such as Bergen auf Rügen, which has a number of houses with thatched roofs, or Putbus with its large Circus (traffic circle) surrounded by neoclassical buildings and with an obelisk at the center. You may veer off the route at km 42 (mi 26) to Binz, which used to be called the "Nice of the East" (as in the former East Germany), and Prora with its stupefying 3 km (1.9 mi) long complex of holiday apartments, which was built by the Nazis and is currently being renovated. Return by the fast ferry from Glewitz to Stahlbrode.

Distance	E+	Difficulty	Appeal
104 km (65 mi)	**550 m** (1,805 ft)	**2/5**	**3/5**

Rügen Airport (km 24/mi 15) is served only by national flights. Stralsund (pop. 60,000) is 2h40 by train or 2h50 by car (280 km/175 mi) from Berlin-Tegel Airport to the south. To the southwest, Hamburg Airport is 3h30 by train or 3h by car (280 km/175 mi) via Rostock (120 km/75 mi).

If you have not opted for Binz, a good feed stop is Rosencafe in Putbus (next to the imposing Circus). It is housed in a superb villa and has a mouthwatering cake display.

Bahnhofstrasse 1
18581 Putbus
rosencafe-putbus.de

Located 2 km (1.25 mi) from the train station and near Stralsund Airport, Fahrradhandel Heiden is the best bike store and workshop for final adjustments. Retailer of Focus and Stevens.

Maxim-Gorki Strasse 28
18435 Stralsund
fahrradhandel-heiden.de

BELGIUM NETHERLANDS LUXEMBOURG

ETTELBRUCK
MEANDERING DOWN THE SÛRE

- *Hilly / Intermediate*
- *Map strava.com/routes/22162216*
- *Test yourself km 13 (mi 8) strava.com/segments/5490095*
- *Test yourself km 32 (mi 20) strava.com/segments/12813009*

This short loop through tranquil, rustic Luxembourg starts in the little town of Ettelbruck and meanders down the pleasant River Sûre, a tributary of the Moselle, before taking to the hills above it. Pure pleasure on a bike.

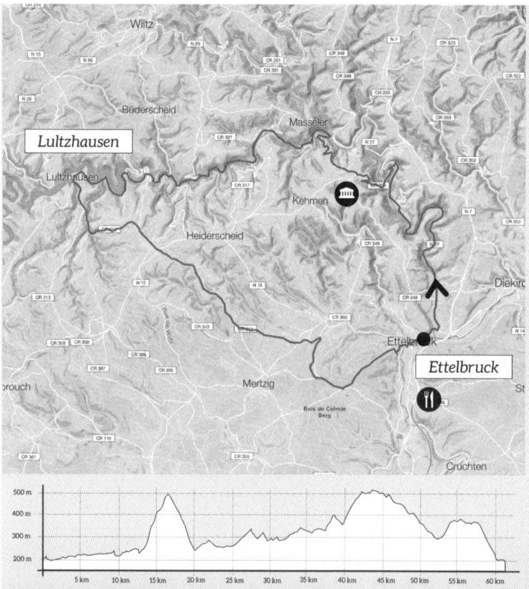

The Grand Duchy of Luxembourg is certainly small. Belgium is less than 10 km (6 mi) from the western edge of the route, Germany is just 15 km (9 mi) from Ettelbruck train station (where we start and finish), and the French town of Metz is barely an hour by car. Yet the countryside is so peaceful, you will feel as if you are miles from anywhere. We follow the River Sûre as it flows through woods and greenery, widening lazily around km 29 (mi 18) near Heiderscheidergrund, with its octagonal chapel. At certain points, the further bank is more than 200 meters/yards away. At km 15 (mi 9), there is a superb view from the rocky promontory of Bourscheid. The 4.5 km (2.8 mi) section after Bourscheid-Moulin rises at a gradient of 7% to nearly 500 m (1,640 ft). Two-thirds of the way up stands the most imposing medieval castle to be found in the area, 150 m (500 ft) above the water.

Distance	E+	Difficulty	Appeal
61 km (38 mi)	1,100 m (3,610 ft)	3/5	4/5

Ettelbruck (pop. 9,000) is only 40 km (25 mi) from the capital, Luxembourg; 35 minutes by train, 30 minutes by car. Liège is 2h by train or 1h40 by car (140 km/87 mi). Cologne is 5h by train (via Liège) or 2h30 by car (180 km/112 mi).

In fine weather, the Brasserie de la Poste "Boffer" sets up a little terrace where you can quench your thirst with a glass of the fine local lager, Bofferding.

Grand-Rue 119
9051 Ettelbruck
bofferding.lu

Bourscheid Castle, a medieval fortress that was constructed and enlarged between 1000 and the late fifteenth century, is the largest monument in the Grand Duchy. It is a majestic sight with eight watchtowers protecting the keep and the Stolzembourg house.

castle-bourscheid.lu

DIEKIRCH
VIEWS OF THE OUR

Very hilly / Advanced

Map strava.com/routes/23387750

Distance	E+	Difficulty	Appeal
72 km (45 mi)	1,350 m (4,450 ft)	3/5	4/5

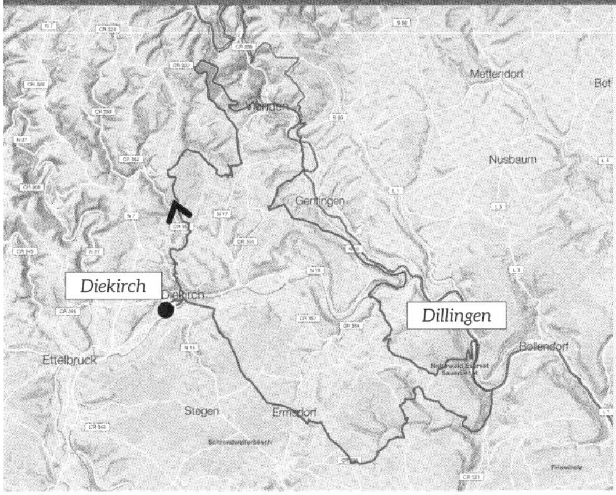

The hills between the Sure and Our rivers in east Luxembourg along the German border are kickers. We climb 1,700 m (5,580 ft) in the course of just 72 km (45 mi)—that is no joke!—on a route starting in the valley town of Diekirch, located 1h15 by train from the capital. The approach to Mont Saint-Nicolas and the reservoir powering the Vianden hydroelectric plant is difficult. At km 15 (mi 9), we are already at 500 m (1,640 ft). We descend to the Our Valley and on toward the ramp of Reisdorf (km 39/mi 24): 3 km (2 mi) at 7%. The scenery of the Grand Duchy is as lovely as the old castles of Vianden and Beaufort that we pass.

LUXEMBOURG
SCHLECK STYLE

Hilly / Intermediate

Map strava.com/routes/22161737

Distance	E+	Difficulty	Appeal
82 km (51 mi)	1,100 m (3,600 ft)	3/5	4/5

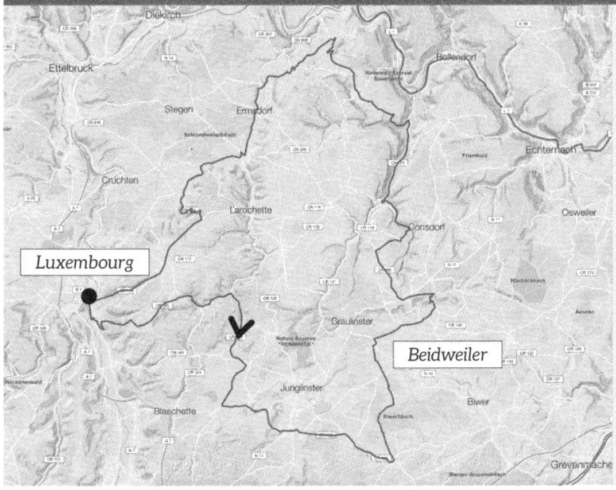

Each year, the Schleck Gran Fondo draws crowds to the Grand Duchy to ride in the slipstream of contemporary cycling icons Frank and Andy. Commencing in Mondorf-les-Bains in the south, our own sporty loop covers part of that race's route north of the capital, Luxembourg. It gets serious from the get-go above Rollingen, then Bourglinster, and Beidweiler—site of the longwave transmitters for RTL radio. Further on in the Mullerthal region, rock formations accentuate the relief. We reach more than 400 m (1,315 ft) above Beaufort and Nommern. You will understand why the Schlecks love climbing so much.

LUXEMBOURG
WHAT A GRAND DUCHY

Hilly / Advanced *Map strava.com/routes/22334827*

Distance	E+	Difficulty	Appeal
97 km (60 mi)	1,500 m (4,920 ft)	3/5	4/5

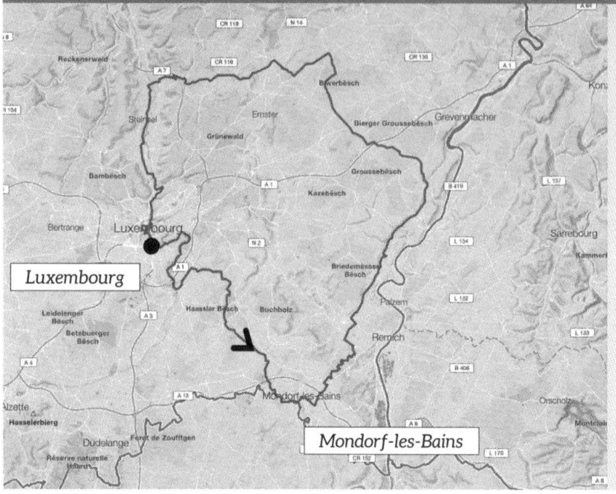

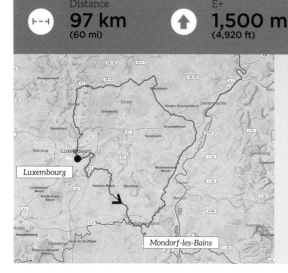

Luxembourg is famous cycling territory. This loop in the southeast of the Grand Duchy heads out of the capital to explore the pocket between France and Germany, returning via the famous cobbled Pfaffenthal climb, the old town, and Adolphe Bridge. Traversing hills planted with vineyards, thick forests, and small valleys, we find little flat terrain as we soar between 150 m (495 ft) and 400 m (1,315 ft). At Greiveldange (km 42/mi 26), veer off the route for a sublime descent to Stadtbredimus and the Moselle Valley. Spare a thought for the Schleck brothers as you ride through their base camps of Itzig and Mondorf-les-Bains.

ESCH-SUR-ALZETTE
LORRAINE SPIRIT

Hilly / Advanced *Map strava.com/routes/23359013*

Distance	E+	Difficulty	Appeal
104 km (65 mi)	1,300 m (4,265 ft)	3/5	4/5

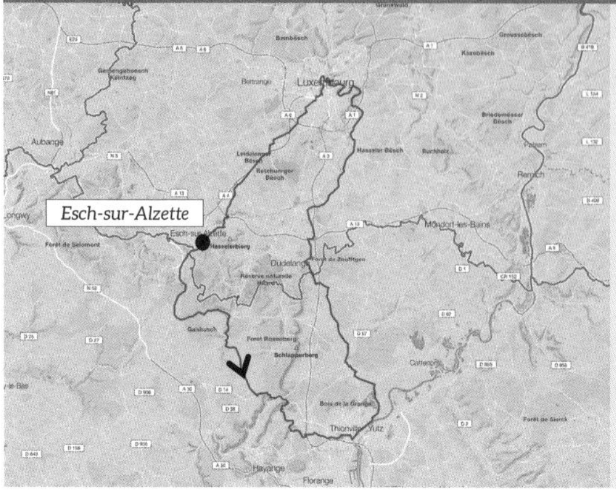

This unusual and varied loop—half in Luxembourg, half in Lorraine, France—starts and finishes in the border town of Esch-sur-Alzette (1h by train from Metz, and 2h from Luxembourg). Before Thionville and the Moselle Valley, we climb above Villerupt, where (at km 19/mi 12) we discover the Ouvrage Rochonvillers—one of the largest fortifications of the Maginot Line. Sweeping through Thionville, we approach green Luxembourg and its buildings of yellow limestone. In Itzig, stop at Andy Schleck Cycles before the historic sites of the capital (Grand Ducal Palace, Place Guillaume II) and the road back to Esch.

SPA

THE HILLS OF "LA DOYENNE"

- *Very hilly / Advanced*
- *Map strava.com/routes/21289925*
- *Test yourself km 36 (mi 22) strava.com/routes/21287772*
- *Test yourself km 60 (mi 37) strava.com/segments/867573*

Liège-Bastogne-Liège, doyenne of the Spring Classics, is legendary among the cycling community for its challenging route. Starting from Spa, you can tackle seven of its best-known climbs in the course of this highly demanding 114 km (71 mi) ride.

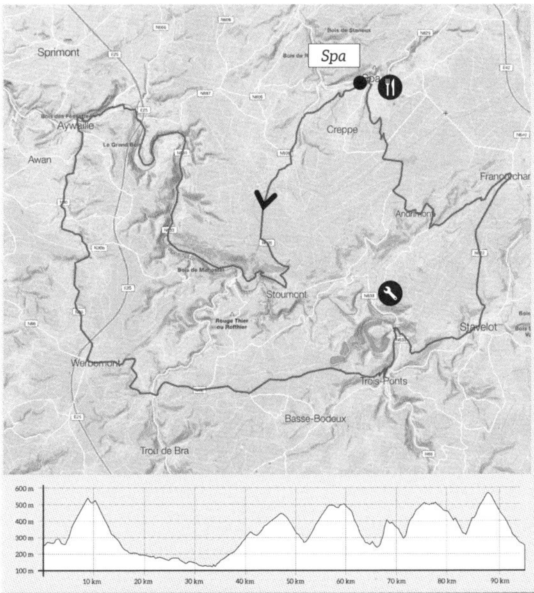

This loop, which starts and ends in Spa, leaves out only the final difficulty (La Roche-aux-Faucons) of what is perhaps the most prestigious—certainly the hilliest—Spring Classic. It tackles, however, the seven preceding climbs, and that is no picnic! We begin with the tough ascent of Francorchamps (not included in the race itinerary). At Stavelot (km 20/mi 12.5), we join the race route and the "wall" of Stockeu—only a kilometer (0.6 mi), but at a gradient of nearly 13%—with a stone to Eddy Merckx at the top. Next, we tackle the grinding Col de la Haute Levée, Col du Rosier, Col de la Vecquée, and Col du Maquisard before Remouchamps at km 75 (mi 47), and the start of a gentle climb toward the well-named Côte de la Redoute: 1,700 m (5,580 ft) at an average gradient of 9.5%, with sections at 14% and then 17% at the top. We finish with the Côte des Forges at km 88 (mi 55).

Distance	E+	Difficulty	Appeal
114 km (71 mi)	2,000 m (6,650 ft)	4/5	5/5

Spa is 1h15 by train from Liège, with a change in Pepinster (15 trains a day). Indeed, you can take the train back from Pepinster (km 107/mi 67). By car, allow 30 minutes (40 km/25 mi) from Liège and 1h40 from Brussels (150 km/93 mi) and Luxembourg (160 km/100 mi).

Back in Spa, celebrate your completed challenge with a glass of Bobeline, the excellent local beer, at the eponymous brewery.

Place Royale 41
4900 Spa
luxeryspa.be

Bicyclic is the go-to bike store chain in the region. This outlet is right at the foot of the Côte de la Redoute.

Square Philippe Gilbert 3
4920 Remouchamps
bicyclic.be

LIÈGE
VINTAGE FINAL

Very hilly / Advanced   *Map* *strava.com/routes/22846200*

Distance	E+	Difficulty	Appeal
81 km (50 mi)	1,150 m (3,800 ft)	4/5	5/5

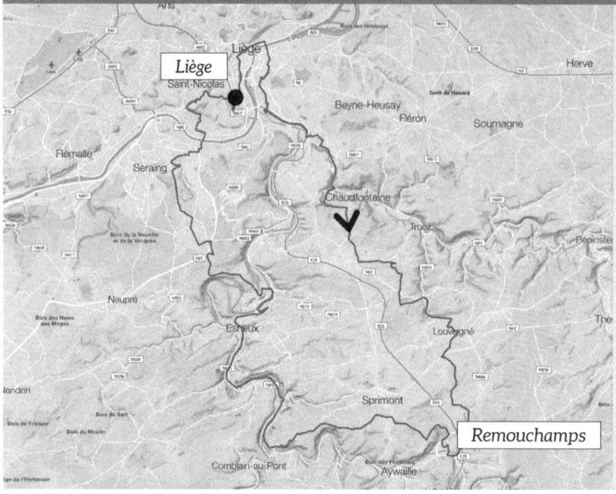

Until quite recently, the Liège–Bastogne–Liège race staged its breathless finale on the ramps of the Côte de Saint-Nicolas and through Ans, suburbs of the "Ardent City." Bartoli, Bettini, Vandenbroucke, Schleck, Valverde, and Gilbert have shone here. "La Doyenne," as the race is known, now finishes on Boulevard de la Sauvenière in the city center. The Côte de Saint-Nicolas (km 76/mi 47) is already legendary: 1.4 km (0.9 mi) at 8%. Our route is a different approach to the race, although it does include the climbs of Chaudfontaine (2 km/1.25 mi at 9%), the classic ascent of La Redoute midway, and the wall of Avister (800 m/2,625 ft at 12%).

CHARLEROI
FOLLOW SPIROU!

Hilly / Intermediate   *Map* *strava.com/routes/22913395*

Distance	E+	Difficulty	Appeal
72 km (45 mi)	800 m (2,625 ft)	2/5	3/5

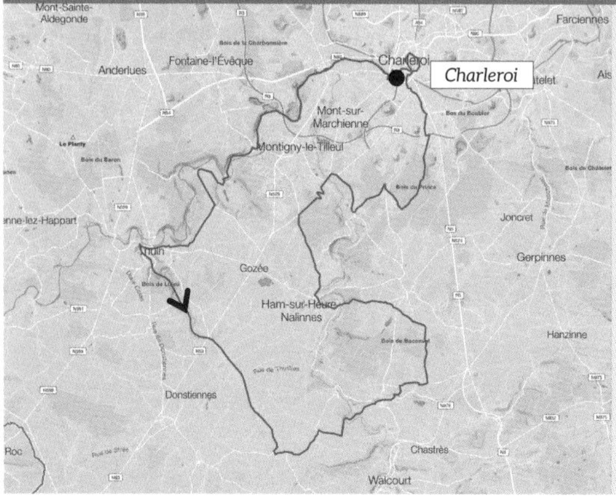

The history of Charleroi, located less than an hour from Brussels, is linked to that of coal extraction as well as comics, two of the finest examples of which are the magazine Spirou and the "Marcinelle school" of cartoonists associated with it. The superb train station and the return via Charleroi center beneath the belfry (74 m/243 ft high) of the town hall are the icing on the cake of this escapade over slag heaps and post-industrial wasteland. The valley of the Sambre, Thuin, the Biesmelle cycle path, and the heights of the Chemin de Panama and the Bois du Prince provide an exciting glimpse of Hainaut province.

NAMUR
FROM WALL TO CITADE

Hilly / Advanced

Map strava.com/routes/21327211

Test yourself km 34 (mi 21) strava.com/segments/14701557

Test yourself km 96 (mi 60) strava.com/segments/715877

Wallonia is a cycling heartland. To the southwest of Liège, you will find such legendary climbs as the Mur de Huy and the Citadel of Namur. They are both on this route along and above the majestic Meuse.

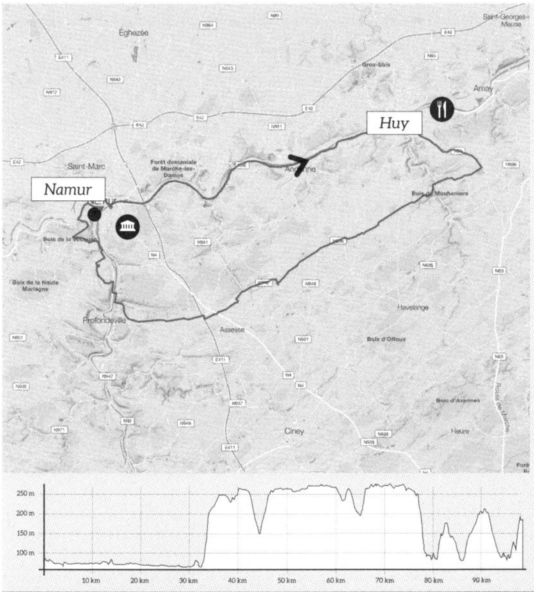

This route includes sections of two Belgian classics well-known to serious cycling fans: the Grand Prix de Wallonie and, above all, La Flèche Wallonne. After rolling along the bank of the Meuse for 30 km (18 mi), we climb the legendary "wall" of Huy (official name: Chemin des Chapelles). It is not easy to get to the top without stopping. The hill is 1,300 m (4,300 ft) long with an average gradient of 9.8%. There is a 17% section 400 m (1,300 ft) from the summit; the last 300 m (1,000 ft) are at between 14% and 15%. The Côte d'Ereffe (km 47/mi 29), is gentler: 2,300 m (7,500 ft) at 6%. After a straight ride back to the Meuse, there is some fun to be had on the surrounding slopes, particularly in the Vecquée Woods. Hold something in reserve for the Citadel of Namur, where the Grand Prix de Wallonie finishes: 1,300 m (4,200 ft) at 6%, with the last 600 m (2,000 ft) at 10%.

Distance	E+	Difficulty	Appeal
99 km (61 mi)	800 m (2,600 ft)	4/5	5/5

Namur is 1h by train from Brussels, and 45 to 55 minutes from Liège. By car, allow 1h10 from Brussels (70 km/43.5 mi), 1h from Liège (65 km/40 mi), and 1h45 from Lille (150 km/93 mi). Nearest airport: Brussels.

Two hundred meters/yards from the foot of the wall is MUR, a bike-themed bar with big TV screens that serves bagels, salads, cakes, and coffee. Headquarters of the jolly Mur Cycling Club.

Place Saint-Séverin, 7
4500 Huy
murcoffee.be

Once you have conquered it on the bike and downed a local Houppe beer, explore the Citadel of Namur and its tower, ramparts, and network of underground passages.

Route Merveilleuse, 64
5000 Namur
citadelle.namur.be

NAMUR
SAMBRE AND MEUSE

Hilly / Intermediate — Map strava.com/routes/23176670

Distance	E+	Difficulty	Appeal
110 km (68 mi)	1,220 m (4,005 ft)	3/5	4/5

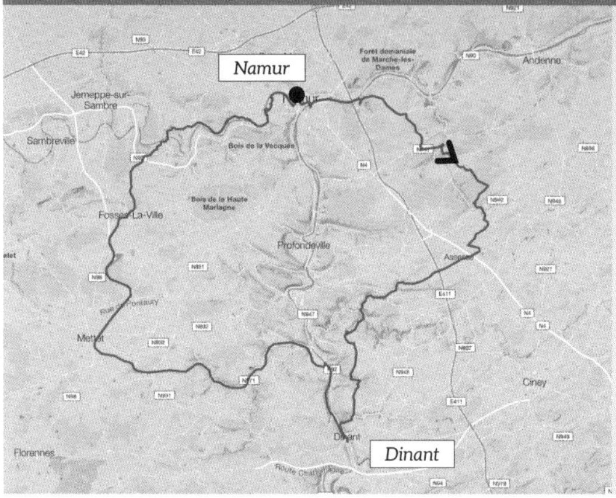

"Sambre et Meuse" has a strong resonance in French military history, being the name of a regiment and a marching tune. This route leaves Namur along the banks of the Meuse and returns along the Sambre River. Between the two lies the magnificent Walloon countryside and hills: Loyers, Gesves, and Évrehailles (km 40/mi 25)—all pretty bumps. After Leffe and its abbey, stop in Dinant (km 49/mi 30) for its rocky cliff and colorful houses. From Anhée to Fosses-la-Ville, the RAVeL L150 cycle path runs along the Molignée River to Montaigle Castle and Maredsous Abbey, and then to Mettet and Bambois Lake.

NAMUR
SAXOPHONE NOTES

Hilly / Intermediate — Map strava.com/routes/23164782

Distance	E+	Difficulty	Appeal
93 km (58 mi)	1,050 m (3,450 ft)	3/5	4/5

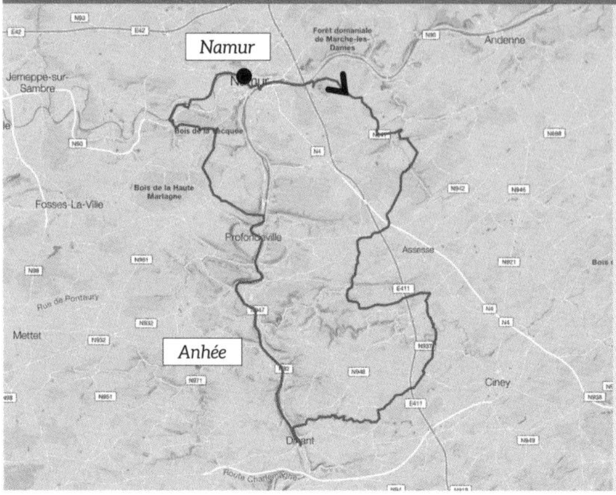

Adolphe Sax, a native son and inventor of the saxophone in the nineteenth century, is still celebrated in Dinant. The town is a surprising discovery for cyclists who arrive here after riding through the Vallée des Fonds de Leffe. Dinant justly deserves its reputation: citadel atop a rocky outcrop, colorful houses on the banks of the Meuse River, and a collegiate church with an onion dome bell tower. Starting in Namur (past its fortifications), we climb the slopes of Grand Pré woods and Durnal before following the meandering course of the Meuse to the Beau Vallon ramp (km 73/mi 46), and then a descent back to the river.

BRUSSELS
BRABANT CHIC

Hilly / Intermediate

Map strava.com/routes/21212906

Test yourself km 57 (mi 35) strava.com/segments/4280753

Test yourself km 65 (mi 40) strava.com/segments/15265351

This loop to the south of Brussels is a surprising mix of the scenic and the sporty, including the peaceful, pretty avenues leading out of the city, the Lion's Mound at Waterloo, and the short climbs around Overijse that feature in the Brabant Arrow—one of the Flanders classics.

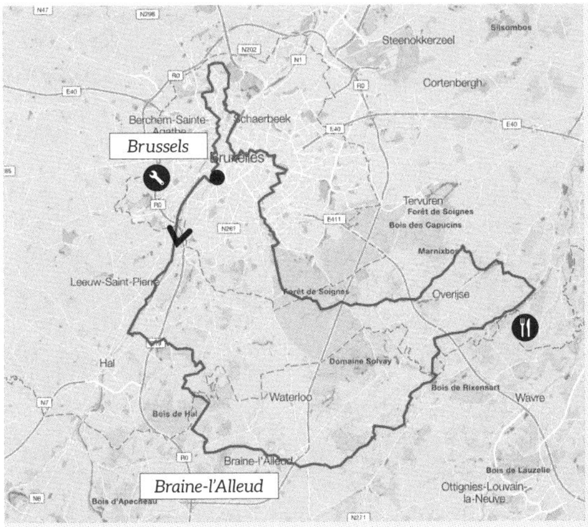

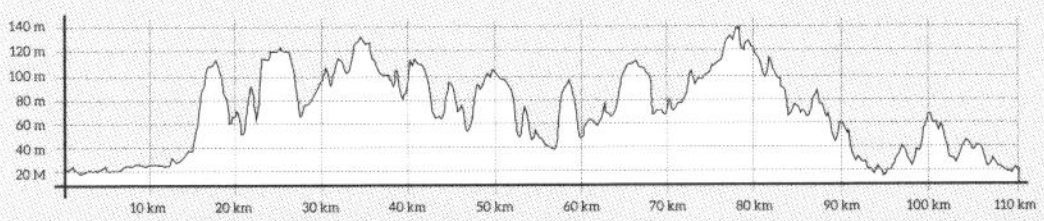

This loop to the south of Brussels highlights the Belgian capital's chic charm and very green surroundings. We depart from Kring Club bike store and ride along the Charleroi Canal before passing the Lion's Mound on the battlefield of Waterloo (km 33/mi 20), then Bois d'Ohain. On the way back, at km 73 (mi 45), we pass the seventeen huge trees of the Arboretum of Groenendaal before pedaling through Sonian Forest and the prestigious Bois de la Cambre park. The "sporty" section essentially comprises 30 km (19 mi) around Overijse, with climbs such as Hagaard, Hertstraat, Holstheide, and Schaveien, which feature in the Brabant Arrow, a beautiful Flanders Classic. The run-in to Brussels begins with a 3 km (2 mi) stretch along Frans Verbeekstraat, named after the plucky Belgian champion of the Merckx generation. Cycling culture is deeply embedded in this part of the world.

Distance	E+	Difficulty	Appeal
110 km (68 mi)	1,000 m (3,300 ft)	3/5	4/5

Brussels is very easy to reach by plane, train, or car from across Europe. Take care when cycling through Brussels; the Belgian capital is a little behind other European countries when it comes to cycling policy/infrastructure.

't Klein Verzet (km 54/mi 33.5) is a traditional Belgian café (the kind you hardly see anymore) in a building frozen in time. Beer, coffee, and snacks. Open every day from 10 am.

Bollestraat 1
3090 Overijse
tkleinverzet.vlaanderen

A mechanical incident? Cyclovia, after the Bois de la Cambre (km 83/mi 52), is a bike shop and Canyon Friendly Store, serving fine Colombian coffee.

Chaussée de Waterloo 521
1050 Ixelles
cicloviastore.com

BRUSSELS

CLIMBING THE MUUR

⊕ *Hilly / Advanced* ⊕ *Map strava.com/routes/23349783*

Distance	E+	Difficulty	Appeal
125 km (78 mi)	1,100 m (3,610 ft)	3/5	4/5

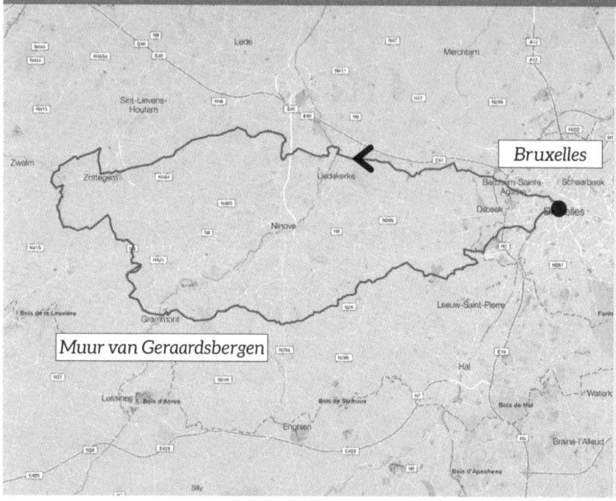

Brussels is a great starting point for your own Tour of Flanders. Members of the Kring Club, who organize social rides each week starting from Brussels, recommended this route. We approach the classic climbs via Zottegem and cobbled Lippenhovestraat. At km 59 (mi 37), we climb the Berendries before the famous Muur van Geraardsbergen road, followed closely by the Bosberg and the Congoberg hills. The "Muur" (wall) is legendary: 1 km (0.6 mi) at an average gradient of more than 9%, with 15% over the last 200 m (656 ft). The small cobbles were laid in such a way as to stop handcarts rolling backward. The ride is worth it just for that.

LOUVAIN

FROM EDDY TO MERCKX

⊕ *Fairly flat / Intermediate* ⊕ *Map strava.com/routes/22919234*

Distance	E+	Difficulty	Appeal
99 km (62 mi)	800 m (2,625 ft)	2/5	4/5

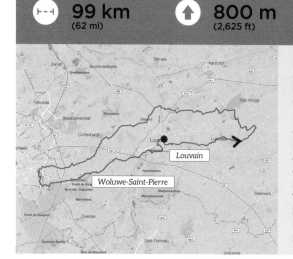

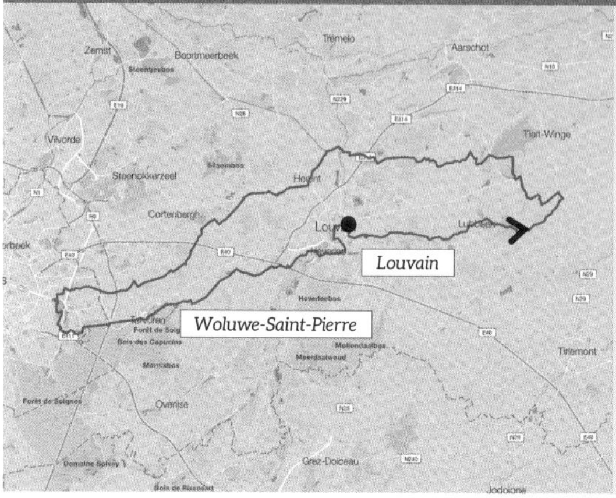

Eddy Merckx was born in Meensel-Kiezegem (km 19/mi 12). He started cycling outside his parents' grocery store before taking his first yellow jersey at Woluwe-Saint-Pierre (km 70/ mi 44). He was living in Tervuren (km 78/mi 49) at the time—a period when the media dubbed him "The Ogre." He still has many admirers of all generations. This loop, which starts and ends in Leuven between Brabant and Brussels, is an ode to Eddy and an homage to Merckx. There are cycle paths, parks and forests, a few kickers, and some cobbled sections, such as Rouge-Cloître (km 71/mi 44), which young Eddy must surely have ridden.

OUDENAARDE
TOUR OF FLANDERS

- *Very hilly / Advanced*
- *Map strava.com/routes/22157444*
- *Test yourself km 13 (mi 8) strava.com/segments/1092383*
- *Test yourself km 26 (mi 16) strava.com/segments/661261*

The Tour of Flanders draws cyclists and fans to Belgium every April. The soul of this race lies in the hills of the Flemish Ardennes, with the famous cobbled sections between Oudenaarde and Geraardsbergen, west of Brussels. It is easy to get to and a delight to explore.

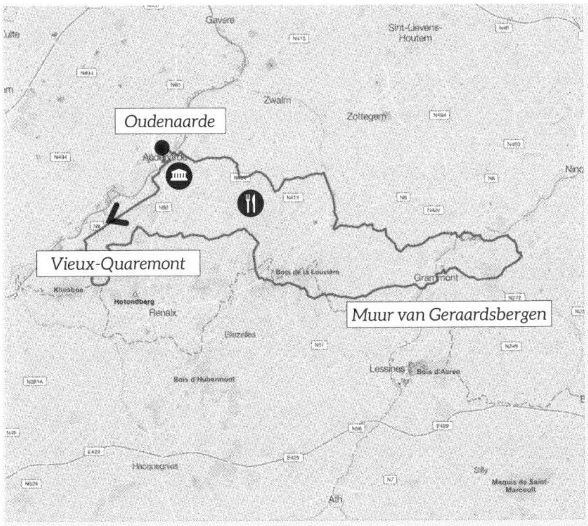

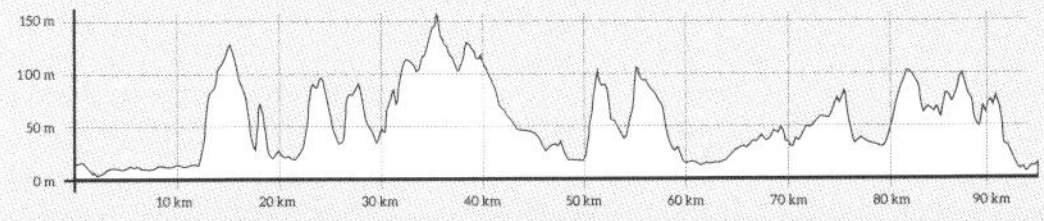

Not only does this route allow you to experience something of the legendary Tour of Flanders, including the fascinating cobbled sections, but in a happy disorder too! This loop of less than 100 km (60 mi) around Oudenaarde is ideal for getting a taste of the classic race, whether on a wooded hill or along a road barely 3 m (10 ft) wide. The route bends and wiggles so much that a GPS is highly recommended. It is quite exhilarating to traverse Oude Kwaremont, Paterberg, Kortekeer, Taaienberg, Steenbeekberg, and Pottelberg in barely 30 km (18 mi), just catching your breath before climbing the Wall of Geraardsbergen, Bosberg, Tenbosse, and Leberg. All that is missing is the fearful Koppenberg. The route does pass by the foot of it at km 7 (mi 4), so you can have a crack at it if you like. Hellish slopes, brutal cobbles, and a sneaky wind—this route has it all. Long live the Ronde van Vlaanderen!

Distance	E+	Difficulty	Appeal
95 km (59 mi)	1,100 m (3,610 ft)	3/5	5/5

Oudenaarde is not far from Ghent, Lille, and Brussels. Ghent is 30 minutes by train, 40 minutes by car (30 km/18 mi). Brussels is 1h05 by train, 1h by car (80 km/50 mi). Lille is 1h15 by train, 50 minutes by car (60 km/37 mi).

Do not wait till Oudenaarde to celebrate this fine day with a local beer. The Rembrandt is a typical Flemish tavern just 300 meters/yards from km 87 (mi 54).

Heerweg 29a
9667 Horebeke
derembrandt.be

The Centrum Ronde van Vlaanderen is an interactive museum with a bike cafe called Peloton, which also hosts cycling events. Well worth dropping in.

Markt 43
9700 Oudenaarde
crvv.be

COURTRAI
VÉLO FOLLIES

Hilly / Intermediate *Map strava.com/routes/23177278*

Distance	E+	Difficulty	Appeal
107 km (67 mi)	850 m (2,790 ft)	3/5	4/5

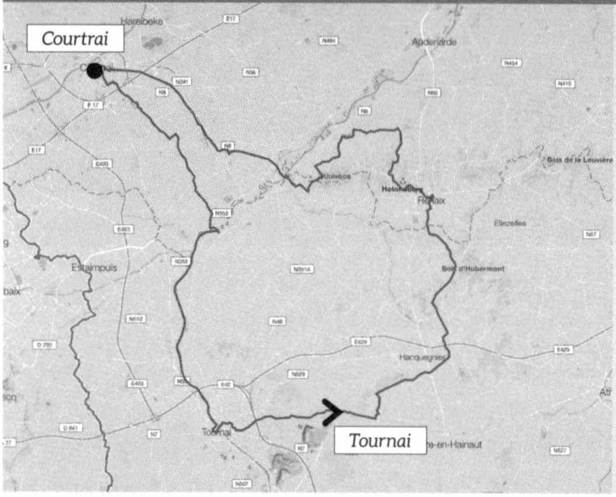

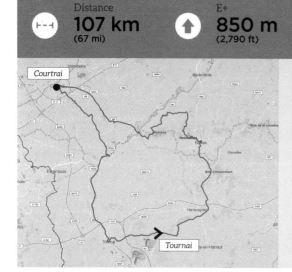

This loop at the edge of the Franco-Belgian border, the Eurometropolis Lille-Courtrai-Tournai, and the route of the Tour of Flanders has the whiff of fries and beer. Indeed, we pass close to several of the breweries (Tournai, Brunehaut, LeFort, Hommel Bier) on our route. If you visit Courtrai in January, you can enjoy the merry cycle show: Velofollies. On the way to Ronse, the woods of Pétrieux, and then Martimont give a foretaste of the West-Flemish Hills: first the Scherpenberg and then the classic Kluisbergen before we return to Courtrai. Yes, there is definitely the whiff of competition cycling too.

YPRES
THE FLAT COUNTRY

Fairly flat / Intermediate *Map strava.com/routes/22181990*

Distance	E+	Difficulty	Appeal
111 km (69 mi)	300 m (985 ft)	2/5	3/5

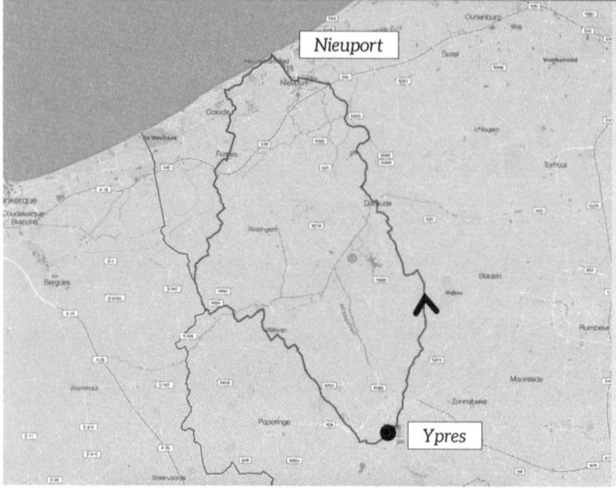

"Le plat pays" (the flat country)—so sang pure Brussels boy Jacques Brel. The town of Ypres, which is very close to France, is barely 120 km (75 mi) from the Belgian capital (2h by train). The flat country is here in the shape of plains that saw some of the deadliest battles of World War I, after which Ypres—a major textile center in the Middle Ages—was faithfully reconstructed, lending it a certain cachet.
We ride to Diksmuide and then to Nieuwpoort on the North Sea. In Veurne, admire the lovely Flemish architecture and taste some chocolate at Verdonck before another stop at Beauvoorde Castle in Vinkem, a little further on, for crepes.

YPRES

FLANDERS EXCURSION

- *Hilly / Intermediate*
- *Map strava.com/routes/22237495*
- *Test yourself km 59 (mi 37) strava.com/segments/5354963*
- *Test yourself km 69 (mi 43) strava.com/segments/2538365*

Western Flanders, at the edge of Belgium and France, has a unique atmosphere. The countryside is pleasantly undulating—a souvenir of the horrors of World War I. The hills straddling the border near Ypres are a delight, with the Kemmel as the icing on the cake.

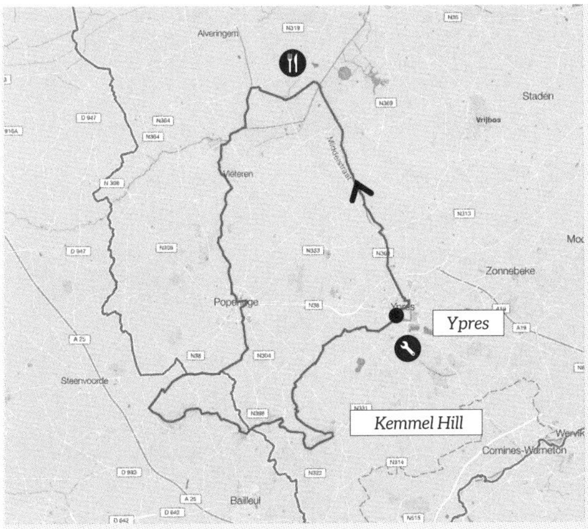

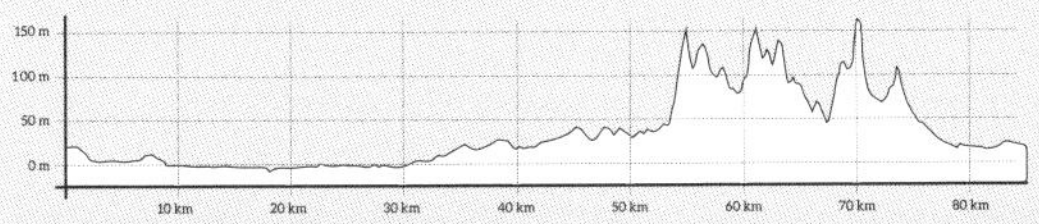

The spectacular Cloth Hall and belfry of Ypres, and its elegant apartment buildings, are testament to the town's wealthy past. But the memory of horror is all around: 170 military cemeteries are in the surrounding area—the final resting place of hundreds of thousands of soldiers of World War I. The best way to explore this region is by bicycle. A 50 km (30 mi) warm-up past Vleteren and Poperinge, with the wind blowing over the hop fields, leads to the first three proper climbs: Mont des Cats, Mont Noir, and Rodeberg. At km 68 (mi 42), Monteberg is the springboard for Kemmelberg, a climb that plays a decisive role in Gent-Wevelgem, one of the "cobbled classics": 1.5 km (1 mi) up to the French Soldiers Monument, with the final (cobbled) third at an average gradient of 11% and one long section at 15%. The descent and ride back to Ypres is magnificent, especially in the light of fall.

Distance	E+	Difficulty	Appeal
85 km (53 mi)	600 m (1,970 ft)	3/5	4/5

Ypres (pop. 35,000) is closer to Lille than the Belgian cities. Lille is 1h35 by train via Courtrai or 40 minutes by car (40 km/25 mi). Gent is 1h by train or car (60 km/37 mi). Brussels is 2h by train via Antwerp and Gent, or 1h30 by car (130 km/80 mi).

Jules Destrooper in Lo (km 23/ mi 14) is the star cookie baker of Western Flanders. Waffles and speculoos like you have never had before!

Gravestraat 5
8647 Lo-Reninge
jules-destrooper.com

Ypres has several good bike stores, but Tommie's Velodroom stands out for its very friendly welcome. Retailer of Giant and Liv bikes.

Zonnebeekseweg 37
8900 Ypres
tommiesvelodroom.be

BRUGES
VENICE OF THE NORTH (SEA)

Flat / Intermediate

Map strava.com/routes/22158506

Test yourself km 12 (mi 7) strava.com/segments/7292655

Test yourself km 86 (mi 53) strava.com/segments/12130216

Bruges is one of Europe's major tourist sites, with its market square, belfry, canals, Minnewaterpark, and chocolate museum. The surrounding countryside and the quaint North Sea coast nearby are reasons enough to explore this part of the world on two wheels.

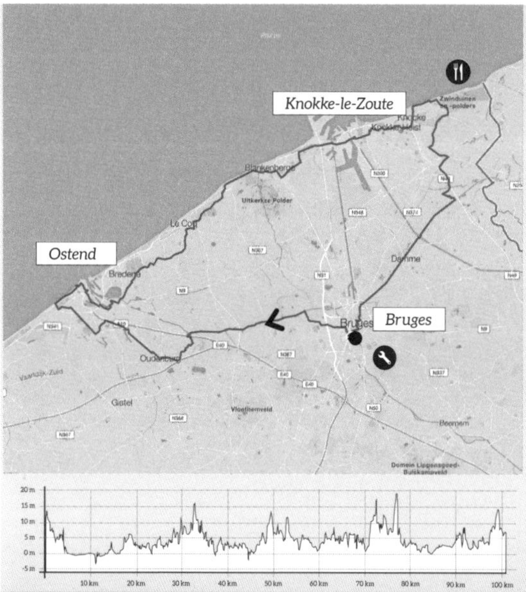

Don't go looking for climbs. This northern part of Flanders close to the Netherlands is beautifully smooth. With a landscape composed of flat roads, canals, and endless sandy beaches, you can glimpse from afar the imposing church spires of each locality. Beware of the wind; there is little shelter. Charming Bruges, the "Venice of the North," needs no further introduction. The 40 km (25 mi) stretch along the coast will more than prove why Jacques Brel was right to sing about it. After passing close to Gistel, home of Belgian cycling great Johan Museeuw, Ostend beckons, with its faded charm and the neoclassical arcade of the Royal Galleries. De Haan, Blankenberge (with its pier), the huge port of Zeebrugge, and finally the exclusive resort of Knokke-le-Zoute are all testament to the rough beauty of this part of the world. We return via picturesque medieval Damme. A delicious 100 km (62 mi).

Distance	E+	Difficulty	Appeal
101 km (63 mi)	250 m (820 ft)	2/5	4/5

Bruges is only 1h15 from Brussels by train, or 1h20 by car (100 km/62 mi). Lille is 2h by train via Ghent, or 1h10 by car (80 km/50 mi). Antwerp is 2h30 by bus or train via Brussels, or 1h20 by car (90 km/55 mi).

The Marie Siska Hotel in Knokke (km 76/mi 47) is one hundred years old. Pop into its tearoom for a coffee and one of its famous heart-shaped waffles—the best on the coast.

Zoutelaan 177
8300 Knokke-Heist
siska-marie.com

Bruges is full of bike stores (after all, we are in Flanders!). Steershop stands out because of its philosophy, aesthetics, and "gravel" culture. Kona bikes.

Koolkerkse Steenweg 7A
8000 Bruges
steershop.be

ANTWERP
FLEMISH TRIPTYCH

Fairly flat / Intermediate

Map strava.com/routes/22206501

Distance **122 km** (76 mi)

E+ **300 m** (985 ft)

Difficulty **3/5**

Appeal **3/5**

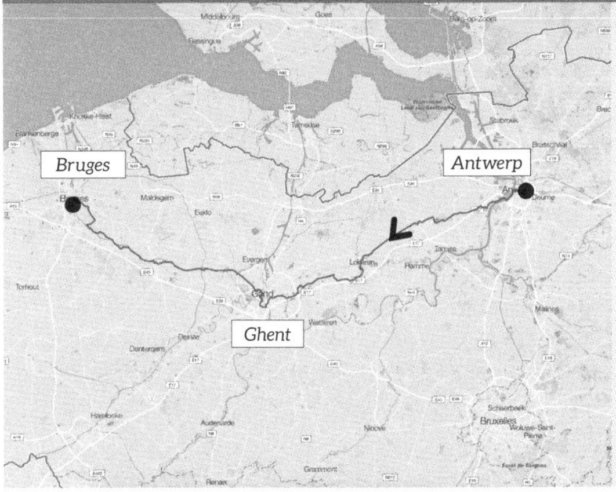

"Flahute" is the term applied to those tough Flemish cyclists who will ride through pain and appalling weather conditions on any kind of road surface for a chance at a few minutes of glory. Races such as Paris-Roubaix are their arenas of predilection, but some have made their mark on pancake-flat routes such as this one from Antwerp to Bruges. In Antwerp (famous for its diamond trade), we take the art deco Saint Anna's Tunnel beneath the Scheldt River. In historic Ghent, we pass the most spectacular velodrome in Europe: the Kuipke, which has a 166 m (548 ft) track. Finally, we ride by the charming canals of Bruges.

HASSELT
GLIMPSES OF LIMBURG

Hilly / Intermediate

Map strava.com/routes/23374824

Distance **70 km** (44 mi)

E+ **300 m** (985 ft)

Difficulty **2/5**

Appeal **3/5**

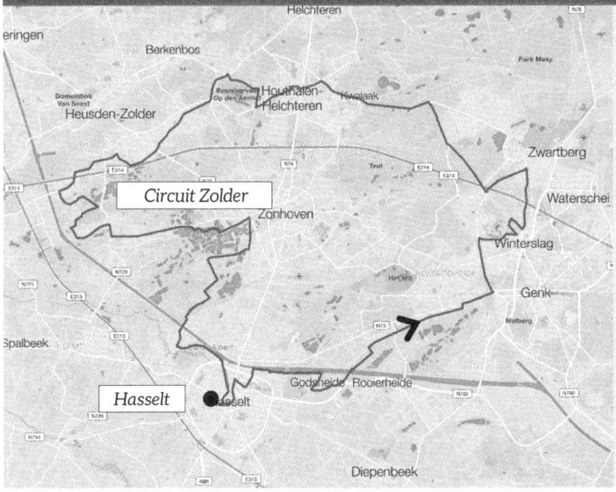

Van Looy, Vanderaerden, Boonen, Van Aert, Wellens. In Limburg, there is no shortage of serious riders, both past and present. Cycling is in the genes. This route from Hasselt, located 1h by train from Brussels or Antwerp, expresses all of the province's diversity: Albert Canal and wetlands, traces of an industrial past (C-Mine in Genk), and the Kievit ponds and their amazing cycle path beside the water. At km 48 (mi 30) is the Zolder motor racing circuit where cyclists have access for €39 ($42) a year. How about recreating Cipollini's sprint in the 2002 world championships?

ROTTERDAM
WINDMILLS OF KINDERDIJK

Flat / Intermediate

Map strava.com/routes/22176192

Test yourself km 33 (mi 21) strava.com/segments/9389454

Test yourself km 103 (mi 64) strava.com/segments/8530719

With its avant-garde architecture, Rotterdam is just an appetizer. This route through southern Holland follows rivers and canals—always on cycle paths, obviously—to the beautiful towns of Gouda and Dordrecht by way of the stunning windmills of Kinderdijk.

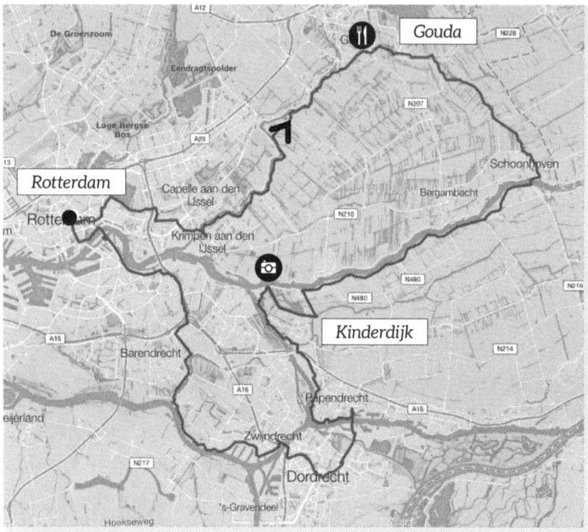

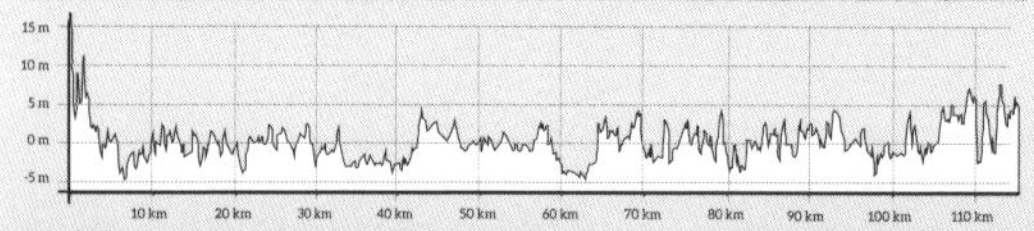

The fabulous line of nineteen windmills (most of them dating from the eighteenth century) of the tiny village of Kinderdijk stands beside canals and polders on which sporty types go speed skating during harsh winters, having left their bicycles in the garage. Here, 15 km (9 mi) east of Rotterdam, the scene is like something from a Dutch fantasy. The route passes alongside and spans some of the most famous rivers in the Netherlands (including the IJssel, Lek, and Noord), crosses umpteen polders, skirts Gouda (home of the eponymous cheese), passes through historic Dordrecht, and explores Rotterdam and its architectural wonders, such as the Markthal, the Erasmus Bridge, the Euromast, and the central station—the starting point for our ride. With a maximum altitude of 12 m (40 ft) over the entire 115 km (71 mi) route—half of which is below sea level—you will not strain a sinew.

Distance	E+	Difficulty	Appeal
115 km (71 mi)	300 m (985 ft)	2/5	4/5

Rotterdam airport is very close to our starting point, Rotterdam central station: 20 minutes by train and 14 minutes by car (8 km/5 mi). Amsterdam is 30 minutes by high-speed train, 1h by regular train, and 1h15 by car (80 km/50 mi). Brussels is 1h20 by train and 2h by car.

Gouda (km 28/mi 17) is located on the other side of the IJssel river. Head for the Gouda Cheese House in the historic center for one of its scrumptious cheese waffles.

Hoogstraat 1
2801 HG Gouda
goudskaashuis.nl

Stam Bakery in Kinderdijk (km 64/mi 40) does fine coffee and cakes, but above all it affords a view of the perfect alignment of windmills.

Molenstraat 143
2961 AK Kinderdijk
bakkerij-stam.nl

The impressive line of windmills of Kinderdijk, Netherlands.

MIDDELBURG
THE WIND OF ZEELAND

- *Flat / Intermediate*
- *Map strava.com/routes/22174460*
- *Test yourself km 34 (mi 21) strava.com/segments/1045009*
- *Test yourself km 57 (mi 35) strava.com/segments/6209270*

Do not be frightened of the wind blowing off the polders, rivers, lakes, and North Sea around Zeeland. You can and you will defy it as you ride due west on the return leg, emulating the valiant competitors of the crazy Tegenwind challenge that takes place during winter storms.

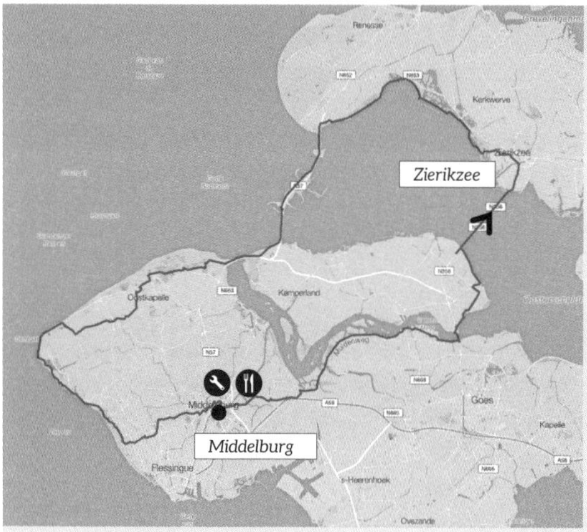

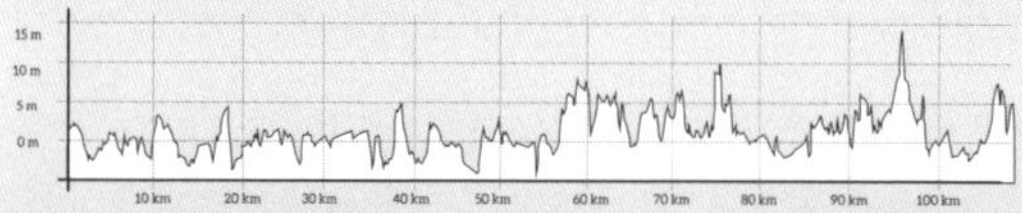

No need to climb 2,000 m (6,500 ft) for a change of scene. Zeeland, in the appropriately named Netherlands, is a striking example. Depart from Middelburg, the provincial capital of the former island of Walcheren, for an exceptional ride along endless cycle paths between sea, polders, lighthouses, and windmills. Follow the Veerse Meer lagoon to the Zandkreekdam lock (km 22/mi 13.5), then cross to the former island of Noord-Beveland. At km 38 (mi 24), you reach Zierikzee on the island of Schouwen-Duiveland. If the wind is blowing from the west, ride on to the Oosterscheldekering storm surge barrier (km 57/mi 35.5) to try your luck at the Tegenwind challenge: an 8.5 km (5.3 mi) ride straight into the wind on a classic Dutch upright bike (the actual competition is held every year during winter storms). The ride back along the Walcheren coast is magical as the sun sets.

Distance	E+	Difficulty	Appeal
109 km (68 mi)	200 m (655 ft)	3/5	4/5

Midden-Zeeland Airport has few connections. Trains from Brussels and Amsterdam go via Rotterdam, which is 1h40 from Middelburg. Add 1h50 from Brussels, 1h20 from Amsterdam. By car, allow 1h30 from Rotterdam, 1h40 from Brussels, and 2h25 from Amsterdam.

Røst is a hip, cozy cafe—the kind the Dutch do so well—right in the center of pretty Middelburg. Its little terrace is perfect for a debrief over a sweet treat.

Sint Janstraat 45
4331 KB Middelburg
www.rostmiddelburg.nl

Vélosport is a specialized store and workshop by the Binnengracht canal. Retailer for Orbea, Merida, and Eddy Merckx.

Beenhouwerssingel 5
4331 MD Middelburg
velosportmiddelburg.nl

TILBURG
FUNNY FRONTIER

Fairly flat / Intermediate

Map strava.com/routes/22939361

Distance	E+	Difficulty	Appeal
54 km (34 mi)	100 m (330 ft)	1/5	3/5

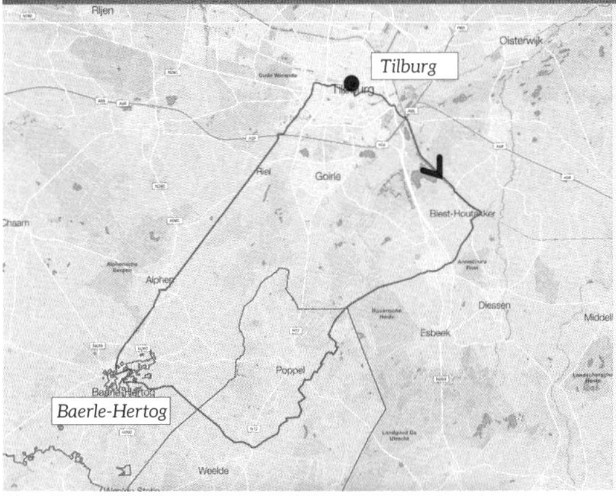

Baerle-Hertog is a Belgian municipality of the province of Antwerp. Part of its territory comprises a mishmash of tiny exclaves in the Dutch municipality of Baerle-Nassau. On the ground, you will see lines of white crosses marking out a border in the middle of a street, or even running straight through a building. Such a curiosity is well worth a two-hour ride from the pretty university town of Tilburg. You will appreciate wandering the pleasant canal sides when you return. Our route crosses countryside and forest with 15 km (9 mi) of dead-straight cycle path on the way back from Alphen.

EINDHOVEN
BRABANT HEATHER

Fairly flat / Intermediate

Map strava.com/routes/22903874

Distance	E+	Difficulty	Appeal
46 km (29 mi)	150 m (495 ft)	1/5	3/5

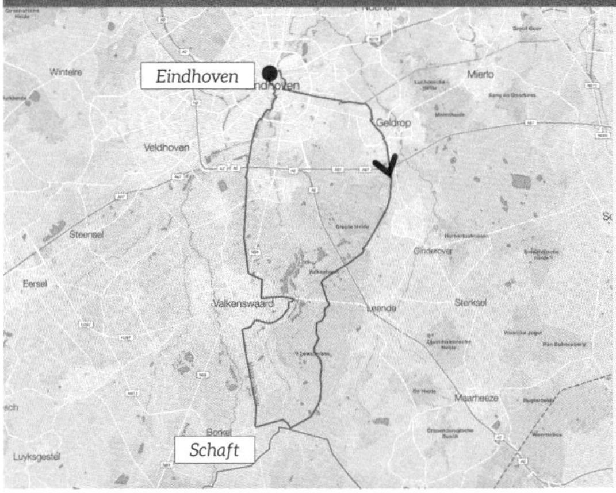

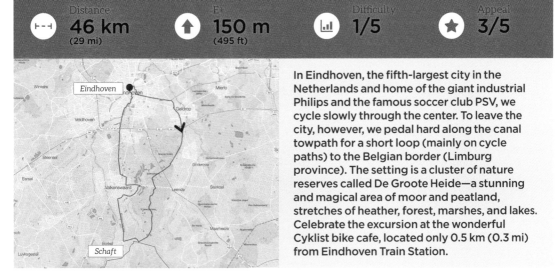

In Eindhoven, the fifth-largest city in the Netherlands and home of the giant industrial Philips and the famous soccer club PSV, we cycle slowly through the center. To leave the city, however, we pedal hard along the canal towpath for a short loop (mainly on cycle paths) to the Belgian border (Limburg province). The setting is a cluster of nature reserves called De Groote Heide—a stunning and magical area of moor and peatland, stretches of heather, forest, marshes, and lakes. Celebrate the excursion at the wonderful Cyklist bike cafe, located only 0.5 km (0.3 mi) from Eindhoven Train Station.

MAASTRICHT
A TASTE OF AMSTEL

Hilly / Intermediate
Map strava.com/routes/22187975
Test yourself km 37 (mi 23) strava.com/segments/7007454
Test yourself km 71 (mi 44) strava.com/segments/1075689

The Amstel Gold Race is a spring classic that follows a convoluted course that explores Limburg province from top to bottom—from Maastricht to the famous Cauberg climb. Limburg is the southernmost of the Netherlands' twelve provinces, and the only one to offer a hilly landscape.

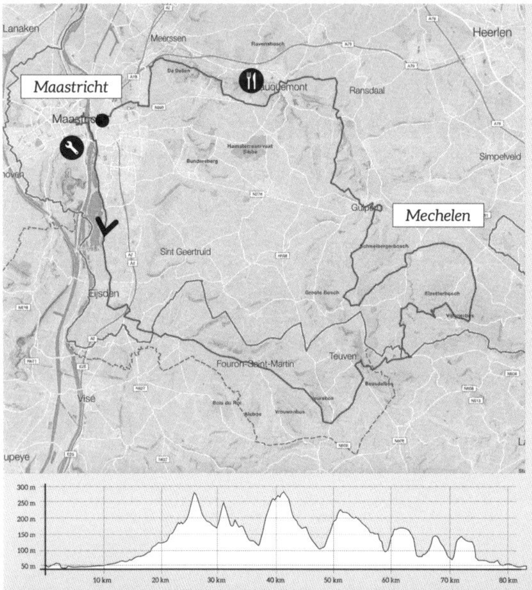

This route does not cover all of the "bergs," those short climbs in the Limburg hills that spice up the Amstel Gold Race. It does, however, take in 20 km (12.5 mi) of Belgian territory, including two precipitous little climbs: Hagelstein (km 24/mi 15), and Beusdael (km 33/mi 20), which passes a thirteenth-century castle on the descent. The route then curls back into the Netherlands for a series of testing traps, starting at km 37 (mi 23) with Camerig (2.4 km/1.5 mi) at an average gradient of over 6%, then Schweiberg (2.6 km/1.6 mi), Gulpen (1.4 km/0.9 mi), and Keutenberg (1.3 km/0.8 mi)—all of them irregular and quite nasty in places. Finally, on the way out of Valkenburg (km 71/mi 44) comes the prestigious Cauberg, where the April race is often decided. Then it's back to Maastricht on the Meuse river, spanned by the Saint Servatius Bridge, which you crossed when you set out.

Distance	E+	Difficulty	Appeal
84 km (52 mi)	1,000 m (3,280 ft)	3/5	4/5

Liège is just 35 minutes by train or 25 minutes by car (35 km/22 mi). Brussels and Cologne are 1h40 and 2h by train (via Liège), and 1h20 (125 km/78 mi) and 1h15 (100 km/62 mi) by car. Amsterdam is further: 2h30 by train or 2h30 (220 km/137 mi) by car.

At the foot of the Cauberg (km 71/mi 44), fuel yourself for the final challenge (or recover after conquering it) amid the bric-a-brac decor of Fixed Gear Coffee.

Daalhemerweg 4
6301 BK Valkenburg
fixedgearcoffee.com

Alley Cat Bikes & Coffee is named in homage to cycle courier culture, but they offer repairs of all kinds of bikes.

Hoenderstraat 15-17
6211 EL Maastricht
alleycatbikescoffee.nl

AMSTERDAM
DUNES AND TULIPS

Fairly flat / Intermediate *Map* strava.com/routes/22178162

Distance	E+	Difficulty	Appeal
100 km (62 mi)	300 m (985 ft)	2/5	3/5

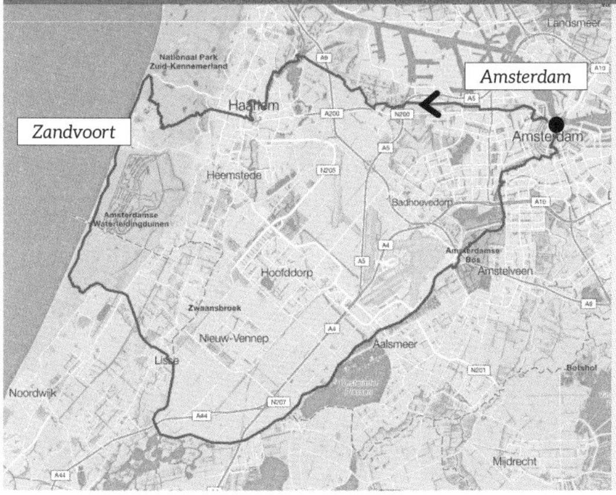

Amsterdam is a cycling city, but it is great to escape it too via the many bridges and cycle paths that run through parks and along canals. We head west to Haarlem and its pretty houses, then through Zuid-Kennemerland National Park to the coast—all dunes and low vegetation. Just before the North Sea resort town of Zandvoort is the famous motor racing track where a popular twenty-four-hour cycling race is held each year. We return by the beautiful town of Lisse and its stunning Keukenhof flower garden (km 56/mi 35), one of the largest in the world. Back in Amsterdam, drop in to Madmen Bicycles Cafe on Steigereiland.

ALKMAAR
POLDER TO POLDER

Fairly flat / Intermediate *Map* strava.com/routes/22936065

Distance	E+	Difficulty	Appeal
90 km (56 mi)	100 m (328 ft)	2/5	3/5

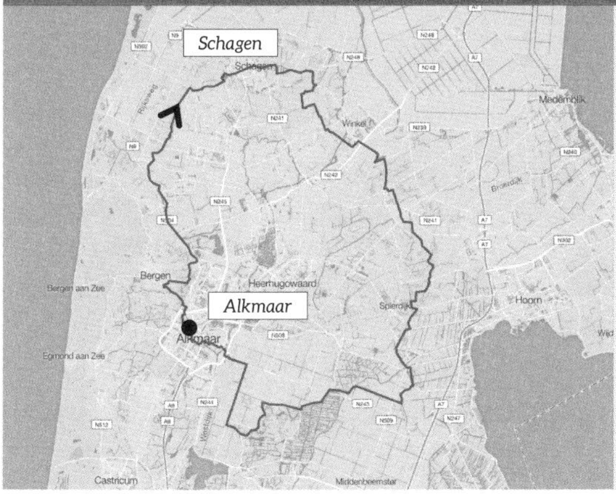

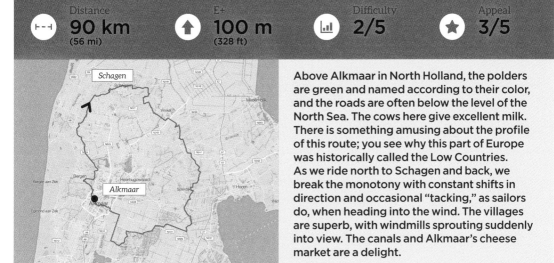

Above Alkmaar in North Holland, the polders are green and named according to their color, and the roads are often below the level of the North Sea. The cows here give excellent milk. There is something amusing about the profile of this route; you see why this part of Europe was historically called the Low Countries. As we ride north to Schagen and back, we break the monotony with constant shifts in direction and occasional "tacking," as sailors do, when heading into the wind. The villages are superb, with windmills sprouting suddenly into view. The canals and Alkmaar's cheese market are a delight.

AMSTERDAM
KOM OP GERRIE! (COME ON GERRIE!)

⊕ *Fairly flat / Intermediate* ⊕ *Map strava.com/routes/23392598*

Distance	E+	Difficulty	Appeal
104 km (64 mi)	200 m (656 ft)	2/5	4/5

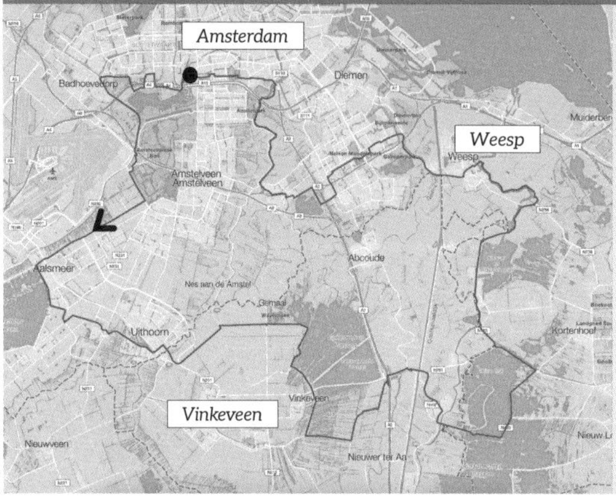

Gerrie Knetemann was a Dutch cycling star of the seventies and eighties, a stalwart of the legendary TI-Raleigh team, and a multiple Yellow Jersey wearer. Born in Amsterdam, he died in 2004. An annual Gran Fondo race is staged in his honor, exploring parks, polders, and cycle paths to the south of the capital. Starting at the 1928 Olympic stadium, we cross little bridges and pass old forts and corners of greenery. The lakes of Westeinder, Vinkeveense, and Loosdrechtse seem huge. On this flat course, we roll fast like Gerrie did. His daughter Roxane, a pro cyclist, is on Strava. Back in Amsterdam, pop into Rapha CC in Jordaan.

OOSTERBEEK
THE INCREDIBLE PARK

⊕ *Fairly flat / Intermediate* ⊕ *Map strava.com/routes/23400396*

Distance	E+	Difficulty	Appeal
99 km (62 mi)	600 m (1,970 ft)	2/5	4/5

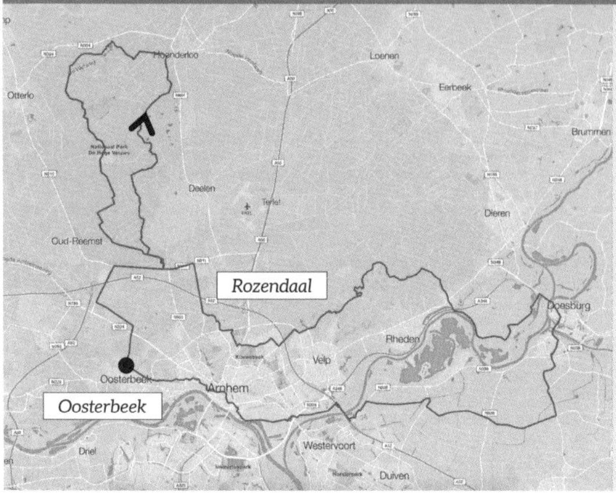

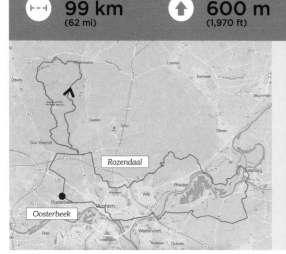

This fairly flat route from Oosterbeek, neighboring Arnhem and the Lower Rhine (1h15 by train from Amsterdam), runs through the fantastic Hoge Veluwe National Park: 5,400 ha (13,345 acres) of woodland, heath, sand dunes, and lakes with deer, wild boar, and wild sheep. Along the 30 km (19 mi) of cycle paths, you will find a multitude of white bicycles provided for visitors to use free of charge. The Kröller-Müller Museum (km 18/ mi 11) has the largest private collection of Vincent van Gogh paintings in the world. Return via some lovely ramps above the IJssel Valley.

SCANDINAVIAN & BALTIC COUNTRIES

ISLANDS OF DENMARK

—

NORWEGIAN FJORDS

—

ARCTIC CIRCLE

—

BLUE LAGOON

—

STOCKHOLM

—

LAKES OF FINLAND

—

FROM TALLINN TO VILNIUS

—

AARHUS
DANISH JOY

- *Hilly / Intermediate*
- *Map strava.com/routes/23540857*
- *Test yourself km 45 (mi 28) strava.com/segments/4354387*
- *Test yourself km 68 (mi 42) strava.com/segments/14968789*

Aarhus must surely qualify as the most livable city in Denmark—the country that is ranked as the best to live in. The surrounding region keeps its promise too, particularly because we reach the highest point in the country midway through our route: 170.77 m (560.3 ft).

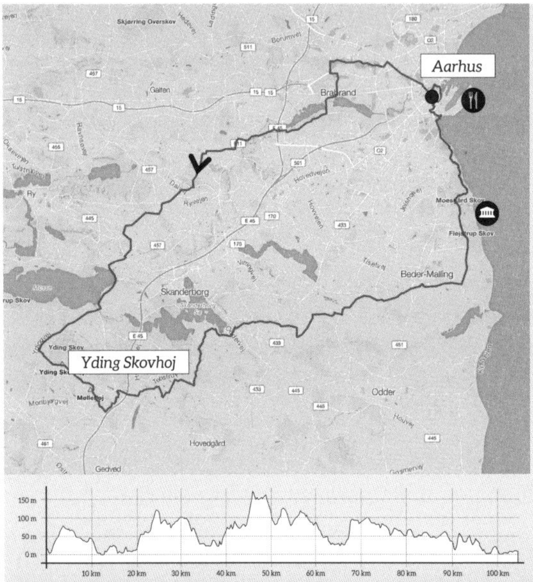

Wonderful Aarhus, the largest city on the continental Jutland peninsula, is a delight. Setting off from the central train station, we ride past the ARoS contemporary art museum, Den Gamle By, and then through several long parks. On the way back, after riding along the wild beaches on the Kattegat, we reenter the city via the futuristic building Dokk1 and the cathedral. Along the route, we explore Lake Mossø—the largest in Jutland—and the surrounding hills, which are pretty low. The toughest ramp in the entire country (1.3 km/0.8 mi at 7%) leads to Yding Skovhøj (km 46/mi 29) at a height of 170.77 m (560.3 ft), a smidgen lower than the highest natural point in Denmark: the neighboring hill of Møllehøj, which we pass 3 km (2 mi) further on. The climb feels like something from the Flanders hills, but the wide expanses of the Jutland countryside exude absolute tranquility.

Distance	E+	Difficulty	Appeal
92 km (57 mi)	800 m (2,600 ft)	3/5	4/5

Aarhus (pop. 265,000) is Denmark's second-largest city, but its airport has few international connections. Copenhagen is 3h by train or car (including a ferry crossing). Hamburg is 4h30 by train or 4h by car (350 km/218 mi).

Before starting out or when you return, pop into Stiller's Coffee in Aarhus's historic center for a cup of some of the finest brew in Denmark.

Klostergade 32E
8000 Aarhus
stillerscoffee.dk

At km 91 (mi 57), stop in Moesgaard Park to visit the MOMU, a museum devoted to Scandinavian archaeology. You will be tempted to cycle up its sloping roof, which is planted with grass.

Moesgård Allé 15
8270 Hojbjerg
moesgaardmuseum.dk

VORDINGBORG
THE CLIFFS OF MØN

Hilly / Intermediate *Map* *strava.com/routes/23550118*

Distance **122 km** (76 mi) | E+ **850 m** (2,790 ft) | Difficulty **3/5** | Appeal **4/5**

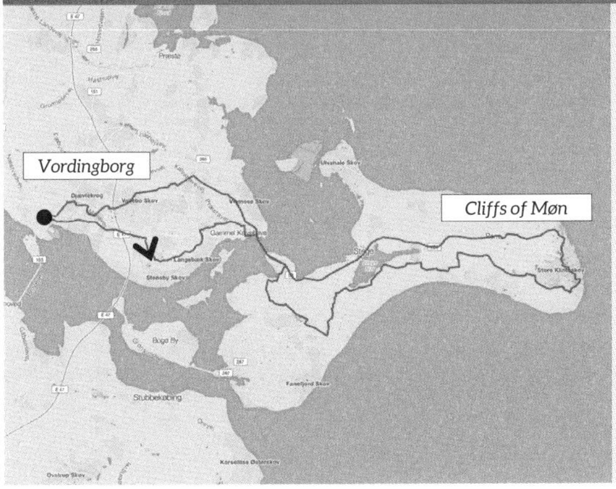

At the southern end of Zealand, Vordingborg (1h25 from Copenhagen by train) is the starting point for our exploration of one of Denmark's natural wonders: the cliffs of the island of Møn. We cross the Queen Alexandrine Bridge and ride through the pretty town of Stege. The cliffs are located at the midway point: a 6 km (4 mi) balcony above the Baltic Sea. The sea becomes so turquoise sometimes that the pebble beaches at the foot of the chalky walls are referred to as the "Cold Caribbean." Stop at km 60 (mi 37), 125 m (410 ft) above the water, to enjoy the panorama to the fullest. Return at night for a wonderfully starry sky.

COPENHAGEN
NOBLE ZEALAND

Fairly flat / Intermediate *Map* *strava.com/routes/23610769*

Distance **131 km** (81 mi) | E+ **700 m** (2,300 ft) | Difficulty **3/5** | Appeal **4/5**

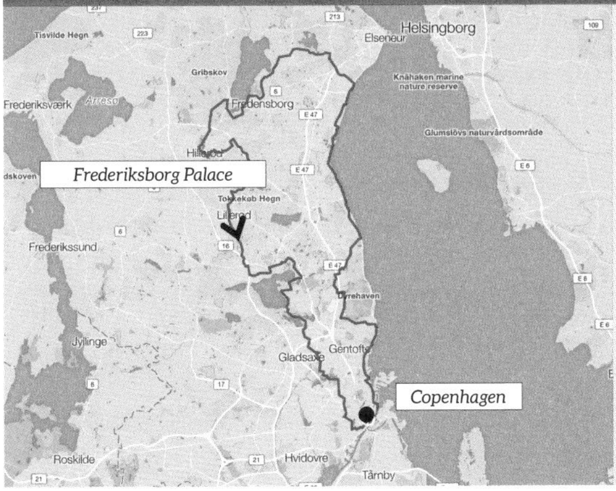

Copenhagen is a very special cycling destination, because it is a world leader for daily bike use. Our fairly flat route explores the northeast of the island of Zealand, heading out along the Øresund strait between parks and beaches, before turning inland to visit the lakes. Along the way, we pass the castles of Gurre (km 45/mi 28), Fredensborg (km 56/mi 35), and Frederiksborg (km 68/mi 42), the largest palace ever built in Scandinavia. Setting out from the Rapha CC store, we take in some of Copenhagen's splendid sights: Nyhavn and its colorful houses, Kastellet citadel, and *The Little Mermaid* statue.

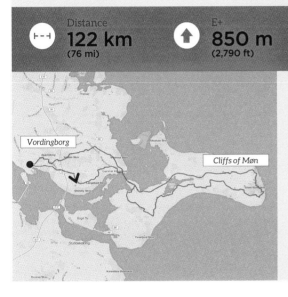

ODDESUND
COLD HAWAII

Fairly flat / Intermediate — *Map* strava.com/routes/23547972

Distance	E+	Difficulty	Appeal
132 km (82 mi)	600 m (1,950 ft)	3/5	4/5

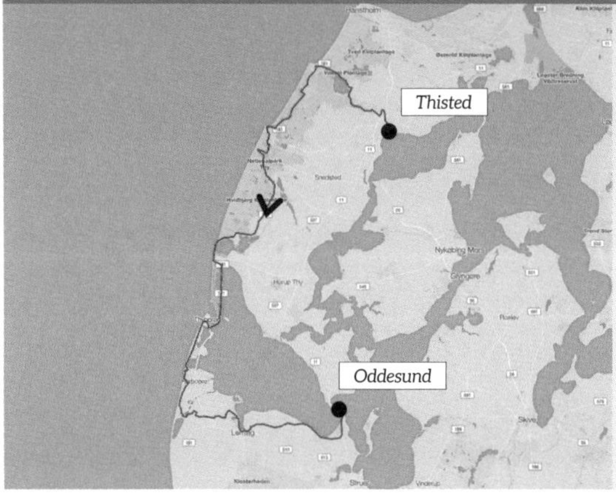

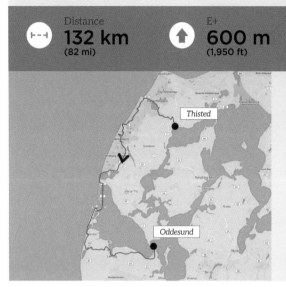

In northwest Denmark, beyond the Limfjord that separates the island of Vendsyssel-Thy from continental Jutland, the wild coast is shaped by the endless winds of the North Sea. Thy National Park comprises dense forest, moorland, and virgin dunes. Deer roam here, and out at sea, blue fishing boats ply their trade. Klitmøller (nicknamed Cold Hawaii) is one of the best surfing spots in Europe. This ride is a total immersion: start at Oddesund North train station (3h from Aarhus) and the bridge over the Limfjord, take the short ferry trip (12 minutes, €6/$6.50) from Thyborøn to Agger, and return by train from Thisted (1h10).

HJÖRRING
WHERE WATERS MEET

Fairly flat / Advanced — *Map* strava.com/routes/23617652

Distance	E+	Difficulty	Appeal
148 km (92 mi)	550 m (1,805 ft)	3/5	4/5

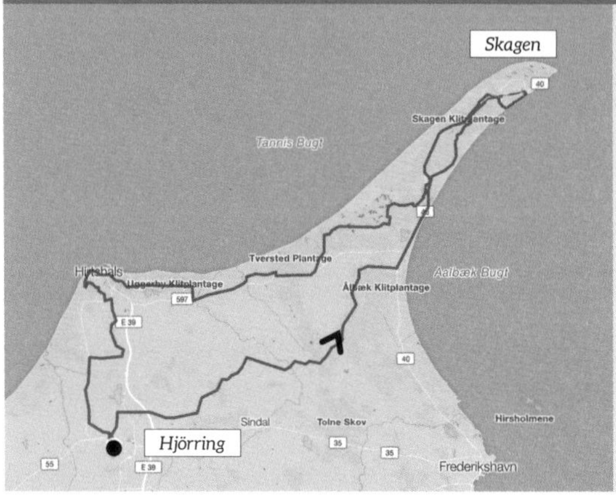

Skagen, located at the northern tip of Jutland, is full of surprises. The light is so beautiful here that it drew a number of artists known as the Skagen Painters, whose work is celebrated in a museum. Two centuries ago, a church was buried by the sand and eventually demolished, leaving only the tower. The sandbar spit at the point of the cap is called Grenen; people flock from all over Denmark to contemplate the curious swirling of the waters of the North and Baltic seas as they meet. Our long route allows us to enjoy both coasts. Stop for lunch at the Port of Skagen and return to Hjørring in the early evening, riding into the setting sun.

OSLO
SETTING SUN

- *Very hilly / Advanced*
- *Map strava.com/routes/23229040*
- *Test yourself km 65 (mi 40) strava.com/segments/7896679*
- *Test yourself km 72 (mi 45) strava.com/segments/17785241*

In the twenty-first century, the Norwegians discovered a fervor for the Tour de France, and cycling really took off in Oslo, the capital. You can enjoy the city's sensible urban planning and huge green spaces in all directions. Here we head south.

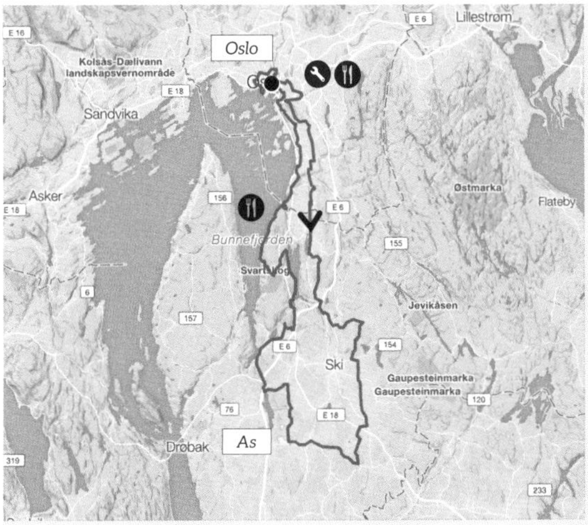

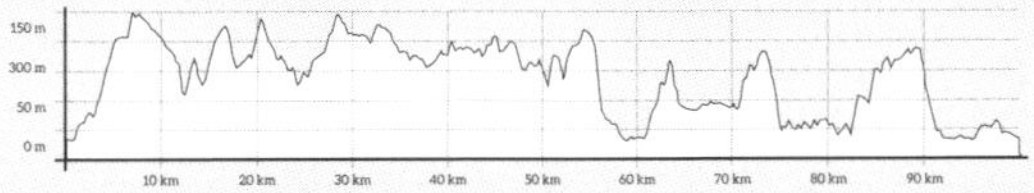

In June and July, this very popular cycling route can become truly enchanting if you finish it in the evening. As you near central Oslo, you see the giant eponymous fjord open out to the west, revealing some unforgettable (and late) sunsets. As you ride south via Ekeberg and its sculpture park (lovely views!), you never feel as if you are quite leaving the suburbs, yet it is not at all oppressive. There are many cycle paths through the numerous forests. It makes you wonder if 1.5 million people really live in the Oslo metropolitan area. At km 59 (mi 37), we hit the Bunnefjorden, the innermost part of the Oslofjord. The ride back is quite idyllic.

Distance	E+	Difficulty	Appeal
100 km (62 mi)	1,450 m (4,760 ft)	3/5	4/5

Oslo Airport is located 35 km (22 mi) northwest of the capital. Take the express train to Oslo Central Station (25 minutes). Gothenburg is 3h40 by train or 3h by car (300 km/185 mi). Kristiansand (ferry connection from Denmark) is 4h15 by train or 3h30 by car (320 km/200 mi).

There are few better ways to enjoy the view over the Bunnefjorden than sitting on the terrace of Ingierstrand Bad Restaurant (km 78/mi 49). It overlooks a beach equipped with a high diving board.

Ingierstrandveien 30
1420 Svartskog
ingierstrandbad.no

Amber and Christian, founders of the exceptional The Service Course bike cafe in Girona, Spain, have opened a branch in Oslo at km 2 (mi 1.25).

Kjølberggata 21
0653 Oslo
theservicecourse.cc

LILLESTRØM
TRANQUIL ØYEREN

- *Hilly / Advanced*
- *Map strava.com/routes/21216479*
- *Test yourself km 7 (mi 4) strava.com/segments/5236403*
- *Test yourself km 67 (mi 41) strava.com/segments/6786989*

Inland Norway is a country on the water. Landscapes stretching into the distance reveal themselves as soon as you rise a little above the many lakes and rivers. This is the case around Øyeren, less than an hour from Oslo.

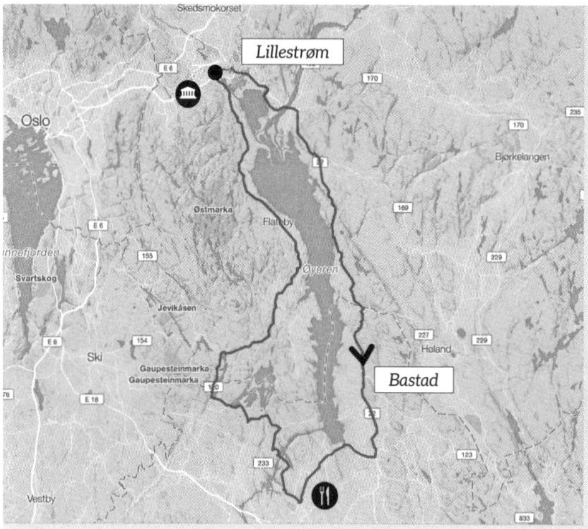

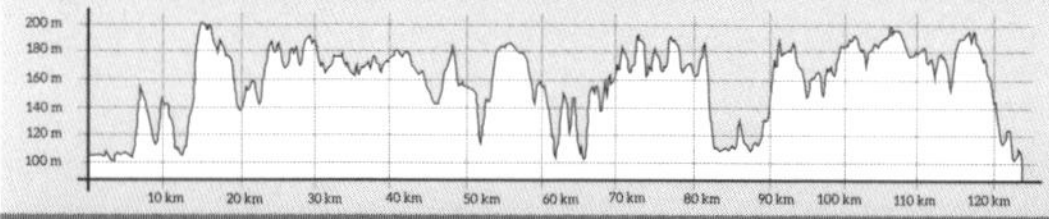

Øyeren is Norway's ninth-largest lake at 85 km² (33 sq mi). It has three things going for it: proximity to the capital and international airport; Norway's longest river, the Glomma, which feeds the lake from the north and flows southward from it down to Oslofjord; and the tranquil roads around it. You will never tire of the peaceful expanses of water, nor the long stretches through forests of spruce, Scots pines, beech, and birch. The route has just enough elevation gain to provide magnificent views over øyeren, as well as Lakes Lyseren and Mjær on the way back to Lillestrøm, our start and end point. Once you cross the Glomma (km 9/mi 5.5), you will find little human habitation until you cross back over it at km 64 (mi 40). Make sure that you take more than the essentials with you, in case you need to repair your bike.

Distance	E+	Difficulty	Appeal
116 km (72 mi)	1,250 m (4,100 ft)	3/5	4/5

Lillestrøm (pop. 85,000) is located 25 km (15.5 mi) northeast of Oslo on the road to Oslo Airport. It is 10 minutes by Airport Express train (every 20 minutes) from Oslo S (center) or the airport. By car, allow 30 minutes from the airport (35 km/22 mi).

If you are feeling hungry at km 59 (mi 37), head to The Coffee Shop in Askim, only 2 km (1.25 mi) off the route. Burgers, salads, and omelets. Open 10 a.m to 8 p.m.

Radhusgata 6
1830 Askim

Next to the train station, Lillestrøm Bicycle Hotel is a fine example of Scandinavian cycling culture. This futuristic building of wood and glass is a very safe bicycle parking lot with space for four hundred bikes. A monthly subscription costs 50Kr ($5.50).

visitnorway.com

STAVANGER
FULL GAS IN ROGALAND

- *Hilly / Intermediate*
- *Map strava.com/routes/23570490*
- *Test yourself km 19 (mi 12) strava.com/segments/11849148*
- *Test yourself km 63 (mi 39) strava.com/segments/6975466*

Winner of the 2014 Milan-San Remo and the 2015 Tour of Flanders, Alexander Kristoff has more than 30,000 followers on Strava (strava.com/pros/9232885). This route follows his favorite roads around Stavanger, where he is from.

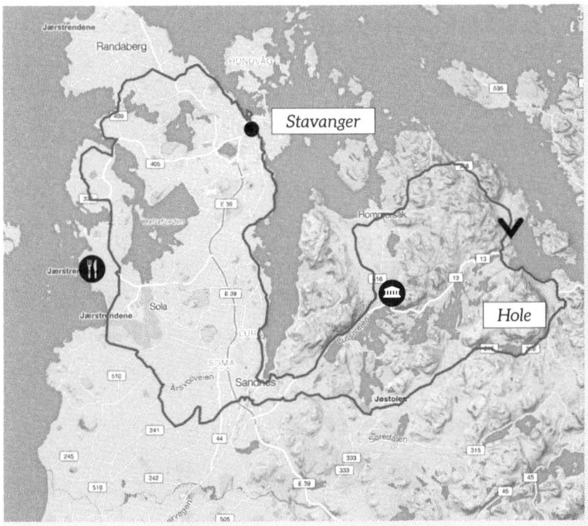

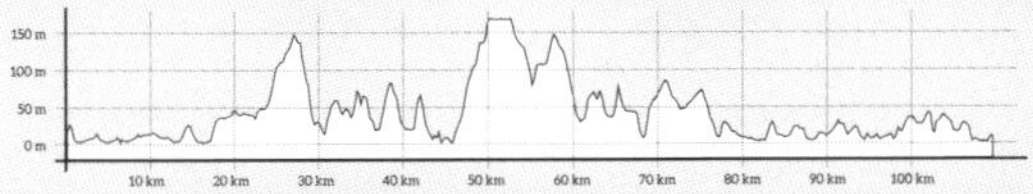

In Norway's far southwest, Rogaland offers only short ramps around Stavanger (pop. 130,000). You have to go a little further north to find the unique sensations of a mountain plunging into the ocean, such as at Preikestolen, an impressive cliff that towers above the Lysefjord. The formidable sprinter/puncher Alexander Kristoff has stayed true to the invigorating air of his native Rogaland. With Norway's oil and gas industry concentrated here, the towns of Stavanger and Sandnes have sprawled; the first challenge is to avoid the galloping urbanization at the start of our route. We ride through Hommersåk at km 31 (mi 19) and on to the shores of the Høgsfjord before exploring the lakes of Sandnes. Further west, you will hardly notice the airport between the beaches of Sola and the Hafrsfjord. Remember to channel your inner Kristoff as you punch your way up the short, intense climbs.

Distance	E+	Difficulty	Appeal
110 km (68 mi)	1,350 m (4,430 ft)	3/5	3/5

Stavanger Airport, which is connected to numerous European cities, is located at Sola: 15 km (9.5 mi) southwest of the city (1h by bus). From Oslo, we recommend the night train (8h). By car, Oslo is 7h (550 km/340 mi).

Located right on the dunes, the Sola Strand Hotel (km 82/mi 51) is a deliciously tranquil establishment with a contemporary design. Heed the call of its terrace —at least, for a coffee.

Axel Lunds veg 27
4055 Sola
sola-strandhotel.no

At km 24 (mi 15), you can opt for the 44 km (27 mi) ride to the vertiginous Preikestolen cliff (E+ 1,000 m/3,280 ft), which may be reached via a 4 km (2.5 mi) hike on foot (E+ 400 m/1,315 ft).

strava.com/routes/23587132

OSLO
ASCENT TO THE TEMPLE

Low mountain / Intermediate — *Map* strava.com/routes/23236621

Distance	E+	Difficulty	Appeal
30 km (19 mi)	550 m (1,805 ft)	3/5	5/5

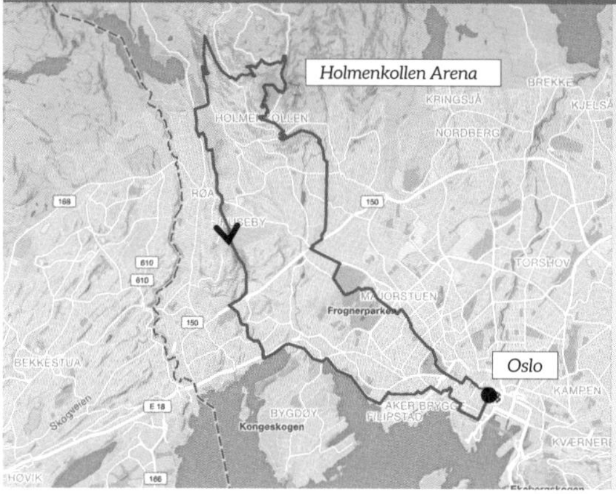

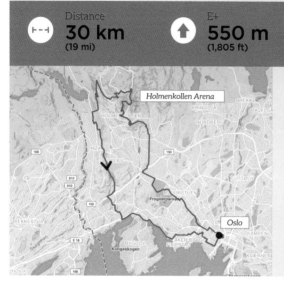

A ride to Holmenkollen is a pilgrimage—at least, that is how any Oslo cyclist feels as they climb this 6 km (3.7 mi) slope (at gradients of between 6% and 8%) up to the impressive ski jump originally built nearly 130 years ago—a temple of the sport ever since the Winter Olympics of 1952. The out-run is used for ice skating in winter and for roller-skating and roller-skiing in summer. No bikes though.
The road climbs a little higher, up to 420 m (1,380 ft), which is where you realize how gutsy ski jumpers are. You can even visit the ski jump itself (134 m/440 ft high) and its museum.
The view over the Oslofjord is astounding.

LILLEHAMMER
OLYMPIC FLAME

Low mountain / Intermediate — *Map* strava.com/routes/23616455

Distance	E+	Difficulty	Appeal
62 km (39 mi)	1,300 m (985 ft)	3/5	4/5

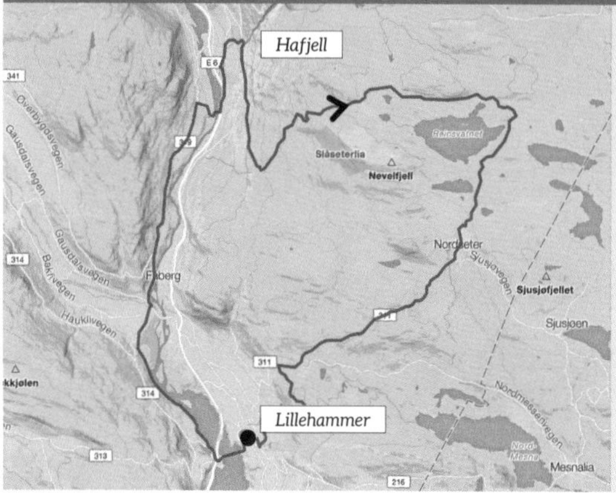

Never had the Winter Olympics been as popular as they were at Lillehammer in 1994. The Norwegian people showed their vibrant passion for togetherness and winter sports. From the bridge over Lake Mjøsa (the largest in the country), we pursue an Olympic tour: Hafjell slalom stadium (km 22/mi 14), the area of the Birkebeiner cross-country ski marathon (km 52/mi 32), above the Lysgards Ski Arena, and past Håkons Hall (ice-skating/hockey) and the Norwegian Olympic Museum.
To visit the Olympic sites of Hamar (to the south) and Kvitfjell (further north) will require two more (longer) rides.

EIDFJORD
EXTREME NORWAY

- *Low mountain / Advanced*
- *Map strava.com/routes/23209425*
- *Test yourself km 18 (mi 11) strava.com/segments/5256391*
- *Test yourself km 92 (mi 57) strava.com/segments/1611526*

Non-athletes beware! This amazing route through the land of fjords is the ultimate adventure, but it should only be undertaken over two days and with careful planning. We follow the route of the cycling section of the Norseman, an extreme annual triathlon contested by elite sportspeople.

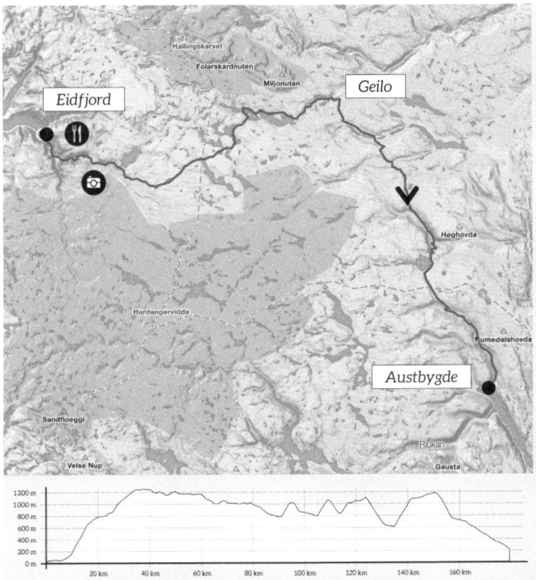

Better have a good think before throwing yourself into this. Remember that competitors in the Norseman swim for nearly 4 km (2.5 mi) in the cold waters of Eidfjord before jumping on their bikes to cycle 180 km (112 mi), then running 42 km (26 mi) to the summit of Gaustatoppen. As the race's founder, Paal Hårek Stranheim, said: "I want to create a completely different race, make it a journey through the most beautiful nature of Norway, let the experience be more important than the finish time." This adventure east of Bergen, from Eidfjord to Austbygde, which skirts Hardangervidda National Park, will be unforgettable if you complete it. Logistic preparations are important, given that you will be all on your own out on the high Hordaland plateau, a landscape of rocks and low vegetation dotted with countless lakes. This may be the most extraordinary ride of your life.

Distance	E+	Difficulty	Appeal
179 km (111 mi)	3,150 m (10,335 ft)	5/5	5/5

Logistic backup with a motor vehicle is recommended. There is a possible rail option: to get to Eidfjord from Bergen, take the train to Voss (1h10), then travel 70 km (44 mi) by bike and 1h by ferry. From Austbygde, it is a 97 km (60 mi) cycle ride to Kongsberg Train Station.

Fjell & Fjord is the perfect place in Eidfjord to spend a comfortable day and night before undertaking the trek. The only disadvantage? Norwegian prices.

Lægreidsvegen 7
5783 Eidfjord
eidfjordhotel.no

Stranheim was right: there is some stunning scenery on his Norseman, including Vøring Falls (km 15/mi 9.5), after an awful 5 km (3 mi) ramp at nearly 10%; Lake Sysen (km 26/mi 16); and the succession of lakes and hamlets with thatched-roof houses on the way to Ustaoset.

BERGEN
TWO MOUNTAINS

Hilly / Advanced — Map strava.com/routes/23422883

Distance	E+	Difficulty	Appeal
34 km (21 mi)	550 m (1,805 ft)	3/5	4/5

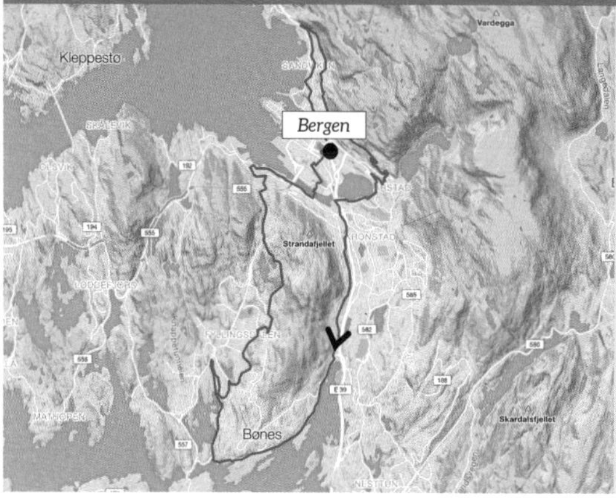

After Norway's second city, Bergen (pop. 280,000), warmly welcomed the UCI Road World Championships in 2017, this gateway to the big fjords was seized by cycling fervor. The symbol of Bergen remains the number "7," for the seven mountains that surround the city. These peaks may be low—Ulriken, the highest, is only 643 m (2,110 ft)—but they make wonderful cycling territory with challenging gradients of between 8% and 11%. Our route begins just above the historic center and its wooden houses, and climbs two of the peaks: Sandviksfjellet and Løvstakken. Bergen is 6h by train from Oslo (480 km/300 mi).

MYRDAL
THE WORKERS' WAY

Hilly / Intermediate — Map strava.com/routes/23220067

Distance	E+	Difficulty	Appeal
64 km (40 mi)	950 m (3,120 ft)	3/5	5/5

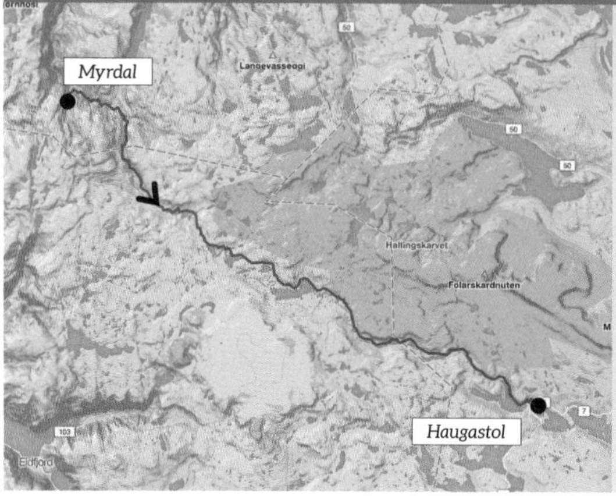

We are in the middle of nowhere, between mountains and fjords, in a grandiose landscape, yet we are not alone—at least, not in summer. It is estimated that 20,000 cyclists ride the very popular Rallarvegen, a road named for the workers who built the Oslo-Bergen railway line in the early twentieth century. Running from Myrdal to Haugastøl (5h by train from Oslo), the Rallarvegen is a favorite with "gravel" fans. More athletic still: start from Flåm and ride through the gorgeous Flåmsdalen valley to reach Myrdal all warmed up, then climb the twenty switchbacks of Myrdalsberget: 1.4 km (0.9 mi) at an average gradient of 18%.

RORA

THE GOLDEN ROAD

Very hilly / Advanced *Map strava.com/routes/23633100*

Distance	E+	Difficulty	Appeal
105 km (65 mi)	1,550 m (5,085 ft)	3/5	5/5

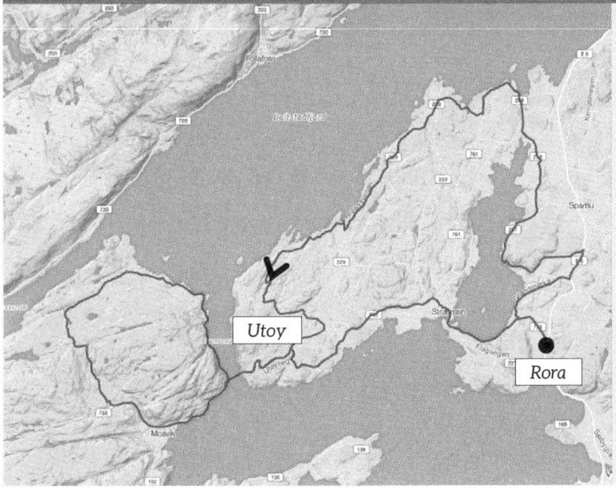

Inderøy (the Interior Island) is a municipality covering two peninsulas locked deep within a fjord 600 km (370 mi) north of Oslo. It is a pristine, sublime territory with gentle contours and beautiful colors. They grow strawberries and distill aquavit here. The local tourist board invented a slogan to promote this attractive place: "The Golden Road." This road, which is dotted with many little kickers, runs around Borgenfjorden and explores the peninsulas on each side of the Skarnsund strait. You can also enjoy the fruits of the local farmers, artisans, and artists. Start from Røra Train Station on the Trondheim-Steinkjer line.

SVOLVÆR

LOFOTEN EXPRESS

Hilly / Advanced *Map strava.com/routes/23623608*

Distance	E+	Difficulty	Appeal
184 km (114 mi)	1,900 m (6,250 ft)	4/5	5/5

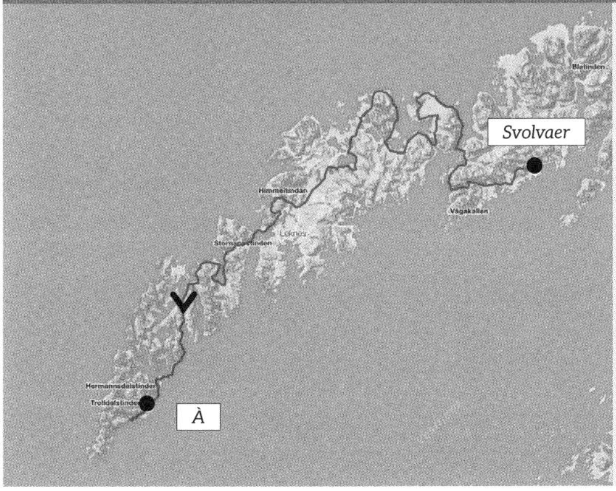

Located above the Arctic Circle, the Lofoten Islands are one of the most inspiring places to experience by bike. Our route should be undertaken over a weekend in June, when the sun never sets over the archipelago. A flight to Bodø via Oslo leads to the ferry for Svolvær, from where we set off for 184 km (114 mi) of magical cycling along a southwest axis toward the light of the star that refuses to drop into the Norwegian Sea. Stretches of pristine nature, white sandy beaches, and fishing villages pass against the extraordinary backdrop of Alps rising from the water. We end in the village of À before taking the ferry back from Moskenes.

The mountains and sheltered bays of the fabulous Lofoten Islands, Norway.

REYKJAVIK
HOT ICELAND

- *Hilly / Advanced*
- *Map strava.com/routes/23533166*
- *Test yourself km 5 (mi 3) strava.com/segments/11793872*
- *Test yourself km 25 (mi 13) strava.com/segments/20824364*

If you are in Reykjavik with a bicycle, then it usually means that you are about to set off on a long-distance adventure. Before you do so, ride this enjoyable loop to the famous hot springs of the Blue Lagoon, which is a foretaste of the Icelandic pleasures to come.

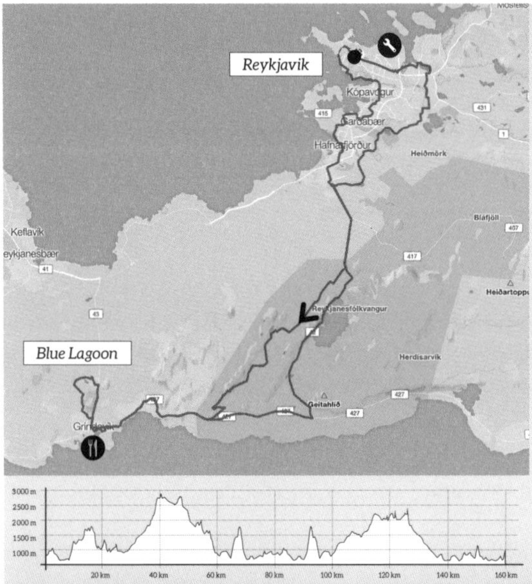

Iceland is one of the most exhilarating cycling destinations there is. A complete circuit of the island is a must, to be undertaken only in June and July because of the weather, and with steely determination—so harsh and bare is this vast territory in the North Atlantic. Two-thirds of the country's total population (360,000) live in Reykjavik. From the capital and its amazing Lutheran parish church Hallgrímskirkja, this route is a sort of gentle first contact with the Icelandic dream before heading off to explore geysers, volcanoes, and glaciers. It is a fair distance, but the relief is nothing special. There is one obligation: a dip in the warm waters of the renowned Blue Lagoon (km 80/mi 50). Book a timeslot online for around $50, and do not forget your swimming gear.

Distance **160 km** (100 mi)

E+ **1,700 m** (5,580 ft)

Difficulty **3/5**

Appeal **5/5**

Many airlines, including the low-cost national carrier Icelandair, fly to Keflavík International Airport (1h by bus southwest of Reykjavik) from Europe and North America. Iceland has no rail network.

Rather than the very expensive establishments at the Blue Lagoon, make a stop in the port of Grindavík (km 87/ mi 54) on the way back. Cafe Bryggjan is open all day.

Miðgarður 2
240 Grindavík
bryggjan.com

There are many bike rental stores in the Icelandic capital. Kría Hjól (2 km/1.25 mi from Hallgrímskirkja) is the best for sports cycling.

Skeifan 11
108 Reykjavík
kriacycles.com

SÄLEN
GRAVEL "VASA"

Hilly / Advanced

Map strava.com/routes/23600520

Distance	E+	Difficulty	Appeal
111 km (69 mi)	1,300 m (4,265 ft)	3/5	5/5

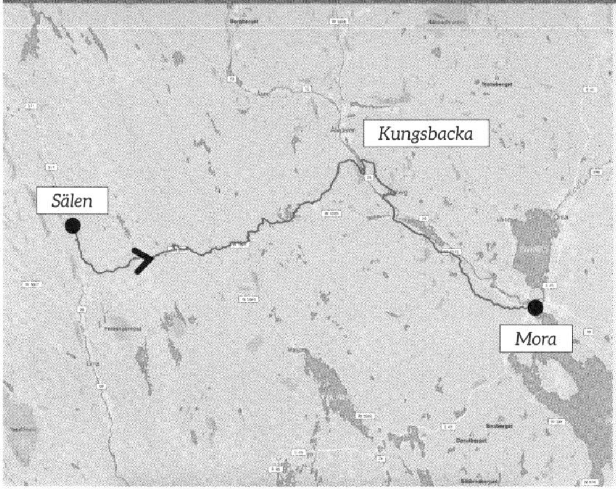

The legendary Vasaloppet remains the event for hardcore cross-country skiers: 90 km (56 mi) between Sälen and Mora in the remote Dalarna region (9 inhabitants per km²/0.4 sq mi). In summer, it is also a mountain bike event on nearby trails. Our route is a variant (requiring the use of a gravel bike), which starts from Berga: 27 km (17 mi) of asphalt, then 20 km (12.5 mi) on the marked Vasaloppsspåret trail before another 33 km (20 mi) of asphalt, past Vasa and up to Blyberg, then 26 km (16 mi) of dirt trail. Proper road is never far if you feel the need. Add a 2h bus ride from Mora to Berga or Sälen in addition to 3h45 on the train from Stockholm.

GOTHENBURG
A CHARMING PORT

Hilly / Intermediate

Map strava.com/routes/23105775

Distance	E+	Difficulty	Appeal
105 km (65 mi)	700 m (2,300 ft)	2/5	4/5

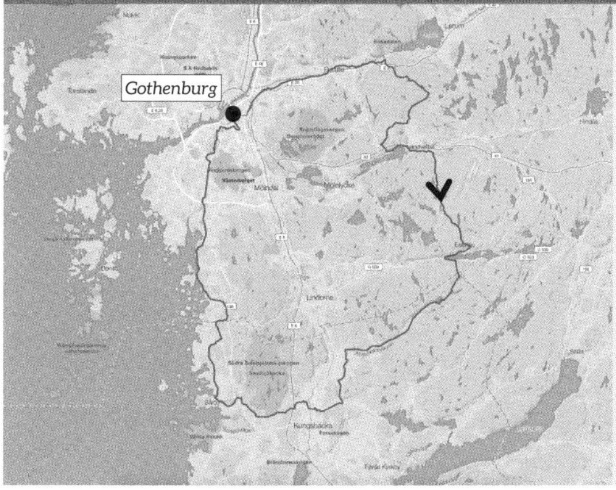

Gothenburg is a maritime destination, suffused with the atmosphere of the Kattegat, which separates it from Denmark. It is Sweden's second city, lying halfway between Copenhagen and Oslo. Home to the carmaker Volvo, Gothenburg is known as being a very livable place. The surrounding countryside is very pleasant too; the woods and cycle paths are dotted with lovely brick houses. The hills ramp up as we approach Göteborg Landvetter Airport. After historic Kungsbacka, we ride back up the coast until we glimpse the granite islands of the Gothenburg Archipelago, including Styrsö, which is worth exploring.

MALMÖ
GREEN SWEDEN

- *Fairly flat / Intermediate*
- *Map strava.com/routes/23151570*
- *Test yourself km 38 (mi 24) strava.com/segments/8081458*
- *Test yourself km 67 (mi 42) strava.com/segments/6588310*

Malmö is Sweden's third-largest city, and it seems the most obvious destination, being the southernmost and facing Copenhagen. It is linked to the continent by the impressive Øresund Bridge. The city also has a region-wide environmental program.

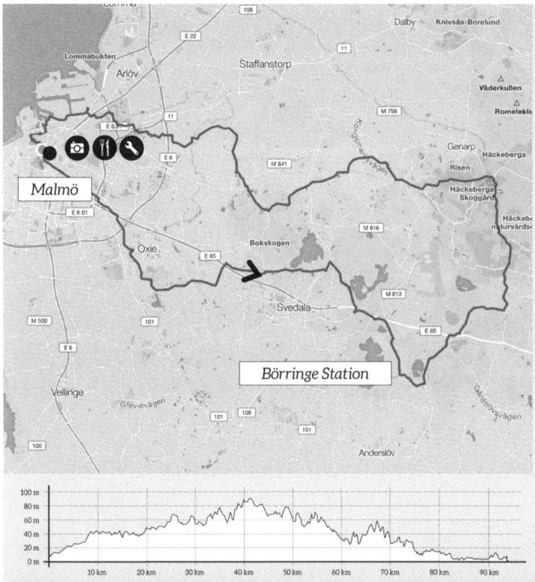

It is not surprising that cycling culture is so developed in Malmö (pop. 320,000). The city is an ideal first point of contact with Sweden—and not just because it is easy to access. Musette bike cafe, an impeccable base camp, is surrounded by local symbols: the medieval Malmöhus Castle, its park, and Ribersborgs beach, from where you can admire Øresund Bridge on one side and, on the other, the amazing Turning Torso skyscraper, which stands in the heart of the avant-garde eco-neighborhood of Västra Hamnen. The tone is set: the experience will be a laid-back one, if not a little twisted. Bike paths snake between fields of crops and wooded areas. Häckeberga Nature Reserve is typical of the Swedish countryside, as is its castle (km 52/mi 32) and that of Torup (km 69/mi 43).

Distance	E+	Difficulty	Appeal
94 km (58 mi)	600 m (1,970 ft)	2/5	4/5

Malmö Airport has plenty of connections in the summer season. It takes 40 minutes to get into town by taxi or bus. Copenhagen is 40 minutes by train or 45 minutes by car (45 km/28 mi) via Øresund Bridge. Gothenburg is 2h30 by train or 3h by car (280 km/175 mi).

It is very tempting to cross the bridge which links Malmö and Copenhagen for the panorama over the Øresund. The only problem is that it is a highway and, therefore, closed to cyclists. There are two options: the train or the special bike ferry, which has room for thirty-six bikes and takes 1h.

Located close to Malmö Castle, Musette is one of the most perfect bike cafe concepts in Europe, with a workshop, clothing brand, events, and house-roasted coffee.

Helmfeltsgatan 1
211 48 Malmö
musette.se

JÖNKÖPING
A LAKE TO RIDE

- *Fairly flat / Intermediate*
- *Map strava.com/routes/23017731*
- *Test yourself near to km 6 (mi 4) strava.com/segments/1680806*
- *Test yourself km 58 (mi 36) strava.com/segments/8399166*

Jönköping is a medium-sized student town (pop. 85,000) with a strong cycling culture. It is also the setting for major sporting events such as a Half Ironman and the Vätternrundan. The surrounding hills reveal a bucolic Sweden with a gentle relief.

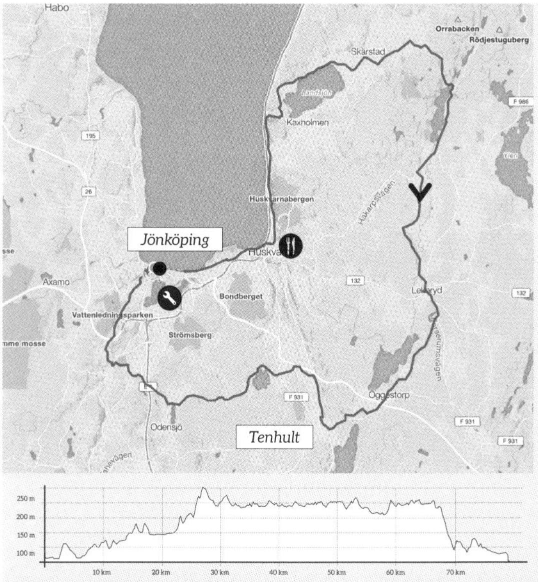

Each summer, thousands of cyclists complete the circuit of Lake Vättern, of which Jönköping is the southernmost point, covering a distance of 300 km (185 mi) from Motala. Thousands of triathletes also give their best in the well-regarded Jönköping Half Ironman, from which our route borrows part of the cycling course. Hundreds of enthusiasts also take part in the 30 km (19 mi) Cycling Tempo, riding against the clock. They certainly love cycling in Småland (literally, "small lands"), a historical province in southern Sweden. Lake Vättern is very pleasant not only to ride around, but also to enjoy from a little higher up among the wooded hills after Huskvarna, which are dotted with the pointed steeples of churches. In Jönköping, do not miss the delightful Match Museum (housed in Jönköping's first match factory) close to the train station. The city was a major producer of matches.

Distance	E+	Difficulty	Appeal
79 km (49 mi)	900 m (2,955 ft)	2/5	4/5

Jönköping Airport has few connections outside of Scandinavia. Stockholm is 4h by train or 3h by car (300 km/185 mi). Gothenburg is 3h by train or 2h by car (150 km/93 mi). Malmö is 2h40 by train or 3h15 by car (300 km/185 mi).

Landhs Teashop (km 7/mi 4.5) is the place to go on Lake Vättern for a very good coffee and a *semla* (sweet roll), either on the way out or coming back.

Grännavägen 21
561 33 Huskvarna
landhs.se

Close to km 74 (mi 46), you can't miss the house painted floor to roof with nature imagery in bright greens: Cykelköket, a community bike repair shop with tools and friendly tips.

Syrgasvägen 7
553 02 Jönköping
cykelkoketjonkoping.se

STOCKHOLM
ROYAL WEST

Fairly flat / Intermediate   *Map* strava.com/routes/23603951

Distance	E+	Difficulty	Appeal
96 km (60 mi)	800 m (2,600 ft)	2/5	4/5

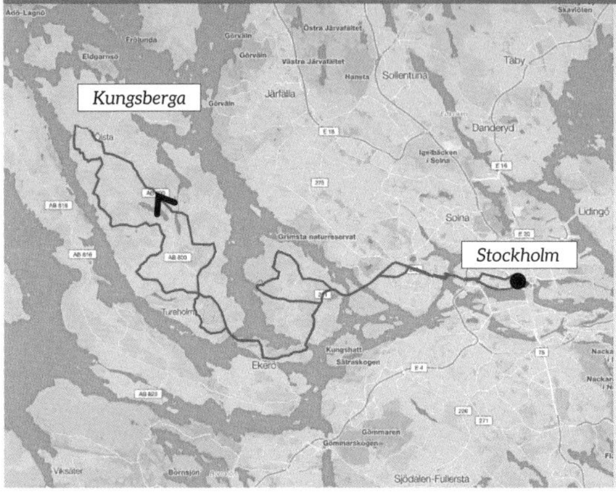

The city of Stockholm is caught between tentacular Lake Mälar and a swirl of islands on the Baltic. Its sprawling urban area numbers no fewer than 24,000 territories surrounded by water. Any exploration of the region necessitates crossing many bridges, and our discovery of the city's western reaches is no exception. We traverse five on the way out and as many on the way back. Before we reach rural Färingsö, the island of Lovön offers us Drottningholm and its magnificent royal residence. On the way back, on Kungsholmen island, we pass Stockholm City Hall (km 92/ mi 57). What a capital!

STOCKHOLM
AROUND AN ARCHIPELAGO

Hilly / Intermediate   *Map* strava.com/routes/23609279

Distance	E+	Difficulty	Appeal
115 km (65 mi)	1,150 m (3,750 ft)	3/5	5/5

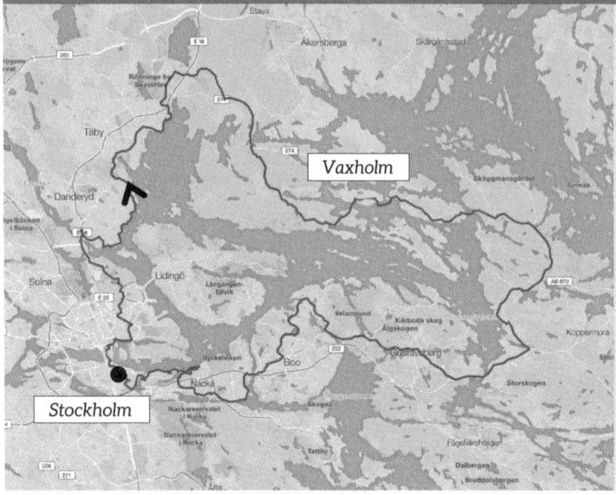

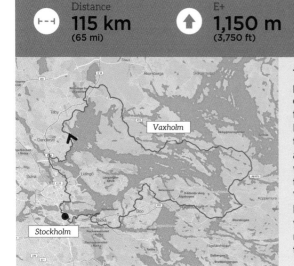

This route east of the Swedish capital over perfect cycle paths is a jewel. It allows us to explore the Stockholm archipelago. We start from Cykelcafé Le Mond and ride past The Royal Palace (km 2/mi 1.25) on Stadsholmen, the founding island. We cross five bridges and five islands to get to Vaxholm, where we have two options: continue by bike and take two short ferry crossings (to Rindö and Värmdö), or enjoy a sumptuous hour on a boat back across the archipelago to Stockholm, which means that although you will have ridden barely 50 km (31 mi), you will get to enjoy a cruise into the setting sun.

The Parliament building viewed from Stadsholmen in Stockholm, Sweden.

TAMPERE
HELLO, NOKIA!

- *Hilly / Intermediate*
- *Map strava.com/routes/23536177*
- *Test yourself km 35 (mi 22) strava.com/segments/10280805*
- *Test yourself km 80 (mi 50) strava.com/segments/5269184*

Finland has more than 180,000 lakes, which were created during the last glacial period. They cover one-third of the country's territory. Our loop from Tampere, which straddles two lakes, is a waterside one, passing Nokia, birthplace of the famous telecoms and technology firm.

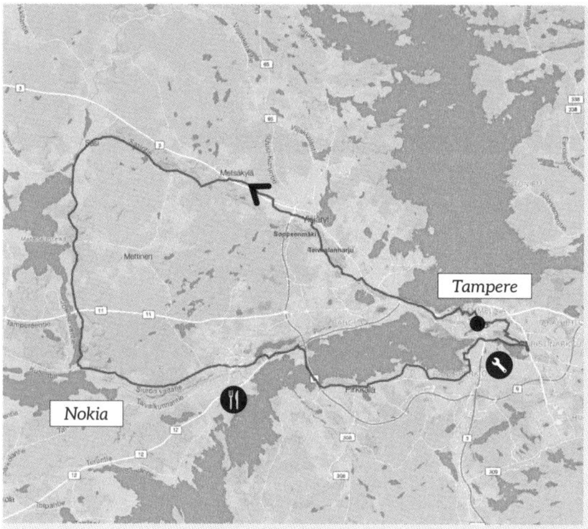

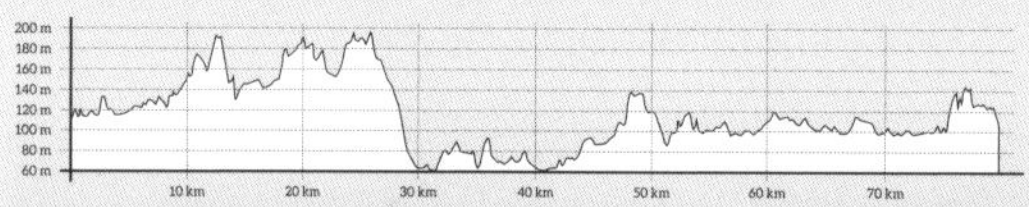

The second-largest urban area in Finland (pop. 320,000), Tampere is a friendly city boasting a mix of architectural styles: neo-Gothic, neo-Renaissance, romantic, and contemporary. There is a geographical curiosity too because Tampere is built between two lakes (the Näsijärvi to the north and the Pyhäjärvi to the south). Because the former is 18 m (60 ft) higher than the latter, a section of rapids flows between them, bisecting the city, and are used for hydroelectric power generation. The rural and lakeside landscape surrounding our route (many cycle paths) is full of gentle hills covered with conifers. We ride past Nokia (pop. 34,000)—proud of its global fame—before crossing the Pyhäjärvi back to Tampere from the south via the Kaleva neighborhood and its parks.

Distance	E+	Difficulty	Appeal
80 km (50 mi)	700 m (2,300 ft)	3/5	3/5

Tampere-Pirkkala Airport has few connections outside of Scandinavia. To the south, Helsinki is 2h by train or by car (170 km/105 mi). To the southwest, Turku is 1h45 by train or 2h by car (160 km/100 mi).

Stop at sleekly designed Kataja Kahvila (km 52/mi 32), the best tea shop in Nokia (located right in the city center) for a coffee and Finnish treat. Cozy and delicious.

Välikatu 19
37100 Nokia
katajakahvila.fi

For a last-minute repair, drop in to Active Bike in the Ruotula neighborhood, located 3 km (2 mi) east of Tampere Central Station.

Jaakonmäenkatu 7
33560 Tampere
active-bike-tampere.business.site

HELSINKI
IN RALLY MODE

Hilly / Advanced *Map strava.com/routes/23614377*

Distance	E+	Difficulty	Appeal
106 km (66 mi)	1,100 m (3,600 ft)	3/5	4/5

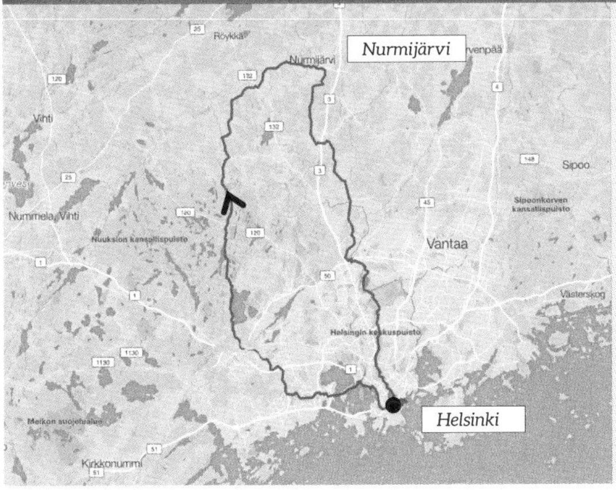

Strava records a total elevation gain of 1 100 m (3 600 ft) for this 106 km (66 mi) ride, and yet the highest point is just 110 m (360 ft). Water features prominently on our undulating route. Indeed, one of the country's nicknames is "land of a thousand lakes." There are, in fact, more than 180,000 lakes. We ride past the skyscrapers of Espoo—the country's second-largest city and headquarters of Nokia. As we reach Lake Bodom (km 26/mi 16), we enter wide open countryside with meadows dotted with flowers. A greenway leads us back to Helsinki via the lively Kruununhaka neighborhood.

TURKU
PROPER FINLAND

Fairly flat / Intermediate *Map strava.com/routes/23623967*

Distance	E+	Difficulty	Appeal
89 km (55 mi)	550 m (1,800 ft)	2/5	3/5

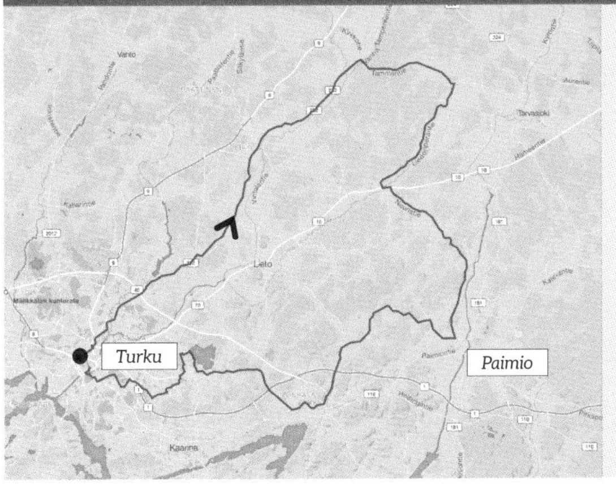

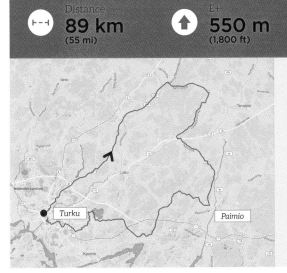

As the oldest town in Finland, Turku and its surrounding area are closely linked to the country's history because it is the site of many major events. Indeed, the region is called *Varsinais-Suomi* in Finnish, which literally means "Finland Proper." Turku has fascinating destinations: the banks of the Aura River, the medieval castle, the cathedral, and the verdant island of Ruissalo. Our route winds between wooded hills with the occasional ski jump appearing. On the way back, we skirt Littoinen Lake and get a view over the Archipelago Sea, which is said to comprise the largest number of islands in the world: 40,000.

TALLINN
CONNECTED JEWEL

Fairly flat / Intermediate

Map strava.com/routes/23632118

Distance	E+	Difficulty	Appeal
79 km (49 mi)	300 m 985 ft)	2/5	3/5

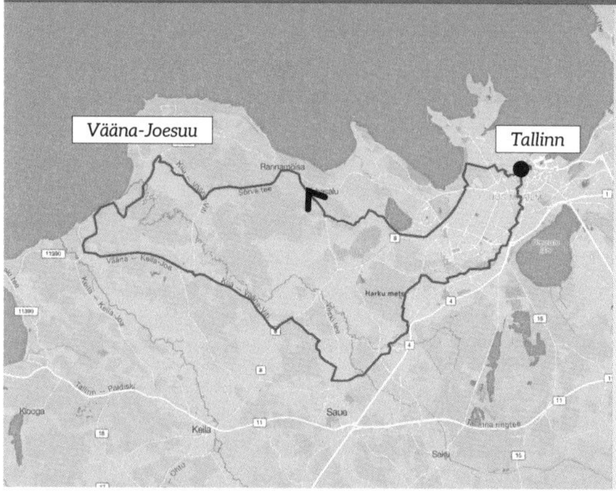

One-third of Estonia's population live in Tallinn (450,000 inhabitants), the most high-tech city in Europe (Skype was developed here). Its historic center is astonishingly well preserved; try cycling its cobbled streets. There are still vestiges of its Soviet past in the hipster neighborhood of Kalamaja: Patarei Prison and Linnahall, where the sailing events of the 1980 Olympics were held. It is also worth riding out of the city to explore the coast and the beautiful countryside (fairly flat with some wooded areas) from the beaches of Stroomi and Tabasalu to the cliffs of Türisalu.

RIGA
LATVIAN ESCAPADE

Fairly flat / Intermediate

Map strava.com/routes/23636533

Distance	E+	Difficulty	Appeal
76 km (47 mi)	400 m (1,315 ft)	2/5	4/5

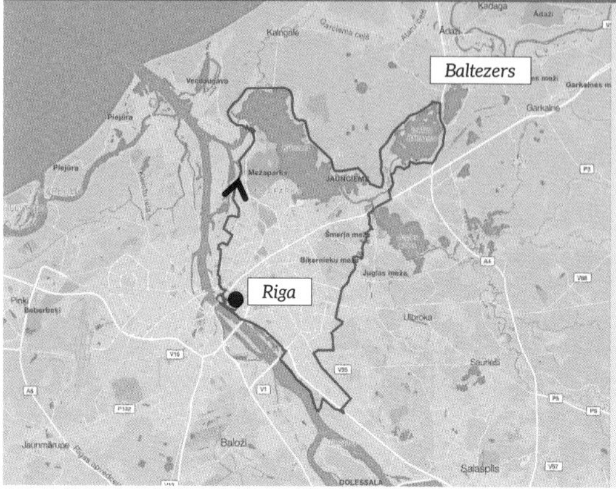

From the bottom of its gulf opposite Stockholm, Riga, the capital of Latvia, is a draw for tourism and industry. Extreme prudence is required when cycling from its historic center—a showcase of art nouveau—to the outskirts. You can, however, escape the bustle, as we do here on our route along the wide Daugava River, then around Lakes Ķīšezers and Baltezers, and past Jugla Lake. You can extend the ride to the long pier at Mangaļsala, located on the Baltic, or cross the Daugava for a panorama over Riga's skyscrapers and a lie on the beach on the island of Ķīpsala before enjoying some of Riga's intense nightlife.

KURESSAARE
BALTIC ISLAND

Fairly flat / Advanced   Map strava.com/routes/23648920

Distance	E+	Difficulty	Appeal
173 km (108 mi)	450 m (1,475 ft)	3/5	4/5

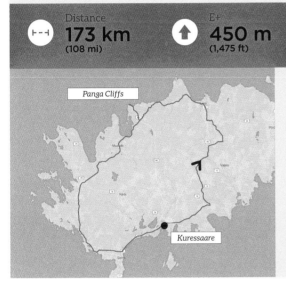

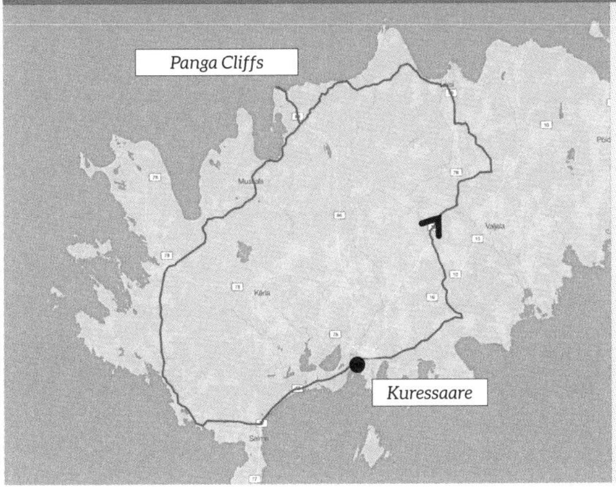

At 173 km (108 mi), this is a long ride, but it is worth it to discover the delights of Saaremaa, the largest island in Estonia, which is slightly bigger in surface area than Luxembourg. It has only 36,000 inhabitants, which means that its roads are quiet even in summer. Saaremaa is not easy to get to though. Fly from Tallinn or Stockholm, or else take the ferry via Virtsu and the island of Muhu. On our route, we explore such treasures as the Kuressaare Episcopal Castle, the Kaali Meteorite Crater Fields, the old windmills of Angla, the Panga cliffs facing the Baltic, Viidumäe Nature Reserve, and the beaches of the south on the Gulf of Riga.

KLAIPEDA
DUNES OF COURLAND

Fairly flat / Intermediate   Map strava.com/routes/23646925

Distance	E+	Difficulty	Appeal
122 km (76 mi)	350 m (1,150 ft)	2/5	5/5

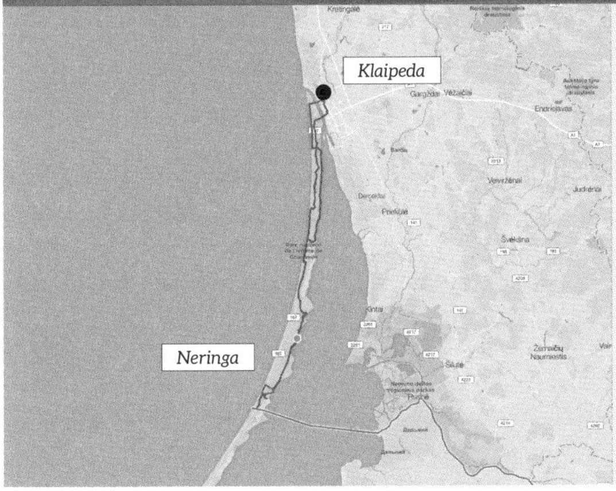

The coast of Lithuania stretches for less than 100 km (62 mi) but has one unbelievable treasure: the seemingly endless curved Curonian Spit. This territory of beaches, pine forests, and sand dunes, which is shared with the Russian semi-exclave of Kaliningrad, is never wider than 2 km (1.25 mi). Just before the border at km 56 (mi 35) is the fine white sandy Parnidis Dune (52 m/170 ft high), the second highest on the continent after France's Pilat Dune (107 m/351 ft). From the Lithuanian side, you can only reach the Curonian Spit via a ten-minute ferry ride from Klaipėda (4h from Vilnius) to Smiltynė.

KAUNAS
LITHUANIAN SOUL

Hilly / Advanced

Map strava.com/routes/23538979

Test yourself km 101 (mi 63) strava.com/segments/9106997

Test yourself km 117 (mi 73) strava.com/segments/12558711

Look out, gravel ahead! There are 35 km (22 mi) of steep packed-dirt tracks in the course of this city-to-city route through the heart of the largest of the Baltic states, from Kaunas to Vilnius (the capital). Lithuania's two major towns are also well worth visiting in their own right.

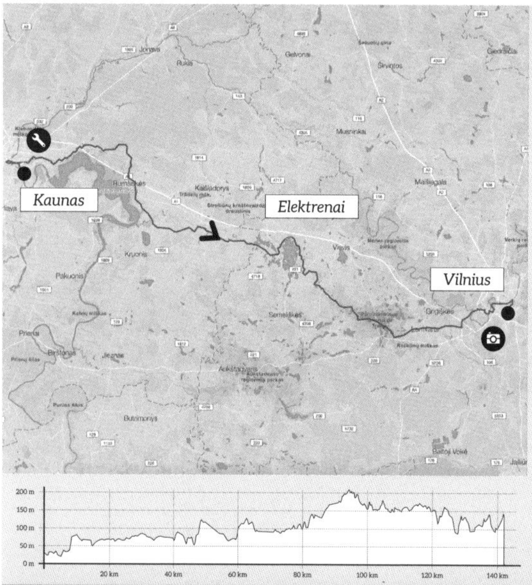

There can be few European nations that have had a more chaotic history than Lithuania, which has been shaped by influences (both good and bad)—Russian, Soviet, German, Polish, Jewish, and Christian—that have modeled, embellished, destroyed, and rebuilt the country. On this day's ride from Kaunas to Vilnius, we explore the soul of Lithuania. In Kaunas, we visit Vytautas the Great Bridge, the House of Perkūnas, the oaks of Ąžuolynas Park, and Pažaislis Monastery. Between Kaunas Reservoir Regional Park (km 18/mi 11) and km 103 (mi 64), there are eight gravel sections of between 4 km (2.5 mi) and 9 km (5.5 mi) in length. We pass Elektrėnai; Trakai and its island castle; and Lentvaris with its Tyszkiewicz Palace. The best is to come: Vilnius—the "Jerusalem of the North" or "City of a Thousand Churches"—in all its gothic, baroque, colorful, and surprising finery.

Distance	E+	Difficulty	Appeal
142 km (88 mi)	**1,300 m** (4,265 ft)	**3/5**	**4/5**

The international airports of Kaunas (15 km/9 mi north of the city, 1h by bus) and Vilnius (7 km/4.5 mi, 15 minutes by bus) are connected to the whole of Europe. Rail access from abroad is difficult. To return to Kaunas from Vilnius is 1h30 by train or 1h15 by car (110 km/68 mi).

Velomanija (1 km/0.6 mi from the train station) is Kaunas's go-to specialist sports bike store, providing route tips. Retailer of Specialized and Orbea.

Laisvės aleja 12
Kaunas 44215
velomanija.lt

Before wandering about the sumptuous historic center (divine coffee at Crooked Nose!), get an overview from up on Gediminas' Tower (km 138/mi 86), Bastion Hill, Three Crosses, and the TV Tower.

govilnius.lt

CARPATHIANS & BALKANS

POLAND

CZECHIA

SLOVAKIA

HUNGARY

CROATIA & MONTENEGRO

BOSNIA & SERBIA

ROMANIA & BULGARIA

GREECE

GDAŃSK
KASHUBIAN ESCAPADE

Fairly flat / Advanced *Map* strava.com/routes/23714099

Distance	E+	Difficulty	Appeal
169 km (105 mi)	1,100 m (3,600 ft)	3/5	4/5

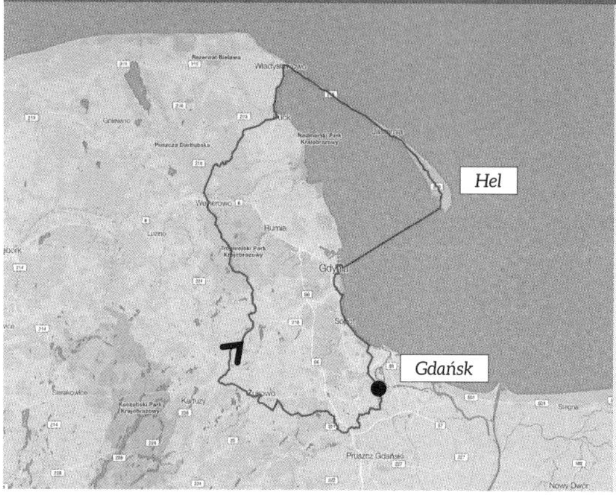

This mega-escapade in northern Poland holds plenty of interest. Quite apart from the modest relief of the Kashubian region and the forests of Pomerania, there is Gdańsk, a major port city on the Baltic with a rich history and range of architectural styles (gothic, renaissance, mannerist, baroque). There is also the incredible 35 km (22 mi) long Hel Peninsula, a sandbar formed by the sea currents, whose width varies from 100 meters/yards to 3 km (2 mi). Previously used for military purposes, Gdańsk's main draw now is tourism because Hel's beaches are superb. Return by ferry via Gdynia or direct to Gdańsk in summer.

JELENIA GÓRA
PRETTY SILESIA

Low mountain / Advanced *Map* strava.com/routes/23724681

Distance	E+	Difficulty	Appeal
94 km (59 mi)	1,550 m (5,100 ft)	3/5	4/5

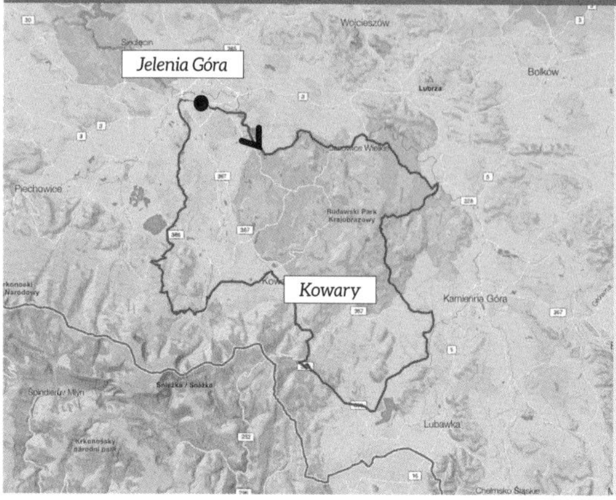

Nestling by the border with the Czechia, Rudawy Landscape Park is a pretty Polish surprise. The bold climbs and elevation gains on this loop, which starts and ends in Jelenia Góra, evoke the low mountains, yet we barely exceed 800 m (2,625 ft). There are three major ramps: Rędzińska (6 km/4 mi at 7%), Koszuta (6 km/4 mi at 4%), and Karpacz (6 km/4 mi at 6%). The backdrop is rocky with beech woods and waterfalls, which all look sumptuous in the fall. To extend your stay in Lower Silesia, you can also start from Świebodzice, close to the famous Książ Castle, and follow a route via pretty Kamienna Góra.

ZAKOPANE
GREATER POLAND

- *Low mountain / Advanced*
- *Map strava.com/routes/21458475*
- *Test yourself km 45 (mi 28) strava.com/segments/12825233*
- *Test yourself km 85 (mi 53) strava.com/segments/18731953*

Zakopane is located at the foot of the Tatra Mountains in the voivodeship of Lesser Poland, south of Kraków, the provincial capital. The surrounding nature and hills are very popular. It is not for nothing that Zakopane is a key European tourist destination in both winter and summer.

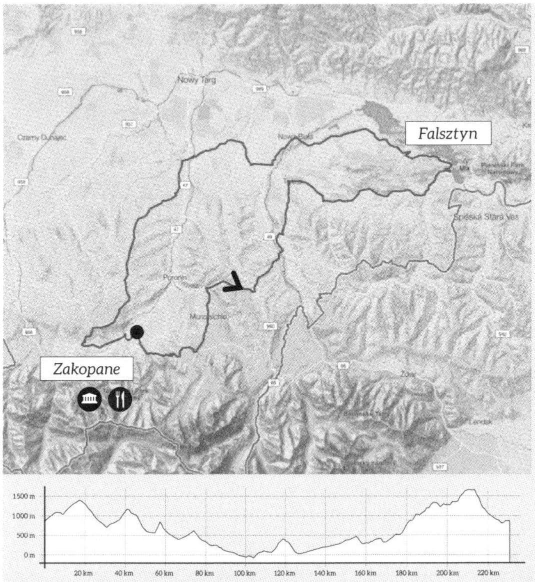

It is estimated that around 2.5 million tourists come to Zakopane in winter and summer each year. Polish mountain bikers and their Czech and Slovak neighbors have long made the area their playground. It is just as nice to explore the surrounding roads, comprising relatively short ramps at pleasing gradients. The final section of our route takes us to a point 300 m (985 ft) above the town, at an altitude of 1,125 m (3,690 ft), via a stiff climb of 3 km (2 mi) to the resort of Gubałówka, where the 2019 Tour de Poland finished. At km 51 (mi 32), after Falsztyn, there is a superb panorama over Lake Czorsztyn. The most amazing thing to discover en route is the wooden architecture that is specific to this region. At km 4 (mi 2.5), you have every right to step off the bike to take a look at the beautiful doll's house-like Jaszczurówka chapel jutting out of the pines.

Distance	E+	Difficulty	Appeal
102 km (63 mi)	1,750 m (5,740 ft)	3/5	4/5

Zakopane (pop. 27,000) is most accessible from Kraków's very well connected John Paul II Airport (110 km/68 mi to the north), the second busiest in Poland: 3h by train, 2h30 by bus, or 1h30 by car. Warsaw is 6h by train or 5h40 by car (470 km/292 mi).

The Europejska cafe in town (0.5 km/0.3 mi from the train station) has retained its striking decor from the Iron Curtain period. It is a friendly and unique place that is open every day.

Krupowski 37
34-500 Zakopane
europejskazakopane.pl

The Villa Atma is a historic chalet that was the home of the Polish composer and pianist Karol Szymanowski. It is now a museum that is a branch of the National Museum in Kraków.

Kasprusie 19
34-500 Zakopane
mnk.pl

PRAGUE
SPIRES AND A "CANYON"

- *Hilly / Intermediate*
- *Map strava.com/routes/23002961*
- *Test yourself km 54 (mi 34) strava.com/segments/8097424*
- *Test yourself km 57 (mi 36) strava.com/segments/8097394*

Even if you do not fancy going all the way to the Krivoklátsko Nature Reserve (a former royal hunting ground) west of the Czech capital, Prague offers some surprising cycling escapades. It is wonderful to ride past the city's fantastic sights on the way out and back.

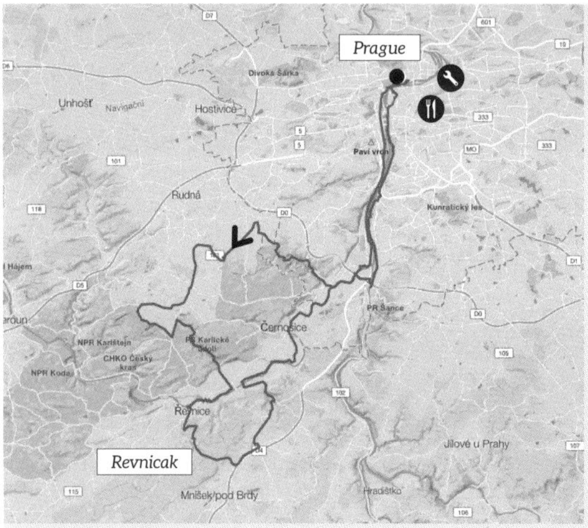

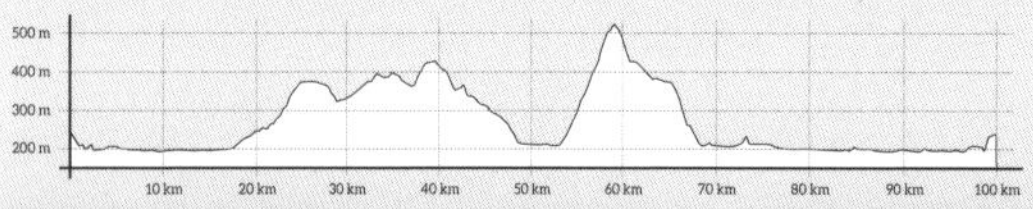

We cycle south out of Prague from KOA bike store near Letná Park along the left bank of the Vltava, saluting the castle (km 3/mi 2) and then the memory of Casanova at the foot of Petřín hill. Follow the course of the Czechia's major river, then that of the Berounka River, which is interrupted by a steep, wooded road leading to an amazing site at km 40 (mi 25): an abandoned limestone quarry with a lake at the bottom called Velká Amerika (Big America) or the Czech Grand Canyon. Next is the ascent of Řevničák at a steady 6% over 5 km (3 mi). We return via the right bank of the Vltava after 15 km (9 mi) along the Berounka. This brings us into authentic Prague through the old town with its gothic spires, old bridges, and narrow cobbled streets. What a great reward!

Distance	E+	Difficulty	Appeal
100 km (62 mi)	900 m (2,950 ft)	2/5	4/5

Václav Havel Airport Prague is located 15 km (9 mi) west of the city. It is well connected to the whole of Europe. The best way to reach the center is to take the number 119 bus from Arrivals and alight at Dejvická station on Line A of the metro.

In the county that consumes the most beer in the world, you absolutely must sample a fine Czech pilsner when you return. We suggest House of Craft Beer, located near km 98 (mi 61).

Navrátilova 1421/11
110 00 Nové Město
craft-beer-prague.business.site

Our route leaves from the well-reputed KOA bike store, which has widened its offer to include all endurance sports, a yoga studio, route tips, and a travel agency.

Jirečkova 1010/5
170 00 Prague 7
koa.cz

KARLOVY VARY
CZECH WATERS

🌐 *Hilly / Intermediate* 🌐 *Map strava.com/routes/23696791*

Distance	E+	Difficulty	Appeal
72 km (45 mi)	700 m (2,300 ft)	2/5	4/5

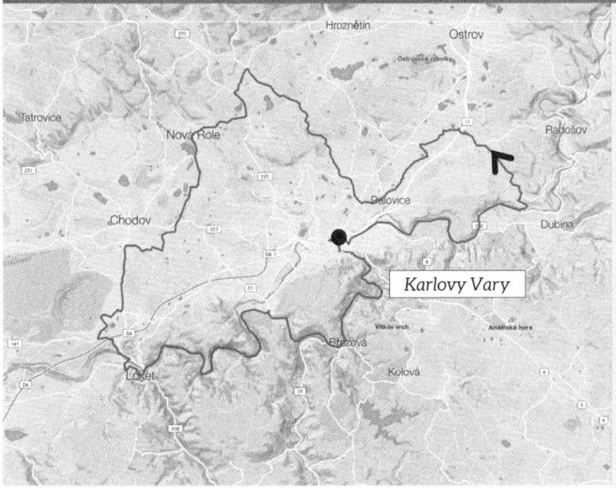

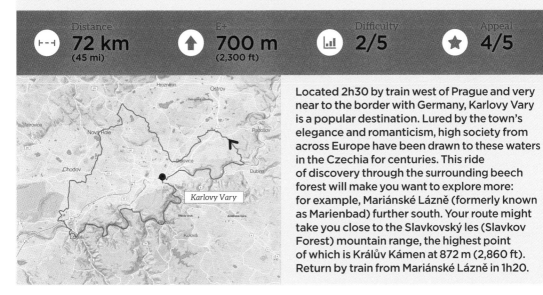

Located 2h30 by train west of Prague and very near to the border with Germany, Karlovy Vary is a popular destination. Lured by the town's elegance and romanticism, high society from across Europe have been drawn to these waters in the Czechia for centuries. This ride of discovery through the surrounding beech forest will make you want to explore more: for example, Mariánské Lázně (formerly known as Marienbad) further south. Your route might take you close to the Slavkovský les (Slavkov Forest) mountain range, the highest point of which is Králův Kámen at 872 m (2,860 ft). Return by train from Mariánské Lázně in 1h20.

ŠUMPERK
STEEP IN THE SUDETES

🌐 *Low mountain / Advanced* 🌐 *Map strava.com/routes/23697952*

Distance	E+	Difficulty	Appeal
108 km (67 mi)	1,500 m (4,900 ft)	3/5	4/5

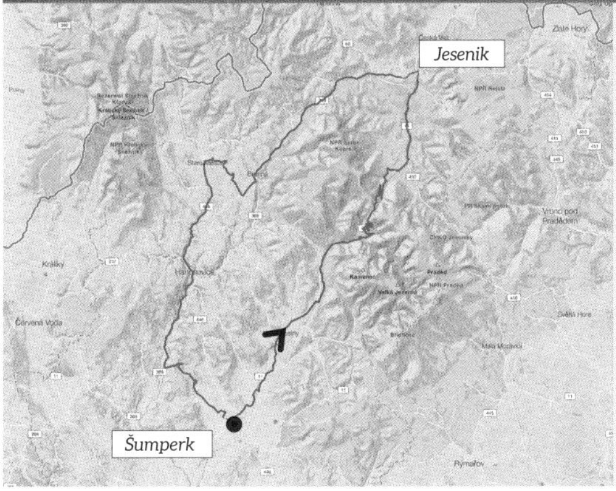

In the Czechia, the Hrubý Jeseník mountain range in the Eastern Sudetes is the setting for some lovely cycling. The backdrop is superb and the climbs do not disappoint. Riding out from Šumperk (2h30 by train from Prague), you hit a 10 km (6 mi) climb at 5% up to the ski resort of Červenohorské (1,000 m/3,280 ft). At km 23 (14.5 mi), you can turn right off the route just before a succession of pretty switchbacks and ride up to the TV transmitter on Praděd (1,492 m/4,895 ft), the highest peak in the Hrubý Jeseník. The return is much easier, although the Ramzová climb is a stiff 4 km (2.5 mi) at 6%.

RUŽOMBEROK
"PETO'S" TATRA

- *Low mountain / Advanced*
- *Map strava.com/routes/23663978*
- *Test yourself km 14 (mi 9) strava.com/segments/17503060*
- *Test yourself km 85 (mi 53) strava.com/segments/5905467*

True cycling enthusiasts cannot come to Slovakia without visiting Žilina, the city where Peter Sagan (or "Peto" as he is known on social media) grew up, and going for a lovely ride in his Tatra Mountains. Our route starts in Ružomberok, 60 km (37 mi) east of "Sagan City."

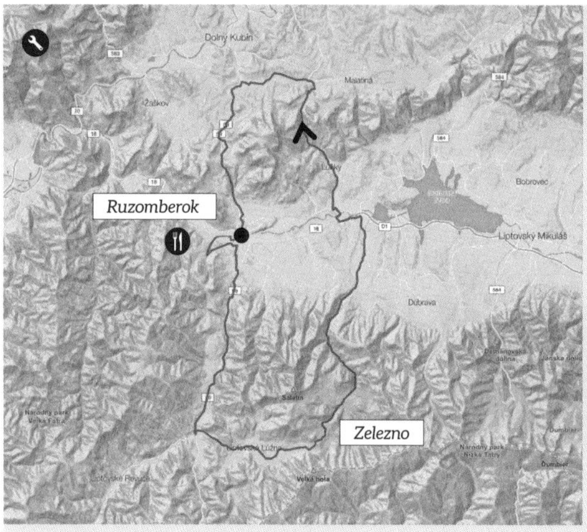

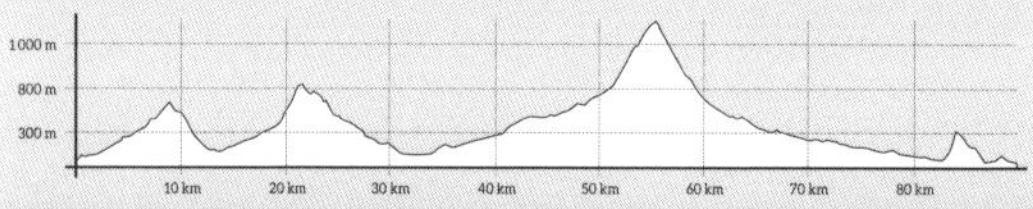

Žilina is just 1h15 by train or 55 minutes by car from Ružomberok, in northern Slovakia. Both towns—bustling Žilina (pop. 80,000) and quieter Ružomberok—share a similar pastoral backdrop, with views over the Tatra Mountains. Žilina is surrounded by ski resorts with dead-end access roads. There are also plenty of challenging climbs in the Veľká Fatra and Low Tatra massifs, the setting for this route. On the way back to Ružomberok, there is a nasty little kicker up to the ski lifts overlooking the town: 0.5 km (0.3 mi) at 13%. The northern part of the loop can be quite challenging, especially around Veľký Choč (1,611 m/5,285 ft). Further south, the scenery is wilder, with canyons, caves, and rocky ridges. The highest point on our route is 1,100 m (3,610 ft) before Liptovská Osada, at the edge of the Veľká Fatra National Park.

Distance	E+	Difficulty	Appeal
90 km (56 mi)	1,350 m (4,450 ft)	3/5	4/5

Ružomberok (pop. 27,000) is 3h15 by train or 2h40 by car (270 km/168 mi) from the capital, Bratislava. Košice (further east) and Ostrava (Czech Republic) are closer: 2h35 by train or 1h50 by car (200 km/125 mi) from the former; 2h15 by train or by car (170 km/105 mi) from the latter.

The place to go in Ružomberok is the cozy Déjà Vu cafe (km 88/mi 55) near the imposing church of Saint Andrew. There is a dress code, so just be sure to look chic on your bike.

Karola Antona Medveckého 3
034 01 Ružomberok
kaviaren-dejavu.business.site

Since it is inconceivable not to visit Žilina, drop in to the Specialized Concept Store. They sell Peter Sagan branded products, so you should at least buy a cycling cap.

Predmestská 1610/86
010 01 Žilina
velosprint.sk

BRATISLAVA
LITTLE CARPATHIANS

⊕ *Very hilly / Advanced* ⊕ *Map strava.com/routes/21453356*

Distance	E+	Difficulty	Appeal
108 km (67 mi)	950 m (3,100 ft)	3/5	4/5

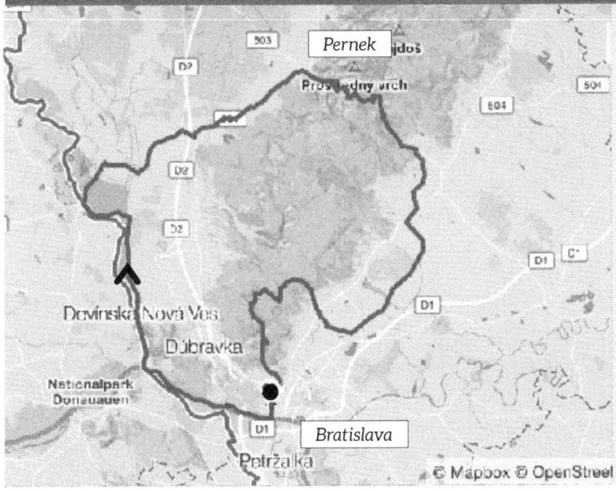

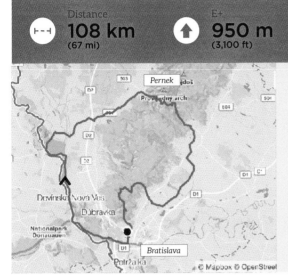

Bratislava, with its baroque buildings, Viennese cafes, and apartment blocks of the former Eastern Bloc is the perfect base from which to explore the low mountains of the Little Carpathians. We ride out past Bratislava Castle and up the Danube river, before turning north along the Austrian border. After glimpsing the Slovak Wine Route, the proper climbing commences in Pernek (km 52/mi 32). You will be warmed up by the time you reach Pezinská Baba, but try to hold something in reserve for the athletic ride back through Bratislava Forest Park and the climb to the Kamzík TV Tower at 437 m (1,434 ft).

ZVOLEN
SLOVAKIAN NATURE

⊕ *Low mountain / Advanced* ⊕ *Map strava.com/routes/23711540*

Distance	E+	Difficulty	Appeal
153 km (85 mi)	1,700 m (5,600 ft)	4/5	4/5

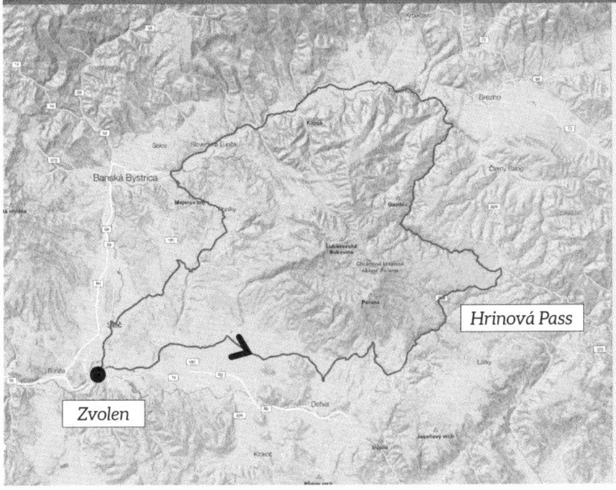

The rich mineral seams of the Slovak Ore Mountains have been exhausted. Nowadays in Zvolen (3h by train east of Bratislava), you meet more tourists than miners. There is much to attract cyclists in neighboring Pol'ana, a small volcanic range that is a protected landscape area. The long Hriňová Pass rises to 1,000 m (3,280 ft) against a backdrop of conifers, rocks, and waterfalls. This is a long route, so hold something back for the Majerov (km 121/mi 75): 3 km (2 mi) at 7% to 10%. Beforehand, you would be wise to make take a break in pretty Banská Bystrica at a cafe terrace on the central square.

TOKAY
THE WINE OF KINGS

Hilly / Advanced

Map strava.com/routes/22455747

Test yourself km 71 (mi 44) strava.com/segments/7529659

Test yourself km 101 (mi 63) strava.com/segments/21548737

The little town of Tokay has barely 4,000 inhabitants, but its reputation extends well beyond Hungary's borders. King Louis XIV of France called the sweet nectar produced here "the wine of kings." Join us for a pleasant pedal up the Tokay wine route that abuts the border with Slovakia.

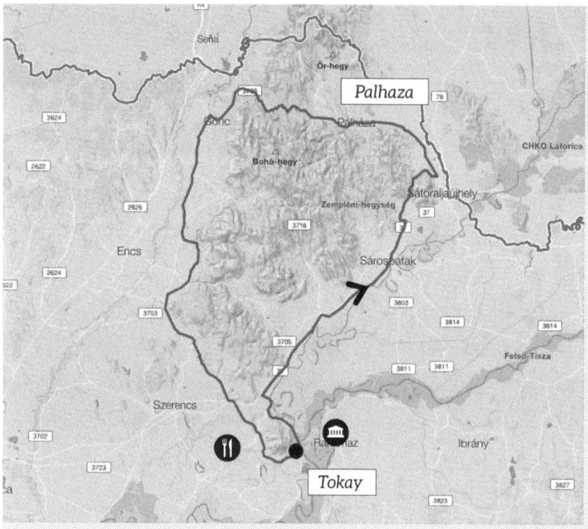

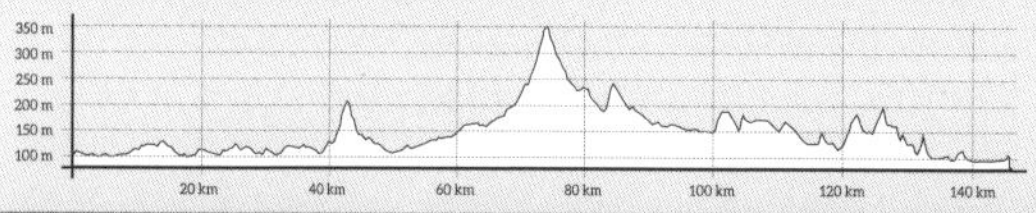

The Tokay region, named after its main town, is not only rich in vineyards. The wine route itself—200 km (125 mi) northeast of Budapest—reveals itself over the first half of our itinerary, out along the River Bodrog, and on the way back. The sweet wine made from local grapes that have been over-ripened before the winemaking process is produced on the opposite bank of the River Bodrog, as well as on that of the River Tisza further east. Midway through our ride, we climb into the densely forested Zemplén Mountains along the Slovakian border. There is nothing too challenging: the Bózsva ramp ascends for 8 km (5 mi) at gradients between 3% and 5%.
The setting is uplifting as we pass the castles of Bodrogolaszi, Sárospatak, and, further on, Boldogkő, as well as Károlyi Palace (3 km/2 mi northeast of Pálháza). In Tokay, nobility is about more than the golden hue of the finest vintages.

Distance **146 km** (91 mi)

E+ **1,150 m** (3,775 ft)

Difficulty **3/5**

Appeal **4/5**

Tokay is 3h by train from Budapest or 2h30 by car (230 km/143 mi). Košice (Slovakia) is 2h30 by train via Miskolc or 1h20 by car (90 km/55 mi). Cluj (Romania) is 4h30 by car (300 km/185 mi).

You are spoiled for choice when it comes to picking a winery from the many that you will pass. Our suggestion for a tasting: Szedmák at km 136 (mi 85).

Keresztúri u. 55
Tarcal 3915
szedmak.pl

The World Heritage Wine Museum (km 2/mi 1.25) in Tokay is a must. It is unquestionably one of the most interesting in Europe on the subject, being interactive and covering wines of the world in addition to the local vintages.

bormuzeum.eu

BUDAPEST
PEARLS OF THE DANUBE

- *Hilly / Advanced*
- *Map strava.com/routes/22457245*
- *Test yourself km 58 (mi 36) strava.com/segments/2517300*
- *Test yourself km 120 (mi 75) strava.com/segments/11343834*

The Danube bisects Budapest—hilly Buda on the right bank, flat Pest on the left. One never tires of the castles, palaces, and the varied architectural styles (baroque, art nouveau, neoclassical). There are many route options for cyclists outside of the Hungarian capital.

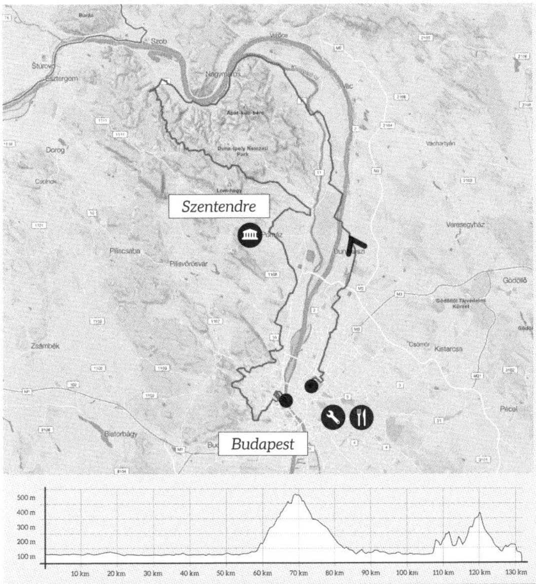

Budapest is a city full of nobility and romanticism, so we might as well commence our ride by passing one of the most beautiful and majestic places: Heroes Square and Vajdahunyad Castle. It is a joy to leave Pest because we will return through Buda, crossing back over the Danube on the Széchenyi Chain Bridge—that nineteenth-century emblem of the "Pearl of the Danube." The most curious and ambitious cyclists will be more than satisfied with this route along the great river, and through the forest. At km 24 (mi 15), we take a short ferry ride over the Danube on our way to explore Duna-Ipoly National Park, and to undertake the 11 km (7 mi) climb (at 4%) of Magas-hegy, reaching a high point of 510 m (1,673 ft) before plunging down to picturesque and colorful Szentendre. We return over the little hills that lead us into Buda, past its Citadella and the Fisherman's Bastion.

Distance	E+	Difficulty	Appeal
139 km (86 mi)	1,200 m (3,950 ft)	4/5	4/5

Budapest Airport is connected to the whole of Europe. It is located 16 km (10 mi) southeast of the city center and is accessible by bus then subway in 30 minutes. Vienna is 2h40 by train or 2h30 by car (250 km/155 mi). Veszprém (Lake Balaton) is 2h20 by train or 1h15 by car (115 km/72 mi).

Located 3 km (2 mi) south of Chain Bridge, Mesterbike is the perfect bike cafe: great workshop, espresso, snacks, and coworking area. Retailer of Specialized, Cannondale, and BMC.

Mester u. 11
Budapest 1095
mesterbike.hu

With its baroque buildings, narrow cobbled streets, and churches of several denominations, Szentendre (meaning Saint Andrew) deserves a return visit. It is renowned for its museums and art galleries.

welovebudapest.com

TOKAY

BLOOD AND GOLD

Hilly / Advanced *Map strava.com/routes/22453959*

Distance **136 km** (85 mi) | E+ **600 m** (2,000 ft) | Difficulty **3/5** | Appeal **4/5**

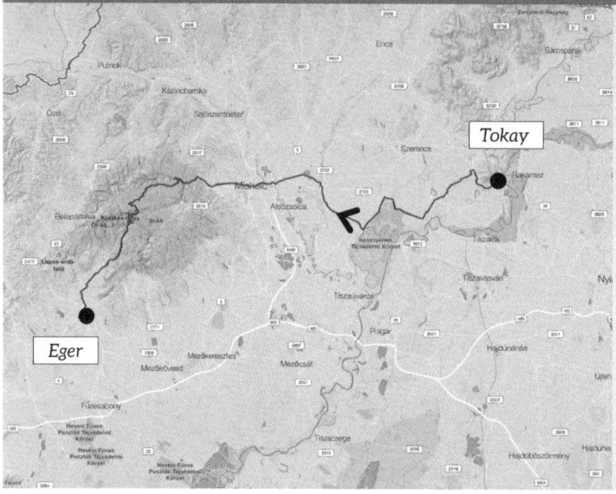

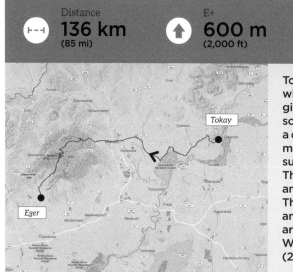

Tokay's renown often leaves other Hungarian winemaking areas in the shade. This route will give you a different perspective. It heads southwest out of the town of Tokaj to Eger, a city of 60,000 inhabitants close to the Mátra mountain range. There is more to Eger than the surprising proximity of a minaret and a basilica. The local red wine, made using primarily Merlot and Pinot Noir grapes, fears no comparison. They call it "Egri bikavér" (bull's blood of Eger), and it goes very well with goulash. The wineries are located in the Valley of the Beautiful Women. On the way, we climb up to 840 m (2,755 ft) in the Bükk Mountains.

BALATONKENESE

THE BALATON 200

Fairly flat / Advanced *Map strava.com/routes/22451808*

Distance **205 km** (127 mi) | E+ **900 m** (2,955 ft) | Difficulty **3/5** | Appeal **4/5**

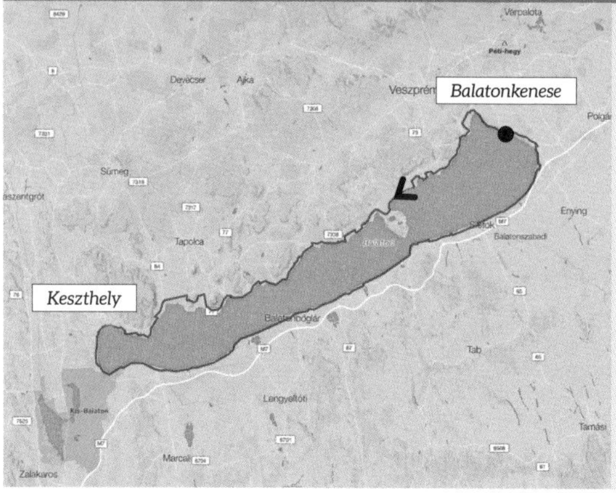

Do not panic. There are plenty of opportunities to cut short our ambitious circuit of Lake Balaton if it gets too hard for you. There are train stations all around the lake to take you back to our start point (2h30 from Budapest); perfect spots to eat, bathe, and sleep; and a ferry across to Tihany Peninsula, which reduces the ride to 78 km (49 mi). With its turquoise waters, fine sandy beaches, and sleek sailboats sliding by, Lake Balaton encourages gentle summer relaxation. Riding out from close to Veszprém (built on five hills), you will want to take your time making the full tour of the lake—that much is sure.

SPLIT
DALMATIA XXL

- *Medium mountain / Advanced*
- *Map strava.com/routes/22445062*
- *Test yourself km 97 (mi 60) strava.com/segments/3559726*
- *Test yourself km 173 (mi 108) strava.com/segments/22716334*

It is not for nothing that Dalmatia, the jewel of Croatia, is one of the most popular destinations in Europe. Its towns laden with history, its mountains, and its coastline are all treasures worth exploring. This route is a tasting menu of the rich cycling options available.

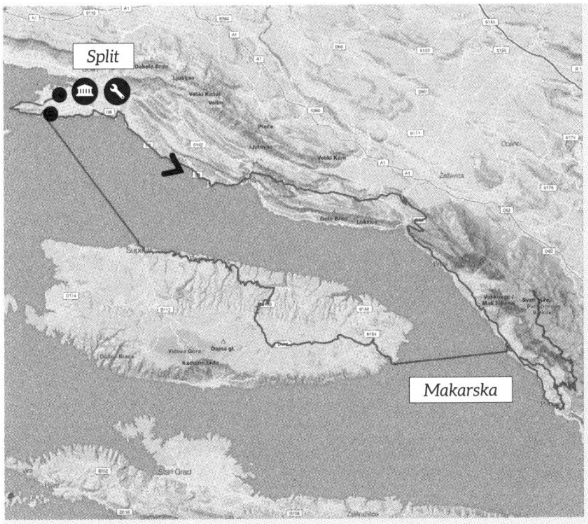

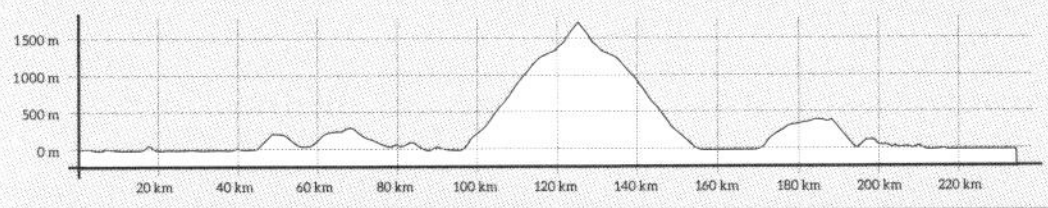

Approach this long Dalmatian route in your own way. As long as you set off in the early morning (between June and September), you will enjoy a lovely long day that is both a superb sporting challenge and an epic exploration of the most beautiful facets of Croatia. Starting from the ancient city of Split, you ride along the Adriatic coast for 85 km (53 mi), with the sea to your right and the mountain to your left, heading for Podgora, where you start the big ascent of the day: the narrow road up the Sveti Jure in the Biokovo massif, part of the Dinaric Alps. You climb for 28 km (17.5 mi) at an average gradient of 6% from sea level to 1,734 m (5,690 ft), with a 1 km (0.6 mi) stretch at nearly 20% in the first third of the climb. The return is much more serene: a ferry from Makarska to the beautiful island of Brač, and another ferry from Supetar to Split, which is 1h20 by train from Makarska.

Distance	E+	Difficulty	Appeal
206 km (128 mi)	2,700 m (8,860 ft)	5/5	5/5

Split Airport is located 20 km (12.5 mi) west of Split Train Station: 25 minutes by taxi, 40 minutes by bus. To the southeast, Dubrovnik is 3h by car (230 km/143 mi) or 5h by train. To the north, Zagreb is 4h by car (400 km/250 mi) or 6h by train.

Peloton Centar, located 1 km (0.6 mi) from the train station and very close to the magnificent Poljud Stadium, is the go-to bike store in Split. Retailer of Wilier Triestina.

Ul. Zrinsko Frankopanska 58
21000 Split
peloton.hr

Split has a finely preserved Roman site: the palace of Diocletian, founder of the city. In the historic center, medieval churches nestle against Renaissance palaces, surrounded by cafe terraces serving wine from the islands of Korčula, Hvar, and Brač.

visitsplit.com

ZAGREB
CROATIAN HERITAGE

Low mountain / Intermediate *Map strava.com/routes/23246668*

Distance 43 km (27 mi) | E+ 1,050 m (3,445 ft) | Difficulty 3/5 | Appeal 4/5

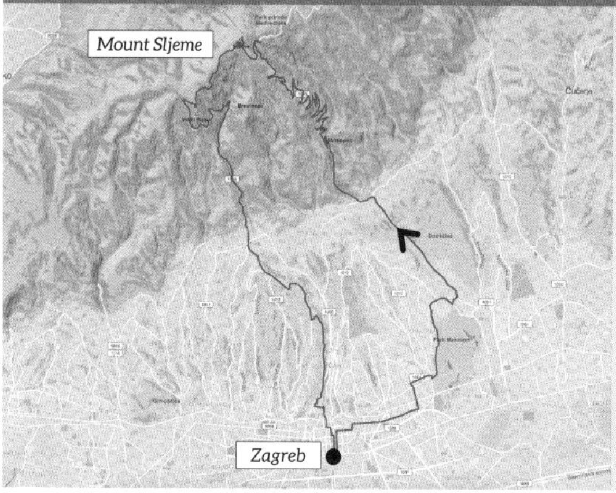

Please, no false modesty at the summit of Sljeme, which overlooks the city of Zagreb. You need a good pair of legs to reach the foot of the TV tower (1,033 m/3,390 ft), from where there is a fantastic view. The ascent (14 km/8.5 mi at 5.5%) via twenty-one switchbacks is the most popular in the Medvednica massif. You will certainly make friends, particularly if you mention that you recall that local skiing idols the Kostelić siblings (Janica and her brother Ivica) learned to ski here before becoming champions in the 2000s. At km 32 (mi 20), take a look at the white fortress of Medvedgrad. They care about their heritage in Croatia.

DUBROVNIK
ENERGIZING JEWEL

Very hilly / Advanced *Map strava.com/routes/23687840*

Distance 47 km (29 mi) | E+ 800 m (2,600 ft) | Difficulty 3/5 | Appeal 5/5

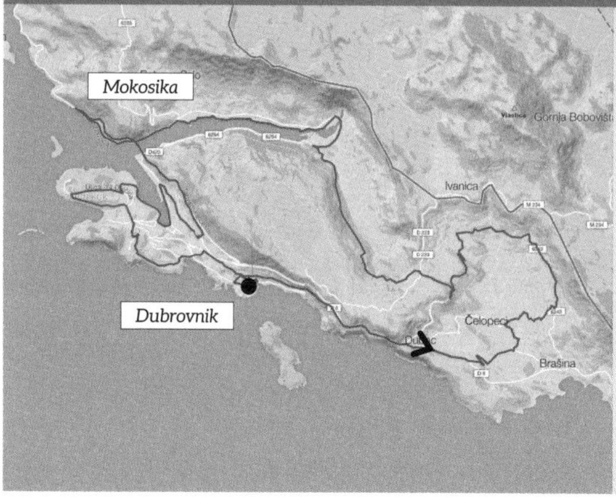

Wandering around Dubrovnik, you can easily forget that nearly thirty years ago the Yugoslav Wars destroyed or damaged two-thirds of the city's buildings. The restoration and reconstruction of Dubrovnik's old town has drawn mass tourism. How can you not fall under the spell of the old stones of the "Pearl of the Adriatic," or, for that matter, the well-surfaced ramps of the surrounding hills? We reach them after riding away from the clock tower on Luža Square down Stradun, the wide main street. This clever, physically demanding route—with slopes at 8%, sometimes 10%—offers magical views over the sea and the city.

BANJA LUKA
BOSNIAN EXCURSION

Low mountain / Intermediate

Map strava.com/routes/23765995

Distance	E+	Difficulty	Appeal
108 km (67 mi)	1,500 m (4,900 ft)	3/5	4/5

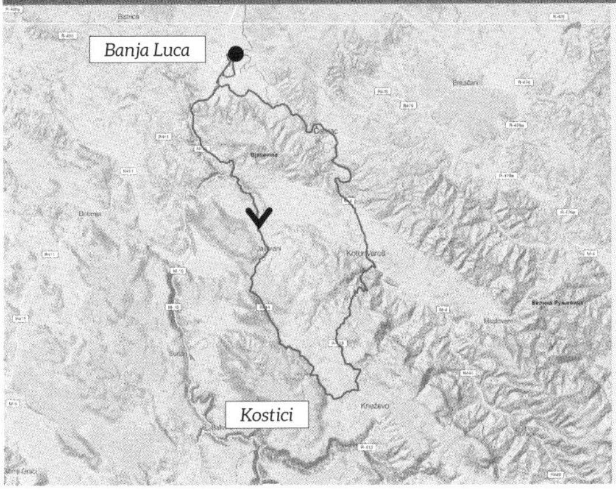

In Banja Luka, the second-largest city in Bosnia and Herzegovina, the street signs are in both the Cyrillic and Roman alphabets, an indication of this region's complex history. Perhaps the only simple thing around here is the stunning beauty of the landscape, as we ride south along the Vrbas River. We turn away from the Vrbas at Karanovac (just before the river enters a canyon) and hit some aggressive climbs up to more than 800 m (2,625 ft), not far from Čemernica mountain (1,339 m/4,393 ft). We return to Banja Luka via its medieval castle. With one bar for every 200 residents, you have many options for your post-ride beer.

NOVI SAD
A FOREST ABOVE THE PLAIN

Hilly / Intermediate

Map strava.com/routes/23751529

Distance	E+	Difficulty	Appeal
73 km (45 mi)	1,150 m (3,775 ft)	3/5	4/5

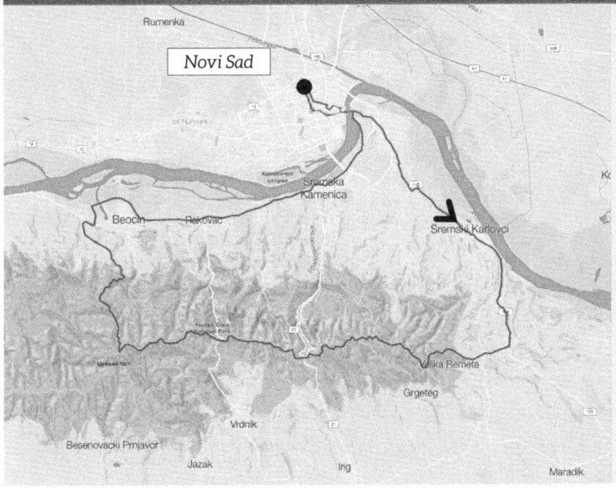

Novi Sad means "new orchard" in Serbian. The country's second-largest city (after Belgrade) has always been a crossroads of peoples and cultures. It has also been called "the Serbian Athens." Our route takes us out of the historic center and across the Danube into Syrmia to climb the wooded massif of Fruška Gora. After an ascent in stages, we ride across the mountain for around 20 km (12 mi) almost to its highest point, Crveni Čot, at 539 m (1,768 ft). Then, we descend and roll pleasantly along the Danube, back to the good vibes of Novi Sad.

KOTOR
MONTENEGRIN GIANT

High mountain / Advanced
Map strava.com/routes/23749055
Test yourself km 31 (mi 19) strava.com/segments/1728715
Test yourself km 52 (mi 32) strava.com/segments/865082

If you had to choose a single destination in Europe for sports cycling, you would absolutely have to choose this spot. Far from the legendary roads of the Tour de France, the Giro, and the Vuelta, the Bay of Kotor and the mountain of Lovćen in Montenegro are pure dream.

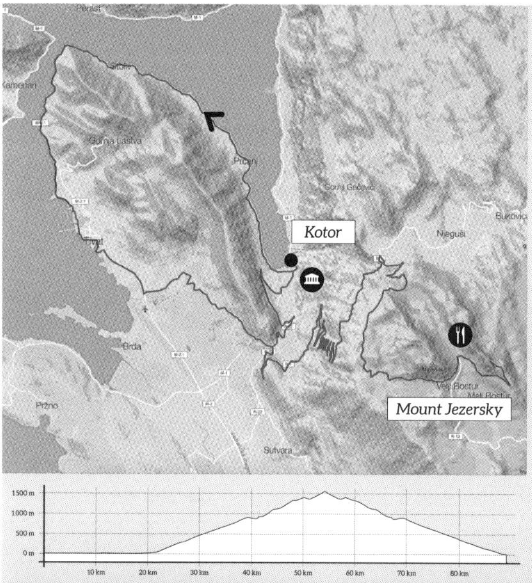

At Kotor, you must take it all in until you cannot manage any more: the little town nestling in seclusion at the end of the bay, the stunningly beautiful villages of Donji Stoliv and Tivat, the tranquil waters that evoke the northern Italian lakes, and then the overview of all that as we climb higher and higher. But another attraction soon appears: the incredible series of twenty-five switchbacks cut into the very rock that overlook Kotor's medieval wall and its fortress. Each switchback is numbered, as on the Stelvio and Alpe d'Huez climbs. Their gradient is a regular 5%. These 8 km (5 mi) of tight bends barely recede before we approach the imposing shape of Lovćen. The last 3 km (2 mi) up to just below Jezerski—one of the mountain's two peaks (1,657 m/5,436 ft)—is at nearly 10%. From the top, there are yet more breathtaking panoramas. A giant dream fulfilled!

Distance **92 km** (57 mi)

E+ **2,300 m** (7,550 ft)

Difficulty **4/5**

Appeal **5/5**

Tivat Airport is 8 km (5 mi) from Kotor (50 minutes by bus), and has many European connections during the summer season. In low season, connect via Belgrade. There is no rail network in this part of Montenegro. By bus, Dubrovnik is 2h30 and Podgorica 2h20. (90 km/55 mi).

Atop Lovćen (km 54/mi 34), you will be unable to resist Vladika Restoran, the only place to sit down and refuel. Located 100 meters/yards higher up is the mausoleum of Petar II Petrović-Njegoš, a Prince-Bishop of Montenegro in the nineteenth century.

Lovćen, Cetinje

There is so much to see around Kotor (Our Lady of the Rocks, the sublime villages of Perast and Stoliv, Mamula Fortress, the Blue Cave) that a bike will not suffice. Take a cruise the day after conquering the twenty-five switchbacks.

visit-montenegro.com

The incredible switchbacks that ascend above Kotor, Montenegro.

PODGORICA
OSTROG PILGRIMAGE

Low mountain / Advanced — *Map strava.com/routes/23749495*

Distance	E+	Difficulty	Appeal
77 km (60 mi)	1,400 m (4,595 ft)	4/5	5/5

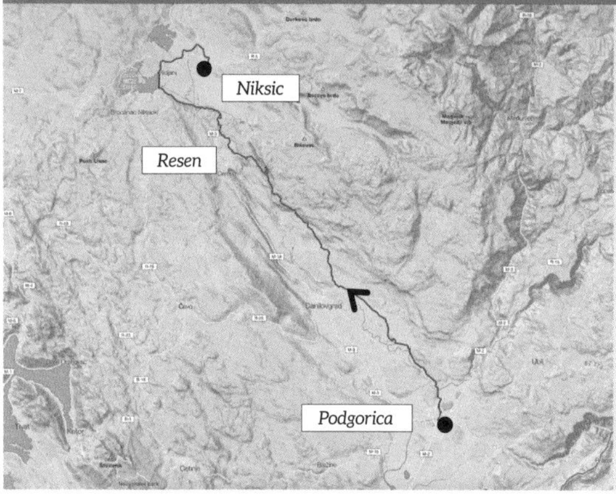

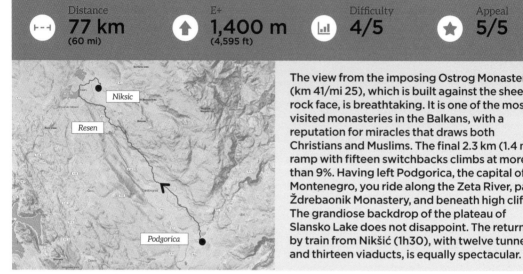

The view from the imposing Ostrog Monastery (km 41/mi 25), which is built against the sheer rock face, is breathtaking. It is one of the most visited monasteries in the Balkans, with a reputation for miracles that draws both Christians and Muslims. The final 2.3 km (1.4 mi) ramp with fifteen switchbacks climbs at more than 9%. Having left Podgorica, the capital of Montenegro, you ride along the Zeta River, past Ždrebaonik Monastery, and beneath high cliffs. The grandiose backdrop of the plateau of Slansko Lake does not disappoint. The return by train from Nikšić (1h30), with twelve tunnels and thirteen viaducts, is equally spectacular.

OHRID
HIGH MACEDONIA

Low mountain / Advanced — *Map strava.com/routes/23684500*

Distance	E+	Difficulty	Appeal
113 km (70 mi)	1,650 m (5,415 ft)	3/5	4/5

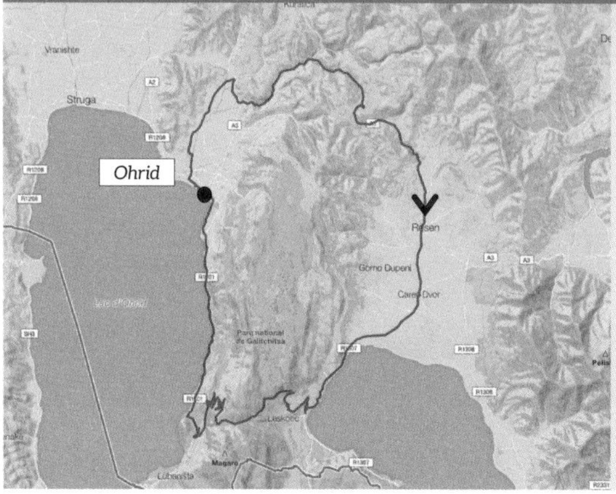

The country of North Macedonia, which is only a little smaller than Belgium, is 80% mountain and has thirty-four peaks above 2,000 m (6,560 ft). We know what to expect on these roads that alternate between concrete and cobbles. Direction: the quiet south (most of the two million Macedonians live in the north). Even on the A3 highway, you encounter more tractors than cars. Galičica National Park and the eponymous pass (1,592 m/5,225 ft) is a must. The panoramic road snakes between low vegetation. From up here, you can fully appreciate the beauty of Lake Prespa to the east and Lake Ohrid to the west.

CLUJ-NAPOCA
VALES OF TRANSYLVANIA

Hilly / Intermediate

Map strava.com/routes/23757359

Distance	E+	Difficulty	Appeal
85 km (53 mi)	1,000 m (3,280 ft)	2/5	4/5

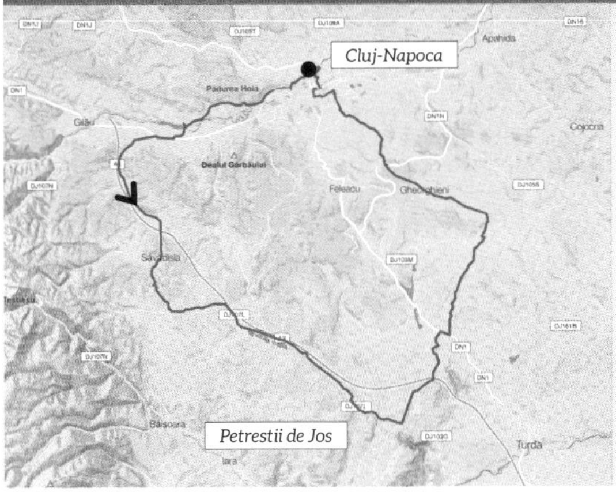

The wooded hills of Cluj set the tone as soon as we ride west out of the city above the Someșul Mic River. Transylvania is no flat country. For the first 15 km (9 mi), we ride toward the Apuseni Mountains, which we will enjoy exploring some other day. We pass the villages of Luna de Sus, Săvădisla, and Petreștii de Jos, which are nestled in the little valleys against a pastoral backdrop, 450 km (280 mi) northwest of Bucharest. The road is sprightly, undulating between 350 m (1,1150 ft) and 650 m (2,135 ft). The ride in to Cluj-Napoca (the country's second-largest city) explores the rich historic center.

SIBIU
ROMANIAN ALPS

Low mountain / Advanced

Map strava.com/routes/23684581

Distance	E+	Difficulty	Appeal
109 km (68 mi)	1,800 m (5,905 ft)	4/5	4/5

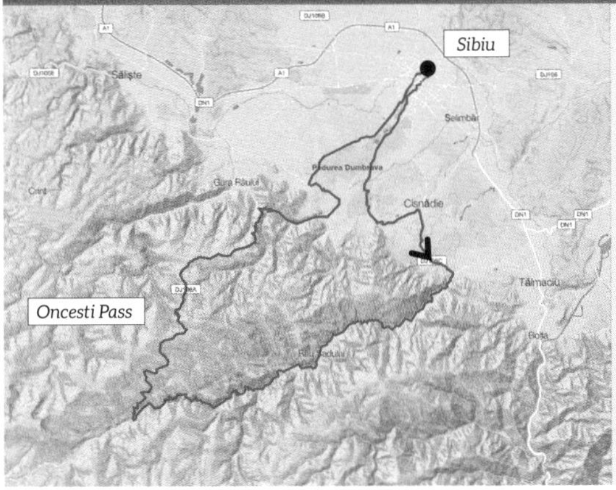

Sibiu (pop. 150,000) escaped the city planning of the Ceaușescu years, retaining examples of Gothic, Renaissance, and baroque architecture, as well as some very old dwellings. The scenery here on the Transylvanian Plateau evokes the fictional Syldavia of the *The Adventures of Tintin* comics. Its proximity to the Southern Carpathians also makes it a popular destination for outdoor activities. To the southwest, Păltiniș (km 72/mi 45) is the highest mountain resort in the country. Just above it is the Oncești Pass at 1,642 m (5,390 ft): an ascent of 26 km (16 mi) through a conifer forest. This corner of Romania has a little Alpine feel.

BRAȘOV

BEAR MOUNTAINS

Low mountain / Intermediate — *Map strava.com/routes/23684155*

Distance	E+	Difficulty	Appeal
74 km (46 mi)	1,300 m (4,265 ft)	3/5	5/5

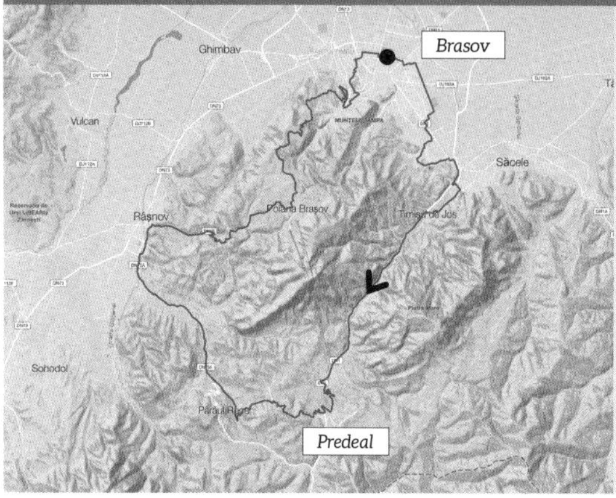

Brașov (pop. 300,000) is 2h30 by train from Bucharest (barely 200 km/125 mi). The city developed the Poiana Brașov Ski Resort (the biggest in Eastern Europe) virtually on its doorstep. The Postăvarul Massif in which the resort sits is where the Southern and Eastern Carpathian Mountains meet. Our route is a tour of the Postăvarul, climbing to 1,200 m (3,940 ft) on the little Trei Brazi road, which skirts the Bucegi Natural Park in a beautiful muddle of ridgelines, canyons, and waterfalls. Keep a lookout for brown bears; there are thousands here, and one might amble out from behind the pines trees or a rock.

PAZARDZHIK

BULGARIAN GRAN FONDO

High mountain / Expert — *Map strava.com/routes/23762424*

Distance	E+	Difficulty	Appeal
105 km (65 mi)	2,300 m (7,545 ft)	4/5	4/5

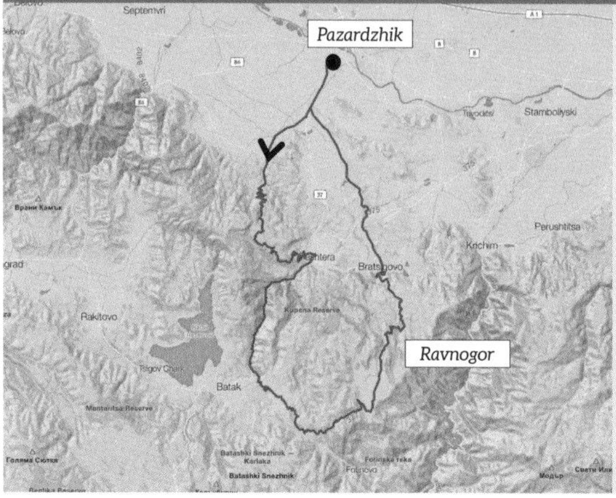

In Bulgaria, you can tackle routes worthy of the high mountains, providing you choose your destination well. The Rhodope Mountain range between Bulgaria and Greece is the perfect terrain. From Pazardzhik (2h20 by train from Sofia), we ride a demanding route similar to a gran fondo, although without approaching the most spectacular gorges closer to the border. Our tour of the Kupena Nature Reserve is lovely enough. The Atoluka climb stretches for more than 20 km (12.5 mi), with the hardest section at the start. After Batak Reservoir, the Peshtera switchbacks wind upward for 10 km (6 mi) at 6%.

CORFU
IONIAN SPLENDORS

- *Low mountain / Advanced*
- *Map strava.com/routes/23682778*
- *Test yourself km 25 (mi 16) strava.com/segments/4873688*
- *Test yourself km 42 (mi 26) strava.com/segments/745401*

There are a thousand exceptional routes to discover on Corfu, the largest of the Ionian Islands. Why not start with the ascent of Mount Pantokrator? From 906 m (2,972 ft) above the sea, you can view the whole of Corfu, continental Greece, and the nearby Albanian coast.

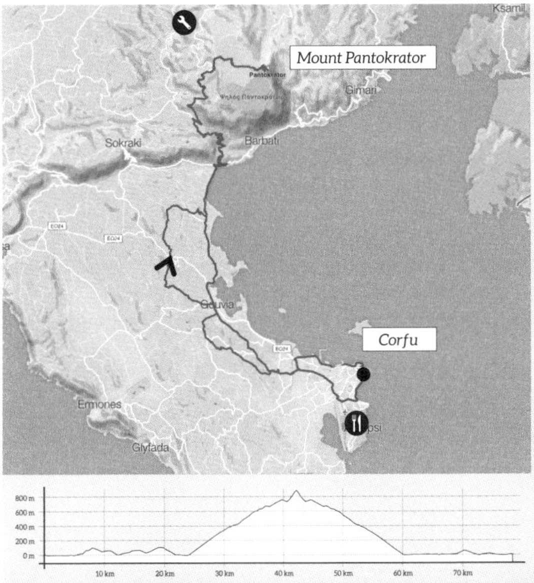

North, south, west—it is worth exploring every corner of the splendid Greek island of Corfu. Covering only 593 km² (229 sq mi), Corfu has some incredible surprises in store along its coasts and up in its hills. Within the cycling community, Corfu is less well known than Mallorca or Tenerife, but so much the better; the roads will be far less crowded. Spring or fall are the best times of year to come; winter is rainy. If you are physically fit enough, commence with Mount Pantokrator, the island's highest point. Our route tackles the long southern ascent: 18 km (11 mi) from Agios Markos beach at an average gradient of 5%, with the last 2 km (1.25 mi) at more than 10%. The 360-degree panorama at the top is the most beautiful of rewards. The sublime beaches and cliffs of the west coast can wait a bit. From the summit of Mount Pantokrator, Corfu seems to belong to you.

Distance	E+	Difficulty	Appeal
78 km (49 mi)	1,500 m (4,920 ft)	4/5	5/5

There are direct flights to Corfu from all over Europe. Corfu International Airport is located 2 km (1.25 mi) south of Corfu Town. Remember that foreign airlines and low-cost carriers focus on the summer season. There are ferries from continental Greece and Italy (Brindisi).

You will be thirsty once you reach the summit; probably hungry too. Fortunately, the inviting terrace of the Pantokrator Cafe Bar awaits. You can even hire a telescope!

Palio Chorio
Pantokrator, Corfu
Facebook/PantokratorCafeBar

You can also climb Mount Pantokrator from the northwest, starting in Acharavi. S-Bikes Cycle Corfu is worth popping into. It offers rentals of Specialized and Cube bikes, and a guide service to Corfu.

Epar. Od. Kassiopis-Sidariou
Acharavi 490 81
cyclecorfu.com

IOANNINA
THE GREEK ABYSS

- *Low mountain / Intermediate*
- *Map strava.com/routes/23607047*
- *Test yourself km 20 (mi 12) strava.com/segments/23607047*
- *Test yourself km 34 (mi 21) strava.com/segments/ 18466723*

The Guinness Book of Records claims that the Vikos Gorge in northwest Greece is the world's "deepest relative to its width." From Ioannina, you may contemplate its 900 m (2,955 ft) abyss in an 83 km (52 mi) ride. Amazing.

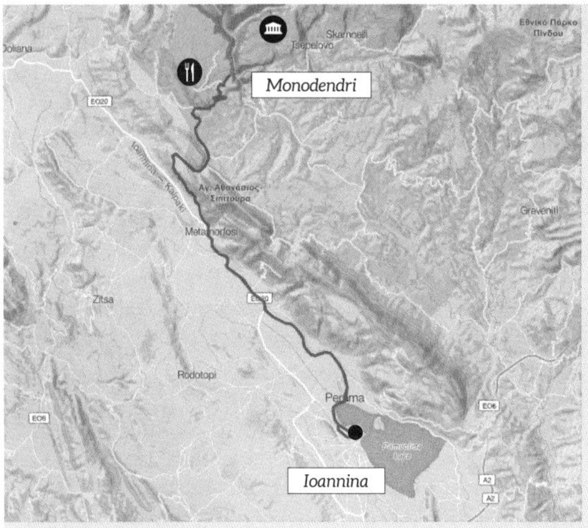

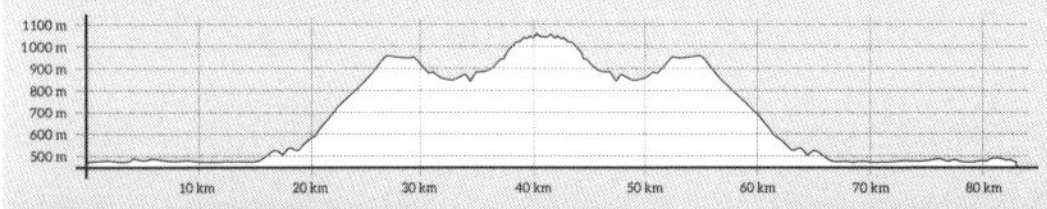

The Voidomatis is a modest river that is only 15 km (9 mi) long. It rises in a magical place: Vikos Gorge, where it has dug a 900 m (2,955 ft) deep furrow through bare cliffs. Starting in Monodendri in the south, the gorge unfurls northward to the village of Papingo. Our route does not go quite that far. Starting from Ioannina, we aim for the old abandoned monastery of Saint Paraskevi (600 m/1,970 ft), reached via a cobbled road above Monodendri. The marvelous view from there, however, must be earned: 7 km (4.5 mi) at 5% from Metamorfosi, and 5 km (3 mi) at a similar gradient through the Vitsa switchbacks. You only see the panorama over the gorge from 600 m (1,970 ft) above the Epirus plain. Getting to Papingo is even more demanding. You can reach the amazing Oxya Viewpoint by climbing 320 m (1,050 ft) higher over a further 16 km (10 mi).

Distance	E+	Difficulty	Appeal
83 km (52 mi)	**1,250 m** (4,100 ft)	**3/5**	**5/5**

Ioannina—often called Yannena—is located 420 km (260 mi) from Athens (4h15 by car or 10h by train). Thessaloniki is 6h20 by train or 3h by car (260 km/160 mi). The major ferry port of Igoumenitsa on the Ionian Sea is 1h10 by car (90 km/55 mi).

For a food stop midway, we recommend the terrace of Mystika Tis Yiayias (the cafe of Vikos Hotel), which is shaded by leafy trees.

Monodendri 440 07
vikoshotel.com

Vikos Gorge should not detract from the splendor of Ioannina. The sublime Ioannina Island is only a 10-minute crossing. Measuring just 0.8 km (0.5 mi) long by 0.5 km (0.3 mi) wide, it counts seven monasteries linked by paved footpaths, and has an adorable little harbor.

travelioannina.com

TRIKALA
HANGING MONASTERIES

- *Hilly / Intermediate*
- *Map strava.com/routes/23588301*
- *Test yourself km 28 (mi 17) strava.com/segments/13442361*
- *Test yourself km 42 (mi 26) strava.com/segments/10130530*

No doubt, you have already seen pictures of the Greek Orthodox monasteries of Meteora, which are perched atop very high natural sandstone pillars right in the middle of Greece. Their conquest by bike begins in Trikala on one of the most fascinating roads in Europe.

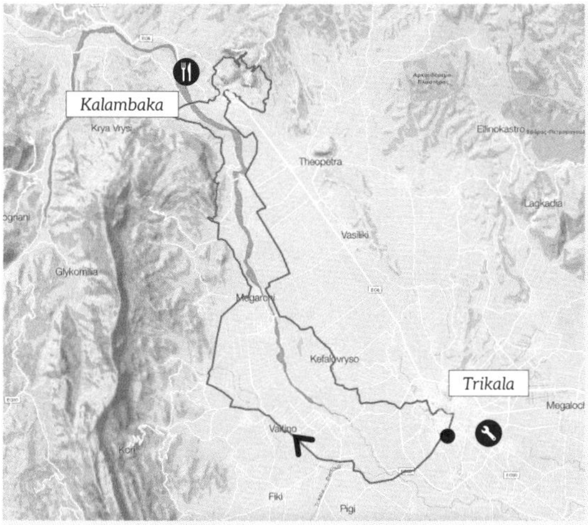

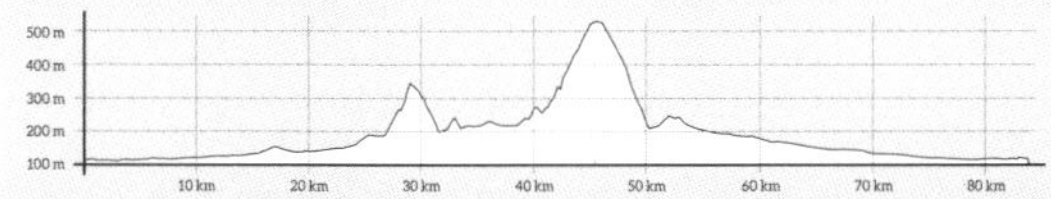

The Meteora are besieged by crowds in summer, and so they are best avoided. For the rest of the year, a departure from Trikala offers an enjoyable approach to this incredible site of huge cliffs and natural sandstone pillars, which rise to 400 m (1,315 ft). On the way, we tackle a 2 km (1.25 mi) ramp at 8% before Kalambaka, which nestles at the foot of our stone sentinels sculpted by erosion. A 12 km (7.5 mi) loop on a superb road that sometimes seems to hover above a sheer drop provides a glimpse of the amazing sight of these monasteries—built and rebuilt in the course of the centuries—atop the summits of the Meteora. Only six of them are still functioning today. These include Varlaam Monastery and Great Meteoron Monastery, which we pass right by at km 44 (mi 27), just before a viewpoint at the very peak of our route, which we reach after a 3 km (2 mi) section at 9%. This is one extraordinary day out!

Distance	E+	Difficulty	Appeal
83 km (52 mi)	850 m (2,790 ft)	3/5	5/5

Trikala (pop. 52,000) is 4h45 by train from Athens or 4h by car (350 km/218 mi). Thessaloniki is 2h50 by train or 2h30 by car (220 km/137 mi). To the west, Ioannina is 2h by car (130 km/81 mi).

With your tour of the Meteora completed, head to the terrace of the Meteoron Panorama, where delicious food is served all day. Return to km 40 (mi 25) or ride on to km 53 (mi 33) and turn right.

Patriarchou Dimitriou 54
Kalambaka 422 00
meteoronpanorama.gr

Located close to Makariou Square and less than 1 km (0.6 mi) from the train station, Vaskos Bikes is Trikala's go-to sports cycling store. Retailer of Bottecchia.

Kapodistriou 20
Trikala 421 31
vaskosbikes.business.site

THESSALONIKI
WHAT A PANORAMA

Very hilly / Intermediate

Map strava.com/routes/23732989

Distance	E+	Difficulty	Appeal
80 km (50 mi)	1,450 m (4,760 ft)	3/5	4/5

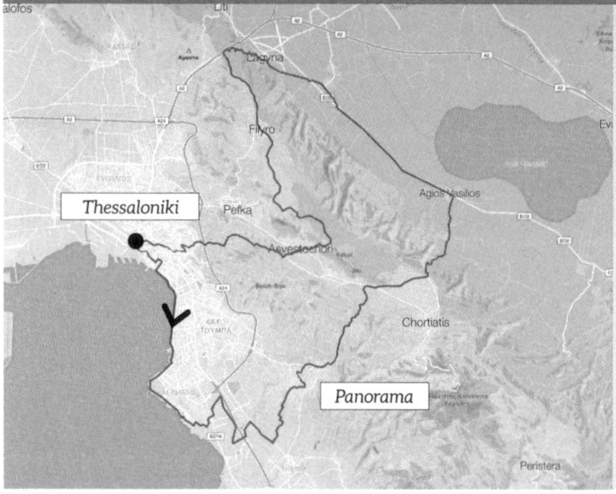

Thessaloniki on the Aegean Sea embraces 4,000 years of history. This former "co-capital" of the Byzantine Empire is the second-largest city in Greece (pop. 800,000), and it remains a major port. There is nothing like the initial 10 km (6 mi) ride along the bay to take it all in before the tempting slopes of Mount Chortiatis, which bring us to 525 m (1,725 ft) by way of the aptly named neighborhood of Panorama. The descent to Lake Koroneia is followed by another climb of more than 10 km (6 mi) at an average gradient of 4%, before dipping down to the red roofs of Asvestochori. Thessaloniki lies at your feet.

HERAKLION
CRETAN DIET

Low mountain / Advanced

Map strava.com/routes/23736383

Distance	E+	Difficulty	Appeal
86 km (54 mi)	1,500 m (4,920 ft)	3/5	5/5

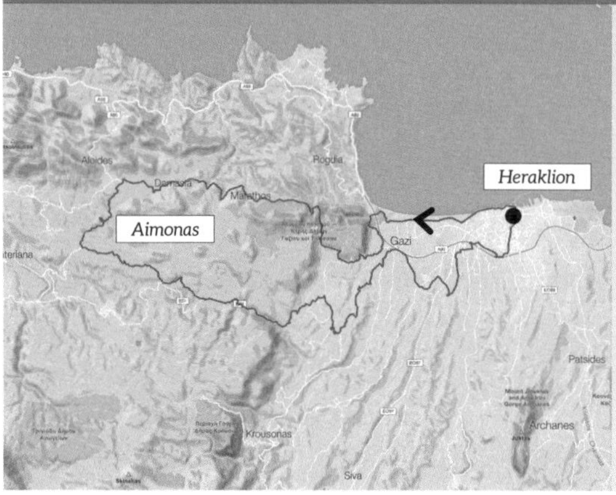

Is Crete the ultimate European cycling destination? Possibly. Its three low mountain ranges promise effort, adventure, and grand spectacle. Our route leaves Heraklion (the airport is 5 km/3 mi away) and the vestiges of its Byzantine and Venetian past, not to mention the Bronze Age site of Knossos. The first ascent, through Almirou Potamou Park, sets the tone as we climb between aromatic plants, rocky formations, caves, and lonely chapels. With the sea for a horizon, the views are vertiginous. We descend between orange and olive plantations. The local olive oil is divine and a key part of the famous Cretan diet.

INDEX

Picture credits : page 11 : © Pajor Pawel/Shutterstock ; **page 21 :** © christographerowens/Shutterstock ; **page 29 :** © orxy/Shutterstock ; **page 35 and cover :** © MNStudio/Shutterstock ; **page 59 :** © Radu Razvan/ Shutterstock ; **pages 64-65 :** © Christophe Lehenaff/Getty Images ; **page 77 :** © Yanis Ourabah/Getty Images ; **page 85 :** © Jon Ingall/Shutterstock ; **page 103 :** © Gi Cristovao Photography/Shutterstock ; **page 121 :** © kovop58/Shutterstock ; **page 135 :** © Marcelo Alex/Shutterstock ; **page 143 :** © iPics/Shutterstock ; **page 161 :** © MC Mediastudio/Shutterstock ; **pages 170-171 :** © Cara-Foto/Shutterstock ; **page 179 :** © kovop58/ Shutterstock ; **page 189 :** © auphoto/Shutterstock ; **page 195 :** © SCK_Photo/Shutterstock ; **pages 208-209 :** © Michael Mantke Shutterstock ; **page 229 :** © Reinhard Tiburzy/Shutterstock ; **page 249 :** © Ionov Vitaly/ Shutterstock ; **pages 266-267 :** © Andrey Armyagov/Shutterstock ; **page 273 :** © MarinaD_37/Shutterstock ; **page 293 :** © Aleksei Kazachok/Shutterstock.